Standard Catalogue of British Coins

COINS OF ENGLAND

AND
THE UNITED KINGDOM

35th Edition

SPINK
LONDON

A Catalogue of the Coins of Great Britain
and Ireland
first published 1929

Standard Catalogue of British Coins
Coins of England and the United Kingdom
35th edition, 2000

© Spink & Son Ltd
5 King Street, St James's
London SW1Y 6QS

Typeset by Data Layout Ltd, 136 Tooley Street, London
Printed in Great Britain by
Cromwell Press
Trowbridge
Wiltshire

ISBN 1 902040 22 8

COINS ILLUSTRATED ON THE FRONT COVER:
ANCIENT BRITISH. CUNOBELIN. Gold Stater
(This coin familiar in the early years of the first Millennium) S.281
AETHELRED II (978-1016) Long Cross Penny of the Winchester Mint
(This type in circulation in the year 1000) S.1151
The Millennium £5 coin in gold (Proof) S.4552

CONTENTS

CONTENTS

PREFACE

This, the 35th edition of our Standard Catalogue of British Coins – Coi
England and the United Kingdom, for the Millennium, has again b
substantially and carefully revised by our in-house numismatic specialists.

This year's edition includes not only illustrations of the coins issued by the
Royal Mint for the year 2000, but also many new or replacement illustrations in
most of the hammered and milled sections of the Catalogue.

Peter Clayton has written a new introductory essay on "Coins and History:
The Changing Face over Two Millennia".

Prices have been extensively revised to reflect current market conditions.

In the hammered series, in addition to including new illustrations
throughout, we have revised and updated the section on the coinages of Edward I,
and II, and early silver of Edward III. In the light of recent research, the
arrangement of the gold coinage of Richard II has been revised. The Oxford Mint
coinages of Charles I have also been reorganised.

In the milled series, as well as replacing and improving illustrations, we
have included additional overdates and varieties.

We would like to say how grateful we are to the many collectors and
specialists who have contacted us with suggestions on how to improve the
sections dealing with their own particular areas of collecting.

Whilst acknowledging the help provided by collectors, the greatest part of
the work involved in revising a work such as this, without doubt, falls heavily on
members of the Coin Department at Spink. We would like to thank Antony
Wilson, now based in our New York office, as Senior Vice-President of Spink
America (Celtic section), May Sinclair (Hammered coins), Steve Hill and Mark
Rasmussen (Milled coins), and Geoff Kitchen (Modern coins).

Don't forget to enter our competition – by doing so you stand a chance of
winning one of the coins featured on the cover of this edition designed for us by
James Shurmer.

Douglas Saville

INTRODUCTION

...gement

arrangement of this catalogue is not completely uniform, but generally it is divided ...o metals (gold, silver, copper, etc) under each reign, then into coinages, denominations and varieties. In the Celtic section the uninscribed coins are listed before the dynastic coins; under Charles II all the hammered coins precede the milled coinage; the reign of George III is divided into coins issued up to 1816 and the new coinage from 1816 to the end of the reign; and under Elizabeth II the decimal issues are separated from the pre-decimal (*£.s.d.*) coinages.

Every major coin type is listed though not every variety. We have endeavoured to give rather more coverage to the varieties of relatively common coins, such as the pennies of Edward I, II and III, than to the very much rarer coins of, for instance, King Offa of Mercia.

Values

The values given represent the range of retail prices at which coins are being offered for sale at the time of going to press and **not** the price which a dealer will pay for those coins. These prices are based on our knowledge of the numismatic market, the current demand for particular coins, recent auction sale prices and, in those cases where certain coins have not appeared for sale for some years, our estimation of what they would be likely to sell at today, bearing in mind their rarity and appeal in relation to somewhat similar coins where a current value is known. Values are given for two grades of preservation from the Celtic period onwards and three to four grades of preservation for coins of the 17th to the 20th century.

Collectors normally require coins in the best condition they can afford and, except in the case of a really rare coin, a piece that is considerably worn is not wanted and has little value. The values given in the catalogue are for the exact state of preservation stated at the head of each column and bearing in mind that a score of identical coins in varying states of wear could be lined up in descending order from mint condition (FDC, *fleur de coin*), through very fine (VF) to *poor* state. It will be realized that only in certain instances will the values given apply to particular coins. A 'fine' (F) coin may be worth anything between one quarter and a half of the price quoted for a 'very fine' (VF); on the other hand, a piece in really mint condition will be valued substantially higher than the price quoted for 'extremely fine' (EF). The designation BV has been adopted for coins whose value on the market has yet to exceed its bullion value. Purchasing sovereigns, catalogued as BV, will attract a dealers' premium.

We emphasize again that the purpose of this catalogue is to give a general value for a particular class of coin in a specified state of preservation, and also to give the collector an idea of the range and value of coins in the English series. The value of any particular piece depends on three things:

Its exact design, legend, mintmark or date.

Its exact state of preservation; this is of prime importance.

The demand for it in the market at any given time.

Some minor varieties are much scarcer than others and, as the number of coins issued varies considerably from year to year, coins of certain dates and mintmarks are rarer and of more value than other pieces of similar type. The prices given for any type are for the commonest variety, mintmark or date of that type.

The Scope

Coin collecting, numismatics, is a fascinating hobby. It requires very little physical exertion and only as much mental effort as one wishes or is able to put into it at any time. There is vast scope and boundless ramifications and byways encompassing not only things historical and geographical, but also touching on economics, metallurgy, heraldry, literature, the fine arts, politics, military history and many other disciplines. This catalogue is solely concerned with British coinage from its earliest times right up to date. From the start the beginner should appreciate that the coinage of our own nation may be seen as a small but very important part of the whole story of world currency.

The first coins, made of electrum, a natural alloy of gold and silver, were issued in western Asia Minor (Lydia) in the later seventh century B.C. Over the next century or so coinage of gold and silver spread across the Aegean to mainland Greece, southwards to the eastern Mediterranean lands and eventually westward to the Greek colonies in southern Italy, Sicily (Magna Graecia) and beyond. The coins of the Greeks are noted for their beautiful, sometimes exquisite craftsmanship, with many of the coin types depicting the patron deities of their cities. Coins of Philip II of Macedon (359-336 B.C.), father of Alexander the Great, circulated amongst the Celtic peoples of the Danubian Basin and were widely copied through central Europe and by the Gauls in France. Gold Gaulish staters were reaching Britain around the beginning of the first century B.C. and the earliest gold to be struck in the island must have been produced shortly afterwards. Although their types and designs copy the Apollo head and racing charioteer of Philip II's gold coins, they are stylistically much removed from the original representation and very individually Celtic in concept.

The coins of the Romans cover some seven centuries and include an enormous number of different types that were current throughout a major part of the civilized world from Spain to Syria and from the Rhine in the north to the Sudan in the south. The Roman province of Britain was part of this vast empire for four hundred years from AD 43 until the early fifth century. Innumerable Roman coins have been recovered from sites in this country, most being made of brass or bronze. Many of these are quite inexpensive and very collectable. In recent years many hoards of gold and silver coins have been found, usually by use of metal detectors.

Following the revival of commerce after the Dark Ages, coinage in Western Europe was virtually restricted to silver until the thirteenth century, though gold was still being minted in Byzantium and in the Islamic world. In the Middle Ages many European cities had their own distinctive coinage and money was issued not only by the kings but also by nobles, bishops and abbots. From the time of the later Crusades gold returned to the West, and the artistic developments of the Renaissance in the fifteenth century brought improved portraiture and new minting techniques.

Large silver crown-size thalers were first minted at Joachimsthal in Bohemia early in the sixteenth century. The substantial shipments of silver coming to Europe from the mines of Spanish America over the next couple of centuries led to a fine series of larger coins being issued by the European states and cities. The larger size allowed greater artistic freedom in the designs and the portraits on the coins.

Both Germany and Italy became unified nation states during the later nineteenth century, thereby substantially reducing the number of mints and coin types. Balancing the reduction in European minting authorities were the new coins that were issued by the independent states of South and Central America. Since the 1950s many new nations have established their independence and their coinage provides a large field for the collector of modern coins.

It can be seen that the scope for the collector is truly vast, but besides the general run of official coinage there is also the large series of token coins—small change unofficially produced to supplement the inadequate supply of authorized currency. These tokens were issued by merchants, innkeepers and manufacturers in many towns and villages in the seventeenth, eighteenth and nineteenth centuries and many collectors specialize in their local issues.

Some coins have designs of a commemorative nature; an example being the Royal Wedding crown of 1981, but there are also large numbers of commemorative medals which, though never intended for use as coinage, are sometimes confused with coins because they are metal objects of a similar shape and sometimes a similar size to coins. This is another interesting field for collectors as these medals often have excellent portraits of famous men or women, or they may commemorate important events or scientific discoveries. Other metallic objects of coin-like appearance that can be confusing for the beginner are reckoning counters, advertising tickets, various other tickets and passes, and items such as brass coin weights.

Minting processes

From the time of the earliest Greek coins in the late seventh century BC to about the middle of the sixteenth century AD, coins were made by hand. The method of manufacture was simple. The obverse and reverse designs were engraved or punched into the prepared ends of two bars of bronze or iron, shaped or tapered to the diameter of the required coin. The obverse die, known as the *pile,* was usually spiked so that it could be anchored firmly into a block of wood or metal. The reverse die, the *trussel,* was held by hand or grasped by tongs.

The coin was struck by placing a metal blank between the two dies and striking the trussel with a hammer. Thus, all coinage struck by this method is known as 'hammered'. Some dies are known to have been hinged so there would be an exact register between the upper and lower die. Usually a 'pair of dies' consisted of one obverse die (normally the more difficult to make because it had the finer detail, such as the ruler's portrait) and two reverse dies. This was because the shaft of iron bearing the reverse design eventually split under the constant hammering; two reverse dies were usually needed to last out the life of the obverse die.

Some time toward the middle of the sixteenth century, experiments, first in Germany and later in France, resulted in the manufacture of coins by machinery.

The term 'milled', which is applied to all machine-made coins, comes from the type of machinery used – the mill and screw press. With this machinery the obverse die was fixed as the lower die and the reverse die brought down into contact with the blank by heavy vertical pressure applied by a screw or worm-drive connected to a cross bar with heavy weights at each end. These weights usually had long leather thongs attached which allowed a more powerful force to be applied by the operators who revolved the arms of the press. New blanks were placed on the lower die and the struck coins were removed by hand. The screw press brought more pressure to bear on the blanks and this pressure was evenly applied, producing a far better and sharper coin.

Various attempts were made during the reigns of Elizabeth I and Charles I to introduce this type of machinery with its vastly superior products. Unfortunately problems associated with the manufacture of blanks to a uniform weight greatly reduced the rate of striking and the hand manufacture of coins continued until the Restoration in 1660, when Charles II brought to London from Holland the Roettiers brothers and their improved screw press.

The first English coins made for circulation by this new method were the silver crowns of 1662, which bore an inscription on the edge, DECVS ET TVTAMEN, 'an ornament and a safeguard', a reference to the fact that the new coins could not be clipped, a crime made easy by the thin and often badly struck hammered coins.

The mill and screw press was used until new steam-powered machinery made by Boulton and Watt was installed in the new mint on Tower Hill in London. This machinery had been used most successfully by Boulton to strike the large 'cartwheel' two- and one-penny pieces of 1797 and other coins, including 'overstriking' Spanish *eight-reale* pieces into Bank of England 'dollars' since the old Mint presses were not able to exert sufficient power to do this. This new machinery was first used at the Mint to strike the 'new coinage' halfcrowns of 1816, and it operated at a far greater speed than the old type of mill and screw presses and achieved a greater sharpness of design.

The very latest coining presses now operating at the Royal Mint at Llantrisant in South Wales, are capable of striking at a rate of up to 800 coins a minute.

Condition

One of the more difficult problems for the beginner is to assess accurately the condition of a coin. A common fault among collectors is to overgrade and, consequently, to overvalue their coins.

Most dealers will gladly spare a few minutes to help new collectors. Many dealers issue price lists with illustrations, enabling collectors to see exactly what the coins look like and how they have been graded.

Coins cannot always be graded according to precise rules. Hammered coins often look weak or worn on the high parts of the portrait and the tops of the letters; this can be due to weak striking or worn dies and is not always attributable to wear through long use in circulation. Milled coins usually leave the Mint sharply struck so that genuine wear is easier to detect. However a x5 or x10 magnifying glass is essential, especially when grading coins of Edward VII and George V where the relief is very low on the portraits and some skill is required to distinguish between an uncirculated coin and one in EF condition.

The condition or grade of preservation of a coin is usually of greater importance than its rarity. By this we mean that a common coin in superb condition is often more desirable and more highly priced than a rarity in poor condition. Coins that have been pierced or mounted as a piece of jewellery generally have little interest to collectors.

One must also be on the lookout for coins that have been 'plugged', i.e. that have been pierced at some time and have had the hole filled in, sometimes with the missing design or letters re-engraved.

Badly cleaned coins will often display a complexity of fine interlaced lines and such coins have a greatly reduced value. It is also known for coins to be tooled or re-engraved on the high parts of the hair, in order to 'increase' the grade of coin and its value. In general it is better to have a slightly more worn coin than a better example with such damage.

Cleaning coins

Speaking generally, *do not* clean coins. More coins are ruined by injudicious cleaning than through any other cause, and a badly cleaned coin loses much of its value. A nicely toned piece is usually considered desirable. Really dirty gold and silver can, however, be carefully washed in soap and water. Copper coins should never be cleaned or washed, they may be lightly brushed with a brush that is not too harsh.

Buying and selling coins

Exchanging coins with other collectors, searching around the antique shops, telling your relatives and friends that you are interested in coins, or even trying to find your own with a metal detector, are all ways of adding to your collection. However, the time will come when the serious collector needs to acquire specific coins or requires advice on the authenticity or value of a coin.

At this point an expert is needed, and the services of a reputable coin dealer are necessary. There are now a large number of coin dealers in the UK, many of whom belong to the B.N.T.A. (The British Numismatic Trade Association) or the I.A.P.N. (The International Association of Professional Numismatists) and a glance through the 'yellow pages' under 'coin dealer' or 'numismatist' will often provide local information. Many dealers publish their own lists of coins. Studying these lists is a good way for a collector to learn about coins and to classify and catalogue their own collections.

The Standard Catalogue of Coins of England and the UK has been published since 1929. It serves as a price guide for all coin collectors. Spink also publish books on many aspects of English, Greek, Roman and Byzantine coins and on British tokens which serve as a valuable source of information for coin collectors. Our books are available directly from Spink or through reputable booksellers. Many branches of W. H. Smith, and other High Street booksellers, stock copies of *The Standard Catalogue*.

Numismatic Clubs and Societies

There are well over one hundred numismatic societies and clubs in the British Isles. For details of how to contact them see page 466. Joining one is the best way to meet fellow enthusiasts, learn about your coins and other series and acquire coins in a friendly and informative way.

Useful suggestions

Security and insurance. The careful collector should not keep valuable coins at home unless they are insured and have adequate protection. Local police and insurance companies will give advice on what precautions may be necessary.

Most insurance companies will accept a valuation based on *The Standard Catalogue*. It is usually possible to have the amount added to a householder's contents policy but particularly valuable individual coins may have to be separately listed. A 'Fire, Burglary and Theft' policy will cover loss only from the insured's address, but an 'All Risks' policy will usually cover accidental damage and loss anywhere within the U.K.

For coins deposited with a bank or placed in a safe-deposit box a lower insurance premium is usually payable.

Keeping a record. All collectors are advised to have an up-to-date record of their collection and, if possible, photographs of the more important and more easily identifiable coins. This should be kept in a separate place from the collection so that a list and photographs can be given to the police should loss occur. Note the price paid, from whom purchased, the date of acquisition and the condition of the coin.

Storage and handling. New collectors should get into the habit of handling coins by the edge. This is especially important as far as highly polished proof coins are concerned.

Collectors may initially keep their coins in paper or plastic envelopes housed in boxes, albums or special containers. Many collectors will eventually wish to own a hardwood coin cabinet in which the collection can be properly arranged and displayed. If a home-made cabinet is being constructed avoid using oak and cedar wood; mahogany, walnut and rosewood are ideal. It is important that coins are not kept in a humid atmosphere; especial care must be taken with copper and bronze coins which are very susceptible to damp or condensation which may result in a green verdigris forming on them.

From beginner to numismatist
The new collector can best advance to becoming an experienced numismatist by examining as many coins as possible, noting their distinctive features and by learning to use the many books of reference that are available. It will be an advantage to join a local numismatic society, as this will provide an opportunity for meeting other enthusiasts and obtaining advice from more experienced collectors. Most societies have a varied programme of lectures, exhibitions and occasional auctions of members' duplicates.

Those who become members of one or both of the national societies, the Royal Numismatic Society and the British Numismatic Society, receive an annual journal containing authoritative papers and have access to the societies' library and programme of lectures.

Many museums have coin collections available for study, although they may not always be displayed, and a number of museum curators are qualified numismatists.

ABBREVIATIONS

Archb.	Archbishop	laur	laureate
Æ	bronze	*mm.*	*mintmark*
Æ	silver	mon.	monogram
Æ	gold	*O., obv.*	obverse
Bp.	Bishop	p.	new penny, pence
BV	bullion value	pl	plume
cuir.	cuirassed	quat.	quatrefoil
d.	penny, pence	qtr.	quarter
diad.	diademed	rad.	radiate
dr.	draped	R., *rev.*	reverse
ex.	exergue	r.	right
grs.	grains	s.	shillings
hd.	head	trun.	truncation
i.c.	inner circle	var.	variety
illus.	illustration	wt.	weight
l.	left		

SOME NUMISMATIC TERMS EXPLAINED

Obverse	That side of the coin which normally shows the monarch's head or name.
Reverse	The side opposite to the obverse, the 'Tails'.
Blank	The coin as a blank piece of metal, i.e. before it is struck.
Flan	The whole piece of metal after striking.
Type	The main, central design.
Legend	The inscription. Coins lacking a legend are called 'mute' or anepigraphic.
Field	That flat part of the coin between the main design and the inscription or edge.
Exergue	That part of the coin below the main design, usually separated by a horizontal line, and normally occupied by the date.
Die	The block of metal, with design cut into it, which actually impresses the coin blank with the design.
Die variety	Coin showing slight variation of design.
Mule	A coin with the current type on one side and the previous (and usually obsolete) type on the other side, or a piece struck from two dies that are not normally used together.
Graining or reeding	The crenellations around the edge of the coin, commonly known as 'milling'.
Proof	Carefully struck coin from special dies with a mirror-like or matt surface. (In this country 'Proof' is *not* a term used to describe the state of preservation, but the method of striking.)
Hammered	Refers to the old craft method of striking a coin between dies hammered by hand.
Milled	Coins struck by dies worked in a coining press. The presses were hand powered from 1560-1800, powered by steam from 1790 and by electricity from 1895.

THE CHANGING FACE OVER TWO MILLENNIA

The 'millennium bug' seems to have been with us now for far too long in all shapes and forms, be they the Millennium Dome, various other structures to tie in with the 'event' such as the Great Court at the British Museum, or more simply things at a lower, perhaps local level. But, really what is it all about – it is all wrong anyway ! Herod the Great, the villain of the piece in the Massacre of the Innocents, reigned in Judaea from 37 to 4 BC – ergo, all the celebrations are at least four years out – we've missed the proverbial boat. Be that as it may, in millennium terms, it is interesting to cast one's eye backwards from the numismatic point of view.

Whilst Britain gets 'geared up' to its millennium celebrations it is as well to remember first that there have been other millennium celebrations outside the Christian one. According to legend Rome was founded in 753 BC, and Roman dates were calculated from that date as auc, *ab urbe condita,* from the founding of the City.

Coins have been used almost from their first appearance to either advertise a local product, shrine, etc, as on Greek coins, or to act as propaganda, literally the 'newspaper headlines of their day', e.g. Roman coins, of which perhaps the most prominent example is the 'EID MAR' denarius of Brutus alluding to the assassination of Julius Caesar on 15 March 44 BC, i.e., the Ides of March, 710 *auc.*

Antoninus Pius emperor of Rome from 138 to 161 rather jumped the millennium gun when he celebrated and commemorated on his coins the 900th anniversary of the foundation of Rome on 21 April AD 147. He issued a remarkable series of coins that alluded on their reverse types to the ancient legends of the foundation of Rome or to the early history of the city. Notable amongst the types were, naturally, Romulus and Remus and the she-wolf that suckled them, but there were references to alternative foundation stories in showing Aeneas carrying his aged father Anchises from the sack of Troy. After various adventures, including dallying with Dido Queen of Carthage, Aeneas arrived in Latium and was seen as an alternative founder of Rome. Anniversary games were held to mark the 900th anniversary and a fifth donative was made by the emperor.

The actual millennium of Rome occurred in the reign of Philip I (244-249), and began on 21 April 248. The celebrations included Secular Games marking the occasion and there was a remarkable series of animals associated with the Games featured on the coins. They included elephants, lions, gazelles, antelopes, goats and stags, as well as, naturally, the Wolf and Twins. The temple of Roma Aeterna with its cult statue also appeared.

It is intriguing to take a look at coins in England over the two millennia, taking year 0 as a starting point and noting them at 500-year intervals. Christ did not start His ministry until late in his life, and he was four years old at least at the year 0. In Britain the rulers issuing Celtic coinage around that date, since none can be definitely dated, are Tincomarus who, until the recent find of the Alton Hoard in 1996, was referred to as Tincommius and identified with the king of that name who fled as a suppliant to Augustus in Rome in the early first century. His coins feature the devolved head of Apollo and the disjointed charioteer as well as some with abbreviated legends in a label – the latter, as with his mounted horseman, copying Roman types. A contemporary, whose reign may have coincided with that of Tincomarus, was Eppillus. His coin types are even more closely modelled on Roman originals and a number carry a mint name identification CALLE for *Calleva Atrebatum* (Silchester in Hampshire). Many of the coins of these two rulers have only come to light in recent years from metal detector finds and do not appear in the older standard works such as Mack.

Coinage in Britain was at its lowest ebb following the recall of the Roman legions by the emperor Honorius in AD 410. What coinage there was in what appears to have reverted to a largely barter economy, were the smaller denomination Roman issues that were still around, getting smaller and smaller until they reached a size that many could fit onto an old halfpenny and were described by their excavator, Dr (later Sir) Mortimer Wheeler, as 'King Arthur's pence'. Merovingian gold coins from the Continent are known from Britain, but not in such quantity that they could be said to have circulated as money. Perhaps the closest dated find of them presently known from Britain is the group of 37 tiny gold tremisses found in a purse in the Sutton Hoo Anglo-Saxon ship burial in Suffolk. It is thought to be the burial of Raedwald, King of East Anglia, who died c. 625. From the evidence of the finds in the ship burial it appears that Raedwald was hedging his bet between paganism and Christianity as both aspects were represented. The coins, minted between 575 and 625, had been carefully selected since each came from a different mint. They are believed, along with the three unstruck gold blanks and two small gold billets in the purse, making a total of 42 pieces of gold, to be payment for the forty oarsmen and crew to row the ghostly ship in the Afterworld.

Pope Gregory I sent St Augustine to convert the 'Angles' in AD 597, which he proceeded to do after landing in Kent. Eventually Canterbury was to become the ecclesiastical focus of Christianity in Britain, achieving even greater prominence as the site of Thomas a Becket's martyrdom on 29 December 1170. However, 170 years before that, Anglo-Saxon England was geared to the end of the first millennium, many believed also that it would either see the end of the world or the Second Coming of Christ.

The first Christian millennium fell in the reign of Aethelred II, 978-1016, who was often better known by the sobriquet of 'the Unready'. This actually comes from the Anglo-Saxon 'unrede', literally 'without counsel' – he lacked good advice. His reign was one fraught with danger for the general populace with the terror of the frequent Danish raids – no wonder then that with the year 1000 approaching many also saw the end of the world as coming with it. His silver pennies were struck at a number of mints, including London, Bath, Cambridge and Thetford. The normal type had the king's bust to the left and a small or a long cross reverse. Reverse types with a more specific Christian significance were the First Hand and Second Hand types with the hand of Providence (S. 1144-6), flanked by the Greek letters for alpha and omega (the beginning and the end), or the hand (presumably of God) giving Benediction (S. 1147). The Hand type was apparently copied from the unique coin of his predecessor, Edward the Martyr, 975-978 (Grueber, p. 29).

Of especial interest for its obverse and reverse types, and struck only shortly after the occurrence of the millennium, in c. 1009, is the very scarce Agnus Dei silver penny (S. 1156). The obverse features the Lamb of God proceeding right with a long processional cross obliquely behind its body, and the reverse shows the Dove in flight. The symbolism of both obverse and reverse type must be a deliberate reference to the millennium and hope for the kingdom in God's hands.

To move forward another 500 years brings us into the reign of Henry VII (1485-1509). Having slain the last of the Plantagenet kings, Richard III, on the field of Bosworth, the Tudor dynasty now took hold. Henry's reign sees the transition from medieval into Renaissance styles in the coinage, especially with the introduction of the German engraver Alexander de Brugsal. He is credited with producing the profile portrait coins of the king that appeared from the London mint in 1504. He also improved the design of the splendid large gold sovereign that had been first produced in 1489 and of which there were eventually four varieties. The other new denomination of the reign was the silver shilling and whilst gold coin was struck at the Tower in London, silver was struck in the provincial mints of Canterbury, Durham and York, as well as at London. Coincidentally, at two of the ecclesiastical mints the incumbents ended their tenure in 1500, Archbishop Thomas Morton (1487-1500) at Canterbury, and infamous for 'Morton's Fork', and Bishop Thomas Rotherham (1480-1500) at York. Each of these primates marked their issues respectively with an M for Morton and a T for Thomas. There do not appear to be any coin types that can be specifically allied to any commemoration of the half millennium.

With the year 2000 rapidly approaching, and looking back over the coinage of the two millennia, the changes seen are enormous. What, one wonders in the event, can be looked for in the coinage for the millennium? The answer seems to be the schoolboy's laconic response, 'Not a lot'. In the last two millennia British coinage has passed from its Roman types into the silver pennies of Anglo-Saxon England, the rich gold and silver coinage of the Middle Ages, from hammered to milled coinage, and to a coinage that no longer supports its intrinsic value and is only a poor token coinage essentially of cupro-nickel. New technology has made new designs, and more intricate ones, possible, but not all meet with common approval. Now, with the Common Market and the postulated single currency, the Euro, it would appear that all nationalistic tendencies and the inherent history in British coinage, let alone that of any other members of the European Union, are to be swept aside in a mad move for 'political correctness' and unity. One of the lessons of history, which politicians and apologists do not seem to be able to grasp, is that you cannot rewrite history – what is past, is past.

So, despite the threats to our national coinage, and no matter what happens to it, numismatics will still continue to be a splendid hobby and subject of study. It was well summed up in November 1753 by George Vertue, a notable engraver, in his 'Observations to the Curious Reader', that prefaces his study of Thomas Simon, perhaps England's greatest coin engraver. Vertue wrote: 'The collecting of coins and medals is known to be a noble amusement; the delight of the curious, a good ornament to history, as well as a necessary appendage to books of that kind. Many nations in former ages, as well as the present, have experience of the subject; and it is allowed and encouraged in all polite nations. From whence it is seen and known the great honour, pleasure and usefulness of such studies; for which no argument need be advanced, where the fact is past dispute.' If only the bureaucrats would take notice of, and act upon, Vertue's last sentence!

Peter A. Clayton

The Celtic or Ancient British issues are amongst the most interesting and varied of all British coins. They are our earliest coins and are the product of a society that left no historical sources of its own. It is therefore often difficult to be specific about for whom, when or where they were produced. Despite only being used for approximately a hundred and fifty years they do provide a rich variety of designs and types in gold, silver and bronze. Collectors looking for a theme to concentrate on may find the coins of one tribe, an individual ruler or a particular phase in the coinage interesting.

Grading Celtic Coins

The majority of Celtic coins were struck by hand, sometimes resulting in a loss of definition through weak striking. In addition, the design on the dies was often bigger than the blank flan employed, resulting in the loss of some of the design. Coins with full legends are generally more valuable than examples with incomplete legends. Bronze coins in good condition (VF or better) and especially toned examples attract a premium. Factors that detract from a coins value are chips, scratches and verdigris on bronze coins. It is important to take into account these factors as well as the amount of wear on a coin when assessing its grade.

Cunobelin Bronze Unit	Epatticus Silver Unit	Cunobelin Gold Stater
Fine		
Very Fine		

Plated Coins

Plated gold staters, quarter staters and silver units are recorded for many known types. They vary considerably in the quality of their production and are usually priced at around a quarter of the substantive types value. Their exact purpose or relation to the type they copy is not fully understood.

References and Select Bibliography.

M   Mack, R.P. (1975) 3rd edition, The Coinage of Ancient Britain.
V   Van Arsdell, R.D. (1989), Celtic Coinage of Britain.
BMC   Hobbs, R. (1996), British Iron Age Coins in the British Museum.

de Jersey, P. (1996), Celtic Coinage in Britain. *A good general introduction to the series.*
Nash, D. (1987), Coinage in the Celtic World. *Sets the coinage in its social context.*

The layout of the following list is derived from the standard works by Mack, Van Arsdell and the British Museum Catalogue by Richard Hobbs. References are made to these works where possible, in the case of the last work it should be noted that the British Museum collection is not exhaustive, and therefore should not be used to assess the rarity of a coin. More detailed information than that given here can be gained from these works.

IMPORTED COINAGE

The earliest coins to circulate in Britain were made in northern Gaul (Belgica) and imported into the south-east of England from around 150 B.C. onwards. They were principally the product of two tribal groups in this region, the Ambiani and Suessiones. In Britain these types are known as Gallo-Belgic A to F. The first type Gallo-Belgic A is ultimately derived from the Macedonian gold staters (M) of Philip II (359-336 B.C.)

The reasons why they were imported are not fully understood. However, the context for their importation is one of close social, political and economic ties between Britain and Gaul. Within this cross-channel relationship they undoubtedly had various functions, such as payment for military service or mercenaries, in exchanges between the elite of each society: in cementing alliances for example, or as gifts in a system of exchange.

Numbers in brackets following each entry refer to numbers employed in previous editions of this catalogue.

GALLO-BELGIC ISSUES

GOLD

M	2	3	5	7

	F	VF
	£	£

From c.150 B.C. – c.50 B.C.

		F	VF
1	**Stater.** Gallo-Belgic A. (Ambiani). Good copy of Macedonian stater, large flan. Laureate head of Apollo r. R. Horse r. *M. 1; V. 10. (1)*	600	1950
2	Similar, but head and horse l. *M. 3; V. 12. (1)*	350	1450
3	B. (Ambiani). Somewhat similar to 1, but small flan and 'defaced' *obv.* die. R. Horse r. *M. 5; V. 30. (3)*	200	500
4	— Similar, but with lyre between horse's legs. *M. 7; V. 33. (3)*	225	525
5	C. (Ambiani), *Stater*. Disintegrated Apollo head. R. horse. *M. 26; V. 44. (5)*	175	375
6	**Quarter Stater.** Gallo-Belgic A. Similar to 1. *M. 2; V .15. (2)*	190	460
7	— Similar to 2. *M. 4; V. 20. (2)*	225	600
8	B. Similar to 3. *M. 6; V. 35. (4)*	160	330
9	— Similar. R. Two horses l. with lyre between legs. *M. 8; V. 37. (4)*	200	450
10	D. Portions of Apollo head R. A mixture of stars, crescents, pellets, zig-zag lines; often referred to as 'Geometric' types,(See also British 'O', S. 46.). *M. 37, 39, 41, 41a, 42; V. 65/7/9/146. (6)*	60	125

From c.50 B.C.

11

		F	VF
		£	£
11	**Stater.** Gallo-Belgic E. (Ambiani). Blank obv. R. Disjointed curved horse r., pellet below, zig-zag in exergue. *M. 27; V. 52, 54. (7)*	120	235
12	F. (Suessiones). Devolved Apollo head r. R. Disjointed horse r. With triple-tail. *M. 34a; V. 85. (8)*	200	375
13	Xc. Blank except for VE monogram at edge of coin, R. S below horse r. *M. 82; V. 87-1. (9)*	250	500

BILLON

Armorican (Channel Islands and N.W. Gaul, c.75–50 B.C.)

14   15

		F	VF
14	**Stater.** Class I. Head r. R. Horse, boar below, remains of driver with Victory above, lash ends in or two loops, or 'gate'. *(12)*	35	85
15	— Class II. Head r. R. Horse, boar below, remains of Victory only, lash ends in small cross of four pellets. *(13)*	35	80
16	— Class III. Head r., anchor-shaped nose. R. Somewhat similar to Class I. *(14)*	35	80
17	— Class IV. Head r. R. Horse with reins, lyre shape below, driver holds vertical pole, lash ends in three prongs. *(15)*	40	80
18	— Class V. Head r. R. Similar to last, lash ends in long cross with four pellets. *(16)*	40	85
19	— Class VI. Head r. R. Horse, boar below, lash ends in 'ladder' *(17)*	45	95
20	**Quarter Stater.** Similar types to above. *(18)*	50	110

20

CELTIC COINS STRUCK IN BRITAIN

Coin production in Britain began at the very end of the second century B.C. with the cast potin coinage of Kent (Nos 62-64). Inspired by Gaulish issues and ultimately derived from the potin coins of Massalia (Marseilles) in southern Gaul, the precise function and period of use of this coinage is not fully understood. The domestic production of gold coins started around 70 B.C., these issues are traditionally known as British A-P and are derived from imported Gallo-Belgic issues. Broadly contemporary with these issues are quarter staters, silver units, and bronze units. Recent work by John Sills has further enhanced our understanding of this crucial early period with the identification of two new British staters (Insular Belgic C or Kentish A and the Ingoldisthorpe type) and their related quarters and a Westerham quarter stater. The Insular Belgic C or Kentish A type derived from Gallo-Belgic C now becomes the first British stater.

EARLY UNINSCRIBED COINAGE

GOLD

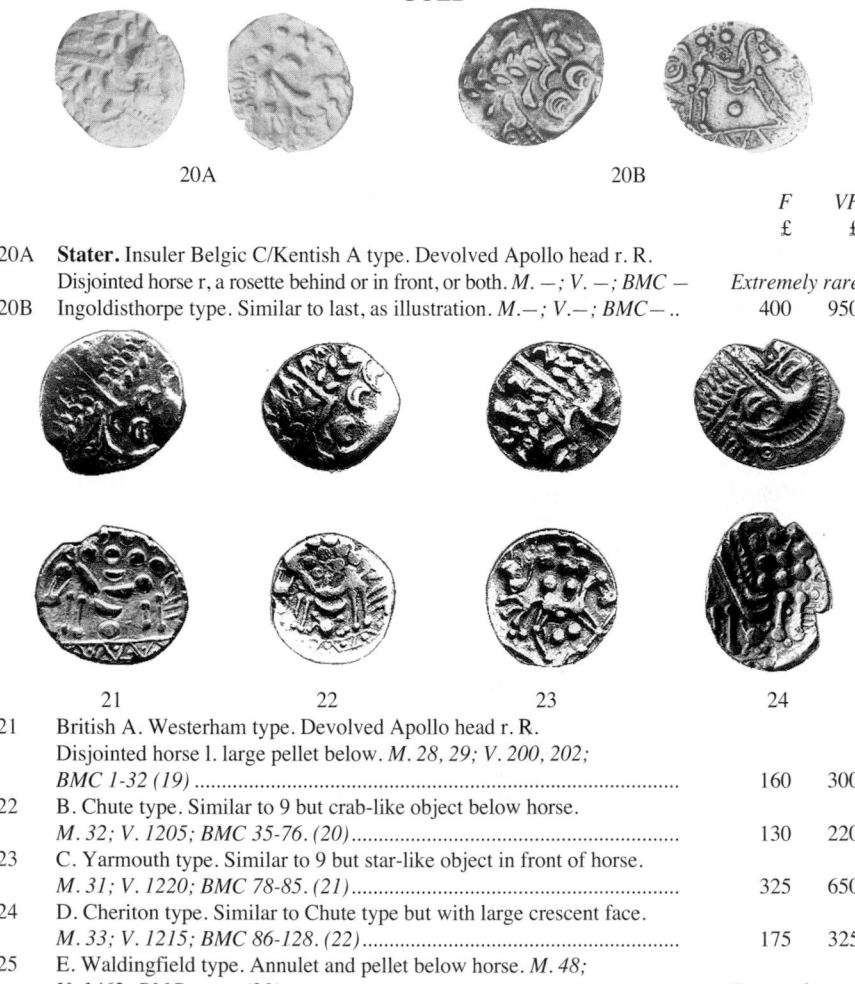

	20A		20B	

		F	VF
		£	£
20A	**Stater.** Insuler Belgic C/Kentish A type. Devolved Apollo head r. R. Disjointed horse r, a rosette behind or in front, or both. *M. —; V. —; BMC —*	*Extremely rare*	
20B	Ingoldisthorpe type. Similar to last, as illustration. *M.—; V.—; BMC—* ..	400	950

	21	22	23	24

21	British A. Westerham type. Devolved Apollo head r. R. Disjointed horse l. large pellet below. *M. 28, 29; V. 200, 202; BMC 1-32 (19)*	160	300
22	B. Chute type. Similar to 9 but crab-like object below horse. *M. 32; V. 1205; BMC 35-76. (20)*	130	220
23	C. Yarmouth type. Similar to 9 but star-like object in front of horse. *M. 31; V. 1220; BMC 78-85. (21)*	325	650
24	D. Cheriton type. Similar to Chute type but with large crescent face. *M. 33; V. 1215; BMC 86-128. (22)*	175	325
25	E. Waldingfield type. Annulet and pellet below horse. *M. 48; V. 1462; BMC — —. (23)*	*Extremely rare*	

26   27

		F £	VF £

26 F. Clacton type 1. Similar to Westerham type but rosette below horse. *M. 47; V. 1458; BMC 137-44. (24)* 275 500

27 G. Clacton type 2. Similar but horse r., with pellet, or pellet with two curved lines below. *M. 46, 46a; V. 30, 1455; BMC 145-79. (25)* 260 480

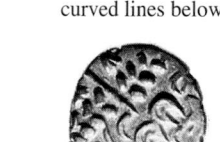   

28   30

28 H. North-East Coast type. Variety of 9, pellet or rosette below horse to r. *M. 50, 50a, 51, 51a; V. 800; BMC 182-191. (26)* 185 375

29 I. — Similar, horse l., pellet, rosette or star with curved rays below. *M. 52-57; V. 804, 805, 807; BMC 193-211. (27)* 175 325

30 J. Norfolk Wolf type. R. Crude wolf to r. *M. 49; V. 610-1; BMC 212-16. (28)* 225 475

31 — Similar but wolf to l. Usually base gold. *M. 49a/b; V. 610-2/3; BMC 217-78. (28A)* 90 200

32 L. Whaddon Chase type. R. Spirited horse r. of new style, various symbols below. *M. 133-138a, 139a; V. 1470-6; 1485/7/9/93; BMC 279-343. (31)* 175 350

33 — Plain. R. Horse r. With ring ornament below or behind. *M. 140-143; V. 1498-1505; BMC 344-46. (32)* 200 425

34 Lx. NorthThames group. Blank apart from reversed SS. R. Similar to last. *M. 146; V. 1509; BMC 350. (33)* .... *Extremely rare*

35 Lz. Weald group. Blank with some traces of Apollo head. R. Horse r., large wheel ornament below. *M. 144-145; V. 1507; BMC 347-49. (36)* .. 325 720

36

36 Ma. Wonersh type. Crossed wreath design with crescents back to back in centre. R. Spiral above horse, wheel below. *M. 148; V. 1520; BMC 351-56. (37)* 250 650

37   38

		F £	VF £

37	Mb. Savernake Forest type. Similar but *obv.* plain or almost blank. *M. 62; V. 1526; BMC 361-64*	200	425
38	Qa. British 'Remic' type. Crude laureate head. R. Triple-tailed horse, wheel below. *M. 58, 60, 61; V. 210-124; BMC 445-58. (41)*	225	450
39	Qb. — Similar, but *obv.* blank. *M. 59; V. 216; BMC 461-76. (42)*	175	300
39A	**Quarter Stater.** Insuler Belgic C/Kentish A type. Similar to Gallo-Belgic D, but with rosette in field on obverse. *M. —; V.—; BMC—*	*Extremely rare*	
39B	Ingoldisthorpe type. Similar to last but with sperm-like objects in field. *M.—; V.—; BMC—*	*Extremely rare*	
39C	British A. Westerham type. Similar to last but of cruder style, or with L-shapes in field on rev. *M.—; V.—; BMC—*	*Extremely rare*	
40	British D. Cheriton type. Similar to Stater, large crescent face. R. Cross motif with pellets. *M. —; V. 143 var; BMC 129-136*	145	325
41	F/G. Clacton type. Plain, traces of pattern. R. Ornamental cross with pellets. *M. 35; V. 1460; BMC 180-1. (43A)*	175	350
42	H. Crescent design and pellets. R. Horse r. *M. —; V. —; BMC 192*	150	325
43	Lx. N.Thames group. Floral pattern on wreath. R. Horse l. or r. *M. 76; V. 234; BMC 365-370. (44)*	100	275

43   44   45

| 44 | Ly. N.Kent group. Blank. R. Horse l. or r. *M. 78; V. 158; BMC 371-3. (45)* | 100 | 200 |
| 45 | Lz. Weald group. Spiral design on wreath. R. Horse l. or r. *M. 77; V. 250; BMC 548-50. (46)* | 120 | 240 |

46   47   48

46	O. Geometric type. Unintelligible patterns (some blank on obv.). *M. 40, 43-45; V. 143, 1225/27/29; BMC 410-32. (49)*	60	125
47	P.Trophy type. Blank. R. Trophy design. *M. 36, 38; V. 145-7; BMC 435-44. (50)*	70	165
48	Qc.British 'Remic' type. Head or wreath pattern. R. Triple-tailed horse, l. or r. *M. 63-67; 69-75; V. 220-32, 36, 42-6, 56; BMC 478-546. (51)*	90	190
49	Xd. Head l. of good style, horned serpent behind ear. R. Horse l. *M. 79; V. 78; BMC 571-575. (11)*	225	450

SILVER

Units (unless otherwise stated)

50 52

		F £	VF £
50	Lx. Head l.or r. R. Horse l. or r. *M. 280, 435, 436, 438, 441; V. 80, 1546, 1549, 1555; BMC 376-382. (53)*	45	125
51	— Head l. R. Stag r. with long horns. *M. 437; V. 1552; BMC 383-7. (54)*	75	225
52	— **Half Unit.** Two horses or two beasts. *M. 272, 442, 443, 445; V. 474, 1626, 1643, 1948; BMC 389-400. (55)*	110	275
53	Lz. Danebury group. Head r. with hair of long curves. R. Horse l., flower above. *M. 88; V. 262; BMC 580-82*	100	225

54 54A

54	— Helmeted head r. R. Horse r wheel below. *M. 89; V. 264; BMC 583 -592. (58)*	100	250
54A	Cruciform pattern with ornaments in angles. R. Horse l., ear of corn between legs, crescents and pellets above, *M.—; V.—; BMC—*	80	175
55	— **Quarter Unit.** As last. *M. 90; V. 268; BMC 642-43. (59)*	65	125
56	— Head r. R. Horse r. star above, wheel below. *M. —; V. 280; BMC 595-601*	75	150
57	— Head l., pellet in ring in front. R. Horse l. or r. *M. —; V. 284; BMC 610-630*	85	175
58	— Serpent looking back. R. Horse l. *M. —; V. 286; BMC 631-33*	100	220
59	— **Quarter Unit.** Cross pattern. R. Two-tailed horse. *M. 119; V. 482; BMC 654-56. (56C). (Formerly attributed to Verica)*	45	125

BRONZE

60	**Unit.** Lx. Winged horse l. R. Winged horse l. *M. 446; V. 1629; BMC 401 (78)*	85	275
61	Chichester Cock type. Head r. R. Head r. surmounted by cock. *M. —; V. — BMC 657-59*	40	125

POTIN
(Cast Copper/Tin alloy)

62

	F £	VF £
62	**Unit.** Thurrock type.Head l. R. Bull butting l. or r. *M. —; V. 1402-42;* *BMC 660-666. (84A)*	40	100

63   64

63	Class I type. Crude head. R. Lines representing bull *(Allen types A-L.)* *M. 9-22a; V. 104, 106, 108, 112, 114, 115, 117, 119, 120, 122, 123, 125,* *127, 129, 131, 133; BMC 667-714. (83)*	30	80
64	Class II type. Smaller flan, large central pellet. *(Allen types M-P.)* *M. 23-25; V. 135-39; BMC 715-23. (84)*	40	90

CELTIC DYNASTIC AND LATER UNINSCRIBED COINAGE

From Julius Caesars expeditions to Britain in 55/54 B.C. and his conquest of Gaul in 52 B.C. to the Claudian invasion in 43 A.D., southern Britain was increasingly drawn into the orbit of the Roman world. This process is reflected not only in the coins but also in what we know about their issuers and the tribes they ruled. Latin legends begin to appear for the first time and increasingly accompany objects and designs drawn from the classical world. A lot of what we know about the Celtic tribes and their rulers, beyond just their names on coins, is drawn from contemporary and slightly later Roman historical sources. A great deal however is still uncertain and almost all attributions to either tribes or historically attested individuals have to be seen as tentative.

The coin producing tribes of Britain can be divided into two groups, those of the core and those of the periphery. The tribes of the core, the Atrebates/Regni, Trinovantes/Catuvellauni and Cantii, by virtue of their geographical location controlled contact with the Roman world. Unlike the tribes of the periphery they widely employed Latin legends, classical designs and used bronze coinage in addition to gold and silver.

Following the Roman invasion of 43 A.D. it is likely that some coinage continued to be produced for a short time. However in 61 A.D. with the death of King Prasutagus and the suppression of the Boudiccan revolt that followed, it is likely that Celtic coinage came to an end.

TRIBAL/MINT MAP

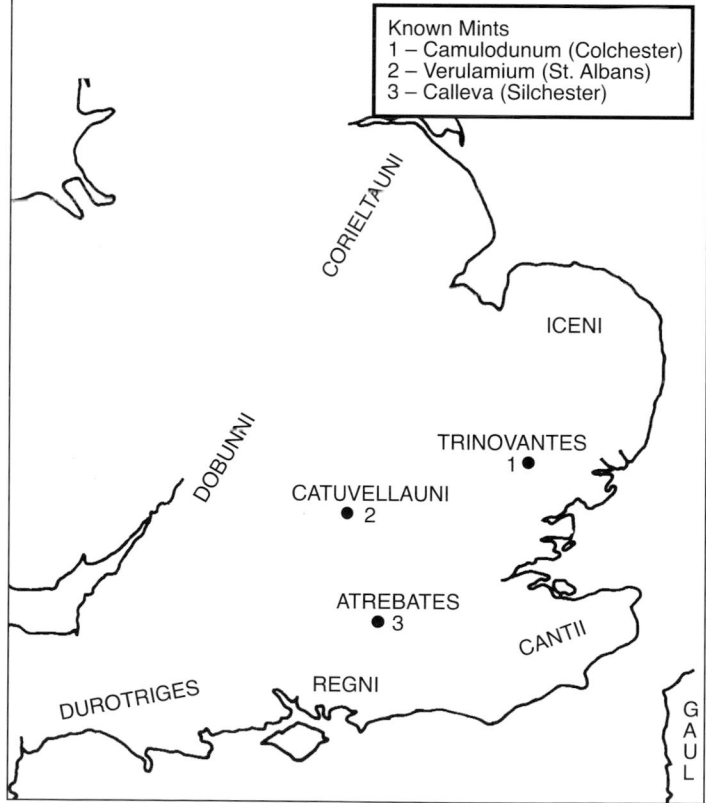

Known Mints
1 – Camulodunum (Colchester)
2 – Verulamium (St. Albans)
3 – Calleva (Silchester)

ATREBATES AND REGNI

The joint tribal area of these two groups corresponds roughly with Berkshire and Sussex and parts of northern and eastern Hampshire. The Atrebatic portion being in the north of this region with its main centre at Calleva (Silchester). The Regni occupying the southern part of the region centred around Chichester.

COMMIUS

(Mid to Late 1st Century B.C.)

The first inscribed staters to appear in Britain, closely resemble British Q staters (no.38) and are inscribed 'COMMIOS'. Staters and silver units with an inscribed 'E' are also thought to be related. Traditionally this Commius was thought to be the Gaulish chieftain who Caesar refers to in De Bello Gallico, as firstly serving him in his expeditions to Britain and finally fleeing to Britain c.50 B.C. This attribution does however present chronological problems, and the appearance of a few early staters reading 'COM COMMIOS' suggests that the Commius who issued coins is more likely to have been the son of Caesar's Commius.

GOLD

65

		F £	VF £
65	**Stater.** Devolved Apollo head r. R. COMMIOS around triple tailed horse r., wheel below. *M. 92; V. 350; BMC 724-29. (85)*	425	1350

66   67

66	Similar, but 'E' symbol above horse instead of legend. *M. —;V. 352.* *BMC 730*	450	1600
67	**Quarter Stater.** Blank except for digamma. R. Horse l. *M. 83; V. 353-5;* *BMC —. (10)*	125	250

SILVER

69

69	**Unit.** Head l. R. Horse l. Mostly with 'E' symbol above. *M. —;V. 355;* *BMC 731-58. (57)*	35	100

70

		F £	VF £
70	**Minim.** Similar to Unit. *M. —; V. 358-5; BMC 759-60*	25	55

TINCOMARUS or TINCOMMIUS
(Late 1st Century B.C. – Early 1st Century A.D.)

Successor to Commius and on his coins styled as 'COM.F' (son of Commius). Early coins of the reign like his predecessors are very obiviously Celtic in their style. However later coins exhibit an increasing tendancy towards Roman designs. Indeed Tincommius is recorded as a supliant king of the Roman emperor Augustus (Res Gestae, xxxii), finally fleeing to Rome in the early 1st century A.D. The discovery of the Alton Hoard in 1996 brought to light gold staters with the new legend TINCOMARVS.

GOLD

71   73

71	**Stater.** *Celtic style.* Devolved Apollo head r. R. TINC COMM. F. around horse. *M. 93; V. 362; BMC —. (86)*	400	900
72	Similar but legend reads TINCOMARVS. *M. 94; V. 363; BMC 761-765. (86)*	600	1650
73	**Quarter Stater.** Spiral with pellet centre. R. Horse r. T above. *M. 81; V. 366; BMC 781-797. (46)*	110	240

74   75

74	TINCOM, zig-zag ornament below. R. Horse l. *M. 95; V. 365; BMC 798-810. (87)*	185	450
75	**Stater.** *Classical style.* TINC(O) on a sunk tablet. R. Horseman with javelin r. often with CF in field. *M. 96-98; V. 375-76; BMC 765-769. (88)*	250	550

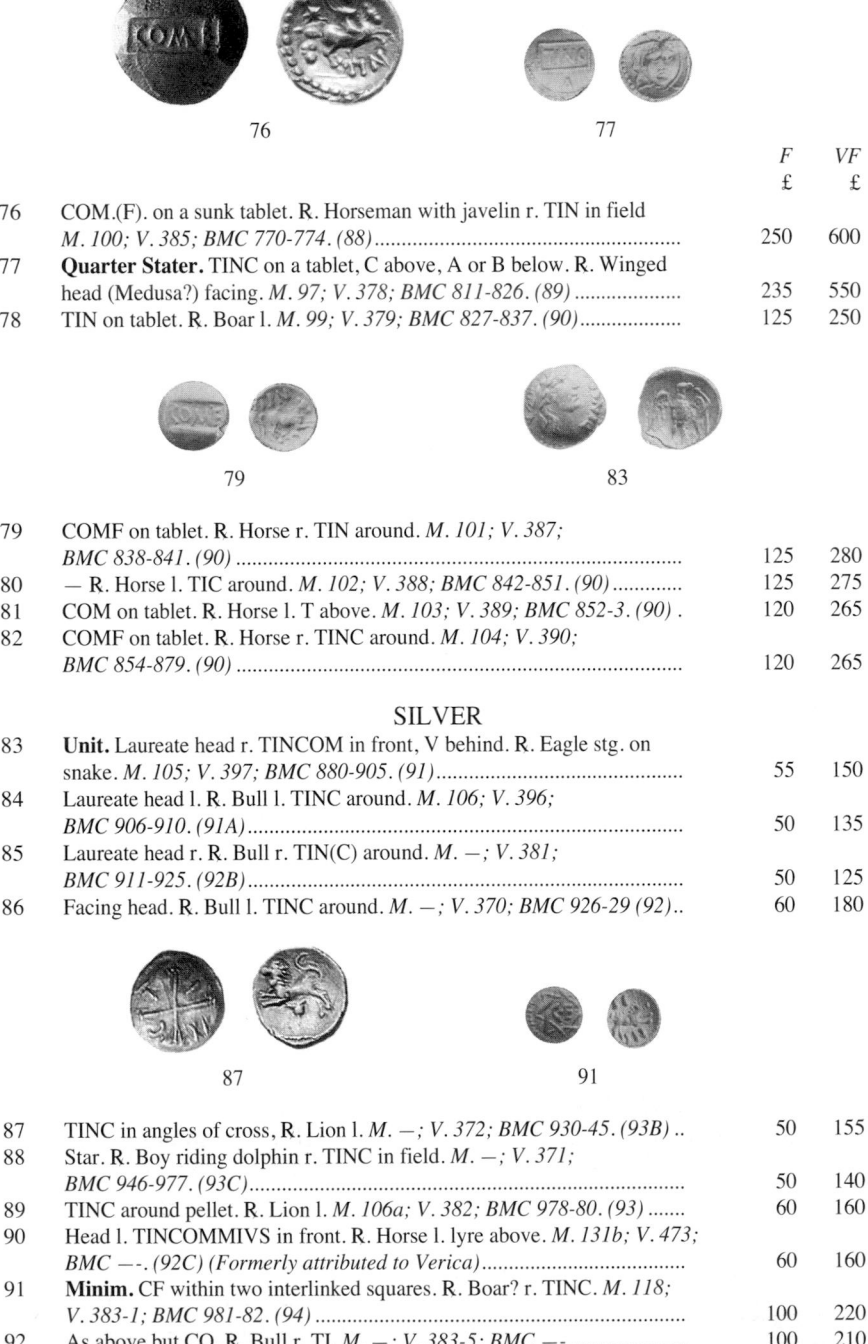

76 77

		F £	VF £

76 COM.(F). on a sunk tablet. R. Horseman with javelin r. TIN in field
M. 100; V. 385; BMC 770-774. (88) 250 600
77 **Quarter Stater.** TINC on a tablet, C above, A or B below. R. Winged
head (Medusa?) facing. *M. 97; V. 378; BMC 811-826. (89)* 235 550
78 TIN on tablet. R. Boar l. *M. 99; V. 379; BMC 827-837. (90)* 125 250

79 83

79 COMF on tablet. R. Horse r. TIN around. *M. 101; V. 387;*
BMC 838-841. (90) 125 280
80 — R. Horse l. TIC around. *M. 102; V. 388; BMC 842-851. (90)* 125 275
81 COM on tablet. R. Horse l. T above. *M. 103; V. 389; BMC 852-3. (90)* . 120 265
82 COMF on tablet. R. Horse r. TINC around. *M. 104; V. 390;*
BMC 854-879. (90) 120 265

SILVER
83 **Unit.** Laureate head r. TINCOM in front, V behind. R. Eagle stg. on
snake. *M. 105; V. 397; BMC 880-905. (91)* 55 150
84 Laureate head l. R. Bull l. TINC around. *M. 106; V. 396;*
BMC 906-910. (91A) 50 135
85 Laureate head r. R. Bull r. TIN(C) around. *M. —; V. 381;*
BMC 911-925. (92B) 50 125
86 Facing head. R. Bull l. TINC around. *M. —; V. 370; BMC 926-29 (92)* .. 60 180

87 91

87 TINC in angles of cross, R. Lion l. *M. —; V. 372; BMC 930-45. (93B)* .. 50 155
88 Star. R. Boy riding dolphin r. TINC in field. *M. —; V. 371;*
BMC 946-977. (93C) 50 140
89 TINC around pellet. R. Lion l. *M. 106a; V. 382; BMC 978-80. (93)* 60 160
90 Head l. TINCOMMIVS in front. R. Horse l. lyre above. *M. 131b; V. 473;*
BMC —-. (92C) (Formerly attributed to Verica) 60 160
91 **Minim.** CF within two interlinked squares. R. Boar? r. TINC. *M. 118;*
V. 383-1; BMC 981-82. (94) 100 220
92 As above but CO. R. Bull r. TI. *M. —; V. 383-5; BMC —-* 100 210

		F £	VF £

93 C inside box, box above and below. R. Bull r. TIN. *M. −; V. 383-7;*
 BMC 983 .... 90 200
94 Cross, T? in angles. R. uncertain object. *M. 120; V. 483; BMC 984-85.*
 (Formerly attributed to Verica) 80 190

EPPILLUS
(Later 1st Century B.C. – Early 1st Century A.D.)

His reign is likely to have coincided with that of Tincommius's, who also claimed to be a son of Commius. Two coinages appear in his name, one for Kent and one minted at Calleva (Silchester, Hants.) in the northern part of the territory of the Atrebates and Regni. The coins of Calleva conform to the southern denominational structure of gold and silver with fractions of each, whilst the Kentish series is distinctly tri-metallic, replacing the silver minim with bronze. A joint coinage was issued by Eppillus and Verica. It is not understood if Eppillus held both territories simultaneously.

COINAGE STRUCK AT CALLEVA
GOLD

95 **Stater.** Devolved Apollo head r. R. EPPI COMMI F around horse.
 M. −; V. 405; BMC − .... *Extremely rare*

96

96 **Quarter Stater.** CALLEV, star above and below. R. Horse r. EPPI.
 M. 107; V. 407-08; BMC 986-1005. (95) 110 275

97   98

97 COMM F EPPILV, around crescent. R. Hound r. *M. −; V. 409;*
 BMC 1006-1009. (95A) 135 350
98 EPPI COMF in two lines. R. Winged horse r. *M. 302; V. 435;*
 BMC 1010-15. (129) 100 250

SILVER

99   100

99 **Unit.** Crescent REX CALLE above and below. R. Eagle r. EPP. *M. 108;*
 V. 415. BMC 1016-1060. (96) 35 95
100 Bearded hd. r. in wreath. R. Boar r. EPPI(L) F CO(M). *M. −; V. 416;*
 BMC 1061-87. (96A) 50 130

			F	VF
			£	£

101   Bearded hd. in pellet border. R. Lion r. EPP COMF. *M. 305; V. 417;*
      BMC 1088-1115. (131) 45 130
102   **Minim.** Floral cross. R. Eagle r. EPPI. *M. —; V. 420; BMC 1116-17* 75 180
103   Spiral and pellets. R. Ram r. EPP. *M. —; V. 421; BMC 1118-20. (96C)* . 80 200
104   Bulls head facing. R. Ram r. EPP. *M. —; V. 422; BMC 1121-24. (96D)* . 80 200
105   Wreath pattern. R. Boar r. EPP. *M. —; V. 423; BMC —-* 75 190
106   Crescent cross. R. Hand holding trident. *M. —; V. 487; BMC —. (111C)* 75 200

KENTISH TYPES
GOLD

107   **Stater.** COMF within wreath. R. Horseman l. EPPILLVS above.
      M. 300; V. 430; BMC 1125-26. (127) .... *Extremely rare*

108   107

108   Victory holding wreath l., within wreath. R. Horseman r. holding
      carnyx, F EPPI COM below. *M. 301; V. 431; BMC 1127-28. (128)* .... *Extremely rare*
109   **Quarter Stater.** Crossed wreaths, EPPI in angles. R. Horse l. *M. 303;*
      V. 436; BMC 1129. (130) 160 425
110   COMF in pellet border. R. Horse r. EPPI. *M. 304; V. 437;*
      BMC 1130-31. (130) 160 380

SILVER

111   **Unit.** Head l. EPPIL in field. R. Horseman holding carnyx, EPPILL.
      M. 306; V. 441; BMC 1132. (131) 60 200

BRONZE

112   **Unit.** Bow cross, EPPI COMF around. R. Eagle facing. *M. 309; V. 450;*
      BMC 1137-38. (134) 55 200
113   Bull r., EPPI COF around. R. eagle facing. *M. 310; V. 451;*
      BMC 1139-41. (134) 50 200
114   Head l., EPPI in front. R. Victory l. holding wreath and standard.
      M. 311; V. 452; BMC 1142. (133) 60 220
115   Bearded hd. r., EPPI CF. R. Biga r. CF. *M. 312; V. 453; BMC —* 60 220

JOINT TYPES OF EPPILUS AND VERICA
SILVER

		F £	VF £

116   **Unit.** Head l. CO VIR in front. R. Victory, EP. *M. 307; V. 442;*
BMC 1133-34. (132)   125   400

117

117   Head r. VIR CO in front. R. Capricorn l. EPPI COMF. *M. 308/a; V. 443;*
BMC 1135-36. (132)   110   400

VERICA
(*c*.10.-*c*.40 A.D.)

The exact details of Verica's succession and relationship to Eppillus and Tincommius are not fully understood. However by c.10 A.D. it seems likely that Verica was the sole ruler of the southern region. His close contact with Rome, both political and economic, seen in the increasing use of classical designs on his coins, culminated in his flight to Rome in c.42 A.D. to seek assistance from Claudius.

GOLD

118   **Stater.** COM:F on tablet. R. Horseman r. holding spear, VIR below.
M. 109; V. 460; BMC 1143-44. (97)...   200   450
119   COM.F. on tablet, pellet in ring ornament above and below. R.
Similar to last. *M. 121; 461; BMC 1146-53. (97)*....................................   200   450

120   121

120   COM.F on tablet. R. Horseman r. holding spear, VIR above, REX below.
M. 121 var; V. 500; BMC 1155-58. (98)   150   325
121   Vine-leaf dividing VI RI. R. Horseman r. with shield and spear. COF in
field. *M. 125; V. 520-1; BMC 1159-73. (99)*   275   600
122   Similar, reads VE RI. *M. 125; V. 520-5/7; BMC 1174-76. (99)*..............   285   575
123   **Quarter Stater.** COMF on tablet. R. Horse l. VIR. *M. 111; V. 465;*
BMC 1177-78. (100)   110   200

124

124   COMF on tablet, pellet in ring ornament above and below R. Horse
r. VI. *M. 112; V. 466; BMC 1179-1206. (100)*   100   180

		F	VF
		£	£
125	COMF on tablet, pellet border. R. Horse r. VI above. *M. 113; V. 467;* *BMC 1207-16. (100)*	100	175

126

128

126	COM FILI. in two lines, scroll in between. R. Horse r. VIR(I) above. *M. 114; V. 468; BMC 1217-22. (100)*	140	280
127	VERI COMF, crescent above, star below. R. Horse r. REX below. *M. 122; V. 501; BMC 1223-36. (101)*	125	225
128	VERI beneath vine-leaf. R. Horseman r. with sword and shield, FRX in field. *M. 124; V. 525; BMC 1237-38. (102)*	250	650
129	COM, horseman r. R. Seated figure, VERICA around. *M. 126; V. 526; BMC 1239. (103)*	300	700
130	Similar to last. R. Laureate bust r., VIRI in front. *M. 127; V. 527; BMC 1240. (103)*	300	700

SILVER

131	**Unit.** COMF, crescent and or pellet in ring above and below. R. Boar r. VI(RI) below. *M. 115; V. 470/72; BMC 1241-1331. (104)*	30	85

132

133

132	VERICA COMMI F around pellet in ring. R. Lion r. REX below. *M. 123; V. 505; BMC 1332-1359. (105)*	40	120
133	COMMI F, horseman with shield r. R. VERI CA, mounted warrior with spear r. *M. 128; V. 530; BMC 1360-92. (106)*	40	125

134

137

134	Two cornucopiae, COMMI F. R. Figure seated r. VERICA. *M. 129; V. 531; BMC 1393-1419. (107)*	35	100
135	Bust r. VIRI. R. Figure seated l. *M. 130; V. 532; BMC 1420. (108)*	65	200
136	Naked figure l. R. Laureate bust r., COMMI F. *M. 131; V. 533; BMC 1421-49. (108)*	35	100
137	VERICA REX, bull r. R. Figure stg. l., COMMI F. *M. —; V. 506; BMC 1450-84. (108B)*	35	110
138	COMF, in tablet and scroll. R. Eagle facing, VI RI. *M. —; V. 471; BMC 1485-1505. (104A)*	30	90

		F	*VF*
		£	£
139	VIRIC across field,ornaments above and below. R. Pegasus r., star design below. *M. —; V. —; BMC —. (104B)*	55	175
140	Head r. Verica. R. COMMI F., eagle l. *M. 131A; V. 534; BMC —. (108A)*	65	200
141	**Minim.** COF in tablet, R. Facing head (Medusa?), VE below. *M. —; V. 384; BMC 1506.(94A). (Formerly attributed to Tincommius)*	60	160
142	Head r. R. Horse r., VIRICO. *M. 116; V. 480; BMC —. (109)*	45	110
143	Pellet and ring pattern. R. Lion r. VIR. *M. 120a/c; V. 484; BMC 1514-17. (109)*	35	110
144	VIRIC reversed. R. Boar r. *M. —; V. 485; BMC 1518*	40	110
145	Cross. R. Trident. *M. —; V. 486-1; BMC —-*	60	170
146	Uncertain. R. Boar r. *M. 120b; V. 510-1; BMC —. (109)*	40	110
147	Crescent cross. R. Boar r. *M. —; V. 510-5; BMC 1521-23. (109)*	50	130
148	VIR VAR in tablets. R. Winged horse r. CO. *M. 120d; V. 511; BMC 1507-12. (109)*	45	125

149   150

149	Vine-leaf, CFO. R. Horse r. VERI CA. *M. —; V. 550; BMC 1524-25*	50	135
150	CF in torc. R. Head r. VERIC. *M. 132; V. 551; BMC 1526-33. (111A)*	40	110
151	Altar, CF, R. Bulls head facing, VERICA. *M. 120e; V. 552; BMC 1534-37. (109)*	55	175
152	Temple, CF. R. Bull r, VER REX. *M. —; V. 553; BMC 1538-41*	45	125

153   154

153	Cornucopia, VER COM. R. Lion r. *M. —; V. 554; BMC 1542*	45	145
154	Two cornucopiae. R. Eagle l. *M. —; V. 555; BMC 1543-58*	40	100
155	Floral pattern, CF. R. Lion r. *M.—; V. 556; BMC 1559-63. (111E)*	50	135
156	Sphinx r., CF, R. dog curled up, VERI. *M. —; V. 557; BMC 1564-68. (109B)*	40	110
157	VERI. R. Urn, COMMI F. *M. —; V. 559; BMC —-*	45	125
158	A in star. R. Bird r. *M. 316; V. 561; BMC 1569-71*	50	130
159	Urn, Rex. R. Eagle r., VERRICA COMMI F. *M. —; V. 563; BMC 1572-78. (109C)*	40	135
160	VIR inside tablet. R. Boars head r. *M. 117; V. 564; BMC 1579-81. (109A)*	40	120
161	Cross. R. bull l. *M. —; V. —; BMC 1582*	45	125
162	Boars head r., CF, R. Eagle, VE. *M. —; V. —; BMC 1583-86*	40	110

163

163	Head r, COMM IF., R. Sphinx, R VE. *M. —; V. —; BMC 1587-89*	40	125

		F	VF
		£	£
164	A in tablet. R. Boar r. VI CO. *M. —; V. —; BMC 1590*	60	160
	The two following coins are possibly issues of Epatticus.		
165	Bull r. R. Eagle with snake l. *M. —; V. 512; BMC 2366-70*.......	35	100
166	Bust r. R. dog r. *M. —; V. 558; BMC 2371-74*	40	110

CANTII

The Cantii who gave their name to Kent, occupied a similar area to that of the modern county.
Caesar considered this the most civilised part of Britain and the early production of potin units in
Kent can be seen as an indicator of this. A number of Kentish rulers for whom we have coins, appear
to be dynasts from the two neighbouring kingdoms, who were involved in struggles to acquire
territory. Eppillus (see Atrebates and Regni) produced coins specifically for circulation in Kent and
like those of Cunobelin they circulated widely.

EARLY UNINSCRIBED
GOLD

167	**Stater.** Ly. Blank. R. Horse l. numerous ring ornaments in field.		
	M. 293; V. 142; BMC 2472. (34)	275	675
168	Blank. R. Horse r. numerous ornaments in field. *M. 294; V. 157;*		
	BMC— (34)	250	600

169

169	Lz. Blank. R. Horse l., box with cross hatching below. *M. 84, 292;*		
	V. 150, 144; BMC 2466-68. (35)	300	750

170   171

170	**Quarter Stater.** Ly. Blank. R. Horse r., pentagram below. *M. 285;*		
	V. 163; BMC 2473-74. (45)	100	200
171	Blank. R. Horse r., 'V' shape above. *M. 284; V. 170; BMC 2475-77. (45)*	100	200
172	Lz. Blank. R. Horse l., 'V' shape above. *M. 85; V. 151; BMC 2469-70. (47)*	100	220

SILVER

173	**Unit.** Curved star. R. Horse r. Pentagram below. *M. 272a; V. 164;*		
	BMC—. (56)	90	200
174	Serpent torc. R. Horse r., box with cross hatching below. *cf Mossop 8;*		
	BMC 2478	110	375
175	**Half Unit.** Spiral of three arms. R. Horse l. *M. —; V. —; BMC 2479*......	60	175

BRONZE

176   **Unit.** Various animal types, R. Various animal types. *M. 295-96,*
316a-d; V. 154/167; BMC 2480-91. (80/141-44) 70   250

DUBNOVELLAUNUS
(Late 1st Century B.C.)

Likely to be the same Dubnovellaunus recorded on coins in Essex (see Trinovantes / Catuvellauni).
The two coinages share the same denominational structure and have some stylistic similarities. It has
been suggested that Dubnovellaunus is the British king of that name mentioned along with
Tincommius as a client king in the Res Gestae of the Roman emperor Augustus.

GOLD

177

	F £	VF £

177   **Stater.** Blank. R. Horse r., bucranium above, serpent like object below,
DUBNOV[ELLAUNUS] or similar around. *M. 282; V. 169;*
BMC 2492-96. (118) 250   450
178   — R. Horse r., but without bucranium and with wheel below.
M. 283; V. 176; BMC 2497-98. (118) 300   700

SILVER

179   **Unit.** Winged animal r. R. Horse l., DVBNO. *M. 286; V. 171;*
BMC 2499-2501. (119) 110   265

180

180   Winged animal l. R. Seated fig. l., holding hammer, DVBNO.
M. 287; V. 178; BMC 2502-03. (119) 125   320

BRONZE

181   **Unit.** Horse r. R. Lion l., DVBN. *M. 290; V. 166; BMC 2504-06. (122).*   75   250
182   Boar l., DVBNO. R. Horseman r. *M. 291; V. 181; BMC 2507-08. (121).*   70
220
183   Boar r., DVBNO. R. Eagle facing. *M. 289; V. 180; BMC 2509-10. (121)*   70   220

VOSENOS
(Late 1st Century B.C./ Early 1st Century A.D.)
Little is known of this ruler who issued coins in a characteristically Kentish style similar to those of
Dubnovellaunus.

GOLD

		F	VF
		£	£
184	**Stater.** Blank. R. Horse l., bucranium above, serpent like object below., [VOSE]NOS. *M. 297; V. 184; BMC 2511-12. (123)*		*Extremely rare*

185

| 185 | **Quarter Stater.** Blank. R. Horse r., VOSI below. *M. 298; V. 185; BMC 2514-15. (124)* | 325 | 850 |

SILVER

| 186 | **Unit.** Horse and griffin. R. Horse r., retrograde legend. *M. 299a; V. 186; BMC —. (125)* | 175 | 450 |

"SA" or "SAM"
(Late 1st Century B.C./ Early 1st Century A.D.)
An historically unattested individual whose coins are stylistically associated with those of
Dubnovellaunus and Vosenos. His coins have been predominantly found in north Kent

SILVER
| 187 | **Unit.** Head l., R. Horse l., SA below. *M. —; V. —; BMC —* | 150 | 475 |

BRONZE
| 187A | **Unit.** Boar l., R. Horse l., SA below. *M. 299; V. 187; BMC 2516-19. (126)* | 125 | 300 |

187B

| 187B | Horse l., SAM below. R. Horse l., SAM below. *M. —; V. —; BMC —* ... | 125 | 300 |

AMMINUS

(Early 1st Century A.D.)

Issued a coinage stylistically distinct from other Kentish types and with strong affinities to those of Cunobelin. Indeed it has been suggested that he is the Adminius recorded by Suetonius, as a son of Cunobelin. The enigmatic legend DVN or DVNO may be an unknown mint site.

SILVER

188

	F £	VF £
188 **Unit.** Plant, AMMINIUS around. R. Winged horse r., DVN. *M. 313; V. 192; BMC 2522-23. (136)*	140	350

190

190 A in wreath. R. Capricorn r., S AM. *M. 314; V. 194; BMC 2520-21. (137)*	140	300

BRONZE

189

189 AM in wreath. R. Horse r., DVNO. *M. —; V. 193; BMC — —*	160	325
191 **Unit.** Head r. R. Hippocamp r., AM. *M. 315; V. 195; BMC 2524. (139)*.	90	285

TRINOVANTES AND CATUVELLAUNI

Occupying the broad area of Essex, southern Suffolk, Bedfordshire, Buckinghamshire, Hertfordshire, parts of Oxfordshire, Cambridgeshire and Northamptonshire, they are likely to have been two separate tribes for most of their history. The Trinovantes were originally located in the eastern half of this area, with their main centre at Camulodunum (Colchester). The original Catuvellauni heartland being further west, with their main centre at Verulamium (St.Albans). The whole area eventually came under the control of Cunobelin at the end of the period.

TRINOVANTES

ADDEDOMAROS

(Late 1st Century B.C.)

Unknown to history he appears to have been a contemporary of Tasciovanus. The design of his staters is based on the Whaddon Chase type (No.32) which circulated widely in this region.

GOLD

200

		F	VF
		£	£
200	**Stater.** Crossed wreath. R. Horse r., wheel below, AθθDIIDOM above. *M. 266; V. 1605; BMC 2390-94. (148)*	165	400

201   202

201	Six armed spiral. R. Horse r., cornucopia below, AθθDIIDOM above. *M. 267; V. 1620; BMC 2396-2404. (148)*	130	275
202	Two opposed crescents. R. Horse r., branch below, spiral or wheel above, AθθDIIDOM. *M. 268; V. 1635; BMC 2405-2415. (149)*	165	425
203	**Quarter Stater.** Circular flower pattern. R. Horse r. *M. 271; V. 1608; BMC 2416. (44)*	150	350
204	Cross shaped flower pattern. R. Horse r. *M. 270; V. 1623; BMC 2417-21. (44)*	125	275
205	Two opposed crescents. R. Horse r., AθθDIIDOM around. *M. 269; V. 1638; BMC 2422-24. (150)*	175	450

BRONZE

206	**Unit.** Head l. R. Horse l. *M. 274; V. 1615/46 BMC 2450-60. (77)*	40	95

DUBNOVELLAUNUS
(Late 1st Century B.C./ Early 1st Century A.D.)

Dubnovellaunus is likely to have been the successor to Addedomaros, with whom his coins are stylistically related. It is not clear if he was the same Dubnovellaunus who also issued coins in Kent (see Cantii) or if he is the same Dumnobeallaunos mentioned in the Res Gestae of the emperor Augustus c.AD14.

GOLD

207 208

		F £	VF £
207	**Stater.** Two crescents on wreath. R. Horse l., leaf below, pellet in ring, DVBNOVAIIAVNOS above. *M. 275; V. 1650; BMC 2425-40. (152)*....	200	475
208	**Quarter Stater.** Similar. *M. 276; V. 1660; BMC 2442. (153)*.................	135	260

SILVER

209	Unit. Head l., DVBNO. R. Winged horse r., lattice box below. *M. 288; V. 165; BMC 2443-44. (120)*	125	260
210	Head l., legend ?, R. Horse l. DVB[NOV]. *M. 278; V. 1667; BMC 2445. (154)*	50	120

BRONZE

211	**Unit.** Head l., R. Horse l., DVBNO above. *M. 281; V. 1669; BMC 2446-48. (154)*	45	130
212	Head r., R. Horse l. *M. 277; V. 1665; BMC 2461-65. (154)*...................	45	100

DIRAS
(Late 1st Century B.C./ Early 1st Century A.D.)

An historically unattested ruler, responsible for a gold stater related stylistically to Dubnovellaunus's.

GOLD

213	**Stater.** Blank. R. Horse r., DIRAS? above, yoke like object above. *M. 279; V. 162; BMC 2449. (151)*	*Extremely rare*

CATUVELLAUNI

TASCIOVANUS

(Late 1st Century B.C./ Early 1st Century A.D.)

The early gold coins of Tasciovanus like those of his contemporary Addedomaros are based on the Whaddon Chase stater. Verulamium (St.Albans) appears to have been his principal mint, appearing as VER or VERL on the coinage. Staters and quarter staters inscribed CAM (Camulodunum/Colchester) are known and perhaps suggest brief or weak control of the territory to the east. The later coins of Tasciovanus use increasingly Romanised designs. The adoption of the title RICON, perhaps a Celtic equivalent to the Latin REX (King), can be seen as a parallel move to that of his contemporary Tincommius to the south.

GOLD

214   217

		F £	VF £
214	**Stater.** Crescents in wreath. R. TASCIAV and bucranium over horse r. *M. 149; V. 1680; BMC 1591-1603. (157)*	250	500
215	— R. Similar reads TAXCIAV. *M. 150; V. 1682; BMC 1604-05. (157)*.	265	550
216	— R. Similar reads TASCIOVAN above, CAM below. *M. 186/a; V. 1684; BMC 1606-07. (160)*	375	850
217	— R. Horseman r. helmeted and with carnyx, TASC in field. *M. 154-55/57; V. 1730-32; BMC 1608-1613. (158)*	240	500
218	Crescents in wreath, with V or VER in design. R. Similar to last. *M. 156-57; V. 1734-35; BMC 1623-24. (158)*	275	600

219   221

		F £	VF £
219	TASCIO(V) RICON in panel. R. Horseman l., wearing armour and holding sword and shield. *M. 184; V. 1780; BMC 1628-36. (161)*	475	1250
220	**Quarter Stater.** Floral design. R. Horse r. *M. —; V. —; BMC 1638-39*.	190	425
221	Crossed Wreath. R. Horse l. *M. 151; V. 1688; BMC 1651-53. (44)*	120	225
222	— R. Horse r., CAM. *M. 187; V. 1694; BMC 1640. (164)*	200	425
223	Similar, TASCI in wreath. R. Horse r., TASC. *M. 153; V. 1692; BMC 1641. (163)*	120	250

224 226

		F £	VF £
224	Similar, VERO in wreath. R. Horse l., TAS. *M. 152; V. 1690; BMC 1642-43. (163)*	200	400
225	TASCIO on tablet. R. Horse l. *M. 195; V. 1848; BMC 1646. (166)*	165	350
226	TASC on tablet. R. Horse l. *M. 185; V. 1786; BMC 1647-50. (165)*	100	200

SILVER

227	**Unit.** Head l. R. Horse r. *M. —; V. 1698; BMC 1654*	60	135
228	Cross and box. R. Horse r., VER in front. *M. —; V. —; BMC 1655*	70	185
229	Cross and crescent. R. Horse l., TASCI. *M. —; V. —; BMC 1665-57*	65	175
230	Bearded head l. R. Horseman r., TASCIO. *M. 158; V. 1745; BMC 1667-68. (167)*	70	225
231	Winged horse l., TAS. R. Griffin r., within circle of pellets. *M. 159; V. 1790; BMC 1660. (168)*	70	200
232	Eagle stg. l., TASCIA. R. Griffin r. *M. 160; V. 1792; BMC 1658-59. (169)*	75	225
233	VER in beaded circle. R. Horse r., TASCIA. *M. 161; V. 1699; BMC 1670-73. (170)*	75	225
234	— R. Naked horseman. *M. 162; V. 1747; BMC 1674-76. (171)*	100	245

235 238 242

235	Laureate hd. r., TASCIA. R. Bull l. *M. 163; V. 1794; BMC 1681-82. (172)*	70	190
236	Cross and box, VERL. R. Boar r. TAS. *M. 164; V. 1796; BMC 1661-62. (173)*	75	250
237	TASC in panel. R. Winged horse l. *M. 165; V. 1798; BMC 1664-65. (174)*	65	150
238	— R. Horseman l., carrying long shield. *M. 166; V. 1800; BMC 1677-79. (174)*	65	150
239	Two crescents. R. Winged griffin, VIR. *M. —; V. —; BMC 1666*	75	225
240	Head r., TAS?. R. Horseman r. *M. —; V. —; BMC 1669*	70	200

BRONZE

241

241	**Double Unit.** Head r., TASCIA, VA. R. Horseman r. *M. 178; V. 1818; BMC 1685-87. (190)*	150	475

	F £	VF £
242 **Unit.** Two heads in profile, one bearded. R. Ram l., TASC. *M. 167; V. 1705; BMC 1711-13. (178)*	70	200
243 Bearded head r. VER(L). R. Horse l., VIIR or VER. *M. 168; V. 1707; BMC 1714-21. (179)*	55	175
244 Bearded head r. R. Horse l., TAS. *M. 169; V. 1709; BMC 1722-23. (179)*	65	190
245 Head r., TASC. R. Winged horse l., VER. *M. 170; V. 1711; BMC 1688-89. (180)*	60	185
246 — R. Horseman r., holding carnyx, VIR. *M. 171; V. 1750; BMC 1724-27. (182)*	65	190

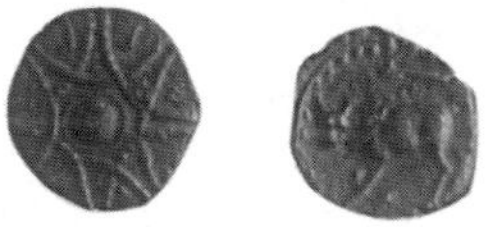

247

	F £	VF £
247 VERLAMIO between rays of star. R. Bull l. *M. 172; V. 1808; BMC 1745-51. (183)*	60	185
248 Similar without legend. R. Bull r. *M. 174; V. 1810; BMC 1752-55. (185)*	55	175
249 Similar. R. Horse l., TASCI. *M. 175; V. 1812; BMC 1709-10. (186)*	60	185
250 Head r., TASCIO. R. Lion r., TA SCI. *M. 176; V. 1814; BMC 1736-38. (188)*	55	175
251 Head r. R. Figure std. l., VER below. *M. 177; V. 1816; BMC 1739-44. (189)*	65	200
252 Cross and Crescents. R. Boar r., VER. *M. 179; V. 1713; BMC 1702-05. (191)*	65	200
253 Laureate head r. R. Horse l., VIR. *M. 180; V. 1820; BMC 1706-08. (192)*	60	185
254 Raised band across centre, VER or VERL below. R. Horse grazing r. *M. 183a; V. 1717; BMC —. (193)*	75	250
255 **Fractional Unit.** Animal r. R. Sphinx l. *M. 181; V. 1824; BMC 1760-61. (198)*	65	160
256 Head l., VER. R. Goat r. *M. 182; V. 1715; BMC 1765-68. (199)*	40	130
257 Head r. R. Boar r, *M. 183; V. 1826; BMC 1762-64. (199)*	40	130
258 Head l. R. Animal with curved tail. *M. 183b, c; V. 1822; BMC 1759. (200)*	40	125

ASSOCIATES OF TASCIOVANUS

(Early 1st Century A.D.)

Towards the end of his reign, a number of joint issues bearing his name and the name of either Sego or Dias appear. In addition coins similar in style to those of Tasciovanus appear with either the name Andoco or Rues. It has been suggested that these issues belong to a period of struggle following the death of Tasciovanus and are all rival contestants for the throne. Another theory is that they are associates or sub-kings of Tasciovanus responsible for areas within the wider territory.

SEGO

GOLD

259

	F £	VF £

259   **Stater.** TASCIO in tablet, annulets above. R. Horseman with carnyx r., SEGO. *M. 194; V. 1845; BMC 1625-27. (162)* .... *Extremely rare*

SILVER

260

260   **Unit.** SEGO on panel. R. Horseman r. *M. 196; V. 1851; BMC 1684. (176)*   160   525

BRONZE

261   **Unit.** Star shaped pattern. R. Winged sphinx l., SEGO. *M. 173; V. 1855; BMC 1690. (184)*...   110   375

ANDOCO

GOLD

262

262   **Stater.** Crescents in wreath. R. Bucranium over horse r., AND below. *M. 197; V. 1860; BMC 2011-14. (202)*......................................   500   1250

	F £	VF £
263 **Quarter Stater.** Crossed wreaths, ANDO in angles. R. Horse l. *M. 198;* *V. 1863; BMC 2015-17. (203)*	135	375

SILVER

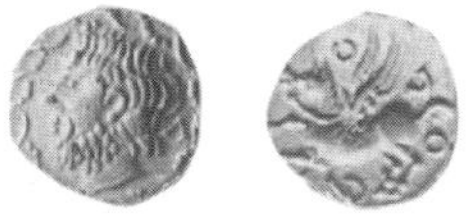

264

| 264 **Unit.** Bearded head l. R. Winged horse l., ANDOC. *M. 199; V. 1868;*
BMC 2018. (204).. | 135 | 325 |

BRONZE

265

| 265 **Unit.** Head r., ANDOCO. R. Horse r., ANDOCO. *M. 200; V. 1871;*
BMC 2019-20. (205) .... | 65 | 175 |
| 266 Head r., TAS ANDO. R. Horse r. *M. 175a; V. 1873; BMC* —. *(187)* ...... | 80 | 235 |

DIAS
SILVER

267    268

| 267 **Unit.** Saltire over cross within square. R. Boar r., TASC DIAS.
M. —; *V.* —; *BMC 1663. (173A)*... | 150 | 425 |
| 268 DIAS CO, in star. R. Horse l., VIR. *M. 188; V. 1877; BMC 1683. (177).* | 125 | 325 |

BRONZE

269

| 269 **Unit.** Bearded head r., DIAS TASC. R. Centaur r., playing pan pipes.
M. 192; V. 1882; BMC 1728-35. (197)... | 100 | 275 |

RUES
BRONZE

		F	VF
		£	£
270	**Unit.** Lion r., RVII. R. Eagle. *M. 189; V. 1890; BMC 1691. (194)*.........	120	300
271	— R. Similar reads RVE. *M. 189; V. 1890-3; BMC 1692. (194)*.............	110	290

272   273

272	Bearded head r., RVIIS. R. Horseman r., VIR. *M. 190; V. 1892;* *BMC 1698-1701. (195)*	125	325
273	RVIIS on tablet. R. Winged sphinx l. *M. 191; V. 1895;* *BMC 1693-97. (196)*	120	300
274	**Fractional Unit.** Annulet within square with curved sides. R. Eagle l., RVII. *M. 193; V. 1903; BMC 1756-58. (201)*..........................	100	275

CUNOBELIN
(Early 1st Century A.D. to *c*.40 A.D.)

Styled as son of Tasciovanus on some of his coins, Cunobelin appears to have ruled over the unified territories of the Trinovantes and Catuvellauni, with additional territory in Kent. His aggressive policy of expansion that involved members of family eventually lead to Roman concern over the extent of his power. Following his death just prior to 43 AD, the emperor Claudius took the decision to invade Britain.

During his long reign an extensive issue of gold, silver and bronze coins used ever increasingly Romanised designs. It has been estimated from a study of known dies that around one million of his gold corn ear staters were produced. His main centre and mint was at Camulodunum (Colchester) appearing as the mint signature CAMV. The names SOLIDV and AGR appear on a few coins associated with Cunobelin and are likely to represent personal names.

GOLD

280   281

280	**Stater.** Biga type. CAMVL on panel. R. Two horses l., wheel below, CVNOBELIN. *M. 201; V. 1910; BMC 1769-71. (207)*............................	650	1500
281	Linear type. Corn ear dividing CA MV. R. Horse r., branch above., CVN. *M. 210; V. 1925; BMC 1772-76. (208)*	200	415
282	— Similar, privy mark 'x' above a letter in *obv.* legend. *M. 210a; VA 1925-3/5; BMC 1777-81. (208)*..	210	450

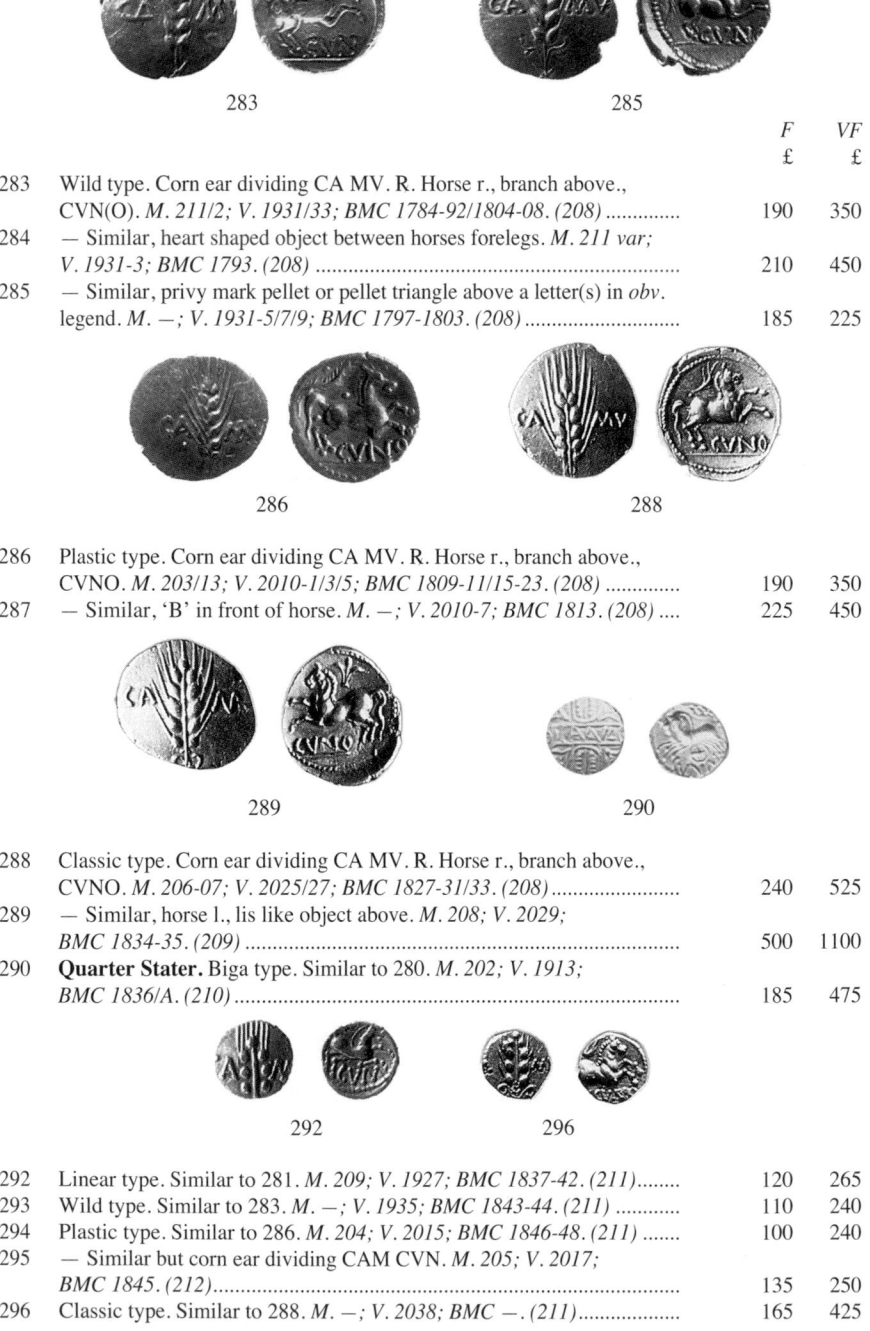

283   285

		F £	VF £
283	Wild type. Corn ear dividing CA MV. R. Horse r., branch above., CVN(O). *M. 211/2; V. 1931/33; BMC 1784-92/1804-08. (208)*	190	350
284	— Similar, heart shaped object between horses forelegs. *M. 211 var; V. 1931-3; BMC 1793. (208)*	210	450
285	— Similar, privy mark pellet or pellet triangle above a letter(s) in *obv.* legend. *M. —; V. 1931-5/7/9; BMC 1797-1803. (208)*	185	225

286   288

286	Plastic type. Corn ear dividing CA MV. R. Horse r., branch above., CVNO. *M. 203/13; V. 2010-1/3/5; BMC 1809-11/15-23. (208)*	190	350
287	— Similar, 'B' in front of horse. *M. —; V. 2010-7; BMC 1813. (208)*	225	450

289   290

288	Classic type. Corn ear dividing CA MV. R. Horse r., branch above., CVNO. *M. 206-07; V. 2025/27; BMC 1827-31/33. (208)*	240	525
289	— Similar, horse l., lis like object above. *M. 208; V. 2029; BMC 1834-35. (209)*	500	1100
290	**Quarter Stater.** Biga type. Similar to 280. *M. 202; V. 1913; BMC 1836/A. (210)*	185	475

292   296

292	Linear type. Similar to 281. *M. 209; V. 1927; BMC 1837-42. (211)*	120	265
293	Wild type. Similar to 283. *M. —; V. 1935; BMC 1843-44. (211)*	110	240
294	Plastic type. Similar to 286. *M. 204; V. 2015; BMC 1846-48. (211)*	100	240
295	— Similar but corn ear dividing CAM CVN. *M. 205; V. 2017; BMC 1845. (212)*	135	250
296	Classic type. Similar to 288. *M. —; V. 2038; BMC —. (211)*	165	425

SILVER

299

		F £	VF £

299 **Unit.** Two bull headed serpents, inter twined. R. Horse l., CVNO.
M. 214; V. 1947; BMC 1856. (213) 100 375
300 Curled serpent inside wheel. R. Winged horse l., CVN. M. —; V. —;
BMC 1857 .... 90 325
301 CVN on panel R. Horse l., (C)M. M. 255; V. 1949; BMC 1858-59. (228) 80 240
302 CVNO BELI on two panels. R. CVN below horseman r. M. 216/7;
V. 1951/53; BMC 1862. (215).. 70 210
303 Head l., CAMVL. R. CVNO beneath Victory std. r. M. 215; V. 2045;
BMV 1863-65. (214) 85 240

304 305

304 Two leaves dividing CVN. R. Horseman r., CAM. M. 218; V. 2047;
BMC 1866-67. (216) 100 350
305 Flower dividing CAMV. R. CVNO below horse r. M. 219; V. 2049;
BMC1867A. (217) 90 275
306 CVNO on panel. R. CAMV on panel below griffin. M. 234; V. 2051;
BMC 1868-69. (218) 85 250
307 CAMVL on panel. R. CVNO below centaur l. carrying palm. M. 234a;
V. 1918; BMC —. (219) 80 240
308 CAMVL on panel. R. Figure seated l. holding wine amphora, CVNOBE.
M. —; V. —; BMC —. (219A) 85 275
309 Plant, CVNOBELINVS. R. Figure stg. r. holding club and thunderbolt
dividing CA MV. M. —; V .—; BMC 1897. (219B) 90 275
310 Laur. hd. r., CVNOBELINVS. R. Winged horse springing l., CAMV
below. M. —; V. —; BMC —. (219C).. 90 275
311 CVNO on panel, wreath around. R. Winged horse r., TASC F. M. 235;
V. 2053; BMC 1870. (220)... 80 240

312 313

312 Head r., CVNOBELINI. R. Horse r., TASCIO. M. 236; V. 2055;
BMC 1871-73. (221) 70 225
313 Winged bust r., CVNO. R. Sphinx std. l., TASCIO. M. 237; V. 2057;
BMC 1874-78. (222) 60 140

314   316

		F £	VF £
314	Draped female fig. r., TASCIIOVAN. R. Figure std. r. playing lyre, tree behind. *M. 238; V. 2059; BMC 1879-82. (223)*	80	250
315	Figure stg. l., holding club and lionskin., CVNO. R. Female rider r., TASCIOVA. *M. 239; V. 2061; BMC 1884-85. (224)*	70	200
316	Female head r., CVNOBELINVS. R. Victory r., TASCIO(VAN). *M. —; V. —; BMC 1883. (224A)*	75	225
317	Fig. r. carrying dead animal, CVNOBELINVS. R. Fig. stg. holding bow, dog at side, TASCIIOVANI. *M. 240; V. 2063; BMC 1886-88. (225)*	90	275
318	CVNO on panel, horn above, dolphin below. R. Fig. stg. r. altar behind. *M. 241/41a; V. 2065; BMC 1889-90. (226)*	90	275

319

		F £	VF £
319	CVN on panel. R. Fig. holding club walking r., CVN. *M. 254; V. 2067; BMC 1891-92. (227)*	80	240
320	CVN in wreath. R. CAM, dog? trampling on serpent r. *M. 256; V. 2069; BMC 1893. (229)*	100	300
321	Winged horse l., CVN. R. Std. fig. r. *M. 258; V. 2071; BMC 1896. (230)*	90	275
322	CVNO in angles of cross. R. Capricorn r., CVNO. *M. —; V. —; BMC 1898*	95	285

BRONZE

		F £	VF £
323	Head l., CVNO. R. Boar l., branch above. *M. 220; V. 1969; BMC—. (232)*	40	175
324	CVNOB ELINI in two panels. R. Victory std. l., TASC. *M. 221; V. 1971; BMC 1921-27. (233)*	40	120
325	Winged horse l., CAM. R. Winged Victory stg l., CVN. *M. 222; V. 1973; BMC 1938-43. (234)*	35	140

326

		F £	VF £
326	Bearded head facing R. Boar l., CVN. *M.223; V.1963; BMC 1904-05. (235)*	35	165
327	Ram-headed animal coiled up in double ornamental circle. R. Animal l., CAM. *M. 224; V. 1965; BMC —. (236)*	70	200
328	Griffin r., CAMV. R. Horse r., CVN. *M. 225; V. 2081; BMC 1909-12. (237)*	35	150

		F £	VF £
329	Bearded head l., CAMV. R. CVN or CVNO below horse l. *M. 226, 229; V. 2085/2131; BMC 1900-01. (238)*	35	140
330	Laureate head r., CVNO. R. CVN below bull butting l. *M. 227; V. 2083; BMC 1902-03. (239)*	40	175
331	Crude head r., CVN. R. Figure stg. l., CVN. *M. 228; V. 2135; BMC —. (240)*	40	175

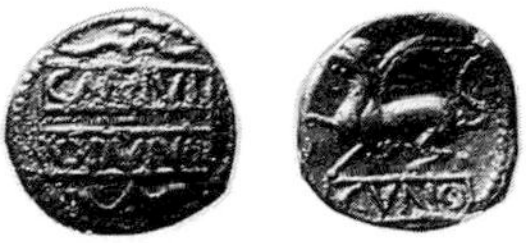

332

		F £	VF £
332	CAMVL / ODVNO in two panels. R. CVNO beneath sphinx crouching l. *M. 230; V. 1977; BMC 1928-30. (241)*	35	150
333	Winged horse l., CAMV. R. Victory stg. r. divides CV NO. *M. 231; V. 1979; BMC 1931-34. (242)*	40	140
334	Victory walking r. R. CVN below, horseman r. *M. 232; V. 1981; BMC 1935. (243)*	50	165
335	Head l., CAM. R. CVNO below eagle. *M. 233; V. 2087; BMC —. (244)*	40	170

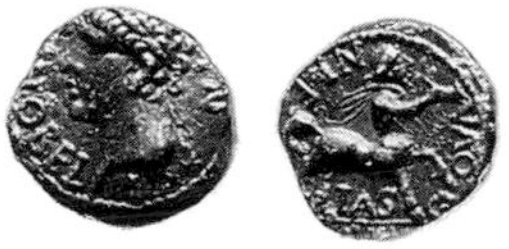

336 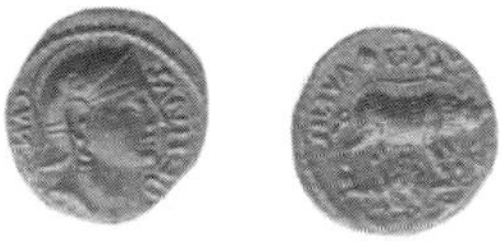   337

		F £	VF £
336	Head l., CVNOBELINI. R. Centaur r., TASCIOVANI.F. *M. 242; V. 2089; BMC 1968-71. (245)*	30	120
337	Helmeted bust r. R. TASCIIOVANII above, sow stg. r., F below. *M. 243; V. 2091; BMC 1956-60. (246)*	40	120
338	Horseman galloping r. holding dart and shield, CVNOB. R. Warrior stg. l., TASCIIOVANTIS. *M. 244; V. 2093; BMC 1961-67. (247)*	30	110

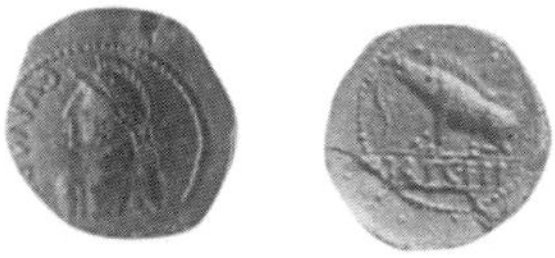

339

		F £	VF £
339	Helmeted bust l., CVOBELINVS REX. R. TASC FIL below boar l., std. on haunches. *M. 245; V. 1983; BMC 1952-55. (248)*	50	180
340	Bare head r., CVNOBELINVS REX. R. TASC below bull butting r. *M. 246; V. 2095; BMC 1944-51. (249)*	40	120
341	Bare head l., CVNO. R. TASC below bull stg. r. *M. 247; V. 1985; BMC —. (250)*	35	150

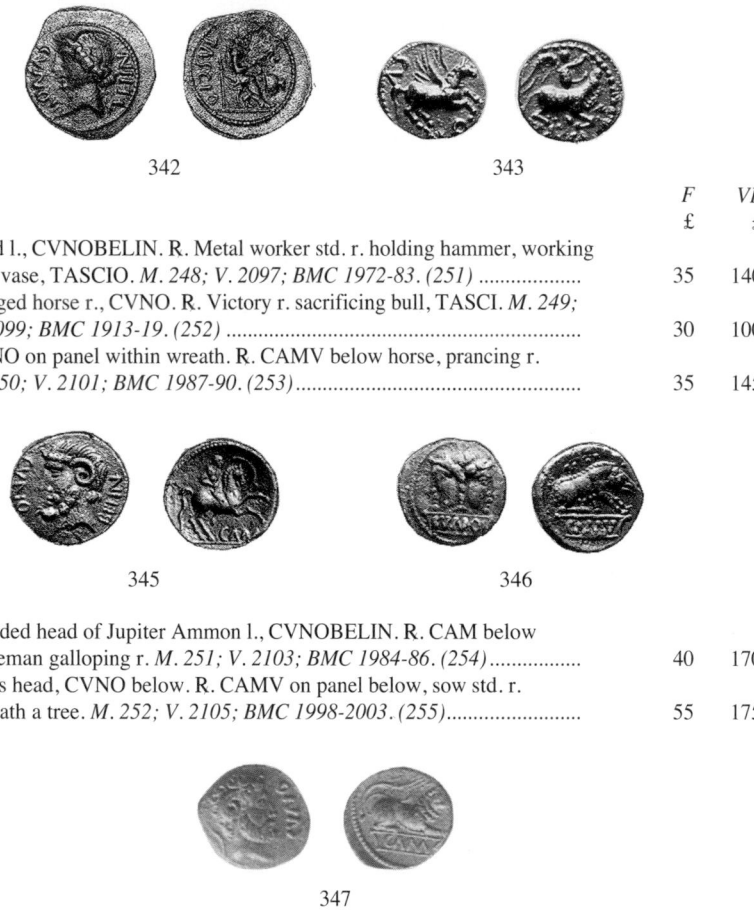

342   343

	F £	VF £
342 Head l., CVNOBELIN. R. Metal worker std. r. holding hammer, working on a vase, TASCIO. *M. 248; V. 2097; BMC 1972-83. (251)*	35	140
343 Winged horse r., CVNO. R. Victory r. sacrificing bull, TASCI. *M. 249; V. 2099; BMC 1913-19. (252)*	30	100
344 CVNO on panel within wreath. R. CAMV below horse, prancing r. *M. 250; V. 2101; BMC 1987-90. (253)*	35	145

345   346

345 Bearded head of Jupiter Ammon l., CVNOBELIN. R. CAM below horseman galloping r. *M. 251; V. 2103; BMC 1984-86. (254)*	40	170
346 Janus head, CVNO below. R. CAMV on panel below, sow std. r. beneath a tree. *M. 252; V. 2105; BMC 1998-2003. (255)*	55	175

347

347 Bearded head of Jupiter Ammon r., CVNOB. R. CAM on panel below lion crouched r. *M. 253; V. 2107; BMC 1991-97. (256)*	45	140
348 Sphinx r., CVNO. R. Fig stg. l. divides CA M. *M. 260; V. 2109; BMC 2004-09. (257)*	40	170
349 Horse r. R. CVN below horseman r. *M. 261; V. 1987; BMC 1936-47. (258)*	60	180
350 Animal l. looking back. R. CVN below horse l. *M. 233a; V. 1967; BMC— . (259)*	70	190
350A Ship, CVN below. R. Fig. r. dividing S E. *M. —; V. 1989; BMC 2010.* ..	110	350

"SOLIDV"

SILVER

351

F	*VF*
£	£

351   **Unit.** SOLIDV in centre of looped circle. R, Stg. fig. l., CVNO.
M. 259; V. 2073; BMC 1894-95. (231)..   175   475

"AGR"

GOLD

352   Quarter Stater. Corn ear dividing CAM CVN. R. Horse r., branch
above., AGR below *M. —; V. —; BMC 1854*..   250   675

353

353   — R. Horse r., branch above., cross and A below. *M. —; V. —;*
BMC 1855..   240   600

SILVER

354   **Unit.** AGR inside wreath. R. Female dog r., AGR below. *M. —; V. —;*
BMC 1899..   170   525

EPATICCUS
(1st Half 1st Century A.D.)

Epaticcus styled as a son of Tasciovanus on his coins, was most probably a brother of Cunobelin. The corn ear employed on his staters is similar to that of his brother's produced at Colchester. His coins appear in northern Atrebatic territory and conform to the area's denominational structure. It seems likely that Epaticcus's coinage reflects an incursion into Atrebatic territory by the Trinovantian/Catuvellaunian dynasty.

GOLD

355

355   **Stater.** Corn ear dividing TAS CIF. R. Horseman r., with spear and
shield. EPATI. *M. 262; V. 575; BMC 2021-23. (112)*..............................   *Extremely rare*

SILVER

356   357

		F £	VF £
356	**Unit.** Head of Hercules r., EPAT(I). R. Eagle stg. on snake. *M. 263/a; V. 580; BMC 2024-2268/2270-76. (113)*	25	60
357	Victory seated r. TASCIOV. R. Boar r., EPAT. *M. 263; V. 581; BMC 2294-2328. (114)*	35	85

358

358	Bearded head l., TASCIO. R. EPATI below lion r. *M. —; V. 582; BMC 2329*	110	300
359	EPATI inside panel. R. Lion r. *M. —; V. 583; BMC 2330. (114A)*	110	300

360   361

360	**Minim.** EPATI. R. Boars head r., TA. *M. 264; V. 585; BMC 2331-46. (115)*	50	110
361	TA inside star. R. Winged horse r., EPA below. *M. —; V. 560; BMC 2351-57. (116)*	60	130
362	Helmeted head r. R. Horse r., E below. *M. —; V. —; BMC 2358-63*	65	145
363	EPATI. R. Winged horse r., cross below. *M. —; V .—; BMC 2365*	65	165

CARATACUS
(1st Half 1st Century A.D.)

Coins inscribed CARA have been traditionally associated with the historically attested son of Cunobelin, Caratacus the leader of British resistance against Rome. His coins appear in the same area as those of Epaticcus and he may have been his successor.

SILVER

364   364A

364	**Unit.** Head of Hercules r., CARA. R. Eagle stg. on snake. *M. 265; V. 593; BMC 2376-84. (117)*	125	265
364A	**Minim.** CARA around pellet in ring. R. Winged horse r. *M. —; V. 595; BMC 2385-89. (117A)*	90	250

DUROTRIGES

(Mid 1st Century B.C. to Mid 1st Century A.D.)

The Durotriges inhabited West Hampshire, Dorset and adjoining parts of Somerset and Wiltshire. Their coinage is one of the most distinctive in Britain due to its rapid debasement. The disappearance of precious metals from the coinage should perhaps be linked to the declining trade between the south-west and western Gaul, following the Roman conquest of the Gaul. Hengistbury Head is the probable mint site of the cast bronzes. Coins inscribed CRAB have been traditionally associated with the tribe.

UNINSCRIBED

SILVER

		F £	VF £
365	**Stater.** White Gold type. Derived from Westerham stater (no. 21). *M. 317; V. 1235, 52, 54, 55; BMC 2525-2731. (60)*	70	165

366

368

366	Silver type. Similar. *M. 317; V. 1235, 52, 54, 55; BMC 2525-2731. (60)*	50	100
367	Billon type. Similar. *M. 317; V. 1235, 52, 54, 55; BMC 2525-2731. (60)*	30	65
368	**Quarter Stater.** Geometric type. Crescent design. R. Zig-zag pattern. *M. 319; V. 1242/29; BMC 2734-79. (61). Quality of metal varies, obv. almost blank on later issues*	40	110

369

369	Starfish type. Spiral. R. Zig-zag pattern. *M. 320; V. 1270; BMC 2780-81 (61A)*	60	135
370	Hampshire Thin Flan type. Crude head of lines and pellets. R. Stylised horse l. *M. 321; V. 1280; BMC 2782-87. (62)*	70	140

BRONZE

371	**Stater.** Struck Bronze type. Similar to No.365-67. *M. 318; V. 1290; BMC 2790-2859. (81)*	20	45

372

		F £	VF £
372	Cast Bronze type. Many varities, as illustration. *M. 322-70;* *V. 1322-70; BMC 2860-2936. (82)*	30	75

"CRAB"

SILVER

373

373	**Unit.** CRAB in angles of cross. R. Eagle. *M. 371; V. 1285;* *BMC 2788. (145)*	*Extremely rare*
373A	**Minim.** CRAB on tablet. R. Star shape. *M. 372; V. 1286; BMC 2789.* *(146)*	*Extremely rare*

DOBUNNI
(Mid 1st Century B.C. to Mid 1st Century A.D.)

Dobunnic territory stretched over Gloucestershire, Hereford and Worcester and into parts of Somerset, Wiltshire and Gwent. The earliest Dobunnic coins are developed from the British Q stater, and have the distinctive tree-like motif of the tribe on the obverse. The inscribed coinage is difficult to arrange chronologically and it may be that some of the rulers named held different parts of the territory simultaneously.

UNINSCRIBED
GOLD

374	**Stater.** Plain except for tree-like object. R. Three tailed horse r., wheel below. *M. 374; V. 1005; BMC 2937-40. (43)*	275	600
375	**Quarter Stater.** Plain with traces of wreath pattern. R. Horse r. *M. 68; V. 1010-3; BMC 2942-46. (52)*	135	275
376	Wreath pattern. R. Horse l., pellet in ring motifs in field. *M. 74; V. 1015; BMC 2949. (51)*	125	275

SILVER

377   378

377 **Unit.** Allen types A-F/I-J. Regular series. Head r. R. Triple-tailed horse
l. or r. *M. 374a, b/75/76, 378a-384; V. 1020/45/49/74/78/95/1135/1137;
BMC 2950-3011. (63-64). Style becomes progressively more abstract,
from-* 30 80
378 Allen types L-O. Irregular series. Similar to last. *M. 377-384d;
V. 1170-85; BMC 3012-22. (63-64)* 40 95

INSCRIBED
The following types are not arranged chronologically.

ANTED
GOLD

379 **Stater.** Dobunnic emblem. R. ANTED or ANTEDRIG over triple
tailed horse r., wheel below. *M. 385-86; V. 1062-69;
BMC 3023-3031. (260)* 300 625

SILVER

380 **Unit.** Crude head r. R. ANTED over horse. *M. 387; V. 1082;
BMC 3032-38. (261)* 80 175

EISV
GOLD

381

381 **Stater.** Dobunnic emblem. R. EISV or EISVRIG over triple tailed horse
r., wheel below. *M. 388; V. 1105; BMC 3039-42. (262)* 475 1100

SILVER

382

382 **Unit.** Crude head r. R. Horse l., EISV. *M. 389; V. 1110;
BMC 3043-55. (263)* 65 150

INAM or INARA

GOLD

		F £	VF £
383	**Stater.** Dobunnic emblem. R. INAM or INARA over triple tailed horse r., wheel below. *M. 390; V. 1140; BMC 3056. (264)*	*Extremely rare*	

CATTI

GOLD

384

384	**Stater.** Dobunnic emblem. R. CATTI over triple tailed horse r., wheel below. *M. 391; V. 1130; BMC 3057-60. (265)*	250	525

COMUX

GOLD

385	**Stater.** Dobunnic emblem. R. COMVX retrograde, over triple tailed horse r., wheel below. *M. 392; V. 1092; BMC 3061-63. (266)*	650	1450

CORIO

GOLD

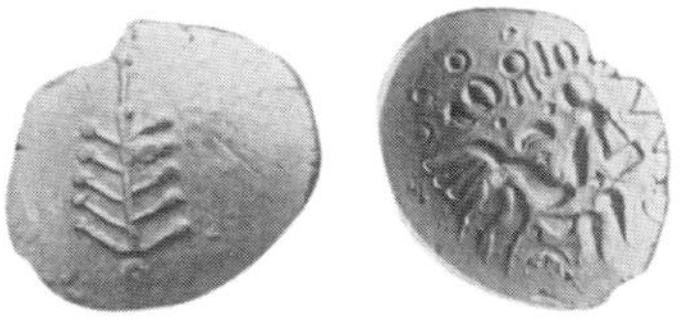

386  387

386	**Stater.** Dobunnic emblem. R. CORIO over triple tailed horse r., wheel below. *M. 393; V. 1035; BMC 3064-3133. (267)*	375	675
387	**Quarter Stater.** COR in centre. R. Horse r., without legend. *M. 394; V. 1039; BMC 3134. (268)*	550	1200

BODVOC

GOLD

	388		389	

		F £	VF £
388	**Stater.** BODVOC across field. R. Horse r., without legend. *M. 395; V. 1052; BMC 3135-42. (269)*	650	1350

SILVER

389	**Unit.** Head l., BODVOC. R. Horse r., without legend. *M. 396; V. 1057; BMC 3143-45. (270)*	125	270

CORIELTAUVI

The Corieltauvi formerly known as the Coritani, occupied Lincolnshire and adjoining parts of Yorkshire, Northamptonshire, Leicestershire and Nottinghamshire. The earliest staters, the South Ferriby type, are developed from Gallo-Belgic C staters, and are associated with the silver Boar/Horse types. The distinctive dish shaped scyphate coinages have no parallels in Britain and stand apart from the main series. The later inscribed issues present a complex system of inscriptions. It has been suggested that some of the later inscriptions refer to pairs of names, possibly joint rulers or moneyers and rulers.

EARLY UNINSCRIBED
(Mid to Late 1st Century B.C.)

GOLD

	390		393	

390	**Stater.** South Ferriby type. Crude laureate head. R. Disjointed horse l., rosette or star below, anchor shape and pellets above. *M. 449-50; V. 809-815/19; BMC 3146-3179. (30)*	125	250
391	Wheel type. Similar, but wheel below horse. *M. 449c; V. 817; BMC 3180*	225	450
392	Kite type. Similar to 390, but diamond shape containing pellets above, spiral below horse. *M. 447; V. 825; BMC 3181-84. (29)*	200	400
393	Domino type. Similar to last, but with rectangle containing pellets. *M. 448; V. 829; BMC 3185-86. (29)*	200	375

                     394   395

		F £	VF £
394	Trefoil type. Trefoil with central rosette of seven pellets. R. Similar to 390. *M. 450a; V. 821; BMC —. (30A)*	*Extremely rare*	
395	North Lincolnshire Scyphate type. Stylised boar r. or l. R. Large S symbol with pellets and rings in field. *M. —; V. —; BMC 3187-93*	300	650

* chipped or cracked specimens are often encountered and are worthless

SILVER

                          396

396	**Unit.** Boar/Horse type I.Boar r., large pellet and ring motif above, reversed S below. R. Horse l. or r., pellet in ring above. *M. 405-06,* *451; V. 855-60, 864, 867; BMC 3194-3214. (66)*	65	165
397	Boar Horse type II. Vestiges of boar on obv. R. Horse l. or r. *M. 410,* *452-53; V. 875-877; BMC 3214-27. (68)*	40	95

                     398   399

398	Boar Horse type III. Blank. R. Horse l.or r. *M. 453-54; V. 884-77;* *BMC 3228-35. (69)*	30	65
399	**Fractional Unit.** Similar to 396-97. *M. 406a, 451a; V. 862/66;* *BMC 3236-3250. (67)*	50	110
400	Similar to 398. *M. —; V. 877-81; BMC 3251-55. (70/71)*	25	60
401	Pattern/Horse. Flower pattern. R. Horse l. *M. —; V. —; BMC 3256-57*	50	110

INSCRIBED
(Early to Mid 1st Century A.D.)
The following types are not arranged chronologically.

AVN COST

GOLD

		F £	VF £
402	**Stater.** Crude wreath design. R. Disjointed horse l., AVN COST. *M. 457; V. 910; BMC 3258. (286)*	475	1150

SILVER

403

403	**Unit.** Remains of wreath or blank. R. AVN COST, horse l. *M. 458; V. 914; BMC 3261-66. (287)*	40	95
404	**Fractional Unit.** Similar. *M. —; l V. 918; BMC 3267-68. (288)*	35	85

ESVP RASV

GOLD

405	**Stater.** Crude wreath design. R. Disjointed horse l., IISVP RASV. *M. 456b; V. 920; BMC 3269. (289)*	400	950

SILVER

406	**Unit.** Similar. *M. 456c; V. 924; BMC 3272-73. (290)*	80	175

VEP

GOLD

407	**Stater.** Blank or with traces of wreath. R. Disjointed horse l., VEP. *M. —; V. 905; BMC 3274-75. (296)*	425	1050

SILVER

408	**Unit.** Blank or with traces of wreath. R. VEP, horse r. *M. —; V. 963; BMC 3277-82. (297)*	65	140
409	**Half Unit.** Similar. *M. 464b; V. 967; BMC 3283-3295. (298)*	60	125

VEP CORF

GOLD

410

		F £	VF £

410 **Stater.** Crude wreath design. R. Disjointed horse l., VEP CORF.
M. 459, 460; V. 930/40/60; BMC 3296-3304. (291) 375 825

SILVER

411 **Unit.** Similar. *M. 460b/464; V. 934/50; BMC 3305-14. (292)* 60 125

412

412 Similar but VEPOC (M)ES, pellet in ring below horse. *M. —; V. 955;*
BMC —. (294) 70 150
413 **Half Unit.** Similar. *M. 464a; V. 938/58; BMC 3316-24. (293/95)* 50 120

DVMNO TIGIR SENO

GOLD

414

414 **Stater.** DVMN(OC) across wreath. R. Horse l., TIGIR SENO. *M. 461;*
V. 972; BMC 3325-27. (299) 700 1500

SILVER

415

415 **Unit.** DVMNOC in two lines. R. Horse r., TIGIR SENO. *M. 462;*
V. 974; BMC 3328-29. (300) 175 400

VOLISIOS DVMNOCOVEROS

GOLD

416

		F £	VF £
416	**Stater.** VOLISIOS between three lines in wreath. R. Horse r. or l., DVMNOCOVEROS. *M. 463/a; V. 978-80; BMC 3330-3336. (301)*.......	400	850

SILVER

417	**Unit.** Similar. R. Horse r., DVMNOCO. *M. 463a; V. 980; BMC 3339. (302)*..................	150	340
418	**Half Unit.** Similar. *M. 465; V. 984; BMC 3340-41. (303)*......................	95	210

VOLISIOS DVMNOVELLAUNOS

GOLD

419	**Stater.** VOLISIOS between three lines in wreath. R. Horse r. or l., DVMNOVELAVNOS. *M. 466; V .988; BMC 3342-43. (304)*	700	1650

SILVER

420	**Half Unit.** As last but DVMNOVE. *M. 467; V. 992; BMC 3344-46. (305).*	175	375

VOLISIOS CARTIVEL

SILVER

421	**Half Unit.** VOLISIOS between three lines in wreath. R. Horse r., CARTILEV. *M. 468; V. 994; BMC 3347-48. (306)*	200	425

IAT ISO E

SILVER

422	**Unit.** IAT ISO (retrograde)on tablet, rosettes above and below. R. Horse r., E above. *M. 416; V. 998; BMC 3349-51. (284)*	190	375

CAT

SILVER

422A	**Unit.** Boar r., pellet ring above, CAT above. R. Horse r. *M. —; V. —; BMC 3352*	*Extremely rare*	

LAT ISON

GOLD

423

		F	VF
		£	£

423   **Stater.** LAT ISO(N) in two lines retrograde. R. Horse r., ISO in box
above, N below. *M. —; V. —; BMC —. Only recorded as an AE/AV
plated core, as illustrated*...   *Extremely rare*

ICENI

The Iceni centered on Norfolk but also occupying neighbouring parts of Suffolk and
Cambridgeshire, are well attested in the post conquest period as the tribe who under Boudicca
revolted against Roman rule. Their earliest coins are likely to have been the British J staters, Norfolk
Wolf type (no.30/31), replaced around the mid first century B.C. by the Snettisham, Freckenham and
Irstead type gold staters and quarter staters. Contemporary with these are silver Boar/Horse and
Face/Horse units and fractions. The introduction of legends around the beginning of the millennia
led to the adoption of a new obverse design of back to back crescents. The continuation of the
coinage after the Roman invasion is attested by the coins of King Prasutagus. Some of the
Face/Horse units (no.434) have been attributed to Queen Boudicca.

EARLY UNINSCRIBED
(Mid to Late 1st Century B.C.)
GOLD

424   425

424   **Stater.** Snettisham type. Blank or with traces of pellet cross. R. Horse
r., serpent like pellet in ring motif above. *M. —; V .—; BMC 3353-59....*   250   550
425   Similar. Blank or with 3 short curved lines. R. Horse r., symbol above
more degraded. *M. —; V. —; BMC 3360-83*   220   500

426 427

	F £	VF £
426 Freckenham type. Two opposed crescents with stars or pellets in field. R. Horse r., various symbols in field. *M. 397/99; V. 620; BMC 3384-89. (38)*	185	425
427 Similar. Blank or with traces of pellet cross. R. Horse r., wheel or arch containing pellets above. *M. 400; V. 624; BMC 3390-95. (40)*	210	425

428

428 Similar. Trefoil on cross design. R. Similar. *M. 401-03; V. 626; BMC 3396-3419. (39)*	200	400

429 430

429 **Quarter Stater.** Snettisham type. Wreath cross. R. Horse r. *M. —; V. —; BMC 3420-35*	100	200
430 Irstead type. Hatched box, wreaths at sides. R. Horse r. *M. 404; V. 628; BMC 3436-39. (48)*	80	160

SILVER

431 432

431 **Unit.** Boar / Horse type. Boar r. R. Horse r. *M. 407-09; V. 655-59; BMC 3440-3512. (72)*	25	60
432 Bury type. Head l. or r. R. Horse l. or r. *M. —; V. —; BMC 3524-35*	65	150

433   433

	F £	VF £
433 Early Face / Horse type. Celticised head l. or r. R. Horse l. or r. M. 412/413a-c/e; BMC 3536-3555. (74)	50	125

434   435

| 434 Face / Horse Regular type. Head r. R. Horse r. M. 413/d; V. 790-94; BMC 3556-3759. (74). Attributed to Queen Boudicca by R.D. van Arsdell | 35 | 125 |
| 435 Early Pattern / Horse type. Cross of two opposed crescents. R. Horse l. or r. M. 414-15; V. 675-79; BMC 3763-74. (75) | 20 | 45 |

436

436 ECEN symbol type. Two opposed crescents. R. Horse r. M. 429; V. 752; BMC 4297-4325	20	50
437 **Half Unit.** Boar / Horse type. Similar to 431. M. 411; V. 661; BMC 3513-20. (73)	25	60
438 **Fractional Unit.** Early Pattern / Horse type. Similar to 435. M. 417/a; V. 681-83; BMC 3775-89. (76/A)	35	70

INSCRIBED
(Early to Mid 1st Century A.D.)
The following types are not arranged chronologically.

CAN DVRO

SILVER

439

| 439 **Unit.** Boar. R. Horse r., CAN(S) above, DVRO below. M. 434; V. 663; BMC 3521-23. (271) | 100 | 225 |

ANTED

GOLD

440

		F £	VF £
440	**Stater.** Triple crescent design. R. Horse r., ANTED monongram below. *M. 418; V. 705; BMC 3790. (272)*	400	850

SILVER

441

441	**Unit.** Two opposed crescents. R. Horse r., ANTED. *M. 419-21; V. 710-11/15; BMC 3791-4025. (273)*.	25	60
442	**Fractional Unit.** Similar to last. *M. 422; V. 720; BMC 4028-31. (274)* ..	30	65

ECEN

GOLD

443

443	**Stater.** Triple crescent design. R. Horse r., ECEN below. *M. —; V. 725; BMC 4032.*	*Extremely rare*	

SILVER

443A	**Unit.** Two opposed crescents. R, Horse r., ECEN. *M. 424; V. 730; BMC 4033-4215. (275)*	20	50
443B	**Half Unit.** Similar to last. *M. 431; V. 736; BMC 4216-17. (276)*	25	60

EDN

SILVER

		F £	VF £

444   **Unit.** Two opposed crescents. R, Horse r., ED, E, ꓱJ or EDN. *M. 423, 425b; V. 734/40; BMC 4219-81. (277)*   30   65

ECE

SILVER

445

445   **Unit.** Two opposed crescents. R, Horse r., ECE. *M. 425-28; V. 761-66; BMC 4348-4538. (278-80)*   25   50

SAENU

SILVER

446   **Unit.** Two opposed crescents. R. Horse r., SAENV. *M. 433; V. 770; BMC 4540-57. (281)*   45   110

AESU

SILVER

447

447   **Unit.** Two opposed crescents. R. Horse r., AESV. *M. 432; V. 775; BMC 4558-72. (282)*   50   125

ALE SCA

SILVER

448   **Unit.** Boar r., ALE. R. Horse r., SCA. *M. 469; V. 996; BMC 4576*   175   350

AEDIC SIA

SILVER

		F	VF
		£	£

449   **Unit.** AEDIC in two lines. R. Horse r., SIA? below. *M.—; V.—;*
       BMC 4581 ....   *Extremely rare*

PRASUTAGUS

SILVER

450

450   **Unit.** Romanised head l., SUB RII PRASTO. R. Rearing horse r.,
       ESICO FECIT. *M. 434a; V. 780; BMC 4577-80. (283)*   600   1200
       This legend translates as "Under King Prasto, Esico made me", giving the name of both
       King and moneyer.

The systematic conquest of Britain by the Romans began in A.D. 43 when the Emperor Claudius (41-54), anxious to enhance his military reputation, authorized an invasion in which he personally participated, albeit in a purely symbolic role. The initial military contact between the two cultures had taken place almost a century before when Julius Caesar, during the course of his conquest of Celtic Gaul, led expeditions to the island in 55 and 54 B.C. Although no actual Roman occupation of Britain resulted from Caesar's reconnoitring campaigns commercial intercourse was certainly accelerated, as evidenced by the 'Romanization' of the British Celtic coinage in the final decades of its production.

The Claudian conquest, commencing in A.D. 43, brought about a complete change in the nature of the currency circulating in Britain and ushered in a period lasting more than three and a half centuries during which Roman coinage was the only official medium of exchange. Local copies of the money brought with them by the four legions of the invasion army began to appear at a very early stage, the most popular type for imitation being the well-known Claudian copper as with reverse type fighting Minerva. Some of these copies are well-executed and of a style not much inferior to the prototype, suggesting that their local minting may have been officially sanctioned by the Roman government in order to make good a shortage of currency in the newly-conquered territory. Other examples are of much poorer style and execution and are frequently well below the normal weight of a Claudian as (usually between 10 and 11 grams). These copies must have been issued unofficially and provide evidence of the huge demand for this type of currency in a population which had never before experienced the benefits of having base metal coins available for small everyday transactions.

In the decades that followed, the boundaries of the Roman province of Britannia were continually pushed further north and west until, under the celebrated Flavian governor Gnaeus Julius Agricola, the Roman army even penetrated to northern Scotland (A.D. 83/4). A few years later, under Trajan, the northern frontier was established along the Tyne-Solway line, a barrier made permanent by the construction of Hadrian's Wall following the emperor's visit to the province in 122. For a brief period in the mid-2nd century the frontier was temporarily advanced to the Forth-Clyde line with the building of the Antonine Wall, though this seems to have been abandoned early in the reign of Marcus Aurelius (ca. 163) when the Hadrianic barrier was re-commissioned and became the permanent frontier. The security thus provided to the now-peaceful province in the south facilitated urban expansion and the development of commerce. The new prosperity brought a flood of Roman coinage into the island-province and it was no longer necessary for shortages to be made good by large scale local imitation.

Until the mid-3rd century the production of Roman coinage remained the prerogative of the mint in the capital, with only occasional issues from provincial centres to serve short-term local needs. But with the deepening political and economic crisis in the third quarter of the century there was a dramatic decentralization of minting operations, with permanent establishments being set up in many important cities in the western as well as the eastern provinces. Britain, however, still remained without an official mint at this time and in the dark days of the 270s, when the separatist Gallic Empire to which Britain belonged was close to collapse, large scale production of imitative antoniniani (commonly called 'barbarous radiates') occurred in the province. The integrity and prestige of the Empire was, to some extent, restored by a rapid succession of Illyrian 'soldier emperors', until the situation was finally stabilized by Diocletian (A.D. 284-305) who established the tetrarchy system under which governmental responsibility was shared by four rulers. By the end of the 3rd century Britain had been reorganized into a civil diocese of four provinces: it had already been subdivided into Britannia Superior and Britannia Inferior almost a hundred years before, under Septimius Severus or Caracalla.

It was left to the colourful and enigmatic usurper Carausius (A.D. 287-293) to establish mints in Britain. It was, of course, vital for him to do so as his dominion was mostly confined to the island-province. Londinium (London) was his principal mint, with a secondary establishment at a place usually signing itself 'C' (probably Camulodunum, modern Colchester). After the downfall of Carausius' murderer and successor Allectus (293-296) Britain was restored to the central government, an event commemorated by the celebrated gold medallion of Constantius I showing the Caesar riding alongside the Thames approaching the gateway of the city of Londinium. At this point the mysterious 'C' mint disappears from the picture. Londinium, on the other hand, retained its status as an official mint under Diocletian's tetrarchy and its successors down to A.D. 325, when it was closed by Constantine the Great who regarded it as superfluous to his needs. In nearly four decades of existence as a Roman mint Londinium had produced a varied and extensive coinage in the names of almost all the emperors, empresses and Caesars of the period. It was destined never again to be active during Roman times, unless the extremely rare gold and silver issues of the late 4th century usurper Magnus Maximus, signed AVG, AVGOB and AVGPS, are correctly attributed to Londinium under its late Roman name of Augusta.

The termination of Roman rule in the British provinces is traditionally dated to A.D. 410 when the emperor Honorius, in response to an appeal for aid from his British subjects, told them to arrange for their own defence as best they might ('Rescript of Honorius'). In reality, the end probably came quite gradually. As the machinery of government ground to a halt and the soldiers stopped receiving their pay there would have been a steady drift of population away from the semi-ruinous cities and military installations to the countryside, where they could better provide for themselves through farming. Under these conditions the need for coinage would have been drastically reduced, as a primitive economy based on barter would largely have replaced the complex monetary economy of the late Roman period. In any case the supply of coinage from the Continent would now have dried up. The few monetary transactions which still took place were made with worn-out coins from earlier periods augmented by local imitations, production of which in Britain had resumed in the mid-4th century. Such was the pitiful end of the long tradition of Roman coinage in the remote island-province of Britannia. More than two centuries of 'Dark Ages' were to elapse before England's new rulers, the Anglo-Saxons, commenced the issue of gold thrymsas, the designs of many of which were based on late Roman types.

As Rome's Imperial coinage provided the currency needs of this country over a period of almost four centuries no representative collection of British coins is complete without some examples of these important issues. The following listing is divided into four categories: 1. Regular Roman issues, all of which would have been legal tender in Britain after A.D. 43; 2. Issues with types referring specifically to the province of Britannia, usually in commemoration of military campaigns in the north; 3. Official Roman coinage struck in Britain; 4. Imitations of Roman coins produced in Britain, all but possibly some of the earliest being of unofficial origin. The reference 'R.R.C.' is to the listing of the type in Michael Crawford's *Roman Republican Coinage* (Cambridge, 1974); and 'R.I.C.' to *The Roman Imperial Coinage* (London, 1923-1994, in ten volumes).

For more detailed collectors' information on Roman coinage, including a more comprehensive listing of types, the reader is referred to *Roman Coins and their Values* by David R. Sear (4th revised edition). A complete catalogue of silver issues may be found in the 5 volumes of *Roman Silver Coins* (H.A. Seaby and C.E. King) which provides a quick and convenient reference and is especially aimed at the collector. Gilbert Askew's *The Coinage of Roman Britain* (2nd edition) concentrates on those issues which are particularly associated with the Roman province of Britannia, but does not provide valuations. A more recent work on this subject is R. Reece's *Coinage in Roman Britain*. Newly published is David R. Sear's *The History and Coinage of the Roman Imperators, 49–27 BC* which is devoted to the vital two decades of transition from Republic to Empire.

The standard works on the coinages of the Roman Republic and the Roman Empire have already been mentioned *(Roman Republican Coinage and Roman Imperial Coinage)*. These monumental publications are essential to the advanced collector and student and their importance cannot be overstated. The British Museum Catalogues (3 volumes of Republican, 6 volumes of Imperial) are also vital. They contain superb interpretive material in their introductions and are very fully illustrated. A similar work is Anne S. Robertson's *Roman Imperial Coins in the Hunter Coin Cabinet*, in 5 volumes (volume 4 is especially important for the later 3rd century coinage). For more general reading we may recommend J.P.C. Kent and M. & A. Hirmer's *Roman Coins,* undoubtedly the most lavishly illustrated book on the subject; C.H.V. Sutherland's *Roman Coins;* and R.A.G. Carson's *Coins of the Roman Empire*. Finally, for a most useful single-volume work on interpretation and background information we would suggest A *Dictionary of Ancient Roman Coins* by John Melville Jones.

1. REGULAR ROMAN ISSUES

A token selection of the types of Roman coins which might be found on Romano-British archaeological sites. Many of the rarer emperors and empresses have been omitted and the types listed often represent only one of hundreds of variant forms which might be encountered.

		F £	VF £
451	**THE REPUBLIC: P. Aelius Paetus** (moneyer), 138 B.C. Æ *denarius.* Helmeted hd. of Roma r. Rev. The Dioscuri galloping r. R.R.C. 233/1 ... *Although dating from long before the Roman conquest many Republican coins circulated well into the Imperial period and found their way to Britain where they are often represented in early hoards.*	20	50
452	**L. Thorius Balbus** (moneyer), 105 B.C. Æ denarius. Hd. of Juno Sospita r., clad in goat's skin. Rev. Bull charging r. *R.R.C. 316/1*.......................	25	60
453	**Q. Antonius Balbus** (moneyer), 83-82 B.C. Æ *denarius.* Laur. hd. of Jupiter r. Rev. Victory in quadriga r. *R.R.C. 364/1*.................................	20	55

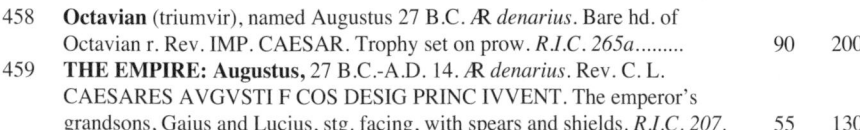

454   456

		F £	VF £
454	**C. Calpurnius Piso** (moneyer), 67 B.C. Æ *denarius.* Laur. hd. of Apollo r. Rev. Horseman galloping r., holding palm-branch. *R.R.C. 408/1a*.......	25	60
455	**Mn. Acilius Glabrio** (moneyer), 49 B.C. Æ *denarius.* Laur. hd. of Salus r. Rev. Valetudo stg. l., holding snake and resting on column. *R.R.C. 442/1.*	20	55
456	**Julius Caesar** (dictator), visited Britain 55 and 54 B.C., died 44 B.C. Æ *denarius.* CAESAR. Elephant r. Rev. Priestly emblems. *R.R.C. 443/1....*	75	150
456A	— Wreathed hd. of Caesar r. Rev. P. SEPVLLIVS MACER. Venus stg. l., holding Victory and sceptre. *R.R.C. 480/9.*	300	700
457	**Mark Antony** (triumvir), died 30 B.C. Æ *denarius.* Galley r. Rev. LEG. II. Legionary eagle between two standards. *R.R.C. 544/14*..........................	50	125

458   459

		F £	VF £
458	**Octavian** (triumvir), named Augustus 27 B.C. Æ *denarius.* Bare hd. of Octavian r. Rev. IMP. CAESAR. Trophy set on prow. *R.I.C. 265a*.........	90	200
459	**THE EMPIRE: Augustus,** 27 B.C.-A.D. 14. Æ *denarius.* Rev. C. L. CAESARES AVGVSTI F COS DESIG PRINC IVVENT. The emperor's grandsons, Gaius and Lucius, stg. facing, with spears and shields. *R.I.C. 207.* *Almost all the coins in the Roman Imperial series have a head or bust of the emperor, empress or prince as their obverse type. Therefore, in most instances only the reverses will be described in the following listings.*	55	130

		F	VF
		£	£
460	Æ as. ROM. ET AVG. The altar of Lugdunum. *R.I.C. 230.*	50	125
460A	Æ quadrans. Obv. Anvil. Rev. Moneyers' inscription around large S. C. *R.I.C. 443.*	15	35
461	**Augustus and Agrippa,** general and designated heir of Augustus, died 12 B.C. Æ *dupondius.* Obv. Their hds. back to back. Rev. COL. NEM. Crocodile r., chained to palm-branch. *R.I.C. 159.* .... *See also no. 468.*	55	140
462	**Divus Augustus,** deified A.D. 14. Æ as. PROVIDENT S. C. Large altar. *R.I.C. 81.*	60	150
463	**Tiberius,** A.D. 14-37. *N aureus.* PONTIF MAXIM. Livia (?) seated r., holding sceptre and branch. *R.I.C. 29.*	350	850

464   467

464	Æ denarius. Similar. *R.I.C. 30.* .... *This type is commonly referred to as the 'Tribute Penny' of the Bible (Matthew 22, 17-21).*	70	150
464A	Æ *as.* Inscription around large S. C. *R.I.C. 44.*	55	140
465	**Livia,** wife of Augustus, mother of Tiberius. Æ *dupondius.* Obv. Veiled bust of Livia as Pietas r. Rev. Inscription of Drusus Caesar around large S. C. *R.I.C. 43.*	120	325
466	**Drusus,** son of Tiberius. Æ *as.* Inscription around large S. C. *R.I.C. 45.*	65	165
467	**Caligula,** A.D. 37-41. Æ *as.* VESTA S. C. Vesta seated l. *R.I.C. 38.*.......	85	225

468

468	**Agrippa,** grandfather of Caligula, died 12 B.C. Æ *as.* S. C. Neptune stg. l., holding dolphin and trident. *R.I.C. 58.* .... *See also no. 461 and under Category 4.*	50	150
469	**Germanicus,** father of Caligula, brother of Claudius, died A.D. 19. Æ *as.* Inscription of Caligula around large S. C. *R.I.C. 35.*	65	165
470	**Agrippina Senior,** mother of Caligula, died A.D. 33. Æ *sestertius.* S.P.Q.R. MEMORIAE AGRIPPINAE. Carpentum drawn l. by two mules. *R.I.C. 55.*	250	850

471   474

		F	VF
		£	£

471 **Claudius,** A.D. 41-54, initiated the conquest of Britain by his invasion in
A.D. 43. Æ *as*. LIBERTAS AVGVSTA S. C. Libertas stg. r., holding pileus.
R.I.C. 113. .... 55 140

471A Æ *quadrans*. Obv. Hand holding scales. Rev. Inscription around large
S. C. *R.I.C. 85.* 15 35
See also under Categories 2 and 4.

472 **Nero Claudius Drusus,** father of Claudius, died 9 B.C. Æ *sestertius*.
TI. CLAVDIVS CAESAR AVG. P. M. TR .P. IMP. P. P. S. C. Claudius seated
l. on curule chair amidst arms. *R.I.C. 109*................................ 130 450
See also under Category 4.

473 **Antonia,** mother of Claudius, died A.D. 37. Æ *dupondius*. TI. CLAVDIVS
CAESAR AVG P.M. TR. P. IMP. S. C. Claudius stg. l., holding simpulum.
R.I.C. 92. .... 100 275
See also under Category 4.

474 **Nero,** 54-68, emperor at the time of Queen Boudicca's rebellion in Britain.
Ν *aureus*. SALVS. Salus seated l. *R.I.C. 66.* 450 1,050

475 Æ *denarius*. IVPPITER CVSTOS. Jupiter seated l. *R.I.C. 53.* 85 250

476 Æ *sestertius*. ROMA S. C. Roma seated l., holding Victory and parazonium.
R.I.C. 274. .... 100 350

476A Æ as. S. C. Victory hovering l., holding shield inscribed S. P. Q. R. *R.I.C. 312.* 50 125

477 **Galba,** 68-69. Æ *denarius*. S.P.Q.R. / OB / C.S. within oak-wreath. *R.I.C. 167.* 90 275

478 **Otho,** 69. Æ *denarius*. SECVRITAS P. R. Securitas stg. l. *R.I.C. 10*...... 200 500

479 **Vitellius,** 69. Æ denarius. CONCORDIA P. R. Concordia seated l. *R.I.C. 90.* 90 275

480 **Vespasian,** 69-79, commanded Legio II in the Claudian invasion of Britain
(43) and appointed Agricola to governorship of the province in 77/8. Ν *aureus*.
ANNONA AVG. Annona seated l. *R.I.C. 131a* 500 1,200

481

481 Æ *denarius*. VICTORIA AVGVSTI. Victory advancing r., crowning standard.
R.I.C. 52. .... 22 65

481A Æ *dupondius*. FELICITAS PVBLICA S. C. Felicitas stg. l. *R.I.C. 554...* 40 100

482 **Titus,** 79-81 (Caesar 69-79). Æ *denarius*. TR. P. IX. IMP. XV. COS. VIII.
P. P. Thunderbolt on throne. *R.I.C. 23a*................................ 40 120

483   485

		F	VF
		£	£
483	**Domitian,** 81-96 (Caesar 69-81), recalled Agricola in 83/4 and abandoned the conquest of northern Scotland (ca. 87). *Æ denarius*. IMP. XIX. COS. XIIII. CENS. P. P. P. Minerva stg. l., resting on spear. *R.I.C. 140.*	22	55
484	*Æ dupondius*. VIRTVTI AVGVSTI S. C. Virtus stg. r. *R.I.C. 393*..........	30	75
484A	*Æ as*. MONETA AVGVSTI S. C. Moneta stg. l. *R.I.C. 354b*..................	30	75
485	**Nerva,** 96-98. *Æ denarius*. AEQVITAS AVGVST. Aequitas stg. l. *R.I.C. 13.*	40	100
485A	*Æ as*. LIBERTAS PVBLICA S. C. Libertas stg. l. *R.I.C. 86.*	55	140
486	**Trajan,** 98-117, established the northern frontier in Britain along the Tyne-Solway line (ca. 100). *N aureus*. P. M. TR. P. COS. VI. P. P. S. P. Q. R. Genius stg. l., holding patera and corn-ears. *R.I.C. 347.*	400	900

487   490

		F	VF
487	*Æ denarius*. COS. V. P. P. S. P. Q. R. OPTIMO PRINC. Military trophy. *R.I.C. 147.*	22	55
488	*Æ sestertius*. S. P. Q. R. OPTIMO PRINCIPI S. C. Spes walking l., holding flower. *R.I.C. 519*...	40	150
488A	*Æ dupondius*. SENATVS POPVLVSQVE ROMANVS S. C. Emperor advancing between two trophies. *R.I.C. 676*...	25	65
489	**Hadrian,** 117-138, visited Britain in 122 and initiated the construction of a fortified frontier line (Hadrian's Wall). *N aureus*. HISPANIA. Hispania reclining l. *R.I.C. 305*...	500	1,100
490	*Æ denarius*. P. M. TR. P. COS. III. Roma stg. l., holding Victory and spear. *R.I.C. 76.*	25	60
491	*Æ sestertius*. COS. III. S. C. Neptune stg. r., holding dolphin and trident, foot on prow. *R.I.C. 632*..	50	175
491A	*Æ as*. FELICITATI AVG COS. III. P. P. S. C. Galley travelling l. over waves. *R.I.C. 719.* .... *See also under Category 2.*	40	100
492	**Sabina,** wife of Hadrian. *Æ denarius*. IVNONI REGINAE. Juno stg. l. *R.I.C. 395a.*	40	100
493	**Aelius Caesar,** heir of Hadrian, 136-138. *Æ denarius*. CONCORD. TR. POT. COS. II. Concordia seated l. *R.I.C. 436.*	75	200
493A	*Æ as*. TR. POT. COS. II. S. C. Spes walking l., holding flower. *R.I.C. 1067.*	50	130

	F	VF
	£	£

494 **Antoninus Pius,** 138-161, ordered the expansion of the Roman province
to include southern Scotland and constructed the Antonine Wall on the
Forth-Clyde line (beginning ca. 143). An uprising in northern Britain in the
150s results in a permanent withdrawal to the Hadrianic frontier early in
the next reign. *N aureus.* COS. IIII. Togate emperor stg. l., holding globe.
R.I.C. 233b. 350 750

495 *R denarius.* PIETATI AVG. COS. IIII. Pietas stg. l. between two children,
holding two more in her arms. *R.I.C. 313c.* 20 50

496

496 *Æ sestertius.* SALVS AVG. S. C. Salus stg. l. at altar, feeding snake.
R.I.C. 635. .... 32 120

496A *Æ dupondius.* TR. POT. XX. COS. IIII. S. C. Providentia stg. l., pointing
at globe at her feet and holding sceptre. *R.I.C. 2025.* 24 60
See also under Categories 2 and 3.

497 **Antoninus Pius and Marcus Aurelius Caesar**. *R denarius.* Obv. Laur.
hd. of Antoninus Pius r. Rev. AVRELIVS CAESAR AVG PII F. COS. Bare
hd. of young Marcus Aurelius r. *R.I.C. 417a* 50 120

498   501

498 **Divus Antoninus Pius,** deified 161. *R denarius.* CONSECRATIO.
Four-storeyed crematorium of Antoninus Pius. *R.I.C. 436.* 24 60

499 **Diva Faustina Senior,** wife of Antoninus Pius, deified 141. *R denarius.*
AETERNITAS. Aeternitas stg. l., holding globe and billowing veil. *R.I.C. 351.* 20 50

499A *Æ sestertius.* AVGVSTA S. C. Ceres stg. l., holding two torches. *R.I.C. 1120.* 30 110

500 **Marcus Aurelius,** 161-180 (Caesar 139-161), re-established Hadrian's Wall
as the permanent northern frontier of the province, ca. 163. *N aureus.*
PROV. DEOR. TR. P. XV. COS. III. Providentia stg. l., holding globe and
cornucopiae. *R.I.C. 19* 400 900

501 *R denarius.* PIETAS AVG. Priestly emblems. *R.I.C. 424a.* 24 60

501A — SALVTI AVG. COS. III. Salus stg. l. at altar, feeding snake. *R.I.C. 222.* 20 55

502 *Æ sestertius.* CONCORD. AVGVSTOR. TR. P. XVI. COS. III. S. C. Marcus
Aurelius and Lucius Verus stg. face to face, clasping hands. *R.I.C. 826.* 35 120

502A *Æ as.* HONOS TR. POT. II. COS. II. S. C. Honos stg. r. *R.I.C. 1271a.* .. 30 75

		F £	VF £

503   **Divus Marcus Aurelius,** deified 180. Æ *denarius*. CONSECRATIO.
Eagle stg. r. on altar. *R.I.C. 272.*   28   70

504   506A

504   **Faustina Junior,** daughter of Antoninus Pius, wife of Marcus Aurelius.
Æ *denarius*. FECVNDITAS. Fecunditas stg. r., holding sceptre and child.
R.I.C. 677.   20   50
504A Æ *sestertius*. HILARITAS S. C. Hilaritas stg. l. *R.I.C. 1642.*   30   110
505   **Diva Faustina Junior,** deified 175. Æ *as*. S. C. Crescent and seven stars.
R.I.C. 1714.   30   75
506   **Lucius Verus,** 161-169. Æ denarius. PAX TR. P. VI. IMP. IIII. COS. II.
Pax stg. l. *R.I.C. 561.*   25   65
506A Æ *dupondius*. TR. P. IIII. IMP. II. COS. II. S. C. Mars stg. r., resting on
spear and shield. *R.I.C. 1387.*   30   75
507   **Lucilla,** daughter of Marcus Aurelius, wife of Lucius Verus. Æ *denarius*.
IVNONI LVCINAE. Juno stg. l., holding child in swaddling clothes.
R.I.C. 771.   25   65
507A Æ *sestertius*. PIETAS S. C. Pietas stg. l., altar at feet. *R.I.C. 1756.*   35   120
508   **Commodus,** 177-192 (Caesar 175-177), major warfare on the British
frontier early in the reign; situation restored by Ulpius Marcellus in 184/5,
followed by unrest in the British legions. Æ *denarius*. LIB. AVG. IIII. TR.
P. VI. IMP. IIII. COS. III. P. P. Liberalitas stg. l. *R.I.C. 22.*   20   50

509   511

509   Æ *sestertius*. IOVI VICTORI IMP. III. COS. II. P. P. S. C. Jupiter seated l.
R.I.C. 1612.   35   110
509A Æ *as*. ANN. AVG. TR. P. VII. IMP. IIII. COS. III. P. P. S. C. Annona stg. l.,
modius at feet. *R.I.C. 339*   24   60
      See also under Category 2.
510   **Crispina,** wife of Commodus. Æ *denarius*. CONCORDIA. Clasped hands.
R.I.C. 279.   30   75
511   **Pertinax,** January-March 193, formerly governor of Britain, ca. 185-7. Æ
denarius. PROVID. DEOR. COS. II. Providentia stg l., reaching up to star.
R.I.C. 11a.   250   550

512   513A

	F	VF
	£	£

512 **Didius Julianus,** March-June 193. Æ *denarius*. CONCORD MILIT.
Concordia Militum stg. l., holding standards. *R.I.C. 1.*   375   850
513 **Clodius Albinus,** 195-197 (Caesar 193-195), governor of Britain (from
191/2) at the time of his imperial proclamation by his troops. Æ *denarius*.
MINER. PACIF. COS. II. Minerva stg. l. *R.I.C. 7.*   55   125
513A — FIDES LEGION. COS. II. Clasped hands holding legionary eagle.
R.I.C. 20b.   75   175

514   516

514 **Septimius Severus,** 193-211, restored the frontier forts in northern Britain
following the downfall of Clodius Albinus; later repaired Hadrian's Wall,
and spent the years 208-11 in Britain campaigning in Scotland; divided
Britannia into two provinces, Superior and Inferior; died at York, February
211. Æ *denarius*. VIRT AVGG. Roma stg. l., holding Victory, spear and
shield. *R.I.C. 171a*..   15   35
514A — P.M. TR. P. XVIII. COS. III. P. P. Jupiter stg. l. between two children.
R.I.C. 240.   15   35
See also under Category 2.
515 **Julia Domna,** wife of Septimius Severus, mother of Caracalla and Geta,
accompanied her husband and sons on the British expedition, 208-211, and
probably resided in London during the northern campaigns. Æ *denarius*.
VENERI VICTR. Venus stg. r., resting on column. *R.I.C. 536.*   15   40
515A — VESTA. Vesta stg. l., holding palladium and sceptre. *R.I.C. 390.*   15   40
516 **Caracalla,** 198-217 (Caesar 196-198), accompanied his father and brother
on the British expedition, 208-211, and led the final campaign in Scotland
in 210 during Severus' illness; made frontier dispositions before returning
to Rome and finalized his father's arrangements for the division of Britain
into two provinces. Æ *antoninianus* (*double denarius,* introduced in 215).
VENVS VICTRIX. Venus stg. l., holding Victory and resting on shield.
R.I.C. 311c.   25   65
517 Æ *denarius*. PART. MAX. PONT. TR. P. IIII. Trophy with two captives at
base. *R.I.C. 54b.*   15   40
517A — P. M. TR. P. XV. COS. III. P. P. Hercules stg. l., holding olive-branch
and club. *R.I.C. 192*..   15   35
See also under Category 2.

| | | F | VF |
| | | £ | £ |

518 **Plautilla,** wife of Caracalla. Æ *denarius.* PROPAGO IMPERI. Caracalla
and Plautilla clasping hands. *R.I.C. 362.* 25 65

519 522A

519 **Geta,** 209-212 (Caesar 198-209), accompanied his father and brother on
the British expedition, 208-211, and took charge of the civil administration
in London during the northern campaigns. Æ *denarius.* PRINC. IVVENTVTIS.
Prince stg. l. beside trophy, holding branch and spear. *R.I.C. 18.* 20 50

519A — FORT RED TR. P. III. COS. II. Fortuna seated l. *R.I.C. 75* 25 65
See also under Category 2.

520 **Macrinus,** 217-218. Æ *denarius.* PROVIDENTIA DEORVM. Providentia
stg. l., globe at feet. *R.I.C. 80.* 30 75

521 **Diadumenian,** 218 (Caesar 217-218). Æ *denarius.* PRINC. IVVENTVTIS.
Prince stg. l., two standards behind. *R.I.C. 109.* 70 175

522 **Elagabalus,** 218-222. Æ *antoninianus.* MARS VICTOR. Mars advancing r.
R.I.C. 122. .... 22 55

522A Æ *denarius.* P. M. TR. P. III. COS. III. P. P. Jupiter seated l., eagle at feet
R.I.C. 27. .... 15 35

523 **Julia Paula,** first wife of Elagabalus. Æ *denarius.* CONCORDIA.
Concordia seated l. *R.I.C. 211.* 40 100

524 **Aquilia Severa,** second wife of Elagabalus. Æ *denarius.* CONCORDIA.
Concordia stg. l., altar at feet. *R.I.C. 226.* 60 150

525 **Julia Soaemias,** mother of Elagabalus. Æ *denarius.* VENVS CAELESTIS.
Venus seated l., child at feet. *R.I.C. 243.* 30 75

526 **Julia Maesa,** grandmother of Elagabalus and Severus Alexander. Æ
denarius. SAECVLI FELICITAS. Felicitas stg. l., altar at feet. *R.I.C. 271.* 22 55

527 **Severus Alexander,** 222-235 (Caesar 221-222). Æ *denarius.*
PAX AETERNA AVG. Pax stg. l. *R.I.C. 165.* 15 35

527A — P. M. TR. P. XIII. COS. III. P. P. Sol advancing l., holding whip. *R.I.C. 123.* 15 35

528

528 Æ *sestertius.* MARS VLTOR S. C. Mars advancing r., with spear and shield.
R.I.C. 635. .... 25 75

		F £	VF £

529   **Orbiana,** wife of Severus Alexander. Æ *denarius.* CONCORDIA AVGG.
Concordia seated l. *R.I.C. 319.*   70   175

530   **Julia Mamaea,** mother of Severus Alexander. Æ *denarius.* VESTA.
Vesta stg. l. *R.I.C. 362.*   20   45

530A   Æ *sestertius.* FELICITAS PVBLICA S. C. Felicitas stg. facing, hd. l.,
resting on column. *R.I.C. 676.*   30   85

531

531   **Maximinus I,** 235-238. Æ *denarius.* PAX AVGVSTI. Pax stg. l. *R.I.C. 12.*   20   45

531A   Æ *sestertius.* SALVS AVGVSTI S. C. Salus seated l., feeding snake arising
from altar. *R.I.C. 85.*   30   85

532   **Maximus Caesar,** son of Maximinus I. Æ *denarius.* PRINC IVVENTVTIS.
Prince stg. l., two standards behind. *R.I.C. 3.*   50   125

533   **Gordian I Africanus,** March-April 238, governor of Britannia Inferior
late in the reign of Caracalla. Æ *denarius.* P. M. TR. P. COS. P. P. Togate
emperor stg. l. *R.I.C. 1.*   250   600

534   **Gordian II Africanus,** March-April 238. Æ *denarius.* VIRTVS AVGG.
Virtus stg. l., with shield and spear. *R.I.C. 3.*   250   600

535   **Balbinus,** April-July 238. Æ *antoninianus.* FIDES MVTVA AVGG.
Clasped hands. *R.I.C. 11.*   75   175

535A   Æ *denarius.* PROVIDENTIA DEORVM. Providentia stg. l., globe at feet.
R.I.C. 7.   50   125

536   **Pupienus,** April-July 238. Æ *antoninianus.* AMOR MVTVVS AVGG.
Clasped hands. *R.I.C. 9a.*   75   175

536A   Æ *denarius.* PAX PVBLICA. Pax seated l. *R.I.C. 4.*   50   120

537   **Gordian III,** 238-244 (Caesar 238). Æ *antoninianus.* LAETITIA AVG. N.
Laetitia stg. l. *R.I.C. 86.*   12   25

538   Æ *denarius.* DIANA LVCIFERA. Diana stg. r., holding torch. *R.I.C. 127.*   15   30

538A

538A   Æ *sestertius.* AETERNITATI AVG. S.C. Sol stg. l., holding globe. *R.I.C. 297a.*   22   65

539

		F	VF
		£	£

539 **Philip I,** 244-249. Æ *antoninianus*. ROMAE AETERNAE. Roma seated l.
R.I.C. 65. .... 12 25

539A Æ *sestertius*. SECVRIT. ORBIS S. C. Securitas seated l. *R.I.C. 190*. 22 65

540 **Otacilia Severa,** wife of Philip I. Æ *antoninianus*. PIETAS AVGVSTAE.
Pietas stg. l. *R.I.C. 125c* .,........ 15 35

540A Æ *sestertius*. CONCORDIA AVGG. S. C. Concordia seated l. *R.I.C. 203a*. 25 75

541 **Philip II,** 247-249 (Caesar 244-247). Æ *antoninianus*. PRINCIPI IVVENT.
Prince stg. l., holding globe and spear. *R.I.C. 218d*.............. 15 35

541A Æ *sestertius*. PAX AETERNA S. C. Pax stg. l. *R.I.C. 268c*. 25 75

542 543

542 **Trajan Decius,** 249-251. Æ *antoninianus*. DACIA. Dacia stg. l., holding
staff with ass's hd. *R.I.C. 12b*. ...., ..., ... 12 30

542A Æ *sestertius*. PANNONIAE S. C. The two Pannoniae stg., each holding
standard. *R.I.C. 124a*................................., ... 25 75

543 **Herennia Etruscilla,** wife of Trajan Decius. Æ *antoninianus*. PVDICITIA
AVG. Pudicitia stg. l. *R.I.C. 58b*................., ,.... 15 35

544 **Herennius Etruscus,** 251 (Caesar 250-251). Æ *antoninianus*. PIETAS
AVGG. Mercury stg. l., holding purse and caduceus. *R.I.C. 142b*.......... 25 65

545 **Hostilian,** 251 (Caesar 251). Æ *antoninianus*. PRINCIPI IVVENTVTIS.
Apollo seated l., holding branch. *R.I.C. 180*............ 35 85

546 **Trebonianus Gallus,** 251-253. Æ *antoninianus*. FELICITAS PVBLICA.
Felicitas stg. l., resting on column. *R.I.C. 34A*.............. 12 30

546A Æ *sestertius*. SALVS AVGG S. C. Salus stg. r., feeding snake held in her
arms. *R.I.C. 121a*. 25 75

547 **Volusian,** 251-253 (Caesar 251). Æ *antoninianus*. VIRTVS AVGG.
Virtus stg. l. *R.I.C. 186*. 12 30

548 **Aemilian,** 253. Æ *antoninianus*. PACI AVG. Pax stg. l., resting on column.
R.I.C. 8. .... 50 120

549 **Valerian,** 253-260. Billon antoninianus. FIDES MILITVM. Fides stg. r.,
holding two standards. *R.I.C. 241*............ 8 20

550 **Diva Mariniana,** wife of Valerian, deified 253. Billon *antoninianus*.
CONSECRATIO. Empress seated on peacock flying r. *R.I.C. 6*. 45 110

			F	VF
			£	£

551   **Gallienus,** 253-268, during whose reign Rome temporarily lost control
over Britain when Postumus rebelled and established the independent
Gallic Empire in 260. Billon *antoninianus*. VIRT GALLIENI AVG.
Emperor advancing r., captive at feet. *R.I.C. 54.* 10   25

552

552   — DIANAE CONS. AVG. Doe l. *R.I.C. 176.*... 8   20
552A — SOLI INVICTO. Sol stg. l., holding globe. *R.I.C. 658.*....................... 8   18
553   **Salonina,** wife of Gallienus. Billon *antoninianus*. VENVS FELIX. Venus
seated l., child at feet. *R.I.C. 7.* 8   20
553A — IVNONI CONS. AVG. Doe l. *R.I.C. 16.*... 8   20
554   **Valerian Junior,** son of Gallienus, Caesar 256-258. Billon *antoninianus*.
IOVI CRESCENTI. Infant Jupiter seated on goat r. *R.I.C. 13.* 15   35
555   **Divus Valerian Junior,** deified 258. Billon *antoninianus*. CONSECRATIO.
Large altar. *R.I.C. 24.*.. 12   30
556   **Saloninus,** 260 (Caesar 258-260). Billon *antoninianus*. PIETAS AVG.
Priestly emblems. *R.I.C. 9.*.. 12   30
557   **Macrianus,** usurper in the East, 260-261. Billon *antoninianus*. SOL.
INVICTO. Sol stg. l., holding globe. *R.I.C. 12.*....................................... 35   85
558   **Quietus,** usurper in the East, 260-261. Billon *antoninianus*.
INDVLGENTIAE AVG. Indulgentia seated l. *R.I.C. 5.* 35   85
559   **Postumus,** usurper in the West, 260-268, founder of the 'Gallic Empire'
which temporarily detached Britain from the rule of the central government,
a state of affairs which continued until Aurelian's defeat of Tetricus in
273. Billon *antoninianus*. HERC. DEVSONIENSI. Hercules stg. r. *R.I.C. 64.* 12   30

560

560   — MONETA AVG. Moneta stg. l. *R.I.C. 75.* 10   25
560A Æ *sestertius*. FIDES MILITVM. Fides stg. l., holding two standards.
R.I.C. 128. 50   140
561   **Laelianus,** usurper in the West, 268. Billon *antoninianus*. VICTORIA AVG.
Victory advancing r. *R.I.C. 9.*... 110   275
562   **Marius,** usurper in the West, 268. Billon *antoninianus*. CONCORDIA
MILITVM. Clasped hands. *R.I.C. 7.* 35   85
563   **Victorinus,** usurper in the West, 268-270. Billon *antoninianus*. INVICTVS.
Sol advancing l. *R.I.C. 114.* 8   20

		F £	VF £

564 **Tetricus,** usurper in the West, 270-273, defeated by Aurelian, thus ending
the 'Gallic Empire' and the isolation of Britain from the authority of Rome.
Billon *antoninianus*. LAETITIA AVGG. Laetitia stg. l. *R.I.C. 87*.......... 8 20
See also under Category 4.

565 **Tetricus Junior,** son of Tetricus, Caesar 270-273. Billon *antoninianus*.
SPES PVBLICA. Spes walking l., holding flower *R.I.C. 272*.................. 8 20
See also under Category 4.

566 **Claudius II Gothicus,** 268-270. Billon *antoninianus*. IOVI STATORI.
Jupiter stg. r. *R.I.C. 52*. 8 18

567 **Divus Claudius II,** deified 270. Billon *antoninianus*. CONSECRATIO.
Large altar. *R.I.C. 261*............. 8 20
See also under Category 4.

568 **Quintillus,** 270. Billon *antoninianus*. DIANA LVCIF. Diana stg. r.,
holding torch. *R.I.C. 49*..... 18 45

569 **Aurelian,** 270-275, restored Britain to the rule of the central government
through his defeat of Tetricus in 273; possibly began construction of the
chain of 'Saxon Shore' forts on the eastern and southern coastlines. Billon
antoninianus. ORIENS AVG. Sol stg. l. between two captives. *R.I.C. 63*. 10 25

569A — RESTITVT. ORBIS. Female stg. r., presenting wreath to emperor stg. l.
R.I.C. 399. .... 10 25

570 **Aurelian and Vabalathus,** ruler of Palmyra 267-272 and usurper in the
East from 271. Billon *antoninianus*. Obv. Laur. bust of Vabalathus r. Rev.
Rad. bust of Aurelian r. *R.I.C. 381*. 25 65

571   574A

571 **Severina,** wife of Aurelian. Billon *antoninianus*. PROVIDEN. DEOR.
Concordia (or Fides) Militum stg. r., facing Sol stg. l. *R.I.C. 9*. 18 45

572 **Tacitus,** 275-276. Billon *antoninianus*. SECVRIT. PERP. Securitas stg. l.,
leaning on column. *R.I.C. 163*. 15 35

573 **Florian,** 276. Billon *antoninianus*. LAETITIA FVND. Laetitia stg. l.
R.I.C. 34. .... 30 75

574 **Probus,** 276-282, suppressed governor's revolt in Britain and lifted
restrictions on viticulture in Britain and Gaul. Billon *antoninianus*.
ADVENTVS PROBI AVG. Emperor on horseback l., captive seated
before. *R.I.C. 160*............ 10 25

574A — VICTORIA GERM. Trophy between two captives. *R.I.C. 222*. 15 40

575 **Carus,** 282-283. Billon *antoninianus*. PAX EXERCITI. Pax stg. l., holding
olive-branch and standard. *R.I.C. 75*..... 15 40

576 **Divus Carus,** deified 283. Billon *antoninianus*. CONSECRATIO. Eagle
facing, hd. l. *R.I.C. 28*. 18 45

577 **Carinus,** 283-285 (Caesar 282-283). Billon *antoninianus*. SAECVLI
FELICITAS. Emperor stg. r. *R.I.C. 214*. 12 30

	F £	VF £

578 **Magnia Urbica,** wife of Carinus. Billon *antoninianus*. VENVS VICTRIX.
Venus stg. l., holding helmet, shield at feet. *R.I.C. 343* 60 150

579 **Numerian,** 283-284 (Caesar 282-283). Billon *antoninianus*. CLEMENTIA
TEMP. Emperor stg. r., receiving globe from Jupiter stg. l. *R.I.C. 463*. .. 12 35

580 **Diocletian,** 284-305. Æ *argenteus*. VIRTVS MILITVM. The four tetrarchs
sacrificing before gateway of military camp. *R.I.C. 27a (Rome)*. 100 250

581 Billon *antoninianus*. IOVI CONSERVAT AVGG. Jupiter stg. l. *R.I.C. 162*. 10 25

582 Æ *follis*. GENIO POPVLI ROMANI. Genius stg. l. R.I.C. 14a *(Alexandria)*. 10 30

582A — (post-abdication coinage, after 305). PROVIDENTIA DEORVM QVIES
AVGG. Quies and Providentia stg. facing each other. *R.I.C. 676a (Treveri)*. 22 65
See also under Category 3.

583 **Maximian,** 286-305 and 306-308, failed in his attempts to suppress the
usurpation of Carausius in Britain. Æ *argenteus*. VICTORIA SARMAT. The
four tetrarchs sacrificing before gateway of military camp. *R.I.C. 37b (Rome)*. 100 250

584

584 Billon *antoninianus*. SALVS AVGG. Salus stg. r., feeding snake held in
her arms. *R.I.C. 417*. 8 20

585 Æ *follis*. SAC. MON. VRB. AVGG. ET CAESS. NN. Moneta stg. l.
R.I.C. 105b (Rome). 12 35

585A — (second reign). CONSERVATORES VRB SVAE. Roma seated in
hexastyle temple. *R.I.C. 84b (Ticinum)*. 12 35
See also under Category 3.

*[For coins of the usurpers **Carausius** and **Allectus** see under Category 3]*

586 **Constantius I,** 305-306 (Caesar 293-305), invaded Britain 296 and defeated
the usurper Allectus, thus restoring the island to the rule of the central
government; Britain now divided into four provinces and the northern
frontier defences reconstructed; died at York, July 306. Æ *argenteus*.
PROVIDENTIA AVGG. The four tetrarchs sacrificing before gateway
of military camp. *R.I.C. 11a (Rome)* 110 275

587

587 Æ *follis*. GENIO POPVLI ROMANI. Genius stg. l. *R.I.C. 26a (Aquileia)*. 12 35

587A — SALVIS AVGG. ET CAESS. FEL. KART. Carthage stg. l., holding
fruits. *R.I.C. 30a (Carthage)*. 15 40
See also under Category 3.

588

| | | F | VF |
| | | £ | £ |

588 **Galerius,** 305-311 (Caesar 293-305). Æ argenteus. VIRTVS MILITVM.
The four tetrarchs sacrificing before gateway of military camp.
R.I.C. 15b (Ticinum). 100 250
588A — XC / VI in wreath. *R.I.C. 16b (Carthage)*............................ 150 400
589 *Æ follis.* GENIO AVGG ET CAESARVM NN. Genius stg. l. *R.I.C. 11b
(Cyzicus)*................................ 12 35
589A — GENIO IMPERATORIS. Genius stg. l. *R.I.C. 101a (Alexandria)*...... 8 25
See also under Category 3.
590 **Galeria Valeria,** wife of Galerius. *Æ follis.* VENERI VICTRICI. Venus
stg. l. *R.I.C. 110 (Alexandria).* 35 85
591 **Severus II,** 306-307 (Caesar 305-306). *Æ follis.* FIDES MILITVM. Fides
seated l. *R.I.C. 73 (Ticinum).* 35 85
See also under Category 3.
592 **Maximinus II,** 310-313 (Caesar 305-310). *Æ follis.* GENIO CAESARIS.
Genius stg. l. *R.I.C. 64 (Alexandria)*........................ 8 25
592A — GENIO POP. ROM. Genius stg. l. *R.I.C. 845a (Treveri)*.................... 8 20
See also under Category 3.

593

593 **Maxentius,** 306-312 (Caesar 306). *Æ follis.* CONSERV. VRB. SVAE.
Roma seated in hexastyle temple. *R.I.C. 210 (Rome)*............................. 10 30
594 **Romulus,** son of Maxentius, deified 309. *Æ quarter follis.* AETERNAE
MEMORIAE. Temple with domed roof. *R.I.C. 58 (Ostia).* 35 85
595 **Licinius,** 308-324. *Æ follis.* GENIO AVGVSTI. Genius stg. l. *R.I.C. 198b
(Siscia).* 8 20
595A *Æ 3.* IOVI CONSERVATORI AVGG. Jupiter stg. l. *R.I.C. 24 (Nicomedia).* 8 20
See also under Category 3.
596 **Licinius Junior,** son of Licinius, Caesar 317-324. *Æ 3.* CAESARVM
NOSTRORVM around wreath containing VOT. / V. *R.I.C. 92 (Thessalonica).* 8 22
597 **Constantine I, the Great,** 307-337 (Caesar 306-307), campaigned with
his father Constantius I against the Picts in northern Britain, summer 306,
and proclaimed emperor by the legions at York on Constantius' death
in July; closed the London mint early in 325 ending almost four decades
of operation. *Æ follis.* GENIO POP ROM. Genius stg. l. *R.I.C. 719b (Treveri).* 12 35
598 — SOLI INVICTO COMITI. Sol stg. l. *R.I.C. 307 (Lugdunum)*............. 6 18
598A *Æ 3.* PROVIDENTIAE AVGG. Gateway of military camp. *R.I.C. 153
(Thessalonica).*........................ 5 15

599   600

		F £	VF £
599	— VIRTVS EXERCIT. Trophy between two captives. *R.I.C. 280 (Treveri)*.	12	30
599A	Æ 3/4. GLORIA EXERCITVS. Two soldiers stg. either side of two standards. *R.I.C. 518 (Treveri)*.	4	12
	See also under Category 3.		
600	**'Urbs Roma'**, after 330. Æ 3/4. Obv. Helmeted bust of Roma l. Rev. She-wolf l., suckling twins. *R.I.C. 195 (Nicomedia)*.	5	15

601   604

601	**'Constantinopolis'**, after 330. Æ 3/4. Obv. Helmeted bust of Constantinopolis l. Rev. Victory stg. l., foot on prow. *R.I.C. 339 (Rome)*.	5	15
602	**Fausta**, wife of Constantine I. Æ 3. SALVS REIPVBLICAE. Empress stg. l., holding two children. *R.I.C. 459 (Treveri)*.	18	45
	See also under Category 3.		
603	**Helena**, mother of Constantine I. Æ 3. SECVRITAS REIPVBLICE. Empress stg. l., holding branch. *R.I.C. 38 (Alexandria)*.	18	40
603A	Æ 4 (posthumous issue, 337-340). PAX PVBLICA. Pax stg. l. *R.I.C. 78 (Treveri)*.	10	25
	See also under Category 3.		
604	**Theodora**, second wife of Constantius I. Æ 4 (posthumous issue, 337-340). PIETAS ROMANA. Pietas stg. r., holding child. R.I.C. 43 (Treveri).	12	30
605	**Crispus**, eldest son of Constantine I, Caesar 317-326. Æ 3. CAESARVM NOSTRORVM around wreath containing VOT. / V. *R.I.C. 68 (Aquileia)*.	8	20
	See also under Category 3.		
606	**Delmatius**, nephew of Constantine I, Caesar 335-337. Æ 3/4. GLORIA EXERCITVS. Two soldiers stg. either side of two standards. *R.I.C. 90 (Antioch)*.	18	45
607	**Hanniballianus**, nephew of Constantine I, Rex 335-337. Æ 4. SECVRITAS PVBLICA. River-god Euphrates reclining r. *R.I.C. 147 (Constantinople)*.	100	250
608	**Constantine II**, 337-340 (Caesar 317-337). Æ 3. BEATA TRANQVILLITAS. Altar inscribed VOT / IS / XX. *R.I.C. 312 (Treveri)*.	8	20
608A	Æ 3/4. GLORIA EXERCITVS. Two soldiers stg. either side of standard. *R.I.C. 392 (Rome)*.	4	10
	See also under Category 3.		
609	**Constans**, 337-350 (Caesar 333-337), visited Britain in 343, the last reigning emperor to do so. Æ 2. FEL. TEMP. REPARATIO. Soldier r., dragging barbarian from hut beneath tree. *R.I.C. 103 (Aquileia)*.	10	30

609A   611B

		F	VF
		£	£

609A — FEL. TEMP. REPARATIO. Emperor stg. l. on galley steered by Victory.
R.I.C. 219 (Treveri).. 10 30

609B Æ 4. VICTORIAE DD. AVGG. Q. NN. Two Victories stg. face to face.
R.I.C. 195 (Treveri).. 4 10

610 **Constantius II,** 337-361 (Caesar 324-337). Æ 3/4. GLORIA EXERCITVS.
Two soldiers stg. either side of two standards. *R.I.C. 85 (Cyzicus)*.......... 4 12

611 Æ *siliqua*. VOTIS / XXX. / MVLTIS / XXXX in wreath. *R.I.C. 207 (Arelate)*. 25 60

611A Æ 2. FEL. TEMP. REPARATIO. Emperor stg. l. on galley. *R.I.C. 218*
(Treveri). 10 30

611B Æ 3. FEL. TEMP. REPARATIO. Soldier advancing l., spearing fallen
horseman. *R.I.C. 189 (Lugdunum)*... 5 15
See also under Categories 3 and 4.

612   616

612 **Magnentius,** usurper in the West, 350-353, temporarily detached Britain
from the rule of the legitimate Constantinian dynasty. Æ 1. SALVS DD.
NN. AVG. ET CAES. *Chi-Rho* Christian monogram between Alpha
and Omega. *R.I.C. 34 (Ambianum)*... 75 175

612A Æ 2. FELICITAS REIPVBLICE. Emperor stg. l., holding Victory and
labarum. *R.I.C. 264 (Treveri)*.. 15 40
See also under Category 4.

613 **Decentius,** brother of Magnentius, Caesar 351-353. Æ 2. VICTORIAE DD.
NN. AVG. ET CAE. Two Victories supporting between them shield
inscribed VOT. / V. / MVLT. / X. *R.I.C. 146 (Lugdunum)*. 20 50
See also under Category 4.

614 **Vetranio,** 'usurper' in the Balkans, 350. Æ 2. CONCORDIA MILITVM.
Emperor stg. l., holding two labara. *R.I.C. 281 (Siscia)*. 50 125

615 **Constantius Gallus,** Caesar under Constantius II, 351-354. Æ 2. FEL.
TEMP. REPARATIO. Soldier advancing l., spearing fallen horseman.
R.I.C. 94 (Cyzicus). 15 40

616 **Julian II,** 360-363 (Caesar 355-360). Æ *siliqua*. VOT. / X. / MVLT. / XX.
in wreath. *R.I.C. 309 (Arelate)*... 25 60

	F	*VF*
	£	£

617 Æ 1. SECVRITAS REIPVB. Bull stg. r. *R.I.C. 411 (Siscia)*.................... 45 140

617A Æ 3. VOT. / X. / MVLT. / XX. in wreath. *R.I.C. 108 (Sirmium)*............. 8 25

618 **Jovian,** 363-364. Æ 3. VOT. / V. / MVLT. / X. in wreath. *R.I.C. 426 (Siscia)*. 12 35

619 **Valentinian I,** 364-375 (in the West), during whose reign the Roman
province of Britannia was devastated by the simultaneous attack of hordes
of invaders on several fronts (the 'Barbarian Conspiracy'); order eventually
restored by Count Theodosius, father of the future emperor . *N solidus.*
RESTITVTOR REIPVBLICAE. Emperor stg. r., holding standard and
Victory. *R.I.C. 2b (Antioch)*... 100 250

619A Æ 3. GLORIA ROMANORVM. Emperor advancing r., dragging
barbarian and holding labarum. *R.I.C. 14a (Siscia)*. 5 15

619B

619B — SECVRITAS REIPVBLICAE. Victory advancing l. *R.I.C. 32a (Treveri)*. 5 15

620 **Valens,** 364-378 (in the East). *R siliqua*. VRBS ROMA. Roma seated l.
R.I.C. 27e (Treveri)... 25 60

620A Æ 3. SECVRITAS REIPVBLICAE. Victory advancing l. *R.I.C. 42b
(Constantinople)*.. 5 15

621 **Procopius,** usurper in the East, 365-366. Æ 3. REPARATIO FEL. TEMP.
Emperor stg. r., holding standard and shield. *R.I.C. 17a (Constantinople)*. 50 125

622 **Gratian,** 367-383 (in the West), overthrown by Magnus Maximus who
had been proclaimed emperor by the army in Britain. *R siliqua*. VRBS
ROMA. Roma seated l. *R.I.C. 27f (Treveri)*. 25 65

623 **Valentinian II,** 375-392 (in the West). Æ 2. REPARATIO REIPVB.
Emperor stg. l., raising kneeling female figure. *R.I.C. 20c (Arelate)*. 10 30

623A Æ 4. SALVS REIPVBLICAE. Victory advancing l., dragging barbarian.
R.I.C. 20a (Alexandria)... 4 12

624 **Theodosius I,** the Great, 379-395 (in the East), son of the Count Theodosius
who had cleared Britain of barbarian invaders in the reign of Valentinian I;
the Emperor Theodosiua twice restored Britain to the rule of the central
government, by his defeat of the usurpers Magnus Maximus (in 388) and
Eugenius (in 394). *R siliqua*. CONCORDIA AVGGG. Constantinopolis
enthroned facing, foot on prow. *R.I.C. 55a (Treveri)*. 30 75

624A

624A — VIRTVS ROMANORVM. Roma enthroned facing. *R.I.C. (Aquileia) 28d*. 30 75

624B Æ 2. VIRTVS EXERCIT. Emperor stg. r., foot on captive, holding
labarum and globe. *R.I.C. 24b (Heraclea)*.. 12 35

		F £	*VF* £

625 **Aelia Flaccilla,** wife of Theodosius I. Æ 2. SALVS REIPVBLICAE.
Victory seated r., inscribing Christian monogram on shield set on cippus.
R.I.C. 81 (Constantinople). 25 65

626 627

626 **Magnus Maximus,** usurper in the West, 383-388, proclaimed emperor
by the army in Britain, invaded Gaul, and overthrew the legitimate western
emperor Gratian; possibly reopened the London mint for a brief issue of
precious metal coinage (Rudyard Kipling presented a rather fanciful
version of his career in "Puck of Pook's Hill"). Æ *siliqua.* VIRTVS
ROMANORVM. Roma enthroned facing. *R.I.C. 84b (Treveri).* 30 75
See also under Category 3.

627 **Flavius Victor,** son of Magnus Maximus, co-emperor 387-388. Æ 4.
SPES ROMANORVM. Gateway of military camp. *RIC 55b (Aquileia).* 40 100

628 **Eugenius,** usurper in the West, 392-394, recognized in Britain until his
defeat by Theodosius the Great. Æ *siliqua.* VIRTVS ROMANORVM.
Roma seated l. on cuirass. *R.I.C. 106d (Treveri).* 120 275

629 **Arcadius,** 395-408 (in the East, co-emperor with his father Theodosius I
from 383). Æ *solidus.* VICTORIA AVGGG. Emperor stg. r., foot on
captive, holding standard and Victory. *R.I.C. 1205 (Milan).* 90 225

629A 631

629A Æ 2. GLORIA ROMANORVM. Emperor stg. l., holding standard and
shield, captive at feet. *R.I.C. 41 (Antioch).* 15 40

630 **Honorius,** 395-423 (in the West, co-emperor with his father Theodosius I
and brother Arcadius from 393), this reign saw the end of Roman rule in
Britain following a succession of usurpations in the province, culminating
in that of Constantine III against whom the Britons rebelled in 409;
Honorius' celebrated 'Rescript' of the following year instructed the
provincials to look to their own defence as he was no longer able to assist
them. Æ *solidus.* VICTORIA AVGGG. Emperor stg. r., foot on captive,
holding standard and Victory. *R.I.C. 1287 (Ravenna)* 90 225

630A Æ *siliqua.* VIRTVS ROMANORVM. Roma seated l. on cuirass.
R.I.C. 1228 (Milan). 35 85

631 **Constantine III,** usurper in the West, 407-411, proclaimed emperor by the
army in Britain, but his authority rejected by the Romano-Britons two years
later, thus effectively ending 366 years of Roman rule in Britain. Æ *siliqua.*
VICTORIA AVGGG. Roma enthroned l. *R.I.C. 1532 (Treveri)* 125 300

F	*VF*
£	£

632   **Valentinian III,** 425-455 (in the West), during whose reign the Saxon
conquest of the former Roman province commenced, following the final
unsuccessful appeal of the Romano-Britons for help addressed to the general
Aetius in 446. *N solidus*. VICTORIA AVGGG. Emperor stg. facing, foot
on human-headed serpent. *R.I.C. 2010 (Ravenna)*.   125   300

632A   Æ 4. VOT. PVB. Gateway of military camp. *R.I.C. 2123 (Rome)*.   25   75

2. ISSUES WITH TYPES REFERRING SPECIFICALLY
TO THE PROVINCE OF BRITANNIA

Struck in Rome, unless otherwise indicated. These usually commemorate military operations in the
northern frontier region of the province or beyond.

633   635

F	*VF*
£	£

633   **Claudius,** A.D. 41-54. AV aureus, celebrating the early stages of the
Roman conquest of Britain which commenced in A.D. 43. DE BRITANN
on architrave of triumphal arch. *R.I.C. 33*.   900   2250

634   Æ *denarius*. Similar. *R.I.C. 34*   275   650

634A   Æ *didrachm* of Caesarea in Cappadocia. DE BRITANNIS. Emperor in
triumphal quadriga r. *R.I.C. 122*.   300   750

635   **Hadrian,** 117-138. Æ as, commemorating the restoration of order in the
province following a serious uprising (or invasion) in the north, probably
early in the governorship of Q. Pompeius Falco (118-122). BRITANNIA
PONT. MAX. TR. POT. COS. III. S. C. Britannia seated facing on rock.
R.I.C. 577a.   125   325

636   Æ *sestertius,* commemorating Hadrian's visit to the province in 122, when
he planned and initiated the construction of the northern frontier system
which bears his name. ADVENTVI AVG. BRITANNIAE S.C. Emperor
and Britannia stg. either side of altar. *R.I.C. 882* ....   *Extremely rare*

637

637   — BRITANNIA S. C. Britannia seated facing, foot resting on rock.
R.I.C. 845. ....   *Extremely rare*

| | F | VF |
| | £ | £ |

637A Æ *dupondius* or as. *Similar. R.I.C. 846*.. *Extremely rare*

638 Æ *sestertius*, commemorating Hadrian's attention to the legionary garrison
strength of the province, principally his transfer of *VI Victrix* from
Germany in 122. EXERC. BRITANNICVS S. C. Emperor on horseback
r., addressing gathering of troops. *R.I.C. 912.* .... *Extremely rare*

638A — EXERC. BRITANNICVS S.C. Emperor stg. r. on tribunal, addressing
gathering of troops. *R.I.C. 913*... *Extremely rare*

639 **Antoninus Pius,** 138-161. *N aureus,* commemorating the conquests in
Scotland by the governor Q. Lollius Urbicus (138/9-142/3) at which time
construction of the Antonine Wall was begun. BRITAN. IMPERATOR II.
Victory stg. l. on globe. *R.I.C. 113.* 600   1500

640

640 Æ *sestertius*. BRITANNIA S. C. Britannia seated l. on rock, holding
standard. *R.I.C. 742*... 400   1000

641 — BRITAN. IMPERATOR II. S. C. Helmeted Britannia seated l., foot on
rock. *R.I.C. 743.* 450   1200

642 — BRITAN. IMPERATOR II. S. C. Britannia seated l. on globe above
waves, holding standard. *R.I.C. 744.* 500   1400

643 — BRITAN. IMPERATOR II. S. C. Victory stg. l. on globe. *R.I.C. 719.*   175
450

643A — BRITANNIA IMPERATOR II. S. C. Britannia seated l. on rock,
holding standard. *R.I.C. 745.* 450   1200

644 Æ *as*. IMPERATOR II. S. C. Victory hovering l., holding shield inscribed
BRI / TAN. *R.I.C. 732.*   90   225

645 Æ *dupondius,* commemorating the quelling of a serious uprising in the
north, ca. 154/5, necessitating the evacuation of the recently constructed
Antonine Wall in Scotland. BRITANNIA COS. IIII. S. C. Britannia seated
l. on rock, shield and vexillum in background. *R.I.C. 930.*   75   185

	F	VF
	£	£

646   Æ *as*. Similar. *R.I.C. 934.*   60   150
Many specimens of this type are carelessly struck on inadequate flans.
Moreover, they have been found in significant quantities on Romano-British
sites, notably in Coventina's Well at Carrawburgh fort on Hadrian's Wall,
raising the interesting possibility that they may have been issued from a
temporary mint in Britain. The style of the engraving is quite regular,
indicating that even if locally produced these coins would have been struck
from normal Roman dies brought to Britain especially for this purpose.
See under Category 3.

647   **Commodus,** 177-192. Æ *sestertius,* commemorating the victories in
Scotland of the governor Ulpius Marcellus in 184/5. These were in
retribution for a major barbarian invasion several years earlier resulting
in serious damage to Hadrian's Wall, which had been temporarily overrun,
and the defeat and death of an unknown governor. BRITT. P. M. TR. P.
VIIII. IMP. VII. COS. IIII. P. P. S. C. Britannia stg. l., holding curved
sword and helmet. *R.I.C. 437.*..   *Extremely rare*

648

648   — VICT. BRIT. P. M. TR. P. VIIII. (or X.) IMP. VII. COS. IIII. P. P. S. C.
Victory seated r., about to inscribe shield. *R.I.C. 440, 452*   90   240

649

649   **Septimius Severus,** 193-211. *N aureus,* commemorating the success of
the punitive Roman campaigns in Scotland during 209 and 210 culminating
in the illness and death of Severus at York in Feb. 211. VICTORIAE BRIT.
Victory advancing l. *R.I.C. 334.*   1200   3000

650   — VICTORIAE BRIT. Victory advancing r., leading child by hand.
R.I.C. 302.   1400   3500

651   Æ *denarius.* VICTORIAE BRIT. Victory advancing r. *R.I.C. 332*..........   35   75

651A   — VICTORIAE BRIT. Victory stg. facing beside palm-tree with shield
attached. *R.I.C. 336.*...   40   85

651B   — VICTORIAE BRIT. Victory stg. l. *R.I.C. 333*....................................   40   85

651C   — VICTORIAE BRIT. Victory seated l., holding shield. *R.I.C. 335.*   40   80

652

	F	VF
	£	£

652 Æ *sestertius*. VICTORIAE BRITTANNICAE S. C. Two Victories placing
shield on palm-tree with captives at base. *R.I.C. 818.* 300 750

653 — P. M. TR. P. XVIII. COS. III. P. P. S. C. Similar. *R.I.C. 796.* 150 375

654 Æ *dupondius.* VICT. BRIT. P. M. TR. P. XIX. COS. III. P. P. S. C. Victory
stg. r. between two captives, holding vexillum. *R.I.C. 809.* 100 275

655 Æ *as*. VICTORIAE BRITTANNICAE S. C. Similar. *R.I.C. 837a.* 100 275

656 Billon *tetradrachm* of Alexandria in Egypt. NEIKH KATA BRET. Nike
flying l. *Milne 2726*.. *Extremely rare*

657 **Caracalla,** 198-217. *N aureus,* commemorating the victories achieved
by the Romans in Scotland during the campaigns led jointly by Severus
and Caracalla in 209, and by Caracalla alone the following year during
his father's illness. VICTORIAE BRIT. Victory seated l., holding shield.
R.I.C. 174. .... 1200 3000

658   659A

658 Æ *denarius*. VICTORIAE BRIT. Victory advancing l. *R.I.C. 231*.......... 40 80

658A — VICTORIAE BRIT. Victory advancing r., holding trophy. *R.I.C. 231A.* 40 80

659 Æ *sestertius*. VICTORIAE BRITTANNICAE S. C. Victory stg. r., erecting
trophy to r. of which Britannia stands facing, captive at feet. *R.I.C. 464.* 250 650

659A — VICT. BRIT. TR. P. XIIII. COS. III. S.C. Similar. *Cf. R.I.C. 483c.* 225 550

660 Æ *dupondius*. VICTORIAE BRITTANNICAE S. C. Victory stg. r.,
inscribing shield set on palm-tree. *R.I.C. 467.*... 100 275

661 Æ *as*. VICT. BRIT. TR. P. XIIII. COS. III. S. C. Similar. *R.I.C. 490*...... 100 250

662 **Geta,** 209-212. *Æ denarius,* commemorating the victories achieved by
his father and brother in Scotland in 209-10 while he and his mother were
resident in London. VICTORIAE BRIT. Victory stg. l. *R.I.C. 92.* 40 85

662A — VICTORIAE BRIT. Victory advancing r. *R.I.C. 91*............................ 40 85

663

	F	VF
	£	£

663　Æ *sestertius*. VICTORIAE BRITTANNICAE S. C. Victory seated r.,
inscribing shield set on knee. *R.I.C. 166*. ....　250　650

663A　— VICT. BRIT. TR. P. III. COS. II. S. C. Similar. *R.I.C. 172b*. ....　225　550

664　Æ *as*. VICTORIAE BRITTANNICAE S. C. Victory seated l., balancing
shield on knee. *R.I.C. 191a*. ....　100　275

665　Billon *tetradrachm* of Alexandria in Egypt. NEIKH KATA BRETAN.
Nike advancing l. *B.M.C. (Alexandria) 1481*. ....　*Extremely rare*

3. OFFICIAL ROMAN COINAGE STRUCK IN BRITAIN

The London mint, and the associated 'C' mint (possibly Colchester), were created by the usurper Carausius soon after his seizure of Britain in 287. Prior to this, in the mid-2nd century, there may have been minting of 'Britannia' asses of Antoninus Pius in the province using dies brought from Rome, though this has not been firmly established. After the downfall of the rebel British regime in 296 the minting establishment in London (though not the subsidiary mint) was retained by the tetrarchal government and the succeeding Constantinian administration. Early in 325, however, Constantine the Great closed the London mint after almost four decades of operation. A possible brief revival under the usurper Magnus Maximus has been postulated for gold and silver coins marked 'AVG', 'AVGOB' and 'AVGPS', though the attribution has not received universal acceptance.

	F	VF
	£	£

666　**Antoninus Pius,** 138-161. Æ *as,* struck in northern Britain (?) in 155.
BRITANNIA COS. IIII. S. C. Britannia seated l. on rock, shield and
vexillum in background. *R.I.C. 930.* ....　50　125
Many poorly struck examples of this type have been found on Romano-British sites, notably at Brocolitia (Carrawburgh) fort on Hadrian's Wall in Northumberland, where no fewer than 327 specimens were discovered in the great votive deposit in the well which formed part of the shrine of the water-nymph Coventina. There appears to be a very real possibility that many of these 'Britannia' asses had been issued from a temporary mint in Britain, most likely situated in the north. The dies, however, are quite regular, and would thus have been brought from Rome to the island province for the express purpose of supplementing the money supply at a time of crisis.

667　**Carausius,** usurper in Britain and northwestern Gaul, A.D. 287-293. *N
aureus,* London. CONSERVAT. AVG. Jupiter stg. l., eagle at feet, ML in
ex. *R.I.C. 1.* ....　5000　12500

668　Æ *denarius,* London. EXPECTATE VENI. Britannia stg. r. and emperor l.,
clasping hands, RSR in ex. *R.I.C. 555.* ....　450　1200

669 672A

		F	VF
		£	£
669	— RENOVAT. ROMANO. She-wolf r., suckling twins, RSR in ex. *R.I.C. 571.*	400	1000
670	Billon *antoninianus,* London. COMES AVG. Victory stg. l., S—P in field, ML in ex. *R.I.C. 14.*	40	100
670A	— HILARITAS AVG. Hilaritas stg. l., B—E in field, MLXXI in ex. *R.I.C. 41.*	25	60
671	— LAETITIA AVG. Laetitia stg. l., F—O in field, ML in ex. *R.I.C. 50.*	25	60
671A	— LEG. II. AVG. Capricorn l., ML in ex. *R.I.C. 58.*	70	175
	Legio II Augusta was stationed at Isca (Caerleon in South Wales).		
672	— LEG. XX. V. V. Boar stg. r. *R.I.C. 82.*	70	175
	Legio XX Valeria Victrix was stationed at Deva (Chester in the northwest Midlands).		
672A	— PAX AVG. Pax stg. l., F—O in field, ML in ex. *R.I.C. 101.*	22	55
673	— Similar, but without mint mark. *R.I.C. 880*	20	50
673A	— PROVIDENT. AVG. Providentia stg. l., B—E in field, MLXXI in ex. *R.I.C. 149.*	25	60
674	— SALVS AVGGG. Salus stg. r., feeding snake held in her arms, S—P in field, ML in ex. *R.I.C. 164.*	25	65
	The reverse legends with triple-ending (AVGGG.) presumably are subsequent to Carausius' recognition by Diocletian and Maximian in 289 following the failure of the latter's attempt to dislodge the usurper from his island stronghold.		
674A	— TEMPORVM FELICITAS. Felicitas stg. l., B—E in field, ML in ex. *R.I.C. 172.*	20	60
675	— VIRTVS AVGGG. Mars (or Virtus) stg. r., holding spear and shield, S—P in field, MLXXI in ex. *R.I.C. 183.*	25	65
676	Billon *antoninianus,* Colchester (?). CONCORDIA MILIT. Emperor stg. r. and Concordia l., clasping hands, C in ex. *R.I.C. 205.*	50	120
676A	— EXPECTATE VENI. Britannia stg. r. and emperor l., clasping hands, MSC in ex. *R.I.C. 216.*	100	250
677	— FELICITAS AVG. Galley with mast and rowers, CXXI in ex. *R.I.C. 221.*	80	200
677A	— FORTVNA RAEDVX. Fortuna seated l., SPC in ex. *R.I.C. 237.*	40	100
678	— LAETITIA AVG. Laetitia stg. l., globe at feet, S—P in field, C in ex. *R.I.C. 255.*	25	60
678A	— MONETA AVG. Moneta stg. l., CXXI in ex. *R.I.C. 287*	25	60
679	— ORIENS AVG. Sol stg. l., C in ex. *R.I.C. 293.*	30	75
679A	— PAX AVGGG. Pax stg. l., S—P in field, MC in ex. *R.I.C. 335.*	25	60

680

		F	VF
		£	£

680	— PROVID. AVG. Providentia stg. l., S—P in field, C in ex. *R.I.C. 353.*	25	60
680A	— SALVS AVG. Salus stg. l. at altar, feeding snake, S—C in field, C in ex. *R.I.C. 396.*	25	60
681	— SPES PVBLICA. Spes walking l., holding flower, S—P in field, C in ex. *R.I.C. 413.*	25	60
681A	— VICTORIA AVG. Victory advancing l., captive at feet, MC in ex. *R.I.C. 429.*	30	75
682	**Carausius, Diocletian and Maximian,** after 289. Billon *antoninianus,* Colchester (?). Obv. CARAVSIVS ET FRATRES SVI. Conjoined busts of the three emperors l. Rev. PAX AVGGG. Pax stg. l., S—P in field, C in ex. *R.I.C. 1.*	800	2000

682A   684A

682A	— MONETA AVGGG. Moneta stg. l., S—P in field, C in ex. *R.I.C. —.* *See also nos. 693-4 and 698-700 as well as regular Carausian types with the triple-ending 'AVGGG.' on reverse.*	1000	2500
683	**Allectus,** usurper in Britain, 293-296. *N̄ aureus,* London. ORIENS AVG. Sol stg. l. between two captives, ML in ex. *R.I.C. 4.*	7000	17500
684	Æ *antoninianus,* London. LAETITIA AVG. Laetitia stg. l., S—A in field, MSL in ex. *R.I.C. 22.*	25	65
684A	— PAX AVG. Pax stg. l., S—A in field, ML in ex. *R.I.C. 28.*	30	70
685	— PROVID. AVG. Providentia stg. l., holding globe and cornucopiae, S—P in field, ML in ex. *R.I.C. 36.*	30	75
685A	— SALVS AVG. Salus stg. r., feeding snake held in her arms, S—A in field, MSL in ex. *R.I.C. 42.*	25	65
686	— TEMPOR. FELICITAS. Felicitas stg. l., S—A in field, ML in ex. *R.I.C. 47.*	25	60
686A	— VICTORIA AVG. Victory advancing l., S—P in field, ML in ex. *R.I.C. 48.*	25	60
687	Æ *antoninianus,* Colchester (?). AEQVITAS AVG. Aequitas stg. l., S—P in field, C in ex. *R.I.C. 63.*	25	65
687A	— FIDES MILITVM. Fides stg. l., holding two standards, S—P in field, C in ex. *R.I.C. 69.*	25	65

688A

		F	VF
		£	£
688	— LAETITIA AVG. Laetitia stg. l., S—P in field, CL in ex. *R.I.C. 79.*.	40	100
	This form of mint mark has given rise to the alternative identification of		
	this mint as Clausentum (Bitterne, Hants.)		
688A	— MONETA AVG. Moneta stg. l., S—P in field, C in ex. *R.I.C. 82.*.....	35	85
689	— PAX AVG. Pax stg. l., S—P in field, C in ex. *R.I.C. 86.*	30	70
689A	— PROVIDENTIA AVG. Providentia stg. l., globe at feet, S—P in field,		
	C in ex. *R.I.C. 111.*	25	65
690	— TEMPORVM FELIC. Felicitas stg. l., S—P in field, CL in ex. *R.I.C. 117.*	40	100
690A	— VIRTVS AVG. Mars stg. r., holding spear and shield, S—P in field,		
	C in ex. *R.I.C. 121.*	25	65
691	Æ *'quinarius'*, London. VIRTVS AVG. Galley l., QL in ex. *R.I.C. 55.*...	25	65
	An experimental denomination issued only during this reign, the types of		
	the so-called 'quinarius' would seem to indicate that it was in some way		
	associated with the operations of the fleet upon which the survival of the		
	rebel regime in Britain was totally dependent.		

692   693

692	Æ *'quinarius'*, Colchester (?). LAETITIA AVG. Galley r., QC in ex.		
	R.I.C. 124.	25	65
692A	— VIRTVS AVG. Galley l., QC in ex. *R.I.C. 128.*	30	70
693	**Diocletian,** 284-305. Billon *antoninianus* of London, struck by Carausius		
	between 289 and 293. PAX AVGGG. Pax stg. l., S—P in field, MLXXI		
	in ex. *R.I.C. 9.*	35	85
694	Billon *antoninianus* of Colchester (?), same date. PROVID AVGGG.		
	Providentia stg. l., globe at feet, S—P in field, C in ex. *R.I.C. 22.*...........	35	85

695

| | F | VF |
| | £ | £ |

695 Æ *follis*, London. GENIO POPVLI ROMANI. Genius stg. l., LON in ex.
R.I.C. 1a. 100 250
*By the time the central government had recovered control of Britain in 296
the antoninianus had been replaced by the larger follis under Diocletian's
sweeping currency reform. London was retained as an official imperial
mint, but the secondary British establishment (at Colchester?) was now
abandoned. Except for its initial issue in 297 (marked 'LON') the London
mint under the tetrarchic government produced only unsigned folles
throughout its first decade of operation. Perhaps Constantius did not
wish to draw attention to his employment of a mint which had been the
creation of a rebel regime.*

696

696 — Similar, but without mint mark. *R.I.C. 6a*.. 10 25
697 — (post-abdication coinage, after 305). PROVIDENTIA DEORVM
QVIES AVGG. Quies and Providentia stg. facing each other (no mint mark).
R.I.C. 77a. 25 55
697A — QVIES AVGG. Quies stg. l., holding branch and sceptre, PLN in ex.
R.I.C. 98. .... 18 45
698 **Maximian,** 286-305 and 306-308. *N aureus* of London, struck by
Carausius between 289 and 293. SALVS AVGGG. Salus stg. r., feeding
snake held in her arms, ML in ex. *R.I.C. 32*. .... *Extremely rare*
699 Billon *antoninianus* of London, same date. PROVIDENTIA AVGGG.
Providentia stg. l., S—P in field, MLXXI in ex. *R.I.C. 37*. 35 85
700 Billon *antoninianus* of Colchester (?), same date. PAX AVGGG. Pax stg.
l., S—P in field, C in ex. *R.I.C. 42*... 35 85
701 Æ *follis,* London. GENIO POPVLI ROMANI. Genius stg. l., LON in ex.
R.I.C. 2. .... 100 250
702 — Similar, but without mint mark. *R.I.C. 23b*... 10 25
703 — (post-abdication coinage, after 305). PROVIDENTIA DEORVM
QVIES AVGG. Quies and Providentia stg. facing each other (no mint mark).
R.I.C. 77b. 25 55

704

	F	VF
	£	£
704 — (second reign). GENIO POP. ROM. Genius stg. l., PLN in ex. *R.I.C. 90.*	15	35
704A — HERCVLI CONSERVATORI. Hercules stg. l., resting on club, PLN in ex. *R.I.C. 91*	25	65
705 **Constantius I,** 305-306 (Caesar 293-305). Æ *follis,* London (as Caesar). GENIO POPVLI ROMANI. Genius stg. l., LON in ex. *R.I.C. 4a.*	110	275

706

706 — Similar, but without mint mark. *R.I.C. 30*	12	30
707 — (as Augustus). Similar. *R.I.C. 52a.*	15	40
708 **Divus Constantius I,** deified 306. Æ *follis,* London. MEMORIA FELIX. Altar flanked by eagles, PLN in ex. *R.I.C. 110*	18	45
709 **Galerius,** 305-311 (Caesar 293-305). Æ *follis,* London (as Caesar). GENIO POPVLI ROMANI. Genius stg. l., LON in ex. *R.I.C. 4b.*	110	275
710 — Similar, but without mint mark. *R.I.C. 15*	10	25
711 — (as Augustus). Similar. *R.I.C. 42.*	12	30
711A — GENIO POP. ROM. Genius stg. l., PLN in ex. *R.I.C. 86.*	18	45
712 **Severus II,** 306-307 (Caesar 305-306). Æ *follis,* London (as Caesar). GENIO POPVLI ROMANI. Genius stg. l. (no mint mark). *R.I.C. 58a*	35	85
713 — (as Augustus). Similar. *R.I.C. 52c.*	35	85
714 **Maximinus II,** 310-313 (Caesar 305-310). Æ *follis,* London (as Caesar). GENIO POPVLI ROMANI. Genius stg. l. (no mint mark). *R.I.C. 57.*	15	40
715 — GENIO POP. ROM. Genius stg. l., PLN in ex. *R.I.C. 89a.*	15	40
716 — (as Augustus). Similar, but with star in r. field. *R.I.C. 209b*	12	30
717 **Licinius,** 308-324. Æ *follis,* London. GENIO POP. ROM. Genius stg. l., star in r. field, PLN in ex. *R.I.C. 209c.*	12	30
717A — Similar, but with S—F in field. *R.I.C. 3.*	8	20
718 — SOLI INVICTO COMITI. Sol stg. l., holding globe, S—P in field, MSL in ex. *R.I.C. 79.*	10	25
719 **Constantine I, the Great,** 307-337 (Caesar 306-307). Æ *follis,* London (as Caesar). GENIO POPVLI ROMANI. Genius stg. l. (no mint mark). *R.I.C. 72.*	25	65
719A — GENIO POP. ROM. Genius stg. l., PLN in ex. *R.I.C. 88b*	15	35

	F	VF
	£	£

720 — PRINCIPI IVVENTVTIS. Prince stg. l., holding standards, PLN in ex.
R.I.C. 97. .... 25 60

721 — (as Augustus). ADVENTVS AVG. Emperor on horseback l., captive
on ground before, star in r. field, PLN in ex. R.I.C. 133........................... 22 55

722

722 — COMITI AVGG. NN. Sol stg. l., holding globe and whip, same mint
mark. R.I.C. 155. .... 18 45

723 — CONCORD. MILIT. Concordia stg. l., holding standards, same mint
mark. R.I.C. 195. .... 15 40

724 — MARTI CONSERVATORI. Mars. stg. r., holding spear and shield,
star in l. field, PLN in ex. R.I.C. 254. .... 15 35

724A — SOLI INVICTO COMITI. Sol stg. l., holding globe, S—F in field,
MLL in ex. R.I.C. 27. .... 8 20

725 Æ 3, London. VICTORIAE LAETAE PRINC. PERP. Two Victories
supporting shield, inscribed VOT. / P. R., over altar, PLN in ex. R.I.C. 159. 10 25

726 — VIRTVS EXERCIT. Vexillum, inscribed VOT. / XX., between two
captives, PLN in ex. R.I.C. 191. .... 10 25

727 — BEAT. TRANQLITAS. Altar, inscribed VOT / IS / XX., surmounted
by globe and three stars, PLON in ex. R.I.C. 267. .... 8 20

727A — SARMATIA DEVICTA. Victory advancing r., trampling captive,
PLON and crescent in ex. R.I.C. 289. .... 18 45

728 — PROVIDENTIAE AVGG. Gateway of military camp, PLON in ex.
R.I.C. 293. .... 8 20

729 Fausta, wife of Constantine I. Æ 3, London. SALVS REIPVBLICAE.
Empress stg. l., holding two children, PLON in ex. R.I.C. 300. .... 60 150

730 Helena, mother of Constantine I. Æ 3, London. SECVRITAS REIPVBLICE.
Empress stg. l., holding branch, PLON in ex. R.I.C. 299. .... 60 150

731 Crispus, eldest son of Constantine I, Caesar 317-326. Æ 3, London.
SOLI INVICTO COMITI. Sol stg. l., holding globe, crescent in l. field,
PLN in ex. R.I.C. 144... 12 30

731A — VIRTVS EXERCIT. Vexillum, inscribed VOT. / XX., between two
captives, PLN in ex. R.I.C. 194... 12 30

732 — BEATA TRANQVILLITAS. Altar, inscribed VOT / IS / XX.,
surmounted by globe and three stars, P—A in field, PLON in ex. R.I.C. 211. 10 25

733 — CAESARVM NOSTRORVM around wreath containing VOT. / X.,
PLON and crescent in ex. R.I.C. 291... 10 25

734 737A

	F £	VF £

734 — PROVIDENTIAE CAESS. Gateway of military camp, PLON in ex.
R.I.C. 295. .... 10 25

735 **Constantine II,** 337-340 (Caesar 317-337). Æ 3, London (as Caesar).
CLARITAS REIPVBLICAE. Sol stg. l., holding globe, crescent in l. field,
PLN in ex. *R.I.C. 131.* 12 30

736 — VICTORIAE LAETAE PRINC. PERP. Two Victories supporting shield,
inscribed VOT. / P. R., over altar ornamented with wreath, PLN in ex.
R.I.C. 182. .... 12 30

737 — VIRTVS EXERCIT. Vexillum, inscribed VOT. / XX., between two
captives, PLON in ex. *R.I.C. 190.* 12 30

737A — BEATA TRANQVILLITAS. Altar, inscribed VOT / IS / XX.,
surmounted by globe and three stars, PLON in ex. *R.I.C. 236.* 10 25

738 — CAESARVM NOSTRORVM around wreath containing VOT. / X.,
PLON and crescent in ex. *R.I.C. 292.* 10 25

738A — PROVIDENTIAE CAESS. Gateway of military camp, PLON in ex.
R.I.C. 296. .... 10 25

739 **Constantius II,** 337-361 (Caesar 324-337). Æ 3, London (as Caesar).
PROVIDENTIAE CAESS. Gateway of military camp, PLON in ex.
R.I.C. 298. .... 25 60

740 **Magnus Maximus,** usurper in the West, 383-388. *N solidus,* London (?).
RESTITVTOR REIPVBLICAE. Emperor stg. r., holding labarum and
Victory, AVG in ex. *R.I.C. 1.* .... *Unique*
The attribution to London of this rare series has not been firmly established,
though Maximus was certainly proclaimed emperor in Britain and it is
well attested that the principal city of the British provinces bore the name
'Augusta' in the late Roman period (Ammianus Marcellinus XXVII, 8, 7;
XXVIII, 3, 7).

741

741 — VICTORIA AVGG. Two emperors enthroned facing, Victory hovering
in background between them, AVGOB in ex. *R.I.C. 2b.* 5000 10000
Maximus appears to have struck a similar type in the name of the eastern
emperor Theodosius I (cf. R.I.C. 2a), though it is presently known only
from a silver-gilt specimen preserved in the British Museum.

	F	VF
	£	£

742 Æ *siliqua*, London (?). VOT. / V. / MVLT. / X. within wreath, AVG below.
R.I.C. 4. .... 850 2000
742A — VICTORIA AVGG. Victory advancing l., AVGPS in ex. *R.I.C. 3.*.... 750 1750

4. IMITATIONS OF ROMAN COINS PRODUCED IN BRITAIN

At certain periods during the three and a half centuries of its occupation Roman Britain seems to have been the source of much local imitation of the official imported coinage. This began soon after the Claudian invasion in A.D. 43 when significant quantities of sestertii, dupondii and asses (especially the last) were produced in the newly conquered territory, as evidenced by the frequency of their occurrence in archaeological finds. The technical excellence of many of these 'copies', together with the surprising extent of their minting, would seem to indicate that some, at least, of these coins were produced with official sanction in order to make good an unexpected deficiency in the currency supply. Others are much poorer and well below weight, representing the 'unofficial' branch of this operation, some of it probably emanating from territory as yet unconquered. As conditions in the new province settled down rapid Romanization and urbanization of British society brought a general increase in wealth, and with it a much greater volume of currency flowing into the country. Local imitation now virtually ceased, except for the occasional activities of criminal counterfeiters, and this state of affairs lasted down to the great political crisis and financial collapse of the second half of the 3rd century. At this point large scale minting of imitations of the debased antoniniani of the late 260s and early 270s began in Britain and in the other northwestern provinces, all of which had been serioulsy affected by the political dislocation of this turbulent era. This class of imitations is usually referred to as 'barbarous radiates', the emperor's spiky crown being a constant and conspicuous feature of the obverses. Most frequently copied were the antoniniani of the Gallic rulers Tetricus Senior and Tetricus Junior (ca. 270-273) and the posthumous issues of Claudius Gothicus (died 270). The quality of the 'barbarous radiates' is variable in the extreme, some exhibiting what appears to be a revival of Celtic art forms, others so tiny that it is virtually impossible to see anything of the design. Their production appears to have ended abruptly with Aurelian's reconquest of the western provinces in 273. A similar phenomenon, though on a lesser scale, occurred in the middle decades of the following century when normal life in Britain was again disrupted, not only by usurpation but additionally by foreign invasion. With supplies of currency from the Continent temporarily disrupted local imitation, particularly of the 'Æ 2' and 'Æ 3' issues of Constantius II and the usurper Magnentius, began in earnest. How long this continued is difficult to determine as life in the island province was now subject to increasingly frequent episodes of dislocation. By now urban life in Britain was in serious decline and when Roman rule ended early in the 5th century, bringing a total cessation of currency supplies, the catastrophic decline in monetary commerce in the former provinces rendered it no longer necessary for the deficiency to be made good.

	F	VF
	£	£

743 **Agrippa,** died 12 B.C. Æ as, of irregular British mintage, imitating the Roman issue made under Agrippa's grandson Caligula, A.D. 37-41.
S. C. Neptune stg. l., holding dolphin and trident.................................... 40 100
The large official issue of Agrippa asses was made shortly before the Claudian invasion of Britain in A.D. 43 and would thus have comprised a significant proportion of the 'aes' in circulation at this time. In consequence, it would soon have become familiar to the new provincials providing an ideal prototype for imitation.

744 **Claudius,** 41-54. Æ *sestertius,* of irregular British mintage. SPES AVGVSTA S. C. Spes walking l., holding flower. 75 250

745 Æ *dupondius,* of irregular British mintage. CERES AVGVSTA S. C. Ceres enthroned l., holding corn- ears and torch. 35 100

Grading of Hammered Coins

As the name suggests, hammered coins were struck by hand with a hammer. This can lead to the coin being struck off centre, double struck, weak in the design, suffer cracks or flan defects. It is important to take these factors into account when assessing the grade of this series. Value is considerably reduced if the coin is holed, pierced, plugged or mounted.

Extremely Fine
Design and legends
sharp and clear.

Very Fine
Design and legends
still clear but with
slight evidence of wear
and/or minor damage.

Fine
Showing quite a lot of
wear but still with
design and legends
distinguishable.

Anglo-Saxon 'Porcupine' Sceat

Gold Noble

Silver Crown

EARLY & MIDDLE ANGLO-SAXON KINGDOMS & MINTS (C.650-973)

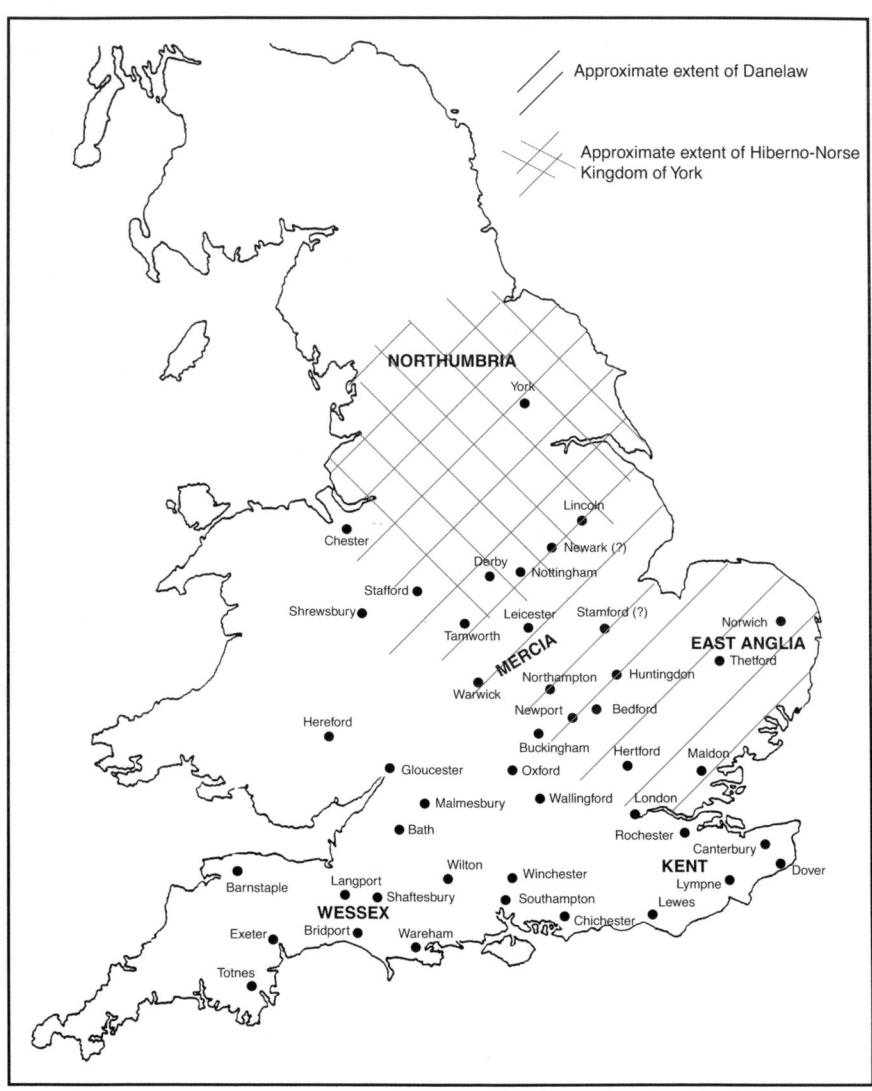

EARLY ANGLO-SAXON PERIOD, *c*. 600-*c*. 775

The withdrawal of Roman forces from Britain early in the 5th century A.D. and the gradual decline of central administration resulted in a rapid deterioration of the money supply. The arrival of Teutonic raiders and settlers hastened the decay of urban commercial life and it was probably not until late in the 6th century that renewed political, cultural and commercial links with the kingdom of the Merovingian Franks led to the appearance of small quantities of Merovingian gold *tremisses* (one-third solidus) in England. A purse containing such pieces was found in the Sutton Hoo ship-burial. Native Anglo-Saxon gold *thrymsas* were minted from about the 630s, initially in the style of their continental prototypes or copied from obsolete Roman coinage and later being made in pure Anglo-Saxon style. By the middle of the 7th century the gold coinage was being increasingly debased with silver, and gold had been superseded entirely by about 675.

These silver coins, contemporary with the *deniers or denarii* of the Merovingian Franks, are the first English pennies, though they are commonly known today as *sceattas* (a term more correctly translated as 'treasure' or 'wealth'). They provide important material for the student of Anglo-Saxon art.

Though the earliest sceattas are a transition from the gold thrymsa coinage, coins of new style were soon developed which were also copied by the Frisians of the Low Countries. Early coins appear to have a standard weight of 20 grains (1.29 gms) and are of good silver content, though the quality deteriorates early in the 8th century. These coins exist in a large number of varied types, and as well as the official issues there are mules and other varieties which are probably contemporary imitations. Many of the sceattas were issued during the reign of Aethelbald of Mercia, but as few bear inscriptions it is only in recent years that research has permitted their correct dating and the attribution of certain types to specific areas. Some silver sceats of groups II and III and most types of groups IV to X were issued during the period (A.D. 716-757) when Aethelbald, King of Mercia, was overlord of the southern English. In Northumbria very debased sceattas or *stycas* continued to be issued until the middle of the ninth century. Though a definitive classification has not yet been developed, the arrangement given below follows the latest work on the series: this list is not exhaustive.

This section has been catalogued in line with research published by Dr D. M. Metcalf. Wherever possible the Seaby number previously in use has been retained. Where it has been necessary to allocate a new and different number, the 'old' S. number is listed, in brackets, at the end of the entry. New entries are given a new number. The primary sceattas are followed by the secondary sceattas and, finally, the continental sceattas. This is not chronologically correct but has been adopted for ease of reference and identification. The reference 'B.M.C.' is to the type given in *British Museum Catalogue: Anglo-Saxon Coins*. Other works of reference include:

North, J. J. *English Hammered Coinage*, Vol. 1, *c*. 650-1272 (1994).
Metcalf, D.M. *Thrymsas and Sceattas in the Ashmolean Museum,* Vols I-III.
Rigold, S. E. 'The two primary series of sceattas', *B.N.J.,* xxx (1960).
Sutherland, C. H. V. *Anglo-Saxon Gold Coinage in the light of the Crondall Hoard* (1948).

ᚠ ᚩ ᚦ ᚯ ᚱ ᚳ · ᚷ ᚹ ᚻ ᚾ ᛁ ᛄ ᛡ ᛈ ᛉ ᛋ ᛏ ᛒ ᛖ ᛗ ᛚ ᛝ ᛞ ᛟ ᚪ ᚫ ᛠ ᚣ

f u th o r k .z w h n i j ih p x s t b e m l ng d oe a Æ ea y

Early Anglo-Saxon Runes

GOLD

		F	VF
		£	£

A.   Early pieces, of uncertain monetary status

| 751 | Thrymsa. Name and portrait of Bishop Leudard (chaplain to Queen Bertha of Kent). R. Cross. *(S.751)* | *Extremely rare* |
| 752 | Solidus. Imitating solidi of Roman rulers. Blundered legends, some with runes. *(S.757)* | *Extremely rare* |

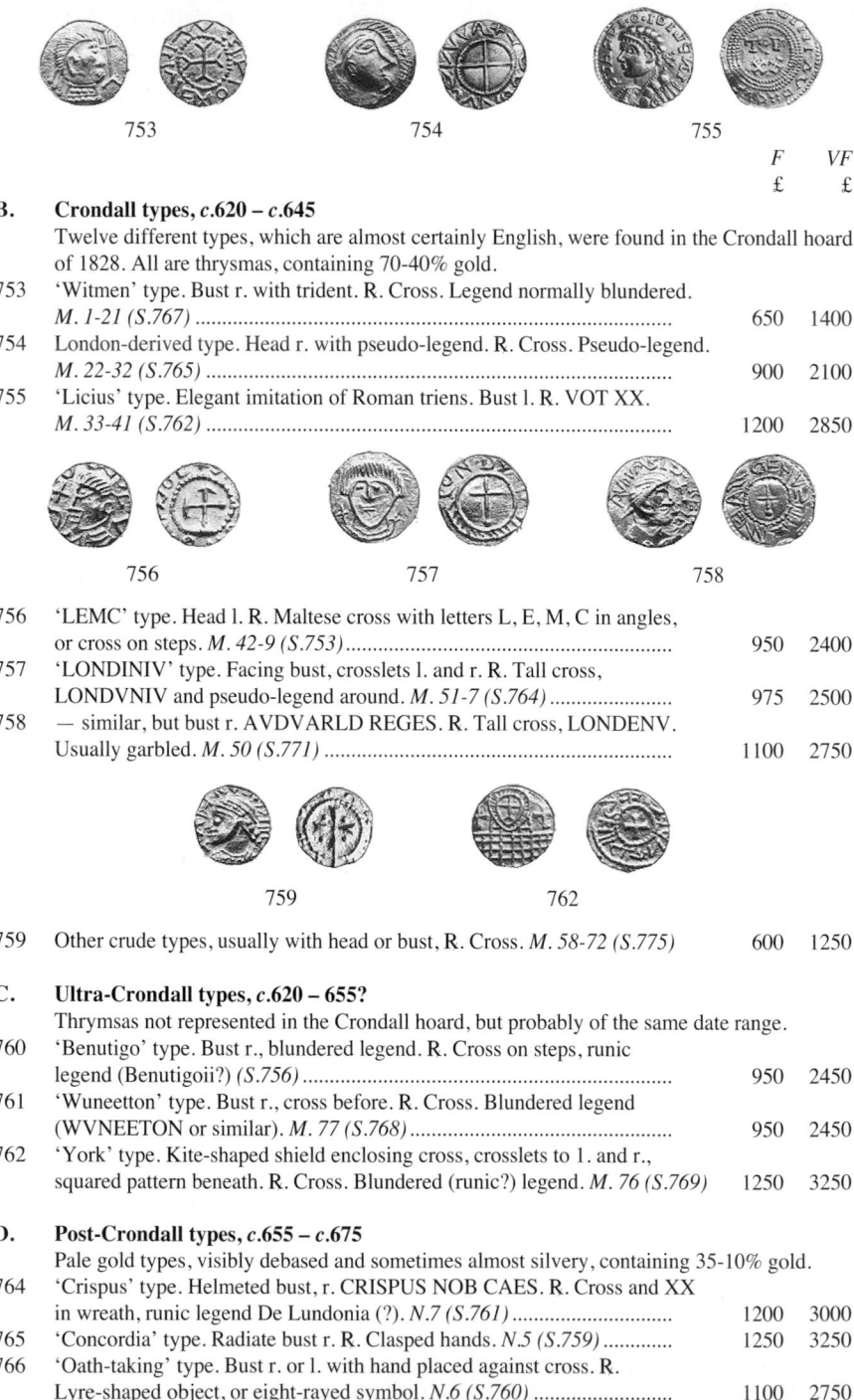

753   754   755

	F £	VF £

B.   **Crondall types, *c*.620 – *c*.645**

Twelve different types, which are almost certainly English, were found in the Crondall hoard of 1828. All are thrysmas, containing 70-40% gold.

753   'Witmen' type. Bust r. with trident. R. Cross. Legend normally blundered.
     M. 1-21 (S.767) 650   1400
754   London-derived type. Head r. with pseudo-legend. R. Cross. Pseudo-legend.
     M. 22-32 (S.765) 900   2100
755   'Licius' type. Elegant imitation of Roman triens. Bust l. R. VOT XX.
     M. 33-41 (S.762) 1200   2850

756   757   758

756   'LEMC' type. Head l. R. Maltese cross with letters L, E, M, C in angles,
     or cross on steps. *M. 42-9 (S.753)* 950   2400
757   'LONDINIV' type. Facing bust, crosslets l. and r. R. Tall cross,
     LONDVNIV and pseudo-legend around. *M. 51-7 (S.764)* 975   2500
758   — similar, but bust r. AVDVARLD REGES. R. Tall cross, LONDENV.
     Usually garbled. *M. 50 (S.771)* 1100   2750

759   762

759   Other crude types, usually with head or bust, R. Cross. *M. 58-72 (S.775)* 600   1250

C.   **Ultra-Crondall types, *c*.620 – 655?**

Thrymsas not represented in the Crondall hoard, but probably of the same date range.

760   'Benutigo' type. Bust r., blundered legend. R. Cross on steps, runic
     legend (Benutigoii?) *(S.756)* 950   2450
761   'Wuneetton' type. Bust r., cross before. R. Cross. Blundered legend
     (WVNEETON or similar). *M. 77 (S.768)* 950   2450
762   'York' type. Kite-shaped shield enclosing cross, crosslets to l. and r.,
     squared pattern beneath. R. Cross. Blundered (runic?) legend. *M. 76 (S.769)* 1250   3250

D.   **Post-Crondall types, *c*.655 – *c*.675**

Pale gold types, visibly debased and sometimes almost silvery, containing 35-10% gold.

764   'Crispus' type. Helmeted bust, r. CRISPUS NOB CAES. R. Cross and XX
     in wreath, runic legend De Lundonia (?). *N.7 (S.761)* 1200   3000
765   'Concordia' type. Radiate bust r. R. Clasped hands. *N.5 (S.759)* 1250   3250
766   'Oath-taking' type. Bust r. or l. with hand placed against cross. R.
     Lyre-shaped object, or eight-rayed symbol. *N.6 (S.760)* 1100   2750

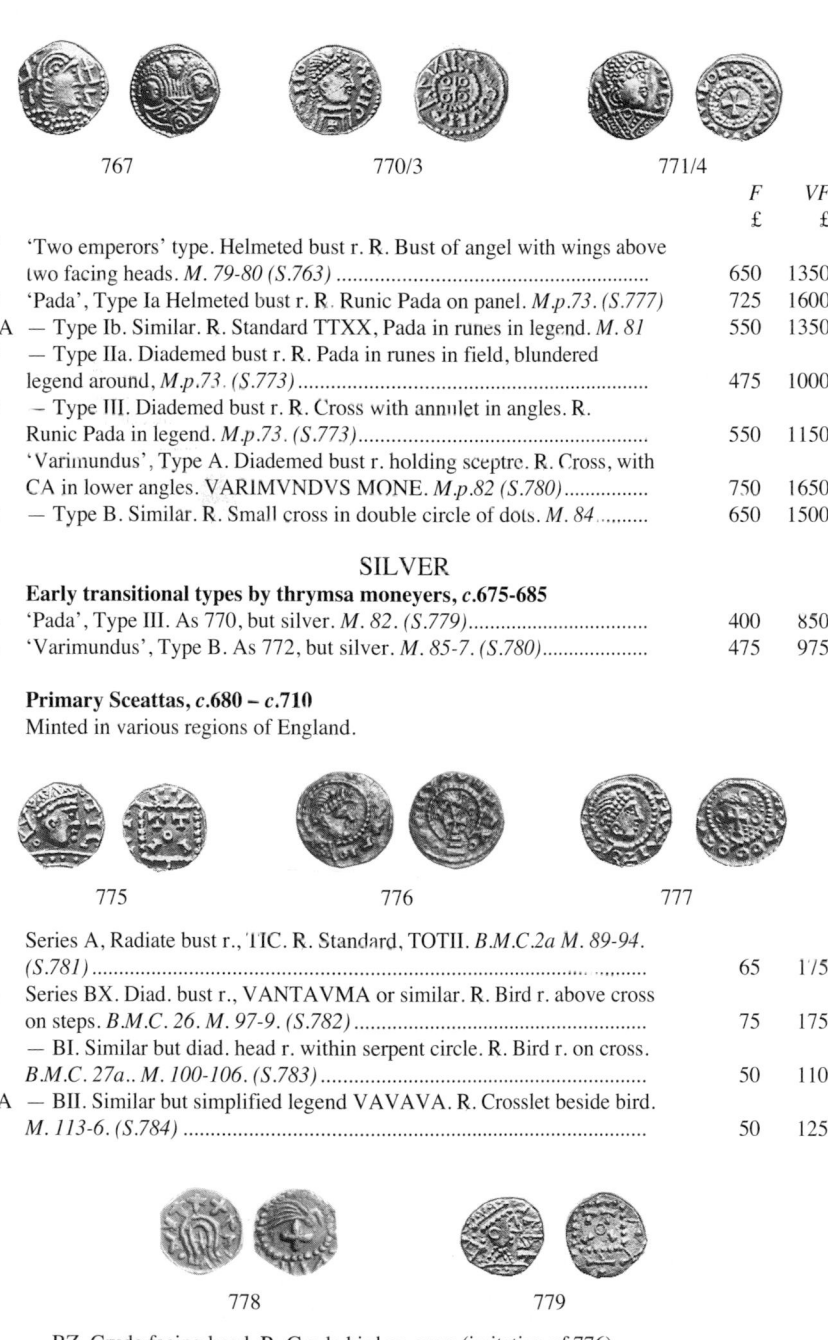

767   770/3   771/4

		F	VF
		£	£
767	'Two emperors' type. Helmeted bust r. R. Bust of angel with wings above two facing heads. *M. 79-80 (S.763)*	650	1350
768	'Pada', Type Ia Helmeted bust r. R. Runic Pada on panel. *M.p.73. (S.777)*	725	1600
768A	— Type Ib. Similar. R. Standard TTXX, Pada in runes in legend. *M. 81*	550	1350
769	— Type IIa. Diademed bust r. R. Pada in runes in field, blundered legend around, *M.p.73. (S.773)*	475	1000
770	— Type III. Diademed bust r. R. Cross with annulet in angles. R. Runic Pada in legend. *M.p.73. (S.773)*	550	1150
771	'Varimundus', Type A. Diademed bust r. holding sceptre. R. Cross, with CA in lower angles. VARIMVNDVS MONE. *M.p.82 (S.780)*	750	1650
772	— Type B. Similar. R. Small cross in double circle of dots. *M. 84*	650	1500

SILVER

A.   Early transitional types by thrymsa moneyers, *c.*675-685

773	'Pada', Type III. As 770, but silver. *M. 82. (S.779)*	400	850
774	'Varimundus', Type B. As 772, but silver. *M. 85-7. (S.780)*	475	975

B.   Primary Sceattas, *c.*680 – *c.*710
Minted in various regions of England.

775   776   777

775	Series A, Radiate bust r., TIC. R. Standard, TOTII. *B.M.C.2a M. 89-94. (S.781)*	65	175
776	Series BX. Diad. bust r., VANTAVMA or similar. R. Bird r. above cross on steps. *B.M.C. 26. M. 97-9. (S.782)*	75	175
777	— BI. Similar but diad. head r. within serpent circle. R. Bird r. on cross. *B.M.C. 27a.. M. 100-106. (S.783)*	50	110
777A	— BII. Similar but simplified legend VAVAVA. R. Crosslet beside bird. *M. 113-6. (S.784)*	50	125

778   779

778	— BZ. Crude facing head. R. Crude bird on cross (imitation of 776). *M. 138-9. (S.784A)*	80	185
779	Series C. Radiate bust r., similar to 775 but runic aepa replaces TIC. R. Standard, TOTII. *B.M.C. 2b. M. 117-125. (S.785)*	40	90

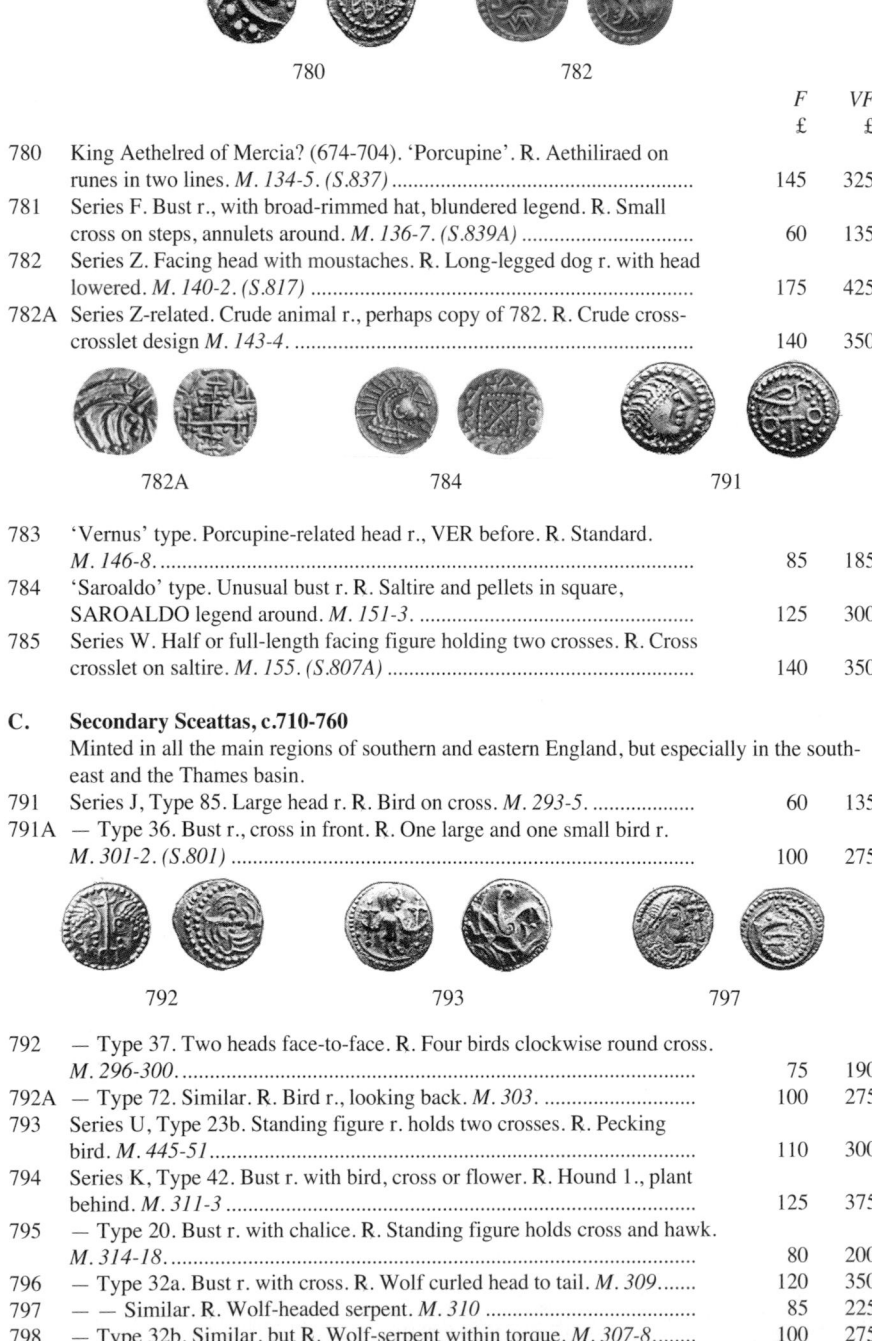

780   782

		F £	VF £
780	King Aethelred of Mercia? (674-704). 'Porcupine'. R. Aethiliraed on runes in two lines. *M. 134-5. (S.837)*	145	325
781	Series F. Bust r., with broad-rimmed hat, blundered legend. R. Small cross on steps, annulets around. *M. 136-7. (S.839A)*	60	135
782	Series Z. Facing head with moustaches. R. Long-legged dog r. with head lowered. *M. 140-2. (S.817)*	175	425
782A	Series Z-related. Crude animal r., perhaps copy of 782. R. Crude cross-crosslet design *M. 143-4.*	140	350

782A   784   791

		F £	VF £
783	'Vernus' type. Porcupine-related head r., VER before. R. Standard. *M. 146-8.*	85	185
784	'Saroaldo' type. Unusual bust r. R. Saltire and pellets in square, SAROALDO legend around. *M. 151-3.*	125	300
785	Series W. Half or full-length facing figure holding two crosses. R. Cross crosslet on saltire. *M. 155. (S.807A)*	140	350

C.   Secondary Sceattas, c.710-760

Minted in all the main regions of southern and eastern England, but especially in the south-east and the Thames basin.

		F £	VF £
791	Series J, Type 85. Large head r. R. Bird on cross. *M. 293-5.*	60	135
791A	— Type 36. Bust r., cross in front. R. One large and one small bird r. *M. 301-2. (S.801)*	100	275

792   793   797

		F £	VF £
792	— Type 37. Two heads face-to-face. R. Four birds clockwise round cross. *M. 296-300.*	75	190
792A	— Type 72. Similar. R. Bird r., looking back. *M. 303.*	100	275
793	Series U, Type 23b. Standing figure r. holds two crosses. R. Pecking bird. *M. 445-51*	110	300
794	Series K, Type 42. Bust r. with bird, cross or flower. R. Hound l., plant behind. *M. 311-3*	125	375
795	— Type 20. Bust r. with chalice. R. Standing figure holds cross and hawk. *M. 314-18.*	80	200
796	— Type 32a. Bust r. with cross. R. Wolf curled head to tail. *M. 309.......*	120	350
797	— — Similar. R. Wolf-headed serpent. *M. 310*	85	225
798	— Type 32b. Similar. but R. Wolf-serpent within torque. *M. 307-8........*	100	275

		F £	VF £

799   — Type 33. Bust r., cross in front. R. Wolf's head with long tongue, l. or r.
      M. 306.   125   350

800   801   802   803

800   'Archer' type. Kneeling archer r. R. Bird on branch r., head turned back.
      M. 349. (S.800A)   400   950
801   'Carip' group. Bust r., CARIP. R. Pecking bird, wolf-serpent, or standing
      figure. *M. 336-40.*   150   450
802   Series O, Type 38. Bust r. in cable border. R. Bird r. in torque. *M. 373-5.*   95   250
803   — Type 21. Similar, but bust l. R. Standing figure with two crosses. *M. 376*   145   425

804   805   806

804   'Triquetras' eclectic group. Facing bust, man and crosses, winged figure,
      or bird and branch. R. Interlace pattern. *M.p.425.*   150   450
805   Series H, Type 39. Pecking bird. R. Round shield with bosses. *M. 283-4.*   85   200
806   — Type 49. 'Wodan' head, annulets around. R. Pecking bird. *M. 285-8.*   85   225
807   — Type 48. Whorl of 3 wolf heads. R. Round shield with bosses.
      M. 289-92.   85   225

808   809A   810

808   Series G. Bust r., cross before. R. Standard with 3 or 4 X's.
      (Minted in Northern France?) M. 267-70..   60   135
809   — crude copies, some with bird or bird on cross. *M. 271-4.*....................   45   100
809A   Series M. Prancing dog l. or r. R. Spiral branch. *M. 363-6. (S.836c.)*   100   275
810   Series N. Two standing figures. R. Monster looking back r. or l. *M. 368-72.*   75   180

811   813   815

811   Series O, Type 40. Standing figure holds two crosses. R. As last. *M. 379-81.*   80   200
812   — Type 43. Interlace shield. R. As last. *M.p.482.*   125   350
813   — Type 57. Bust r. in cable border. R. Monster looking back l. *M. 377..*   135   375
814   'Animal mask' group. Facing animal (lion?) mask. R. Bird, figure, monster
      or cross. *M. 354-6. (S.814v).*   250   650
815   Series V. Wolf and twins. R. Bird in vine. *M. 453.*   150   425

816   818   822

		F	VF
		£	£
816	Series T. Diad. bust r., +LEL. R. 'Porcupine' l. *M. 442-4*.	125	350
818	Series L, Type 12. Bust r., LVNDONIA. R. Standing figure holds two crosses. *M. 319-22*.	125	350
820	— Type 13. Similar. R. Seated figure holds hawk and cross. *M.p.409*.	225	650
821	— Type 14. Similar, but bust l. R. Celtic cross. *M.p.427*.	135	400
822	— Type 15. Bust r. with cross, no legend. R. Standing figure holds two crosses. *M. 323-6*.	85	250
825	— Type 16. Bust r. with floral scroll. R. Standing figure holds branch and cross, or two branches. *M. 329-30*.	100	275
827	— Type 18. Bust r. with cross. R. Standing figure holds cross and bird. *M. 331-3*.	85	235
828	— Type 19. Similar, but bust l. *M. 335*.	100	275
828A	— Type 34. Bust r. with cross or sceptre. R. Celtic cross. *M. 345-6*. (*S.800*)	125	350
828B	Series L-related. Bust r. rosettes in field. R. Standing figure holds two crosses. *M. 347*.	175	475

829   831   832

829	Type 22. Victory standing with wreath. R. Winged figure, or standing figure holding two crosses. *M. 350-1*.	200	550
830	Type 23e. Standing figure holds two crosses. R. Whorl of 3 wolf heads. *M. 359-62*.	100	250
831	Series S. Female centaur. R. Whorl of 4 wolf heads. *M. 438-41*.	90	235
832	Series R. Bust r. or l. Epa, Wigraed, Spi, etc in runes. R. Standard. *M. 391-428*.	40	90

833   834A   836

832B	Series Q(R), Type 73. Crude radiate bust r. or l. R. Quadruped r. *M. 388*.	100	275
833	'Saltire Standard' types. Bust l. or r. with cross, two standing figures, or double croix ancree. R. Saltire and pellets in square. *M. 432-5*	75	175
834	'Monita Scorum' type. Small bird looking back, MONITA SCORUM. R. Standard with saltire of annulets. *M.p.436*.	325	750
834A	— Bust r., MONITA SCORUM. R. 'porcupine' l., figure with two crosses, or triquetra. *M. 348*.	375	900
835	Type 70. Saltire-standard. R. Standard. *M. 436-7*	50	110
836	Series Q, Types QII-IVd Bird l. or r. R. Quadruped l. or r. *M. 386-7*.	110	285
836A	— Type QIVe Quadruped both sides. *M.p.501*	120	325
836B	— Type QIe Bust r. with cross. R. Walking bird l. *M. 383*.	125	350

		F	VF
		£	£

836C — Type QIf Standing figure with two crosses. R. Walking bird l. *M. 384.*   150 450

836D — Type QIg Facing head. R. Long-legged quadruped looking back. *M.p.492.* 200 575

844   844A

844 Type 30. Facing 'Wodan' head. R. Two standing figures, or standard. *M. 429-31.* 135 375

844A — Type 53. 'Porcupine', similar to 787. R. Stepped cross, annulet at centre. *Mint? M. 258-62.* 85 200

C. Continental Sceattas, c.695-c.740
Most are from the Rhine area, or Frisia

786

786 Series E. Porcupine-like figure, body with annulet at one end, triangle at other. R. 'Standard' with four pellets around central annulet. *Dorestad. M. 209-11.* 35 80

787   789   790

787 — Similar, with triangular fore-leg. R. 'Standard' with four lines and central annulet. *M. 200-5.* 30 65

788 — Similar, with parallel lines in curve of body. R. 'Standard' with VICO. *M. 194-8.* 35 75

789 — Figure developed into plumed bird. R. Standard. *M. 190-3* 45 100

790 Later issues. R. 'Standard' 'Porcupine'. Innumerable varieties. *M. 214-53.*   30 60

832A Type 10. Bust r., AEPA or APA. R. Porcupine modified into profile face. *Mint? M.p.248.* 175 350

838 'Porcupine' R. Small cross, S E D E in angles. *Mint? M. 263.* 175 525

839   840   843

839 Series D, Type 2c. Bust r., pseudo-runes. R. Plain cross with pellets in angles. *Domburg? M. 158-80.* 35 75

840 — Type 8. Standard. R. As 839. *M. 183-6.* 30 65

841 'Maastricht' Type. Crude head l. R. Quatrefoil interlace. *M. 265-6* 150 375

843 Series X. Facing 'Wodan' head. R. Monster l. *Ribe, Jutland, M. 275-81.*   95 225

843A — cruder copies. *English, M. 282* 125 350

In the North a series of silver sceats was struck with the king's name on the obverse and a fantastic animal on the reverse. Towards the end of the eighth century the coinage degenerated to one of base silver and finally to copper or brass; from the second reign of Aethelred I the design becomes standardised with the king's name retained on the obverse but with the moneyer's name on the reverse and in the centre of both sides a cross, pellet or rosette., etc. A parallel series of ecclesiastical coins was struck by the Archbishops of York.

The coinage continued until the conquest of Northumbria by the Danes and the defeat of Osbert in 867, almost a century after introduction of the broad silver penny in Southern England.

		F	VF
		£	£
846	**Aldfrith** (685-705). Æ *sceat*. Pellet in annulet. R. Fantastic animal l. with trifid tail..	300	650
852	**Eadberht** (737-758). Æ *sceat*. Small cross. R. Fantastic quadruped to l. or r.	100	250

853   858A

853	**Alcred** (765-774). Æ *sceat*. As 852...	200	450
854	**Aethelred I,** first reign (774-779). Æ *sceat*. As last	250	550
855	**Aelfwald I** (779-788). Æ *sceat*. As last.................................	225	500
856	— — Small cross. R. With name of moneyer CVDBEVRT	200	450
857	**Aethelred I,** second reign (789-796). Æ *sceat*. Similar. R. SCT CVD (St. Cuthbert), shrine...	350	800
858	— Small cross. R. With moneyer's name	120	250
858A	**Eardwulf** (796-806). Æ sceat. pellet in centre. R. CVDHEARD around small cross		

The last and the rest of the sceats, except where otherwise stated, have on the obv. the king's name,and on the rev. the moneyer's name: in the centre on both sides is a cross, a pellet, a rosette, etc. During the following reign the silver sceat becomes debased and later issues are only brass or copper.

859	**Eanred** (810-c. 854). Base Æ *sceat*	40	90
860	— Æ *sceat*...	15	40

859   861

861	**Aethelred II,** first reign (*c*. 854-858). Æ *sceat*	15	35
862	— R. Quadruped	175	450
863	**Redwulf** (c. 858). Æ *sceat*.	35	85
864	**Aethelred II,** second reign (*c*. 858-*c*. 862). Æ *sceat*, mainly of the moneyer EARDWVLF	15	35
865	**Osbert** (*c*. 862-867). Æ *sceat*	50	125

Coins with blundered legends are worth less than those with normal readings, and to this series have been relegated those coins previously attributed to Eardwulf and Aelfwald II.

866

		F	VF
		£	£
866	**Ecgberht** (732 or 734-766). Æ *sceat*, with king Eadberht. As illustration, or holds cross and crozier	175	475
866A	— — with Aethelwald Moll. Cross each side	375	850
867	— — with Alchred. Cross each side	275	600

868   870   871

868	**Eanbald II** (796-*c*. 830). Æ *sceat*. R. With name of moneyer	75	200
869	— Æ *sceat*, as last	60	150
870	**Wigmund** (837-854). Gold *solidus*. Facing bust. R. Cross in wreath	*Extremely rare*	
871	— Æ *sceat*, various	20	50
872	**Wulfhere** (854-900). Æ *sceat*	75	160

In the kingdom of the Franks a reformed coinage of good quality *deniers* struck on broad flans had been introduced by Pepin in 755 and continued by his son Charlemagne and his descendants. A new coinage of *pennies* of similar size and weighing about 20 grains (1.3 gms) was introduced into England, probably by Offa, the powerful king of Mercia, about 755/780, though early pennies also exist of two little known kings of Kent, Heaberht and Ecgberht, of about the same period.

The silver penny (*Lat*. 'denarius', hence the *d*. of our £ *s*. *d*.) remained virtually the sole denomination of English coinage for almost five centuries, with the rare exception of occasional gold coins and somewhat less rare silver halfpence. The penny reached a weight of 24 grains, i.e., a 'pennyweight' during the reign of Alfred the Great. Silver pennies of this period normally bear the ruler's name, though not always his portrait, and the name of the moneyer responsible for their manufacture.

Pennies were issued by various rulers of the Heptarchy for the kingdoms of Kent, Mercia, East Anglia and Wessex (and possibly Anglian Northumbria), by the Danish settlers in the Danelaw and the Hiberno-Norse kings of York, and also by the Archbishops of Canterbury and a Bishop of London. Under Eadgar, who became the sole ruler of England, a uniform coinage was instituted throughout the country, and it was he who set the pattern for the 'reformed' coinage of the later Anglo-Saxon and Norman period.

Halfpence were issued by most rulers from Alfred to Eadgar between 871-973 for S. England, and although all are rare today, it is probable that reasonable quantities were made.

Nos. 873-1387 are all silver pennies except where stated.

NB. Many pennies of the early part of this period have chipped flans and prices should be reduced accordingly.

KINGS OF KENT

		F	VF
		£	£
873	**Heaberht** (*c*. 765). Monogram for REX. R. Five annulets, each containing a pellet, joined to form a cross	*Extremely rare*	
874	**Ecgberht** (*c*. 780). Similar. R. Varied	850	2000

875   877

875	**Eadberht Praen.** Type 1. (796-798). As illustration. R. Varied..............	975	2500
875A	— Type 2. (*c*. 798). His name around Ⓜ , in centre, R. Moneyer's name in angles of a tribrach..	1100	2750
876	**Cuthred** (798-807). *Canterbury*. Various types without portrait.............	375	825
877	— — Portrait. R. Cross and wedges or A	475	1100

878   879

	Anonymous (*c*. 822-823). *Canterbury*. As illustration or 'Baldred' style head	600	1450
	Baldred (*c*. 823-825). *Canterbury*. Head or bust r. R. Varied	800	2100

		F	VF
		£	£
880	— Cross each side	625	1750
881	*Rochester*. Diademed bust r. R. Varied	725	1900

ARCHBISHOPS OF CANTERBURY

882

881A	**Jaenberht** (765-792). New type (early). Under Ecgberht II of Kent (?). (before *c*. 780 ?) His name around small cross of pellets in centre. R. PONTIFEX in three lines	1250	2750
882	Under Offa of Mercia (*c*. 780-792) His name around central ornament or cross and wedges. R. OFFA REX in two lines	750	1850
883	— His name in three lines. R. OFFA or OFFA REX between the limbs of Celtic cross	900	2250
884	**Aethelheard** (el. 792, cons. 793, d. 805). With Offa as overlord. First issue (792-?), with title *Pontifex*	900	2250

![885] ![887]

885   887

885	— Second issue (?-796), with title *Archiepiscopus*	850	2000
885A	— Third issue (*c*. 796-798), with title *Archiepiscopus*. His name and AR around EP in centre. R. Moneyer's name, EADGAR or CIOLHARD	975	2500
886	— With Coenwulf as overlord. (798-800 ?) Fourth Issue. As last. R. King's name in the angles of a tribrach	850	2000
886A	— Fifth issue (*c*. 798-805?). As last R. Coenwulf's name around Ⓜ in centre	625	1650
887	**Wulfred** (805-832). group I (805-*c*. 810). As illustration. R. Crosslet, alpha-omega	650	1750
888	— Group II (*c*. 810). As last. R. DOROVERNIA C monogram	575	1400
889	— Group III (pre- 823). Bust extends to edge of coin. R. As last	475	1150
890	— Groups IV and V (*c*. 822-823). Anonymous under Ecgberht. Moneyer's name in place of the Archbishop's. R. DOROBERNIA CIVITAS in three or five lines	575	1400
891	— Group VI (*c*. 823-825). Baldred type. Crude portrait. R. DRVR CITS in two lines	850	2000
892	— Group VII (*c*. 832). Second monogram (Ecgberht) type. Crude portrait r., PLFRED. R. DORIB C. Monogram as 1035	650	1750

893    894

		F	VF
		£	£
893	**Ceolnoth** (833-870). Group I with name CIALNOD. Tonsured bust facing. R. Varied	350	750
894	— Group II. Similar but CEOLNOD. R. Types of Aethelwulf of Wessex	350	750
895	— Group III. Diad. bust r. R. Moneyer's name in and between lunettes .	450	975

896    898

896	**Aethelred** (870-889). Bust r. R. As illustration or with long cross with lozenge panel	1050	2750
897	— Cross pattee. R. ELF / STAN	1200	3000
898	**Plegmund** (890-914). DORO in circle. R. As illustration above, various moneyers	425	1000
899	— Similar, but title EPISC, and XDF in centre	450	1050
900	— Small cross pattee. R. Somewhat as last	325	700
901	— Crosses moline and pommee on *obv*	600	1350
901A	— Halfpenny. As 900	1300	3250

KINGS OF MERCIA

Until 825 Canterbury was the principal mint of the Kings of Mercia and some moneyers also struck coins for the Kings of Kent and Archbishops of Canterbury.

GOLD

902   903

902	**Offa** (757-796). Gold *dinar*. Copy of Arabic dinar of Caliph Al Mansur, dated 157 A.H. (A.D. 774), with OFFA REX added on *rev*	*Extremely rare*
903	Gold *penny*. Bust r., moneyer's name. R. Standing figure, moneyer's name	*Extremely rare*

A copy of a solidus with a diademed bust appears to read CIOLHEARD and is probably Mercian of this or the following reign.

SILVER

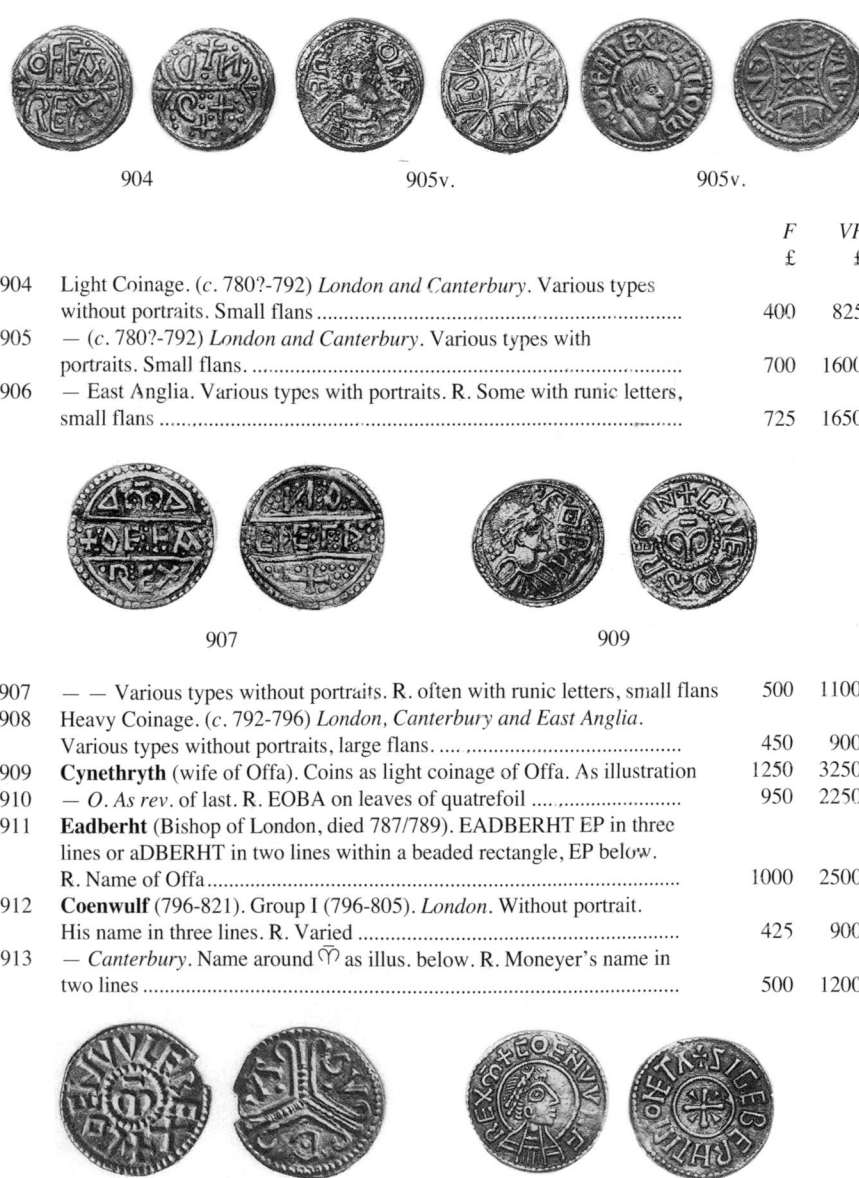

904   905v.   905v.

		F	*VF*
		£	£
904	Light Coinage. (*c.* 780?-792) *London and Canterbury.* Various types without portraits. Small flans	400	825
905	— (*c.* 780?-792) *London and Canterbury.* Various types with portraits. Small flans.	700	1600
906	— East Anglia. Various types with portraits. R. Some with runic letters, small flans	725	1650

907   909

907	— — Various types without portraits. R. often with runic letters, small flans	500	1100
908	Heavy Coinage. (*c.* 792-796) *London, Canterbury and East Anglia.* Various types without portraits, large flans.	450	900
909	**Cynethryth** (wife of Offa). Coins as light coinage of Offa. As illustration	1250	3250
910	— *O. As rev.* of last. R. EOBA on leaves of quatrefoil	950	2250
911	**Eadberht** (Bishop of London, died 787/789). EADBERHT EP in three lines or aDBERHT in two lines within a beaded rectangle, EP below. R. Name of Offa	1000	2500
912	**Coenwulf** (796-821). Group I (796-805). *London.* Without portrait. His name in three lines. R. Varied	425	900
913	— *Canterbury.* Name around ᛗ as illus. below. R. Moneyer's name in two lines	500	1200

914   915

| 914 | — *Both mints.* Tribrach type | | |
| 915 | — Group II (*c.* 805-810). *Canterbury.* With portrait. Small flans. R. Varies but usually cross and wedges | | |

		F	VF
		£	£
916	— Groups III and IV (*c*. 810-820). *Canterbury*. Similar but larger flans. R. Varied	350	800
917	— *Rochester*. Large diad. bust of coarse style. R. Varied. (Moneyers: Dun, Ealhstan)	425	975
918	— *London*. With portrait generally of Roman style. R. Crosslet	425	950
919	— *E. Anglia*. Crude diad. bust r. R. Moneyer's name LVL on leaves in arms of cross	350	750
920	— — *O*. as last. R. Various types	400	850

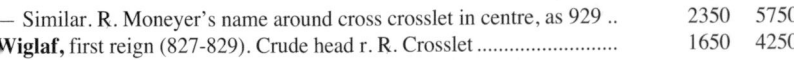

921   929

921	**Ceolwulf I** (821-823). Canterbury. Group I. Bust r. R. Varied. (Moneyers: Oba, Sigestef)	675	1600
922	— — Group II. Crosslet. R. Varied	625	1450
923	— — Group III. Tall cross with MERCIORŪ. R. Crosslet. SIGESTEF DOROBERNIA	750	1850
924	— *Rochester*. Group I. Bust r. R. Varied	675	1600
925	— — Group IIA. As last but head r.	675	1600
926	— — Group IIB. Ecclesiastical issue by Bp. of Rochester. With mint name, DOROBREBIA, but no moneyer	900	2000
927	— *East Anglia*. Crude style and lettering with barbarous portrait. R. Varied	525	1200
928	**Beornwulf** (823-825). Bust r. R. Moneyer's name in three lines	750	1850
929	— R. Cross crosslet in centre	700	1650
930	Crude copy of 928 but moneyer's name in two lines with crosses between	975	2500
931	**Ludica** (825-827). Bust r. R. Moneyer's name in three lines as 928	2250	5500

932   933

	— Similar. R. Moneyer's name around cross crosslet in centre, as 929 ..	2350	5750
	Wiglaf, first reign (827-829). Crude head r. R. Crosslet	1650	4250

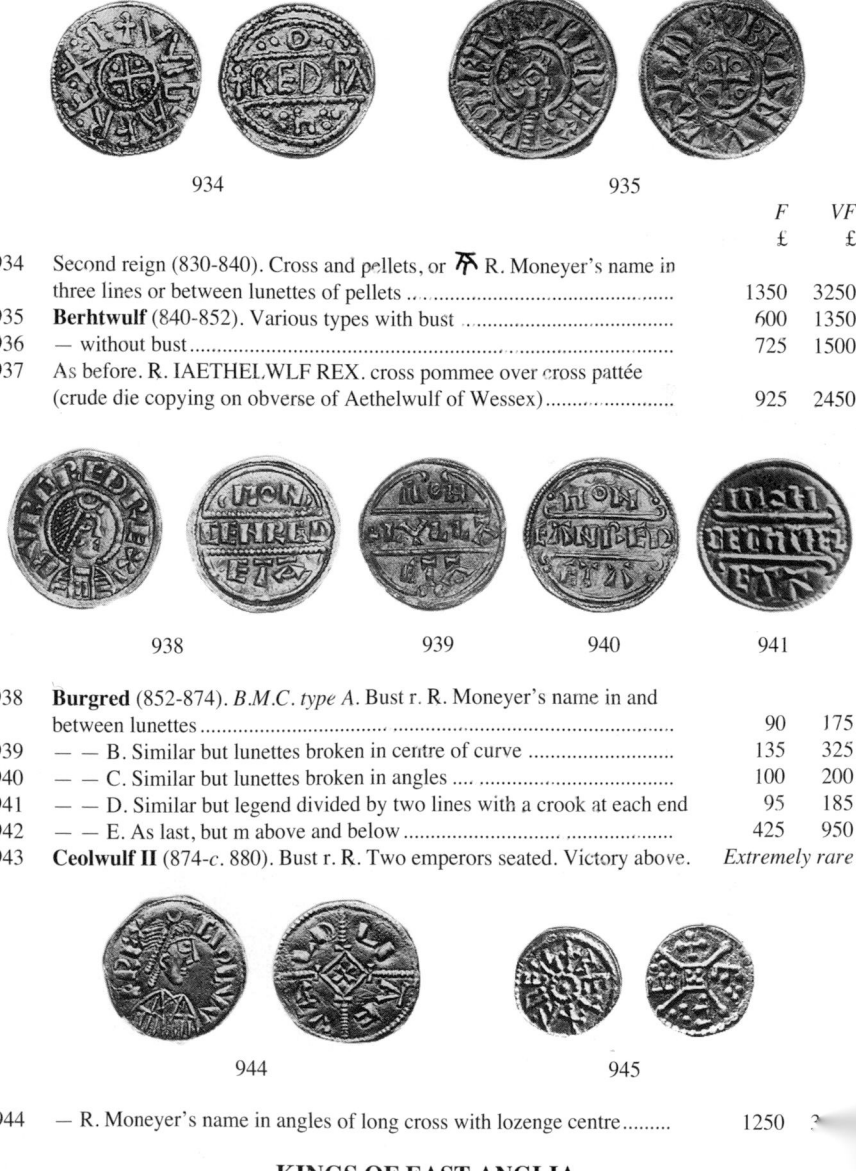

934 935

		F £	VF £

934 Second reign (830-840). Cross and pellets, or 𐰴 R. Moneyer's name in three lines or between lunettes of pellets 1350 3250

935 **Berhtwulf** (840-852). Various types with bust 600 1350

936 — without bust.. 725 1500

937 As before. R. IAETHELWLF REX. cross pommee over cross pattée (crude die copying on obverse of Aethelwulf of Wessex)........................ 925 2450

938 939 940 941

938 **Burgred** (852-874). *B.M.C. type A.* Bust r. R. Moneyer's name in and between lunettes 90 175

939 — — B. Similar but lunettes broken in centre of curve 135 325

940 — — C. Similar but lunettes broken in angles 100 200

941 — — D. Similar but legend divided by two lines with a crook at each end 95 185

942 — — E. As last, but m above and below......................... .... 425 950

943 **Ceolwulf II** (874-c. 880). Bust r. R. Two emperors seated. Victory above. *Extremely rare*

944 945

944 — R. Moneyer's name in angles of long cross with lozenge centre......... 1250 ?

KINGS OF EAST ANGLIA

945 **Beonna,** King of East Anglia, *c.* 758. Æ sceat. Pellet in centre, Runic inscription. R. EFE in Roman characters around saltire cross ....

945A — Similar. R. WILRED in runic around pellet or cross ....

945B — Similar. R. Interlace pattern (large flans)...

945C **Alberht** (749-?). Pellet in centre, AETHELBERT (runic) around R. Rosette in circle, TIAELRED (runic) around. ....

946

		F	VF
		£	£
946	**Aethelberht** (d. 794). As illustration	*Extremely rare*	
947	**Eadwald** (*c.* 798). King's name in three lines. R. Moneyer's name in quatrefoil or around cross	650	1500
947A	— King's name around cross or ⋔ in centre. R. Moneyer's name in quatrefoil	750	1600

948   951

948	**Aethelstan I** (*c.* 825-840). Bust r. or l. R. Crosslet or star	650	1650
949	Bust r. R. Moneyer's name in three or four lines.....................................	650	1650
950	Alpha or A. R. Varied	275	575
951	*O.* and *rev.* Cross with or without wedges or pellets in angles	300	625
952	— Similar, with king's name both sides	400	850
952A	Name around ship in centre. R. Moneyer Eadgar, around cross of pellets or in two lines (Possibly the earliest of his coins.)...................................	1350	3500

953   954

953	**Aethelweard** (*c.* 840-*c.* 855), A. Omega or cross and crescents. R. Cross with pellets or wedges..	400	825
	Edmund (855-870). Alpha or A. R. Cross with pellets or wedges	175	350
	— *O.* Varied. R. Similar	175	350

*St. Edmund coins and the Danish issues struck in East Anglia bearing the name of Aethelred
~ish East Anglia.*

Danish East Anglia, *c*. 885-915

957

		F	VF
		£	£
956	**Aethelstan II** (878-890), originally named Guthrum? Cross pattee. R. Moneyer's name in two lines	850	2000
957	**Oswald** (unknown except from his coins). Alpha or A. R. Cross pattee..	1350	3500
958	— Copy of Carolinigian 'temple' type. R Cross and pellets	1500	4000
959	**Aethelred I.** (*c*.870) As last, with name of Aethelred I. R. As last, or cross-crosslet	1250	3000
959A	— As 954	975	2350
960	**St. Edmund,** memorial coinage, *Æ penny*, type as illus. below, various legends of good style	75	150

961   962

961	— Similar, but barbarous or semi-barbarous legends	70	135
962	*Halfpenny*. Similar	325	725

963   966

963	**St. Martin of Lincoln.** As illustration	1350	3500
964	**Alfred.** (Viking imitations, usually of very barbarous workmanship.) Bust r. R. *Londonia* monogram	450	1200
965	— Similar, but *Lincolla* monogram	850	2000
966	— Small cross, as Alfred group II (*Br. 6*), various legends, some read REX DORO	190	40C
967	— Similar. R. 'St. Edmund type' A in centre	450	10C
968	— Two emperors seated. R. As 964. (Previously attributed to Halfdene.)	*Extremely r*	
969	*Halfpenny*. As 964 and 965	325	

970

	F £	VF £
970 — As 966	300	675

DANELAW, *c.* 898-915

971   975

971	**Alfred** (Imitations). ELFRED between ORSNA and FORDA. R. Moneyer's name in two lines (occasionally divided by horizontal long cross)	275	550
972	— *Halfpenny*. Similar, of very crude appearance	425	1050
973	**Alfred/Plegmund.** *Obv.* ELFRED REX PLEGN	625	1350
974	**Plegmund.** Danish copy of 900	325	675
975	**Earl Sihtric.** Type as 971. SCELDFOR between GVNDI BERTVS. R SITRIC COMES in two lines	1650	4250

Viking Coinage of York?
References are to 'The Classification of Northumbrian Viking Coins in the Cuerdale hoard', by
C. S. S. Lyon and B. H. I. H. Stewart, in Numismatic Chronicle, 1964, p. 281 ff.

975A	**Guthfrith.** GU DE F. RE Small cross. R. Moneyer's name in two lines.	*Extremely rare*	
976	**Siefred.** C. SIEFRE DIIS REX in two lines. R. EBRAICE CIVITAS (or contractions), small cross. *L. & S. Ia, Ie, Ii*	185	450
977	— Cross on steps between. R. As last. *L. & S. If, Ij*	275	675
978	— Long cross. R. As last. *L. & S. Ik*	300	700
979	SIEFREDVS REX, cross crosslet within legend. R. As last. *L. & S. Ih...*	140	300

980   984

980	SIEVERT REX, cross crosslet to edge of coin. R. As last. *L. & S. Ic, Ig, Im*	150	325
	— Cross on steps between. R. As last. *L. & S. Il*	250	575
	— Patriarchal cross. R. DNS DS REX, small cross. *L. & S. Va*	200	475
	— — R. MIRABILIA FECIT, small cross. *L. & S. VIb*	225	525
	REX, at ends of cross crosslet. R. SIEFREDVS, small cross. *L. & S. IIIa, b*	175	37 5

		F	VF
		£	£
985	— Long cross. **R.** As last. *L. & S. IIIc*	165	350
986	*Halfpenny*. Types as 977, *L. & S. Ib; 980, Ic; and 983, VIb*	475	950
987	**Cnut.** CNVT REX, cross crosslet to edge of coin. **R.** EBRAICE CIVITAS, small cross. *L. & S. Io, Iq*	145	300
988	— — **R.** CVNNETTI, small cross. *L. & S. IIc*	135	275
989	— Long cross. **R.** EBRAICE CIVITAS, small cross. *L. & S. Id, In, Ir*	90	175
990	— — **R.** CVNNETTI, small cross. *L. & S. IIa, IId*	80	150
991	— Patriarchal cross. **R.** EBRAICE CIVITAS, small cross. *L. & S. Ip, Is*	80	150
992	— — **R.**— *Karolus* monogram in centre. *L. & S . It*	525	1250

993   995

993	— — **R.** CVNNETTI, small cross. *L. & S. IIb, IIe*	70	130
994	*Halfpenny*. Types as 987, *L. & S. Iq; 989, Id; 991, Is; 992, Iu; 993, IIb and e*	300	625
995	As 992, but CVNNETTI around *Karolus* monogram. *L. & S. IIf*	325	650
996	**Cnut and/or Siefred.** CNVT REX, patriarchal cross. **R.** SIEFREDVS, small cross. *L. & S. IIId*	125	250
997	— — **R.** DNS DS REX, small cross. *L. & S. Vc.*	200	450

998

998	— — **R.** MIRABILIA FECIT. *L. & S. VId*	120	240
999	EBRAICE C, patriarchal cross. **R.** DNS DS REX, small cross. *L. & S. Vb*	175	350

1000   1002

1000	— — **R.** MIRABILIA FECIT. *L. & S. VIc*	120	240
1001	DNS DS REX in two lines. **R.** ALVALDVS, small cross. *L. & S. IVa*	650	1450
1002	DNS DS O REX, similar. **R.** MIRABILIA FECIT. *L. & S. VIa*	240	475
1003	*Halfpenny*. As last. *L. & S. VIa*	450	975
1004	**'Cnut'.** Name blundered around cross pattée with extended limbs. **R.** QVENTOVICI around small cross. *L. & S. VII*	275	550

| | F | VF |
| | £ | £ |

1005 *Halfpenny*. Similar. *L. & S. VII* 450 975
      Possibly not Northumbrian; the reverse copied from the Carolingian coins
      of Quentovic, N. France.

York, early tenth century issues

1006   1009

1006 **St. Peter coinage.** Early issues. SCI PETRI MO in two lines. R. Cross
      pattee 175 375
1007 — similar. R. 'Karolus' monogram 825 1850
1008 *Halfpenny*. Similar. R. Cross pattee 550 1250
1009 **Regnald** (blundered types). RAIENALT, head to l. or r. R. EARICE CT,
      'Karolus' monogram 1450 3750

1010

1010 — Open hand. R. Similar 975 2500
1011 — Hammer. R. Bow and arrow 1350 3750
1012 Anonymous R. Sword 1100 3250

ENGLISH COINS OF THE HIBERNO-NORSE VIKINGS

Early period, *c*. 919-925
1013 **Sihtric** (921-927). SITRIC REX, sword. R. Cross, hammer or T 1250 3250
1014 **St. Peter coinage.** Late issues SCI PETRI MO, sword and hammer. R.
      EBORACEI, cross and pellets 500 1100

1015   1016

1015 — Similar. R. Voided hammer 450 925
1016 — Similar. R. Solid hammer 575 1250
      St. Peter coins with blundered legends are rather cheaper.

Later period, 939-954 (after the battle of Brunanburh). Mostly struck at York.

1017	**Anlaf Guthfrithsson,** 939-941. Flower type. Small cross, ANLAF REX TO D. R. Flower above moneyer's name	2000	4500
1018	**Olaf Guthfrithsson.** Circumscription type, with small cross each side, ANLAF CVNVNC, M in field on reverse *(Derby)*	1750	4250
1018A	— Two line type. ONLAF REX. Large letter both sides *(Lincoln?)*	1750	4250

1019   1020

		F	VF
		£	£
1019	— Raven type. As illustration, ANLAF CVNVNC..................................	1200	2650
1020	**Olaf Sihtricsson,** first reign, 941-944. Triquetra type. As illus., CVNVNC. R. Danish standard	1250	3500
1021	— Circumscription type (a). Small cross each side, CVNVNC	1200	3250
1022	— Cross moline type, CVNVN C. R. Small cross	1250	3500
1023	— Two line type. Small cross. R. ONLAF REX. R. Name in two lines ..	1200	3250
1024	**Regnald Guthfrithsson,** 943-944. Triquetra type. As 1020. REGNALD CVNVNC..	1800	4500

1025   1030

1025	— Cross moline type. As 1022, but REGNALD CVNVNC	1750	4250
1026	**Sihtric Sihtricsson,** *c.* 942. Triquetra type. As 1020, SITRIC CVNVNC	1800	4500
1027	— Circumscription type. Small cross each side	1650	4000
1027A	**Anonymous?** Two line type. Small cross ELTANGERHT. R. RERNART in two lines	1750	4500
1028	**Eric Blood-axe,** first reign, 948. Two line type. Small cross, ERICVC REX A; ERIC REX AL; or ERIC REX EFOR. R. Name in two lines..............	2000	4750
1029	**Olaf Sihtricsson,** second reign, 948-952. Circumscription type (b). Small cross each side. ONLAF REX	1250	3500
1029A	— Flower type. small cross ANLAF REX R. Flower above moneyer's name..	2000	4500
1029B	— Two line type. Small cross, ONLAF REX. R. Moneyer's name in two lines	1200	3250
1030	**Eric Blood-axe,** second reign, 952-954. Sword type. ERIC REX in two lines, sword between. R. Small cross...	2250	5500

Later, KINGS OF ALL ENGLAND FROM 959
All are silver pennies unless otherwise stated

BEORHTRIC, 786-802
Beorhtric was dependent on Offa of Mercia and married a daughter of Offa.

1031

		F	VF
		£	£
1031	As illustration	*Extremely rare*	
1032	Alpha and omega in centre. R. Omega in centre	*Extremely rare*	

ECGBERHT, 802-839
King of Wessex only, 802-825; then also of Kent, Sussex, Surrey, Essex and East Anglia, 825-839, and of Mercia also, 829-830.

1033	*Canterbury.* Group I. Diad. hd. r. within inner circle. R. Various	900	2250
1034	— II. Non-portrait types. R. Various	600	1450

1035

1035	— III. Bust r. breaking inner circle. R. DORIB C	625	1500
1036	*London.* Cross potent. R. LVN / DONIA / CIVIT	975	2500
1037	— — R. REDMVND MONE around TA	850	2350
1038	*Rochester,* royal mint. Non-portrait types with king's name ECGBEO RHT	625	1500
1039	— — Portrait types, ECGBEORHT	750	1750
1040	*Rochester,* bishop's mint. Bust r. R. SCS ANDREAS (APOSTOLVS)...	975	2500
1041	*Winchester.* SAXON monogram or SAXONIORVM in three lines. R. Cross	750	1750

Son of Ecgberht; sub-King of Essex, Kent, Surrey and Sussex, 825-839; King of all southern England, 839-855; King of Essex, Kent and Sussex only, 855-858. No coins are known of his son Aethelbald who ruled over Wessex proper, 855-860.

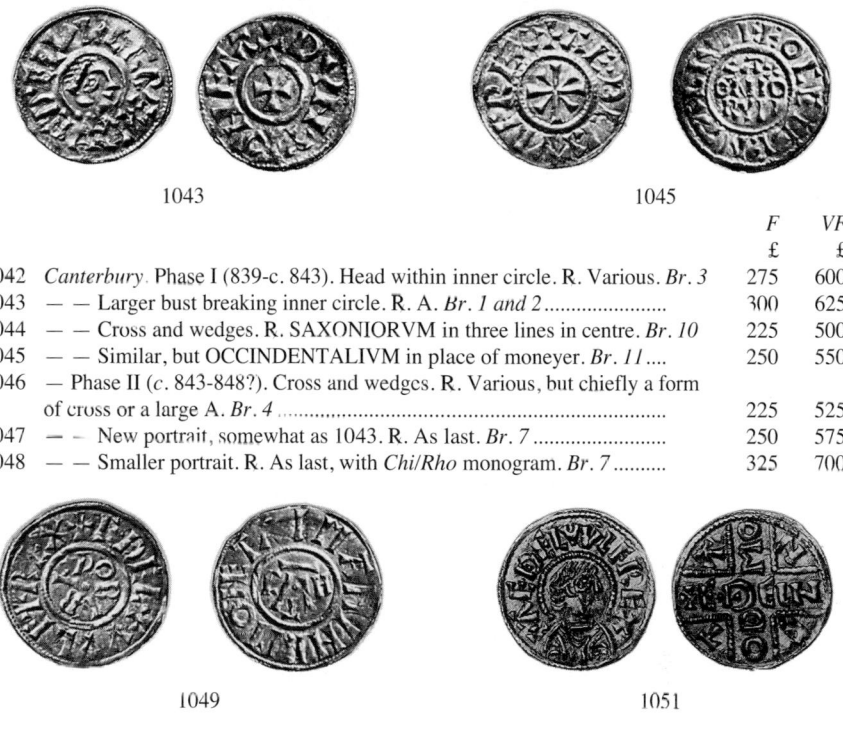

1043   1045

		F £	VF £
1042	*Canterbury.* Phase I (839-c. 843). Head within inner circle. R. Various. *Br. 3*	275	600
1043	— — Larger bust breaking inner circle. R. A. *Br. 1 and 2*	300	625
1044	— — Cross and wedges. R. SAXONIORVM in three lines in centre. *Br. 10*	225	500
1045	— — Similar, but OCCINDENTALIVM in place of moneyer. *Br. 11*	250	550
1046	— Phase II (*c.* 843-848?). Cross and wedges. R. Various, but chiefly a form of cross or a large A. *Br. 4*	225	525
1047	— — New portrait, somewhat as 1043. R. As last. *Br. 7*	250	575
1048	— — Smaller portrait. R. As last, with *Chi/Rho* monogram. *Br. 7*	325	700

1049   1051

1049	— Phase III (*c.* 848/851-*c.* 855). DORIB in centre. R. CANT mon. *Br. 5*	250	550
1050	— — CANT mon. R. CAN M in angles of cross. *Br. 6*	325	675
1051	— Phase IV (*c.* 855-859). Type as Aethelberht. New neat style bust R. Large voided long cross. *Br. 8*	250	525
1052	*Winchester.* SAXON mon. R. Cross and wedges. *Br. 9*	375	850

A unique Penny with a portrait resembling some of Aethelwulf and reading EANRED REX is attributed with some reservations to the Northumbrian King of that name.

Son of Aethelwulf; sub-King of Kent, Essex and Sussex, 858-860; King of all southern England, 860-865/6.

1053

	F	*VF*
	£	£
1053 As illustration above	225	475
1054 *O*. Similar, R. Cross fleury over quatrefoil	525	1250

AETHELRED I, 865/866-871

Son of Aethelwulf; succeeded his brother Aethelberht.

1055

1055 As illustration	275	625
1056 Similar, but moneyer's name in four lines	525	1250

For another coin with the name Aethelred see 959 under Viking coinages.

Brother and successor to Aethelred, Alfred had to contend with invading Danish armies for much of his reign. In 878 he and Guthrum the Dane divided the country, with Alfred holding all England south and west of Watling Street. Alfred occupied London in 886.

Types with portraits

	1057		1058		

1057	Bust r. R. As Aethelred I. *Br. 1* (*name often* AELBRED)	275	625
1058	— R. Long cross with lozenge centre, as 944, *Br. 5*	1000	2750
1059	— R. Two seated figures, as 943. *Br. 2*	*Extremely rare*	
1060	— R. As Archbp. Aethered; cross within large quatrefoil. *Br. 3*	*Extremely rare*	

	1061		1062		

1061	*London*. Bust. r. R. LONDONIA monogram	625	1400
	Copies made of tin at the Wembley Exhibition are common		
1062	— R. Similar, but with moneyer's name added	675	1650
1063	— *Halfpenny*. Bust r. or rarely l. R. LONDONIA monogram as 1061	350	850
1064	*Gloucester*. R. Æ GLEAPA in angles of three limbed cross	*Extremely rare*	

Types without portraits

1065	King's name on limbs of cross, trefoils in angles. R. Moneyer's name in quatrefoil. *Br. 4.*	*Extremely rare*	

	1066		1069		

1066	Cross pattée. R. Moneyer's name in two lines. *Br. 6*	250	465
1067	— As last, but neater style, as Edw, the Elder	260	500
1068	— *Halfpenny*. As 1066	325	700
1069	*Canterbury*. As last but DORO added on *obv. Br. 6a*	275	750
1070	*Exeter?* King name in four lines. R. EXA vertical	2250	5250
1071	*Winchester?* Similar to last, but PIN	2500	6250
1071A	*Oxford*. Elfred between OHSNA and FORDA. R. Moneyer's name in two lines (much commoner as a Viking Imitation see 971)	650	1450
1072	'Offering penny'. Very large and heavy. AELFRED REX SAXORVM in four lines. R. ELIMO in two lines i.e. (*Elimosina*, alms)	*Extremely rare*	

For other pieces bearing the name of Alfred see under the Viking coinages.

Edward, the son of Alfred, aided by his sister Aethelflaed 'Lady of the Mericians', annexed all England south of the Humber and built many new fortified boroughs to protect the kingdom.

1074   1078

	F £	VF £

Rare types

		F £	VF £
1073	*Br. 1. Bath?* R. BA	1300	3250
1074	— *2. Canterbury.* Cross moline in pommee. R. Moneyer's name	850	2000
1075	— *3. Chester?* Small cross. R. Minster	1100	2750
1076	— *4.* — Small cross. R. Moneyer's name in single line	700	1600
1077	— *5.* — R. Two stars	850	2000

1081   1082

		F £	VF £
1078	— *6.* — R. Flower above central line, name below	1000	2650
1079	— *7.* — R. Floral design with name across field	1000	2650
1080	— *8.* — R. Bird holding twig	1750	4750
1081	— *9.* — R. Hand of Providence, several varieties	1350	3500
1082	— *10.* — R. City gate of Roman style	1250	3000
1083	— *11.* — R. Anglo-Saxon burg	975	2500

Ordinary types

1084   1087

		F £	VF £
1084	*Br. 12.* Bust l. R. Moneyer's name in two lines	400	950
1085	— — As last, but in *gold*	*Extremely rare*	
1086	— *12a.* Similar, but bust r. of crude style	525	1200
1087	— *13.* Small cross. R. Similar (to 1084)	135	300
1088	*Halfpenny.* Similar to last	625	1350
1088A	— — R. Hand of Providence	900	2400

Aethelstan, the eldest son of Eadward, decreed that money should be coined only in a borough, that every borough should have one moneyer and that some of the more important boroughs should have more than one moneyer.

1089

		F	VF
		£	£
1089	**Main issues.** Small cross. R. Moneyer's name in two lines	145	325
1090	Diad. bust r. R. As last	550	1350
1091	— R. Small cross	500	1250
1092	Small cross both sides	225	475

1093   1094

1093	— Similar, but mint name added	210	425
1094	Crowned bust r. As illustration. R. Small cross	375	900
1095	— Similar, but mint name added	350	850
1096	**Local Issues.** *N. Mercian mints.* Star between two pellets. R. As 1089	650	1500
1097	— Small cross. R. Floral ornaments above and below moneyer's name	700	1750
1098	— Rosette of pellets each side	250	525
1099	— Small cross one side, rosette on the other side	275	550

1100   1104

1100	*N.E. mints.* Small cross. R. Tower over moneyer's name	950	2500
1101	Similar, but mint name added	1000	2650
1102	— Bust in high relief r. or l. R. Small cross	550	1250
1103	— Bust r. in high relief. R. Cross-crosslet	550	1250
1104	'Helmeted' bust or head r. R. As last or small cross	600	1450
1104A	Halfpenny, small cross. R. Moneyer's name in two lines	675	1450

Eadmund, the brother of Aethelstan, extended his realm over the Norse kingdom of York.

1105   1107

		F	VF
		£	£
1105	Small cross, rosette or annulet. R. Moneyer's name in two lines with crosses or rosettes between	145	335
1106	Crowned bust r. R. Small cross	425	975
1107	Similar, but with mint name	450	1000
1108	Small cross either side, or rosette on one side	225	475
1109	Cross of five pellets. R. Moneyer's name in two lines	225	475
1110	Small cross. R. Flower above name	900	2450
1111	'Helmeted' bust r. R. Cross-crosslet	675	1650

1111   1112

1112	*Halfpenny*. small cross, R. Moneyer's name in two lines or one line between rosettes	600	1350
1112A	— Flower. R. As 1105	725	1650

EADRED, 946-955

Eadred was another of the sons of Eadward. He lost the kingdom of York to Eric Bloodaxe.

1113   1115

1113	As illustration. R. Moneyer's name in two lines	130	275
1114	— Similar, but mint name after REX	300	750
1115	Crowned bust r. As illustration	300	650
1116	— R. Similar, with mint name added	375	800

	F	*VF*
	£	£
1117 Rosette. R. As 1113	200	425
1118 Small cross. R. Rosette	225	475
1119 — R. Flower enclosing moneyer's name. *B.M.C. II*	1100	2650
1120 *Halfpenny*. Similar to 1113	475	1000

HOWEL DDA, d. 949/950

Grandson of Rhodri Mawr, Howel succeeded to the kingdom of Dyfed *c*. 904, to Seisyllog *c*. 920 and became King of Gwynedd and all Wales, 942.

1121

1121 HOPÆL REX, small cross or rosette. R. Moneyer's name in two lines ..   *Extremely rare*

EADWIG, 955-959

Elder son of Eadmund, Eadwig lost Mercia and Northumbria to his brother Eadgar in 957.

1122   1123

1122 *Br. 1*. Type as illustration	185	375
1123 — — Similar, but mint name in place of crosses	375	825
1124 — 2. As 1122, but moneyer's name in one line	700	1800
1125 — 3. Similar. R. Floral design	1100	2650
1126 — 4. Similar. R. Rosette or small cross	275	625
1127 — 5. Bust r. R. Small cross	1750	4500

1128

1128 *Halfpenny*. Small cross. R. Flower above moneyer's name	900	2250
1128A — Similar. R. PIN (Winchester) across field	975	2450
1128B — Star. R. Moneyer's name in two lines	800	1750

King in Mercia and Northumbria from 957; King of all England 959-975.

It is now possible on the basis of the lettering to divide up the majority of Eadgar's coins into issues from the following regions: N.E. England, N.W. England, York, East Anglia, Midlands, S.E. England, Southern England, and S.W. England. (See 'Anglo-Saxon Coins', ed. R. H. M. Dolley.)

1129   1135

	F	VF
	£	£
1129 *Br I*. Small cross. R. Moneyer's name in two lines, crosses between, trefoils top and bottom	85	185
1130 — — R. Similar, but rosettes top and bottom (a N.W. variety)	110	235
1131 — — R. Similar, but annulets between	125	275
1132 — — R. Similar, but mint name between (a late N.W. type)	165	375
1133 — *2*. — R. Floral design	900	2250
1134 — *4*. Small cross either side	95	210
1135 — — Similar, with mint name	175	400
1136 — — Rosette either side	125	275
1137 — — Similar, with mint name	225	500
1138 — *5*. Large bust to r. R. Small cross	525	1200
1139 — — Similar, with mint name	575	1250
1140 *Halfpenny*. (8.5 grains.) *Br. 3*. Small cross. R. Flower above name	850	2000
1140A — — R. Mint name around cross (Chichester)	900	2250
1140B — Bust r. R. 'Londonia' monogram	450	975

For Eadgar 'reform' issues see overleaf

In 973 Eadgar introduced a new coinage. A royal portrait now became a regular feature and the reverses normally have a cruciform pattern with the name of the mint in addition to that of the moneyer. Most fortified towns of burghal status were allowed a mint, the number of moneyers varying according to their size and importance: some royal manors also had a mint and some moneyers were allowed to certain ecclesiastical authorities. In all some seventy mints were active about the middle of the 11th century (see list of mints pp. 127-8).

     The control of the currency was retained firmly in the hands of the central government, unlike the situation in France and the Empire where feudal barons and bishops controlled their own coinage. Coinage types were changed at intervals to enable the Exchequer to raise revenue from new dies and periodic demonetization of old coin types helped to maintain the currency in a good state. No halfpence were minted during this period. During the latter part of this era, full pennies were sheared into 'halfpennies' and 'farthings'. They are far rarer than later 'cut' coins.

Eadgar, 959-975 *continued*

1141

	F	VF
	£	£
1141 **Penny.** Type 6. Small bust l. R. Small cross, name of moneyer and mint.	575	1200

EDWARD THE MARTYR, 975-978

Son of Eadgar and Aethelflaed, Eadward was murdered at Corfe castle, reputedly on the orders of his stepmother Aelfthryth.

1142

| 1142 Type as illustration above .... | 675 | 1425 |

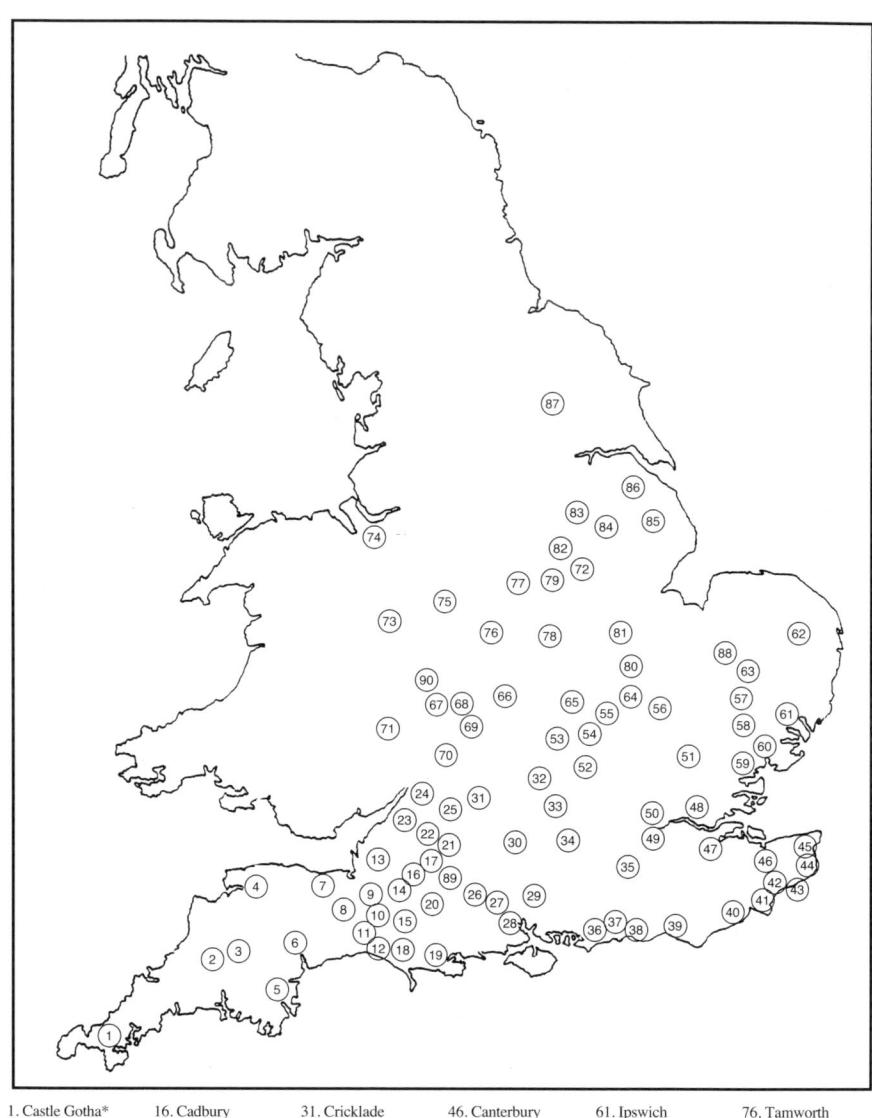

1. Castle Gotha*	16. Cadbury	31. Cricklade	46. Canterbury	61. Ipswich	76. Tamworth
2. Launceston	17. Bruton	32. Oxford	47. Rochester	62. Norwich	77. Derby
3. Lydford	18. Dorchester	33. Wallingford	48. Horndon	63. Thetford	78. Leicester
4. Barnstaple	19. Wareham	34. Reading	49. Southwark	64. Huntingdon	79. Nottingham
5. Totnes	29. Shaftesbury	35. Guildford	50. London	65. Northampton	80. Peterborough
6. Exeter	21. Warminster	36. Chichester	51. Hertford	66. Warwick	81. Stamford
7. Watchet	22. Bath	37. Cissbury	52. Aylesbury	67. Worcester	82. Torksey
8. Taunton	23. Bristol	38. Steyning	53. Buckingham	68. Pershore	83. Lincoln
9. Langport	24. Berkeley	39. Lewes	54. Newport Pagnell*	69. Winchcombe	84. Lincoln
10. Petherton	25. Malmesbury	40. Hastings	55. Bedford	70. Gloucester	85. Horncastle
11. Crewkerne	26. Wilton	41. Romney	56. Cambridge	71. Hereford	86. Caistor
12. Bridport	27. Salisbury	42. Lympne	57. Bury St Edmunds	72. Grantham*	87. York
13. Axbridge	28. Southampton	43. Dover	58. Sudbury	73. Shrewsbury	88. Wilton. Norfolk*
14. Ilchester	29. Winchester	44. Dover	59. Maldon	74. Chester	89. Frome*
15. Miborne Port	30. Bedwyn	45. Sandwich	60. Colchester	75. Stafford	90. Droitwich

Possible location of uncertain mint

He was the son of Eadgar and Aelfthryth. His reign was greatly disturbed by incursions of Danish fleets and armies which massive payments of money failed to curb. He was known as 'The Unready', from UNREDE, meaning 'without counsel', ie. he was without good advice.

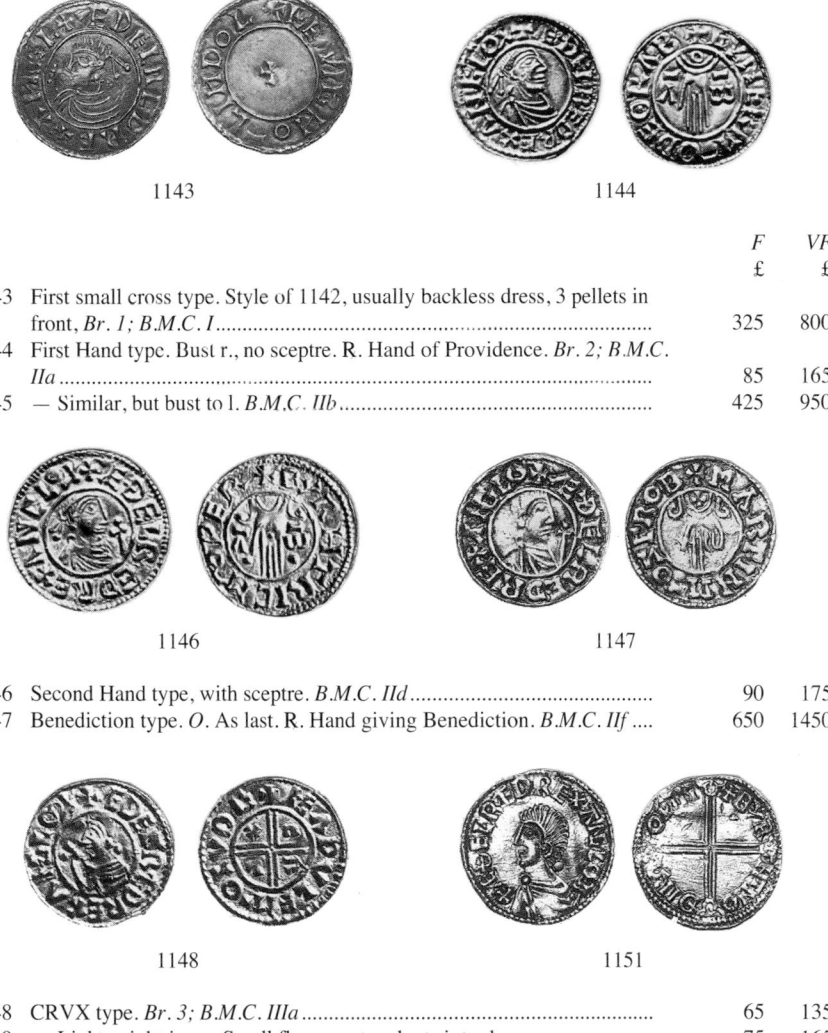

1143   1144

	F £	VF £
1143 First small cross type. Style of 1142, usually backless dress, 3 pellets in front, *Br. 1; B.M.C. I*	325	800
1144 First Hand type. Bust r., no sceptre. R. Hand of Providence. *Br. 2; B.M.C. IIa*	85	165
1145 — Similar, but bust to l. *B.M.C. IIb*	425	950

1146   1147

1146 Second Hand type, with sceptre. *B.M.C. IId*	90	175
1147 Benediction type. *O.* As last. R. Hand giving Benediction. *B.M.C. IIf*	650	1450

1148   1151

1148 CRVX type. *Br. 3; B.M.C. IIIa*	65	135
1149 — Lightweight issue. Small flan, sceptre slants into drapery	75	165
1150 Intermediate small cross type. Somewhat as 1143, no pellets, similar bust to CRVX type (1148) but no sceptre	525	1250
1151 Long cross type. *Br. 5; B.M.C. IVa*	70	135

1152

		F	*VF*
		£	£
1152	Helmet type. *Br. 4; B.M.C. VIII*	80	165
1153	— — Similar, but struck in **gold**	*Extremely rare*	

1154   1156

1154	Last small cross type. As 1143, but different style	65	130
1154A	Similar, but bust r.	175	425
1155	— Similar, but bust to edge of coin. *B.M.C. Id*	250	575
1156	Agnus Dei type. *c*. 1009. *Br. 6; B.M.C. X*	3000	7250

Son of Swegn Forkbeard, King of Denmark, Cnut was acclaimed King by the Danish fleet in England in 1014 but was forced to leave. He returned in 1015 and in 1016 agreed on a division of the country with Eadmund Ironsides, the son of Aethelred. No coins of Eadmund are known and on his death in November 1016 Cnut secured all England, marrying Emma of Normandy, widow of Aethelred.

Main types

| 1157 | 1158 | 1159 | 1160 |

	F	VF
	£	£
1157 Quatrefoil type. *Br. 2; B.M.C. VIII*	60	130
1158 Helmet type. *Br. 3; B.M.C. XIV*	50	100
1159 Short cross type. *Br. 4; B.M.C. XVI*	45	90
1159A — Similar, but with banner in place of sceptre	525	1250
1160 Jewel cross type. *Br. 6; B.M.C. XX.* Type as *1163*	325	750

This type is now considered to be a posthumous issue struck under the auspices of his widow, Aelgifu Emma.

HAROLD I, 1035-1040

Harold, the son of Cnut and Aelgifu of Northampton, initially acted as regent for his half-brother Harthacnut on Cnut's death, was then recognised as King in Mercia and the north, and King throughout England in 1037.

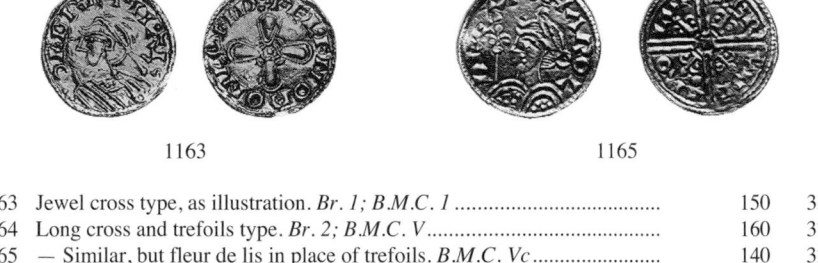

| 1163 | 1165 |

1163 Jewel cross type, as illustration. *Br. 1; B.M.C. 1*	150	350
1164 Long cross and trefoils type. *Br. 2; B.M.C. V*	160	375
1165 — Similar, but fleur de lis in place of trefoils. *B.M.C. Vc*	140	325

He was heir to Cnut but lost the throne to his half-brother Harold owing to his absence in Denmark. On Harold's death he recovered his English realm.

	F £	VF £
1166 **Early period, 1036.** Jewel cross type, as 1163; bust l. *Br. 1; B.M.C. I* ...	800	2000

1167   1168

1167 — Similar, but bust r. *B.M.C. Ia*	700	1650
1168 **Restoration, 1040-1042.** Arm and sceptre type, with name Harthacnut. *Br. 2; B.M.C. II*	675	1500

1169   1170

1169 — Similar, but with name 'Cnut'..	275	600
1170 **Danish types,** of various designs, some of English type mostly struck at Lund, Denmark (now Sweden)	150	350

EDWARD THE CONFESSOR, 1042-1066

Edward was the son of Aethelred II and Emma of Normandy. A number of new mints were opened during his reign.

1171   1173

1170A Arm and Sceptre type. B.M.C. iiic..	800	1750
1171 PACX type, cross extends to edge of coin. *Br. 4; B.M.C. IV*	120	250
1172 — Similar, but cross ends at legend. *B.M.C. IVa*	140	300
1173 Radiate type. *Br. 2; B.M.C. I*	75	140

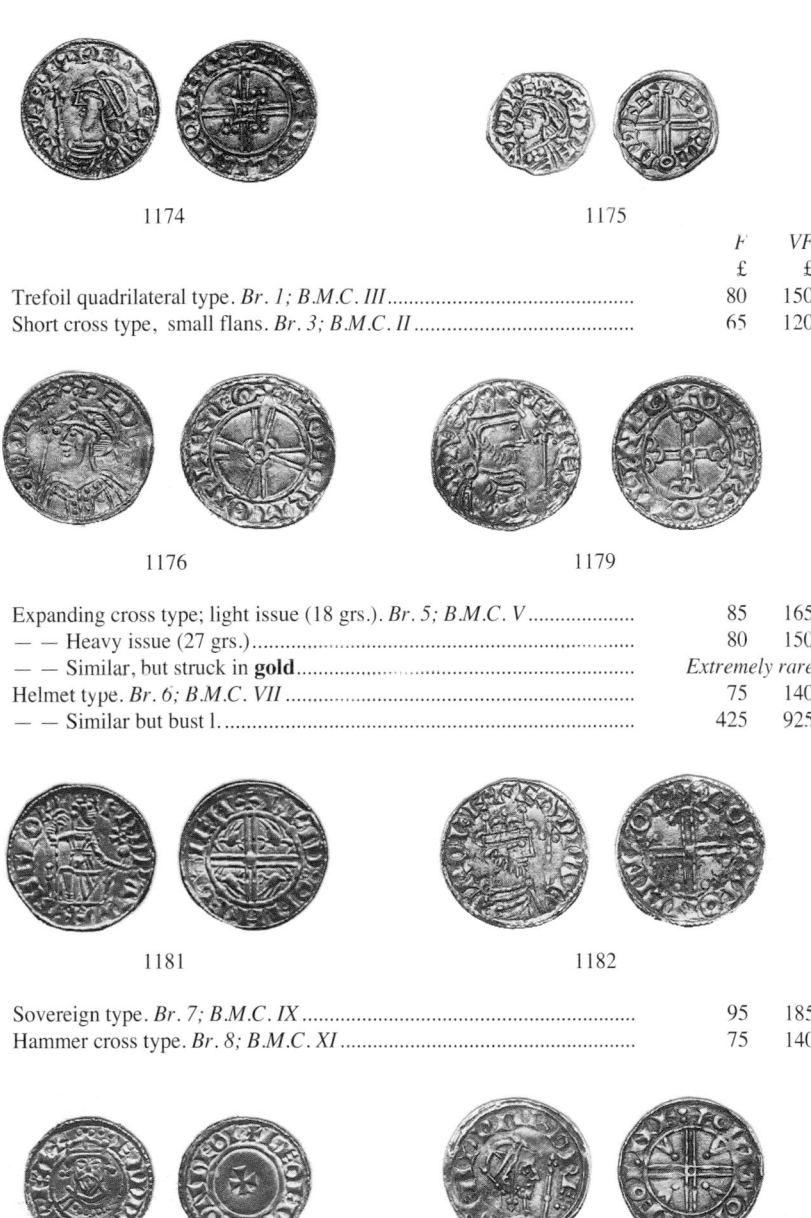

1174   1175

	F £	VF £
1174 Trefoil quadrilateral type. *Br. 1; B.M.C. III*	80	150
1175 Short cross type, small flans. *Br. 3; B.M.C. II*	65	120

1176   1179

1176 Expanding cross type; light issue (18 grs.). *Br. 5; B.M.C. V*	85	165
1177 — — Heavy issue (27 grs.)	80	150
1178 — — Similar, but struck in **gold**	*Extremely rare*	
1179 Helmet type. *Br. 6; B.M.C. VII*	75	140
1180 — — Similar but bust l.	425	925

1181   1182

1181 Sovereign type. *Br. 7; B.M.C. IX*	95	185
1182 Hammer cross type. *Br. 8; B.M.C. XI*	75	140

1183   1184

1183 Facing bust type. *Br. 9; B.M.C. XIII*	70	135
1184 Pyramids type. *Br. 10; B.M.C. XV*	90	160

1185

	F	VF
	£	£
1185 Transitional Pyramids type. *B.M.C. XIV*	850	2000

Most York coins of this reign have an annulet in one quarter of the reverse.

HAROLD II, 1066

Harold was the son of Godwin Earl of Wessex. He was the brother-in-law of Edward the Confessor and was recognised as King on Edward's death. He defeated and killed Harald of Norway who invaded the north, but was himself defeated and killed at the Battle of Hastings by William of Normandy.

1186   1187

1186 Bust l. with sceptre. R. PAX across centre of *rev. B.M.C. I*	350	725
1187 Similar, but without sceptre. *B.M.C. Ia*	425	900
1188 Bust r. with sceptre *B.M.C. Ib*	625	1450

ANGLO-SAXON, NORMAN AND EARLY PLANTAGENET MINTS

In Anglo-Saxon times coins were struck at a large number of towns. The place of mintage is normally given on all coins from the last quarter of the 10th century onwards, and generally the name of the person responsible (e.g. BRVNIC ON LVND). Below we give a list of the mints, showing the reigns (Baronial of Stephen's reign omitted), of which coins have been found. After the town names we give one or two of the spellings as found on the coins, although often they appear in an abbreviated or extended form. On the coins the Anglo-Saxon and Norman w is like a P or T and the th is D. We have abbreviated the kings' names, etc.:

Alf	—	Alfred the Great	Wi	—	William I
EE	—	Edward the Elder	Wii	—	William II
A'stan	—	Aethelstan	He	—	Henry I
EM	–	Edward the Martyr	St	—	Stephen (regular issues)
Ae	—	Aethelred II	M	—	Matilda
Cn	—	Cnut	HA	—	Henry of Anjou
Hi	—	Harold I	WG	—	William of Gloucester
Ht	—	Harthacnut	T	—	'Tealby' coinage
ECfr	—	Edward the Confessor	SC	—	Short cross coinage
Hii	—	Harold II	LC	—	Long cross coinage

Abergavenny (FANI), Wi.
Axbridge (ACXEPO, AGEPOR) Ae, Cn, Ht.
Aylesbury (AEGEL) Ae, Cn, ECfr.
Barnstaple (BEARDA, BARDI), Edwig, Ae-Hi, ECfr, Wi, He.
Bath (BADAN) EE-Edmund, Edwig-ECfr, Wi, He, St.
Bedford (BEDANF, BEDEF) Edwig-T.
Bedwyn (BEDE CIN) ECfr, Wi.
Berkeley (BEORC) ECfr, Wi.
Bramber ? (BRAN) St.
Bridport (BRIPVT, BRIDI) A'stan, Ae, Cn, Ht, ECfr, Wi.
Bristol (BRICSTO) Ae T, M. HA, LC.
Bruton (BRIVT) Ae-Cn, ECfr
Buckingham (BVCIN) EM-Hi, ECfr.
Bury St. Edmunds (EDMVN, SEDM, SANTEA) A'stan?, ECfr, Wi, He-LC.
Cadbury CADANB) Ae, Cn
Caistor (CASTR) EM, Ae, Cn.
Cambridge (GRANTE) Edgar-He.
Canterbury (DORO, CAENT, CANTOR, CANT CAR) Alf, A'stan, Edgar-LC.
Cardiff (CAIRDI, CARDI, CARITI) Wi, He, St, M.
Carlisle (CAR, CARDI, EDEN) He-LC.
Castle Gotha ? (GEOĐA, IOĐA) Ae-Ht.
Castle Rising (RISINGE) St.
Chester (LEIGECES, LEGECE, CESTRE) A'stan, Edgar-T.
Chichester (CISSAN CIV, CICES, CICST) A'stan, Edgar-St, SC
Chippenham ? (CIPEN) St.
Christchurch, see Twynham.
Cissbury (SIĐEST) Ae, Cn.
Colchester (COLEAC, COLECES) Ae-Hi, ECfr-T.
Crewkerne (CRVCERN) Ae, Cn.
Cricklade (CROCGL, CRIC, CREC) Ae-Wii.
Derby (DEOR, DIORBI, DERBI) A'stan, Edgar-ECfr, Wi-St.
Dorchester (DORCE, DORECES) Ae-ECfr, Wi-He, WG.
Dover (DOFER) A'stan, Edgar-St.
Droitwich (PICC, PICNEH) ECfr, Hii.
Dunwich (DVNE) St.
Durham (DVRE, DVRHAN) Wi, St-LC.
Exeter (EAXANC, EXEC, XECST) Alf, A'stan, Edwig-LC.

Fye (EI, EIE) St.
Frome ? (FRO) Cn-ECfr.
Gloucester (GLEA C EC, GLE C , G C) Alf, A'stan, Edgar-St, HA, T, LC.
Grantham (GRE) Ae
Guildford (GILDEF) EM-Cn, Ht-Wii.
Hastings (HAESTIN) Ae-St.
Hedon, near Hull (HEDVN) St.
Hereford (HERFFOR) A'stan, Ae-St, HA, T, LC.
Hertford (HEORTF) A'stan, Edwig-Hi, ECfr, Wi, Wii.
Horncastle ? (HORN) EM, Ae.
Horndon ? (HORNIDVNE) ECfr.
Huntingdon (HVNTEN) Edwig-St.
Hythe (HIĐEN) ECfr, Wi, Wii.
Ilchester (IVELCE, GIFELCST, GIVELC) Edgar, E M-He, T, LC.
Ipswich (GIPES C IC) Edgar-SC.
Kings Lynn (LENN, LENE) SC.
Langport (LANCPOR) A'stan, Cn, Hi, ECfr.
Launceston (LANSTF, SANCTI STEFANI) Ae, Wi, Wii, St. T.
Leicester (LIGER, LIHER, LEHRE) A'stan, Edgar-T.
Lewes (LAEPES) A'stan, Edgar-T.
Lichfield (LIHFL) SC.
Lincoln (LINCOLNE, NICOLE) Edgar-LC.
London (LVNDENE) Alf-LC.
Lydford (LYDAN) EM-Hi, ECfr.
Lympne (LIMEN) A'stan, Edgar-Cn.
Maldon (MAELDVN, MAELI) A'stan, Ae-Hi, ECfr, Wii.
Malmesbury (MALD, MEALDMES) Ae-Wii, HA.
Marlborough (MAERLEB) Wi, Wii.
Milbourne Port (MYLE) Ae, Cn.
Newark (NEPIR, NIPOR) Edwig, Eadgar, Ae, Cn.
Newcastle (NEWEC, NIVCA) St, T, LC.
Newport (NIPAN, NIPEP) Edgar, ECfr.
Northampton (HAMTVN, NORHANT) Edwig, Edgar-Wi, He-LC.
Norwich (NORPIC) A'stan-LC.
Nottingham (SNOTINC) A'stan, Ae-St.
Oxford (OXNAFOR, OXENEF) Alf A'stan, Edmund, Edred, Edgar-St, M, T-LC.
Pembroke (PAN, PAIN) He-T.
Pershore (PERESC) ECfr.

Peterborough (MEDE, BVR) Ae, Cn, Wi.
Petherton (PEDÐR) ECfr.
Pevensey (PEFNESE, PEVEN) Wi, Wii, St.
Reading (READIN) ECfr.
Rhuddlan (RVDILI, RVLA) Wi, SC.
Rochester (ROFEC) A'stan, Edgar-He, SC.
Romney (RVME, RVMNE) Ae-Hi, ECfr-He.
Rye (RIE) St.
Salisbury (SAEREB, SALEB) Ae-ECfr, Wi- T.
Sandwich (SANPIC) ECfr, Wi-St.
Shaftesbury (SCEFTESB, SCEFITI) A'stan, Ae-St.
Shrewsbury (SCROBES, SALOP) A'stan, Edgar-LC.
Southampton (HAMWIC, HAMTVN) A'stan, Edwig-Cn.
Southwark (SVDGE, SVD C EEORC) Ae-St.
Stafford (STAFF, STAEF) A'stan, Ae-Hi, ECfr, Wi, Wii, St, T.
Stamford (STANFOR) Edgar-St.
Steyning (STAENIG) Cn-Wii.
Sudbury (SVDBI, SVB) Ae, Cn, ECfr, Wi- St.

Swansea (SWENSEI) HA?
Tamworth (TOMPEARÐGE, TAMPRÐ) A'stan, Edwig-Hi, ECfr, Wi-St.
Taunton (TANTVNE) Ae, Cn, Ht-St.
Thetford (ÐEOTFOR,, TETFOR) Edgar-T.
Torksey (TORC, TVRC) EM-Cn.
Totnes (DARENT VRB, TOTANES, TOTNESE) A'stan, Edwig-Cn, Wii.
Twynham, now Christchurch (TPIN, TVEHAM) Wi, He.
Wallingford (PELING, PALLIG) A'stan, Edgar-He, T, LC.
Wareham (PERHAM) A'stan, Ae, Cn, Ht-St, M, WG.
Warminster (PORIME) Ae-Hi, ECfr.
Warwick (PAERING, PERPIC) A'stan, Edgar-St.
Watchet (PECEDPORT, PICEDI) Ae-ECfr, Wi-St.
Wilton (PILTVNE) Edgar-LC.
Winchcombe (PINCELE, PINCL) Edgar-Cn, Ht-Wi.
Winchester (PINTONIA, PINCEST) Alf-A'stan, Edwig -LC.
Worcester (PIHRAC, PIHREC) Ae-Hi, ECfr-Sc.
York (EBORACI, EOFERPIC) A'stan, Edmund, Edgar-LC

The location of the following is uncertain.
AESTHE *(? Hastings)* Ae.
DERNE, DYR *(E. Anglian mint East Dereham?)* ECfr.
DEVITVN *(? Welsh Marches or St. Davids)* Wi.
MAINT, Wi.
WEARDBYRIG *(? Warborough)* A'stan, Edgar.

BRYGIN *(? Bridgnorth*, but die-links with NIPAN and with *Shaftesbury)* Ae.
EANBYRIG, Cn.
ORSNAFORDA *(Danelaw imitation)*
'WILTV' *(?Wilton, Norfolk)* Ae

EDWARDIAN AND LATER MINTS

Aberystwyth: Chas. I.
Aberystwyth: -Furnace: Chas. I.
Ashby de la Zouche: Chas. I.
Berwick-on-Tweed: Edw. I-Edw. III.
Birmingham, Heaton: Vic., Geo. V.
Birmingham, King's Norton: Geo. V.
Birmingham, Soho: Geo. III.
Bombay, India (branch mint): Geo. V.
Bridgnorth: Chas. I.
Bristol: Edw. I, Edw. IV, Hen. VI rest., Hen. VIII-Edw. VI, Chas. I, Wm. III.
Bury St. Edmunds: Edw. I-Edw. III.
Calais: Edw. III-Hen. IV, Hen. VI.
Canterbury: Edw. I-Edw. III, Edw. IV, Hen. VII-Edw. VI.
Carlisle: Chas. I.
Chester: Edw. I, Chas. I, Wm. III.
Colchester: Chas. I.
Coventry: Edw. IV.
Durham: Edw. I-Edw. IV, Rich. III-Hen. VIII.
Exeter: Edw. I, Chas. I, Wm. III.
Hartlebury Castle, Worcs.: Chas. I.
Hereford: Chas. I.
Kingston-upon-Hull: Edw. I.
Lincoln: Edw. I.

Llantrisant: Eliz. II (decimal coinage).
London, Tower: Edw. I-Geo. III.
London, Tower Hill: Geo. III-Eliz. II.
London, Durham House: Hen. VIII (posth.)-Edw. VI.
Melbourne, Australia (branch mint): Vic.-Geo. V.
Newark: Chas. I.
Newcastle-upon-Tyne: Edw. I.
Norwich: Edw. IV, Wm. III.
Ottawa, Canada (branch mint): Edw. VII-Geo. V.
Oxford: Chas I.
Perth, Australia (branch mint): Vic.-Geo. V.
Pontefract: Chas. I.
Pretoria, South Africa (branch mint): Geo. V.
Reading: Edw. III.
Scarborough: Chas. I.
Shrewsbury: Chas. I.
Southwark: Hen. VIII-Edw. VI.
Sydney, Australia (branch mint): Vic.-Geo. V.
Tournai, Belgium: Hen. VIII.
Truro: Chas. I.
Welsh Marches: Chas I
Worcester: Chas I.
York: Edw. I, Edw. III-Edw. IV, Rich. III-Edw. VI, Chas. I, Wm. III.

NORMAN MINTS (WILLIAM I TO HENRY I)

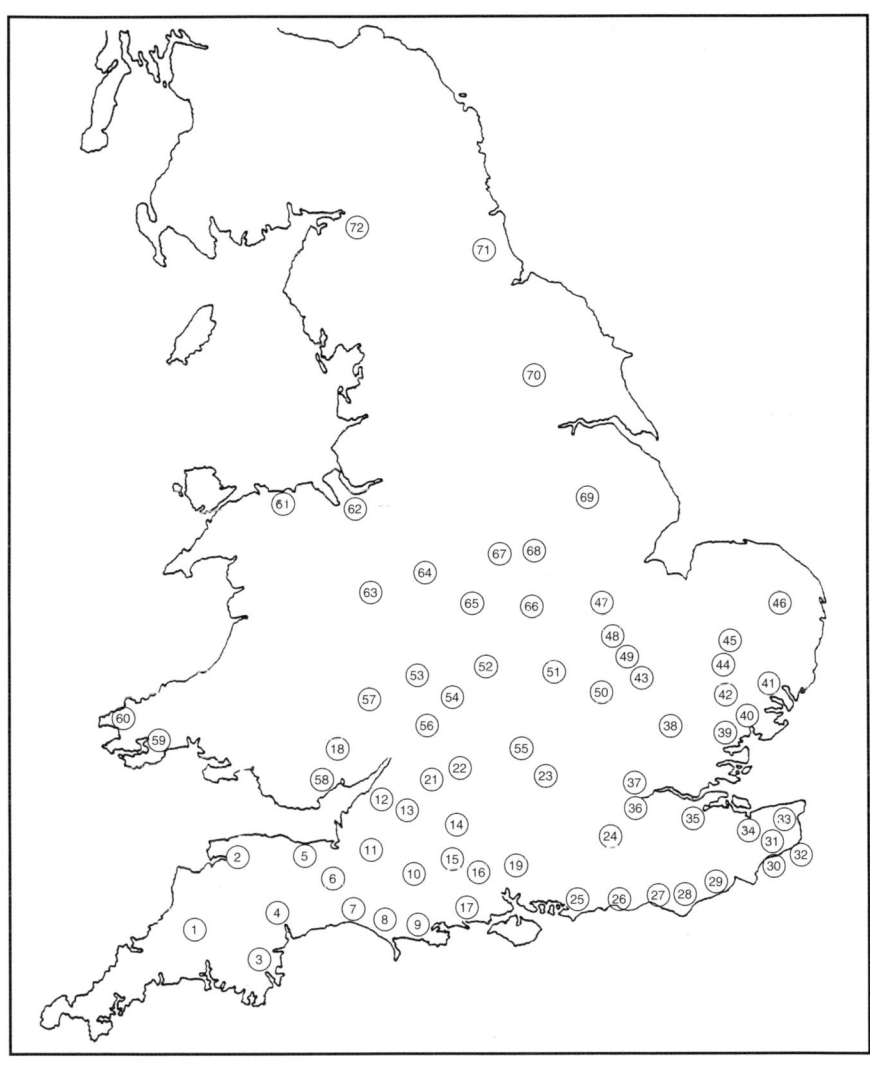

1. Launceston	13. Bath	25. Chichester	37. London	49. Huntingdon	61. Rhuddlan
2. Barnstaple	14. Marlborough	26. Steyning	38. Hertford	50. Bedford	62. Chester
3. Totnes	15. Wilton	27. Lewes	39. Maldon	51. Northampton	63. Shrewsbury
4. Exeter	16. Salisbury	28. Pevensey	40. Colchester	52. Warwick	64. Stafford
5. Watchet	17. Chirstchurch	29. Hastings	41. Ipswich	53. Worcester	65. Tamworth
6. Taunton	18. Abergavenny*	30. Romney	42. Sudbury	54. Winchcombe	66. Leicester
7. Bridport	19. Winchester	31. Hythe	43. Cambridge	55. Oxford	67. Derby
8. Dorchester	20. Bedwyn	32. Dover	44. Bury	56. Gloucester	68. Nottingham
9. Wareham	21. Malmesbury	33. Sandwich	45. Thetford	57. Hereford	69. Lincoln
10. Shaftesbury	22. Cricklade	34. Canterbury	46. Norwich	58. Cardiff	70. York
11. Ilchester	23. Wallingford	35. Rochester	47. Stamford	59. Pembroke	71. Durham
12. Bristol	24. Guildford	36. Southwark	48. Peterborough	60. St Davids*	72. Carlisle

* Possible location of uncertain mint

There were no major changes in the coinages following the Norman conquest. The controls and periodic changes of the type made in the previous reigns were continued. Nearly seventy mints were operating during the reign of William I; these had been reduced to about fifty-five by the middle of the 12th century and, under Henry II, first to thirty and later to eleven. By the second half of the 13th century the issue of coinage had been centralized at London and Canterbury, with the exception of two ecclesiastical mints. Of the thirteen types with the name PILLEMVS, PILLELM, etc. (William), the first eight have been attributed to the Conqueror and the remaining five to his son William Rufus. Cut 'halfpennies' and 'farthings' were still made in this period and are scarce until the later issues of Henry I and Stephen.

From William I to Edward II inclusive all are silver pennies unless otherwise stated.

WILLIAM I, 1066-1087

William Duke of Normandy was the cousin of Edward the Confessor. After securing the throne of England he had to suppress several rebellions.

1250    1251

		F	VF
		£	£
1250	*Penny*. Profile left type. *Br. I*	160	375

1252    1253

| 1251 | Bonnet type. *Br. II* | 120 | 240 |
| 1252 | Canopy type. *Br. III* | 210 | 475 |

1254    1255

1253	Two sceptres type. *Br. IV*	140	325
1254	Two stars type. *Br. V*	110	230
1255	Sword type. *Br. VI*	175	390

	1256		1257		

				F	VF
				£	£
1256	Profile right type. *Br VII*			240	550
1257	PAXS type. *Br. VIII*			95	165

WILLIAM II, 1087-1100

William Rufus was the second son of William I, his elder brother Robert succeeded to the Dukedom of Normandy. He was killed while hunting in the New Forest.

	1258		1259		

1258	Penny. Profile type. *Br. 1*	300	700
1259	Cross in quatrefoil type. *Br. 2*	275	575

	1260		1261		

1260	Cross voided type. *Br. 3*	275	600
1261	Cross pattée and fleury type. *Br. 4*	300	650

	1262	

1262	Cross fleury and piles type. *Br. 5*	350	750

Fifteen types were minted during this reign. In 1106-7 provision was made for minting round halfpence again, none having been struck since the time of Eadgar, but relatively few can have been made. The standard of coinage manufacture was now beginning to deteriorate badly. Many genuine coins were being cut to see if they were plated counterfeits and there was a reluctance by the public to accept such damaged pieces. About 1107-8 an extraordinary decision was taken to order the official mutilation of all new coins by snicking the edges, thus ensuring that cut coins had to be accepted. Pennies of types VII to XII (Nos. 1268-1273) usually have a cut in the flan that sometimes penetrated over a third of the way across the coin.

At Christmas 1124 the famous 'Assize of the Moneyers' was held at Winchester when all the moneyers in England were called to account for their activities and a number are said to have been mutilated for issuing coins of inferior quality.

The dates and the order of Henry's issues have been modified several times since Brooke. The main changes are as follows: BMC 11 preceded 10 and BMC 9 follows 6. The order of BMC 7 and 8 remains uncertain. The issues were not made for equal periods of time, as BMC 15 began in early 1125. The contemporary chronicles mention the round halfpenny (and farthings) and the order to snick whole coins under 1107 or 1108. The halfpennies are now dated to agree with these references when BMC 6 and 9 pennies were current. A few pennies of BMC 6 are snicked as are most of the halfpennies. Snicks continue to be used on coins of BMC 13 and 14, thought the cut is smaller and only a quarter to a half of the coins are snicked. [Brooke 1916; Archibald and Conté SNC 1990; Blackburn RNS 1990.]

1263   1263A

		F	VF
		£	£
1263	**Penny.** *Br*. I. Annulets type	300	650
1263A	— II. Profile l. R. Cross fleury..	225	475

1264   1265

| 1264 | — III. PAX type.. | 210 | 450 |
| 1265 | — IV. Facing bust. R. Five annulets and four piles................................ | 275 | 550 |

1266   1267

| 1266 | — V. — R. Voided cross with fleur in each angle .... | 450 | 950 |
| 1267 | — VI. Pointing bust and stars type .... | 600 | 1250 |

1268

		F	*VF*
		£	£
1268	*Br*. VII. Facing bust. R. Quatrefoil with piles	225	475

1269   1270

| 1269 | — VIII. Large bust l. R. Cross with annulet in each angle .... | 750 | 1750 |
| 1270 | — IX. Facing bust. R. Cross in quatrefoil .... | 450 | 900 |

1271   1272

| 1271 | — X. Small facing bust in circle. R. Cross fleury .... | 140 | 325 |
| 1272 | — XI. Very large bust l. R. 'Double inscription' around small cross pattee | 325 | 725 |

1273   1274

| 1273 | — XII. Small bust l. R. Cross with annulet in each angle .... | 250 | 550 |
| 1274 | — XIII. Star in lozenge fleury type .... | 225 | 500 |

● = Regular mints of Stephen.

⊕ = Mints striking irregular coins including Angevin.

+ = Mints striking regular and irregular coins.

N.B.   Attribution to some of the towns shown is uncertain.

1275    1276

	F £	VF £
1275 Br. XIV. Pellets in quatrefoil type	135	300
1276 — XV. Quadrilateral on cross fleury type	100	225

1277

	F	VF
1277* *Halfpenny.* Facing head. R. Cross potent with pellets in angles	900	2250
1277A — As above R. Struck from a penny die of type IX	1750	4000

STEPHEN, 1135-1154
and the Civil War and Anarchy, 1138-1153

Stephen of Blois, Count of Boulogne and a nephew of Henry I, hastily crossed the Channel on his uncle's death and secured the throne for himself, despite Henry's wishes that his daughter Matilda should succeed him. She was the widow of the German emperor Henry V, and was then married to Geoffrey, Count of Anjou. Two years later Matilda arrived in England to claim the throne, supported by her half-brother Robert of Gloucester.

During the protracted civil war that ensued Matilda and later her son, Henry of Anjou, set up an alternative court at Bristol and held much of the west of England, striking coins at mints under their control. Many irregular coins were struck during this troubled period, some by barons in their own name. Particularly curious are the coins from the Midlands and E. Anglia which have Stephen's head defaced, now believed to have been issued during the Interdict of 1148. In 1153, following the death of Stephen's son, Eustace, a treaty between the two factions allowed for the succession of Matilda's son Henry and a uniform coinage was once more established throughout the kingdom.

B.M.C. Norman Kings, 2 vols. (1916). *M.—* Mack, R. P., 'Stephen and the Anarchy 1135-54', *BNJ, XXXV* (1966), pp. 38-112.

Regular regal issuess

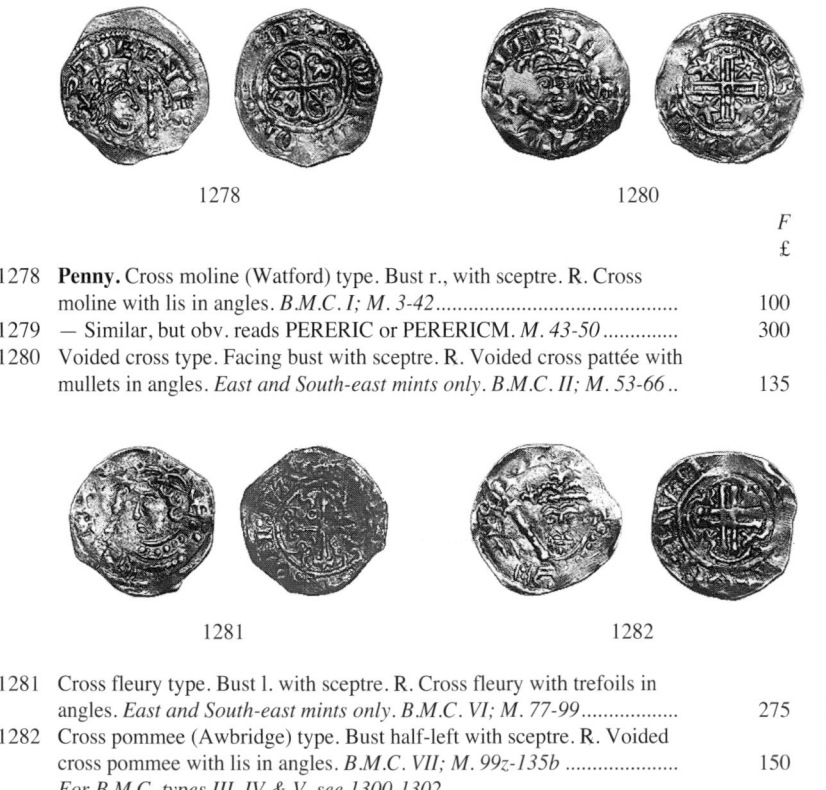

1278   1280

		F	VF
		£	£
1278	**Penny.** Cross moline (Watford) type. Bust r., with sceptre. R. Cross moline with lis in angles. *B.M.C. I; M. 3-42*.....	100	250
1279	— Similar, but obv. reads PERERIC or PERERICM. *M. 43-50*..............	300	650
1280	Voided cross type. Facing bust with sceptre. R. Voided cross pattée with mullets in angles. *East and South-east mints only. B.M.C. II; M. 53-66*..	135	325

1281   1282

1281	Cross fleury type. Bust l. with sceptre. R. Cross fleury with trefoils in angles. *East and South-east mints only. B.M.C. VI; M. 77-99*..................	275	650
1282	Cross pommee (Awbridge) type. Bust half-left with sceptre. R. Voided cross pommee with lis in angles. *B.M.C. VII; M. 99z-135b*	150	375
	For B.M.C. types III, IV & V, see 1300-1302.		

LOCAL AND IRREGULAR ISSUES OF THE CIVIL WAR

A. Coins struck from erased or defaced dies (interdict of 1148)

1283

		F	VF
		£	£
1283	As 1278, with king's bust defaced with long cross. *East Anglian Mints. M. 137-147*	450	975
1284	— Similar, but king's bust defaced with small cross. *Nottingham. M. 149*	400	850
1285	— Similar, but sceptre defaced with bar or cross. *Nottingham, Lincoln and Stamford. M. 148 and 150-154*	400	825
1286	— Similar, but king's name erased. *Nottingham. M. 157*	325	700
1286A	— Other defacements	400	850

B. South-Eastern variant

1287	As 1278, but king holds mace instead of sceptre. *Canterbury. M. 158*	900	2500

C. Eastern variants

1288

1288	As 1278, but roundels in centre or on limbs of cross or in angles. *Suffolk mints. M. 159-168*	575	1250
1288A	As 1278, but star before sceptre and annulets at tips of *fleurs on reverse. Suffolk mints. M. 188*	650	1500
1289	As 1278, but thick plain cross with pellet at end of limbs, lis in angles. *Lincoln. M. 169-173*	600	1350
1290	— Similar, but thick plain cross superimposed on cross moline. *M. 174.*	600	1450
1290A	As 1278. R. Quadrilateral over voided cross. *M. 176*	850	2250
1290B	As 1278. R. Long cross to edge of coin, fleurs outwards in angles. *Lincoln. M. 186-187*	800	2000

			F £	VF £

D. Southern variants

1291 As 1278, but with large rosette of pellets at end of obverse legend.
      M. 184-185 .... 650 1500
1292 — Similar, but star at end of obverse legend. *M. 187y* 600 1450
1293 Crowned bust r. or l. with rosette of pellets before face in place of sceptre.
      R. As 1280, but plain instead of voided cross. *M. 181-183* 700 1650

1291    1295

1295 As 1278, but usually collar of annulets. R. Voided cross moline with
      annulet at centre. *Southampton. M. 207-212* 225 525

E. Midland variants

1296

1296 As 1278, but cross moline on reverse has fleured extensions into legend.
      Leicester. M. 177-178 .... 800 2000
1297 As 1278 but crude work. R. Voided cross with lis outwards in angles.
      Tutbury. M. 179 .... 750 1750

1298    1300

1298 Somewhat similar. R. Voided cross with martlets in angles. *Derby. M. 175*   1200 3250
1299 As 1278. R. Plain cross with T-cross in each angle. *M. 180* 800 2000
1300 Facing bust with three annulets on crown. R. Cross pattée, fleurs inwards
      in angles. *Northampton or Huntingdon (?). B.M.C. III; M. 67-71* 975 2500

1301   1302

	F	VF
	£	£
1301 Facing bust with three fleurs on crown. R. Lozenge fleury, annulets in angles. *Lincoln or Nottingham. B.M.C. IV; M. 72-75*	1000	2650
1302 Bust half-right with sceptre. R. Lozenge with pellet centre, fleurs inwards in angles. *Leicester. B.M.C. V; M. 76*	1250	3250
1303 **Robert**, Earl of Leicester(?). As 1280, but reading ROBERTVS. *M. 269*	1750	4750

F. North-east and Scottish border variants

1304 As 1278, but star before sceptre and annulets at tips of fleurs on reverse. *M. 188*	650	1500
1305 As 1278, but a voided cross extending to outer circle of reverse. *M. 189-192*	800	2000
1306 As 1278, but crude style, with Stephen's name. *M. 276-279 and 281-282*	450	975
1307 — Similar. R. Cross crosslet with cross-pattée and crescent in angles. *M. 288*	1000	2500
1308 David I (K. of Scotland). As 1305, but with name DAVID REX. *M. 280*	1250	3000
1309 **Henry** (Earl of Northumberland, son of K. David). hENRIC ERL. As 1278. *M. 283-285*	1050	2750
1310 — Similar. R. Cross fleury. *M. 286-287*	950	2250
1311 — As 1307, but with name NENCI : COM on obverse. *M. 289*	1050	2750

G. 'Ornamented' series. *So-called 'York Group' but probably minted in Northern France*

1312 As 1278, with obverse inscription NSEPEFETI, STEFINEI or RODBDS. R. WISĐ. GNETA, etc., with ornament(s) in legend (sometimes retrograde). *M. 215-216 and 227*	1350	3250

1313   1315

1313 Flag type. As 1278, but king holds lance with pennant, star to r. R. As 1278, mostly with four ornaments in legend. *M. 217*	850	2100
1313A — Similar, but with eight ornaments in reverse inscription. *M. 217*	850	2100
1314 As 1278, but STIEN and ornaments, sceptre is topped by pellet in lozenge. R. Cross fleury over plain cross, ornaments in place of inscription. *M. 218*	1350	3250
1314A King stg. facing, holding sceptre and long standard with triple-tailed pennon. R. Cross pattee, crescents and quatrefoils in angles, pellets around, ornaments in legend	1750	4750
1315 **Stephen and Queen Matilda.** Two standing figures holding sceptre, as illustration. R. Ornaments in place of inscription. *M. 220*	1650	4250

1316   1320

		F £	VF £
1316	**Eustace.** EVSTACIVS, knight stg. r. holding sword. R. Cross in quatrefoil, EBORACI EDTS (or EBORACI TDEFL). *M. 221-222*	1500	4000
1317	— Similar, but ThOMHS FILIuS VIF. *M. 223*	1500	4000
1318	— Similar, but mixed letters and ornaments in *rev.* legend. *M. 224*	1350	3750
1319	[EVSTA] CII . FII . IOANIS, lion passant r, collonnade (or key?) below. R. Cross moline with cross-headed sceptres in angles, mixed letters and ornaments in legend. *M. 225*	1650	4250
1320	Lion rampant r., looped object below, EISTAOhIVS. R. Cross fleury with lis in angles, mostly, ornaments in legend. *M. 226*	1350	3500

1321   1322

1321	**Rodbert.** Knight on horse r., RODBΕRTVS IESTV (?). R. As 1314. *M. 228*	2250	5250
1322	**Bishop Henry.** Crowned bust r., crozier and star to r., HΕNRICVS ΕPC. R. Somewhat as last, STΕPhANVS RΕX. M. 229	2500	6000

H. Uncertain issues

1323	Crowned bust r. with sceptre, -NEΓ:. R. Cross pattée with annulets in angles (as Hen. I type XIII). *M. 272*	750	1650
1324	Crowned facing bust with sceptre, star to r. (as Hen. I type XIV). R. As last. *M. 274 Extr*	1350	3250
1325	Other types	650	1400

1326

1326	**Matilda,** Dowager Empress, Countess of Anjou (in England 1139-1148). As 1278, but cruder style, MATILDI IMP. etc. *M. 230-240*	850	2000
1326A	Obv. similar. R. Cross pattee over cross fleury (Cardiff hoard)	850	2000
1326B	Similar, but triple pellets or plumes at end of cross (Cardiff hoard)	950	2250
1326C	**Henry of Neubourg,** Bust r., R. As 1276A or 1278	2250	5000

	F £	VF £
1327 **Duke Henry,** son of Matilda and Geoffrey of Anjou, Duke of Normandy from 1150 (in England 1147-1149-1150 and 1153-1154). As 1278 but hENRICVS, etc. *M. 241-245*	1650	3750
1327A As 1295 but hENRIC. *M. 246*	1650	3750
1327B As 1326B, but hENNENNVS R, etc	1750	4000
1328 Obverse as 1278. R. Cross crosslet in quatrefoil. *M. 254*	1750	4000
1329 Crowned bust r. with sceptre. R. Cross fleury over quadrilateral fleury. *M. 248-253*	1750	4000

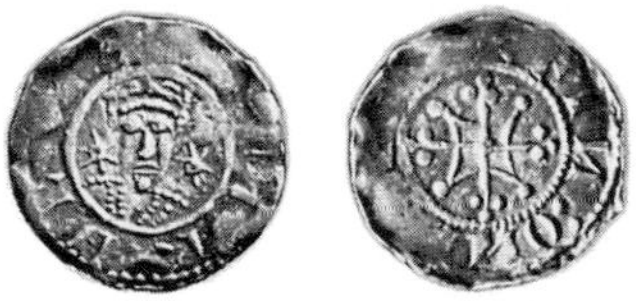

1330 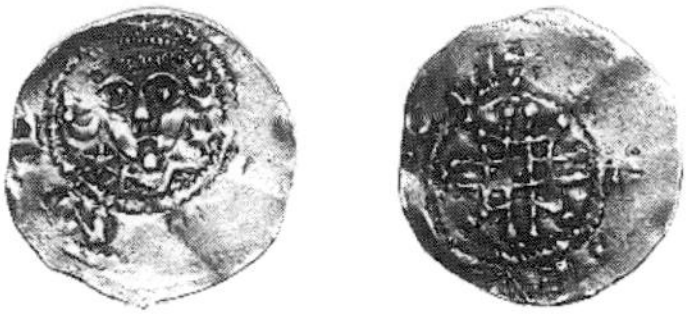   1331

	F £	VF £
1330 Crowned facing bust, star each side. R. Cross botonnée over a quadrilateral pommée. *M. 255-258*	2000	4500
1331 Obverse as 1330. R. Voided cross botonnée over a quadrilateral pommée. *M. 259-261*	2000	4500
1331A **Robert, Earl of Gloucester,** 1143-7, Lion. r. R. Cross fleury	1500	3750
1332 **William,** Earl of Gloucester (succeeded his father, Earl Robert, in 1147). Type as Henry of Anjou, no. 1329. *M. 262*	2000	4500
1333 Type as Henry of Anjou, no. 1330. *M. 263*	2250	4750
1334 Type as Henry of Anjou, no. 1331. *M. 264-268*	2000	4500
1334A – Lion. R. Cross fleury	1450	3500
1335 **Brian Fitzcount,** Lord of Wallingford (?). Type as Henry of Anjou, no. 1330. *M. 270*	2750	6500
1336 **Patrick,** Earl of Salisbury (?). Helmeted bust r. holding sword, star behind. R. As Henry of Anjou, no. 1329. *M. 271*	3000	6750

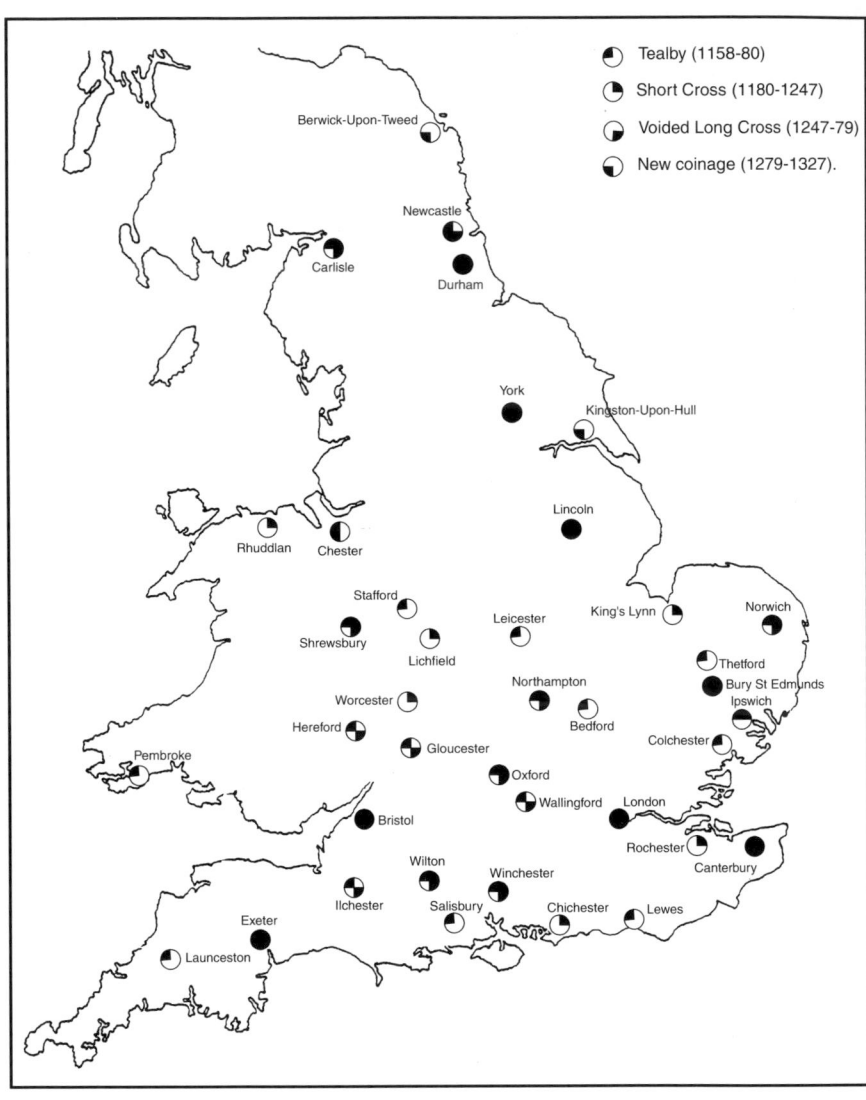

Tealby (1158-80)

Short Cross (1180-1247)

Voided Long Cross (1247-79)

New coinage (1279-1327).

HENRY II, 1154-1189

Cross-and-crosslets ('Tealby') Coinage, 1158-1180

Coins of Stephen's last type continued to be minted until 1158. Then a new coinage bearing Henry's name replaced the currency of the previous reign which contained a high proportion of irregular and sub-standard pennies. The new Cross and Crosslets issue is more commonly referred to as the 'Tealby' coinage, as over 5000 of these pennies were discovered at Tealby, Lincolnshire, in 1807. Thirty mints were employed in this re-coinage, but once the re-minting had been completed not more than a dozen mints were kept open. The issue remained virtually unchanged for twenty-two years apart from minor variations in the king's portrait. The coins tend to be poorly struck on irregular plans.

Cut coins occur with varying degrees of frequency during this issue, according to the type and local area.

The price quoted for coins in this section allows for the usual poor quality strike.

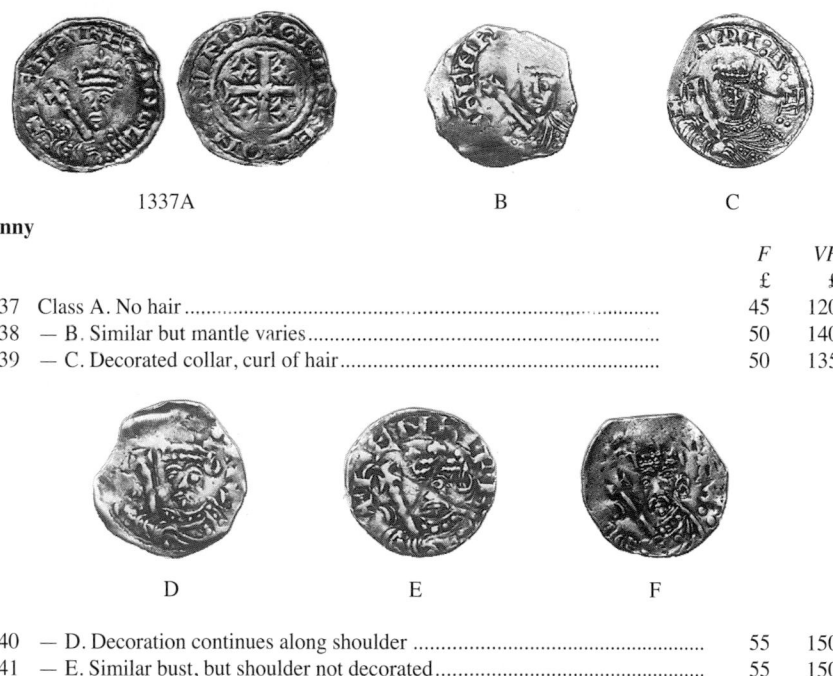

| | | 1337A | | B | | C |

Penny

		F	VF
		£	£
1337	Class A. No hair	45	120
1338	— B. Similar but mantle varies	50	140
1339	— C. Decorated collar, curl of hair	50	135

| D | E | F |

1340	— D. Decoration continues along shoulder	55	150
1341	— E. Similar bust, but shoulder not decorated	55	150
1342	— F. Hair in long ringlet to r. of bust	55	165

Mints and classes of the Cross-and-Crosslets coinage

Approximate dates for the various classes are as follows:

A 1158-1161, B and C 1161-1165, D 1165-1168, E 1168-1170 and F 1170-1180.

Mint	Classes	Mint	Classes	Mint	Classes
Bedford	A - - - - -	Ilchester	A B C D - F	Pembroke	A - - - - -
Bristol	A B C D E F	Ipswich	- B C D E F	Salisbury	A - - - - -
Bury St. Edmunds	A B C D E F	Launceston	A - - - - -	Shrewsbury	A - - - - -
Canterbury	A B C D E F	Leicester	A - - - - -	Stafford	A - C - - -
Carlisle	A - C D E F	Lewes	- - - - ? F	Thetford	A - C D - F
Chester	A - - D - -	Lincoln	A B C D E F	Wallingford	A - - - - -
Colchester	A - C - E -	London	A B C D E F	Wilton	A - - - - -
Durham	A B C - - -	Newcastle	A - C D E F	Winchester	A - C D ? -
Exeter	A B C D - -	Northampton	A - C ? - -	York	A - C D - -
Gloucester	A - - - - -	Norwich	A B C D - F		
Hereford	A - C - - -	Oxford	A - - D E -		

The publishers would like to thank Prof. Jeffrey Mass for re-organising and updating the short cross series. All illustrations have kindly been supplied by Prof. Mass.

'Short Cross' coinage of Henry II (1180-1189)

In 1180 a coinage of new type, known as the Short Cross coinage, replaced the Tealby issue. The new coinage is remarkable in that it covers not only the latter part of the reign of Henry II, but also the reigns of his sons Richard and John and on into the reign of his grandson Henry III, and the entire issue bears the name 'hENRICVS'. There are no English coins with the names of Richard or John. The Short Cross coins can be divided chronologically into various classes: ten mints were operating under Henry II and tables of mints, moneyers and classes are given for each reign.

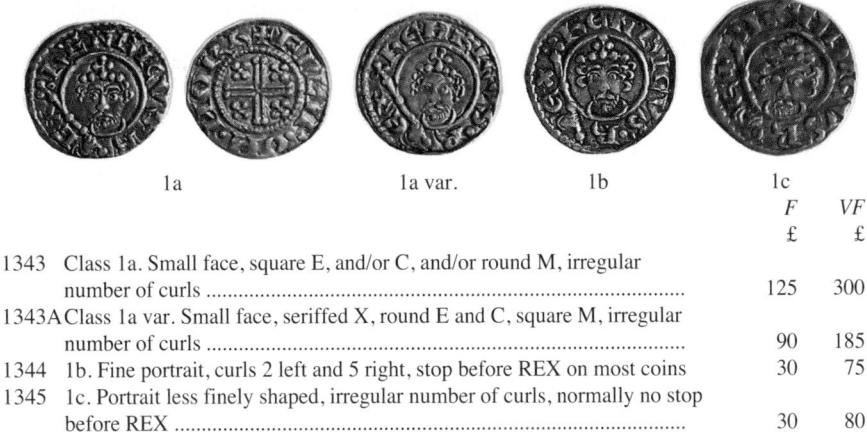

	1a	1a var.	1b	1c

		F	VF
		£	£
1343	Class 1a. Small face, square E, and/or C, and/or round M, irregular number of curls	125	300
1343A	Class 1a var. Small face, seriffed X, round E and C, square M, irregular number of curls	90	185
1344	1b. Fine portrait, curls 2 left and 5 right, stop before REX on most coins	30	75
1345	1c. Portrait less finely shaped, irregular number of curls, normally no stop before REX	30	80

RICHARD I, 1189-1199

Pennies of Short Cross type continued to be issued throughout the reign, all bearing the name hENRICVS. The coins of class 4, which have very crude portraits, continued to be issued in the early years of the next reign. The only coins bearing Richard's name are from his territories of Aquitaine and Poitou in western France.

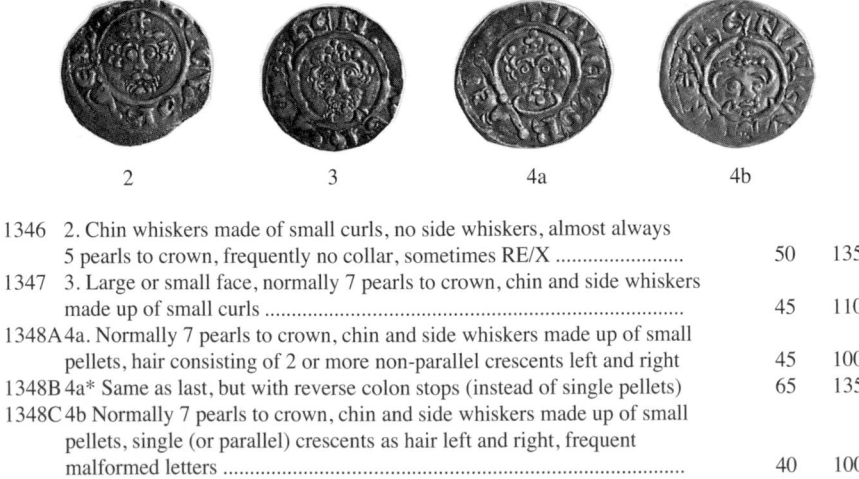

	2	3	4a	4b

		F	VF
1346	2. Chin whiskers made of small curls, no side whiskers, almost always 5 pearls to crown, frequently no collar, sometimes RE/X	50	135
1347	3. Large or small face, normally 7 pearls to crown, chin and side whiskers made up of small curls	45	110
1348A	4a. Normally 7 pearls to crown, chin and side whiskers made up of small pellets, hair consisting of 2 or more non-parallel crescents left and right	45	100
1348B	4a* Same as last, but with reverse colon stops (instead of single pellets)	65	135
1348C	4b Normally 7 pearls to crown, chin and side whiskers made up of small pellets, single (or parallel) crescents as hair left and right, frequent malformed letters	40	100

'Short Cross' coinage *continued*. All with name hENRICVS

The Short Cross coins of class 4 continued during the early years of John's reign, but in 1205 a re-coinage was initiated and new Short Cross coins of better style replaced the older issues. Coins of classes 5a and 5b were issued in the re-coinage in which sixteen mints were employed. Only ten of these mints were still working by the end of class 5. The only coins to bear John's name are the pennies, halfpence and farthings issues for Ireland.

4c   5a1   5a2

5b   5c   6a

		F	VF
		£	£
1349	4c. Reversed S, square face at bottom, 5 pearls to crown, normally single crescents as hair left and right...	65	135
1350A	5a1 Reversed or regular S, irregular curved lines as hair (or circular curls containing no pellets), cross pattee as initial mark on reverse, *London and Canterbury* only	65	135
1350B	5a2 Reversed S, circular curls left and right (2 or 3 each side) containing single pellets, cross pomme as initial mark on reverse	50	110
1350C	5a/5b or 5b/5a...	45	100
1351	5b. Regular S, circular pelleted curls, cross pattee as initial mark on reverse	30	75
1352	5c. Slightly rounder portrait, letter X in the form of a St. Andrew's cross	30	70
1353	6a. Smaller portrait, with smaller letter X composed of thin strokes or, later, short wedges..	30	65

'Short Cross' coinage *continued* (1216-47)
The Short Cross coinage continued for a further thirty years during which time the style of portraiture and workmanship deteriorated. By the 1220s minting had been concentrated at London and Canterbury, one exception being the mint of the Abbot of Bury St. Edmunds.

Halfpenny and farthing dies are recorded early in this issue; a few halfpennies and now farthings have been discovered. See nos 1357 D-E.

6b	6c	6c orn.	6x	6d

	F	VF
	£	£
1354 6b. Very tall lettering and long rectangular face......................................	30	60
1355 6c. Lettering now shorter, face narrow and triangular..............................	30	60
1355A 6c. orn. Various letters now ornamental in design, curls 3/3 left and right	60	125
1355B 6x. Canterbury mint only, RE/X, curls 2/2, nostril pellets outside nose...	110	240
1355C 6d. Face less distinct in shape, N's containing a pellet along the crossbar	35	70

7a	7b	7c

1356A 7a. Small compact face, letter A with top coming to a point under crossbar	20	45
1356B 7b. Letter A with square top, M appears as H..	20	40
1356C 7c. Degraded portrait, letter A and M as in 7b, large lettering	15	35

8a	8b	8c

1357A 8a. New portrait; letter X in shape of curule; cross pattee as initial mark on reverse (early style), or cross pommee (late style)...............................	60	125
1357B 8b. Degraded portrait, wedge-shaped X, cross pomme as initial mark	30	75
1357C 8c. Degraded portrait, cross pomme X, cross pomme as initial mark	30	75
1357D Round halfpenny in style of class 7, initial mark in shape of up-turned crescent, London mint only..	750	1750
1357E Round farthing in style of class 7, initial mark in shape of up-turned crescent, London mint only..	800	2000

1357D   1357E

Moneyer tables for the short cross coinage

Fine

Henry II:

London: Aimer (1a-b), Alain (1a-b), Alain V (1a-b), Alward (1b), Davi (1b-c), Fil Aimer (1a-b), Gefrei (1c), Gilebert (1c), Godard (1b), Henri (1a-b), Henri Pi (1a), Iefrei (1a-b), Iohan (1a-b), Osber (1b), Pieres (1a-c), Pieres M (1a-b), Randvl (1a-b), Ravl (1b-c), Reinald (1a-b), Willelm (1a-b)   *From*   30
Carlisle: Alain (1b-c)   *From*   70
Exeter: Asketil (1a-b), Iordan (1a-b), Osber (1a-b), Ravl (1b), Ricard (1b-c), Roger (1a-c)   *From*   65
Lincoln: Edmvnd (1b-c), Girard (1b), Hvgo (1b), Lefwine (1b-c), Rodbert (1b), Walter (1b), Will. D.F. (1b), Willelm (1b-c)   *From*   50
Northampton: Filip (1a-b), Hvgo (1a-b), Ravl (1a-c), Reinald (1a-c), Simvn (1b), Walter (1a-c), Willelm (1a-b)   *From*   35
Oxford: Asketil (1b), Iefrei (1b), Owein (1b-c), Ricard (1b-c), Rodbert (1b), Rodbt. F. B. (1b), Sagar (1b)   *From*   60
Wilton: Osber (1a-b), Rodbert (1a-b)   *From*   65
Winchester: Adam (1a-c), Clement (1a-b), Gocelm (1a-c), Henri (1a), Osber (1a-b), Reinier (1b), Rodbert (1a-b)   *From*   35
Worcester: Edrich (1b), Godwine (1b-c), Osber (1b-c), Oslac (1b)   *From*   60
York: Alain (1a-b), Efrard (1a-c), Gerard (1a-b), Hvgo (1a-c), Hunfrei (1a-b), Isac (1a-b), Tvrkil (1a-c), Willelm (1a-b)   *From*   35

Richard I

London: Aimer (2-4a), Fvlke (4a-b), Henri (4a-b), Ravl (2), Ricard (2-4b), Stivene (2-4b), Willelm (2-4b)   *From*   40
Canterbury: Goldwine (3-4b), Hernavd (4b), Hve (4b), Ioan (4b), Meinir (2-4b), Reinald/Reinavd (2-4b), Roberd (2-4b), Samvel (4b), Simon (4b), Vlard (2-4b)   *From*   40
Carlisle: Alein (3-4b)   *From*   90
Durham: Adam (4a), Alein (4a-b), Pires (4b)   *From*   100
Exeter: Ricard (3)   *From*   95
Lichfield: Ioan (2)   *Extremely rare*
Lincoln: Edmvnd (2), Lefwine (2), Willelm (2)   *From*   75
Northampton: Giferei (4a), Roberd (3), Waltir (3)   *From*   80
Northampton or Norwich: Randvl (4a-b), Willelm (4a-b)   *From*   70
Shrewsbury: Ive (4a-b), Reinald/Reinavd (4a-b), Willem (4a)   *From*   165
Winchester: Adam (3), Gocelm (3), Osbern (3-4a), Pires (4a), Willelm (3-4a)   *From*   55
Worcester: Osbern (2)   *From*   200
York: Davi (4a-b), Efrard/Everard (2-4b), Hvgo/Hve (2-4a), Nicole (4a-b), Tvrkil (2-4a)   *From*   50

John

London: Abel (5c-6a), Adam (5b-c), Beneit (5b-c), Fvlke (4c-5b), Henri (4c-5b/5a), Ilger (5b-6a), Ravf (5c-6a), Rener (5a/b-5c), Ricard (4c-5b), Ricard B (5b-c), Ricard T (5a/b-5b), Walter (5c-6a), Willelm (4c-5b), Willelm B (5a/b-5c), Willelm L (5b-c), Willelm T (5b-c)   *From*   30
Canterbury: Goldwine (4c-5c), Hernavd/Arnavd (4c-5c), Hve (4c-5c), Iohan (4c-5c), Iohan B (5b-c), Iohan M (5b-c), Roberd (4c-5c), Samvel (4c-5c), Simon (4c-5c)   *From*   30
Bury St Edmunds: Fvlke (5b-c)   *From*   65
Carlisle: Tomas (5b)   *From*   80
Chichester: Pieres (5b/a-5b), Ravf (5b/a-5b), Simon (5b/a-5b), Willelm (5b)   *From*   50
Durham: Pieres (5a-6a)   *From*   60
Exeter: Gileberd (5a-b), Iohan (5a-b), Ricard (5a-b)   *From*   50

Ipswich: Alisandre (5b-c), Iohan (5b-c) — From 40

Kings Lynn: Iohan (5b), Nicole (5b), Willelm (5b) — From 100

Lincoln: Alain (5a), Andrev (5a-5c), Hve (5a/b-5c), Iohan (5a), Ravf (5a/b-5b),
Ricard (5a-5b/a), Tomas (5a/b-5b) — From 30

Northampton: Adam (5b-c), Roberd (5b), Roberd T (5b) — From 40

Northampton or Norwich: Randvl (4c) — From 80

Norwich: Gifrei (5a/b-5c), Iohan (5a-c), Renald/Renavd (5a-c) — From 40

Oxford: Ailwine (5b), Henri (5b), Miles (5b) — From 50

Rochester: Alisandre (5b), Hvnfrei (5b) — From 80

Winchester: Adam (5a-c), Andrev (5b-c), Bartelme (5b-c), Henri (5a), Iohan (5a-c),
Lvkas (5b-c), Miles (5a-c), Ravf (5b-c), Ricard (5a-b) — From 30

York: Davi (4c-5b), Nicole (4c-5c), Renavd (5b), Tomas (5a/b-5b) — From 35

Henry III

London: Abel (6b-7a), Adam (7b-c), Elis (7a-b), Giffrei (7b-c), Ilger (6b-7b),
Ledvlf (7b-c), Nichole (7c-8c), Ravf (6b-7b), Ricard (7b), Terri (7a-b),
Walter (6b-c) — From 20

Canterbury: Arnold (6c/6x, 6x), Henri (6b-6c/d, 7a-c), Hivn/Ivn (6b-7b),
Iohan (6b-7c, 8b-c), Ioan Chic (7b-c), Ioan F. R. (7b-c), Nichole (7c, 8b-c),
Osmvnd (7b-c), Robert (6b, 7b-c), Robert Vi (7c), Roger (6b-7b),
Roger of R (7a-b), Salemvn (6x, 7a-b), Samvel (6b-d, 7a), Simon (6b-d, 7a-b),
Tomas (6d, 7a-b), Walter (6b-7a), Willem (7b-c, 8b-c), Willem Ta (7b-c) — From 20

Bury St Edmunds: Iohan (7c-8c), Norman (7a-b), Ravf (6c-d, 7a), Simvnd (7b-c),
Willelm (7a) — From 30

Durham: Pieres (7a) — From 80

Winchester: Henri (6c) — From 85

York: Iohan (6c), Peres (6c), Tomas (6c), Wilam (6c) — From 85

Irregular Local Issue
Rhuddlan (in chronological order) — From 75
Group I (c. 1180 – pre 1205) Halli, Tomas, Simond
Group II (c.1205 – 1215) Simond, Henricus

Rhuddlan

'Long Cross' coinage (1247-72)

By the middle of Henry's reign the coinage in circulation was in a poor state, being worn and clipped. In 1247 a fresh coinage was ordered, the new pennies having the reverse cross extended to the edge of the coin to help safeguard the coins against clipping. The earliest of these coins have no mint or moneyers' names. A number of provincial mints were opened for producing sufficient of the Long Cross coins, but these were closed again in 1250, only the royal mints of London and Canterbury and the ecclesiastical mints of Durham and Bury St. Edmunds remained open.

In 1257, following the introduction of new gold coinages by the Italian cities of Brindisi (1232), Florence (1252) and Genoa (1253), Henry III issued a gold coinage in England. This was a gold 'Penny' valued at 20 silver pence and twice the weight of the silver penny. The coinage was not a success, being undervalued, and it ceased to be minted after a few years; few coins have survived.

Cut halfpennies and farthings are common for this period, with a greater concentration in the early part. They are up to 100 times commoner than in late Anglo-Saxon times.

Without sceptre

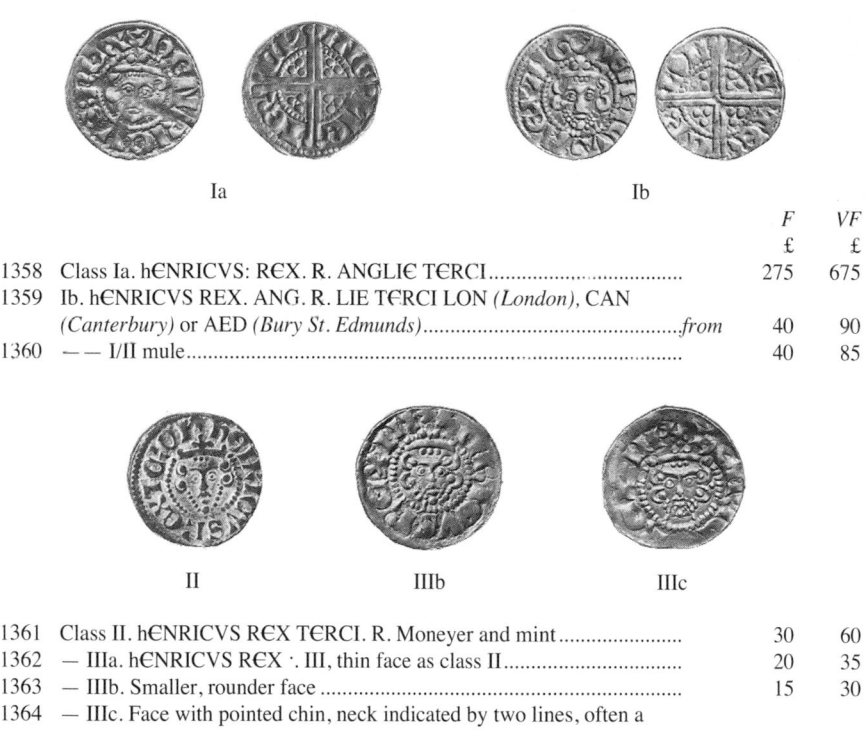

Ia   Ib

		F	VF
		£	£
1358	Class Ia. hENRICVS: REX. R. ANGLIE TERCI	275	675
1359	Ib. hENRICVS REX. ANG. R. LIE TERCI LON *(London)*, CAN *(Canterbury)* or AED *(Bury St. Edmunds)* ....*from*	40	90
1360	— — I/II mule	40	85

II   IIIb   IIIc

1361	Class II. hENRICVS REX TERCI. R. Moneyer and mint	30	60
1362	— IIIa. hENRICVS REX ·. III, thin face as class II	20	35
1363	— IIIb. Smaller, rounder face	15	30
1364	— IIIc. Face with pointed chin, neck indicated by two lines, often a pellet between curls, usually REX: III	20	35

With sceptre

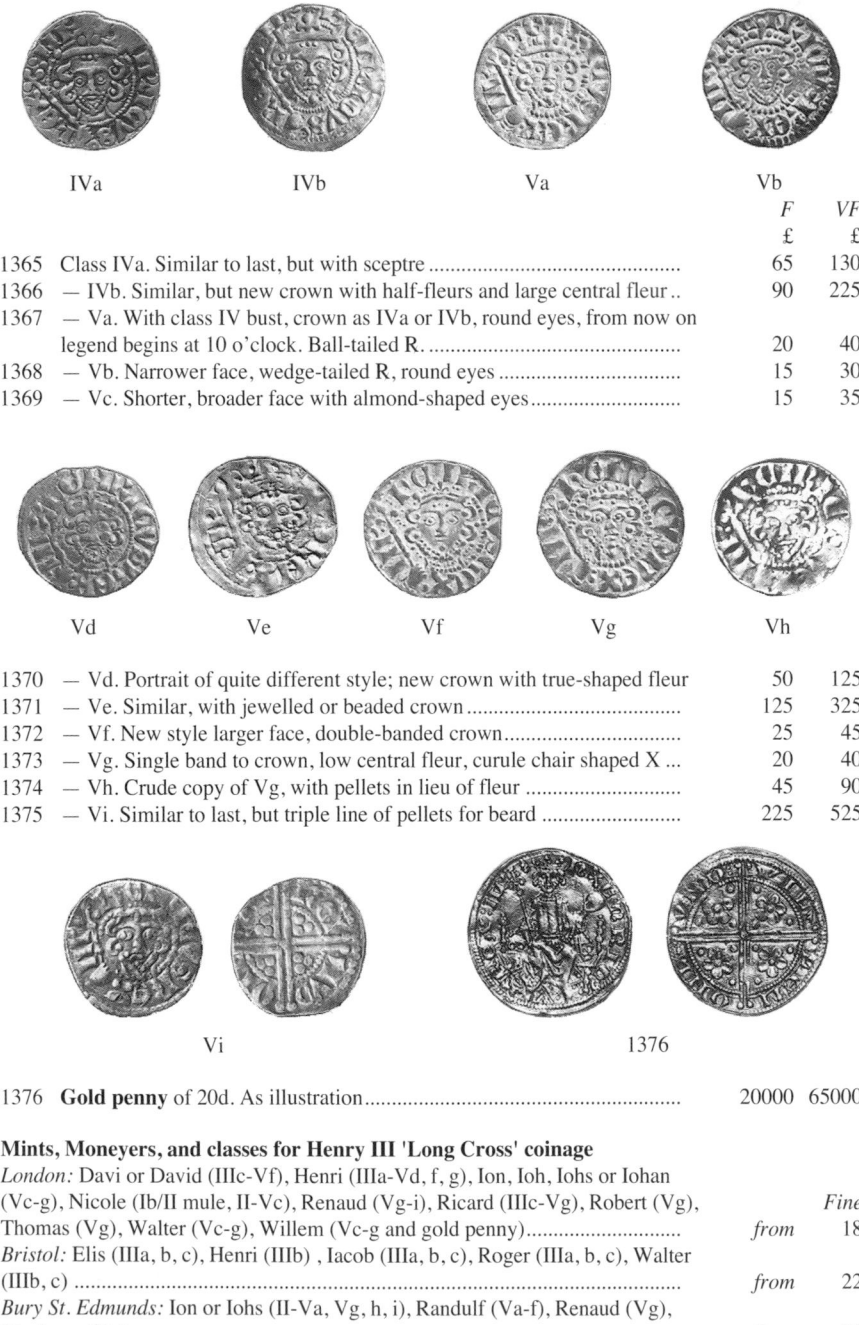

IVa	IVb	Va	Vb

		F	VF
		£	£
1365	Class IVa. Similar to last, but with sceptre	65	130
1366	— IVb. Similar, but new crown with half-fleurs and large central fleur ..	90	225
1367	— Va. With class IV bust, crown as IVa or IVb, round eyes, from now on legend begins at 10 o'clock. Ball-tailed R.	20	40
1368	— Vb. Narrower face, wedge-tailed R, round eyes	15	30
1369	— Vc. Shorter, broader face with almond-shaped eyes...........................	15	35

Vd	Ve	Vf	Vg	Vh

1370	— Vd. Portrait of quite different style; new crown with true-shaped fleur	50	125
1371	— Ve. Similar, with jewelled or beaded crown	125	325
1372	— Vf. New style larger face, double-banded crown.................................	25	45
1373	— Vg. Single band to crown, low central fleur, curule chair shaped X ...	20	40
1374	— Vh. Crude copy of Vg, with pellets in lieu of fleur	45	90
1375	— Vi. Similar to last, but triple line of pellets for beard	225	525

Vi	1376

1376	**Gold penny** of 20d. As illustration..	20000	65000

Mints, Moneyers, and classes for Henry III 'Long Cross' coinage

London: Davi or David (IIIc-Vf), Henri (IIIa-Vd, f, g), Ion, Ioh, Iohs or Iohan (Vc-g), Nicole (Ib/II mule, II-Vc), Renaud (Vg-i), Ricard (IIIc-Vg), Robert (Vg), Thomas (Vg), Walter (Vc-g), Willem (Vc-g and gold penny)............................

Bristol: Elis (IIIa, b, c), Henri (IIIb) , Iacob (IIIa, b, c), Roger (IIIa, b, c), Walter (IIIb, c) ....

Bury St. Edmunds: Ion or Iohs (II-Va, Vg, h, i), Randulf (Va-f), Renaud (Vg), Stephane (Vg)..

	Fine
from	18
from	22
from	20

Fine

Canterbury: Alein (Vg, h), Ambroci (Vg), Gilbert (II-Vd/c mule, Vf, g), Ion, Ioh,
Iohs, or Iohanes (IIIe-Vd, f, g), Nicole or Nichole (Ib/II mule, II-Vh), Ricard
(Vg, h), Robert (Vc-h), Walter (Vc-h), Willem or Willeme (Ib/II mule, II-Vd, f, g)   *from*   15
Carlisle: Adam (IIIa, b), Ion (IIIa, b), Robert (IIIa, b), Willem (IIIa, b) ....   *from*   45
Durham: Philip (IIIb), Ricard (V, b, c), Roger (Vg), Willem (Vg) ....   *from*   60
Exeter: Ion (II-IIIc), Philip (II-IIIc), Robert (II-IIIc), Walter (II-IIIb)................   *from*   30
Gloucester: Ion (II-IIIc), Lucas (II-IIIc), Ricard (II-IIIc), Roger (II-IIIc) ....   *from*   30
Hereford: Henri (IIIa, b), Ricard (IIIa, b, c), Roger (IIIa, b, c), Walter (IIIa, b, c)   *from*   40
Ilchester: Huge (IIIa, b, c), Ierveis (IIIa, b, c), Randulf (IIIa, b, c), Stephe
(IIIa, b, c)...   *from*   65
Lincoln: Ion (II-IIIc), Ricard (II-IIIc), Walter (II-IIIc), Willem (II-IIIc)............   *from*   25
Newcastle: Adam (IIIa, b), Henri (IIIa, b, c), Ion (IIIa, b, c), Roger (IIIa, b, c) ..   *from*   22
Northampton: Lucas (II-IIIb), Philip (II-IIIc), Tomas (II-IIIc), Willem (II-IIIc)   *from*   25
Norwich: Huge (II-IIIc), Iacob (II-II Ic), Ion (II-IIIc), Willem (II-IIIc) ....   *from*   30
Oxford: Adam (II-IIIc), Gefrei (II-IIIc), Henri (II-IIIc), Willem (II-IIIc) ....   *from*   30
Shrewsbury: Lorens (IIIa, b, c), Nicole (IIIa, b, c), Peris (IIIa, b, c), Ricard (IIIa,
b, c)   ....   *from*   40
Wallingford: Alisandre (IIIa, b), Clement (IIIa, b), Ricard (IIIa, b), Robert (IIIa,
b)   ....   *from*   60
Wilton: Huge (IIIb, c), Ion (IIIa, b, c), Willem (IIIa, b, c) ....   *from*   35
Winchester: Huge (II-IIIc), Iordan (II-IIIc), Nicole (II-IIIc), Willem (II-IIIc) ....   *from*   22
York: Alain (II-IIIb), Ieremie (II-IIIb), Ion (II-IIIc), Rener (II-IIIc), Tomas (IIIb, c)   *from*   25

EDWARD I, 1272-1307

'Long Cross' coinage (1272-79). With name hENRICVS
The earliest group of Edward's Long Cross coins are of very crude style and known only of Durham
and Bury St. Edmunds. Then, for the last class of the type, pennies of much improved style were
issued at London, Durham and Bury, but in 1279 the Long Cross coinage was abandoned and a
completely new coinage substituted.

Cut halfpennies and farthings also occur for this issue, and within this context are not especially rare.

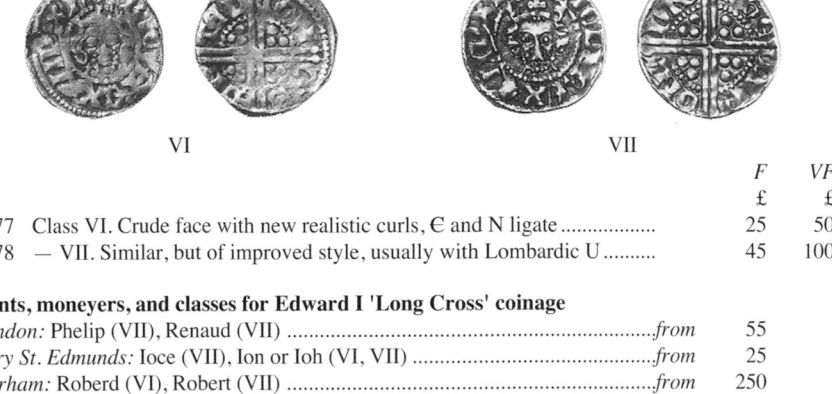

VI   VII

	F	VF
	£	£
1377 Class VI. Crude face with new realistic curls, Є and N ligate	25	50
1378 — VII. Similar, but of improved style, usually with Lombardic U	45	100

Mints, moneyers, and classes for Edward I 'Long Cross' coinage
London: Phelip (VII), Renaud (VII) ....*from*   55
Bury St. Edmunds: Ioce (VII), Ion or Ioh (VI, VII) ....*from*   25
Durham: Roberd (VI), Robert (VII) ....*from*   250

The publishers would like to thank Jeffrey North for re-organising and updating the coinage of Edward I and II and early silver of Edward III.

New Coinage (from 1279).

A major re-coinage was embarked upon in 1279 which introduced new denominations. In addition to the penny, halfpence and farthings were also minted and, for the first time, a fourpenny piece called a 'Groat' (from the French *Gros*).

As mint administration was now very much centralized, the practice of including the moneyer's name in the coinage was abandoned (except for a few years at Bury St. Edmunds). Several provincial mints assisted with the re-coinage during 1279-81, then minting was again restricted to London, Canterbury, Durham and Bury.

The provincial mints were again employed for a subsidiary re-coinage in 1299-1302 in order to remint lightweight coins and the many illegal *esterlings* (foreign copies of the English pennies, mainly from the Low Countries), which were usually a poorer quality than the English coins.

1379

	F	VF
	£	£
1379 **Groat.** (=4d.; wt. 89 grs.). Type as illustration but several minor varieties	900	3000

Extant specimens often show traces of having been mounted on the obverse and gilded on the reverse; such coins are worth less.

1a   1b   1c

1380	**Penny.** *London*. Class 1a. Crown with plain band, ЄDW RЄX; Lombardic Π on *obv;* pellet 'barred' S on rev. A with sloping top	250	625
1381	— 1b. — ЄD RЄX; no drapery on bust, Roman N	450	1050
1382	— 1c. — ЄDW RЄX; Roman N, normal or reversed; small lettering	20	50
1383	— 1d. — ЄDW R;—; large lettering and face	20	45

1d(1384)   2a   2b

1384	— — — Annulet below bust (for the Abbot of Reading)	125	300
1385	— 2a. Crown with band shaped to ornaments; usually broken left petal to central fleur portraits as 1d. N usually reversed	15	40
1386	— 2b. — tall bust; long neck; N reversed	15	40

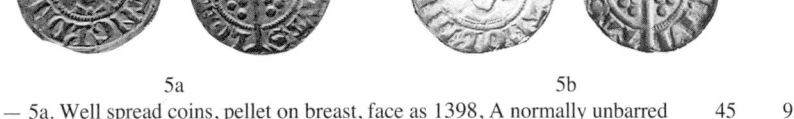

3a 3b 3c

	F	VF
	£	£

1387 — 3a. Crescent-shaped contraction marks; pearls in crown, drapery is foreshortened circle with hook ends 30 70

1388 — 3b. — — drapery is segment of a circle, pearls in crown 20 45

1389 — 3c. — normal crown; drapery in one piece, hollowed in centre 15 35

3e 3f 3g 4a

1390 — 3d. — — drapery in two pieces, broad face 15 35

1391 — 3e. — long narrow face (Northern mints) 15 40

1392 — 3f. — broad face, large nose, rougher work, late S first used 30 65

1393 — 3g. — Spread crown small neat bust, narrow face 12 30

4b 4c 4d 4e

1394 — 4a. Comma-shaped contraction mark, late S always used, C and Є open 15 40

1395 — 4b. Similar, but face and hair shorter 12 30

1396 — 4c. Larger face with more copious hair; nick to band of crown 20 45

1397 — 4d. Pellet at beginning of *obv.* and *rev.* inscription 15 35

1398 — 4e. Three pellets on breast, ropy hair, pellet in *rev.* legend
(no pellets on Bury or Durham) 15 40

5a 5b

1399 — 5a. Well spread coins, pellet on breast, face as 1398, A normally unbarred 45 95

1400 — 5b. Coins more spread, tall lettering, long narrow face, pellet on breast 35 80

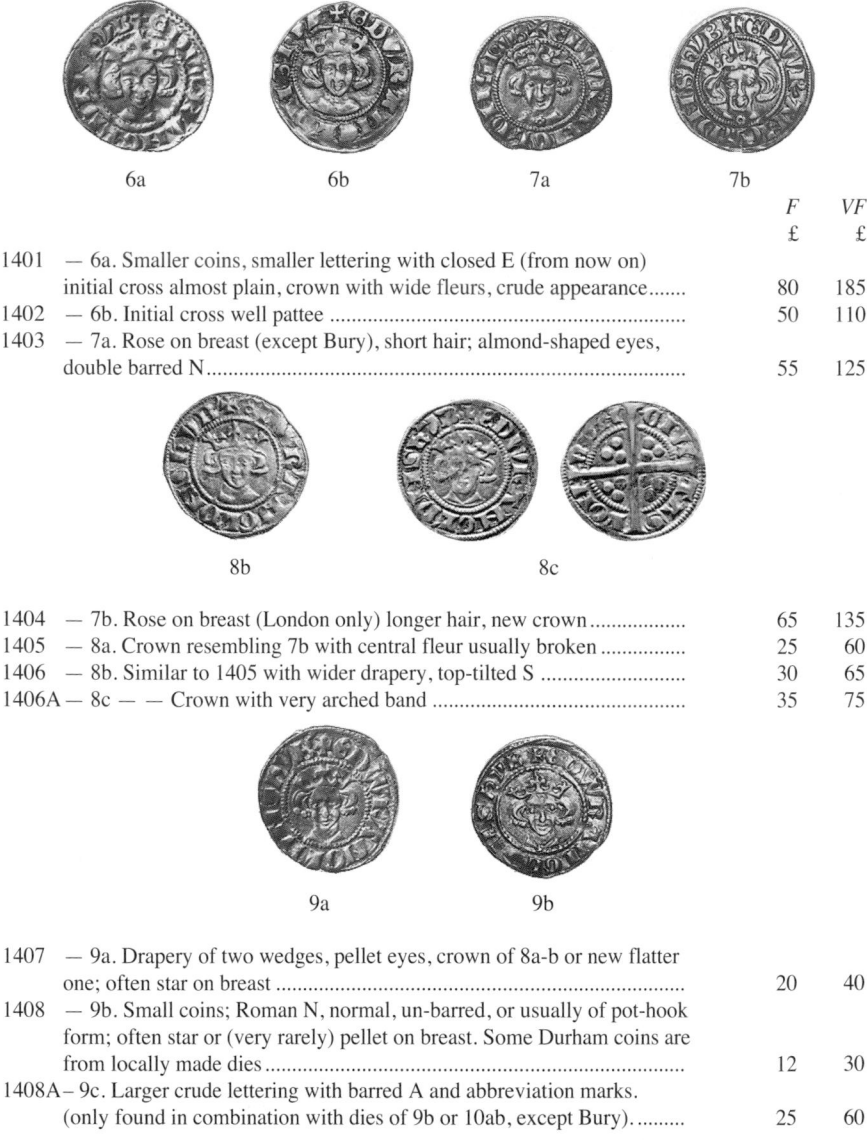

6a   6b   7a   7b

	F £	VF £
1401 — 6a. Smaller coins, smaller lettering with closed E (from now on) initial cross almost plain, crown with wide fleurs, crude appearance.......	80	185
1402 — 6b. Initial cross well pattee	50	110
1403 — 7a. Rose on breast (except Bury), short hair; almond-shaped eyes, double barred N..	55	125

8b   8c

	F £	VF £
1404 — 7b. Rose on breast (London only) longer hair, new crown..................	65	135
1405 — 8a. Crown resembling 7b with central fleur usually broken................	25	60
1406 — 8b. Similar to 1405 with wider drapery, top-tilted S	30	65
1406A — 8c — — Crown with very arched band	35	75

9a   9b

	F £	VF £
1407 — 9a. Drapery of two wedges, pellet eyes, crown of 8a-b or new flatter one; often star on breast	20	40
1408 — 9b. Small coins; Roman N, normal, un-barred, or usually of pot-hook form; often star or (very rarely) pellet on breast. Some Durham coins are from locally made dies..	12	30
1408A — 9c. Larger crude lettering with barred A and abbreviation marks. (only found in combination with dies of 9b or 10ab, except Bury).	25	60

10ab

		F £	*VF* £
1409	— 10ab. ЄDWARD. Bifoliate crown (converted 9b or new taller one). Narrow incurved lettering.	15	40
1409A	— 10ab. Similar with annulet on breast or a pellet each side of head and on breast	70	150
1409B	— 10ab. ЄDWAR (rarely ЄDWR). Similar to 1409. A few early coins have the trifoliate crown of 9b.	15	40

10cf1   10cf2

Crown 1   Crown 2   Crown 3   Crown 4   Crown 5

1410	— 10cf1. Crown 1 (Axe-shaped central fleur, wedge-shaped petals). ЄDWA from now on. Stub-tailed. R	12	30
1411	— 10cf2. Crown 2 (Well-shaped central lis, no spearheads). Spreading hair.	12	30

10cf3   10cf4   10cf5

1412	— 10cf3. Crown 3 (Left-hand arrowhead inclines to right). Early coins have the broken lettering of 10cf2; later have new lettering with round-backed Є.	12	30
1413	— 10cf4. Crown 4 (Neat with hooked petal to right-hand side fleur).	30	65
1414	— 10cf5. Crown 5 (taller and more spread, right-hand ornament inclines to left). Later coins are on smaller flans	15	40

For a more detailed classification of Class 10, see 'Sylloge of British Coins, 39, The J. J. North Collection, Edwardian English Silver Coins 1279-1351', The Classification of Class 10, c. 1301-10, by C. Wood.

Prices are for full flan, well struck coins.
The prices for the above types are for London. For coins of the other mints see following pages; types are in brackets, prices are for the commonest type of each mint.

Berwick Type 1   Type II   Type III   Type IV

		F £	VF £
1415	*Berwick-on-Tweed.* (Blunt types I-IV) Local dies ....*from*	15	45
1416	*Bristol.* (2; 3b; c, d; 3f, g; 9b).........................*from*	15	40
1417	*Bury St. Edmunds.* Robert de Hadelie (3c, d, g; 4a, b, c)........*from*	50	110
1418	— Villa Sci Edmundi (4e; 5b; 6b; 7a; 8ab, 9a – 10 cf 5).....*from*	20	45
1419	*Canterbury.* (2; 3b-g; 4; 5; 7a; 9;10)...................*from*	12	25
1420	*Chester.* (3g; 9b) ....*from*	35	75
1421	*Durham.* Plain cross mm (9b; 10ab; 10cf 2-3; 10cf 5) ....*from*	15	40
1422	— Bishop de Insula (2; 3b, c, e, g; 4a)................*from*	20	45
1423	— Bishop Bec (4b-e; 5b; 6b; 7b; 9a, 9b, 10) with *mm.* cross moline ......*from*	20	45
1424	— — (4b) cross moline in one angle of *rev*.............................	125	325
1425	*Exeter.* (9b)..	70	150
1426	*Kingston-upon-Hull.* (9b).................................	55	110
1427	*Lincoln.* (3c, d, f, g)...................................*from*	15	35
1428	*Newcastle-upon-Tyne.* (3e; 9b; 10ab) ....*from*	25	55
1429	*York.* Royal mint (2; 3b, c, d, f; 9b) ....*from*	15	35
1430	— Archbishop's mint (3e, f; 9b). R. Quatrefoil in centre ....*from*	20	40
1431	**Halfpenny,** *London.* Class 3b. Drapery as segment of circle.............	30	80
1432	3c-e Drapery as two wedges or hollowed	20	50

1434A   1433

1433	— 3g. Similar, larger letters usually thick-waisted S, wider crown	20	55
1433A	— — 4c. Crown less spread; smaller lettering	25	65
1433B	— — Pellet before LON	35	85
1434	— 4e. Three pellets on breast, one on *rev*............................	40	100
1434A	— 6. Large coarse crown, small face, short hair.....................	40	95
1435	— 7. Larger face, open C and Є, double-barred N	40	90
1436	— 8. Tall crown, small neat lettering............................	30	75
1437	— 10. ЄDWAR R ANGL DNS hYB, thick waisted letters	30	70

The above prices are for London; halfpence of the mints given below were also struck.

		F	*VF*
		£	£
1438	*Berwick-on-Tweed.* (Blunt types I, II and III)...........................*from*	65	175
1439	*Bristol.* (3c; 3g) ....*from*	30	70
1440	*Lincoln.* (3c)	40	100
1441	*Newcastle.* (3e). With single pellet in each angle of *rev.*....................	60	150
1442	*York.* (3b)	40	100

1443A   1445

1443	**Farthing,** *London.* Class 1a. Heavy weight (6.65 grains), €DWARDVS REX. R. LONDONI€NSIS, (very rarely LONDRI€NSIS), bifoliate crown	30	100
1443A	— — 1b. trifoliate crown without intermediate jewels.	30	90
1444	— 2. trifoliate crown with jewels, narrow face, reversed Ns (6.62 grs.) ..	20	60
1445	— 3c. flatter crown, longer face with bushy hair.....................................	20	50
1445A	— 3d/e. € R ANGLI€ without inner circle. (5.5 grs.)	15	35
1446	— 3g. Similar with spread sidefleurs to crown..	15	35
1446A	— 4de. Similar, neat appearance. CIVITAS LONDON (from now on) ..	30	100
1446B	— 5. Wider crown...	30	100
1447	— 6-7. Small crown, conspicuous pellet or almond eyes.......................	35	110
1448	— 8. € R ANGL DN. Tall crude crown, closed €	30	85
1449	9a. Flatter crown, smaller face, unbarred Ns.	30	90
1449A	— 9b. Wide flat crown, bushy hair, Initial cross patte.	35	110
1450	— 10 or 11. (Edward II) €DWARDVS REX A or AN inner circle both sides	12	30
	Type 1450 often appears on oval flans.		

The above prices are for London; farthings of the mints given below were also struck.

1446   1452

1451	*Berwick-on-Tweed.* (Blunt type I, IIIb)......................................	110	275
1452	*Bristol.* (2; 3c (heavy), 3 (light))	35	90
1453	*Lincoln.* (3)	45	100
1453A	*Newcastle.* (3e), triple pellet in *rev.* quarters	175	475
1454	*York.* (2; 3)	65	150

For further information see J. J. North 'Sylloge of British Coins, 39, The J. J. North Collection, Edwardian English Silver Coins 1279-1351'.

The coinage of this reign differs only in minor details from that of Edward I. No groats were issued in the years *c*. 1282-1351.

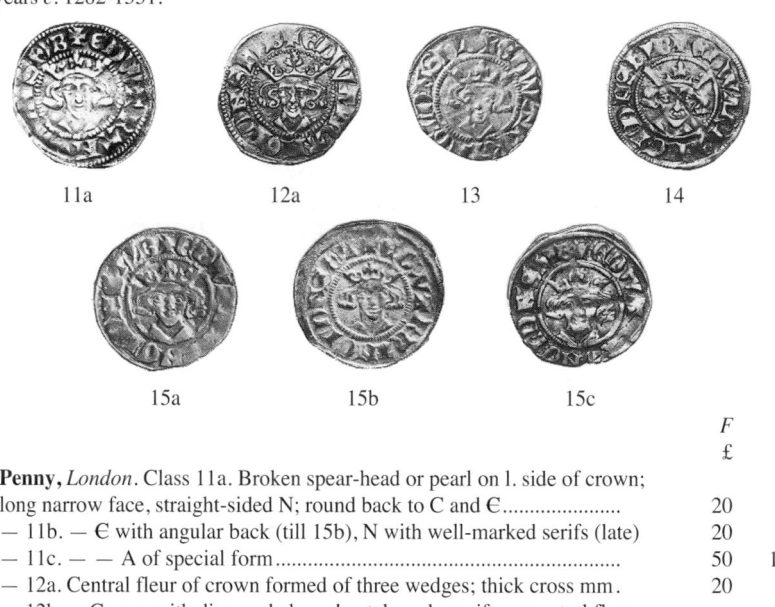

11a   12a   13   14

15a   15b   15c

		F £	VF £
1455	**Penny,** *London*. Class 11a. Broken spear-head or pearl on l. side of crown; long narrow face, straight-sided N; round back to C and Є	20	45
1456	— 11b. — Є with angular back (till 15b), N with well-marked serifs (late)	20	45
1457	— 11c. — — A of special form	50	120
1458	— 12a. Central fleur of crown formed of three wedges; thick cross mm.	20	60
1458A	— 12b — Crown with diamond-shaped petals and cruciform central fleur; cross of four wedges mm	40	90
1458B	— 12c — Crown with heart-shaped petals; cross patte mm	45	100
1459	— 13. Central fleur of crown as Greek double axe	20	50
1460	— 14. Crown with tall central fleur; large smiling face with leering eyes	20	45
1461	— 15a. Small flat crown with both spear-heads usually bent to l.; face of 14	20	50
1462	— 15b. — very similar, but smaller face	20	45
1463	— 15c. — large face, large Є	20	45

Berwick Type V   Type VI   Type VII

		F	VF
1464	*Berwick-on-Tweed*. (Blunt types V, VI and VII) Local dies except V	35	85
1465	*Bury St. Edmunds*. (11; 12; 13; 14; 15)	20	45
1466	*Canterbury*. (11; 12a; 13; 14; 15)	20	45
1467	*Durham*. King's Receiver (11a), *mm*. plain cross	25	50
1468	— Bishop Bec. (11a), *mm*. cross moline	25	55
1469	— Bishop Kellawe (11; 12a; 13), crozier on *rev*.	25	50
1470	— Bishop Beaumont (13; 14; 15), *mm*. lion with lis	30	65
1471	*mm*. plain cross (11a, 14, 15c)	45	100
1472	**Halfpenny** of *London*. ЄDWARDVS REX A(NG) Bifoliate or trifoliate crown	50	140
1473	— — *Berwick-on-Tweed*. (Blunt type V)	95	225
1474	**Farthing** of *London*. ЄDWARDVS REX (AN)	40	90
1475	— *Berwick-on-Tweed*. (Blunt type V)	125	325

During Edward's early years small quantities of silver coin were minted following the standard of the previous two reigns, but in 1335 halfpence and farthings were produced which were well below the .925 Sterling silver standard. In 1344 an impressive gold coinage was introduced comprising the Florin or Double Leopard valued at six shillings, and its half and quarter, the Leopard and the Helm. The design of the Florin was based on the contemporary gold of Philip de Valois of France.

The first gold coinage was not successful and it was replaced later the same year by a heavier coinage, the Noble, valued at 6s. 8d, i.e., 80 pence, half a mark or one third of a pound, together with its fractions. The Noble was lowered in weight in two stages over the next few years, being stabilized at 120 grains in 1351. With the signing of the Treaty of Bretigni in 1360 Edward's title to the Kingdom of France was omitted from the coinage, but it was resumed again in 1369.

In 1344 the silver coinage had been re-established at the old sterling standard, but the penny was reduced in weight to just over 20 grains in 1351 to 18 grains. Groats were minted again in 1351 and were issued regularly henceforth until the reign of Elizabeth.

Subsequent to the treaty with France which gave England a cross-channel trading base at Calais, a mint was opened there in 1363 for minting gold and silver coins of English type. In addition to coins of the regular English mints, the Abbot of Reading also minted silver pence, halfpence and farthings with a scallop shell in one quarter of the reverse while coins from Berwick display one or two boars' or bears' heads.

There is evidence of re-use of dies at later periods, e.g. 3rd coinage halfpennies.

For further study of the English Hammered Gold Coinage see: Sylloge of Coins of the British Isles, 47, the Herbert Schneider Collection Volume One, by Peter Woodhead. 1996.

Mintmarks

| 6 | 1 | 2 | 3 | 74 | 4 | 5 | 7a |

1334-51	Cross pattée (6)		1356	Crown (74)
1351-2	Cross 1 (1)		1356-61	Cross 3 (4)
1351-7	Crozier on cross end (76a, *Durham*)		1361-9	Cross potent (5)
1352-3	Cross 1 broken (2)		1369-77	Cross pattée (6)
1354-5	Cross 2 (3)			Plain cross (7a)

The figures in brackets refer to the plate of mintmarks in Appendix III.

GOLD

Third coinage, 1344-51
First period, 1344

| 1476 | 1477 | 1478 |

	F	*VF*
	£	£

1476 **Florin** or **Double Leopard.** (=6s.; wt. 108 grs.). King enthroned beneath
canopy; crowned leopard's head each side. R. Cross in quatrefoil.......... *Extremely rare*
1477 **Half-florin** or **Leopard.** Leopard sejant with banner l. R. Somewhat as last *Extremely rare*
1478 **Quarter-florin** or **Helm.** Helmet on fleured field. R. Floriate cross .... *Extremely rare*

Second period, 1344-46

1479

1479 **Noble** (=6s. 8d., wt. 138.46 grs.). King stg. facing in ship with sword and
shield. R. L in centre of royal cross in tressure .... *Extremely rare*
1479A Half-noble. Similar... *Extremely rare*
1480 **Quarter-noble.** Shield in tressure. R. As last... 1250   3000

Third period, 1346-51
1481 **Noble** (wt. 128.59 grs.). As 1479, but Є in centre; large letters 750   1700
1482 **Half-noble.** Similar... 1500   3750
1483 **Quarter-noble.** As 1480, but Є in centre 275   575

Fourth coinage, 1351-77
Reference: L. A. Lawrence, *The Coinage of Edward III from 1351.*
Pre-treaty period, 1351-61. With French title.
1484 **Noble** (wt. 120 grs.), series B (1351). Open Є and C, Roman M; *mm.*
cross 1 (1)... 375   800
1485 — — *rev.* of series A (1351). Round lettering, Lombardic M and N; closed
inverted Є in centre 425   925

		F	VF
		£	£
1486	C (1351-1352). Closed Є and C, Lombardic M; *mm.* cross 1 (1)............	325	675
1487	D (1352-1353). *O.* of series C. R. *Mm.* cross 1 broken (2).....................	600	1350

1488   1498

1488	E (1354-1355). Broken letters, V often has a nick in r. limb; *mm.* cross 2 (3)..	325	675
1489	F (1356). *Mm.* crown (74)..	450	925
1490	G (1356-1361). *Mm.* cross 3 (4). Many varieties......................................	325	650
1491	**Half-noble,** B. As noble with *rev.* of series A, but closed Є in centre not inverted..	300	625
1492	C. *O.* as noble. *Rev.* as last..	375	750
1493	E. As noble...	475	1100
1494	G. As noble. Many varieties..	275	525
1495	**Quarter-noble,** B. Pellet below shield. R. Closed Є in centre................	170	350
1496	C. *O.* of series B. *Rev.* details as noble	200	450
1497	E. *O.* as last. *Rev.* details as noble, pellet in centre	180	375
1498	G. *Mm.* cross 3 (4). Many varieties...	150	310

Transitional treaty period, 1361. French title omitted, replaced by that of Aquitaine on the noble and (rarely) on the half-noble, but not on the quarter-noble; irregular sized letters; *mm.* cross potent (5).

1499

1499	**Noble.** R. Pellets or annulets at corners of central panel	385	800

1500   1503

		F £	VF £
1500	**Half-noble.** Similar..	225	475
1501	**Quarter-noble.** Similar. Many varieties. Pellet and rarely Є in centre....	150	310

Treaty period, 1361-69. Omits FRANC, new letters, usually curule-shaped X; *mm.* cross potent(5).

1502	**Noble.** *London.* Saltire or nothing before ЄDWARD	350	675
1503	— Annulet before ЄDWARD (with, rarely, crescent on forecastle)........	325	625
1504	*Calais.* C in centre of *rev.*, flag at stern of ship	375	750
1505	— — without flag	400	775

1506   1508

1506	**Half-noble.** *London.* Saltire before ЄDWARD	235	465
1507	— Annulet before ЄDWARD	245	500
1508	*Calais.* C in centre of *rev.*, flag at stern of ship	350	800
1509	— — without flag	400	850
1510	**Quarter-noble.** *London.* As 1498. R. Lis in centre	140	280
1511	— — annulet before ЄDWARD	145	290
1512	*Calais.* R. Annulet in centre	150	350
1513	— — cross in circle over shield..	175	375
1514	— R. Quatrefoil in centre; cross over shield..	225	465
1515	— — crescent over shield...	300	625

Post-treaty period, 1369-1377. French title resumed.

1516	**Noble.** *London.* Annulet before ЄD. R. Treaty period die......................	475	1100
1517	— — — crescent on forecastle	450	900
1518	— — post-treaty letters. R. Є and pellet in centre	375	750
1519	— — — R. Є and saltire in centre..	425	850
1520	*Calais.* Flag at stern. R. Є in centre	400	825

1521

		F	*VF*
		£	£
1521	— — *Rev.* as 1518, with Є and pellet in centre	375	750
1522	— As 1520, but without flag. R. Є in centre	425	850
1523	**Half-noble.** *London. O.* Treaty die. *Rev.* as 1518...............................	850	1750
1524	*Calais.* Without AQT, flag at stern. R. Є in centre................................	575	1200
1525	— — R. Treaty die with C in centre	625	1250

SILVER

First coinage, 1327-35 (.925 fineness)

1526   1530

1526	**Penny.** *London.* As Edw. II; class XVd with Lombardic n's	350	750
1527	*Bury St. Edmunds.* Similar	450	1000
1528	*Canterbury; mm.* cross pattée with pellet centre.....................................	275	600
1529	— — three extra pellets in one quarter	250	550
1530	*Durham.* R. Small crown in centre	375	850
1531	*York.* As 1526, but quatrefoil in centre of *rev;* three extra pellets in TAS quarter..	250	525
1532	— — — pellet in each quarter of *mm.*	275	650
1534	— — — Roman N's on *obv.*	275	650
1535	*Berwick* (1333-1342, Blunt type VIII). Bear's head in one quarter of *rev.*	375	900
1536	**Halfpenny.** *London.* Indistinguishable from EDWARD II (cf. 1472)	50	140
1537	*Berwick* (Bl. VIII). Bear's head in one or two quarters	50	130
1538	**Farthing.** *London.* Indistinguishable from those of EDWARD II (cf. 1474)	40	90
1539	*Berwick* (Bl. VIII). As 1537..	50	130

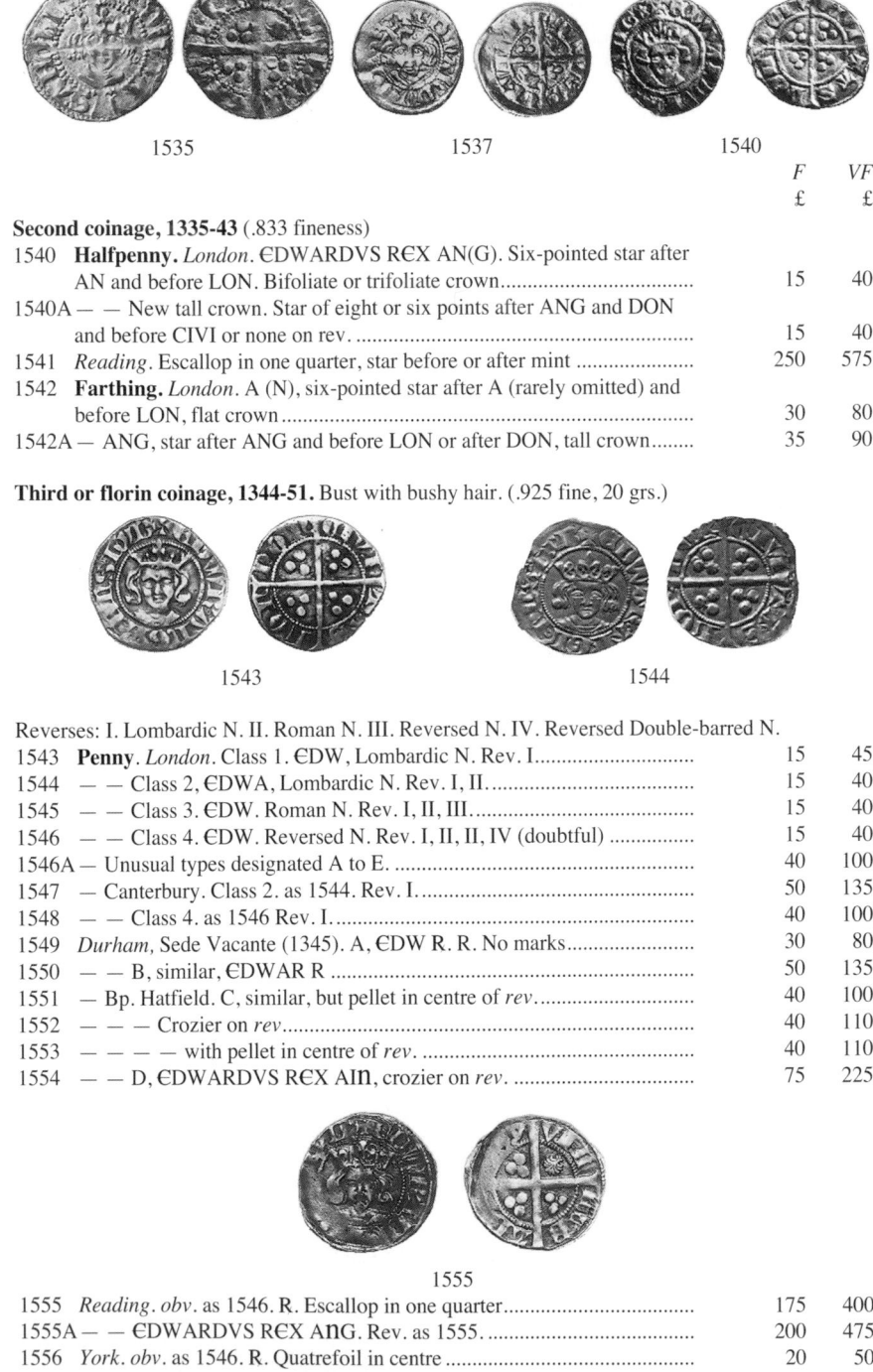

1535   1537   1540

	F £	VF £

Second coinage, 1335-43 (.833 fineness)
1540 **Halfpenny.** *London.* ЄDWARDVS RЄX AN(G). Six-pointed star after
   AN and before LON. Bifoliate or trifoliate crown.................................... 15   40
1540A — — New tall crown. Star of eight or six points after ANG and DON
   and before CIVI or none on rev. 15   40
1541 *Reading.* Escallop in one quarter, star before or after mint 250   575
1542 **Farthing.** *London.* A (N), six-pointed star after A (rarely omitted) and
   before LON, flat crown.. 30   80
1542A — ANG, star after ANG and before LON or after DON, tall crown........ 35   90

Third or florin coinage, 1344-51. Bust with bushy hair. (.925 fine, 20 grs.)

1543   1544

Reverses: I. Lombardic N. II. Roman N. III. Reversed N. IV. Reversed Double-barred N.
1543 **Penny.** *London.* Class 1. ЄDW, Lombardic N. Rev. I............................. 15   45
1544 — — Class 2, ЄDWA, Lombardic N. Rev. I, II................................... 15   40
1545 — — Class 3. ЄDW. Roman N. Rev. I, II, III.................................. 15   40
1546 — — Class 4. ЄDW. Reversed N. Rev. I, II, II, IV (doubtful) 15   40
1546A — Unusual types designated A to E. 40   100
1547 — Canterbury. Class 2. as 1544. Rev. I.. 50   135
1548 — — Class 4. as 1546 Rev. I... 40   100
1549 *Durham,* Sede Vacante (1345). A, ЄDW R. R. No marks...................... 30   80
1550 — — B, similar, ЄDWAR R 50   135
1551 — Bp. Hatfield. C, similar, but pellet in centre of *rev.*......................... 40   100
1552 — — — Crozier on *rev.* 40   110
1553 — — — — with pellet in centre of *rev.* 40   110
1554 — — D, ЄDWARDVS RЄX AIn, crozier on *rev.* 75   225

1555

1555 *Reading. obv.* as 1546. R. Escallop in one quarter................................... 175   400
1555A — — ЄDWARDVS RЄX AnG. Rev. as 1555. 200   475
1556 *York. obv.* as 1546. R. Quatrefoil in centre 20   50

	F £	VF £
1557 **Halfpenny.** *London.* ЄDWARDVS RЄX	15	35
1558 — — ЄDWARDVS RЄX Aᴨ.	15	35
1559 — — as 1558 with pellet or small saltire each side of crown and/or in one reverse quarter	25	60
1560 — *Reading.* as 1557. Rev. Escallop in one quarter................................	200	475
1561 — — as 1558. Rev. as 1560..	225	500
1562 **Farthing.** *London.* ЄDWARDVS RЄX	25	55
1562A *Reading.* As S.1562. Rev. as 1560.	300	650
1562B — — ЄDWARDVS RЄX Aᴨ. Rev. as 1560	325	675

Fourth coinage, 1351-77

Reference: L. A. Lawrence, *The Coinage of Edward III from 1351.*
Pre-treaty period, 1351-61. With French title.

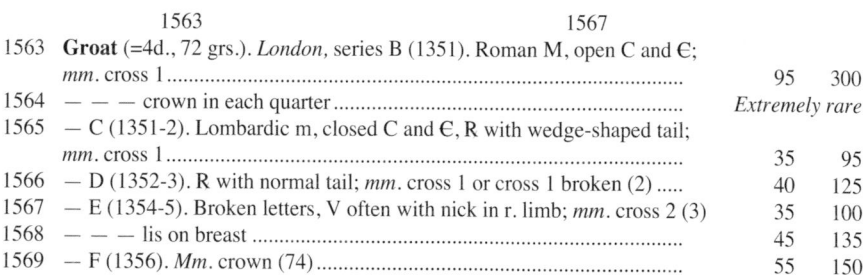

        1563   1567

1563 **Groat** (=4d., 72 grs.). *London,* series B (1351). Roman M, open C and Є; *mm.* cross 1	95	300
1564 — — — crown in each quarter...	*Extremely rare*	
1565 — C (1351-2). Lombardic m, closed C and Є, R with wedge-shaped tail; *mm.* cross 1...	35	95
1566 — D (1352-3). R with normal tail; *mm.* cross 1 or cross 1 broken (2)	40	125
1567 — E (1354-5). Broken letters, V often with nick in r. limb; *mm.* cross 2 (3)	35	100
1568 — — — lis on breast	45	135
1569 — F (1356). *Mm.* crown (74)...	55	150

        1570   1572

1570 — G (1356-61). Usually with annulet in one quarter and sometimes under bust, *mm.* cross 3 (4). Many varieties	30	85
1571 *York,* series D. As London	90	250
1572 — E. As London	40	120

    1573   1574

	F £	VF £
1573 **Halfgroat.** *London,* series B. As groat	75	175
1574 — C. As groat	20	55
1575 — D. As groat	25	65
1576 — E. As groat	25	65
1577 — F. As groat	30	80
1578 — G. As groat	25	65
1579 — — — annulet below bust	30	75
1580 *York,* series D. As groat	60	140
1581 — E. As groat	35	85
1582 — — — lis on breast	50	125
1583 **Penny.** *London.* Series A (1351). Round letters, Lombardic m and n, annulet in each quarter; *mm.* cross pattee	50	125

   1584   1587   1591

1584 — C. Details as groat, but annulet in each quarter	15	35
1585 — D. Details as groat, but annulet in each quarter	15	40
1586 — E. Sometimes annulet in each quarter	15	40
1587 — F. Details as groat	20	45
1588 — G. Details as groat	15	35
1589 — — — annulet below bust	20	45
1590 — — — saltire in one quarter	25	60
1591 *Durham,* Bp. Hatfield. Series A. As 1583, but extra pellet in each quarter, VIL LA crozier DVRRЄM	90	235
1592 — C. Details as groat. R. Crozier, CIVITAS DVNЄLMIЄ	20	45
1593 — D — — —	25	65
1594 — E — — —	25	65
1595 — F — R. Crozier, CIVITAS DVRЄMЄ	25	65
1596 — G — — —	20	60
1597 — — — — — annulet below bust	25	65
1598 — — — — — saltire in one quarter	35	80
1599 — — — — — annulet on each shoulder	35	80
1600 — — — — — trefoil of pellets on breast	35	8(
1601 — — — R. Crozier, CIVITAS DVRЄLMIЄ	40	8

		£	
1602	*York*, Royal Mint. Series D	25	
1603	— — E	20	4.
1604	— Archb. Thoresby. Series D. R. Quatrefoil in centre	25	60
1605	— — G —	20	45
1606	— — — annulet or saltire on breast	30	65
1607	**Halfpenny.** *London.* Series E. ЄDWARDVS RЄX Aᴨ	95	225
1608	— G, but with *obv.* of F (*mm.* crown). Annulet in one quarter	125	325
1609	**Farthing.** *London.* Series E. ЄDWARDVS RЄX	95	225
1609A	— — Series G. Annulet in one quarter	100	250

Transitional treaty period, 1361. French title omitted, irregular sized letters; *mm.* cross potent (5).

1610	**Groat.** *London.* Annulet each side of crown	150	450

1611	1612

1611	**Halfgroat.** Similar, but only seven arches to tressure	90	225
1612	**Penny,** *London.* Omits RЄX, annulet in two upper qtrs. of *mm.*	75	175
1613	*York*, Archb. Thoresby. Similar, but quatrefoil enclosing pellet in centre of *rev.*	60	145
1614	*Durham.* Bp. Hatfield. Similar. R. Crozier, CIVITAS DORЄLMЄ	65	150
1615	**Halfpenny.** Two pellets over *mm.*, ЄDWARDVS RЄX Aᴨ	80	200

Treaty period, 1361-69. French title omitted, new letters, usually 'Treaty' X, rarely curule chair X *mm.* cross potent (5).

1616	**Groat,** *London.* Many varieties	55	140
1617	— Annulet before ЄDWARD	60	165
1618	— Annulet on breast	95	250

1617	1619

1619	*Calais.* As last	135	350

1621   1635

		F £	VF £
1620	**Halfgroat,** *London*. As groat	30	75
1621	— — Annulet before ЄDWARDVS	30	75
1622	— — Annulet on breast	45	110
1623	*Calais*. As last	110	250
1624	**Penny,** *London*. ЄDWARD AnGL R, etc	25	65
1625	— — — pellet before ЄDWARD	25	70
1626	*Calais*. R. VILLA CALЄSIE	100	240
1627	*Durham*. R. CIVITAS DVnЄLMIS	55	125
1628	— R. Crozier, CIVITAS DVRЄMЄ	50	110
1629	*York,* Archb. Thoresby. Quatrefoil in centre of *rev.*, ЄDWARDVS DЄI G RЄX An	35	95
1630	— — — ЄDWARDVS RЄX AnGLI	20	60
1631	— — — — quatrefoil before ЄD and on breast	25	70
1632	— — — — annulet before ЄD	25	70
1633	— — — ЄDWARD AnGL R DnS HYB	30	80
1634	**Halfpenny.** ЄDWARDVS RЄX An, pellet stops	25	65
1635	— Pellet before ЄD, annulet stops	25	70
1636	**Farthing.** ЄDWARDVS RЄX, pellet stops	95	250

Post-treaty period, 1369-77. French title resumed, X like St. Andrew's cross; *mm*. 5, 6, 7a.

1637   1639

		F	VF
1637	**Groat.** Various readings, *mm*. cross pattee	65	185
1638	— — row of pellets across breast (chain mail)	150	475
1639	— row of annulets below bust (chain mail); *mm*. cross potent with four pellets	165	500
1640	**Halfgroat.** Various readings	90	245

1640A

	F	VF
	£	£
1640A — Thin portrait of Richard II	125	225
1641 — row of pellets one side of breast (chain mail)	135	375
1642 **Penny,** *London*. No marks on breast	35	100
1643 — Pellet or annulet on breast	45	120
1644 — Cross or quatrefoil on breast	40	110
1645 *Durham*, Bp. Hatfield. *Mm*. 7a, CIVITAS DVnOLM, crozier	40	110
1646 — — — — annulet on breast	50	125
1647 — — — — lis on breast	40	110
1648 *York*. Archb. Thoresby or Neville. R. Quatrefoil in centre	30	80
1649 — — — lis on breast	35	95
1650 — — — annulet on breast	35	90
1651 — — — cross on breast	35	95

1652

1652 **Farthing.** ЄDWARD RЄX ANGL, large head without neck	130	325

was no change in the weight standard of the coinage during this reign and the coins evolve
n early issues resembling those of Edward III to late issues similar to those of Henry IV.

There is no overall, systematic classification of the coins of Richard II but a coherent scheme
for the gold coinage has been worked out and is published in the Schneider Sylloge (SCBI 47). This
classification has been adopted here.

Reference: *Silver coinages of Richard II, Henry IV and V*. (B.N.J. 1959-60 and 1963).

Mintmark: cross pattée (6)

	F	VF
	£	£

GOLD

		F	VF
1653	**Noble**, *London*. Style of Edw. III. IA. Lis over sail (1654)	600	1250

1654   1658

		F	VF
1654	— IB. Annulet over sail (1655)	475	950
1655	French title omitted. IIA. Crude style, saltire over sail. IIB. Fine style, trefoil over sail. IIC. Porcine style, no mark over sail (1656, 58)	500	975
1656	French title resumed. IIIA. Fine style, no marks (1656)	525	1100
1657	— IIIB. Lis on rudder. IIIC. Trefoil by shield (1656, 1658)	650	1300
1658	Henry IV style. IVA. Escallop on rudder. IVB. Crescent on rudder (1658)	700	1450
1659	*Calais*. Mule with *obv.* of Edw. III (1659)	650	1300
1660	Style of Edw. III. IB. Voided quartrefoil over sail (1660)	600	1250

1661   1662

		F	VF
1661	French title omitted. IIA. Crude style, no marks. IIB. Fine style, trefoil over sail. IIC. Porcine style, no marks (1661, 63)	500	975
1662	French title resumed. IIIA. Fine style, no marks (1661)	550	1050
1663	— IIIB. Lion on rudder. IIIC. Two pellets by shield (1662)	650	1300
1664	**Half-noble**, *London*. With altered *obv.* of Edw. III. Usually muled with *rev.* or altered *rev.* of Edw. III (1664)	700	1450

1665 1673

		F	VF
		£	£
1665	Style of Edw. III. IB. No marks or saltire over sail (1665)	625	1300
1666	French title omitted. IIA. New style, no marks (1665)	675	1400
1667	French title resumed. IIIA. No marks. IIIB. Lion on rudder (1666)	650	1350
1668	Henry IV style. IVB. Crescent on rudder (1667)	750	1500
1669	*Calais*. Mule with *obv*. or *rev*. of Edw. III (1668)	975	2500
1670	Style of Edw. III. IB. Quatrefoil over sail (1669)	950	2300
1671	Late style. French title. IIIA. No marks. IIIB. Saltire by rudder (1671)	950	2250
1672	**Quarter-noble,** *London*. IA. R in centre of *rev*. (1672)	325	625
1673	IB Lis in centre of *rev*. (1673)	250	500
1674	— lis or cross over shield (1677)	300	600

1675 1677

1675	IIIA. Pellet in centre of *rev*. (1673)	275	525
1676	IIIB. Trefoil of annulets over shield or trefoils in spandrels (1676)	350	725
1677	IVA. Escallop over shield (1675)	325	675

SILVER

1679 1682

1678	**Groat.** I. Style of Edw. III, F (*i.e. et*) before FRANC, etc.	275	750
1679	II. New lettering, retrograde Z before FRANC, etc.	210	550
1680	III. Bust with bushy hair, 'fishtail' serifs to letters	275	800
1681	IV. New style bust and crown, crescent on breast	900	2750
1682	**Halfgroat.** II. New lettering	165	400
683	III. As 1680	250	600
24	— — with *obv*. die of Edw. III (1640A)	275	625

		F	*VF*
		£	£
1685	IV. As 1681, but no crescent..	625	1450
1686	**Penny,** *London*. I Lettering as 1678, RICARDVS REX ANGLIE..........	225	600
1688	— II. As 1679, Z FRANC lis on breast	250	625

1689   1692

1689	— III. As 1680, RICARD REX AnGLIE, fish-tail letters	265	650
1690	*York*. I. Early style, usually with cross or lis on breast, quatrefoil in centre of *rev*	45	145
1691	— II. New bust and letters, no marks on breast..	50	150
1692	— Local dies. Pellet above each shoulder, cross on breast, REX ANGLIE or ANGILIE..	40	130
1693	— — — REX DNS EB	70	200
1694	— — — REX ANG FRANC..	70	200
1695	— III. As 1680, REX ANGL Z FRANC (scallop after TAS)	55	145
1696	— IV. Very bushy hair, new letters, no crescent. R. R in centre of quatrefoil	250	575
1697	*Durham*. Cross or lis on breast, DVNOLM	135	425

1698   1699   1701   1704

1698	**Halfpenny.** Early style. LONDON, saltire or annulet on breast	55	150
1699	Intermediate style. LONDON, no marks on breast..................................	30	70
1700	Type III. Late style. Similar, but fishtail letters	35	80
1700A	Type IV. Short, stubby lettering..	35	90
1701	**Farthing.** Small bust and letters	120	275
1703	Similar but no neck	110	250
1704	Rose in each angle of *rev*. instead of pellets	150	425
1704A	Large head with broad face as Henry IV	175	450

HENRY IV, 1399-1413

In 1412 the standard weights of the coinage were reduced, the noble by 12 grains and the penny by 3 grains, partly because there was a scarcity of bullion and partly to provide revenue for the king, as Parliament had not renewed the royal subsidies. As in France, the royal arms were altered, three fleur-de-lis taking the place of the four or more lis previously displayed.

Mintmark: cross pattée (6)

GOLD

Heavy coinage, 1399-1412

	1707		1705		
				F	VF
				£	£
1705	**Noble** (120 grs.), *London*. Old arms with four lis in French quarters; crescent or annulet on rudder			3560	8750
1706	— New arms with three lis; crescent, pellet or no marks on rudder			3560	8750
1707	*Calais*. Flag at stern, old arms; crown on or to l. of rudder			4750	10500

	1708		1710		
1708	— — new arms; crown or saltire on rudder			4500	10000
1709	**Half-noble,** *London*. Old arms			3250	6500
1710	— new arms			3000	6000
1711	*Calais*. New arms			3500	7000
1712	**Quarter-noble,** *London*. Crescent over old arms			800	1750
1713	— — — new arms			750	1650
1714	*Calais*. New arms. R. *Mm.* crown			975	2500

1715

	F	VF
	£	£

Light coinage, 1412-13

1715 **Noble** (108 grs.). Trefoil, or trefoil and annulet, on side of ship. R. Trefoil
　　in one quarter .... 875　　1850

1716 **Half-noble.** Similar, but always with annulet.. 2250　　5000

1717

1717 **Quarter-noble.** Trefoils, or trefoils and annulets beside shield, lis above. R.
　　Lis in centre... 375　　750

SILVER

Heavy coinage, 1399-1412

1718　　　　　　　　　　1722　　　　　　　　　　1723

		F	VF
1718	**Halfgroat** (36 grs.). Star on breast	1250	2500
1718A	— Muled with Edw. III (1640A) *obv*.	750	1750
1719	**Penny,** *London*. Similar, early bust with long neck...................................	550	1250
1720	— later bust with shorter neck, no star	550	1250
1722	*York* Bust with broad face, round chin..	250	600
1723	**Halfpenny.** Early small bust...	125	325
1724	— later large bust, with rounded shoulders, ...	140	350
1725	**Farthing.** Face without neck	475	1100

	F £	VF £
1750 — — Mullet over shield, broken annulet on *rev.*	375	750
1751 — F. Similar, but no annulet on ship, usually trefoil by shield	600	1300

1752

1752 — F/E. As last, but pellet in 1st and annulet in 2nd quarter	625	1350
1753 — G. As noble, but quatrefoil over sail, mullet sometimes omitted after first word of *rev*	475	1000
1754 **Quarter-noble.** A. Lis over shield and in centre of *rev*. Short broad letters; quatrefoil and annulet beside shield, stars at corners of centre on *rev*	400	850
1755 — C. Ordinary letters; quatrefoil to l., quat. and mullet to r. of shield	275	525

1756   1759

1756 — — — annulet to l., mullet to r. of shield	210	425
1757 — F. Ordinary letters; trefoil to l., mullet to r. of shield	235	475
1758 — G. — no marks, except mullet after first word	235	475

SILVER

1759 **Groat.** A. Short broad letters; 'emaciated' bust	575	1450
1760 — — muled with Hen. IV *obv.* or *rev*	650	1500
1761 — — muled with later *rev.* of Hen. V	550	1350

1762   1765

1762 B. Ordinary letters; 'scowling' bust	240	550
1762A — — mullet in centre of breast	275	600
1762B — — mullet to r. of breast	300	725
1763 — — muled with Hen. IV or later Hen. V	325	750
1764 C. Normal bust	120	275
1765 — — mullet on r. shoulder	75	185

		F	*VF*
		£	£
1766	— — R muled with Hen. IV	375	900
1767	G. Normal bust; no marks	150	375
1768	**Halfgroat.** A. As groat, but usually with annulet and pellet by crown	525	1250
1769	B. Ordinary letters; no marks	250	575
1770	— — muled with Hen. IV or class C (HV) *obv*	225	525
1771	C. Tall neck, broken annulet to l. of crown	65	175
1772	— — — mullet on r. shoulder	75	225

1773   1774

1773	— — — mullet in centre of breast	70	200
1774	F. Annulet and trefoil by crown, mullet on breast	75	210
1775	G. New neat bust: no marks.	80	225
1776	**Penny.** *London*. A. Letters, bust and marks as 1768	300	675
1777	— Altered Hen. IV *obv*. with mullet added to l. of crown	375	900

1778   1791

1778	— C. Tall neck, mullet and broken annulet by crown	20	60
1779	— D. Similar, but whole annulet	25	75
1780	— F. Mullet and trefoil by crown	30	80
1781	— G. New neat bust, no marks, DI GRA	35	90
1782	*Durham*. C. As 1778 but quatrefoil at end of legend	45	100
1783	— D. As 1779	35	90
1784	— G. Similar, but new bust. R. Annulet in one qtr.	45	110
1785	*York*. C. As 1778, but quatrefoil in centre of *rev*.	20	60
1786	— D. Similar, but whole annulet by crown	25	70
1787	— E. As last, but pellet above mullet	40	95
1788	— F. Mullet and trefoil by crown	25	60
1789	— — Trefoil over mullet to l., annulet to r. of crown	45	100
1790	— G. Mullet and trefoil by crown (London dies)	25	75
1791	— — Mullet and lis by crown, annulet in one qtr. (usually local dies)	25	75
1792	**Halfpenny.** A. Emaciated bust, annulets by crown	60	150
1793	— altered dies of Hen. IV	95	275
1794	C. Ordinary bust, broken annulets by crown	20	50
1795	D. Annulets, sometimes broken, by hair	20	50

1796

1798

		F	VF
		£	£
1796	F. Annulet and trefoil by crown	20	50
1797	G. New bust; no marks, (usually muled with Henry VI annulet *rev.*)	45	110
1798	**Farthing.** G. Small face with neck	110	300

The supply of gold began to dwindle early in the reign, which accounts for the rarity of gold after 1426. The Calais mint was reopened in 1424 and for some years a large amount of coin was struck there. It soon stopped minting gold; the mint was finally closed in 1440. A royal mint at York was opened for a short time in 1423/4.

Marks used to denote various issues become more prominent in this reign and can be used to date coins to within a year or so.

Reference: C. A. Whitton Heavy Coinage of Henry VI. (B.N.J. 1938-41).

Mintmarks

136	7a	105	18	133	8	9	15

1422-7	Incurved pierced cross (136)	1422-34	Cross pommee (133)
1422-3	Lis (105, York)	1427-34	Cross patonce (8)
1422-60	Plain cross (7a, intermittently		Cross fleury (9)
	Lis (105, on gold)	1434-35	Voided cross (15)
1422-27	Pierced cross (18)	1435-60	Cross fleury (9)
1460	Lis (105, on rev. of some groats)		

For Restoration mintmarks see page 196.

GOLD

1799

		F	VF
	Annulet issue, 1422-7	£	£
1799	**Noble.** *London.* Annulet by sword arm, and in one spandrel on *rev.;* trefoil stops on *obv.* with lis after hЄnRIC, annulets on *rev.*, with mullet after IhC	350	675
1800	— Similar, but *obv.* from Henry V die	700	1400
1801	— As 1799, but Flemish imitative coinage...	300	575
1802	*Calais.* As 1799, but flag at stern and C in centre of *rev*	475	925

1803

		F	VF
		£	£
1803	— — with h in centre of *rev.*	425	825
1804	*York.* As London, but with lis over stern	450	875

1805

1805	**Half-noble.** *London.* As 1799	235	475
1806	— Similar, but *obv.* from Henry V die	625	1350
1807	*Calais.* As noble, with C in centre of *rev.*	525	1100
1808	— — with h in centre of *rev.*	475	975
1809	*York.* As noble	525	1100
1810	**Quarter-noble.** *London.* Lis over shield; *mm.* large lis	145	295
1811	— — — trefoil below shield	175	350
1812	— — — pellet below shield	225	450
1813	*Calais.* Three lis over shield; *mm.* large lis	235	475

1814   1819

1814	— Similar but three lis around shield	225	450
1815	— As 1810, but much smaller *mm.*	200	425
1816	*York.* Two lis over shield	235	475

| | *F* | *VF* |
| | £ | £ |

Rosette-mascle issue, 1427-30

1817	**Noble.** *London.* Lis by sword arm and in *rev.* field; stops, rosettes, or rosettes and mascles	700	1450
1818	*Calais.* Similar, with flag at stern	825	1800
1819	**Half-noble.** *London.* Lis in *rev.* field; stops, rosettes and mascles...........	925	2250
1820	*Calais.* Similar, flag at stern; stops, rosettes	1200	2750
1821	**Quarter-noble.** *London.* As 1810; stops, as noble	425	825
1822	— without lis over shield	450	925
1823	*Calais.* Lis over shield, rosettes r. and l., and rosette stops	475	1000

Pinecone-mascle issue, 1430-4

1824

1824	**Noble.** *London.* Stops, pinecones and mascles	650	1300
1825	**Half-noble.** *London.* *O.* Rosette-mascle die. R. As last	1350	3250
1826	**Quarter-noble.** As 1810, but pinecone and mascle stops	675	1450

Leaf-mascle issue, 1434-5

1827	**Noble.** Leaf in waves; stops, saltires with two mascles and one leaf	1500	3500
1828	**Half-noble.** (Fishpool hoard and Reigate hoard).....................................	1750	4250
1829	**Quarter-noble.** As 1810; stops, saltire and mascle; leaf on inner circle of *rev.*	800	1650

Leaf-trefoil issue, 1435-8

1830	**Noble.** Stops, leaves and trefoils..	2000	4500
1830A	**Half-noble.**	2250	4750
1831	**Quarter-noble.** Similar	925	2000

Trefoil issue, 1438-43

| 1832 | **Noble.** Trefoil to left of shield and in *rev.* legend.................................... | 1750 | 4250 |

Leaf-pellet issue, 1445-54

| 1833 | **Noble.** Annulet, lis and leaf below shield .... | 1750 | 4250 |

Cross-pellet issue, 1454-60

| 1834 | **Noble.** Mascle at end of *obv.* legend... | 2500 | 6250 |

SILVER

Annulet issue, 1422-7

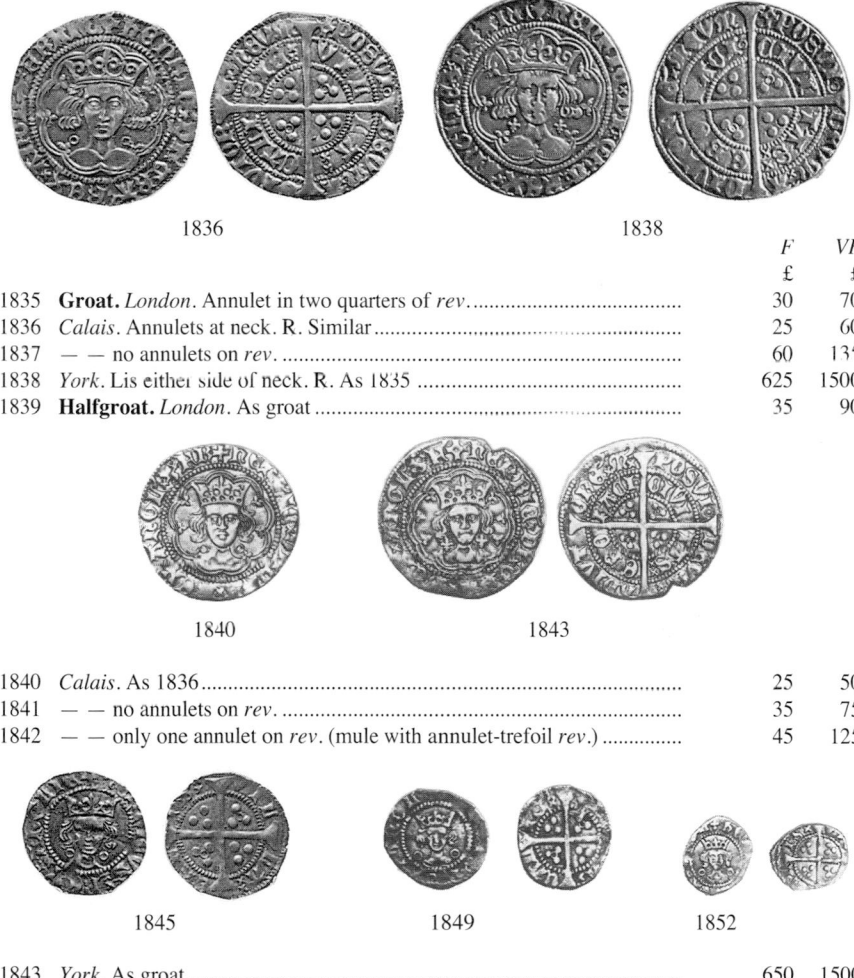

1836   1838

		F	VF
		£	£
1835	**Groat.** *London*. Annulet in two quarters of *rev.*	30	70
1836	*Calais*. Annulets at neck. R. Similar	25	60
1837	— — no annulets on *rev.*	60	135
1838	*York*. Lis either side of neck. R. As 1835	625	1500
1839	**Halfgroat.** *London*. As groat	35	90

1840   1843

1840	*Calais*. As 1836	25	50
1841	— — no annulets on *rev.*	35	75
1842	— — only one annulet on *rev.* (mule with annulet-trefoil *rev.*)	45	125

1845   1849   1852

1843	*York*. As groat	650	1500
1844	**Penny.** *London*. Annulets in two qtrs.	20	55
1845	*Calais*. Annulets at neck. R. As above	20	50
1846	— — only one annulet on *rev.*	30	75
1847	*York*. As London, but lis at neck	600	1350
1848	**Halfpenny.** *London*. As penny	15	35
1849	*Calais*. Similar, but annulets at neck	15	35
1850	*York*. Similar, but lis at neck	325	750
1851	**Farthing.** *London*. As penny, but *mm*. cross pommée	95	235
1852	*Calais*. Similar, but annulets at neck	175	425
1852A	*York*. Similar, but lis at neck	450	950

| | *F* | *VF* |
| | £ | £ |

Annulet-trefoil sub-issue

1854	**Groat.** *Calais,* as 1836 but trefoil to l. of crown.	45	110
1855	**Halfgroat.** *Calais.* Similar, but usually with ann. or rosette mascle *rev.*.	65	145
1856	**Penny.** *Calais.* Similar..	60	140
1857	— — only one annulet on *rev*	70	150

Muling exists in Henry VI coins spanning two or three issues. Full flan coins in the smaller denominations are difficult to find.

Rosette-mascle issue, 1427-30. All with rosettes (early) or rosettes and mascles somewhere in the legends.

| 1858 | **Groat.** *London.* .... | 50 | 125 |

1859   1861

1859	*Calais*	30	65
1860	— mascle in two spandrels (as illus. 1863)	45	95
1861	**Halfgroat.** *London.*..	65	140
1862	*Calais*	25	55

1863   1872

1863	— mascle in two spandrels, as illustrated	35	80
1864	**Penny.** *London.*...	65	175
1865	*Calais*	30	70
1866	*York.* Archb. Kemp. Crosses by hair, no rosette	25	65
1867	— — Saltires by hair, no rosette	30	70
1868	— — Mullets by crown	25	65
1869	*Durham,* Bp. Langley. Large star to l. of crown, no rosette, DVnOLMI	45	120
1870	**Halfpenny,** *London*	15	40
1871	*Calais*	15	40
1872	**Farthing,** *London*	135	300
1873	*Calais. Mm.* cross pommee	165	375

Pinecone-mascle issue, 1430-4. All with pinecones and mascles in legends.

	1874	1876/7	1879

			F	VF
			£	£
1874	**Groat,** London		30	75
1875	*Calais*		30	65
1876	**Halfgroat,** *London*		35	90
1877	*Calais*		25	60
1878	**Penny,** *London*		40	100
1879	*Calais*		30	70
1880	*York,* Archb. Kemp. Mullet by crown, quatrefoil in centre of *rev.*		25	65
1881	— — rosette on breast, no quatrefoil		25	65
1882	— — mullet on breast, no quatrefoil		30	70
1883	*Durham,* Bp. Langley. DVnOLMI		40	100

	1884		1888

1884	**Halfpenny,** *London*	15	40
1885	*Calais*	20	45
1886	**Farthing,** *London*	135	300
1887	*Calais. Mm.* cross pommée	165	375

Full flan coins are difficult to find in the smaller denominations.

Leaf-mascle issue, 1434-5. Usually with a mascle in the legend and a leaf somewhere in the design.

1888	**Groat.** *London.* Leaf below bust, all appear to read DOnDOn	100	275
1889	— — *rev.* of last or next coinage	85	225
1890	*Calais.* Leaf below bust, and usually below MЄVM	70	165
1891	**Halfgroat.** *London.* Leaf under bust, pellet under TAS and DON	85	225

1892   1897

	F £	VF £
1892 *Calais*. Leaf below bust, and sometimes on *rev.*	75	185
1893 **Penny.** *London*. Leaf on breast, no stops on *rev*	50	125
1894 *Calais*. Leaf on breast and below SIЄ	60	140
1895 **Halfpenny.** *London*. Leaf on breast and on *rev*	30	65
1896 *Calais*. Leaf on breast and below SIЄ	60	135

Leaf-trefoil issue, 1435-8. Mostly with leaves and trefoil of pellets in the legends.

	F £	VF £
1897 **Groat.** *London*. Leaf on breast	50	120
1898 — without leaf on breast	50	110
1899 *Calais*. Leaf on breast	350	850
1900 **Halfgroat.** *London*. Leaf on breast; *mm.* plain cross	45	110
1901 — *O. mm.* cross fleury; leaf on breast	45	110
1902 — — without leaf on breast	50	125
1902A *Calais*. leaf on breast, mule with leaf mascle *rev.*	95	225
1903 **Penny.** *London*. Leaf on breast	50	125
1903A *Calais*. Similar	250	575
1904 *Durham,* Bp. Neville. Leaf on breast. R. Rings in centre, no stops, DVnOLM	100	240
1905 **Halfpenny.** *London*. Leaf on breast	20	45
1906 — without leaf on breast	20	50
1907 **Farthing.** *London*. Leaf on breast; stops, trefoil and saltire on *obv.*	150	350

Trefoil issue, 1438-43. Trefoil of pellets either side of neck and in legend, leaf on breast.

1909   1911A

	F	VF
1908 **Groat.** *London*. Sometimes a leaf before LON.	55	145
1909 — Fleurs in spandrels, sometimes extra pellet in two qtrs.	80	200
1910 — Trefoils in place of fleurs at shoulders, none by neck, sometimes extra pellets	60	165
1911 *Calais*	165	400
1911A **Halfgroat,** *London* Similar, but trefoil after DEUM and sometimes after POSUI Mule only with leaf trefoil *obv*	135	325
1911B — *Calais Obv.* Similar to 1911, mule with leaf mascle *rev.*	300	700
1912 **Halfpenny,** *London*	25	6(

Trefoil pellet issue, 1443-5

1912	1913	1915	1917		

		F	*VF*
		£	£
1913	**Groat.** Trefoils by neck, pellets by crown, small leaf on breast; sometimes extra pellet in two quarters	70	180

Leaf-pellet issue, 1445-54. Leaf on breast, pellet each side of crown, except where stated.

1914	**Groat.** ANGL; extra pellet in two quarters	45	125
1915	*Similar,* but ANGLI	40	100
1916	— — trefoil in *obv.* legend	60	145
1917	Leaf on neck, fleur on breast, often extra pellet in two quarters	40	100
1918	As last, but two extra pellets by hair	110	275
1919	**Halfgroat.** As 1914 *mm.*Cross patonce	50	125
1920	Similar, but *mm.* plain cross, some times no leaf on breast, no stops	45	110
1921	**Penny.** *London.* Usually extra pellets in two quarters	40	95
1922	— — pellets by crown omitted	45	100
1923	— — trefoil in legend	50	125
1924	*York,* Archb. Booth. R. Quatrefoil and pellet in centre	30	90
1925	— — two extra pellets by hair (local dies)	30	85
1926	*Durham,* Bp. Neville. Trefoil in *obv.* legend. R. Two rings in centre of cross	65	160

1927	1932		

1927	— — Similar, but without trefoil	65	165
1928	**Halfpenny.** Usually extra pellet in two quarters	15	40
1929	— *mm.* plain cross	15	40
1930	**Farthing.** As last	135	325

Unmarked issue, 1453-4

1931	**Groat.** No marks on *obv.;* two extra pellets on *rev.*	300	725
1932	— four extra pellets on *rev.*	350	850
1933	**Halfgroat.** As 1931	200	525

	F	VF
	£	£

Cross-pellet issue, 1454-60

1934 **Groat.** Saltire either side of neck, pellets by crown, leaf and fleur on breast,
extra pellets on *rev.* 250 600

1935 Saltire on neck, no leaf, pellets by crown, usually mullets in legend; extra
pellets on *rev.* 65 165

1935   1940

1936 — Similar, but mascles in place of mullets on *obv.* 70 185

1937 — — pellets by hair instead of by crown 125 325

1938 **Halfgroat.** Saltire on neck, pellets by crown and on *rev.*, mullets in legend 200 475

1939 **Penny.** *London.* Saltire on neck, pellets by crown and on *rev.*, mascle(s),
or mullet and mascle in legend 200 475

1940 *York,* Archb. Wm. Booth. Saltires by neck, usually leaf on breast, pellets
by crown. R. Cross in quatrefoil in centre. 30 75

1941 *Durham,* Bp. Laurence Booth. Saltire and B or B only at neck, pellets by
crown. R. Rings in centre 65 165

1942 **Halfpenny.** Saltires by neck, usually two extra pellets on *rev.* 50 120

1943 Similar, but saltire on neck, sometimes mullet after hЄПRIC 25 65

1944 **Farthing.** Saltire on neck, usually pellets by crown and on *rev.*, but known
without either. 150 400

Lis-pellet issue, 1456-60

1945

1945 **Groat.** Lis on neck; pellets by crown. R. Extra pellets 165 450

EDWARD IV, First Reign, 1461-70

In order to increase the supply of bullion to the mint the weight of the penny was reduced to 12 grains in 1464, and the current value of the noble was raised to 8s. 4d. Later, in 1465, a new gold coin was issued, the Ryal or 'Rose Noble', weighing 120 grains and having a value of 10s. However, as 6s. 8d. had become the standard professional fee the old noble was missed, and a new coin was issued to take its place, the Angel of 80 grains.

Royal mints were opened at Canterbury and York to help with the re-coinage, and other mints were set up at Bristol, Coventry and Norwich, though they were not open for long.

Reference: C. E. Blunt and C. A Whitton, *The Coinage of Edward IV and Henry VI (Restored),* B.N.J. 1945-7.

Mintmarks

105	9	7a	33	99	28	74	11

1461-4	Lis (105)	1467-70	Lis (105, *York*)	
	Cross fleury (9)	1467-8	Crown (74)	(often
	Plain cross (7a)		Sun (28)	combined)
1464-5	Rose (33 and 34)	1468-9	Crown (74)	(sometimes
1464-7	Pall (99, *Canterbury*)		Rose (33)	combined)
1465-6	Sun (28)	1469-70	Long cross	
1466-7	Crown (74)		fitchee (l.c.f) (11)	(often
			Sun (28)	combined)

GOLD

Heavy coinage, 1461-4

		F	VF
		£	£
1946	**Noble** (=6s. 8d., wt. 108 grs.). Normal type, but *obv.* legend commences at top left, lis below shield; *mm.*-/lis (Spink's sale May 1993)	2250	5500
1947	— Quatrefoil below sword arm; *mm.* rose/lis	2750	6500
1948	— R. Roses in two spandrels; *mm.* rose	3250	7500
1949	**Quarter-noble**	*Extremely rare*	

1946   1950

| | *F* | *VF* |
| | £ | £ |

Light coinage, 1464-70

1950   **Ryal** or rose-noble (=10s., wt. 120 grs.), *London*. As illustration. Large
      fleurs in spandrels; *mm*. 33-74   325   675

1951   — — Small trefoils in spandrels; *mm*. 74-11   325   675

1952

1952 — Flemish imitative coinage (mostly 16th cent. on a large flan)	300	550
1953 *Bristol*. B in waves, large fleurs; *mm*. sun, crown	425	850
1954 — — small fleurs in spandrels; *mm*. sun, crown	450	900
1955 *Coventry*. C in waves; *mm*. sun	800	1700
1956 *Norwich*. Π in waves; *mm*. sun, rose	950	2100
1957 *York*. Є in waves, large fleurs in spandrels, *mm*. sun, lis	400	825
1958 — — small fleurs, *mm*. sun. lis	450	925
1959 **Half-ryal.** *London*. As 1950	285	575
1960 *Bristol*. B in waves; *mm*. sun, sun/crown	475	950
1961 *Coventry*. C in waves; *mm*. sun	1850	4750
1962 *Norwich*. n in waves; *mm*. rose	1600	3750

1963   1965

1963 *York*. Є in waves; *mm*. 28, 105, 33/105	310	625
1963 Similar but lis instead of Є in waves (probably York)	375	800
1964 **Quarter-ryal.** Shield in tressure of eight arcs, rose above. R. Somewhat as half ryal; *mm*. sun/rose	600	1250
1965 Shield in quatrefoil, R. Є above, rose on l., sun on r.; *mm*. 33/28-74/33 ..	200	425
1966 — — sun on l., rose on r.; *mm*. 74-11	200	450

1967

| | | *F* | *VF* |
| | | £ | £ |

| 1967 | **Angel** (=6s. 8d., wt. 80 grs.). St. Michael spearing dragon. R. Ship, rays of sun at masthead, large rose and sun beside mast; *mm.*-/33 | 3000 | 6250 |
| 1968 | — — small rose and sun at mast; *mm.*-/74 | 3250 | 7000 |

SILVER

Heavy coinage, 1461-4

1969	**Groat** (60 grs.). Group I, lis on neck, pellets by crown; *mm.* 9, 7a, 105, 9/105	110	275
1970	— Lis on breast, no pellets; *mm.* plain cross, 7a/105	120	315
1971	— — with pellets at crown; *mm.* plain cross	125	325

1972

1972	II, quatrefoils by neck, crescent on breast; *mm.* rose	110	250
1973	III, similar but trefoil on breast; *mm.* rose	100	235
1974	— — — eye in *rev.* inner legend, *mm.* rose	95	220
1975	— Similar, but no quatrefoils by bust	145	375
1976	— — Similar, but no trefoil on breast	140	350
1977	IV, annulets by neck, eye after TAS; *mm.* rose	150	400

1973   1978

| 1978 | **Halfgroat.** I, lis on breast, pellets by crown and extra pellets in two qtrs.; *mm.* 9, 7a | 375 | 900 |

		F	*VF*
		£	£
1979	II, quatrefoils at neck, crescent on breast; *mm.* rose	300	650
1980	III, similar, but trefoil on breast, eye on rev.; *mm.* rose	265	550
1981	— Similar, but no mark on breast	265	550
1982	IV, annulets by neck, sometimes eye on *rev.; mm.* rose	300	675
1983	**Penny** (15 grs.), *London*. I, marks as 1978, but mascle after RЄX; *mm.* plain cross	500	1100
1984	II, quatrefoils by neck; *mm.* rose	425	900

1985

1985	III, similar, but eye after TAS; *mm.* rose	250	525
1986	IV, annulets by neck; *mm.* rose	375	800
1987	*York,* Archb. Booth. Quatrefoils by bust, voided quatrefoil in centre of *rev.; mm.* rose	135	300
1988	*Durham. O.* of Hen. VI. R. DVПOLIП	150	350
	Some of the Durham pennies from local dies may belong to the heavy coinage period, but if so they are indistinguishable from the light coins.		
1989	**Halfpenny.** I, as 1983, but no mascle	100	250
1990	II, quatrefoils by bust; *mm.* rose	60	135
1991	— saltires by bust; *mm.* rose	50	110
1992	III, no marks by bust; *mm.* rose	55	125
1993	IV, annulets by bust; *mm.* rose	65	150
1994	**Farthing.** I, as 1989	300	650
1994A	II. saltires by bust; *mm.* rose	325	700
1994B	III, no marks by bust; mm. rose	275	600

Light coinage, 1464-70. There is a great variety of groats and we give only a selection. Some have pellets in one quarter of the reverse, or trefoils over the crown; early coins have fleurs on the cusps of the tressure, then trefoils or no marks on the cusps, while the late coins have only trefoils.

1995	**Groat** (48 grs.), *London*. Annulets at neck, eye after TAS; *mm.* 33 (struck from heavy dies, IV)	75	185
1996	— — — Similar, but new dies, eye after TAS or DOП	80	195
1997	— Quatrefoils at neck, eye; rose (heavy dies, III)	65	145
1998	— — — Similar, but new dies, eye in *rev.* legend	70	160
1999	— No marks at neck, eye; rose	120	275

2000	2002

Light coinage, silver, *continued*.

		F £	VF £
2000	— Quatrefoils at neck, no eye; *mm*. 33, 74, 28, 74/28, 74/33, 11/28	35	85
2001	— — — rose or quatrefoil on breast; *mm*. 33, 74/28...............	40	90
2002	— No marks at neck; *mm*. 28, 74, 11/28, 11..........................	50	120
2003	— Trefoils or crosses at neck; *mm*. 11/33, 11/28, 11................	45	110
2004	*Bristol*. B on breast, quatrefoils at neck; *mm*. 28/33, 28, 28/74, 74, 74/28	40	95
2005	— — trefoils at neck; *mm*. sun	65	165
2006	— — no marks at neck; *mm*. sun	75	200
2007	— Without B, quatrefoils at neck; *mm*. sun	90	225

Bristol is variously rendered as BRESTOLL, BRISTOLL, BRESTOW, BRISTOW.

		F	VF
2008	*Coventry*. C on breast, quatrefoils at neck, COVETRE; *mm*. 28/33, 28 ...	70	165
2009	— — Local dies, similar; *mm*. rose	90	225
2010	— — — as last, but no C or quatrefoils.......................	120	275
2011	Norwich. ꞃ on breast, quatrefoils at neck, ꞃORWIC or ꞃORVIC, *mm*. 28/33, 28..	60	135
2012	*York*. Є on breast, quatrefoils at neck, ЄBORACI; *mm*. 28, 105/74, 105, 105/28..	40	100
2013	— Similar, but without Є on breast, *mm*. lis....................	60	150
2014	— Є on breast, trefoils at neck; *mm*. 105/28, 105.............	50	125
2015	**Halfgroat.** *London*. Annulets by neck (heavy dies); *mm*. 33	250	550
2016	— Quatrefoils by neck; *mm*. 33/-, 28/-, 74, 74/28	45	110
2017	— Saltires by neck; *mm*. 74, 74/28	50	120
2018	— Trefoils by neck; *mm*. 74, 74/28, 11/28	50	125
2019	— No marks by neck; *mm*. 11/28	85	185
2020	— *Bristol*. Saltires or crosses by neck; *mm*. 33/28, 28, 74, 74/-	135	300
2021	— Quatrefoils by neck; *mm*. 28/-, 74, 74/-	125	275
2022	— Trefoils by neck; *mm*. crown...................................	150	350
2023	— No marks by neck; *mm*. 74/28	160	375
2024	*Canterbury*, Archb. Bourchier (1464-7). Knot below bust; quatrefoils by neck; *mm*. 99/-, 99, 99/33, 99/28...........................	25	65
2025	— — — quatrefoils omitted *mm*. 99............................	25	65
2026	— — — saltires by neck; *mm*. 99/-, 99/28	30	70
2026A	— — — trefoils by neck; *mm*. 99	40	95

2027   2030

	F	VF
	£	£
2027 — — — wedges by hair and/or neck; *mm*. 99, 99/33, 99/28....................	35	80
2028 — — As 2024 or 2025, but no knot...	35	85
2029 — Royal mint (1467-9). Quatrefoils by neck; *mm*. 74, 74/-	30	80
2030 — — Saltires by neck; *mm*. 74/-, 74	30	80
2031 — — Trefoils by neck; *mm*. 74, 74/-, 74/28, 33	25	65
2032 — No marks by neck; *mm*. sun	60	145
2033 *Coventry*. Crosses by neck; *mm*. sun...	700	1750
2034 *Norwich*. Saltires by neck; *mm*. sun	675	1650
2035 *York*. Quatrefoils by neck; *mm*. sun, lis, lis/-	60	135
2036 — Saltires by neck; *mm*. lis	55	125
2037 — Trefoils by neck; *mm*. lis, lis/-...	65	145
2038 — Є on breast, quatrefoils by neck; *mm*. lis/-...................................	70	150
2039 **Penny** (12 grs.), *London*. Annulets by neck (heavy dies); *mm*. rose	200	475
2040 — Quatrefoils by neck; *mm*. 74, sun. crown...................................	30	75
2041 — Trefoil and quatrefoil by neck; *mm*. crown....................................	35	100
2042 — Saltires by neck; *mm*. crown	35	90
2043 — Trefoils by neck; *mm*. crown, ll	35	90
2044 — No marks by neck; *mm*. ll	110	275
2045 *Bristol*. Crosses, quatrefoils or saltires by neck, BRISTOW; *mm*. crown	150	400
2046 — Quatrefoils by neck; BRI(trefoil)STOLL	150	400
2047 — Trefoil to r. of neck BRISTOLL	165	450
2048 *Canterbury, Archb.* Bourchier. Quatrefoils or saltires by neck, knot on breast; *mm*. pall	70	165
2049 — — Similar, but no marks by neck	75	175
2050 — — As 2048, but no knot	75	175
2051 — — Crosses by neck, no knot...	75	175
2052 — Royal mint. Quatrefoils by neck; *mm*. crown	200	525
2053 — *Durham*, King's Receiver (1462-4). Local dies, mostly with rose in centre of *rev*.; *mm*. 7a, 33	25	65
2054 — Bp. Lawrence Booth (1465-70). B and D by neck, B on *rev*.; *mm*. 33	35	90
2055 — — Quatrefoil and B by neck; *mm*. sun..	30	80
2056 — — B and quatrefoil by neck; *mm*. crown	35	100
2057 — — D and quatrefoil by neck; *mm*. crown	35	90
2058 — — Quatrefoils by neck; *mm*. crown	30	85
2059 — — Trefoils by neck; *mm*. crown..	30	85
2060 — Lis by neck; *mm*. crown	30	80
2061 *York*, Sede Vacante (1464-5). Quatrefoils at neck, no quatrefoil in centre of *rev*.; *mm*. sun, rose	50	125
2062 — Archb. Neville (1465-70). Local dies, G and key by neck, quatrefoil on *rev*.; *mm*. sun, plain cross..	25	70

2063

2068

		F	VF
		£	£
2063	— — London-made dies, similar; *mm*. 28, 105, 11	25	75
2064	— — Similar, but no marks by neck; *mm*. large lis	40	120
2065	— — — Quatrefoils by neck; *mm*. large lis	30	85
2066	— — — Trefoils by neck; *mm*. large lis	30	80
2067	**Halfpenny,** *London*. Saltires by neck; *mm*. 34, 28, 74	20	65
2068	— Trefoils by neck; *mm*. 28, 74, 11	20	65
2069	— No marks by neck; mm. 11	50	135
2070	*Bristol*. Crosses by neck; *mm*. crown	100	250
2071	— Trefoils by neck; *mm*. crown	95	225
2072	*Canterbury*. Archb. Bourchier. No marks; *mm*. pall	90	200
2072A	— — — Trefoils by neck, *mm*. pall	90	200
2073	— Royal mint. Saltires by neck; *mm*. crown	80	165
2074	— — Trefoils by neck; *mm*. crown	60	135
2074A	*Norwich*. Quartrefoils by neck., *mm*. Sun	225	525
2075	*York*. Royal mint. Saltires by neck; *mm*. lis/-, sun/-	65	145
2076	— — Trefoils by neck; *mm*. lis/-	60	135
2077	**Farthing,** *London*. ЄDWARD DI GRA RЄX, no marks at neck, *mm*. rose	275	625
2077A	— Trefoils by neck, *mm*. crown	325	750

Full flan coins are difficult to find in the smaller denominations.

The coinage of this short restoration follows closely that of the previous reign. Only angel gold was issued, the ryal being discontinued. Many of the coins have the king's name reading henRICV — another distinguishing feature is an R that looks like a B.

Mintmarks

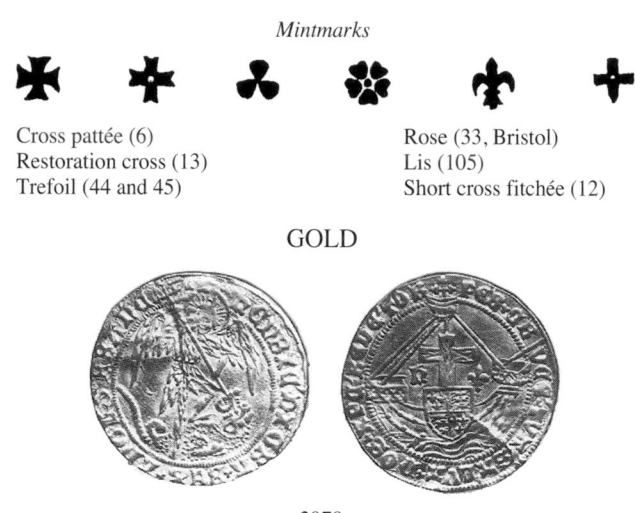

Cross pattée (6)   Rose (33, Bristol)
Restoration cross (13)   Lis (105)
Trefoil (44 and 45)   Short cross fitchée (12)

GOLD

2079

		F	*VF*
		£	£
2078	**Angel,** *London.* As illus. but no B; *mm.* -/6, 13, -/105, none	650	1350
2079	*Bristol.* B in waves; *mm.* -/13, none	1000	2500
2080	**Half-angel,** *London.* As 2078; *mm.* -/6, -/13, -/105	1500	3250
2081	*Bristol.* B in waves; *mm.* -/13	2000	4500

SILVER

2082   2084

2082	**Groat,** *London.* Usual type; *mm.* 6, 6/13, 6/105, 13, 13/6, 13/105, 13 /12	120	300
2083	*Bristol.* B on breast; *mm.* 13, 13/33, 13/44, 44, 44/13, 44/33, 44/12	150	425
2084	*York.* C on breast; *mm.* lis, lis/sun	135	325
2085	**Halfgroat,** *London.* As 2082; *mm.* 13, 13/-	200	450
2086	*York.* C on breast; *mm.* lis	425	900
2087	**Penny,** *London.* Usual type; *mm.* 6, 13, 12..	325	775

	F	VF
	£	£
2087A *Bristol.* Similar; *mm.* 12	600	1250
2088 *York.* G and key by neck; *mm.* lis	225	500
2089 **Halfpenny,** *London.* As 2087; *mm.* 12, 13, ...	75	185
2090 *Bristol.* Similar; *mm.* cross	400	925

EDWARD IV, Second Reign, 1471-83

The Angel and its half were the only gold denominations issued during this reign. The main types
and weight standards remained the same as those of the light coinage of Edward's first reign. The
use of the 'initial mark' as a mintmark to denote the date of issue was now firmly established.

Mintmarks

33	105	12	55	44	55	28	56	17

30	37	6	18	19	20	31	11	38

1471-83	Rose (33, *York & Durham*)	1473-7	Cross pattée (6)
	Lis (105, *York*)		Pierced cross 1 (18)
1471	Short cross fitchee (12)	1477-80	Pierced cross and
1471-2	Annulet (large, 55)		pellet (19)
	Trefoil (44)		Pierced cross 2 (18)
	Rose (33, *Bristol*)		Pierced cross, central
1471-3	Pansy (30, *Durham*)		pellet (20)
1472-3	Annulet (small, 55)		Rose (33, *Canterbury*)
	Sun (28, *Bristol*)	1480-3	Heraldic cinquefoil (31)
1473-7	Pellet in annulet (56)		Long cross fitchee
	Cross and four pellets (17)		(11, *Canterbury*)
	Cross in circle (37)	1483	Halved sun and rose (38)
			(Listed under Ed. IV/V.)

GOLD

2091   2093

	F	VF
	£	£
2091 **Angel.** *London.* Type as illus.; *mm.* 12, 55, 56, 17, 18, 19, 31	275	550
2092 *Bristol.* B in waves; *mm.* small annulet......................................	1300	2750
2093 **Half-angel.** As illus.; *mm.* 55, cross in circle, 19, 20/19, 31	265	525

		F	*VF*
		£	£
2094	King's name and title on rev.; *mm*. 12/-	325	650
2095	King's name and the title both sides; *mm*. 55/-	350	700

SILVER

2096   2101

2096	**Groat,** *London*. Trefoils on cusps, no marks by bust; *mm*. 12-37	35	90
2097	— — roses by bust; *mm*. pellet in annulet	50	145
2098	— Fleurs on cusps; no marks by bust; *mm*. 18-20	40	95
2099	— — pellets by bust; *mm*. pierced cross	70	180
2100	— — rose on breast; *mm*. 31	40	100
2101	*Bristol*. B on breast no marks by bust; *mm*. 33, 33/55, 28/55, 55, 55/-, 28	70	180
2102	*York*. Є on breast no marks by bust; *mm*. lis	80	190
2103	**Halfgroat,** *London*. As 2096; *mm*. 12-31	40	90
2104	*Bristol*. B on breast; *mm*. 33/12	275	650
2105	*Canterbury* (Royal mint). As 2103; *mm*. 33, 11, 11/31, 31	35	80

2106

2106	— C on breast; *mm*. rose	25	70
2107	— — R. C in centre; *mm*. rose	25	70
2108	— — R. Rose in centre; *mm*. rose	30	75
2109	*York*. No. Є on breast; *mm*. lis	100	275
2110	**Penny,** *London*. No marks by bust; *mm*. 12-31	30	90
2111	*Bristol*. Similar; *mm*. rose	225	525
2112	*Canterbury* (Royal). Similar; *mm*. 33, 11	65	165
2113	— C on breast; *mm*. rose	90	225
2114	*Durham,* Bp. Booth (1471-6). No marks by neck; *mm*. 12, 44	20	65

2115   2116

2115	— — D in centre of *rev.;* B and trefoil by neck; *mm*. 44, 33, 56	25	70
2116	— — — two lis at neck; *mm*. rose	25	75
2117	— — — crosses over crown, and on breast; *mm*. rose	25	70

	F	VF
	£	£

2118 — — — crosses over crown, V under CIVI; *mm.* rose, pansy 25 70
2119 — — — B to l. of crown, V on breast and under CIVI 20 65
2120 — — — As last but crosses at shoulders 20 65
2121 — Sede Vacante (1476). R. D in centre; *mm.* rose 30 95
2122 — Bp. Dudley (1476-83). V to r. of neck; as last 25 70

2123   2125   2134

2123 — — D and V by neck; as last, but *mm.* 31 .... 25 70
Nos. 2117-2123 are from locally-made dies.
2124 *York*, Archb. Neville (1471-?). Quatrefoils by neck. R. Quatrefoil; *mm.*
   12 (over lis) 70 175
2125 — — Similar, but G and key by neck; *mm.* 12 (over lis) 20 60
2126 — Neville suspended (1472-5). As last, but no quatrefoil in centre of *rev.* 30 75
2126A — — no marks by bust, similar; *mm.* annulet 70 200
2127 — — No marks by neck, quatrefoil on *rev.; mm.* 55, cross in circle, 33 . 20 60
2128 — — Similar but Є and rose by neck; *mm.* rose 20 60
2129 — Archb. Neville restored (1475-6). As last, but G and rose 20 65
2130 — — Similar, but G and key by bust 20 60
2131 — Sede Vacante (1476). As 2127, but rose on breast; *mm.* rose 25 75
2132 — Archb. Lawrence Booth (1476-80). B and key by bust, quatrefoil on
   rev.; mm. 33, 31 .... 20 60
2133 — Sede Vacante (1480). Similar, but no quatrefoil on rev.; mm. rose 25 70
2134 — Archb. Rotherham (1480-3). T and slanting key by neck, quatrefoil
   on *rev.; mm.* 33 .... 20 60
2135 — — — Similar, but star on breast 70 165
2136 — — — Star on breast and to r. of crown 65 150
2137 **Halfpenny**, *London.* No marks by neck; *mm.* 12-31 .... 20 50
2138 — Pellets at neck; *mm.* pierced cross 35 100
2139 *Canterbury* (Royal). C on breast and in centre of *rev.; mm.* rose 90 200
2140 — C on breast only; *mm.* rose 80 175
2141 — Without C either side; *mm.* 11 .... 70 160
2142 *Durham,* Bp. Booth. No marks by neck. R. DЄR ΛM, D in centre; *mm.*
   rose 135 325
2142A — — Lis either side of neck. R. D or no mark in centre 150 375
2142B — — B to l. of crown, crosses at shoulders. R. D. in centre; *mm.* rose.... 150 375
2143 — — — Bp. Dudley V to l. of neck; as last 145 350

Full flan coins are very difficult to find in the small denominations.

On the death of Edward IV, 9th April, 1483, the 12-year-old Prince Edward was placed under the guardianship of his uncle, Richard, Duke of Gloucester, but within eleven weeks Richard usurped the throne and Edward and his younger brother were confined to the Tower and never seen alive again. The boar's head was a personal badge of Richard, Edward's 'Protector'.

The consensus now favours the last year of Edward IV for the introduction of the halved-sun and rose mintmark, but it is suggested that all the coins of Edward V's reign were also struck from dies bearing this mint mark. The coins are very rare.

Mintmark: Halved sun and rose.

GOLD

		F	VF
		£	£
2144	**Angel.** As 2091	975	2250
2145	**Half-angel.** As 2093	1750	3750

SILVER

2145   2146

2146	**Groat.** As 2098 with or without pellet below bust	475	1200
2147	**Penny.** As 2110..	575	1350
2148	**Halfpenny.** As 2137	125	300

2149

COINS ATTRIBUTABLE TO RICHARD III, 1483

Recent research indicates that coins with the mint marks previously thought to be for Edward V are now attributable to Richard III, even though they bear Edward's name.

Mintmarks: Boar's head on *obv.,* halved sun and rose on *rev.*

GOLD

2149	**Angel.** As 2091	3000	7000
2150	**Half-angel.** Similar..	*Extremely rare*	

SILVER

2151

		F	VF
		£	£
2151	**Groat.** As 2098	1450	3500
2152	**Halfgroat.** As 2103	900	2250
2153	**Penny.** As 2110 (*mm.* uncertain on only known specimen)	*Extremely rare*	

RICHARD III, 1483-85

Richard's brief reign was brought to an end on the field of Bosworth. His coinage follows the pattern of the previous reigns. The smaller denominations of the London mint are all rare.

Mintmarks

38   62   63   105   33

Halved sun and rose, 3 styles (38, 39 and another with the sun more solid, see *North*).
Boar's head, narrow (62) wide (63).
Lis (105, *Durham*)
Rose only (33).

GOLD

| 2154 | **Angel.** Reading ЄDWARD but with R and rose by mast; *mm.* sun and rose .... | *Extremely rare* | |
| 2155 | — Similar, but boar's head *mm.* on *obv* .... | *Extremely rare* | |

2156   2158

2156	Reading RICARD or RICAD. R. R and rose by mast; *mm.* various combinations	925	1850
2157	— Similar, but R by mast over rose	950	1900
2158	**Half-angel.** R. R and rose by mast; *mm.* boar's head	2250	4750

SILVER

2159   2160

		F	VF
		£	£
2159	**Groat,** *London. Mm.* various combinations	275	625
2160	— Pellet below bust	300	650
2161	*York. Mm.* Sun and rose (*obv.*)	625	1450
2162	**Halfgroat.** *Mm.* sun and rose on *obv.* only	425	975
2163	Pellet below bust; *mm.* sun and rose	475	1100

2164   2168

		F	VF
2164	— mm. boar's head (*obv.*)	625	1350
2165	**Penny.** *London. mm.* boar's head (*obv.*)	825	2000
2166	*York,* Archb. Rotherham. R. Quatrefoil in centre; *mm.* sun and rose	225	500
2167	— — T and upright key at neck; *mm.* rose	125	350
2168	— — — *mm.* boar's head	135	375

2169   2170

		F	VF
2169	*Durham,* Bp. Sherwood. S on breast. R. D in centre; *mm.* lis	100	275
2170	**Halfpenny,** *London. Mm.* sun and rose	100	275
2171	— *Mm.* boar's head	135	375
2171A	**Farthing,** *Mm.* boar's head, sun and rose	700	1650

Most small denomination coins are short of flan and unevenly struck.

HENRY VII, 1485-1509

For the first four years of his reign Henry's coins differ only in name and mintmark from those of his predecessors, but in 1489 radical changes were made in the coinage. Though the pound sterling had been a denomination of account for centuries, a pound coin had never been minted. Now a magnificent gold pound was issued, and, from the design of the king enthroned in majesty, was called a 'Sovereign'. The reverse had the royal arms set in the centre of a Tudor rose. A few years later the angel was restyled and St. Michael, who is depicted about to thrust Satan into the Pit with a cross-topped lance, is no longer a feathered figure but is clad in armour of Renaissance style. A gold ryal of ten shillings was also minted again for a brief period.

The other major innovation was the introduction of the shilling in the opening years of the 16th century. It is remarkable for the very fine profile portrait of the king which replaces the representational image of a monarch that had served on the coinage for the past couple of centuries. This new portrait was also used on groats and halfgroats but not on the smaller denominations.

Mintmarks

39	41	40	42	33	11	7a	123

105	76b	31	78	30	91	43	57

85	94	118	21	33	53

1485-7	Halved sun and rose (39)	1495-8	Pansy (30)
	Lis upon sun and rose (41)		Tun (123, *Canterbury*)
	Lis upon half rose (40)		Lis (105, York)
	Lis-rose dimidiated (42)	1498-9	Crowned leopard's head (91)
	Rose (33, *York*)		Lis issuant from rose (43)
1487	Lis (105)		Tun (123, *Canterbury*)
	Cross fitchy (11)	1499-1502	Anchor (57)
1487-8	Rose (33)	1502-4	Greyhound's head (85)
	Plain cross (7a, *Durham*)		Lis (105, profile issue only)
1488-9	No marks		Martlet (94, *York*)
1489-93	Cinquefoil (31)	1504-5	Cross-crosslet (21)
	Crozier (76b, *Durham*)	1504-9	Martlet (94, (*York, Canterbury*)
1492	Cross fitchée (11, gold only)		Rose (33, *York* and
1493-5	Escallop (78)		*Canterbury*)
	Dragon (118, gold only)	1505-9	Pheon (53)
	Lis (105, *Canterbury and York*		
	Tun (123, *Canterbury*)		

GOLD

	F	VF
	£	£

2172 **Sovereign** (20s; wt. 240 gr.). Group I. Large figure of king sitting on
backless throne. R. Large shield crowned on large Tudor rose. *mm*. 31 ..   *Extremely rare*

2173 — Group II. Somewhat similar but throne has narrow back, lis in
background. R. Large Tudor rose bearing small shield. *mm*. -/11 ....   *Extremely rare*

2174

2174 — III. King on high-backed very ornamental throne, with greyhound
and dragon on side pillars. R. Shield on Tudor rose; *mm*. dragon   7750   16000

2175 — IV. Similar but throne with high canopy breaking legend and broad seat,
mm. 105/118, (also with no *obv*. i.c. *mm*. 105/118, very rare)   7000   14500

2176 — Narrow throne with a portcullis below the king's feet (like Henry VIII);
mm. 105/21, 105/53   7250   15000

2177 **Double-sovereign** and **Treble-sovereign** from same dies as 2176. These
piedforts were probably intended as presentation pieces *mm*. 105/21, 105/53   *Extremely rare*

2178

2178 **Ryal** (10s.). As illustration: *mm*. -/11   6750   17000

2179 **Angel** (6s. 8d). I. Angel of old type with one foot on dragon. R. PER
CRVCEM. etc., *mm*. 39, 40, (also muled both ways)..............................   550   1200

2179A — With Irish title, and legend over angel head. mm. 33/-   650   1350

2180 — — Name altered from RICARD? and h on *rev*. from R. mm. 41/39,
41/40, 41/-, 39/?   575   1250

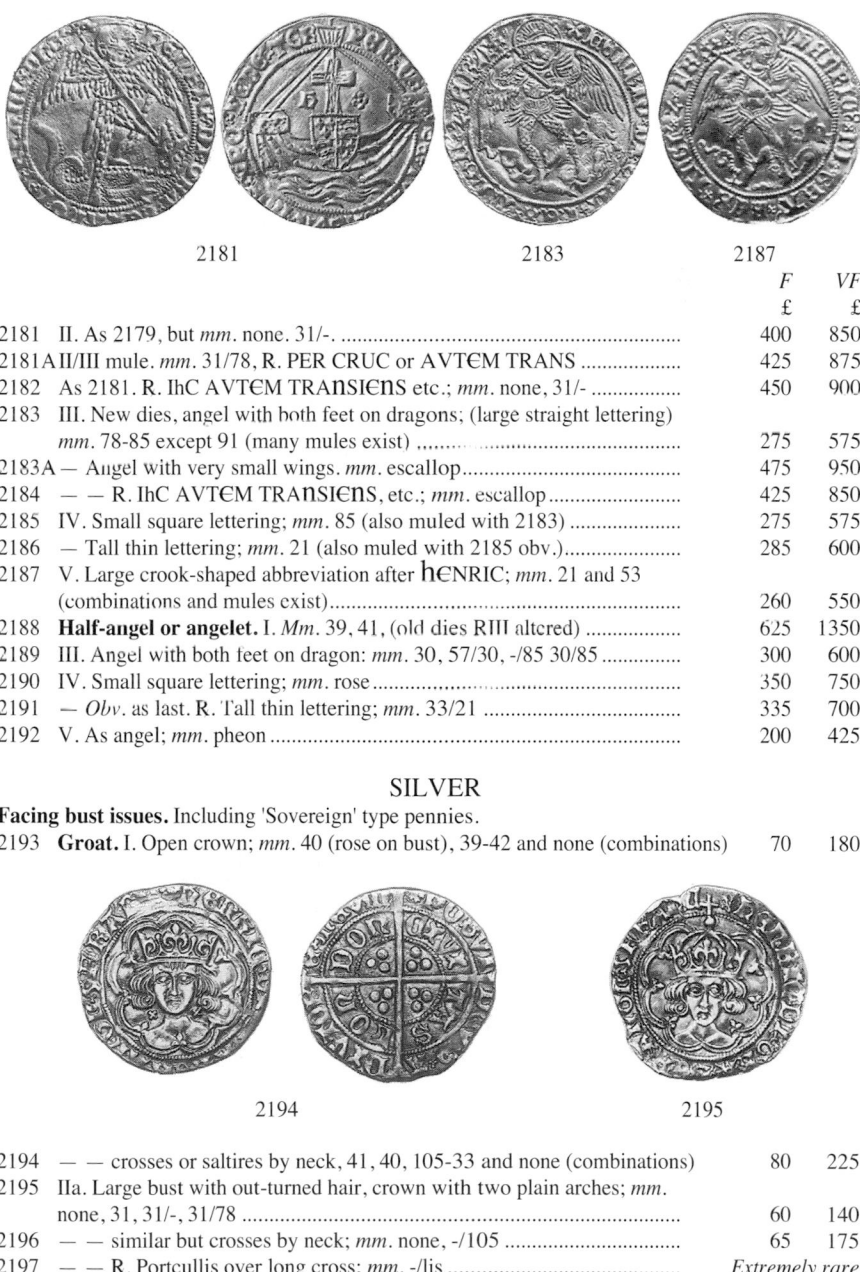

2181   2183   2187

		F £	VF £
2181	II. As 2179, but *mm.* none. 31/-.	400	850
2181A	II/III mule. *mm.* 31/78, R. PER CRUC or AVTEM TRANS	425	875
2182	As 2181. R. IhC AVTEM TRANSIENS etc.; *mm.* none, 31/-	450	900
2183	III. New dies, angel with both feet on dragons; (large straight lettering) *mm.* 78-85 except 91 (many mules exist) ,,........	275	575
2183A	— Angel with very small wings. *mm.* escallop..	475	950
2184	— — R. IhC AVTEM TRANSIENS, etc.; *mm.* escallop	425	850
2185	IV. Small square lettering; *mm.* 85 (also muled with 2183)	275	575
2186	— Tall thin lettering; *mm.* 21 (also muled with 2185 obv.)......................	285	600
2187	V. Large crook-shaped abbreviation after hENRIC; *mm.* 21 and 53 (combinations and mules exist)..	260	550
2188	**Half-angel or angelet.** I. Mm. 39, 41, (old dies RIII altered)	625	1350
2189	III. Angel with both feet on dragon: *mm.* 30, 57/30, -/85 30/85	300	600
2190	IV. Small square lettering; *mm.* rose	350	750
2191	— *Obv.* as last. R. Tall thin lettering; *mm.* 33/21	335	700
2192	V. As angel; *mm.* pheon	200	425

SILVER

Facing bust issues. Including 'Sovereign' type pennies.

2193	**Groat.** I. Open crown; *mm.* 40 (rose on bust), 39-42 and none (combinations)	70	180

2194   2195

2194	— — crosses or saltires by neck, 41, 40, 105-33 and none (combinations)	80	225
2195	IIa. Large bust with out-turned hair, crown with two plain arches; *mm.* none, 31, 31/-, 31/78	60	140
2196	— — similar but crosses by neck; *mm.* none, -/105	65	175
2197	— — R. Portcullis over long cross; *mm.* -/lis	*Extremely rare*	

2198   2199   2201

	F £	VF £
2198 **Groat.** IIIa. Bust as IIa. Crown with two jewelled arches, *mm.* 31, 78? ..	95	275
2198A IIIb. Similar, but new bust with realistic hair *mm.* 78, 30	45	110
2199 IIIc. Bust as IIIb, but crown with one plain and one jewelled arch, *mm.* 30-21 and none	40	100
2199A IIId. As last, but plainer letters. mm 57, 85, 33 and none	45	110
2200 IVa. Wide single arch crown; arch is single or double bar with 4 crockets; *mm.* 85, 85/33, 21	50	125
2201 IVb. — Similar, but arch is double bar with 6 uprights or crockets as jewels; *mm.* 85, 21/85, 21	45	110
2202 **Halfgroat,** *London.* I. Open crown, tressure unbroken; *mm.* 40/-, 40/39 (R. III mule)	275	675
2203 — IIIa. Double arched crown, rosettes on tressure; mm. escallop	60	175
2204 — IIIb. Similar, nothing on tressure. R. Lozenge panel in centre; *mm.* lis	35	90
2205 — — Similar, but also with lis on breast; mm. lis....................................	40	100
2206 — IIIc. Unarched crown with tressure broken. R. Lozenge panel in centre; *mm.* lis	30	70
2206A — — — Similar but smaller dies and much smaller lettering	30	75

2207   2211

2207 *Canterbury,* Archb. Morton. I. Open crown, crosses by neck. R. M in centre; *mm.* tun/-	30	75
2208 — — II. Similar, but double-arched crown; no *mm.*	30	70
2209 III King and Archb. jointly. As last but without M; (a) early lettering, trefoil stops; *mm.* lis, tun and lis/lis	30	75
2210 — — (b) ornate lettering, rosette stops; *mm.* tun, lis in combinations	25	60
2211 — — (c) — saltire or no stops; *mm.* 123, 123 & 30/123	25	60
2212 *York,* Royal mint. (a) Double-arched crown, lis on breast (rarely omitted). R. Lozenge panel in centre; *mm.* lis	40	95
2213 — — (b) Similar, but unarched crown, tressure broken, *mm.* lis.	30	70

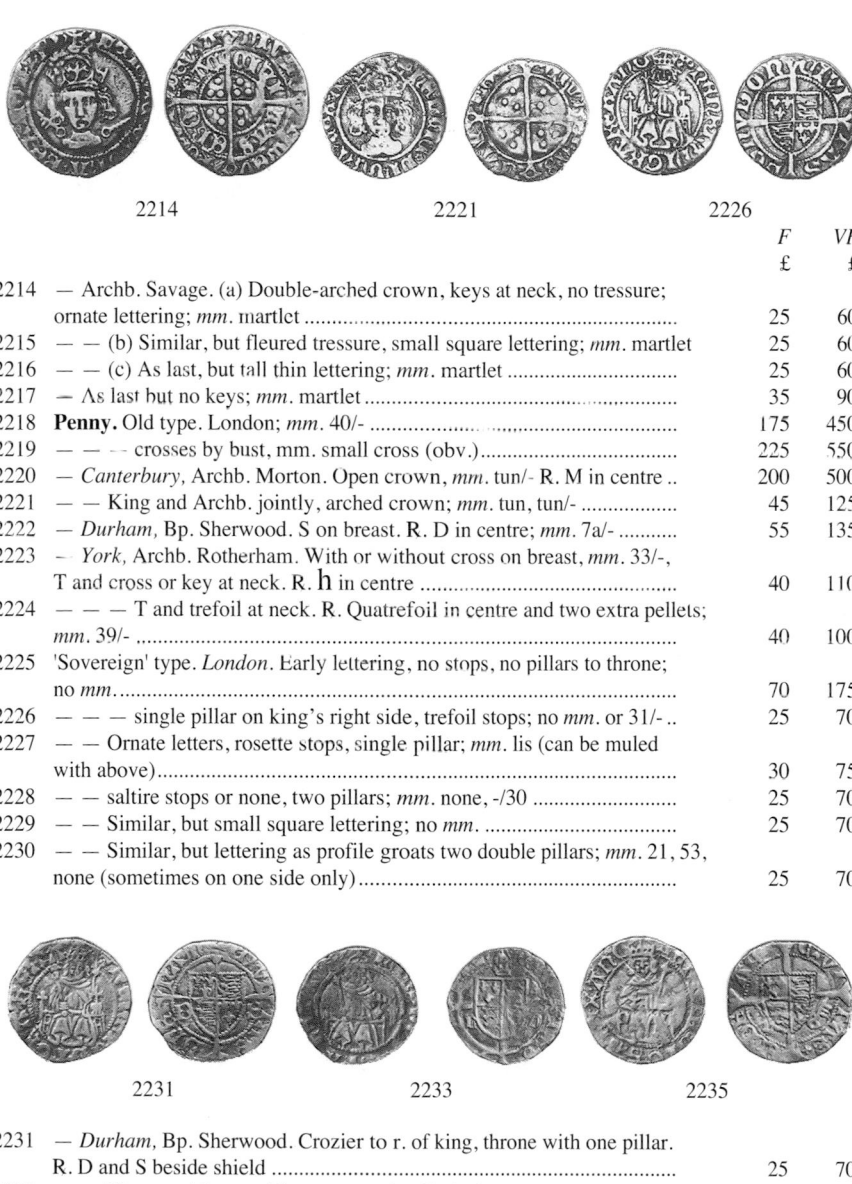

2214   2221   2226

| | F | VF |
| | £ | £ |

2214   — Archb. Savage. (a) Double-arched crown, keys at neck, no tressure;
ornate lettering; *mm.* martlet 25   60

2215   — — (b) Similar, but fleured tressure, small square lettering; *mm.* martlet 25   60

2216   — — (c) As last, but tall thin lettering; *mm.* martlet 25   60

2217   — As last but no keys; *mm.* martlet 35   90

2218   **Penny.** Old type. London; *mm.* 40/- 175   450

2219   — — crosses by bust, mm. small cross (obv.)..................................... 225   550

2220   — *Canterbury,* Archb. Morton. Open crown, *mm.* tun/- R. M in centre .. 200   500

2221   — — King and Archb. jointly, arched crown; *mm.* tun, tun/- 45   125

2222   — *Durham,* Bp. Sherwood. S on breast. R. D in centre; *mm.* 7a/- 55   135

2223   — *York,* Archb. Rotherham. With or without cross on breast, *mm.* 33/-,
T and cross or key at neck. R. h in centre 40   110

2224   — — — T and trefoil at neck. R. Quatrefoil in centre and two extra pellets;
mm. 39/- 40   100

2225   'Sovereign' type. *London.* Early lettering, no stops, no pillars to throne;
no *mm.* 70   175

2226   — — — single pillar on king's right side, trefoil stops; no *mm.* or 31/- .. 25   70

2227   — — Ornate letters, rosette stops, single pillar; *mm.* lis (can be muled
with above)... 30   75

2228   — — saltire stops or none, two pillars; *mm.* none, -/30 25   70

2229   — — Similar, but small square lettering; no *mm.* 25   70

2230   — — Similar, but lettering as profile groats two double pillars; *mm.* 21, 53,
none (sometimes on one side only).. 25   70

2231   2233   2235

2231   — *Durham,* Bp. Sherwood. Crozier to r. of king, throne with one pillar.
R. D and S beside shield 25   70

2232   — — Throne with two pillars, no crozier. R. As last 30   75

2233   — — Bp. Fox. Throne with one pillar. R. Mitre above shield, RD or DR
at sides, no *mm.*.. 25   65

2234   — — Similar, but two pillars... 25   70

		F £	VF £
2235	*York,* Archb. Rotherham. Keys below shield; early lettering, trefoil stops, no pillars to throne, no *mm*	25	65
2236	— — — single pillar	25	60
2237	— — — — ornate lettering, rosette or no stops, ...	25	65
2238	— — — two pillars sometimes with crosses between legs of throne	25	65
2239	**Halfpenny,** *London.* I. Open crown; *mm.* 40, 42	35	100
2240	— — — trefoils at neck; no *mm.*, rose	40	115
2241	— — — crosses at neck; *mm.* rose	35	110
2242	— II. Double arched crown; *mm.* cinquefoil, none	25	60
2243	— — — saltires at neck; no *mm.*	25	60
2244	— III. Crown with single arch, ornate lettering; no *mm.*	20	50

2245   2248

		F £	VF £
2245	— V. Much smaller portrait; *mm.* pheon, lis, none	20	55
2246	*Canterbury,* Archb. Morton. I. Open crown, crosses by neck; R. M in centre	80	175
2247	— — II. Similar, but arched crown, saltires by bust; *mm.* profile eye (82)	70	165
2247A	— — — no marks at neck	85	200
2248	— III. King and Archb. Arched crown; *mm.* lis, none	45	110

2249   2250

		F £	VF £
2249	*York,* Archb. Savage. Arched crown, key below bust	75	175
2250	**Farthing,** *London.* hENRIC DI GRA REX (A), arched crown	125	325

*No.s 2239-49 have *mm.* on *obv.* only.

Profile issue

2251	Testoon (ls.). Type as groat. hENRIC (VS); *mm.* lis	4250	8000
2252	— hENRIC VII; *mm.* lis	4500	8500

2253

2253	— hENRIC SEPTIM; *mm.* lis...	4750	9500

2254 2258

	F	VF
	£	£

2254 **Groat,** *Tentative issue* (contemporary with full-face groats). Double band
to crown, hҽnRIC VII; *mm.* none, 105/-, -/105: 105/85, 105, 85, 21 ..... | 135 | 325
2255 — — — tressure on *obv.*; *mm.* cross-crosslet.. | 2250 | 5000
2256 — — hҽnRIC (VS); *mm.* 105, -/105, 105/ 85, none.............................. | 300 | 750
2257 — — hҽnRIC SҽPTIM; *mm.* -/105 .... | 2350 | 5250
2258 *Regular issue.* Triple band to crown; *mm.* 21, 53
(both *mm.*s may occur on some *obv.* or *rev.*) .... | 65 | 175
2259 **Halfgroat,** *London.* As last; *mm.* 105, 53/105, 105/53, 53...................... | 70 | 200
2260 — — no numeral after King's name, no *mm.,* -/lis................................. | 450 | 975

2261 2262

2261 *Canterbury,* King and Archb. As London, but *mm.* 94, 33, 94/33............ | 35 | 100
2262 *York,* Archb. Bainbridge. As London, but two keys below shield; *mm.*
94, 33, 33/94.. | 30 | 95
2262A — Similar but no keys; *mm.* rose .... | 65 | 175

2263

2263 — — XB beside shield; *mm.* rose/martlet .... | 300 | 750
2263A — — Similar but two keys below shield *mm.* rose(?)/martlet................. | 325 | 800

Henry VIII is held in ill-regard by numismatists as being the author of the debasement of England's gold and silver coinage; but there were also other important numismatic innovations during his reign. For the first sixteen years the coinage closely followed the pattern of the previous issues, even to the extent of retaining the portrait of Henry VII on the larger silver coins.

In 1526, in an effort to prevent the drain of gold to continental Europe, the value of English gold was increased by 10%, the sovereign to 22s. 0d. and the angel to 7s. 4d., and a new coin valued at 4s. 6d.—the Crown of the Rose—was introduced as a competitor to the French *écu au soleil*. The new crown was not a success and within a few months it was replaced by the Crown of the Double Rose valued at 5s but made of gold of only 22 carat fineness, the first time gold had been minted below the standard 23c. At the same time the sovereign was again revalued to 22s. 6d. and the angel to 7s. 6d., with a new coin, the George Noble, valued at 6s. 8d. (one-third pound).

The royal cyphers on some of the gold crowns and half-crowns combine the initial of Henry with those of his queens: Katherine of Aragon, Anne Boleyn and Jane Seymour. The architect of this coinage reform was the chancellor, Cardinal Thomas Wolsey, who besides his other changes had minted at York a groat bearing his initials and cardinal's hat in addition to the other denominations normally authorized for the ecclesiastical mints.

When open debasement of the coinage began in 1544 to help finance Henry's wars, the right to coin of the archbishops of Canterbury and York and of the bishop of Durham was not confirmed. Instead, a second royal mint was opened in the Tower as in subsequent years were six others, at Southwark, York, Canterbury, Bristol, Dublin and Durham House in the Strand. Gold, which fell to 23c. in 1544, 22c. in 1545, and 20c. in 1546 was much less debased than silver which declined to 9oz 2dwt. in 1544, 6oz 2dwt. in 1545 and 4oz 2dwt. in 1546. At this last standard the blanched silver surface of the coins soon wore away to reveal the copper alloy beneath which earned for Henry the nickname 'Old Coppernose'.

Mintmarks

53	69	70	108	33	94	73	11
105	22	23	30	78	15	24	110
52	72a	44	8	65a	114	121	90
36	106	56	S	E	116	135	

1509-26	Pheon (53)		1509-14	Martlet (94, *York*)
	Castle (69)		1509-23	Radiant star (22, *Durham & York*)
	Castle with H (70, gold)		1513-18	Crowned T (135, *Tournai*)
	Portcullis crowned (108)		1514-26	Star (23, *York & Durham*)
	Rose (33, *Canterbury*)			Pansy (30, *York*)
	Martlet (94, *Canterbury*)			Escallop (78, *York*)
	Pomegranate (73, but broader, *Cant.*)			Voided cross (15, *York*)
	Cross fitchée (11, *Cant.*)		1523-26	Spur rowel (24, *Durham*)
	Lis (105, *Canterbury, Durham*)			
1526-44	Rose (33)		1526-32	Cross patonce (8, *Cant.*)
	Lis (105)			T (114, *Canterbury*)

Sunburst 110)
Arrow (52)
Pheon (53)
Lis (106)
Star (23, *Durham*)
1526-9   Crescent (72a, *Durham*)
Trefoil (44 variety, *Durham*)
Flower of eight petals and circle centre (*Durham*)
1526-30   Cross (7a, sometimes slightly voided, *York*)
Acorn (65a, *York*)

Uncertain mark (121, *Canterbury*)
1529-44   Radiant star (22, *Durham*)
1530-44   Key (90, *York*)
1533-44   Catherine wheel (36, *Canterbury*)
1544-7   Lis (105 and 106)
Pellet in annulet (56)
S (Southwark)
C or E (Southwark)
1546-7   WS monogram (116, *Bristol*)

GOLD

First coinage, 1509-26

		F	VF
		£	£
2264	**Sovereign** (20s.). Similar to last sov. of Hen. VII; *mm.* 108	3500	8000
2264A	**Ryal** (10s.) King in ship holding sword and shield. R. Similar to 1950, *mm.*-/108	*Extremely rare*	
2265	**Angel** (6s. 8d.). As Hen. VIII, but hᴇnʀɪc? VIII DI GRA Rᴇx, etc.; *mm.* 53, 69, 70, 70/69, 108, R. May omit h and rose, or rose only; mm. 69, 108	250	525
2266	**Half-angel.** Similar (sometimes without VIII), *mm.* 69, 70, 108/33, 108	225	475

2265

Second coinage, 1526-44

2267

2267	**Sovereign** (22s. 6d.). As 2264, R. single or double tressure *mm.* 110, 105, 105/52	3000	6500
2268	**Angel** (7s. 6d.). As 2265, hᴇnʀɪc VIII D(I) G(RA) R(ᴇx) etc,; mm. 110, 105	425	900
2269	**Half-angel.** Similar; *mm.* lis	575	1200

Second coinage

2270   2272

	F	*VF*
	£	£
2270 **George-noble** (6s. 8d.). As illustration; *mm*. rose	3000	6500
2270A— Similar, but more modern ship with three masts, without initials hR. R. St. George brandishing sword behind head.	5500	12000
2271 **Half-George-noble.** Similar to 2270 *mm* rose, lis	*Extremely rare*	
2272 **Crown of the rose** (4s. 6d., 23 c. 3 ¹/₂ gr.). As illustration; *mm*. rose, two legend varieties	6000	12500
2273 **Crown of the double-rose** (5s., 22 c). Double-rose crowned, hK (Henry and Katherine of Aragon) both crowned in field. R. Shield crowned; *mm*. rose	235	475
2274 — hK both sides; *mm*. rose/lis, lis, arrow	245	500
2275* — hK/hA or hA/hK; *mm*. arrow	600	1250
2276* — hR/hK or hI/hR; *mm*. arrow	525	1050
2277 — hA (Anne Boleyn); *mm*. arrow	500	1050
2278 — hA/hR; *mm*. arrow	600	1250

2279   2285

2279 — hI (Jane Seymour); *mm*. arrow	300	625
2280* — hK/hI; *mm*. arrow	550	1100
2281 — hR/hI; *mm*. arrow	475	975
2282 — hR (Rex); *mm*. arrow	275	575
2283 — — but with hIBERIE REX; *mm*. pheon	575	1200
2284 **Halfcrown.** Similar but king's name henric 8 on *rev*., no initials; *mm*. rose	400	850
2285 — hK uncrowned on *obv*.; *mm*. rose	235	500
2286 — hK uncrowned both sides; *mm*. rose/lis, lis, arrow	250	525
2287 — hI uncrowned both sides; *mm*. arrow	300	650
2288 — hR uncrowned both sides; hIB REX; *mm*. pheon	450	950

*The hK initials may on later coins refer to Katherine Howard (Henry's fifth wife).

Third coinage, 1544-7

2291

		F £	VF £
2289	**Sovereign,** I (20s., Wt. 200 gr., 23 c.). As illustration but king with larger face and larger design; *mm*. lis	4500	10000
2290	II (20s., wt. 200 or 192 grs., 23, 22 or 20 ct.). *Tower*. As illustration; *mm*. lis, pellet in annulet/lis	1600	3750
2291	— *Southwark*. Similar; *mm*. S, Є/S	1500	3500
2292	— — Similar but Є below shield; *mm*. S/Є	2000	4500
2293	— *Bristol*. As London but *mm*. WS/-	2350	5500

2294

2294	**Half-sovereign** (wt. 100 or 96 gr.), *Tower*. As illus.; *mm*. lis, pellet in annulet	275	600
2295	— Similar, but with annulet on inner circle (either or both sides)	300	650
2296	*Southwark. Mm*. S	325	725
2297	— Є below shield; *mm*. S, Є, S/Є, Є/S, (known without sceptre; *mm*. S)	300	700
2298	*Bristol*. Lombardic lettering; *mm*. WS, WS/-	500	1100
2299	**Angel** (8s., 23 c). Annulet by angel's head and on ship; hЄnRIC' 8; *mm*. lis	245	500
2300	— Similar, but annulet one side only or none	250	525
2301	**Half-angel.** Annulet on ship; *mm*. lis	250	500
2302	— No annulet on ship; *mm*. lis	265	575

2303 2304

2303	— Three annulets on ship; *mm*. lis	275	600
2304	**Quarter-angel** Angel wears armour; *mm*. lis	240	500
2304A	— Angel wears tunic; *mm*. lis	250	525

Third coinage

		F £	VF £
2305	**Crown,** *London*. Similar to 2283, but hЄПRIC' 8 ; Lombardic lettering; mm . 56	250	500
2306	— without RVTILAΠS; *mm*. 56	265	550
2307	— — — with annulet on inner circle	265	550
2307A	— King's name omitted. DEI GRA both sides, *mm*. 56	450	950
2308	— *Southwark*. As 2306; *mm*. S, Є, E/S, Є/-, E/Є	325	650
2309	*Bristol*. hЄПRIC VIII. ROSA etc. R. D G, etc.; *mm*.-/WS	250	525
2310	— Similar but hЄПRIC(VS) 8 R. DЄI) G(RA); *mm*. -/WS, WS	250	535
2311	**Halfcrown,** *London*. Similar to 2288; *mm*. 56, 56/-	200	400
2312	— — with annulet on inner circle *mm*. 56	210	425
2313	*Southwark*. As 2311; *mm*. S	275	550
2314	— *O*. hЄПRIC 8 ROSA SINЄ SPIΠ. R. DЄI GRA, etc.; *mm*. Є	285	575
2315	*Bristol. O*. RVTILAΠ S, etc. R. hЄПRIC 8; *mm*. WS/-	275	550

For other gold coins in Henry's name see page 218-19.

SILVER

First coinage, 1509-26

2316   2327

2316	**Groat.** Portrait of Hen. VII. *London mm*. 53, 69, 108, 108 over 135...	60	175
2317	— *Tournai; mm*. crowned T. R. CIVITAS TORΠACЄП*	300	825
2318	**Halfgroat.** Portrait of Hen. VII. London; *mm*. 108, 108/-	70	200
2319	— *Canterbury*, Archb. Warham. POSVI *rev*.; *mm*. rose	75	225
2320	— — — WA above shield; *mm*. martlet	45	135
2321	— — — WA beside shield; *mm*. cross fitchee	45	135
2322	— — CIVITAS CAΠTOR *rev*., similar; *mm*. 73, 105, 11/105	35	100
2323	— *York*, POSVI *rev*., Archb. Bainbridge (1508-14). Keys below shield; *mm*. martlet	40	120
2324	— — — XB beside shield no keys; *mm*. martlet	55	135
2325	— — — Archb. Wolsey (1514-30). Keys and cardinal's hat below shield; *mm*. 94, 22	90	250
2326	— — CIVITAS ЄBORACI *rev*. Similar; *mm*. 22, 23, 30, 78, 15, 15/78	35	100
2327	— — As last with TW beside shield; *mm*. voided cross	65	165
2327A	— *Tournai*. As 2317	975	2650

*Other non-portrait groats and half-groats exist of this mint, captured during an invasion of France in 1513. (Restored to France in 1518.)

2332   2335   2336

		F	VF
		£	£
2328	**Penny,** 'Sovereign' type, *London; mm.* 69, 108 /-	30	85
2329	— *Canterbury.* WA above shield; *mm.* martlet	70	185
2330	— — — WA beside shield; *mm.* 73/-	50	125
2331	— *Durham,* Bp. Ruthall (1509-23). TD above shield; *mm.* lis	25	65
2332	— — — TD beside shield; *mm.* lis, radiant star	25	65
2333	— — Bp. Wolsey (1523-9). DW beside shield, cardinal's hat below; spur rowel	125	300
2334	**Halfpenny.** Facing bust, hЄnRIC DI GRA RЄX (AGL). *London; mm.* 69, 108/-	20	55
2335	— *Canterbury.* WA beside bust; *mm.* 73/-, 11	50	125
2335A	— *York.* Key below bust, *mm.* star.	90	240
2336	**Farthing.** *mm.* 108/-, hЄnRIC DI GRA RЄX, portcullis. R. CIVITAS LOnDON, rose in centre of long cross	250	600

Second coinage, 1526-44

2337   2337D   2337E

		F	VF
2337	**Groat.** His own young portrait. *London;* bust r., with heavy jowls; *mm.* rose, mainly Roman letters, both sides, roses in cross ends	250	675
2337A	— *Obv.* as last. R. Lombardic letters, saltires in cross ends; *mm.* rose	150	400
2337B	Bust as 2337 but Lombardic letters. R. Lombardic letters but roses in cross ends; *mm.* rose	175	475
2337C	— *Obv.* as last. R. As 2337A; *mm.* rose	125	325
2337D	Second bust, Greek profile, longer hair, less heavy jowls; *mm.* rose	65	175
2337E	Third bust, stereotyped as ill. *mm.* 33-53 (muling occurs)	45	120
2338	— — with Irish title HIB; larger flan, saltires in cross ends; *mm.* 53, 105 53/105, 105/53,	265	625
2339	— *York*, Archb. Wolsey. TW beside shield, cardinal's hat below; *mm.* voided cross, acorn, muled (both ways)	75	185
2340	— — — omits TW; *mm.* voided cross	175	475

Second coinage silver

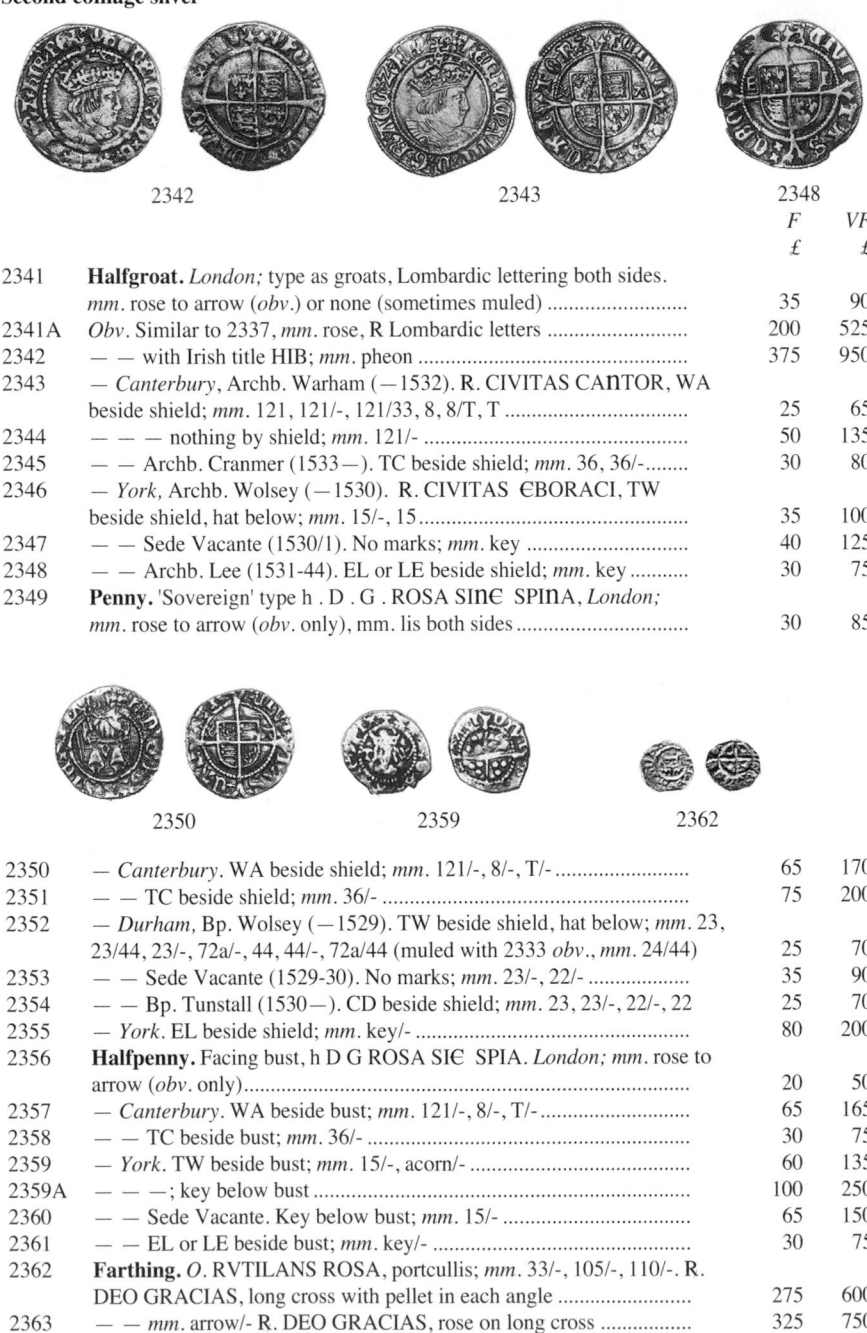

2342   2343   2348

		F £	VF £
2341	**Halfgroat.** *London;* type as groats, Lombardic lettering both sides. *mm.* rose to arrow (*obv.*) or none (sometimes muled)	35	90
2341A	*Obv.* Similar to 2337, *mm.* rose, R Lombardic letters	200	525
2342	— — with Irish title HIB; *mm.* pheon	375	950
2343	— *Canterbury,* Archb. Warham (−1532). R. CIVITAS CAПTOR, WA beside shield; *mm.* 121, 121/-, 121/33, 8, 8/T, T	25	65
2344	— — — nothing by shield; *mm.* 121/-	50	135
2345	— — Archb. Cranmer (1533−). TC beside shield; *mm.* 36, 36/-	30	80
2346	— *York,* Archb. Wolsey (−1530). R. CIVITAS ЄBORACI, TW beside shield, hat below; *mm.* 15/-, 15	35	100
2347	— — Sede Vacante (1530/1). No marks; *mm.* key	40	125
2348	— — Archb. Lee (1531-44). EL or LE beside shield; *mm.* key	30	75
2349	**Penny.** 'Sovereign' type h . D . G . ROSA SIПЄ SPIПA, *London;* *mm.* rose to arrow (*obv.* only), mm. lis both sides	30	85

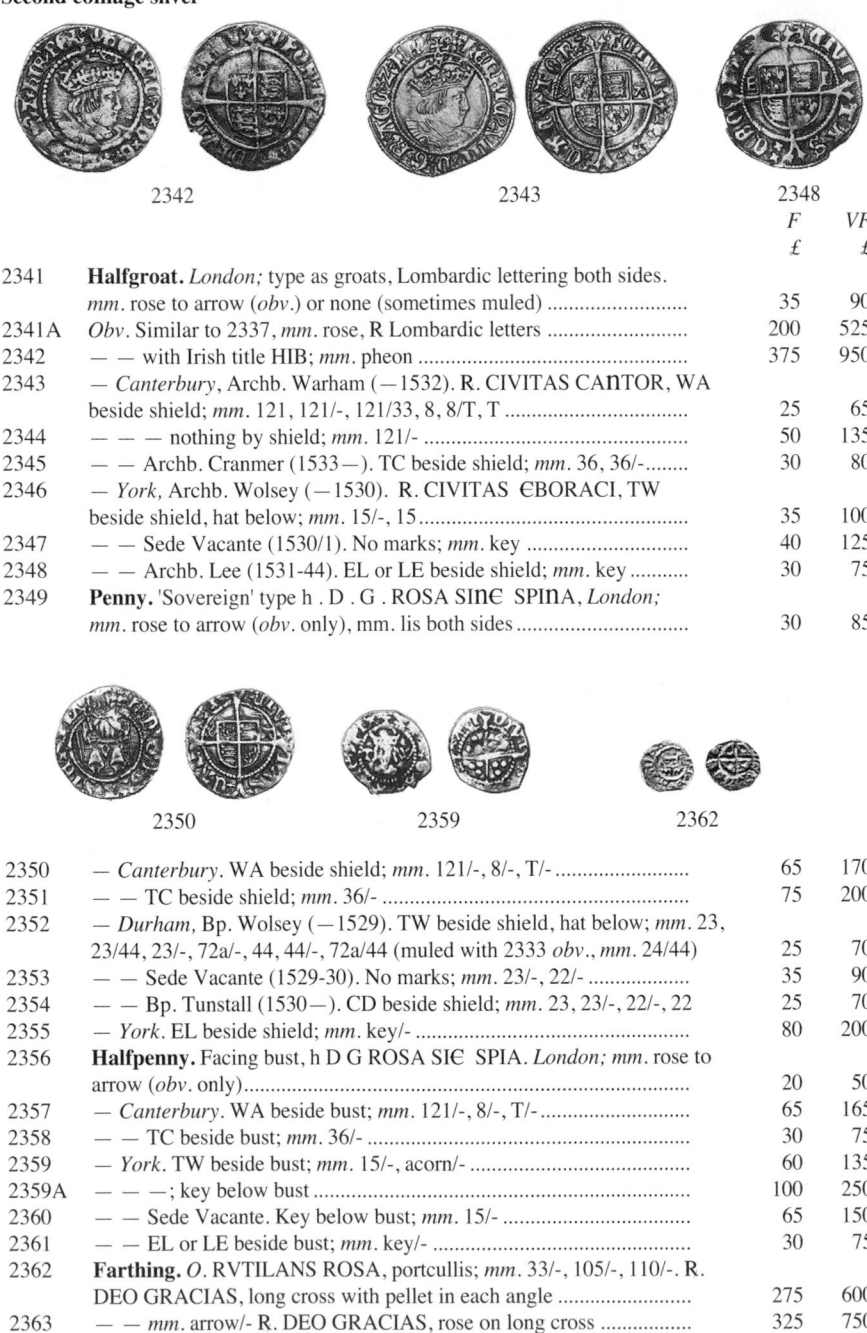

2350   2359   2362

2350	— *Canterbury.* WA beside shield; *mm.* 121/-, 8/-, T/-	65	170
2351	— — TC beside shield; *mm.* 36/-	75	200
2352	— *Durham,* Bp. Wolsey (−1529). TW beside shield, hat below; *mm.* 23, 23/44, 23/-, 72a/-, 44, 44/-, 72a/44 (muled with 2333 *obv.*, *mm.* 24/44)	25	70
2353	— — Sede Vacante (1529-30). No marks; *mm.* 23/-, 22/-	35	90
2354	— — Bp. Tunstall (1530−). CD beside shield; *mm.* 23, 23/-, 22/-, 22	25	70
2355	— *York.* EL beside shield; *mm.* key/-	80	200
2356	**Halfpenny.** Facing bust, h D G ROSA SIЄ SPIA. *London; mm.* rose to arrow (*obv.* only)	20	50
2357	— *Canterbury.* WA beside bust; *mm.* 121/-, 8/-, T/-	65	165
2358	— — TC beside bust; *mm.* 36/-	30	75
2359	— *York.* TW beside bust; *mm.* 15/-, acorn/-	60	135
2359A	— — —; key below bust	100	250
2360	— — Sede Vacante. Key below bust; *mm.* 15/-	65	150
2361	— — EL or LE beside bust; *mm.* key/-	30	75
2362	**Farthing.** *O.* RVTILANS ROSA, portcullis; *mm.* 33/-, 105/-, 110/-. R. DEO GRACIAS, long cross with pellet in each angle	275	600
2363	— — *mm.* arrow/- R. DEO GRACIAS, rose on long cross	325	750
2363A	— *Canterbury.* O. Similar. R. Similar. *mm.* 36/-	450	975

2364 2368

		F	VF
		£	£

Third coinage, 1544-7 (Silver progressively debased. 9oz (2dwt), 6oz (2dwt) 4oz (2dwt)).

2364   **Testoon.** *Tower.* hENRIC'. VIII, etc. R. Crowned rose between h
and R.POSVI, etc.; *mm.* lis, lis and 56, lis/two lis 525   1600

2365   — hENRIC 8, *mm.* 105 and 56, 105/56, 105 and 56/56, 56 425   1350

2366   annulet on inner circle of rev. or both sides; *mm.* pellet in
annulet.. 450   1400

2367   *Southwark.* As 2365. R. CIVITAS LONDON; *mm.* S, Є, S/Є, Є/S 475   1450

2368   *Bristol. Mm.*-/WS monogram. (Tower or local dies.) 600   1750

2384   Bust 1   Bust 2   Bust 3

2369   **Groat.** *Tower.* As ill. above, busts 1, 2, 3; *mm.* lis/-, lis.................. 55   175

2369A   Bust 1, R. As second coinage; i.e. saltires in forks; *mm.* lis 70   225

2370   Bust 2 or 3 annulet on inner circle, both sides or rev. only 65   185

2371   *Southwark.* As 2367, busts 1, 2, 3, 4; no *mm.* or lis/-; S or S and Є or
Є in forks 60   180

2372   *Bristol. Mm.*-/WS monogram, Bristol bust and Tower bust 2 or 3 55   175

2373   *Canterbury.* Busts 1, 2, (2 var); no *mm*, or lis/– 65   200

2374   *York.* Busts 1 var., 2, 3, no *mm.* 55   175

2375   **Halfgroat.** *Tower.* As 2365, bust 1; *mm.* lis, none 50   150

2376   *Southwark.* As 2367, bust 1; no *mm.*; S or Є and S in forks.............. 110   275

2377   *Bristol. Mm.*-/WS monogram.. 45   135

2378   *Canterbury.* Bust 1; no *mm.* 30   100

2379   *York.* Bust 1; no *mm.* 40   135

2380   **Penny.** *Tower.* Facing bust; no *mm.* or lis/- 30   100

2381   *Southwark.* Facing bust; *mm.* S/-, Є/-, -/Є 90   250

2382   *Bristol.* Facing bust; no *mm.* (Tower dies or local but truncated at neck) 35   110

2383   *Canterbury.* Facing bust; no *mm.*... 30   100

2384   *York.* Facing bust; no *mm.* 30   100

2385   **Halfpenny.** *Tower.* Facing bust; no *mm.* or lis/-, pellet in annulet in *rev.*
centre... 45   135

2386   *Bristol.* Facing bust; no *mm.* 55   165

2387   *Canterbury.* Facing bust; no *mm.*, (some read H 8)............................ 40   120

2388   *York.* Facing bust; no *mm.* 30   95

2388A   **Farthing** *obv.* Rose. R. Cross and pellets... 450   975

These coins were struck during the reign of Edward VI but bear the name and portrait of Henry VIII, except in the case of the half-sovereigns which bear the youthful head of Edward.

Mintmarks

56	105	52	K	E	116
66	115	33	122	t	94

GOLD

		F	VF
		£	£
2389	**Sovereign** (20 c), *London*. As no. 2290, but Roman lettering; *mm*. lis	2350	5000
2390	— *Bristol*. Similar but *mm*. WS	2750	6250

2391

2391A

2391	**Half-sovereign.** As 2294, but with youthful portrait with sceptre. *Tower*; *mm*. 52, 105, 94 (various combinations)..	275	600
2391A	— Similar but no sceptre; *mm*. 52, 52/56	300	675
2392	— — — K below shield; *mm*.-/K, none,. E/-	300	675
2393	— — — grapple below shield; *mm*. 122, none, 122/-, -/122................	350	725
2394	— *Southwark. Mm*. E, E/-, -/E, Є /E. Usually Є or E (sometimes retrograde) below shield (sceptre omitted; *mm*. -/E)....................................	300	650
2394A	— — — R. As 2296; *mm*.-/S...	375	800

2395

		F	VF
		£	£
2395	**Crown.** Similar to 2305. *London; mm.* 52, 52/-, -/K, 122, 94, ...	300	650
2396	— Similar but transposed legends without numeral; *mm.* -/arrow	350	750
2396A	-- As 2395, but omitting RVTILANS; *mm.* arrow	375	825
2396B	Similar, but RVTILANS both sides; *mm.* arrow	375	825
2397	— *Southwark.* Similar to 2396; *mm.* E	400	850
2398	— — King's name on *obv.; mm.* E/-, -/E	385	825
2399	**Halfcrown.** Similar to 2311. *London; mm.* 52, K/-, 122/-, 94, -/52	325	675
2399A	As last but E over h on *rev., mm.* 56/52	450	950
2399B	As 2399 but RVTILANS etc. on both sides, *mm.* arrow	375	800
2400	— *Southwark. Mm.* E, E/-, -/E	325	675

SILVER

AR (4oz .333)

2401	**Testoon.** *Tower.* As 2365 with lozenge stops one side; -/56, 56	650	1850
2402	*Southwark.* As 2367; *mm.* S/E	700	1900

Bust 4   Bust 5   Bust 6

Some of the Bristol testoons, groats and halfgroats with WS monogram were struck after the death of Henry VIII but cannot easily be distinguished from those struck during his reign.

2403	**Groat.** *Tower.* Busts 4, 5, 6 (and, rarely, 2). R. POSVI, etc.; *mm.* 105-94 and none (frequently muled)	50	170
2404	*Southwark.* Busts 4, 5, 6. R. CIVITAS LONDON; no *mm.* -/E; lis/-, -/lis, K/E; roses or crescents or S and Є in forks, or rarely annulets	50	165
2405	*Durham House.* Bust 6. R. REDDE CVIQVE QVOD SVVM EST; *mm.* bow	125	400
2406	*Bristol. Mm.* WS on *rev.* Bristol busts A and B, Tower bust 2 and 3 ...	55	175
2407	— — *Mm.* TC on *rev.* Similar, Bristol bust B	80	250
2408	*Canterbury.* Busts 5, 6; no *mm.* or rose/-	55	170
2409	*York.* Busts 4, 5, 6; no *mm.* or lis/-, -/lis	55	170

		F £	VF £
2410	**Halfgroat.** Bust 1. *Tower*. POSVI, etc.; *mm*. 52, 52/-, 52/K , -/K, 52/122, 122, -/122	45	140
2411	— *Southwark*. CIVITAS LONDON; *mm*. E, -/E, none, 52/E, K/E......	30	110
2412	**Halfgroat.** *Durham House*. R. REDD, etc.; *mm*. bow, -/bow	275	650
2413	— *Bristol*. Mm. WS on *rev*.	45	140
2414	— — *mm*. TC on *rev*.	55	160
2415	— *Canterbury*. No *mm*. or t/-, -/t, ...	35	110
2416	— *York*. No *mm*., bust 1 and three quarter facing	45	140

2418   2422   2427

2417	**Penny.** *Tower*. CIVI TAS LONDON. Facing bust; *mm*. 52/-, -/52, -/K, 122/-, -/122, none	30	95
2418	— — three-quarter bust; no *mm*.	35	100
2419	*Southwark*. As 2417; *mm*. E, -/E	55	170
2420	*Durham House*. As groat but shorter legend; *mm*. -/bow	325	825
2421	*Bristol*. Facing busts, as 2382 but showing more body, no *mm*.	50	160
2422	*Canterbury*. Similar to 2417	30	85
2423	— three-quarters facing bust; no *mm*.	35	100
2424	*York*. Facing bust; no *mm*.	30	95
2425	— three-quarters facing bust; no *mm*.	40	120
2426	**Halfpenny.** *Tower*. 52?, none	25	80
2427	*Canterbury*. No *mm*., sometimes reads H8	35	110
2428	*York*. No *mm*.	30	85

Coinage in his own name

The 4 oz. 2.5dwt coins of Henry VIII and those issued under Edward in 1547 and 1548 caused much disquiet, yet at the same time government was prevented by continuing financial necessity from abandoning debasement. A stratagem was devised which entailed increasing the fineness of silver coins, thereby making them appear sound, while at the same time reducing their weight in proportion so that in practice they contained no more silver than hitherto. The first issue, ordered on 24 January 1549, at 8 oz.2 dwt. fine produced a shilling which, at 60 gr., was so light that it was rapidly discredited and had to be replaced in April by another at 6 oz. 2 dwt. Weighing 80 gr., these later shillings proved acceptable.

Between April and August 1551 the issue of silver coins was the worst ever – 3 oz. 2dwt. fine at 72s per lb. before retrenchment came in August, first by a 50% devaluation of base silver coin and then by the issue of a fine standard at 11oz. 1dwt. 'out of the fire'. This was the equivalent of 11oz.3dwt. commixture, and means that since sterling was only 11oz. 2dwt., this issue, which contained four new denominations – the crown, halfcrown, sixpence and threepence – was in effect the finest ever issued under the Tudors.

Some base 'pence' were struck in parallel with the fine silver, but at the devalued rate, they and the corresponding 'halfpence' were used as halfpence and farthings respectively.

The first dates on English coinage appear in this reign, first as Roman numerals and then on the fine issue crowns and halfcrowns of 1551-3, in Arabic numerals.

Mintmarks

66	52	35	115	E	53	122
t	T	111	Y	126	94	91A
92	105	y	97	123	78	26

1548-9	Bow (66, *Durham House*)	1550	Martlet (94)
1549	Arrow (52)	1550	Leopard's head (91A)
	Grapple (122)	1550-1	Lion (92)
	Rose (35, *Canterbury*)		Lis (105, *Southwark*)
	TC monogram (115, *Bristol*)		Rose (33)
	Roman E (*Southwark*)	1551	Y or y (117, *Southwark*)
	Pheon (53)		Ostrich's head (97, gold only)
	t or T (*Canterbury*)	1551-3	Tun (123)
1549-50	Swan (111)		Escallop (78)
	Roman Y (*Southwark*)	1552-3	Pierced mullet (26, *York*)
1549-50	6 (126 gold only)		

GOLD

First period, Apr. 1547-Jan. 1549

2429   2431

		F	VF
		£	£
2429	**Half-sovereign** (20 c). As 2391, but reading EDWARD 6. Tower; *mm.* arrow	625	1350
2430	— *Southwark* (Sometimes with E or Є below shield); *mm.* E	525	1150
2431	**Crown.** RVTILANS, etc., crowned rose between ER both crowned. R. EDWARD 6, etc., crowned shield between ER both crowned; *mm.* arrow, E over arrow/-	2250	5500
2431A	— *Obv.* as last. R. As 2305, *mm.* 52/56	2500	6000
2432	**Halfcrown.** Similar to 2431, but initials not crowned; *mm.* arrow	2000	4500

Second period, Jan. 1549-Apr. 1550

2433

2433	**Sovereign** (22 ct). As illustration; *mm.* arrow, –/arrow, Y,	1800	4250
2434	**Half-sovereign.** Uncrowned bust. *London.* TIMOR etc., MDXLIX on *obv. mm.* arrow	2350	5000

2435

2435	— — SCVTVM, etc., as illustration; *mm.* arrow, **6,** Y	575	1300

	F	VF
	£	£

2436 — *Durham House*. Uncrowned, 1/2 length bust with MDXLVIII at end of
obv. legend; *mm.* bow; SCVTVM etc. 3750 8500

2437 — Normal, uncrowned bust. LVCERNA, etc., on *obv.*; *mm.* bow 3250 7000

2438   2441

2438 — Crowned bust. *London*. EDWARD VI, etc. R. SCVTVM, etc.; *mm.* 52,
122, 111/52, 111, Y, 94.., 500 1150

2439 — *Durham House*. Crowned, half-length bust; *mm.* bow 3500 8000

2440 — — King's name on *obv.* and *rev.*; *mm.* bow (mule of 2439/37) 3000 7500

2441 **Crown.** Uncrowned bust, as 2435; *mm.* 6, Y, 52/-, Y/- 800 1650

2442 — Crowned bust, as 2438; *mm.* 52, 122, 111, Y (usually *obv.* only) 700 1400

2443 **Halfcrown.** Uncrowned bust; R. As 2441, *mm.* arrow, Y, Y/-, 52/- 750 1600

2444 — Crowned bust, as illus. above; *mm.* 52, 52/111, 111, 122, Y, Y/- 650 1350

2445 — Similar, but king's name on *rev.*, *mm.* 52, 122 .... 725 1450

Third period, 1550-3

2446 **'Fine' sovereign** (30s.). King on throne; *mm.* 97, 123 .... 9000 20000

2447 **Double sovereign.** From the same dies, *mm.* 97 .... *Extremely rare*

2444   2448

2448 **Angel** (10s.). As illustration; *mm.* 97, 123 .... 3500 8000

2449 **Half-angel.** Similar, *mm.* 97 .... *Extremely rare*

2450 **Sovereign.** (=20s.). Half-length figure of king r., crowned and holding
sword and orb. R. Crowned shield with supporters; *mm.* y, tun 1100 2650

2450

2451

		F	VF
		£	£
2451	**Half-sovereign**. As illustration above; *mm.* y, tun	725	1500
2452	**Crown**. Similar, but *rev.* SCVTVM etc., *mm.* y, tun	750	1650
2453	**Halfcrown**. Similar, *mm.* tun, y	850	1750

*Small denominations often occur creased or straightened.

SILVER
First period, Apr. 1547-Jan. 1549

2454

		F	VF
2454	**Groat.** Crowned bust r. *Tower*. R. Shield over cross, POSVI, etc.; *mm.* arrow	450	1250
2455	— As last, but EDOARD 6, *mm.* arrow	500	1350
2456	— *Southwark*. *Obv.* as 2454. R. CIVITAS LONDON; *mm.*-/E or none, somethimes S in forks	475	1300
2457	**Halfgroat.** *Tower*. *Obv.* as 2454; *mm.* arrow	425	950
2458	*Southwark*. As 2456; *mm.* arrow, E	450	1000

2459   2460

		F	VF
2459	*Canterbury*. Similar. No *mm.*, reads EDOARD or EDWARD (rare)	175	500
2460	**Penny.** *Tower*. As halfgroat, but E.D.G. etc. R. CIVITAS LONDON; *mm.* arrow	225	600
2461	— *Southwark*. As last, but *mm.* -/E	325	850
2462	*Bristol*. Similar, but reads ED6DG or E6DG no *mm.*	200	525
2463	**Halfpenny.** *Tower*. *O*. As 2460, *mm.* E (?). R. Cross and pellets	325	950
2464	— *Bristol*. Similar, no *mm.* but reads E6DG or EDG	300	900

Second period, Jan. 1549-Apr. 1550

At all mints except Bristol, the earliest shillings of 1549 were issued at only 60 grains but of 8 oz. 2 dwt standard. This weight and size were soon increased to 80 grains., (S.2466 onwards), but the fineness was reduced to 6 oz. 2 dwt so the silver content remained the same.

2465   2466

	F	VF
	£	£

60 gr; 8oz. 2 dwt.

	F	VF
2465 **Shilling**. *Tower*. Broad bust with large crown. *Obv.* TIMOR etc. MDXLIX. R. Small, oval garnished shield dividing ER. EDWARD VI etc., *mm.* 52, no *mm*; slight bust var. *mm.*, –/52	145	525
2465A *Southwark*. As last, *mm.* Y, EY/Y	150	550
2465B *Canterbury*. As last, *mm.* -/rose	250	725
2469 *Durham House*. Bust with elaborate tunic and collar TIMOR etc. MDXLIX. R. Oval shield, very heavily garnished in different style. EDWARD VI etc., *mm.* bow	225	650

80 gr; 6oz. 2 dwt.

	F	VF
2466 *Tower*. Tall, narrow bust with small crown. *Obv.* EDWARD VI etc. MDXLIX or MDL. R. As 2465 but TIMOR etc., *mm.* 52-91a (frequently muled)	80	275
2466A — *Obv.* as last, MDXLIX. R. Heavily garnished shield, Durham House style. *mm.* grapple	165	575
2466B *Southwark*. As 2466, *mm.* Y, Y/swan	85	300
2466C — — — R. as 2466A. *mm.* Y	185	600

2467

	F	VF
2467 *Bristol*. *Obv.* similar to 2466. R. Shield with heavy curved garniture or as 2466, *mm.* TC/rose TC, rose TC	675	1750

2468

	F	VF
2468 *Canterbury*. As 2466, *mm.* T, T/t, t/T, t	100	375

2470	2472	2472C

	F	*VF*
	£	£
2470 *Durham House*. Bust as 2469. INIMICOS etc., no date. R. EDWARD etc.	165	575
2472 — Bust similar to 2466. EDWARD VI etc. R. INIMICOS etc.	125	425
2472A — As last but legends transposed	225	750
2472B *Tower*. Elegant bust with extremely thin neck. R. As 2466, *mm.* martlet	135	450
2472C *Southwark*. As last, *mm.* Y	135	450

For coins of Edward VI countermarked, see p. 236

Third period, 1550-3

Very base issue (1551) 3oz. 2 dwt.

2473	2475

	F	*VF*
2473 **Shilling**, *Tower*. As 2472B. MDL or MDLI, *mm.* lion, rose, lion/rose	90	325
2473A *Southwark*. As last, *mm.* lis/Y, Y/lis, lis	90	325
2474 **Base Penny**. *London. O*. Rose. R. Shield; *mm.* escallop (*obv*.)................	45	135
2475 — — *York. Mm.* mullet (*obv*.) as illustration.............................	40	110
2476 **Base Halfpenny**. As penny, but single rose	150	425

* The base penny and halfpenny were used as halfpenny and farthing respectively.

Fine silver issue, (1551-3) 11oz. 3 dwt.

2478

	F	*VF*
2478 **Crown**. King on horseback with date below horse. R. Shield on cross; *mm.* y. 1551; tun, 1551-3 (1553, wire line inner circle may be missing) .	275	700

2479

		F	VF
		£	£
2479	**Halfcrown**. Walking horse with plume; *mm*. y, 1551	225	575
2480	Galloping horse without plume; *mm*. tun, 1551-3	250	650
2481	Large walking horse without plume; *mm*. tun, 1553	650	1450

2482 2483

2482	**Shilling**. Facing bust, rose l., value XII r. *mm*. y, tun (several bust varieties)	60	185
2483	**Sixpence**. *London*. Similar, as illustration; *mm*. y/-, -/y, y, tun (bust varieties)	75	235
2484	*York*. As last, but CIVITAS EBORACI; *mm*. mullet	120	375

2485 2486

2485	**Threepence**. *London*. As sixpence, but III; *mm*. tun	125	425
2486	*York*. As 2484, but III by bust	225	650

2487 2487A

2487	**Penny**. 'Sovereign' type; *mm*. tun	675	1750
2487A	**Farthing**. *O*. Portcullis, R Cross and Pellets (previously 2477)	650	1650

Mary brought English coins back to the sterling standard and struck all her gold coins at the traditional fineness of 23 c. 3 1/2 gr. The mintmarks usually appear at the end of the first or second word of the legends.

Pomegranate   Halved rose and castle

GOLD

2488

		F	*VF*
		£	£
2488	**'Fine' Sovereign** (30s.). Queen enthroned. R. Shield on rose, MDLIII, MDLIIII and undated, *mm.* pomegranate, half-rose (or mule)	2100	4500
2489	**Ryal** (15s.). As illus, MDLIII. R. As 1950 but A DNO etc. *mm.* pomegranate/-	8000	16500

2489   2490

2490	**Angel** (10s.). Usual type; *mm.* pomegranate, half-rose, none? (Known with rose and M transposed)	625	1250
2491	**Half-angel**. Similar; *mm.* pomegranate, pomegranate/-	1750	3750

SILVER

2492

		F	VF
		£	£
2492	**Groat**. Crowned bust l. R. VERITAS, etc.; *mm.* pomegranate, pomegranate/-	65	235
2493	**Halfgroat**. Similar	475	1350
2494	**Penny**. Similar, but M. D. G. ROSA, etc.	300	850
2495	— As last. R. CIVITAS LONDON; no *mm.*	300	850
2495A	— Base penny. Similar to 2474 but M.D.G. etc.............*All late 19th cent. fabrications*		

The groats and smaller silver coins of this period have Mary's portrait only, but the shillings and sixpences show the bust of the queen's husband, Philip of Spain.

Mintmarks

Lis (105 ⚜ Half-rose and castle ✠

GOLD

2496

		F	VF
		£	£
2496	**Angel**. As illustration; wire line inner circles, calm sea, *mm*. lis............	1700	4000
2496A	— — New-style, large wings, wire line i.c...	1750	4250
2496B	— — As above but beaded i.c..	1800	4500
2497	**Half-angel**. Similar to 2496	4750	9500

SILVER

2498   2500

2498	**Shilling**. Busts face-to-face, full titles, undated, no *mm*.......................	165	550
2499	— — — also without mark of value	175	600
2500	— — 1554..	175	600
2501	— English titles only 1554, 1555...	200	700
2501A	— — undated	225	725
2502	— — without mark of value, 1554, 1555 (rare).....................................	225	725
2503	— — date below bust, 1554, 1555..	700	1650
2504	— — As last, but without ANG., 1555..	750	1750

2505

		F	*VF*
		£	£
2505	**Sixpence**. Similar. Full titles, 1554 (and undated?)	165	600

2506

2506	— English titles only, 1555 (no *mm*., rare), 1557 (*mm*. lis, rounder garnishing)	175	625
2506A	— As last but heavy beaded i.c. on obv. 1555. (Irish 4d. obv. mule)	275	750
2507	— — date below bust, 1554, 1557 (very rare)......................................	475	1000

2508

2508	**Groat**. Crowned bust of Mary 1. R. POSVIMVS etc.; *mm*. lis	70	275
2509	**Halfgroat**. Similar, but POSVIM, *mm*. lis...............................	250	725

2510

2510	**Penny**. Similar to 2495, but P. Z. M. etc.; *mm*. lis.................................	250	700
2510A	**Base penny**. Similar to 2495A, but P. Z. M . etc.; *mm*. halved rose and castle or castle/–, (used as a halfpenny)	45	165

Similar 'pence' of the York mint were made for currency in Ireland

Elizabeth's coinage is particularly interesting on account of the large number of different denominations issued. 'Crown' gold coins were again issued as well as the 'fine' gold denominations. In 1559 the base shillings of Edward VI's second and third coinages were called in and countermarked for recirculation at reduced values. Smaller debased coins were also devalued but not countermarked. The old debased groat became a three halfpence and other coins in proportion. The normal silver coinage was initially struck at .916 fineness as in the previous reign but between 1560 and 1577 and after 1582 the old sterling standard of .925 was restored. Between 1578 and 1582 the standard was slightly reduced and the weights were reduced by 1/32nd in 1601. Gold was similarly reduced slightly in quality 1578-82, and there was a slight weight reduction in 1601.

To help alleviate the shortage of small change, and to avoid the expense of minting an impossibly small silver farthing, a threefarthing piece was introduced to provide change if a penny was tendered for a farthing purchase. The sixpence, threepence, threehalfpence and threefarthings were marked with a rose behind the queen's head to distinguish them from the shilling, groat, half-groat and penny.

Coins of exceedingly fine workmanship were produced in a screw press introduced by Eloye Mestrelle, a French moneyer, in 1561. With parts of the machinery powered by a horse-drawn mill, the coins produced came to be known as 'mill money'. Despite the superior quality of the coins produced, the machinery was slow and inefficient compared to striking by hand. Mestrelle's dismissal was engineered in 1572 and six years later he was hanged for counterfeiting.

Mintmarks

1ST ISSUE   2ND ISSUE   3RD ISSUE

106	21	94	23	53	33	107	92

4TH ISSUE

			74	71	77	65b	27

5TH ISSUE

7	14	113					

6TH ISSUE

			60	54	79	72b	86

1	2	123	124	90	57	0

First Issue
1558-60 Lis (106)
Second Issue
1560-1 Cross crosslet (21)
         Martlet (94)
Third Issue
1560-6 Star (23, milled)
1561-5 Pheon (53)
1565 Rose (33)
1566 Portcullis (107)
1566-7 Lion (92)
1567-70 Coronet (74)

            Lis (105, milled)
1569-71 Castle (71)
1572-3 Ermine (77)
1573-4 Acorn (65b)
1573-7 Eglantine (27)
Fourth Issue
1578-9 Greek cross (7)
1580-1 Latin cross (14)
1582 Sword (113)
Fifth Issue
1582-3 Bell (60)
1582-4 A (54)

1584-6 Escallop (79)
1587-9 Crescent (72b)
1590-2 Hand (86)
1591-5 Tun (123)
1594-6 Woolpack (124)
1595-8 Key (90)
1597-1600 Anchor (57)
1600 **0**
Sixth Issue
1601-2 **1**
1602 **2**

N.B. *The dates for* mms *sometimes overlap. This is a result of using up old dies, onto which the new mark was punched.*

GOLD

Hammered Coinage
First to Third issues, 1559-78. ('Fine' gold of .994. 'Crown' gold of .916 fineness. Sovereigns of 240 gr.). Mintmarks; lis to eglantine.

	F	VF
	£	£

		F	VF
2511	**'Fine' Sovereign** (30 s.) Queen enthroned, tressure broken by throne, reads Z not ET, no chains to portcullis. R. Arms on rose; *mm*. lis.	2000	5250

2512

		F	VF
2512	— — Similar but ET, chains on portcullis; *mm*. crosslet	1750	4250
2513	**Angel**. St. Michael. R. Ship. Wire line inner circles; *mm*. lis.	550	1200
2513A	— Similar, but beaded i.c. on *obv*., *mm*. lis	525	1100
2514	— — Similar, but beaded inner circles; ship to r.; *mm*. 106, 21, 74, 27,..	310	675
2515	— — — Similar, but ship to l.; *mm*. 77-27	335	725
2516	**Half Angel**. As 2513, wire line inner circles; *mm*. lis	1000	2350
2516A	— As last, but beaded i.c.s, legend ends. Z.HIB	550	12150
2517	— As 2514, beaded inner circles; *mm*. 106, 21, 74, 77-27	300	650
2518	**Quarter Angel**. Similar; *mm*. 74, 77-27	275	575

2513   2520A

		F	VF
2519	**Half Pound** (10 s.) Young crowned bust l. R. Arms. Wire line inner circles; *mm*. lis..	1100	2500
2520	— Similar, but beaded inner circles; *mm*. 21, 33-107...............................	425	900
2520A	— — Smaller bust; *mm*. lion	825	1850
2520B	— — Broad bust, ear visible; *mm*. 92, 74, 71	475	1000
2521	**Crown**. As 2519; *mm*. lis..	1350	3250
2522	— Similar to 2520; *mm*. 21, 33-107...	400	850
2522A	— Similar to 2520B; *mm*. 74, 71, 92	425	900
2523	**Half Crown**. As 2519; *mm*. lis..	1050	2500
2524	— Similar to 2520; *mm*. 21, 33-107 (2 busts)	425	900
2524A	— Similar to 2520B; *mm*. 107-71...	450	950

| | F | VF |
| | £ | £ |

Fourth Issue, 1578-82 (`Fine' gold only of .992). *Mms* Greek cross, Latin cross and sword.

2525	**Angel**. As 2514; *mm*. 7, 14, 113	310	675
2526	**Half Angel**. As 2517; *mm*. 7, 14, 113...	300	650
2527	— Similar, but without E and rose above ship; *mm*. latin cross	425	900
2528	**Quarter Angel**. As last; *mm*. 7, 14, 113..	275	550

Fifth Issue, 1583-1600 (`Fine' gold of .979, `crown' gold of .916; pound of 174.5 grs. wt.). Mintmarks: bell to **O**.

2529

| 2529 | **Sovereign** (30 s:). As 2512, but tressure not normally broken by back of throne; *mm*. 54-123 .... | 1600 | 3500 |

2530

| 2530 | **Ryal** (15 s.). Queen in ship. R. Similar to 1950; *mm*. 54-86 (*rev*. only) .. | 3250 | 7500 |

2531

2531	**Angel**. As 2514; *mm*. 60-123, 90-**O**	310	675
2532	**Half Angel**. As 2517; *mm*. 60-86, 90-57...	300	625
2533	**Quarter Angel**. As 2518; *mm*. 60-123, 90-57/–	275	525

| | F | VF |
| | £ | £ |

2534 **Pound** (20 s.). Old bust l., with elaborate dress and profusion of hair; *mm.*,
lion and tun/tun, 123-**O**.. 750 1600

2535

2535 **Half Pound**. Similar; *mm*. tun 600 1300
2535A — Similar but smaller bust with less hair; *mm*. 123-**O** 575 1250

2536

2536 **Crown**. Similar to 2534; *mm*. 123-90. **O** 450 950
2537 **Half Crown**. Similar; *mm*. -/123, 123-0, **O**... 425 900

Sixth Issue, 1601-3 ('Fine' gold of .994, 'crown' gold of .916; Pound of 172 gr.). Mintmarks:
1 and **2**
2538 **Angel**. As 2531; *mm*. **1, 2** 450 975
2539 **Pound**. As 2534; *mm*. **1, 2** 750 1650
2540 **Half Pound**. As 2535A; *mm*. **1, 2**... 675 1450
2541 **Crown**. As 2536; *mm*. **1, 2** 650 1350
2542 **Half Crown**. As 2537; *mm*. **1, 2**.. 650 1350

Milled Coinage, 1561-70

2543

2543 **Half Pound**. Crowned bust l.; *mm*. star, lis 1000 2650
2544 **Crown**. Similar; *mm*. star, lis 950 2400
2545 **Half Crown**. Similar; *mm*. star, lis... 1250 3250

For further details on both AV and AR milled coinage, *see* D. G. Borden *'An introduction to the
milled coinage of Elizabeth I'*. BNJ 1983

SILVER

Hammered Coinage

Countermarked Edward VI base shillings (1559)

2546   2547

		Fair £	*F* £
2546	**Fourpence-halfpenny**. Edward VI 2nd period 6oz and 8oz shillings .... cmkd on obv. with a portcullis; *mm*. 66, –/33, 52, t, 111, Y and 122	650	1350
2547	**Twopence-farthing**. Edward VI 3rd period 3 oz. shillings .... countermarked on obverse with a seated greyhound; *mm*. 92. 105, 35 and 87	750	1600
N.B.	*Occasionally the wrong countermark was used*		

First Issue, 1559-60 (.916 fine, shillings of 96 grs.)

2548   2549

		F £	*VF* £
2548	**Shilling**. Without rose or date. ELIZABET(H), wire line inner circles, pearls on bodice (three similar busts); *mm*. lis.	240	700
2549	— Similar, ELIZABETH, wire line and beaded inner circles, no pearls on bodice (several busts); *mm*. lis..	70	225
2550	**Groat**. Without rose or date, wire line or no inner circles (two busts); *mm*. lis	80	250

2551

2551	— Similar, wire line and beaded inner circles, circles *mm*. lis	45	135
2551A	— — Small bust and shield (from halfgroat punches); *mm*. lis	90	250

	F	VF
	£	£

2552 **Halfgroat**. Without rose or date, wire line inner circles; *mm*. lis .... | 125 | 350
2553 **Penny**. Without rose or date, wire line inner circles; *mm*. lis .... | 165 | 475
2554 — Similar but dated 1558 on *obv*.; *mm*. lis .... | 375 | 950

Second Issue, 1560-1 (.925 fineness, shilling of 96 gr.)

2555   2559   2560

2555 **Shilling**. Without rose or date, beaded inner circles. ET instead of Z
(several bust varieties); *mm*. 21, 94 .... | 60 | 185
2555A— large bust with pearls on bodice as 2548; *mm*. 21, 94 .... | 65 | 225
2556 **Groat**. Without rose or date, bust as 2551; *mm*. 21, 94 .... | 30 | 100
2557 **Halfgroat**. Without rose or date; *mm*. 21, 94 .... | 25 | 75
2558 **Penny**. Without rose or date (three bust varieties); *mm*. 21, 94 .... | 20 | 55

Third Issue, 1561-77 (Same fineness and weight as last)
2559 **Sixpence**. With rose and date, large flan (27 *mm*. or more), large bust with
hair swept back, 1561; *mm*. pheon .... | 110 | 325
2560 — Similar, small bust, 1561; *mm*. pheon .... | 45 | 135
2561 — Smaller flan (26.5 *mm*.). Small regular bust, 1561-6; *mm*. 53-107 ...... | 30 | 90

2561   2561B   2562   2563

2561A— Similar, without rose, 1561; *mm*. pheon .... | 250 | 675
2561B— Similar, very large bust, with rose, 1563-5; *mm*. pheon .... | 50 | 175
2562 — Intermediate bust, ear shows, 1566-74; *mm*. 92-65b (also 1567 *mm*. 71/
74) .... | 30 | 90
2562A— Similar, without date; *mm*. lion, coronet, ermine .... | 325 | 825
2563 — Larger bust, 1573-7; *mm*. 77-27 .... | 30 | 95
2564 **Threepence**. With rose and date 1561, large flan (20.5 *mm*.); *mm*. pheon | 30 | 95
2565 — smaller flan (19 *mm*.). Regular bust, 1561-7; *mm*. 53-92 .... | 20 | 70
2566 — taller bust, ear shows, 1566-77; *mm*. 92-27, 27/-, 27/65b.................... | 20 | 65
2566A— Similar, without rose, 1568; *mm*. coronet .... | 275 | 625

2567   2571

		F £	VF £
2567	**Halfgroat**. Without rose or date; *mm*. 107-71	40	120
2568	**Threehalfpence**. With rose and date 1561, large flan (17 *mm*.) *mm*. pheon	30	90
2569	— — Smaller flan (16 *mm*.); 1561-2, 1564-70, 1572-7; *mm*. 53-27	25	75
2570	**Penny**. Without rose or date; *mm*. 33-71, 65b, 27, 33/107, 92/107, 74/107	20	65
2571	**Threefarthings**. With rose and date 1561-2, 1567, 1568, 1572-7; *mm*. 53, 74, 77-27	45	135

Fourth Issue, 1578-82 (.921 fineness, shilling of 95.6 gr.)

2572

| 2572 | **Sixpence**. As 2563, 1578-82; *mm*. 7-113, 14/113, 14/7 .... | 30 | 90 |

2573   2575

2573	**Threepence**. As 2566, 1578-82; *mm*. 7-113...	20	65
2574	**Threehalfpence**. As 2569, 1578-9, 1581-2; *mm*. 7-113..........................	25	80
2575	**Penny**. As 2570; *mm*. 7-113, 7/14, 14/7	20	60
2576	**Threefarthings**. As 2571, 1578-9, 1581-2; *mm*. 7-113............................	45	135

Fifth Issue, 1582-1600 (.925 fineness, shilling of 96 gr.)

| 2577 | 2578A | 2580 | 2581 |

	F £	VF £
2577 **Shilling**. Without rose or date, ELIZAB; ear concealed (two busts) *mm*. 60-72b, ear shows. *mm*. 79-**0** (mules occur)	55	165
2578 **Sixpence**. As 2572, ELIZABETH, 1582, 1583 *mm*. bell	40	120
2578A — Similar, ELIZAB, 1582-1600; *mm*. 60-**0**, also 1583 *mm*. 79/54	30	95
2579 **Halfgroat**. Without rose or date, two pellets behind bust. R. CIVITAS LONDON; *mm*. 60-**0** (*mm*. bell sometimes without pellets)	15	40
2580 **Penny**. Without rose or date. R. CIVITAS LONDON; *mm*. 60-57, 90/-, 57/-, **0**/-	20	60
2581 **Halfpenny**. Portcullis. R. Cross and pellets; *mm*. none, 54-**0**	20	50

Sixth Issue, 1601-2 (.925 fineness, shilling of 92.9 gr.)

| 2582 | 2583 |

2582 **Crown**. As illustration, *mm*. **1, 2**	525	1200
2583 **Halfcrown**. As illustration, *mm*. **1, 2**	325	750
2584 **Shilling**. As 2577; *mm*. **1, 2**	60	175
2585 **Sixpence**. As 2578A, 1601-2; *mm*. **1, 2**	35	100
2586 **Halfgroat**. As 2579, *mm*. **1, 2, 2**/-	20	50
2587 **Penny**. As 2580, *mm*. **1, 2, 2**/-	20	60
2588 **Halfpenny**. As 2581, *mm*. **1, 2**	25	65

Milled coinage

2589 **Shilling**. Without rose or date; *mm*. star. Plain dress, large size (over 31 *mm*.)	375	1050
2590 — decorated dress, large size	165	600
2591 — — intermediate size (30-31 *mm*.)	100	375
2592 — — small size (under 30 *mm*.)	75	275

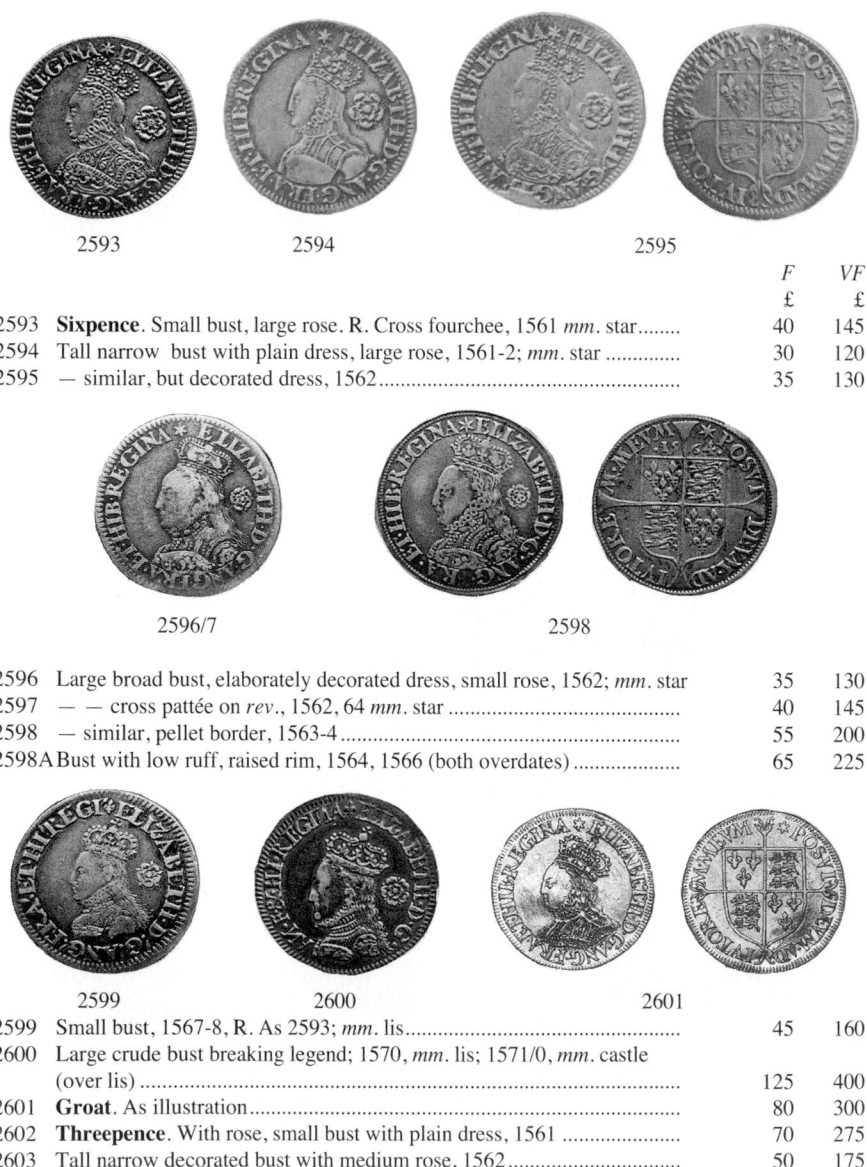

2593 2594 2595

	F	VF
	£	£
2593 **Sixpence**. Small bust, large rose. R. Cross fourchee, 1561 *mm*. star........	40	145
2594 Tall narrow bust with plain dress, large rose, 1561-2; *mm*. star	30	120
2595 — similar, but decorated dress, 1562...	35	130

2596/7 2598

2596 Large broad bust, elaborately decorated dress, small rose, 1562; *mm*. star	35	130
2597 — — cross pattée on *rev*., 1562, 64 *mm*. star	40	145
2598 — similar, pellet border, 1563-4...	55	200
2598A Bust with low ruff, raised rim, 1564, 1566 (both overdates)	65	225

2599 2600 2601

2599 Small bust, 1567-8, R. As 2593; *mm*. lis...	45	160
2600 Large crude bust breaking legend; 1570, *mm*. lis; 1571/0, *mm*. castle (over lis)	125	400
2601 **Groat**. As illustration..	80	300
2602 **Threepence**. With rose, small bust with plain dress, 1561	70	275
2603 Tall narrow decorated bust with medium rose, 1562...............................	50	175
2604 Broad bust with very small rose, 1562..	60	200
2605 Cross pattee on *rev*., 1563, 1564/3...	100	350

2606

		F	VF
		£	£
2606	**Halfgroat**. As groat	80	275
2607	**Threefarthings**. E . D . G . ROSA, etc., with rose. R. CIVITAS LONDON, shield with 1563 above	1250	3000

Portcullis money

Trade coins of 8, 4, 2, and 1 Testerns were coined at the Tower Mint in 1600/1 for the first voyage of the incorporated 'Company of Merchants of London Trading into the East Indies'. The coins bear the royal arms on the obverse and a portcullis on the reverse and have the *mm*. **O**. They were struck to the weights of the equivalent Spanish silver 8, 4, 2 and 1 reales.

2607A

2607A	Eight testerns	800	2000

2607B

2607B	Four testerns	425	975

2607C

		F	VF
		£	£
2607C	Two testerns	400	925

2607D

| 2607D | One testern .... | 350 | 800 |

THE HOUSE OF STUART AND THE COMMONWEALTH, 1603-1714

JAMES I, 1603-25

With the accession of James VI of Scotland to the English throne, the royal titles and coat of arms are altered on the coinage; on the latter the Scottish rampant lion and the Irish harp now appear in the second and third quarters. In 1604 the weight of the gold pound was reduced and the new coin became known as the 'Unite'. Fine gold coins of 23 c. 3 1/2 carat and crown gold of 22 c. were both issued, and a gold four-shilling piece was struck 1604-19. In 1612 all the gold coins had their values raised by 10%; but in 1619 the Unite was replaced by a new, lighter 20s. piece, the 'Laurel', and a lighter rose-ryal, spur-ryal and angel were minted.

In 1613 the king granted Lord Harington a licence to coin farthings of copper as a result of repeated public demands for a low value coinage; this was later taken over by the Duke of Lennox. Towards the end of the reign coins made from silver sent to the mint from the Welsh mines had the Prince of Wales's plumes inserted over the royal arms.

Mintmarks

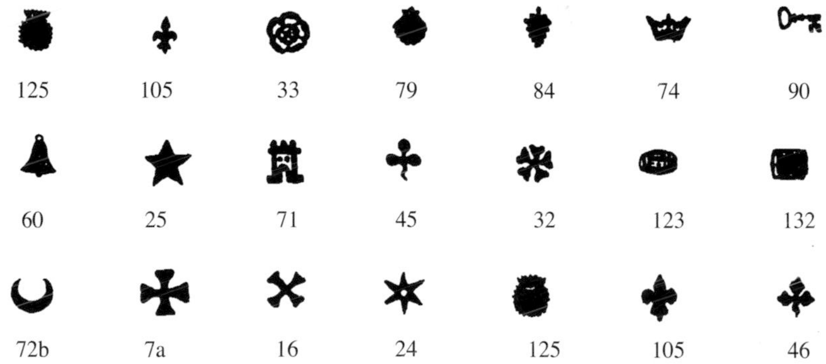

125
105
33
79
84
74
90
60
25
71
45
32
123
132
72b
7a
16
24
125
105
46

First coinage
1603-4 Thistle (125)
1604-5 Lis (105)

Second coinage
1604-5 Lis (105)
1605-6 Rose (33)
1606-7 Escallop (79)
1607 Grapes (84)
1607-9 Coronet (74)
1609-10 Key (90)
1610-11 Bell (60)
1611-12 Mullet (25)
1612-13 Tower (71)
1613 Trefoil (45)
1613-15 Cinquefoil (32)
1615-16 Tun (123)
1616-17 Book on lectern (132)
1617-18 Crescent (72b, gold)
1618-19 Plain cross (7a)
1619 Saltire cross (16, gold)

Third coinage
1619-20 Spur rowel (24)
1620-1 Rose (33)
1621-3 Thistle (125)
1623-4 Lis (105)
1624 Trefoil (46)

GOLD
First coinage, 1603-4 (Obverse legend reads D' . G' . ANG : SCO : etc.)

		F £	*VF* £
2608	**Sovereign** (20s.). King crowned r., half-length, first bust with plain armour. R. EXVRGAT, etc.; *mm*. thistle	700	1500
2609	— second bust with decorated armour; *mm*. thistle, lis	750	1650

2610   2612

2610	**Half-sovereign**. Crowned bust r. R. EXVRGAT, etc.; *mm*. thistle	1650	3750
2611	**Crown**. Similar. R. TVEATVR, etc.; *mm*. 125, 105/125	950	2450
2612	**Halfcrown**. Similar; *mm*. thistle, lis	475	1100

N.B. *The Quarter-Angel of this coinage is considered to be a pattern (possibly a later strike), although coin weights are known.*

Second coinage, 1604-19 (Obverse legend reads D' G' MAG : BRIT : etc.)

2613   2614

2613	**Rose-ryal** (30s., 33s. from 1612). King enthroned. R. Shield on rose; *mm*. 33-90, 25-132	950	2100
2614	**Spur ryal** (15s., 16s. 6d. from 1612). King in ship; *mm*. 33, 79, 74, 25-32, 132	1850	4750
2615	**Angel** (10s., 11s. from 1612). Old type but larger shield; *mm*. 33-74, 60-16	550	1250
2616	— — pierced for use as touch-piece	275	575
2617	**Half-angel** (5s., 5s. 6d. from 1612). Similar; *mm*. 71-132, 7a, 16	1500	3500

Second coinage gold

		F	VF
		£	£
2618	**Unite** (20s., 22s. from 1612). Half-length second bust r. R. FACIAM etc.; *mm*. lis or rose	300	625
2619	— fourth bust; *mm*. rose to cinquefoil	275	550

2620

	2622		11.24		
2620	— fifth bust; *mm*. cinquefoil to saltire		....	285	575
2621	**Double-crown**. Third bust r. R. HENRIC' etc.; *mm*. lis or rose			235	500
2622	Fourth bust; *mm*. rose to bell ....,		\...	225	475
2623	Fifth bust; *mm*. key, mullet to saltire			215	465
2624	**Britain crown**. First bust r.; *mm*. lis to coronet			165	345
2625	Third bust; *mm*. key to cinquefoil			150	325
2626	Fifth bust; *mm*. cinquefoil to saltire			150	325

2627

2627	**Thistle crown** (4s.). As illus.; *mm*. lis to plain cross	160	350
2628	— IR on only one side or absent both sides; *mm*. 79, 74, 71-123	175	375
2629	**Halfcrown**. I' D' G' ROSA SINE SPINA. First bust; *mm*. lis to key	140	275
2630	Third bust; *mm*. key to trefoil, trefoil/tower	145	285
2631	Fifth bust; *mm*. cinquefoil to plain cross..	135	265

Third coinage, 1619-25

2632	**Rose-ryal** (30s.; 196 1/2 grs.). King enthroned. R. XXX above shield; lis, lion and rose emblems around; *mm*. 24, 125, 105	1250	3250
2633	Similar but plain back to throne; *mm*. trefoil	1350	3500

2634   2635

		F	VF
		£	£
2634	**Spur-ryal** (15s.). As illus. R. Somewhat like 2614, but lis are also crowned. *mm*. 24-125, 46	1850	4750
2635	**Angel** (10s.) of new type; *mm*. 24-46	750	1750
2636	— pierced for use as touch-piece	325	650
2637	**Laurel** (20s.; 140 1/2 gr.). First (large) laur, bust l.; *mm*. 24, 24/-	325	650
2638	Second, medium, square headed bust, `SS' tie ends; *mm*. 24, 33	275	550
2638A	Third, small rounded head, ties wider apart; *mm*. 33, 125	250	500

2638B

		F	VF
2638B	Fourth head, very small ties; *mm*. 105, 46	240	475
2638C	Fourth head variety, tie ends form a bracket to value; *mm*. lis	260	525
2639	Fifth, small rather crude bust; *mm*. trefoil	750	1750

2640   2641A

		F	VF
2640	**Half-laurel**. First bust; *mm*. spur rowel	265	550
2641	— As 2638A; *mm*. rose	235	47⁵
2641A	— As 2638B; *mm*. 33-46, 105/-	185	3⁶
2642	**Quarter-laurel**. Bust with two loose tie ends; *mm*. 24-105	135	
2642A	Bust as 2638C; *mm*. 105, 46, 105/46	135	

2642B

	F	VF
	£	£
2642B As last but beaded, i.c. on *rev.* or both sides; *mm.* 105, 46	145	275

Rev. mm. on ¹/₂ *and* ¹/₄ *laurels normally follows REGNA.*

SILVER

2643

First coinage, 1603-4

2643	**Crown**. King on horseback. R. EXVRGAT, etc., shield; *mm.* thistle, lis	500	1200
2644	**Halfcrown**. Similar...	525	1450

2645   2646

2645	**Shilling**. First bust, square-cut beard. R. EXVRGAT, etc.; *mm.* thistle ...	45	200
2646	— Second bust, beard merges with collar; *mm.* thistle, lis	40	145
2647	**Sixpence**. First bust; 1603; *mm.* thistle..	30	135

2648   2650   2651

		F	VF
		£	£
2648	Second bust; 1603-4; *mm*. thistle, lis	30	120
2649	**Halfgroat**. As illustration 2650 but II; *mm*. thistle, lis	20	60
2650	**Penny**. First bust I behind head; *mm*. thistle, lis ?	40	125
2650A	— Second bust; *mm*. thistle, lis..	15	50
2651	**Halfpenny**. As illustration; *mm*. thistle, lis	15	40

Second coinage, 1604-19

2652	**Crown**. King on horseback. R. QVAE DEVS, etc. *rev*. stops; *mm*. 105-84	475	1100
2653	**Halfcrown**. Similar; *mm*. 105-79	825	2250
2654	**Shilling**. Third bust, beard cut square and stands out (*cf*. illus. 2657); *mm*. lis, rose	30	125
2655	— Fourth bust, armour plainer (*cf*. 2658); *mm*. 33-74, 60 over 74	30	130

2656

2656	— Fifth bust, similar, but hair longer; *mm*. 74-7a (several bust varieties)	35	140

2657   2658

2657	**Sixpence**. Third bust; 1604-6; *mm*. lis, rose, escallop	30	100
2658	— Fourth bust; 1605-16; *mm*. rose to book, 90/60, 25/60	30	110
2658A	— Fifth bust, 1618; *mm*. plain cross	575	1250
2659	**Halfgroat**. As illus. but larger crown on *obv*.; *mm*. lis to coronet............	15	40

2660 2663

		F	VF
		£	£
2660	— — Similar, but smaller crown on *obv.*; *mm.* coronet to plain cross	15	40
2660A	As before, but TVEATVR legend both sides; *mm.* plain cross over book?	45	125
2661	**Penny.** As halfgroat but no crowns; *mm.* 105-32,7a and none, -/84, 32/-	15	35
2662	— As before but TVEATVR legend both sides; *mm.* mullet	40	110
2663	**Halfpenny.** As illus.; *mm.* 105- 25, 32; all *mms* on *rev.* only	15	35

Third coinage, 1619-25

| 2664 | **Crown.** As 2652, with plain or grass ground line, colon stops on *obv.*, no stops on *rev.*; *mm.* 33-46 .... | 250 | 550 |

2665

| 2665 | — — plume over shield; *mm.* 125-46... | 300 | 700 |

2666

| 2666 | **Halfcrown.** As 2664 but normally plain ground line only; all have bird-headed harp; *mm.* 33-46 .... | 110 | 275 |
| 2666A | — — Similar but no ground line; *mm.* rose .... | 300 | 750 |

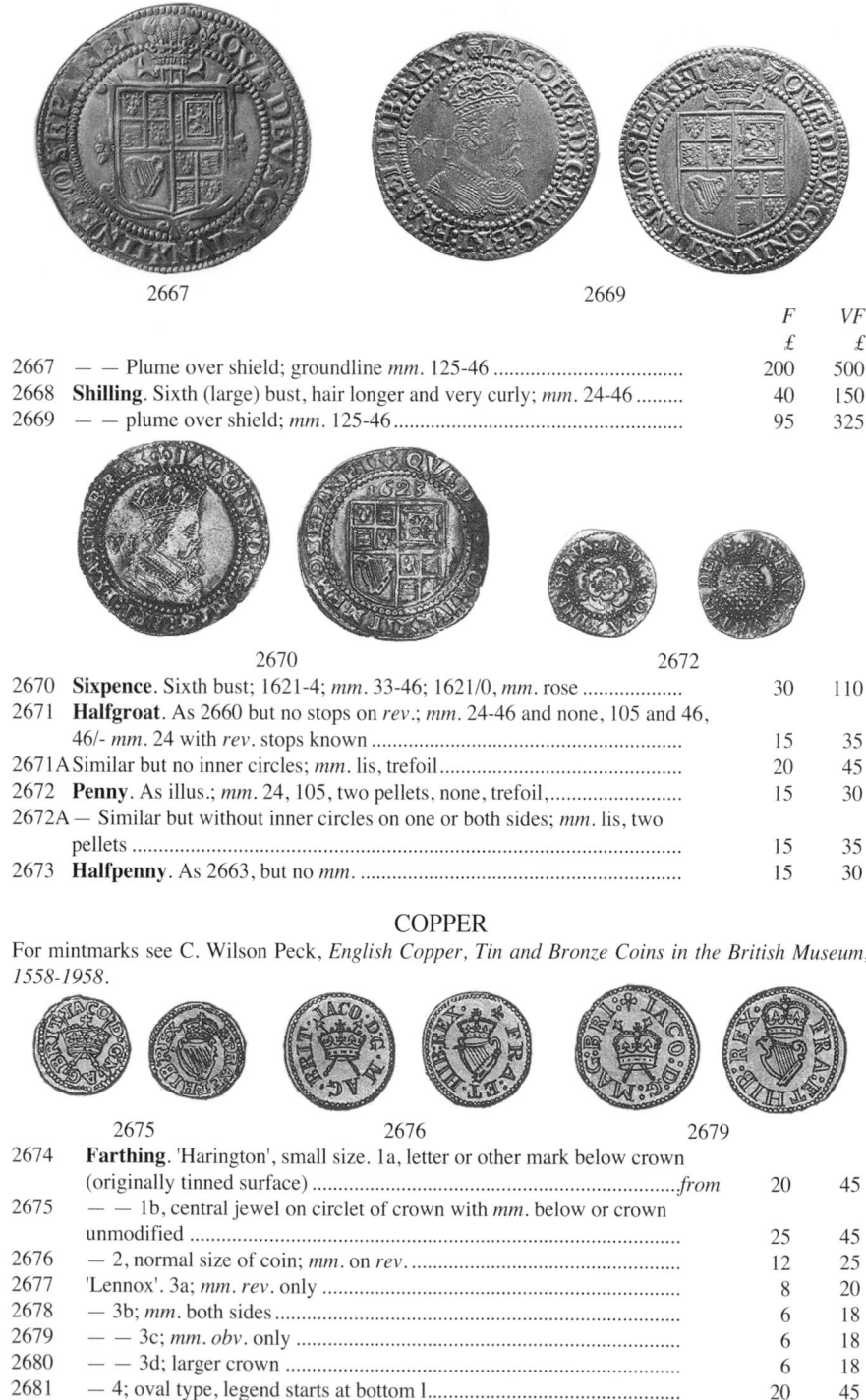

2667   2669

		F	VF
		£	£
2667	— — Plume over shield; groundline *mm*. 125-46	200	500
2668	**Shilling**. Sixth (large) bust, hair longer and very curly; *mm*. 24-46	40	150
2669	— — plume over shield; *mm*. 125-46	95	325

2670   2672

2670	**Sixpence**. Sixth bust; 1621-4; *mm*. 33-46; 1621/0, *mm*. rose	30	110
2671	**Halfgroat**. As 2660 but no stops on *rev*.; *mm*. 24-46 and none, 105 and 46, 46/- *mm*. 24 with *rev*. stops known	15	35
2671A	Similar but no inner circles; *mm*. lis, trefoil...	20	45
2672	**Penny**. As illus.; *mm*. 24, 105, two pellets, none, trefoil,........................	15	30
2672A	— Similar but without inner circles on one or both sides; *mm*. lis, two pellets	15	35
2673	**Halfpenny**. As 2663, but no *mm*.	15	30

COPPER

For mintmarks see C. Wilson Peck, *English Copper, Tin and Bronze Coins in the British Museum, 1558-1958*.

2675   2676   2679

2674	**Farthing**. 'Harington', small size. 1a, letter or other mark below crown (originally tinned surface) ....*from*	20	45
2675	— — 1b, central jewel on circlet of crown with *mm*. below or crown unmodified	25	45
2676	— 2, normal size of coin; *mm*. on *rev*.	12	25
2677	'Lennox'. 3a; *mm*. *rev*. only	8	20
2678	— 3b; *mm*. both sides..	6	18
2679	— — 3c; *mm*. *obv*. only	6	18
2680	— — 3d; larger crown	6	18
2681	— 4; oval type, legend starts at bottom l..	20	45

Numismatically, this reign is one of the most interesting. Some outstanding machine-made coins were produced by Nicholas Briot, a French die-sinker, but they could not be struck at sufficient speed to supplant hand-hammering methods. In 1637 a branch mint was set up at Aberystwyth to coin silver extracted from the Welsh mines. After the king's final breach with Parliament the parliamentary government continued to issue coins at London with Charles's name and portrait until the king's trial and execution. The coinage of copper farthings continued to be manufactured privately under licences held first by the Duchess of Richmond, then by Lord Maltravers and later by various other persons. The licence was finally revoked by Parliament in 1644.

During the Civil War coins were struck at a number of towns to supply coinage for those areas of the country under Royalist control. Many of these coins have an abbreviated form of the 'Declaration' made at Wellington, Shropshire, Sept., 1642, in which Charles promised to uphold the Protestant Religion, the Laws of England and the Liberty of Parliament. Amongst the more spectacular pieces are the gold triple unites and the silver pounds and half-pounds struck at Shrewsbury and Oxford, and the emergency coins, some made from odd-shaped pieces of silver plate during the sieges of Newark, Scarborough, Carlisle and Pontefract.

Mintmarks

| 105 | 10 | 96 | 71 | 57 | 88 | 101 | 35 |

| 87 | 107 | 60 | 75 | 123 | 57 | 119a | 23 |

| 119b | 98 | 112 | 81 | 120 | 109 |

Tower Mint under Charles I		**Tower Mint under Parliament**
1625	Lis (105)	1633-4	Portcullis (107)	
1625-6	Cross Calvary (10)	1634-5	Bell (60)	1643-4	P in brackets (98)
1626-7	Negro's head (96)	1635-6	Crown (75)	1644-5	R in brackets (112)
1627-8	Castle (71)	1636-8	Tun (123)	1645	Eye (81)
1628-9	Anchor (57)	1638-9	Anchor (57)	1645-6	Sun (120)
1629-30	Heart (88)	1639-40	Triangle (119a)	1646-8	Sceptre (109)
1630-1	Plume (101)	1640-1	Star (23)	
1631-2	Rose (35)	1641-3	Triangle in circle	
1632-3	Harp (87)		(119b)	

Mint mark no. 57 is often horizontal to left or right.

| 59 | B | 58 *var* | 58 |

Briot's Mint

1631-2	Flower and B (59)	1638-9	Anchor (57)
1632	B		Anchor and B (58)
			Anchor and mullet (58v)

On mint mark no. 58 the 'B' below the anchor is sometimes shown as ꓭ

61	104	35	92	103	6	65b	71

89	91 *var*	131	84	94 *var*	64	93	34

102	67	127	128	129	25	83	100

134	71	A	B	75

Provincial Mints

1638-42	Book (61, *Aberystwyth*)
1642	Plume (104, *Shrewsbury*)
	Pellets or pellet (*Shrewsbury*)
1642-3	Rose (35, *Truro*)
	Bugle (134, *Truro*)
1642-4	Lion (92, *York*)
1642-6	Plume (103, *Oxford*)
	Pellet or pellets (*Oxford*)
	Lis (105, *Oxford*)
1643	Cross pattee (6, *Bristol*)
	Acorn (65b, *Bristol*)
	Castle (71, *Worcester* or *Shrewsbury*)
	Helmet (89, *Worcester* and *Shrewsbury*)
1643-4	Leopard's head (91 *var. Worcester*)
	Two lions (131, *Worcester*)
	Lis (105, *Worcs.* or *Shrews.*)
	Bunch of grapes (84, *Worcs.* or *Shrews.*)
	Bird (94 *var., Worcs.* or *Shrews.*)

1643-4	Boar's head (64 *Worcs.* or *Shrews.*)
	Lion rampant (93, *Worcs.* or *Shrews.*)
	Rosette (34, *Worcs.* or *Shrews.*)
1643-5	Plume (102, *Bristol*)
	Br. (67, *Bristol*)
	Pellets (*Bristol*)
	Rose (35, *Exeter*)
	Rosette (34, *Oxford*)
1643-6	Floriated cross (127, *Oxford*)
1644	Cross pattee (6, *Oxford*)
	Lozenge (128, *Oxford*)
	Billet (129, *Oxford*)
	Mullet (25, *Oxford*)
1644-5	Gerb (83, *Chester*)
	Pear (100, *Worcester*)
	Lis (105, *Hereford?*)
	Castle (71, *Exeter*)
1645-6	Plume (102, *Ashby, Bridgnorth*)
1645	A (*Ashby*)
1646	B (*Bridgnorth*)
1648-9	Crown (75, *Aberystwyth Furnace*)

GOLD

Tower mint, under the King, 1625-42

Tower Gold

		F £	VF £
2682	**Angel**. As for James I last issue, but *rev*. reads AMOR POPVLI etc; without mark of value; *mm*. lis and cross calvary	900	2750
2683	— — pierced for use as touch-piece	400	850
2684	— X in field to r.; *mm*. 96-88, 71 and 96/71, 57 and 71/57	850	2650
2685	— — — pierced for use as touch-piece	400	850
2686	- X in field to l.; *mm*. 96, 88, 35-23	850	2650

2687

2687	— — — pierced for use as touch-piece	400	850
2688	**Unite** (20s.). First bust with ruff and collar of order, high double-crown. R. Square-topped shield; *mm*. lis.	275	575
2688A	— Similar, but extra garnishing to shield; *mm*. lis	300	625
2689	— Similar, but flat single-arched crown; *mm*. lis, cross calvary	285	600
2689A	R. As 2688A. *mm*. lis	325	650

2690

2690	Second bust with ruff and armour nearly concealed with scarf; R. Square-topped shield with slight garnishing *mm*. 10-88	250	550
2690A	Similar but more elongated bust, usually dividing legend. *mm*. 57-101, 88/101	260	565
2691	— As 2690A but *mm*. anchor below bust	725	1600
2691A	*Obv*. as 2690A. R. As next: *mm*. plume	625	1350
2692	Third bust, more armour visible. R. Oval shield with CR at sides; *mm*. 101, 35.	275	575
2693	Fourth bust, small lace collar with large high crown usually breaking i.c., long hair. Garter ribbon on breast. R. Oval shield with crowned CR at sides; *mm*. harp, portcullis	260	565
2693A	Similar, but unjewelled crown, within or touching i.c.; *mm*. 107-23	250	550
2694	Sixth (Briot's) bust, large lace collar. R. Similar; *mm*. 119a-119b	300	625
2695	Briot's hammered issue, (square-topped shield); *mm*. anchor	2250	5250

2696 2696A 2697

	F	VF
	£	£
2696 **Double-crown**. First bust. As 2688. R. Square-topped shield; *mm*. lis....	300	675
2696A Similar to last but wider flatter double-arched crown; *mm*. 105, 10.........	265	550
*2697 Second bust. R. Similar to 2690; *mm*. 10-57	225	475
*2697A Similar to 2690A: *mm*. 57-101	225	475
2697B *Obv*. as last. R. As next: *mm*. plume	325	675
2698 Third bust. Flat or domed crown. R. Oval shield with CR at		
sides; *mm*. plume, rose	275	550
2699 Fourth bust, large head, high wide crown. R. Oval shield with crowned CR		
at sides; *mm*. portcullis...	250	525
2699A — Similar to last, but flat crown, jewelled outer arch: *mm*. 87-123	225	465
2699B — Similar, but smaller head, unjewelled crown: *mm*. 60-57....................	225	460
2699C — Sim. to 2699, but bust within i.c.; *mm*. bell	310	650
2700 Fifth bust (Early Aberystwyth style). R. Similar; *mm*. anchor	325	700
2700A — (Late Aberystwyth style). R. *mm*. anchor, triangle	310	650
2701 Sixth bust. R. Normal; *mm*. 119a-119b.............................	250	525
2702 — R. Briot's square-topped shield; *mm*. anchor......................................	1100	2750

*For these coins inner circles are sometimes omitted on *obv*., *rev*., or both. *See also 2704, 2704A and 2707*.

2703 2707

2703 **Crown**. First bust with small round crown. R. Square-topped shield; *mm*.		
lis, cross calvary	140	310
2703A As 2696A. *mm*. cross calvary...	160	350
2704 Second bust as 2690. R. Similar; *mm*. 10-71	140	290
2704A As 2690A. *mm*. 57-101, 88/-, 57/-, 101/-..	140	290
2704B As 2691. Wire line i.c.s on *rev*..	250	500
2705 *Obv*. as 2690A. R. As next; 101, 35, 101/-...	160	350
2706 Third bust. R. Oval shield with CR at sides; *mm*. plume	275	600
2707 Fourth bust. R. Oval shield with crowned CR at sides; *mm*. -/87, 87-119b,		
23/119a, 107/60..	140	290
2708 Fifth (Aberystwyth style) bust. R. Similar; *mm*. anchor	265	550
2709 Sixth (Briot's) bust. R. Similar; *mm*. anchor...	725	1500

Tower mint, under Parliament, 1642-9. All Charles I types

		F	VF
		£	£
2710	**Unite**. Fourth bust, as 2693A; *mm*. (P), (P)/-	425	875
2711	Sixth bust, as 2694 but crude style; *mm*. (P), (R), 119b	450	925

2712

2712	Seventh bust, crude r style; *mm*. eye, sun, sceptre	550	1200
2713	**Double-crown**. Fourth bust, as 2699B; *mm*. eye	625	1350
2714	Fifth bust, as 2700A; *mm*. sun, sceptre	450	900
2715	Sixth bust, as 2701; *mm*. (P)	425	850
2716	Eighth, dumpy bust with single flat-arched crown; *mm*. sun	700	1450
2717	**Crown**. Fourth bust, as 2707 jewelled crown; *mm*. -/98 , 98/-, 98-120	225	450
2717A	Sim. but unjewelled crown. R. Small crude shield; *mm*. 81-109	275	575

Nicholas Briot's coinage, 1631-2

2718	**Angel**. Type somewhat as Tower but smaller and neater; *mm*. -/B	3000	7000

2719

2719	**Unite**. As illustration. R. FLORENT etc.; *mm*. flower and B/B	1100	2700
2720	**Double-crown**. Similar but X. R. CVLTORES, etc. *mm*. flower and B/B	825	1800
2720A	Similar but King's crown unjewelled: *mm*. flower and B/B, B	850	1850
2721	**Crown**. Similar; *mm*. B	1500	4250

Briots Hammered Gold: See No. 2695, 2702 and 2709

Provincial issues, 1638-49

Chester mint, 1644

2722	**Unite**. As Tower. Somewhat like a crude Tower sixth bust. R. Crowned, oval shield, crowned CR, *mm*. plume	10000	27500

Shrewsbury mint, 1642 (See also 2749)

2723 **Triple unite**, 1642. Half-length figure l holding sword and olive-branch; *mm*.: R. EXVRGAT, etc., around RELIG PROT, etc., in two wavy lines. III and three plumes above, date below ...... *Extremely rare*

Oxford mint, 1642-6

		F	VF
		£	£
2724	**Triple unite**. As last, but *mm*. plume, tall narrow bust, 1642	2250	5250
2725	Similar, but 'Declaration' on continuous scroll, 1642-3	2650	6500
2725A	Large bust of fine style. King holds short olive branch; *mm*. small lis.....	8000	25000
2726	As last, but taller bust, with scarf behind shoulder, 1643, *mm*. plume	2600	6000

2727

2727	Similar, but without scarf, longer olive branch, 1643..............................	2350	5350
2728	Similar, but OXON below 1643, rosette stops..	4000	9500
2729	Smaller size, olive branch varies, bust size varies, 1644 OXON..............	2650	6250
2730	— Obv. as 2729, 1644 / OX..	2750	6500
2731	**Unite**. Tall thin bust. R. 'Declaration' in two wavy lines, 1642; *no mm*...	800	1600
2732	— R. 'Declaration' in three lines on continuous scroll, 1642-3	825	1650
2733	Tall, well-proportioned bust. R. Similar, 1643, no *mm*.	975	2000
2734	Shorter bust, king's elbow not visible. R. Similar, 1643; *mm*. plume/-	725	1500
2735	Similar but longer olive branch curving to l. 1644 / OX; *mm*. plume	750	1600

2735A

2735A	Similar, but dumpy bust breaking lower i.c., small flan	775	1650
2736	Tall bust to edge of coin. R. Similar, 1643	1300	2750
2737	As 2734. R. 'Declaration' in three straight lines, 1644 / OX	1650	3750
2738	Similar to 2734, but smaller size; small bust, low olive branch. 1645	1000	2250
2739	— R. Single plume above 'Declaration', 1645-6 / OX; *mm*. plume,		
	rosette, none	1100	2350
2740	**Half-unite**. 'Declaration' in three straight lines, 1642	1350	3000
2741	'Declaration' on scroll; *mm*. plume; 1642-3	1200	2450

2742

	F	VF
	£	£
2742 Bust to bottom of coin, 1643; Oxford plumes	775	1600
2743 — 1644 / OX. Three Shrewsbury plumes (neater work)	1400	3250

Bristol mint, 1645

| *2744 **Unite**. Somewhat as 2734; Two busts known. *mm*. Br. or Br/ plumelet.; 1645.. | 7000 | 16500 |
| 2745 **Half-unite**. Similar 1645 .... | *Extremely rare* | |

Truro mint, 1642–3

| 2745A **Half-Unite**. Crowned bust l. (similar to Tower 4th bust). R. CVLT, etc., crowned shield .... | *Extremely rare* | |

Exeter mint, 1643–4

| 2746 **Unite**. *obv*. sim. to early Oxford bust. R. FLORENT, etc., crowned oval shield between crowned CR, *mm*. rose .... | 12000 | 30000 |
| 2747 — R. CVLTORES, etc., similar but no CR .... | 10500 | 27500 |

Worcester mint, 1643–4

| 2748 **Unite**. Crude bust R. FLORENT, etc., double annulet stops, crowned oval shield, lion's paws on either side of garniture, no *mm*............................. | 8500 | 22500 |

Salopia (Shrewsbury) mint, 1644

| 2749 **Unite**. *Obv*. bust in armour. R. Cr. shield, crowned CR. *mm*. lis/- .... | *Extremely rare* | |

Colchester besieged, 1648

| 2750 **Ten Shillings** Gateway of castle between CR; below OBS CO L 16 S/X 48. Uniface – now considered a later concoction .... | | |

Pontefract besieged, 1648-9. After the death of Charles I, in the name of Charles II

| 2751 **Unite**. DVM : SPIRO : SPERO around CR crowned. CAROLVS : SECVИDVS : 16 48, castle, OBS on l., PC above.................................. | *Extremely rare* | |
| 2752 **Unite**. CAROL : II, etc., around HANC : DEVS, etc. R. POST : MORTEM, etc., around castle. *Octagonal*.. | *Extremely rare* | |

SILVER

Tower mint, under the King, 1625-42

2753 **Crown**. King on horseback with raised sword. 1a. Horse caparisoned with plume on head and crupper. R. Square-topped shield over long cross fourchee; *mm*. lis, cross calvary	300	725
2754 — 1b. Similar, but plume over shield, no cross; *mm*. 105, 10, 71	650	1500
2755 — 2a. Smaller horse, plume on hd. only, cross on housings, king holds sword on shoulder. R. Oval garnished shield over cross fourchee, CR above; *mm*. harp	275	625
2756 — 2b¹. — — plume divides CR, no cross; *mm*. plume, rose....................	325	750
2757 — 2b². — — — with cross; *mm*. harp...	425	950

2758

	F	VF
	£	£
2758 — 3a. Horse without caparisons. R. Oval shield without CR; *mm*. 60-23	275	625
2759 — 3b. — — plume over shield; *mm*. 107, 75, 123	300	725
2760 'Briot' horse with ground-line; *mm*. triangle in circle	2500	5250
2761 **Halfcrown**. As 2753. 1a¹. Rose on housings, ground-line; *mm*. lis	135	425
2761A— Similar, but no rose on housings; *mm*. lis	325	750

2762

	F	VF
2762 — 1a². Similar, but no rose or ground-line; *mm*. 105, 10 over 105	95	240
2763 — 1a³. As last but shield not over cross; *mm*. 10 sometimes over lis on one or both sides, 96	100	250
2763A— Similar but only slight garnishing to shield; *mm*. 10, 71	140	375
2763B— As 2763, light weight (204 grains as standard) *mm* 10, (usually over lis)	275	675
2764 — 1a⁴. — — with ground-line; *mm*. lis	400	925
2765 — 1b. Heavy garnishing, plume over shield; *mm*. 105, 10, 96	425	950
2765A— Similar but only slight garnishing; *mm*. 96-57	425	950
2766 — 2/1b. As 2755 but rose on housings. R. As last; *mm*. heart, plume	575	1350
2767 — 2a. As 2755. R. Flattened oval garnished shield without cross; *mm*. 101/ 35 plume, rose, (CR above, divided by rose (rare), lis over rose (rare), lis)	55	160
2768 — 2b. Similar, but large plume between the CR; *mm*. plume, (rare) rose	110	350
2769 — 2c. As 2a, but differently garnished oval shield with CR at sides; *mm*. harp, portcullis, 107/87	40	125
2770 — 2d. Similar, but with plume over shield; *mm*. harp	575	1350

2771   2775

		F £	VF £
2771	— 3a¹. No caparisons on horse, upright sword, scarf flies out from waist. R. Round garnished shield, no CR; *mm*. 60-119a, 60/75	35	110
2772	— 3b. — — plume over shield; *mm*. 107-123	80	265
2773	— 3a². — cloak flies from king's shoulder; R. Shields vary; *mm*. 123-23, 119b, 119b over 119a/119b	35	120
2774	— — — — rough ground beneath horse; R. Shields vary; *mm*. 119a, 23,	40	130
2775	— 4. Foreshortened horse, mane before chest, tail between legs; *mm*. 23, 119b	30	95

Most late Tower halfcrowns have irregular flans.

2776   2776A

2776	**Shilling**. 1. Bust in ruff, high crown, jewelled arches. R. Square-topped shield over cross fourchee; *mm*. lis, (normal weight 92.9 gr.)	55	220
2776A	— Similar but larger crown, plain inner arch; *mm*. 105, 10	45	180
2777	Similar but light weight (81.75 grs.); *mm*. cross calvary	70	225
2778	— 1b¹. As 2776A, but plume over shield, no cross; *mm*. 105, 10	225	600
2779	— 1a. Bust in ruff and armour concealed by scarf. R. As 2776; 10-71	45	175
2780	— — — — light weight; *mm*. cross Calvary (often extremely small XII)	65	200
2781	— 1b². As 2779, but plume over shield, no cross; *mm*. 10-101 (five bust varieties)	90	250
2781A	— — light weight 1b² *mm*. 10	140	375
2782	— 1b³, — — cross; *mm*. negro's head	350	825
2783	— 2a. More armour visible. R. Oval shield, CR above; *mm*. 35, 101, 101 over 88/101, (two bust varieties)	40	140
2784	— 2b. — — plume over shield; *mm*. 101, 35, 101 over 88/101, (three bust varieties)	120	350
2785	— 3¹. Bust with lace collar, (six bust varieties). R. Flattish oval shield, CR at sides; *mm*. harp, portcullis	35	115
2786	— 3². — — plume over shield; *mm*. harp (three bust varieties)	325	750

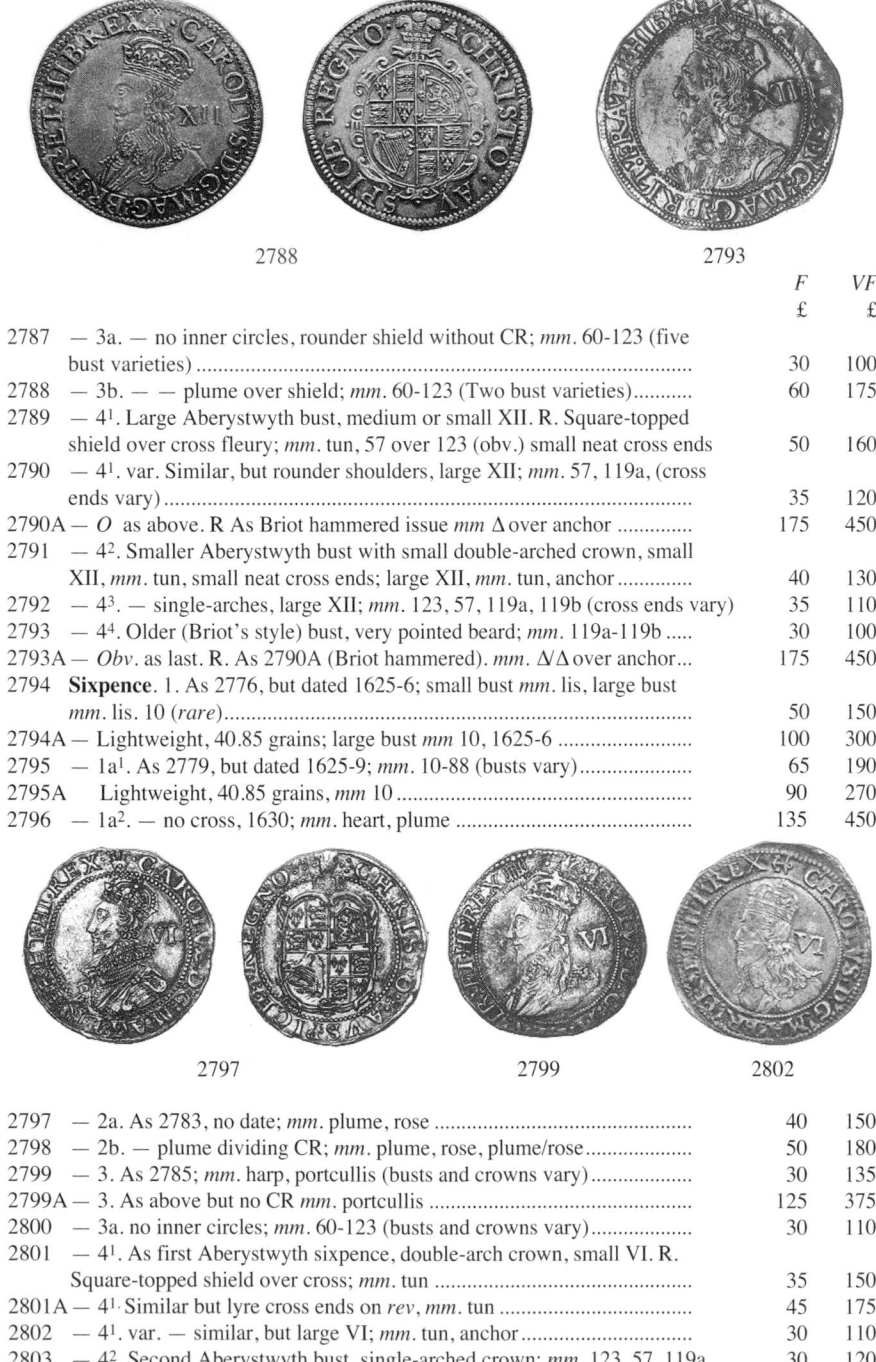

2788   2793

	F £	VF £
2787 — 3a. — no inner circles, rounder shield without CR; *mm*. 60-123 (five bust varieties)	30	100
2788 — 3b. — — plume over shield; *mm*. 60-123 (Two bust varieties)..........	60	175
2789 — 4¹. Large Aberystwyth bust, medium or small XII. R. Square-topped shield over cross fleury; *mm*. tun, 57 over 123 (obv.) small neat cross ends	50	160
2790 — 4¹. var. Similar, but rounder shoulders, large XII; *mm*. 57, 119a, (cross ends vary)	35	120
2790A — *O* as above. R As Briot hammered issue *mm* Δ over anchor	175	450
2791 — 4². Smaller Aberystwyth bust with small double-arched crown, small XII, *mm*. tun, small neat cross ends; large XII, *mm*. tun, anchor	40	130
2792 — 4³. — single-arches, large XII; *mm*. 123, 57, 119a, 119b (cross ends vary)	35	110
2793 — 4⁴. Older (Briot's style) bust, very pointed beard; *mm*. 119a-119b	30	100
2793A — *Obv*. as last. R. As 2790A (Briot hammered). *mm*. Δ/Δ over anchor...	175	450
2794 **Sixpence**. 1. As 2776, but dated 1625-6; small bust *mm*. lis, large bust *mm*. lis. 10 (*rare*)..	50	150
2794A — Lightweight, 40.85 grains; large bust *mm* 10, 1625-6	100	300
2795 — 1a¹. As 2779, but dated 1625-9; *mm*. 10-88 (busts vary)....................	65	190
2795A — Lightweight, 40.85 grains, *mm* 10	90	270
2796 — 1a². — no cross, 1630; *mm*. heart, plume	135	450

2797   2799   2802

2797 — 2a. As 2783, no date; *mm*. plume, rose	40	150
2798 — 2b. — plume dividing CR; *mm*. plume, rose, plume/rose...................	50	180
2799 — 3. As 2785; *mm*. harp, portcullis (busts and crowns vary)..................	30	135
2799A — 3. As above but no CR *mm*. portcullis	125	375
2800 — 3a. no inner circles; *mm*. 60-123 (busts and crowns vary).................	30	110
2801 — 4¹. As first Aberystwyth sixpence, double-arch crown, small VI. R. Square-topped shield over cross; *mm*. tun	35	150
2801A — 4¹. Similar but lyre cross ends on *rev*, *mm*. tun	45	175
2802 — 4¹. var. — similar, but large VI; *mm*. tun, anchor..............................	30	110
2803 — 4². Second Aberystwyth bust, single-arched crown; *mm*. 123, 57, 119a	30	120

		F	*VF*
		£	£
2804	— 4². larger bust, *mm*. triangle	40	150
2805	— 4³. Older (Briot's style) bust; *mm*. 119a-119b (moline cross ends).....	30	135

2806   2808   2818

2806	**Halfgroat**. 1. Crowned rose type. Beaded and/or wire line inner circles on one or both sides. *mm* 105, 105/–, 10..................................	20	50
2807	— 1a. — — similar but without inner circles, *mm* 96–101	20	55
2808	— 2a. King's 2nd bust in ruff and mantle. R. Oval shield; *mm*. plume, rose	20	55
2809	— 2b. Similar, but with plume over shield; *mm*. plume, rose, plume/-	25	75
2809A	— — 2a Var. 3rd bust, with more armour. breaks i.c. at top. R. As last; *mm*. plume, rose	20	55
2809B	— — Sim. but plume over shield; *mm*. plume...............................	25	75
2810	— 3¹. Bust with lace collar. R. Oval shield between CR; no inner circles; *mm*. rose, harp, portcullis, crown	15	40
2811	— 3². — — inner circles *mm*. harp, portcullis...........................	15	40
2812	— 3³. — — inner circle on R. *mm*. harp, portcullis	15	40
2813	— 3⁴. — — inner circle on O. *mm*. harp, portcullis	15	40
2814	— 3⁵. — – no CR, no inner circles; *mm*. portcullis	20	50
2815	— 3⁶. — — — inner circles on *obv*.; *mm*. portcullis, harp..................	20	50
2816	— 3a¹. — R. Rounder shield, different garniture, no i.cs.; *mm*. 60-119a.	15	35
2817	— 3a². — — inner circle on *obv*.; *mm*. triangle, anchor.........................	15	45
2818	— 3a³. — — inner circles both sides; *mm*. 119a-119b..........................	15	40
2819	— 3a⁴. Aberystwyth bust, no inner circles; *mm*. anchor..................	20	60
2820	— 3a⁵. — inner circle on *rev*.; *mm*. anchor	20	60
2821	— 3a⁶. Very small bust, no inner circles; *mm*. anchor..................	25	85

2822   2828   2831

2822	**Penny**. 1. Rose each side; i.cs.; *mm*. 96, :/lis, lis/:, one or two pellets, lis	12	30
2823	— 1a. — no i.cs. — *mm*. lis, one or two pellets, anchor	12	30
2824	— 1b. — i.c. on *rev*.; *mm*. negro's head/two pellets........................	20	65
2825	— 2. Bust in ruff and mantle. R. Oval shield; i.cs.; *mm*. plume, plume/rose, rose	20	50
2826	— 2¹. — — no i.cs.; *mm*. plume, rose	20	50
2827	— 2a¹. More armour visible; no i.cs.; *mm*. plume, rose, plume/rose........	15	40
2828	— 2a². — i.c. on *obv*.; *mm*. plume, rose, plume over rose	15	40
2829	— 2a³. — i.cs. both sides; *mm*. plume, rose	15	40
2830	— 2a⁴. — i.c. on *rev*.; *mm*. rose over plume............................	15	45
2831	— 3¹. Bust in lace collar. R. CR at sides of shield; no i.cs.; *mm*. harp, one or two pellets. ⸳⸳/harp (also *obv*. i.c. *mm*. harp)	12	30
2832	— 3². — similar but no CR; *mm*. 87, 107, 107/⸳⸳, pellets, none	12	30
2833	— 3³. — — i.c. on *obv*.; *mm*. harp,⸳⸳,..	15	30

F	*VF*
£	£

2834 — 3⁴. — — i.c. on *rev.*; *mm.* harp   15   35
2835 — 3a¹. — similar, but shield almost round and with scroll garniture; no
     i.cs.; *mm.* bell, triangle, one to four pellets, none, bell/   12   30
2835A — 3a¹ variety — i.c. on *obv.*, *rev.* or both sides; *mm.* triangle/two pellets,
     Δ,∵, ...   15   40
2836 — 3a³. Aberystwyth bust; i.c. on *obv.* or none; *mm.* one or two pellets or
     triangle or none, or mule of these *mms.*   15   35

2837

2837 **Halfpenny.** Rose each side; no legend or *mm.*   12   35
Many small denominations have uneven irregular flans.

Tower mint, under Parliament, 1642-8. All Charles I type
2838 **Crown**. 4. Foreshortened horse; *mm.* (P) to sun   300   750
2839 — 5. Tall spirited horse; *mm.* sun   425   950
2840 **Halfcrown**. 3a³. As 2773, but coarse work; *mm.* (P) to sun, 81/120   30   100
2841 — 4. Foreshortened horse; *mm.* (P)   125   350
2842 — 5. Tall horse; *mm.* sun, sceptre   50   150
2843 **Shilling**. 4⁴. Briot style bust, *mm.* (P), (R); coarse work; *mm.* eye, sun ...   30   110

2844   2845

2844 — 4⁵. Long narrow coarse bust; *mm.* sun, sceptre   40   140
2845 — 4⁶. Short bust with narrow crown; *mm.* sceptre   40   145

2845A

2845A — — Short broad bust, as illus., broader crown; *mm.* sceptre   45   175
2846 **Sixpence**. 4³. Briot style bust; *mm.* (P) (R)   55   185

2847   2848

		F	VF
		£	£
2847	— 4⁴. Late Aberystwyth bust modified; *mm*. (R) to sceptre	45	150
2848	— 4⁵. Squat bust of crude style; *mm*. eye, sun, sun over eye	85	325
2849	**Halfgroat**. 3a³. Sim. to 2818; *mm*. (P) to eye, sceptre, 98/119b	20	50
2850	— 3a⁷. Older, shorter bust, pointed beard; *mm*. eye to sceptre	15	45
2851	**Penny**. 3a². Older bust; *mm*. pellets, i.c. on *obv*. only	20	50

Nicholas Briot's coinage, 1631-9

First milled issue, 1631-2

2852	**Crown**. King on horseback. R. Crowned shield between CR crowned; *mm*. flower and B / B	375	975
2853	**Halfcrown**. Similar	185	525
2854	**Shilling**. Briot's early bust with falling lace collar. R. Square-topped shield over long cross fourchee; R. Legend starts at top or bottom *mm*. flower and B/B, B	140	425

2855

2855	**Sixpence**. Similar, but VI behind bust; *mm*. flower and B/B, flower and B/-	65	220

	2856		2857		

		F	VF
		£	£
2856	**Halfgroat**. Briot's bust, B below, II behind. R. IVSTITIA, etc., square-topped shield over long cross fourchee	30	70
2856A	Pattern halfgroat. Uncrowned bust in ruff r. R. crowned, interlocked Cs. (North 2687). (Included because of its relatively regular appearance.)	30	70
2857	**Penny**. Similar, but I behind bust, B below bust; position of legend may vary	35	75

Second milled issue, 1638-9

	2858		2859	

2858	**Halfcrown**. As 2853, but *mm*. anchor and B	140	375
2859	**Shilling**. Briot's late bust, the falling lace collar is plain with broad lace border, no scarf. R. As 2854 but cross only to inner circle; *mm*. anchor and B, anchor or muled	60	200
2860	**Sixpence**. Similar, but VI; *mm*. anchor, anchor and mullet/anchor	30	95

The two last often exhibit flan reduction marks.

Briot's hammered issue, 1638-9

2861	**Halfcrown**. King on Briot's style horse with ground line. R. Square-topped shield; *mm*. anchor, triangle over anchor. Also muled with Tower *rev*.	475	1350
2862	**Shilling**. Sim. to 2859; R. Square-topped shield over short cross fleury; usually *mm*. triangle over anchor. Each *mm*. alone is very rare. Often muled with Tower *obv*. (see 2790A, 2793A) *or rev*	275	750

Provincial and Civil War issues, 1638-49
York mint, 1643-4. *Mm*. lion

2863	**Halfcrown**. 1. Ground-line below horse. R. Square-topped shield between CR	275	750
2864	— 2. — R. Oval shield as Tower 3a, groundline grass or dotted	235	600
2865	— 3. No ground-line. R. Similar	235	600
2866	*— 4. As last, but EBOR below horse with head held low. Base metal, often very base	80	250
2867	— 5. Tall horse, mane in front of chest, EBOR below. R. Crowned square-topped shield between CR, floral spray in legend	175	525

These pieces are contemporary forgeries (Besly, English Civil War Hoards BM 51, 1987)

2868

		F	*VF*
		£	£

2868   — 6. As last, but shield is oval, garnished (*rev*. detail variations)   125   350
2869   — 7. Similar, but horse's tail shows between legs. R. Shield as last, but with
     lion's skin garniture, no CR or floral spray   110   300

2870/2

2870 **Shilling**. 1. Bust in scalloped lace collar 3¹. R. EBOR above square-topped
     shield over cross fleury   85   250
2871   — 2. Similar, but bust in plain armour, mantle; coarse work   100   275
2872   — 3. *Obv*. as 2870. — R. EBOR below oval shield   110   325
2873   — 4. — Similar, but crowned oval shield (*obv*. finer style)   80   240
2874   — 5. — As last, but lion's skin garniture   80   240
2875 **Sixpence**. *Obv*. Sim. to 2870. Crowned oval shield   175   450

2876   2877

2876   — — Crowned CR at sides...   140   350
2877 **Threepence**. As type 1 shilling, but III behind bust. R. As 2870............   35   95

	F	VF
	£	£

Aberystwyth mint, 1638/9-42. *Mm*. book.

Plume 1=with coronet and band. Plume 2=with coronet only

2878 **Halfcrown**. Horseman similar to 2773, but plume 2 behind. R. Oval
garnished shield with large plume above. *Obv.* plume 2, *rev.* plume 1.... | 400 | 950

2879 — Similar to 2774, plume 1 behind King, ground below horse. *Obv.* squat
plume 1, *rev.* plume 1.. | 475 | 1250

2880 As 2773 but more spirited horse, no ground. FRAN ET HIB, plume 2/1 | 450 | 1100

2881 **Shilling**. Bust with large square lace collar, plume 2 before, small XII. R.
As before. No inner circles .... | 190 | 550

2881   2884

2882	— inner circle on *rev.*	175	500
2883	As 2881, but large plume 1 or 2, large XII, inner circles, large or	175	525
	small shield		
2884	As last, but small narrow head, square lace collar, large or square plume	200	600
2885	Small Briot style face, small crown, plume 2	350	900
2885A	**Sixpence**. *Obv.* as Tower bust 3a, plume before. R. as 2889; *mm*. book		
	(*obv.* only)	300	675

2886

2886	Somewhat as 2881, but double-arched crown, small VI; no inner circles	150	425
2887	Similar to 2886, but single arched crown, plume 2, inner circle *obv*. Large VI	165	475
2888	Similar, but with inner circles both sides	150	450
2889	— — *Rev*. with small squat-shaped plume above, sometimes no *rev. mm*.	150	450
2890	Bust as the first Oxford sixpence; with crown cutting inner circle...........	225	600

2891   2894   2895

		F £	VF £
2891	**Groat**. Large bust, lace collar, no armour on shoulder. Crown breaks or touches inner circle. R. Shield, plume 1 or 2	30	75
2892	— Similar, armour on shoulder, shorter collar. R. Similar	35	80
2893	— Smaller, neater bust well within circle. R. Similar	30	70
2894	**Threepence**. Small bust, plume 2 before. R. Shield, plume 1 or 2 above, *obv*. legend variations	25	65
2895	— Similar, but crown cuts i.c. squat pl. on *obv*., R. Pl. 2, *Obv*. legend variations	30	70
2900	**Halfgroat**. Bust as Tower type 3. R. Large plume. No inner circles, *mm*. pellet/book,book	35	90

2900A   2905   2907

		F	VF
2900A	Bust as 2886. R. As last, no inner circle	45	125
2901	Bust with round lace collar; single arch crown, inner circles, colon stops	30	85
2902	After Briot's bust, square lace collar: inner circles	35	90
2903	**Penny**. As 2901; CARO; no inner circles	50	140
2904	As 2901; CARO; inner circles	45	125
2905	As last but reads CAROLVS; inner circles	55	160
2906	*Obv*. similar to 2890, tall narrow bust, crown touches inner circle	60	170
2907	**Halfpenny**. No legend. O. Rose. R. Plume	125	375

Aberystwyth-Furnace mint, 1648/9. *Mm*. crown

		F	VF
2908	**Halfcrown**. King on horseback. R. Sim. to 2878	1250	3000
2909	**Shilling**. Aberystwyth type, but *mm*. crown	1500	3750
2910	**Sixpence**. Similar	925	2250

2911   2913

		F	VF
2911	**Groat**. Similar	160	425
2912	**Threepence**. Similar	150	375
2913	**Halfgroat**. Similar. R. Large plume	225	550
2914	**Penny**. Similar	600	1350

Uncertain mint (? Hereford) 1644-5

2915   2930/1

	F	VF
	£	£
2915 **Halfcrown**. As illustration, dated 1645 or undated	1250	2650
2915A — Scarf with long sash ends. CH below horse. R. Oval shield 1644	1650	4250
2915B — R. Crowned oval shield, lion paws	1650	4250

Shrewsbury mint, 1642. Plume without band used as *mm.* or in field.

2917 **Pound**. King on horseback, plume behind, similar to Tower grp. 3 crowns. R. Declaration between two straight lines, XX and three Shrewsbury plumes above, 1642 below; *mm.* pellets, pellets/-.....................................	1250	2850
2918 Similar, but Shrewsbury horse walking over pile of arms; no *mm.*, pellets	1050	2500
2919 As last, but cannon amongst arms and only single plume and XX above Declaration, no *mm.*	1400	3250
2920 **Half-pound**. As 2917, but X; *mm.* pellets	600	1350
2921 Similar, but only two plumes on *rev.*; *mm.*, pellets....................................	850	2000
2922 Shrewsbury horseman with ground-line, three plumes on *rev.*; *mm.*, none, pellets/-...	550	1250
2923 — with cannon and arms or arms below horse; *mm.* pellets/-	600	1300
2924 — no cannon in arms, no plume in *obv.* field; *mm.* plume/pellets, plume/-	475	1100
2925 **Crown**. Aberystwyth horseman, no ground line	6000	15000

2926

2926 Shrewsbury horseman with ground-line; *mm.* -/pellets, pellets/-, none....	450	1050
2927 **Halfcrown**. *O*. From Aberystwyth die; (S2880); *mm.* book. R. Single plume above Declaration, 1642	725	1750
2928 Sim. to Aberystwyth die, fat plume behind. R. Three plumes above Declaration; *mm.* pellets, pellets/-..	325	750

		F	VF
		£	£
2929	Shrewsbury horseman, no ground line. R. As 2927, single plume, no *mm.*	375	950
2929A	— — R. As 2933	300	700
2930	— R. 2: plume; 6, above Declaration	650	1450
2931	— with ground-line. R. Similar	650	1450
2932	— — R. As 2927, single plume	375	1000
2933	— — R. Three plumes above Declaration; *mm.* none or pellets	280	650
2933A	— — R. Aberystwyth die, plume over shield; *mm.* -/book	750	1750
2934	As 2933 but no plume behind king; *mm.* plume/pellets	265	600
2935	**Shilling**. *O.* From Aberystwyth die; S2885 *mm.* book. R. Declaration type	650	1450
2936	*O.* From Shrewsbury die. R. Similar	750	1750

Oxford mint, 1642-6. *Mm.* usually plume with band, except on the smaller denominations when it is lis or pellets. There were so many dies used at this mint that we can give only a selection of the more easily identifiable varieties.

For many years Oxford Halfcrowns and Shillings have been catalogued according to Morrieson obverse die varieties. In many cases, these are very small and difficult to identify. We have, therefore, simplified the obverse classification and used the available space to expand the listing of the more interesting reverse varieties.

Numbers in brackets following each entry refer to numbers employed in previous editions.

2937

2937	**Pound**. Large horseman over arms, no exergual line, fine workmanship. R. Three Shrewsbury plumes and XX above Declaration, 1642 below; *mm.* plume/pellets	1750	4250
2938	— Similar, but three Oxford plumes, 1643; *mm.* as last	1650	4000
2939	Shrewsbury horseman trampling on arms, exergual line. R. As last, 1642	1200	2750
2940	— — cannon amongst arms, 1642-3; *mm.* similar	1050	2450
2941	— as last but exergue is chequered, 1642; *mm.* similar	1350	3000
2942	Briot's horseman, 1643; *mm.* similar	2500	5750
2943	*O.* As 2937. R. Declaration in cartouche, single large plume above, 1644 OX below	2850	7000
2944	**Half-pound**. Shrewsbury horseman over arms, Oxford plume behind. R. Shrewsbury die, 1642; mm. plume/-	450	1050
2945	— R. Three Oxford plumes above, 1642; *mm.* plume/-	425	925
2945A	— — 1643; *mm.* plume/- (2945)	450	975

	F	*VF*
	£	£

2946 **Crown.** Shrewsbury die with groundline. R. Three Oxford plumes,
1642; no mm. 325 700

2946A — — 1643; no *mm.* (2946) 325 700

2947 Oxford horseman, grass below. R. Three Oxford plumes, 1643; *mm.*
plume/- 600 1300

2948 Rawlins' crown. King riding over a view of the city. R. Floral scrolls
above and below Declaration, date in script, 1644 OXON; *mm.*
floriated cross/- *(Electrotypes and copies of this coin are common)* 6250 16500

2949 **Halfcrown.** *O.* Shrewsbury die with groundline, plume behind. R.
Oxford die, declaration in two lines, three Oxford plumes above,
1642 below; no *mm.* 300 750

2950 — no plume behind. R. as last, 1642; *mm.* plume/- (2949) 235 575

2951 Shrewsbury horseman with groundline, Oxford plume behind. R.
Shrewsbury die, 1642; *mm.* plume/- (2950)... 200 475

2952 — R. Three Oxford plumes, 1642; *mm.* plume/- (2951).......................... 100 325

2953 — — without groundline, 1642; *mm.* plume/- (2952) 120 350

2954

2954 Oxford horseman without groundline, 1643; *mm.* plume/-....................... 100 300

2954A — — R. Shrewsbury die, 1642; *mm.* plume/- or no *mm*........................... 210 500

2955 — with groundline. R. Three Oxford plumes, 1643; *mm.* plume/- (2953) 110 325

2956 Briot horseman, grassy, rocky or uneven ground. R. Three Oxford plumes,
1643; *mm.* plume/-, plume & rosette/- (2955, 57) 125 350

2957 — — 1643 OX; *mm.* plume/rosette, rosette (2955, 57) 145 400

2958 — — 1644 OX; *mm.* plume/- (2959, 63, 64) 135 375

2958A — — lozenges by OX, 1644 OX; *mm.* plume/- (2959, 63, 64) 145 400

2959 — — 1645 OX; *mm.* plume/-, plume/rosette (2959, 63, 64, 66, 68) 135 375

2959A — — pellets by date, 1645 OX; *mm.* plume/- (2967)............................... 150 475

2960 — — 1646 OX; *mm.* plume/- (2966, 68)... 135 375

2961 — — pellets or annulets by plumes and date, 1646 OX; *mm.* plume/- (2967) 150 450

2962 — R. Large central plume and two Oxford plumes, 1643; *mm.* plume/- (2956) 150 475

2963 — — 1643 OX; *mm.* plume/-, rosette/-, plume & rosette/rosette, plume
& rosette/- (2956, 58)... 135 375

2964 — — rosettes by OX, 1643 OX; *mm.* rosette/-, plume & rosette/- (2958) 150 475

2965 2965A

	F £	VF £
2965 — — plain, pellets or lozenges by plumes and/or OX, 1644 OX; *mm*. plume/- plume/rosette, rosette (2956, 58, 60, 65)	125	350
2965A — — date in script, 1644 OX; *mm*. plume/- (2961)	145	425
2966 — — rosettes by plume and date, 1644 OX; *mm*. plume & rosette/rosette (2958)	150	475
2967 — — small plumes by date, 1644 OX; *mm*. plume & rosette/-, rosette (2962)	200	525
2968 — R. Large central plume and two small Shrewsbury plumes, lozenges in field, date in script, 1644 OX; *mm*. plume/rosette (2960A)	200	525
2969 — — small plumes by date, pellets by OX, 1644 OX; *mm*. plume/- (2962)	240	575
2970 **Shilling.** *O*. Shrewsbury die. R. Declaration in three lines, three Oxford plumes above, 1642; *mm*. plume/-	300	750
2971 Oxford bust (small). R. Three Oxford plumes, 1642; *mm*. Oxford plume/-,	135	400
2972 Oxford bust (small or large). R. Three Oxford plumes, 1643; *mm*. Oxford plume/-, Oxford plume/rosette (2971, 72, 73, 75)	120	325
2972A — — pellets by date, 1644; *mm*. plume/- (2975)	150	400
2972B — — 1644 OX; mm. plume/rosette (2974)	125	375
2973 — R. Oxford and two Shrewsbury plumes, lozenges by date, 1644 OX; *mm*. plume/- (2976)	175	475

2974

2974 — R. Three Shrewsbury plumes, 1643; *mm*. plume/- (2972, 73)	165	425

2975

		F £	VF £
2975	Fine Oxford bust. R. Three Oxford plumes, lozenges in field, 1644 OX; *mm.* Shrewsbury plume/- (2974)	125	350
2975A	— — large date in script, 1644 OX; *mm.* plume/- (2974A)	145	425
2976	— 1645 OX; *mm.* plume/- (2974)	450	1250
2976A	— R. Oxford and two Shrewsbury plumes, 1644 OX; *mm.* plume/- (2974)	175	475
2977	— R. Three Shrewsbury plumes, 1644 OX; *mm.* plume/- (2974)	165	425
2978	— — annulets or pellets at date, 1646; *mm.* plume/floriated cross, plume/- (2979)	165	450
2979	Rawlins' die. Fine bust with R. on truncation. R. Three Oxford plumes, rosettes or lozenges by plumes, lozenges by date, 1644 OX; *mm.* Shrewsbury plume/rosette, Shrewsbury plume/- (2978)	275	700
2979A	— — pellets by date, no OX, 1644; *mm.* plume/- (2977)	250	650
2979B	R. Oxford and two Shrewsbury plumes, 1644 OX; *mm.* plume/- (2978)	250	650

2980

2980	**Sixpence.** O. Aberystwyth die R. Three Oxford plumes, 1642; *mm.* book/-	175	475
2980A	— — 1643; *mm.* book/- (2980)	135	375
2981	— R. Three Shrewsbury plumes, 1643; *mm.* book/-	125	325
2982	— R. Shrewsbury plume and two lis, 1644 OX (groat rev. die); *mm.* book/-	350	900
2983	**Groat.** O. Aberystwyth die. R. Shrewsbury plume and two lis, 1644 OX; *mm.* book/-	75	225
2984	— R. Three Shrewsbury plumes, 1644 OX; mm. book/-	95	275

2985

2985	Oxford bust within inner circle. R. As 2983, 1644 OX; mm. floriated cross/-	65	180

		F	*VF*
		£	£

2985A — R. Three Shrewsbury plumes, 1644 OX; *mm.* floriated cross/- 85 250

2985B — R. Single plume, Declaration between wavy lines, 1645; *mm.*
floriated cross/- (2989)... 125 325

2986 Large bust to top of coin. R. As 2983, 1644 OX; *mm.* lis/- 125 325

2987 Large bust to bottom of coin. R. As 2983, 1644 OX; no *mm.* 95 275

2988 — R. Single plume, Declaration between wavy lines, 1645; no *mm.* (2990) 75 200

2989 Rawlins' die, no inner circle, R on shoulder. R. As 2983, 1644 OX;
no *mm.* (2988) 110 300

2990 — R. Single plume, Declaration in cartouche, 1645; no *mm.* (2991) 125 350

2990

2991 — — 1646/5; no mm. 110 325

2992 **Threepence.** *O.* Aberystwyth die. R. Three lis over Declaration,
1644 OX; *mm.* book/-.. 60 175

2993 Rawlins; die, R below shoulder. R. Aberystwyth die, oval shield; *mm.*
lis/book 60 175

2994 — R. Three lis over Declaration, 1644; *mm.* lis/- 45 120

2995   2996   3000

2995 Crown breaks inner circle, no R. R. Three lis, 1646/4; *mm.* lis/-.............. 50 145

2996 **Halfgroat.** Small bust, beaded or wireline inner circle. R. Large plume
in field; *mm.* mullet/lis, lis, -/lis 70 165

2997 — R. Three lis over Delcaration, 1644 OX; *mm.* lis............................. 70 175

2998 **Penny.** *O.* Aberystwyth die, CARO. R. Small plume in field; *mm.* book/- 90 240

2999 Aberystwyth die, CAROLVS; R. Large plume; *mm.* book/- 90 240

3000 Rawlins' die, CARO. R. Small plume; *mm.* lis/mullet, lis/- 125 350

3001 Broad bust, CAROL. R. Small plume; *mm.* lis 110 300

3002 — R. Three lis over Declaration, 1644; *mm.* lis 375 950

Bristol mint, 1643-5. *Mm.* usually plume or Br., except on small denominations

3003 **Halfcrown.** *O.* Oxford die with or without ground-line. R. Declaration,
three Bristol plumes above, 1643 below.. 165 525

3004 — Obv. as above. R as above, but *mm.* Br. 1643 .... 175 550

3005 King wears unusual flat crown, *obv. mm.* acorn? between four pellets. R.
As 3003, 1643 .... 175 550

3006 — Obv. as above. R as 3004 but 1643-4 .... 150 475

3007 Shrewsbury plume behind king. R. As last.. 135 300

3008 — Obv. as above. R as 3004 but Br below date instead of as *mm* . 1644. 140 375

3009

		F	VF
		£	£
3009	— Obv. as 3007 but Br below horse. R as above but 1644-5	135	325
3010	— Obv. as above. R as 3004 but Br. as *mm.* as well as 1644-5	140	375
3011	**Shilling**. *O*. Oxford die. R. Declaration, 1643, 3 crude plumes above, no *mm*.	175	525

3012   3014

3012	— — R Similar, but *mm*. Br., 1643-4, less crude plumes	160	425
3013	—Obv. Coarse bust. R. As 3011, no *mm*.	175	525
3014	— — Coarse bust, R. as 3012, *mm*. Br, but 1644	175	500

3015   3017

3015	Obv. Bust of good style, plumelet before face. R. As 3012 *mm*. Br. but 1644-5	140	350
3016	— — R.as 3012, 1644, but Br below date instead of *mm*........................	165	450
3016A	— — R as 3012, 1644 but plume and plumelet either side	140	325
3017	—Obv. Taller bust with high crown, no plumelets before, *mm*. Br. on its side. R As 3016 Br.below 1644-5	175	500
3018	—Obv. As 3017 but no *mm*. R as above but *mm*.. no Br. below 1644-5 ..	185	550
3018A	— — R as above but plume and plumelets, 1645....................................	185	550
3019	**Sixpence**. Small bust, nothing before. R. Declaration surrounded by CHRISTO etc., 1643; *mm*. ./Br...	235	550
3020	Fine style bust. Plumelet before face, 1644; *mm*. ./Br. (on its side)	140	325

	F	VF
	£	£
3021 **Groat**. Bust l. R. Declaration, 1644	135	350
3022 — Plumelet before face, 1644	100	250
3023 — Br. below date, 1644	100	250
3023A — Similar, but larger bust and more spread plume before. Mm. pellet/Br; nothing below 1644	110	275

3024   3026   3027

3024 **Threepence**. *O*. As 2992. Aberystwyth die; *mm*. book. R. Declaration, 1644	135	350
3025 Bristol die, plume before face, no *mm*., 1644	175	450
3026 **Halfgroat**. Br. in place of date below Declaration	175	450
3027 **Penny**. Similar bust, I behind. R. Large plume with bands	275	650

This penny may belong to the late declaration issue. It has the same reverse plume punch as 3044.

Late 'Declaration' issues, 1645-6

(Previously given as Lundy Island and/or Appledore and Barnstaple/Bideford, it seems likely that coins marked A, 1645 may be Ashby de la Zouch and the coins marked B or plumes, 1646 may be Bridgnorth on Severn.)

3028 **Halfcrown**. A below horse and date and as *rev. mm*. 1645	1200	2650
3029 Similar but *rev*. from altered Bristol die (i.e. the A's are over Br.)	1000	2350
3030 As 3028 but without A below date 1645	950	2250
3031 A below horse and as *rev. mm*. Scroll above Declaration, B below 1646	1500	3750
3032 Plumelet below horse struck over A. R. *Mm*. Shrewsbury plumes; scroll above Declaration, 1646	525	1400

3033

3033 — Similar, but plumelet below date	575	1500
3034 **Shilling**. Crowned bust l., *mm*. plume. R. Declaration type; *mm*. A and A below 1645	600	1450

3035

	F £	VF £
3035 — Similar, but plumelet before face	625	1500
3036 — — Scroll above 'Declaration', 1646; *mm* plume/plumelet	250	600
3036A — Bristol obv. die, no plumelet, similar to 3018 *mm*. Br. R. As last but *mm.* pellet. 1646.	325	750
3037 Obv as above, but Shrewsbury plume before face. plume over Br. *mm*. R. As above	275	650
3038 **Sixpence**. *O.* Plumelet before face; *mm*. A; R. 1645, 3 plumelets over 'Dec'	425	950

3039

	F	VF
3039 *O.* Large Shrewsbury plume before face; *mm*. B. R. Scroll above Declaration, 1646, Shrewsbury plume and two plume plumelets	110	275
3040 **Groat**. As 3038	350	825
3041 Somewhat similar, but *obv. mm.* plumelet; R *mm.* pellet or plume,1646 .	85	210
3042 **Threepence**. Somewhat as last but only single plumelet above Declaration, no line below, 1645; no *mm*.	250	575
3043 — Scroll in place of line above, 1646 below	90	225
3044 **Halfgroat**. Bust l., II behind. R. Large plume with bands dividing 1646; no *mm*.	350	750

Truro mint, 1642-3. *Mm.* rose except where stated
Entries from here to 3092 have been revised to follow E. Besly (BNJ 1992). The original catalogue numbers are therefore no longer sequential.

	F	VF
3045 **Crown.** King on horseback, head in profile, sash flies out in two ends. R. CHRISTO, etc., round garnished shield (3048)	225	525
3046 **Halfcrown.** King on walking horse, groundline below, R. Oblong shield, CR above, *mm.* bugle/– (3048A)	950	2250
3047 Galloping horse, king holds baton. R. Oblong shield, CR at sides (3050)	1000	2850

3048   3052

	F	VF
	£	£
3048 Walking horse, king holds sword. R. Similar (3054)	550	1300
3049 — R. Similar, but CR above (3055)	575	1350
3050 Galloping horse, king holds sword. R. Similar, but CR at sides (3051)	850	2350
3051 — R. Similar, but CR above (3052)	825	2250
3052 Trotting horse. R. Similar, but CR at sides (3053)	600	1400
3053 **Shilling**. Small bust of good style. R. Oblong shield (3056)	1650	4500

Exeter mint, 1643-6. Undated or dated 1644-6 *Mm*. rose except where stated

3054 **Half-pound**. King on horseback, face towards viewer, sash in large bow. R. CHRISTO, etc., round garnished shield. Struck from crown dies on a thick flan (3045)	*Extremely rare*	
3055 **Crown**. King on horseback, sash in large bow. R. Round garnished shield (3046)	200	450
3056 — Shield garnished with twelve even scrolls (3047)	225	550
3057 As 3055, R Date divided by *mm*. 16 rose 44 (3070)	275	650
3058 — R Date to l. of *mm*. 1644 (3071)	185	425
3059 — *mm*: rose/EX, 1645 (3072)	225	500
3060 King's sash flies out in two ends; *mm*. castle/rose, 1645 (3073)	350	750
3061 — *mm*. castle/EX, 1645 (3074)	225	475
3062 — *mm*. castle, 1645 (3075)	175	400
3063 **Halfcrown**. King on horseback, sash tied in bow. R. Oblong shield CR at sides (3062)	325	825
3064 — R. Round shield with eight even scrolls (3063)	185	425

3065

3065 — R. Round shield with five short and two long scrolls (3064)	145	350
3066 — R. Oval shield with angular garnish of triple lines	475	975

3067   3071

		F	VF
		£	£
3067	Briot's horseman with lumpy ground. R. As 3064 (3067)	225	525
3068	— R. As 3065 (3069)	200	475
3069	— R. As 3066 (3068)	475	975
3070	— R. As 3065, date to 1. of *mm*. 1644 (3079)	325	700
3071	King on spirited horse galloping over arms. R. Oval garnished shield, 1642 in cartouche below (3049)	1100	3000
3072	— R. As 3070, date to 1. of *mm*. 1644-5 (3076)	1650	4000
3073	— R. *mm*. castle, 1645 (3077)	1750	4250
3074	Short portly king, leaning backwards on ill-proportioned horse, 1644, 16 rose 44 (3078)	475	1250
3075	Horse with twisted tail, sash flies out in two ends R. As 3064 (3065)	275	650
3076—	R. As 3070, date divided by *mm*. 16 rose 44, or date to 1. of *mm*. 1644-5 (3080)	240	550
3077	— R. *mm*. castle, 1645 (3081)	350	775
3078	— R. *mm*. EX, 1645 (3082)	325	750
3079	— R. Declaration type; *mm*. EX. 1644-5 (3083)	1250	2750
3080	— R. Similar, EX also below declaration, 1644 (3084)	1100	2500
3081	**Shilling.** Large Oxford style bust. R. Round shield with eight even scrolls (3057)	650	1450
3082	— R. Oval shield with CR at sides (3058)	600	1300
3083	Normal bust with lank hair. R. As 3081 (3060)	500	1050
3083A	— R. As 3082 (3059)	475	1000
3084	— R. Round shield with six scrolls (3061)	400	850

3085   3087A

3085	— R. Similar, date to r. of *mm*. 1644, divided 16 rose 44, or to left of *mm*. 1644-5	180	500
3086	— R. Declaration type, 1645	650	1450
3087	**Sixpence.** Similar to 3085, large bust and letters 1644 rose	185	475
3087A	— Smaller bust and letters from punches used on 3088, small or large VI, 16 rose 44	175	450

| | *F* | *VF* |
| | £ | £ |

3088 **Groat**. Somewhat similar but 1644 at beginning of *obv*. legend .... | 60 | 145

3089   3091   3092

3089 **Threepence**. Similar. R. Square shield, 1644 above .... | 70 | 165
3090 **Halfgroat**. Similar, but II. R. Oval shield, 1644 .... | 120 | 300
3091 — R. Large rose, 1644 .... | 135 | 350
3092 **Penny**. As last but I behind head .... | 240 | 575

Worcester mint 1643-4
3093 **Halfcrown**. King on horseback l., W below; *mm*. two lions. R. Declaration
         type 1644 altered from 1643 Bristol die; *mm*. pellets .... | 650 | 1650
3094 — R. Square-topped shield; *mm*. helmet, castle .... | 450 | 1150
3095 — R. Oval shield; *mm*. helmet .... | 475 | 1250

3096

3096 Similar but grass indicated; *mm*. castle. R. Square-topped shield; *mm*.
         helmet or pellets. .... | 375 | 1000
3097 — R. Oval draped shield, lis or lions in legend .... | 450 | 1150
3098 — R. Oval shield CR at sides, roses in legend .... | 475 | 1250
3099 — R. FLORENT etc., oval garnished shield with lion's paws each side . | 550 | 1450
3100 Tall king, no W or *mm*. R. Oval shield, lis, roses, lions or stars in legend | 450 | 1150
3101 — R. Square-topped shield; *mm*. helmet .... | 500 | 1250
3102 — R. FLORENT, etc., oval shield; no *mm*. .... | 550 | 1400
3103 Briot type horse, sword slopes forward, ground-line. R. Oval shield, roses
         in legend; *mm*. 91v, 105, none (combinations) .... | 525 | 1300
3104 — Similar, but CR at sides, 91v/- .... | 550 | 1350
3105 Dumpy, portly king, crude horse. R. As 3100; *mm*. 91v, 105, none .... | 475 | 1250

3106

		F	*VF*
		£	£
3106	Thin king and horse. R. Oval shield, stars in legend; *mm.* 91v, none	450	1200

Worcester or Salopia (Shrewsbury) 1643-4

3107	**Shilling**. Bust of king l., adequately rendered. R. Square-topped shield; *mm.* castle	675	1800
3108	— R. CR above shield; *mm.* helmet and lion	675	1800
3109	— R. Oval shield; *mm.* lion, pear..	650	1700
3110	— Bust a somewhat crude copy of last (two varieties); *mm.* bird, lis. R. Square-topped shield with lion's paws above and at sides; *mm.* boar's head, helmet	750	1950

3111

3111	— — CR above..	750	1950
3112	— R. Oval shield, lis in legend; *mm.* lis	650	1650
3113	— R. Round shield; *mm.* lis, 3 lis	600	1600
3114	Bust r.; *mm.* pear/-, pear/lis. R. draped oval shield with or without CR. (Halfcrown reverse dies)	1500	3500
3115	**Sixpence**. As 3110; *mm.* castle, castle/boar's hd	675	1500

3116   3117

3116	**Groat**. As 3112; *mm.* lis/helmet, rose/helmet..	400	850
3117	**Threepence**. Similar; *mm.* lis	225	425
3118	**Halfgroat**. Similar; *mm.* lis (*O.*) various (*R.*)	350	800

Salopia (Shrewsbury) mint, 1644

		F £	VF £
3119	**Halfcrown**. King on horseback l. SA below; *mm*. lis. R. (*mm*. lis, helmet, lion rampant, none). Cr. oval shield; CHRISTO etc. *mm*. helmet	2250	5250
3120	— R. FLORENT, etc., crowned oval shield, no *mm*.	2400	5250
3121	— SA erased or replaced by large pellet or cannon ball; *mm*. lis in legend, helmet. R. As 3119..	1200	2850
3122	Tall horse and king, nothing below; *mm*. lis. R. Large round shield with crude garniture; *mm*. helmet..	575	1350
3123	— R. Uncrowned square-topped shield with lion's paw above and at sides; *mm*. helmet	650	1500
3124	— R. Small crowned oval shield; *mm*. various..	550	1250

3125

3125	— R. As 3120..	650	1450
3126	Finer work with little or no mane before horse. R. Cr. round or oval shield	625	1450
3127	Grass beneath horse. R. Similar; *mm*. lis or rose	700	1650
3128	Ground below horse. R. As 3120	750	1850

Hartlebury Castle (Worcs.) mint, 1646

3129

3129	**Halfcrown**. *O. Mm*. pear. R. HC (Hartlebury Castle) in garniture below shield; *mm*. three pears...	900	2350

Chester mint, 1644

3130

		F	VF
		£	£
3130	**Halfcrown.** As illus. R. Oval shield; *mm.* three gerbs and sword	450	1000
3131	— Similar, but without plume or CHST; R. Cr. oval shield with lion skin; *mm.* prostrate gerb; -/cinquefoil, ⁻/.∴.	525	1100
3132	— R. Crowned square-topped shield with CR at sides both crowned *rev.*; *mm.* cinquefoil...	325	750
3133	As 3130, but without plume or CHST. R. Declaration type, 1644 *rev.*; *mm.* plume...	675	1500
3133A	**Shilling.** Bust l. R. Oval garnished shield; *mm.* .∴. (obv. only)	750	1750
3133B	R. Square-topped shield; *mm.* as last	750	1750
3133C	— R . Shield over long cross	750	1750
3134	**Threepence.** R. Square-topped shield; *mm.*-/ prostrate gerb...................	725	1600

Welsh Marches mint? 1644

3135

3135	**Halfcrown.** Crude horseman, l. R. Declaration of Bristol style divided by a dotted line, 3 plumes above, 1644 below	625	1350

Carlisle besieged, 1644-5

		F £	VF £
3136	**Three shillings**. Large crown above C. R between rosettes / .III. S. *rev.* OBS . CARL / . 1645, rosette below	2750	6000

3137

3137	Similar but :- OBS :/-: CARL :./.1645, rosette above and below	2850	6500
3138	**Shilling**. Similar	1850	4000
3139	R. Legend and date in two lines	1950	4250
	Note. *(3136-39) Round or Octagonal pieces exist.*		

Newark besieged, several times 1645-6, surrendered May 1646

3140   3144

3140	**Halfcrown**. Large crown between CR ; below, XXX. *rev.* OBS / NEWARK / 1645 or 1646	375	725
3141	**Shilling**. Similar but crude flat shaped crown, NEWARKE, 1645	300	625
3142	Similar but normal arched crown, 1645	285	525
3143	— NEWARK, 1645 or 1646	285	525
3144	**Ninepence**. As halfcrown but IX, 1645 or 1646	275	500
3145	— NEWARKE, 1645	285	525

3146

3146	**Sixpence**. As halfcrown but VI, 1646	275	500

Pontefract besieged, June 1648-March 1648-9

F	VF
£	£

3147 **Two shillings** (lozenge shaped). DVM : SPIRO : SPERO around CR
crowned. R. Castle surrounded by OBS, PC, sword and 1648 .... *Extremely rare*

3148

3148 **Shilling** (lozenge shaped, octagonal or round). Similar 675 1600

3149   3150

3149 — Similar but XII on r. dividing PC 625 1350

After the death of Charles I (30 Jan. 1648/9), in the name of Charles II

3150 **Shilling** (octagonal). *O*. As last. R. CAROLVS : SECVИDVS : 1648, castle
gateway with flag dividing PC, OBS on l., cannon protrudes on r........... 675 1550

3151 CAROL : II : etc., around HANC : DE / VS : DEDIT 1648. R. POST :
MORTEM : PATRIS : PRO : FILIO around gateway etc. as last............ 700 1650

Scarborough besieged, July 1644-July 1645

3156	3165	3169

Type I. Large Castle with gateway to left, SC and value Vs below

3152	**Crown.** (various weights)	14500

Type II. Small Castle with gateway, no SC, value punched on flan

3153	**Five shillings and eightpence.**	9250
3154	**Crown.** Similar	12500
3155	**Three shillings.** Similar	8500
3156	**Two shillings and tenpence.** Similar	8500
3157	**Two shillings and sevenpence.** Similar	8500
3158	**Halfcrown.** Similar	9500
3159	**Two shillings and fourpence.** Similar	8250
3161	**One shilling and ninepence.** *Struck from a different punch, possibly of later manufacture*	
3162	**One shilling and sixpence.** Similar to 3159	6500
3163	**One shilling and fourpence.** Similar	6500
3164	**One shilling and threepence.** Similar	6500
3165	**Shilling.** Similar	8500
3166	**Sixpence.** Similar	8500
3167	**Groat.** Similar	5250

Type III. Castle gateway with two turrets, value punched below

3168	**Two shillings and twopence**	5500
3169	**Two shillings.** Castle punched twice	5500
3170	**One shilling and sixpence.** Similar to 3168	5000
3171	**One shilling and fourpence.** Similar	5000
3172	**One shilling and threepence.** Similar	5000
3173	**One shilling and twopence.** Similar	4750
3174	**One shilling and one penny.** Similar	4750
3175	**Shilling.** Similar	5500
3176	**Elevenpence.** Similar	4250
3177	**Tenpence.** Similar	4250
3178	**Ninepence.** Similar	4500
3178A	**Eightpence.** Similar	3750
3179	**Sevenpence.** Similar	3750
3180	**Sixpence.** Similar	5250

COPPER

For mintmarks see C. Wilson Peck, *English Copper, Tin and Bronze Coins in the British Museum, 1558-1958.*

		F £	VF £
3181	**Royal farthing**. 'Richmond' round, colon stops, 1a. CARO over IACO; *mm.* on *obv.*	8	22
3182	— — 1b. CARA; *mm.* on *obv.*	75	150
3183	— — 1c. CARO; *mm.* on *obv.*	5	15

Royal farthing.

3184	'Richmond' round apostrophe stops. 1d. Eagle-headed harp	8	22

	3185	3191		3194	
3185	— 1e. Beaded harp			6	17
3186	— 1f. Scroll-fronted harp, 5 jewels on circlet			12	35
3187	— 1g. — — 7 jewels on circlet			6	17
3188	Transitional issue, double-arched crowns			18	50
3189	'Maltravers' round, 3a; *mm.* on *obv. only*			9	24
3190	— 3b. *Mm.* both sides			5	15
3191	— 3c. Different *mm.* either side			6	18
3192	'Richmond' oval. 4a. CARO over IACO; *mm.* both sides			18	45
3193	— — — *mm.* on *obv.*			18	45
3194	— 4b. CARO, colon stops; *mm.* on *obv.*			15	40
3195	— — — — *mm.* on *rev.*			15	40
3196	— — — — *mm.* both sides			15	40
3197	— 4c. apostrophe stops; *mm.* rose on *obv.*			18	45
3198	— — — *mm.* rose both sides			18	45
3199	— — — *mm.* rose (*obv.*); scroll (*rev.*)			18	45
3200	'Maltravers' oval. 5. CAROLVS; *mm.* lis both sides			22	50

	3201		3207		
3201	**Rose farthing**. 1a. Double-arched crowns; double rose; sceptres within inner circle, BRIT; *mm.* on *obv.* or *rev.* or both sides, or different each side			9	24
3202	— 1b. — — sceptres just break circle, BRIT; *mm.* on *obv.* or both sides or no *mm.*			7	20
3203	— 1c. — — sceptres almost to outer circle, BRIT; *mm.*s as 3201			6	18
3204	— 1d. — — — BRI; *mm.* on *obv.* or both sides, or different each side			6	18
3205	Transitional mules of types 1d/2, with double and single arched crowns; *mm.* as 3204			9	24
3206	— 2. Single-arched crowns; single rose; *mm.* as 3204			4	12
3207	— 3. Sceptres below crown; *mm.* mullet			18	45

The coins struck during the Commonwealth have inscriptions in English instead of Latin which was considered to savour of too much popery. St. George's cross and the Irish harp take the place of the royal arms. The silver halfpenny was issued for the last time. Coins with *mm.* anchor were struck during the protectorship of Richard Cromwell.

Mintmarks

1649-57 Sun   1658-60 Anchor

GOLD

3208   3209

		F	VF
		£	£
3208	**Unite.** As illustration; *mm.* sun, 1649-57	75	975
3209	Similar, *mm.* anchor, 1658, 1660	1350	3000
3210	**Double-crown.** As illus., but X; *mm.* sun, 1649-57	375	775
3211	Similar, *mm.* anchor, 1660	1300	2850
3212	**Crown.** Similar, but V; *mm.* sun, 1649-57	325	650
3213	As illus., *mm.* anchor, 1658, 60	1300	2850

SILVER

3215

3214	**Crown.** Same type; *mm.* sun, 1649, 51-4, 56	350	675
3215	**Halfcrown.** Similar; *mm.* sun, 1649, 1651-7	125	325

		F	VF
		£	£
3216	— *mm*. anchor, 1658-1660	525	1100
3217	**Shilling.** Similar; *mm*. sun, 1649, 1651-7	90	210

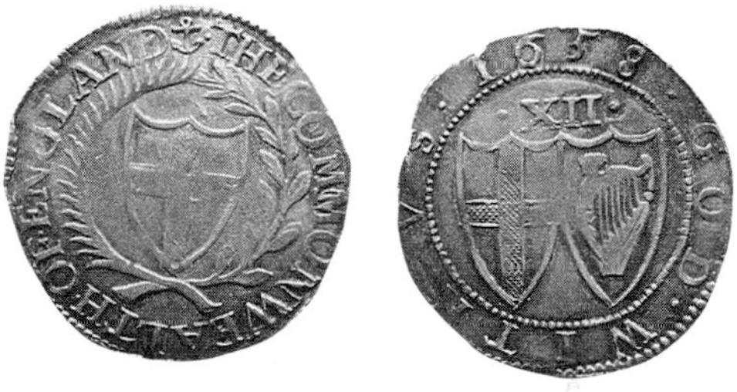

3218

3218	— *mm*. anchor, 1658-60	325	650
3219	**Sixpence.** Similar; *mm*. sun, 1649, 1651-7	75	165
3220	— *mm*. anchor, 1658-60	300	625

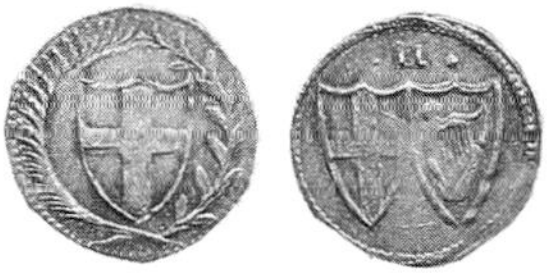

3221 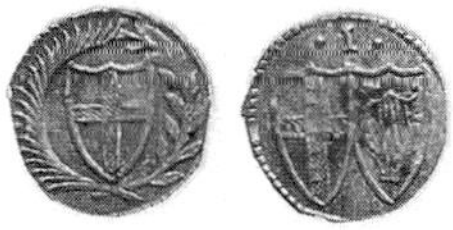   3222

| 3221 | **Halfgroat**.. | 20 | 55 |
| 3222 | **Penny**. Similar, but I above shields .... | 20 | 40 |

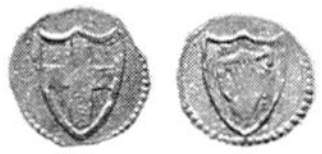

3223

| 3223 | **Halfpenny.** .... | 25 | 50 |

Although often referred to as patterns, there is in fact nothing to suggest that the portrait coins of Oliver Cromwell were not intended for circulation. Authorised in 1656, the first full production came in 1657 and was followed by a second more plentiful one before Cromwell's death. All coins were machine made, struck from dies by Thomas Simon in the presses of the Frenchman, Pierre Blondeau. Later, some of Simon's puncheons were sold in the Low Countries and an imitation Crown was made there. Other Dutch dies were prepared and some found their way back to the Mint, where in 1738 it was decided to strike a set of Cromwell's coins. Shillings and Sixpences were struck from the Dutch dies, and Crowns from new dies prepared by John Tanner. Thomas Simon later died in the Great Plague of 1665.

GOLD

	F £	VF £	EF £
3224 Fifty shillings. laur. head l. R. Crowned Shield of the Protectorate, 1656. Inscribed edge			15000

3225

3225 Broad. of Twenty Shillings, similar, but grained edge 1656.	2000	3500	6000

SILVER

3226

3226 Crown. Dr. bust l. R. Crowned shield, 1658/7. Inscribed edge	800	1250	1950
3227 Halfcrown. Similar, 1656 different obverse legend.....................	1000	2000	—

3227A

	F	VF	EF
	£	£	£
3227A Halfcrown. 1658 Similar legend to 3226......................................	400	750	1250

3228

3228 **Shilling.** Similar, but grained edge, 1658......................................	275	500	850
3229 **Sixpence.** Similar 1658...		*Extremely rare*	

COPPER

3230

3230 **Farthing.** Dr. bust l. R. CHARITIE AND CHANGE, shield	1500	3500	—

There are also other reverse types for this coin.

For the first two years after the Restoration the same denominations, apart from the silver crown, were struck as were issued during the Commonwealth although the threepence and fourpence were soon added. Then, early in 1663, the ancient hand hammering process was finally superceded by the machinery of Blondeau.

For the emergency issues struck in the name of Charles II in 1648/9, see the siege pieces of Pontefract listed under Charles I, nos. 3150-1.

Hammered coinage, 1660-2

Mintmark: Crown.

3301   3302

GOLD

		F	VF
	First issue. Without mark of value	£	£
3301	**Unite** (20s.). Type as illustration	750	1650
3302	**Double-crown**. As illustration	600	1250
3303	**Crown**. Similar	625	1300

3303   3304

	Second issue. With mark of value		
3304	**Unite**. Type as illustration	650	1350
3305	**Double-crown**. As illustration	475	1000
3306	**Crown**. Similar	550	1100

SILVER

		F £	VF £
	First issue. Without inner circles or mark of value		
3307	**Halfcrown**. Crowned bust, as 3308	550	1450

3308 3309

3308	**Shilling**. Similar	175	525
3309	**Sixpence**. Similar	145	400
3310	**Twopence**. Similar	25	70
3311	**Penny**. Similar	25	65
3312	As last, but without mintmark	25	65

3313 3322

	Second issue. Without inner circles, but with mark of value		
3313	**Halfcrown**. Crowned bust	700	1650
3314	**Shilling**. Similar	375	825
3315	**Sixpence**. Similar	800	1750
3316	**Twopence**. Similar, but mm. on obv. only	80	225

3310 3317 3326

3317	Similar, but mm. both sides (machine made)	15	35
3318	Bust to edge of coin, legend starts at bottom l. (machine made, single arch crown)..	15	35
3319	**Penny**. As 3317	15	40
3320	As 3318 (single arch crown)	15	35

		F	*VF*
		£	£
	Third issue. With inner circles and mark of value		
3321	**Halfcrown**. Crowned bust to i.c. (and rarely to edge of coin).............	110	375
3322	**Shilling**. Similar..	75	200
3323	**Sixpence**. Similar..	65	185
3324	**Fourpence**. Similar...	20	55
3325	**Threepence**. Similar..	25	55
3326	**Twopence**. Similar..	20	40
3327	**Penny**. Similar	20	50

Grading of Early and Later Milled Coinage

Milled coinage refers to coins that are struck by dies worked in a mechanical coining press. The early period is defined from the time of the successful installation of Peter Blondeau's hand powered machinery at the mint, initiated to strike the first portrait coins of Oliver Cromwell in 1656. The early period continuing until the advent of Matthew Boulton's steam powered presses from 1790. The coinage of this early period is therefore cruder in it's execution than the latter. When grading coins of the early peiod, we only attribute grades as high as extremely fine, and as high as uncirculated for the latter period. Most coins that occur of the early period in superior grades than those stated will command considerably higher prices, due to their rarity. We suggest the following definitions for grades of preservation:

Milled Coinage Conditions

Proof A very carefully struck coin from speciallly prepared dies, to give a superior definition to the design, with mirror-like fields. Occurs occasionally in the Early Milled Coinage, more frequently in the latter period. Some issues struck to a matt finish for Edward VII.

FDC *Fleur-de-coin*. Absolutely flawless, untouched, without wear, scratches, marks or hairlines. Generally applied to proofs.

UNC *Uncirculated*. A coin in as new condition as issued by the Mint, retaining full lustre or brilliance but, owing to modern mass-production methods of manufacture and storage, not necessarily perfect.

EF *Extremely Fine*. A coin that exhibits very little sign of circulation, with only minimal marks or faint wear, which are only evident upon very close scrutiny.

VF *Very Fine*. A coin that exhibits some wear on the raised surfaces of the design, but really has only had limited circulation.

F *Fine*. A coin that exhibits considerable wear to the raised surfaces of the design, either through circulation, or damage perhaps due to faulty striking

Fair *Fair*. A coin that exhibits wear, with the main features still distinguishable, and the legends, date and inscriptions still readable.

Poor *Poor*. A coin that exhibits considerable wear, certainly with milled coinage of no value to a collector unless it is an extremely rare date or variety.

Examples of Condition Grading

Early Milled

Gold N   Silver Æ   Copper Æ

Extremely Fine

Gold Aʋ

Silver Æ

Copper Æ

Very Fine

Fine

James II
Two Guineas

William III
Crown

George III
Halfpenny

Later Milled

Gold Aʋ

Silver Æ

Copper Æ

Uncirculated

Gold *AV* Silver *AR* Copper *Æ*

Extremely Fine

Very Fine

Fine

Victoria
Sovereign

Victoria
Halfcrown

George III
Twopence

Early in 1663, the ancient hand hammering process was finally superceded by the machinery of Blondeau. John and Joseph Roettier, two brothers, engraved the dies as a safeguard against clipping, the larger coins were made with the edge inscribed DECVS ET TVTAMEN and the regnal year. The medium-sized coins were given a grained edge.

The new gold coins were current for 100s., 20s. and 10s., and they came to be called 'Guineas' as the gold from which some of them were made was imported from Guinea by the Africa Company (whose badge was the Elephant and Castle). It was not until some years later that the Guinea increased in value to 21s. and more. The Africa Co. badge is also found on some silver and so is the plume symbol indicating silver from the Welsh mines. The four smallest silver denominations, though known today as 'Maundy Money', were actually issued for general circulation: at this period the silver penny was probably the only coin distributed at the Royal Maundy ceremonies. Though never part of the original agreement, smaller coins were eventually also struck by machinery.

A good regal copper coinage was issued for the first time in 1672, but later in the reign, farthings were struck in tin (with a copper plug) in order to help the Cornish tin industry.

GOLD

3328

Milled coinage

	F £	VF £	EF £		F £	VF £	EF £
3328 Five Guineas. First laur. bust r., pointed trun., regnal year on edge in words							
(e.g. 1669=VICESIMO PRIMO)							
1668 VICESIMO	950	1950	4800	1675 V. SEPTIMO	950	1950	4800
1669 – PRIMO	950	1950	4800	1676 – OCTAVO	1100	2200	5200
1670 – SECVNDO	950	1950	4800	1676 – SEPTIMO	1000	2000	5000
1671 – TERTIO	1100	2200	5200	1677 – NONO	950	1950	4800
1672 – QVARTO	950	1950	4800	1678/7 – TRICESIMO	950	1950	4800
1673 – QVINTO	950	1950	4800	1678 – TRICESIMO	1000	2000	5000
1674 – SEXTO	1100	2200	5200				
3329 — with elephant below bust							
1668 VICESIMO	950	1750	4500	1675 V. SEPTIMO	1250	2500	6000
1669 – PRIMO	1250	2500	6000	1677/5 – NONO	*Extremely rare*		
3330 — with elephant and castle below bust							
1675 – SEPTIMO	*Extremely rare*			1678/7 – TRICESIMO	1250	2500	5500
1676 – OCTAVO	950	1950	4800	1678 TRICESIMO	1250	2500	5500
1677 – NONO	1100	2200	5200				
3331 Second laur. bust r., rounded trun.							
1678/7 TRICESIMO	1250	2200	5200	1682 T. QVARTO	950	1950	4800
1679 – PRIMO	950	1950	4800	1683 – QVINTO	950	1950	4800
1680 – SECVNDO	950	1950	4800	1684 – SEXTO	950	1950	4800
1681 – TERTIO	950	1950	4800				

| | *F* | *VF* | *EF* | | *F* | *VF* | *EF* |
| | £ | £ | £ | | £ | £ | £ |

3332 Five Guineas. Second laur. bust r., with elephant and castle below

1680 T. SECVNDO.......	*Extremely rare*			1683 T. QVINTO .1200	2400	5500
1681 – TERTIO......1250	2200	5200		1684 – SEXTO.......950	1950	4800
1682 – QVARTO 950	1950	4800				

3333   3335

3333 Two Guineas. First laur. bust r., pointed trun.

| 1664 ....550 | 1200 | 3500 | 1669 .... | *Extremely rare* | |
| 1665 .... | *Extremely rare* | | 1671 ....550 | 1250 | 3750 |

3334 — with elephant below bust

| 1664 ....475 | 1000 | 3250 |

3335 Second laur. bust r., rounded trun.

1675 575	1250	3750	1680 600	1300	4000
1676 475	1000	3250	1681 475	1000	3250
1677 475	1000	3250	1682 475	1000	3250
1678/7 475	1000	3250	1683 475	1000	3250
1679 475	1000	3250	1684 525	1100	3500

3336 — with elephant and castle below bust

1676 475	1000	3250	1682 475	1000	3250
1677	*Extremely rare*		1683 600	1300	4000
1678 475	1000	3250	1684 600	1300	4000

3337 — with elephant only below, 1678 .... *Extremely rare*

Overstruck dates are listed only if commoner than the normal date or if no normal date is known.

3338 Guinea. First laur. bust r., 1663 ....475 | 1250 | 3000

3339 — with elephant below bust, 1663 ....425 | 1200 | 2750

3340 Second laur. bust r., 1664 ....375 | 1000 | 2500

3341 — with elephant below bust, 1664 .... *Extremely rare*

3339   3342

3342 Third laur. bust r.

1664 300	850	2000	1669 300	875	2250
1665 275	750	1750	1670 275	750	1750
1666 275	750	1750	1671 275	750	1750
1667 275	750	1750	1672 325	925	2400
1668 275	750	1750	1673 350	975	2600

3344   3345

	F £	VF £	EF £		F £	VF £	EF £

3343 Guinea. Third laur. bust r., with elephant below

	F	VF	EF		F	VF	EF
1664	400	950	2500	1668		*Extremely rare*	
1665	350	875	2400				

3344 Fourth laur. bust r., rounded trun.

1672	250	625	1650	1679	225	600	1600
1673	250	625	1650	1680	225	600	1600
1674	300	800	2250	1681	280	700	2000
1675	280	700	2000	1682	250	625	1650
1676	225	600	1600	1683	225	600	1600
1677	225	600	1600	1684	250	625	1650
1678	225	600	1600				

3345 Fourth laur. bust r., with elephant and castle below

1674		*Extremely rare*		1680	450	1150	3000
1675	350	850	2250	1681	350	800	2250
1676	275	650	1750	1682	300	750	2000
1677	300	700	1850	1683	450	1150	3000
1678	350	850	2250	1684	300	750	2000
1679	350	850	2250				

3346 — — with elephant below bust

1677		*Extremely rare*		1678		*Extremely rare*	

3347   3348

3347 Half-Guinea. First laur. bust r., pointed trun.

1669	280	650	2000	1671	325	750	2200
1670	250	550	1750	1672	325	750	2200

3348 Second laur. bust r., rounded trun.

1672	260	600	1900	1679	250	550	1750
1673	375	850	2500	1680	375	850	2500
1674	395	900	2750	1681	375	850	2500
1675		*Extremely rare*		1682	375	850	2500
1676	260	550	1750	1683	260	600	1900
1677	260	600	1900	1684	250	550	1750
1678	280	650	2000				

3349 — with elephant and castle below bust

1676	425	1000	—	1681		*Extremely rare*	
1677	380	900	2750	1682	380	900	2750
1678/7	325	750	2200	1683		*Extremely rare*	
1680		*Extremely rare*		1684	280	650	2000

SILVER

3350

	F	VF	EF		F	VF	EF
	£	£	£		£	£	£

3350 Crown. First dr. bust r., rose below, edge undated, 1662 ....85 | 350 | 1500

3351 — — edge dated, 1662 ....95 | 400 | 1600

3352 — no rose, edge dated, 1662 ....100 | 500 | 1750

3353 — — edge not dated, 1662 ....95 | 450 | 1750

3354 — — new reverse, shields altered, 1663, regnal year on edge in
Roman figures ANNO REGNI XV ....100 | 500 | 1750

3355 Second dr. bust r., regnal year on edge in Roman figures (e.g. 1664 = XVI)

1664 edge XVI.......... 75	350	1500	1665 XVII.................500	1000	—
1665 XVI	*Extremely rare*		1666 XVIII 75	400	1650
1665/4 XVII..............500	1000	—	1667 XVIII 1500	—	—

3356

3356 — — elephant below bust, 1666 XVIII ....175 | 650 | —

3357

3357 — regnal year on edge in words (e.g. 1667= DECIMO NONO)

1667 D. NONO.......... 75	300	1500	1669/8 — 180	500	—
1667 AN.· REG.· 75	300	1500	1670 V. SECVNDO ...95	400	1500
1668 VICESIMO...... 60	250	1400	1670/69 — 100	450	1650
1668/7 — 75	300	1500	1671 – TERTIO..........75	350	1600
1668/5	*Extremely rare*		1671 T/R in ET — 500	—	—
1669 – PRIMO..........180	500	—	1671 ET over FR — .750	1750	—

	3358				3359		
	F	VF	EF		F	VF	EF
	£	£	£		£	£	£

3358 Crown. Third dr. bust r.

	F	VF	EF		F	VF	EF
1671 V. TERTIO 70	300	1500		1675 EGNI error 650	—	—
1671 – QVARTO............	*Extremely rare*		1676 V. OCTAVO......70	300	1500
1672 – QVARTO...... 70	300	1500		1676 OCCTAVO........80	400	—
1673 – QVARTO	*Extremely rare*		1677 – NONO............90	400	1750
1673 – QVINTO 70	300	1500		1677/6 — 100	500	—
1673/2 — 100	500	1850		1678/7 TRICESIMO.100	500	—
1674 – SEXTO	*Extremely rare*		1679 – PRIMO 75	300	1500
1675/3 – SEPTIMO ..500	1500	—		1680/79 – SECVNDO.90	325	1600
1675 — 750	2500	—		1680 — 100	450	2000

3359 Fourth dr. bust r.

	F	VF	EF		F	VF	EF
1679 T. PRIMO 70	300	1400		1682 T. QVARTO 500	1250	3500
1680 – SECVNDO 75	300	1500		1682 QVRRTO error.200	750	—
1680/79 — 100	450	—		1683 – QVINTO 300	850	—
1681 – TERTIO 75	300	1500		1684 – SEXTO 200	500	—
1682/1 T. QVARTO ...70	300	1500				

3360 — elephant and castle below bust, 1681 – TERTIO ....1500 3500 —

	3361		3362		3364	

3361 Halfcrown. First dr. bust r., regnal year on edge in Roman figures

		F	VF	EF
1663 XV 75	325	1450
1663 — V/S in CAROLVS 125	500	—
1663 no stops on obverse 100	425	—
3362 Second dr. bust r., 1664 XVI..90	400	1750
3363 Third dr. bust r., 1666 XVIII..550	1950	—
3364 — elephant below bust, 1666 XVIII 400	850	—

	F £	VF £	EF £		F £	VF £	EF £

3365 Halfcrown. Third dr bust r. regnal date on edge in words (eg. 1667=DECIMO NONO)

1667/4 D. NONO............	*Extremely rare*			1669 — R/I in PRIMO ...	*Extremely rare*		
1668/4 VICESIMO ...150	500	—		1670 – SECVNDO 65	250	1350	
1669/1 V. PRIMO.....150	450	—		1670 – MRG for MAG300	—	—	
1669 — 350	800	—					

3366 Third bust variety r.

1671 V. TERTIO 60	250	1100		1672 V. TERTIO	*Extremely rare*		
1671/0 — 85	325	1500		1672 V. QVARTO......60	250	1350	

3367   3369   3370

3367 Halfcrown. Fourth dr. bust r.

1672 V. QVARTO......90	350	1500		1679 — DECNS error 150	450	—	
1673 – QVINTO 60	225	1000		1679 — DNCVS error200	—	—	
1673 —A/R in FRA........	*Extremely rare*			1679 — PRICESIMO			
1673 — B/R in BR	*Extremely rare*			error 200	500	—	
1674 – SEXTO 95	300	1500		1679 — inverted A's for			
1674/3 — 150	—	—		V's on edge 200	—	—	
1675 – SEPTIMO 70	275	1250		1680 – SECVNDO ...120	375	—	
1675 — Retrograde 1 .75	325	1500		1680 — SECVNCIO error	*Extremely rare*		
1676 – OCTAVO........55	200	950		1681 – TERTIO 70	275	1250	
1676 — Retrograde 1 .65	250	1000		1681/0 — 100	—	—	
1677 – NONO.............60	250	1100		1682 – QVARTO 80	325	1350	
1678 TRICESIMO 150	400	—		1682/79 —	*Extremely rare*		
1679 T. PRIMO 60	225	1000		1683 – QVINTO.........60	225	1000	
1679 — GRATTA error .	*Extremely rare*			1684/3 – SEXTO 125	450	—	
1679 — REGЯI error	*Extremely rare*						

3368 — plume below bust

1673 V. QVINTO ...1000	—	—		1683 T. QVINTO	*Extremely rare*		

3369— plume below bust and in centre of *rev*., 1673 V. QVINTO .... *Extremely rare*

3370 — elephant and castle below bust, 1681 T. TERTIO..........................1350   —   —

Shillings

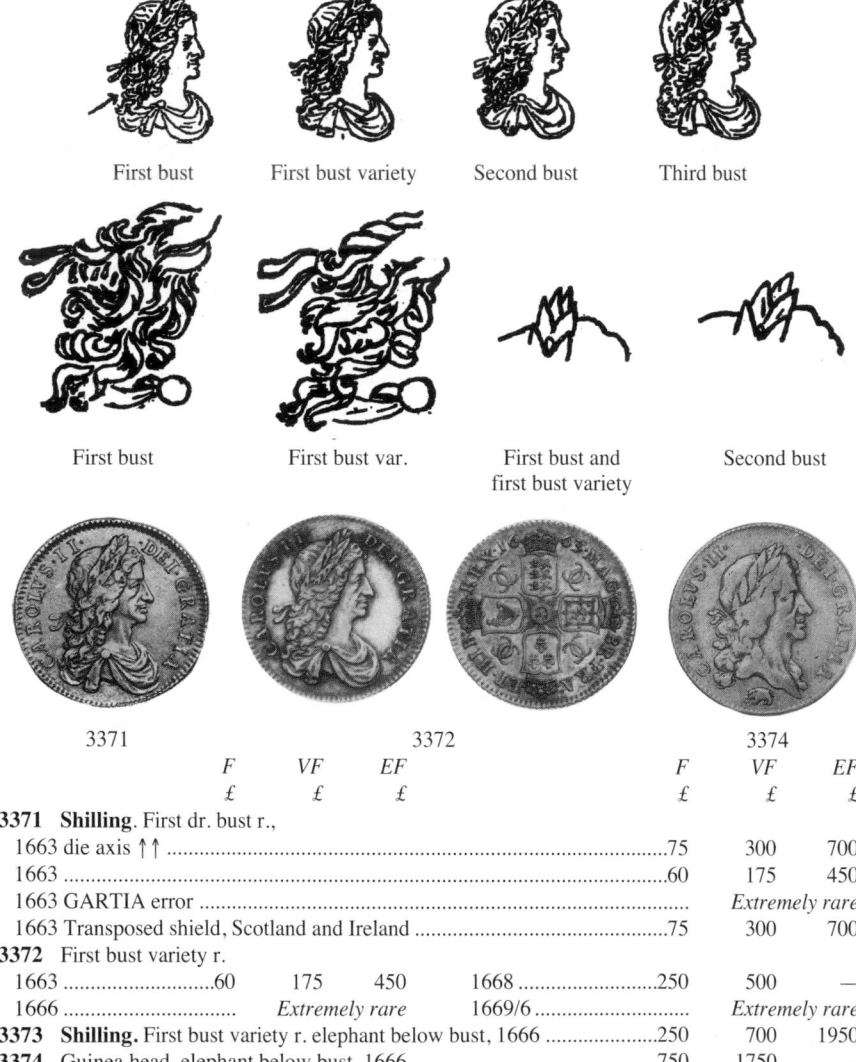

| First bust | First bust variety | Second bust | Third bust |

| First bust | First bust var. | First bust and first bust variety | Second bust |

3371   3372   3374

	F £	VF £	EF £		F £	VF £	EF £

3371   Shilling. First dr. bust r.,

1663 die axis ↑↑ 75   300   700

1663 60   175   450

1663 GARTIA error ....   *Extremely rare*

1663 Transposed shield, Scotland and Ireland 75   300   700

3372   First bust variety r.

1663 60   175   450   1668 250   500   —

1666 ....   *Extremely rare*   1669/6 ....   *Extremely rare*

3373   Shilling. First bust variety r. elephant below bust, 1666 250   700   1950

3374   Guinea head, elephant below bust, 1666...750   1750   —

3375   3376

	F £	VF £	EF £		F £	VF £	EF £

3375 Shilling. Second dr. bust r.

1666	*Extremely rare*			1676	65	200	500
1668	50	150	425	1676/5	75	250	600
1668/7	65	200	550	1677	65	200	500
1669	*Extremely rare*			1678	80	250	700
1670	80	250	700	1678/7	80	250	700
1671	100	325	800	1679	65	200	500
1672	65	200	550	1679/7	80	250	700
1673	100	325	800	1680	*Extremely rare*		
1673/2	150	500	1000	1681	95	325	800
1674	125	400	900	1681/0	95	325	800
1674/3	100	325	800	1682/1	300	650	—
1675	150	500	1000	1683	*Extremely rare*		
1675/4	150	500	1000				

3376 — plume below bust and in centre of *rev.*

1671	150	450	1200	1676	165	475	1300
1673	165	475	1300	1679	200	600	1650
1674	150	450	1200	1680	275	750	1900
1675	165	475	1300	1680/79	275	750	1900

3377 — plume *rev.* only, 1674 200   600   1650

3378 — plume *obv. only*

1677	200	600	1650	1679	185	550	1500

3379 — elephant and castle below bust, 1681/0 900   —   —

3380   3381

3380 Third dr. (large) bust r.

1674	200	550	1650	1675/3	150	375	1100
1675	150	375	1100				

3381 Fourth dr. (large) bust r., older features

1683	120	275	900	1684	100	300	800

3382

	F £	VF £	EF £		F £	VF £	EF £
3382 Sixpence. dr. bust r.							
1674	35	120	300	1679	50	150	350
1675	35	120	300	1680	75	225	500
1675/4	50	175	400	1681	35	100	250
1676	75	225	500	1682	75	200	500
1676/5	75	225	500	1682/1	50	150	350
1677	35	120	300	1683	35	120	300
1678/7	50	150	350	1684	60	150	350

3383 Fourpence. Undated. Crowned dr. bust l. to edge of coin, value
behind. R. Shield 6   15   30

3384   3386

3384 Fourpence. Dated. O. As illustration 3384. R. Four interlinked Cs

1670	10	20	45	1678/6	8	18	40
1671	8	18	40	1678	6	15	300
1672/1	7	16	35	1678/7	8	18	40
1673	7	16	35	1679	6	15	30
1674	7	16	35	1680	6	15	30
1674/4 sideways	10	20	50	1681 B/R in HIB	10	20	50
1674 7 over 6	8	18	40	1681	6	15	30
1675	7	16	35	1681/0	8	18	40
1675/4	8	18	40	1682	6	15	30
1676	7	16	35	1682/1	8	18	40
1676 7 over 6	8	18	40	1683	6	15	30
1676/5	8	18	40	1684	8	18	40
1677	6	15	30	1684/3	6	15	30

3385 Threepence. Undated. As 3383 8   18   40

3386 Threepence. Dated. As illustration

1670	6	12	28	1678	6	10	25
1671	6	10	25	1679	6	10	25
1671 GRⱯTIA	8	15	35	1679 O/A in CAROLVS	8	15	35
1672/1	6	10	25	1680	6	10	25
1673	6	10	25	1681	6	10	25
1674	6	10	25	1681/0	7	14	30
1675	6	12	28	1682	6	10	25
1676/5	7	14	30	1682/1	7	14	30
1676	6	10	25	1683	6	10	25
1676 ERA for FRA	8	15	35	1684	6	10	25
1677	6	12	28	1684/3	7	14	30

	F	VF	EF		F	VF	EF
	£	£	£		£	£	£

3387 Twopence. Undated. As 3383 (double arch crown) 6   10   25

3388   3390

3388 Dated. As illustration

1668	8	14	30	1679	6	10	25
1670	6	10	25	1679 HIB over FRA	8	14	30
1671	6	10	25	1680	6	10	25
1672/1	6	10	25	1680/79	8	14	30
1673	8	14	30	1681	6	10	25
1674	6	10	25	1682/1	8	14	30
1675	6	10	25	1682/1 ERA for FRA	..10	15	35
1676	6	10	25	1683	6	10	25
1677	8	14	30	1683/2	8	14	30
1678	6	10	25	1684	8	14	30
1678/6	8	14	30				

3389 Penny. Undated. As 3383 (double arch crown) 6   16   40

3390 Dated. As illustration

1670	8	14	35	1678 ƆRATIA error	10	20	50
1671	8	14	35	1678	9	18	45
1672/1	8	14	35	1679	9	18	45
1673	8	14	35	1680	8	14	35
1674	8	14	35	1681	10	20	50
1674 ƆRATIA error	...10	20	50	1682/1	10	20	50
1675	8	14	35	1682	9	18	40
1675 ƆRATIA error	...10	20	50	1682 ERA for FRA	10	20	50
1676	9	18	45	1683/1	8	14	35
1676 ƆRATIA error	...10	20	50	1684	9	18	45
1677	8	14	35	1684/3	10	20	50
1677 ƆRATIA error	...10	20	50				

3391 Maundy Set. Undated. The four coins 85   175   275

3392 Maundy Set. Dated. The four coins. Uniform dates

1670	70	120	250	1678	70	150	300
1671	60	100	200	1679	65	110	225
1672	70	120	250	1680	60	100	200
1673	60	100	200	1681	70	150	300
1674	60	100	200	1682	65	110	225
1675	65	110	200	1683	60	100	200
1676	65	110	200	1684	65	110	225
1677	65	110	200				

COPPER AND TIN

3393

	F £	VF £	EF £		F £	VF £	EF £
3393 Copper **Halfpenny** Cuir. bust l.							
1672	50	150	400	1675	45	125	375
1673	40	120	350				

3394   3395

3394 Copper **Farthing.** As illustration							
1672	40	110	275	1675	40	110	275
1673	40	110	275	1679	50	140	325
1674	50	140	325				

	Fair £	F £	VF £	EF £

Prices for tin coinage based on corrosion free examples, and in the top grades with some lustre

3395 Tin **Farthing.** Somewhat similar, but with copper plug, edge inscribed NUMMORVM FAMVLVS, and date on edge only				
1684	35	95	350	950
1685			*Extremely rare*	

During this reign the dies continued to be engraved by John Roettier, the only major difference in the silver coinage being the ommission of the interlinked C's for Carolvs in the angles of the shields on the reverses. Tin halfpence and farthings provided the only base metal coinage during this short reign. All genuine tin coins of this period have a copper plug.

GOLD

	F	VF	EF		F	VF	EF
	£	£	£		£	£	£

3396 **Five Guineas.** First laur. bust l., sceptres misplaced date on edge in
words (e.g. 1686 = SECVNDO), 1686 SECVNDO..........................1300 2500 5500

3397 — sceptres normal.

1687 TERTIO..........1000	2000	5000	1688 QVARTO 1000	2000	5000

3397A

3397A Second laur. bust l.

1687 TERTIO..........1000	2000	5000	1688 QVARTO 1000	2000	5000

3398

3398 First laur. bust l. Elephant and castle below bust

1687 TERTIO..........1250	2500	5500	1688 QVARTO 1250	2500	5500

3399

3399 **Two Guineas.** Similar

1687 650	1800	4500	1688/7 650	1800	4750

	F	*VF*	*EF*			*F*	*VF*	*EF*
	£	£	£			£	£	£

3400 Guinea. First laur. bust l.
1685 275   650   1750   1686 300   750   2000
3401 — elephant and castle below
1685 350   900   2200   1686 ....   *Extremely rare*
3402 Second laur. bust l.
1686 250   600   1500   1688 275   650   1650
1687 250   600   1500

3403

3404

3403 — elephant and castle below
1686 425   1000   2950   1688 300   700   1950
1687 300   700   1950
3404 Half-Guinea laur. bust l.
1686 225   600   1650   1688 275   650   1750
1687 325   750   2000
3405 elephant and castle below, 1686...400   1800   —

SILVER

3406

3406 Crown. First dr. bust, l. regnal year on edge in words (e.g. 1686 = SECVNDO)
1686 SECVNDO 125   550   1750
1686 — No stops on obverse 275   750   —

3407

| | F | VF | EF | | F | VF | EF |
| | £ | £ | £ | | £ | £ | £ |

3407 Crown. Second dr. bust l.

	F	VF	EF		F	VF	EF
1687 TERTIO 100	400	800		1688/7 — 125	550	1250
1688 QVARTO.........100	450	950				

3408   1st bust   2nd bust

3408 Halfcrown. First dr. bust, l. regnal year on edge in words (e.g. 1685 = PRIMO)

	F	VF	EF		F	VF	EF
1685 PRIMO 90	275	800	1686 TERTIO 120	350	1000
1686 SECVNDO 90	275	800	1687 TERTIO 90	275	800
1686/5 — 200	500	—	1687/6 — 120	350	1000
1686 TERTIO Vover S or B			1687 — 6 over 8	*Extremely rare*	
in JACOBVS 150	450	—			

3409 Second dr. bust l.

	F	VF	EF		F	VF	EF
1687 TERTIO.............100	350	950	1688 QVARTO 85	250	800

3410

3410 Shilling. Dr. bust l.

	F	VF	EF		F	VF	EF
1685 90	225	500	1687 120	350	750
1685 no stops on reverse120	350	750	1687/6 100	300	650
1686 90	225	500	1688 100	300	650
1686 V/S in JACOBVS120	350	750	1688/7 120	350	750
1687 G/A in MAG 140	400	850			

	F	*VF*	*EF*		*F*	*VF*	*EF*
	£	£	£		£	£	£

3411 Shilling. plume in centre of *rev.*, 1685 ....Fair £4000

3412   3413

3412 Sixpence. R. Early type shields

1686 75	200	400	1687/6 75	200	400
1687 75	200	400			

3413 Sixpence. R. Late type shields

1687 55	175	350	1687 Later/early shields100	250	500
1687/6 85	225	450	1688 70	200	400

3414   3415

3414 Fourpence. O. As illus. R. IIII crowned

1686 8	15	40	1688 8	15	40
1686 Date over crown...8	15	40	1688 1 over 8 8	15	40
1687/6 6	12	35	1688/7 8	15	40
1687 8 over 7 8	15	40			

3415 Threepence. – R. III crowned

1685 5	14	35	1687/6 5	14	35
1685 Groat flan 12	30	60	1688 5	14	35
1686 5	14	35	1688/7 6	16	40
1687 6	16	40			

3416 Twopence. – R. II crowned

1686 7	14	35	1687 ERA for FRA.......8	16	40
1686 IΛCOBVS 10	20	45	1688 8	16	40
1687 7	14	35	1688/7 8	16	40

3416   3417

3417 Penny. – R. I crowned

1685 8	15	40	1687/8 8	15	40
1686 8	15	40	1688 8	15	40
1687/6 8	15	40	1688/7 8	15	40
1687 8	15	40			

3418 Maundy Set. As last four. Uniform dates

1686 75	150	300	1688 75	150	300
1687 75	150	300			

TIN

3419

	Fair	F	VF	EF
	£	£	£	£

Prices for tin coinage based on corrosion free examples, and in the top grades with some lustre

3419 Halfpenny. Dr. bust r.; date on edge

1685	45	100	300	800
1686	55	120	350	850
1687	45	100	300	800

3420

3420 Farthing. Cuir. bust r.; date on edge

1684			*Extremely rare*	
1685	40	90	250	700
1686	45	100	275	775
1687			*Extremely rare*	
3421 Dr. bust r.; date on edge, 1687	50	100	300	850

Due to the poor state of the silver coinage, much of it worn hammered coin, the Guinea, which was valued at 21s. 6d. at the beginning of the reign, circulated for as much as 30s. by 1694. The tin Halfpennies and Farthings were replaced by copper coins in 1694. The rampant Lion of Nassau is now placed as an inescutcheon on the centre of the royal arms.

GOLD

3422

	F £	VF £	EF £		F £	VF £	EF £
3422 Five Guineas. Conjoined busts r. regnal year on edge in words (e.g. 1691 = TERTIO)							
1691 TERTIO	950	1850	4500	1694/2 SEXTO	1000	2200	5000
1692 QVARTO	950	1850	4500	1694 SEXTO	1200	2500	5500
1693 QVINTO	950	1850	4500				

3423   3424

	F £	VF £	EF £		F £	VF £	EF £
3423 — elephant and castle below							
1691 TERTIO	1100	2250	5000	1694/2 SEXTO	1100	2500	5250
1692 QVARTO	1100	2250	5000	1694 SEXTO	1200	2750	5500
1693 QVINTO	1250	2500	5500				
3424 Two Guineas. Conjoined busts r.							
1693	600	1450	3250	1694/3	600	1450	3250
3425 — elephant and castle below							
1691		*Extremely rare*		1694/3	700	1750	4000
1693	700	1750	4000				
3426 Guinea. Conjoined busts r.							
1689	275	700	1950	1692	300	800	2500
1690	300	750	2200	1693	300	750	2200
1691	300	750	2200	1694	275	725	2000

3427

| F | VF | EF | | F | VF | EF |
| £ | £ | £ | | £ | £ | £ |

3427 Guinea. Conjoined busts r. elephant and castle below

1689	300	750	2250	1692	300	800	2500
1690	375	850	2750	1693		*Extremely rare*	
1691	300	800	2500	1694	300	800	2500

3428 — elephant only below

| 1692 | 375 | 900 | 2750 | 1693 | | *Extremely rare* | |

Overstruck dates are listed only if commoner than the normal date or if no normal date is known.

3429   3430

3429 Half-Guinea. First busts r. 1689 .... 350 · 750 · 2000

3430 Second busts r. R. Second shield

1690	250	625	1850	1693		*Extremely rare*	
1691	275	700	2000	1694	250	625	1850
1692	300	625	1850				

3431 — — elephant and castle below

| 1691 | 250 | 550 | 1650 | 1692 | 275 | 700 | 2000 |

3432 — — elephant only below, 1692 .... *Extremely rare*

SILVER

3433

3433 Crown. Conjoined busts r. regnal year on edge in words (e.g. 1691 = TERTIO)

1691 TERTIO	195	500	1500	1692/ℨ QVARTO	250	750	—
1691 TERTTIO		*Extremely rare*		1692/ℨ QVINTO	195	500	1500
1692 QVARTO	195	500	1500				

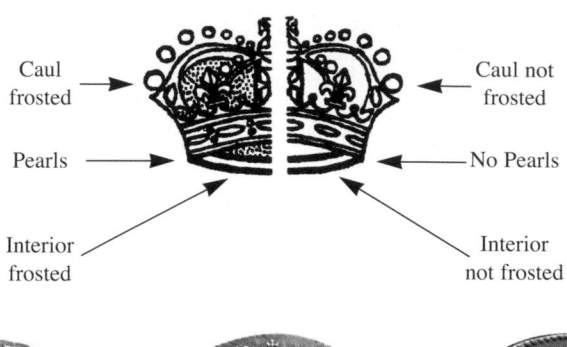

Caul frosted →   ← Caul not frosted

Pearls →   ← No Pearls

Interior frosted   Interior not frosted

3434   3435

	F £	VF £	EF £		F £	VF £	EF £

3434 Halfcrown. First busts, r. R. First shield, 1689 PRIMO R. Crown with caul
and interior frosted, with pearls 50 140 600
1689— 2nd L/M in GVLIELMVS 60 150 625
1689 — 1st V/A in GVLIELMVS, only caul frosted 60 150 625
1689 — — interior also frosted, no pearls 55 145 625
1689 Caul only frosted, pearls 50 140 600
1689 — no pearls 55 145 625
1689 No frosting, pearls 55 145 625
1689 No stops on obverse 60 150 625
1689 FRA for FR 95 200 750

3435 — second shield

1689 PRIMO R. Caul ..	65	175	650	1689 Caul only frosted	.65	175	650
and interior frosted with pearls				1689 no frosting, pearls	60	150	625
1689 — — no pearls	75	200	700	1689 no frosting no			
1689 — — — ŁT for ET error	*Extremely rare*			pearls	60	150	625
1689 GVLIŁMVS error ..	*Extremely rare*			1690 SECVNDO	75	250	750
1689 Caul only				1690 — GRETIA error	150	475	1250
frosted pearls	60	150	625	1690 TERTIO	100	350	950
1689 interior frosted,							
no pearls	65	175	650				

3436

	F	VF	EF		F	VF	EF
	£	£	£		£	£	£

3436 Halfcrown. Second busts r. R. Crowned cruciform shields, WM monogram in angles

1691 TERTIO.............65	185	700		1693 QVINTO...........65	175	650
1692 QVARTO 65	200	700		1693 3 over inverted 375	200	700
1692 R/G in REGINA	*Extremely rare*			1693 inverted 3 125	300	850
1692 QVINTO 125	400	—				

3437

3438

3437 Shilling. Conjoined busts r. R. Similar

1692 85	300	600		1693 9/0 120	350	850
1692 inverted 1 100	350	700		1693 80	275	550

3438 Sixpence. Similar

1693 80	200	375		1694 95	225	500
1693 inverted 3	100	250		550		

3439 Fourpence. First busts, r. no tie to wreath

1689 GV below bust 8	14	35		1690 6 over 5 10	15	40
1689 G below bust 8	14	35		1691 12	20	50
1689 stop befor G........10	16	40		1691/0 11	18	42
1690 10	16	40		1694 12	20	50

3440 Second busts r. tie to wreath

1692 11	18	42		1693 12	25	55
1692/1 12	25	50		1694 12	25	55
1693/2 12	25	50		1694 small lettering 12	25	55

3441 Threepence. First busts, r. no tie to wreath

1689 7	12	30		1690 6 over 5 8	14	35
1689 No stops on rev...10	20	40		1690 Large lettering 8	14	35
1689 LMV over MVS.10	20	40		1690 9 over 6 8	14	35
1689 Hyphen stops on rev.8	14	35		1691 30	60	100
1690 8	14	35				

	F £	VF £	EF £		F £	VF £	EF £

3442 Threepence. Second busts, r. tie to wreath

1691	10	20	45	1693 GV below bust	9	16	40
1692 G below bust	10	20	45	1694 G below bust	9	16	40
1692 GV below bust	10	20	45	1694 — MARIΛ error	10	20	45
1692 GVL below bust	10	20	45	1694 GV below bust	9	16	40
1693 G below bust	9	16	40	1694 GVL below bust	9	16	40
1693/2 G below bust	9	16	40				

3443 Twopence. Conjoined busts r.

1689	8	14	35	1693/2	10	20	45
1691	8	14	35	1694	10	20	45
1692	9	16	40	1694/3	10	20	45
1694 HI for HIB	10	20	45	1694 MARLA error	12	25	50
1693	9	16	40				

3444 Penny. Legend continuous over busts,

| 1689 | 150 | 275 | 400 | 1689 MΛRIΛ | 175 | 300 | 450 |
| 1689 GVIELMVS error | 175 | 300 | 450 | | | | |

3445 Legend broken by busts

1690	14	28	65	1694	12	25	60
1691/0	12	25	60	1694 no stops on obv.	15	30	65
1692	14	28	65	1694 HI for HIB	15	30	65
1692/1	15	30	70	1694 — 9/6	15	30	65
1693	12	25	60				

3446

3446 Maundy Set. As last four. Uniform dates

1689	250	475	750	1693	150	250	450
1691	95	175	350	1694	95	175	350
1692	150	250	450				

TIN AND COPPER

	Fair £	F £	VF £	EF £

Prices for tin coinage based on corrosion free examples, and in the top grades with some lustre

3447 Tin **Halfpenny.** Small dr. busts r.; date on edge 1689 250   500   —   —

3448

3448 Large cuir. busts r.; date only on edge

| 1690 | 60 | 120 | 350 | 800 |

	F	VF	EF		F	VF	EF
	£	£	£		£	£	£

3449 Halfpenny. date in ex. and on edge

1691	50	100	300	750
1692	50	100	300	750

3450 Tin Farthing. Small dr. busts r.

1689	120	300	750	—
1689, edge 1690		*Extremely rare*		

3451

3451 Large cuir. busts r.

1690, edge 1689		*Extremely rare*		
1690	40	100	300	750
1691	40	100	300	750
1692	50	125	350	800

3452

3452 Copper Halfpenny, 1694   50   120   375

3453

3453 Copper Farthing, 1694   60   150   425

In 1696 a great re-coinage was undertaken to replace the hammered silver that made up most of the coinage in circulation, much of it being clipped and badly worn. Branch mints were set up at Bristol, Chester, Exeter, Norwich and York to help with the re-coinage. For a short time before they were finally demonetized, unclipped hammered coins were allowed to circulate freely provided they were officially pierced in the centre. Silver coins with roses between the coats of arms were made from silver obtained from the West of England mines.

GOLD

3454

	F	VF	EF		F	VF	EF
	£	£	£		£	£	£

3454 Five Guineas. First laur. bust r. regnal year on edge in words (e.g. 1699 = UNDECIMO)

1699 UNDECIMO ..1000	2000	4000	1700 DVODECIMO 1100	2200	4500

3455 — elephant and castle below, 1699 UNDECIMO ....1350 | 2950 | 5000

3456    3457

3456 Second laur. bust r. ('fine work'), 1701. Plain or ornamental
sceptres DECIMO TERTIO ....1000 | 2750 | 4800

3457 Two Guineas. ('fine work'), similar 1701..1000 | 1950 | 3750

3458

3458 Guinea. First laur. bust r.

1695 200	550	1500	1697 225	600	1750
1696 225	600	1750			

	F	VF	EF		F	VF	EF
	£	£	£		£	£	£

3459 Guinea. elephant and castle below
1695 250   700   2000   1696 ....   *Extremely rare*

| 3460 | 3463 |

3460 Second laur. bust r. human-headed harp
1697 225   600   1750   1699 250   700   2000
1698 200   500   1350   1700 200   500   1350
3461   — elephant and castle below
1697 500   1250   —   1699 ....   *Extremely rare*
1698 300   750   2000   1700 500   1400   —
3462 Second laur. bust. r. R. Human headed harp. Large lettering and
large date, 1698 200   500   1350
3463 — R. Narrow crowns, plain or ornamented sceptres, 1701 200   500   1350
3464 — elephant and castle below, 1701...   *Extremely rare*
3465 Third laur. bust r. ('fine work'), 1701 350   800   2500

| 3466 | 3468 |

3466 Half-Guinea. R. With early harp, 1695 185   400   1200
3467 — elephant and castle. R. With early harp
1695 275   750   1850   1696 200   600   1500
3468 — R. With late harp
1697 240   650   1750   1700 150   300   900
1698 150   300   900   1701 150   300   900
1699 ....   *Extremely rare*
3469 — elephant and castle, 1698 225   600   1750

SILVER

3470

	F £	VF £	EF £		F £	VF £	EF £

3470 Crown. First dr. bust, r. R.First harp, regnal year on edge in words (e.g. 1696 = OCTAVO)

	F	VF	EF		F	VF	EF
1695 SEPTIMO 60	175	600		1696 G/D IN GRA....250	400	—	
1695 OCTAVO...........65	200	650		1696 — no stops 300	500	—	
1695 OCTA∀O error 100	300	—		1696/5 300	500	—	
1695 TVTA·EN error	*Extremely rare*			1696 GEI for DEI 200	400	—	
1696 OCTAVO...........50	150	500		1696 — no stops 250	—	—	
1696 No stops on obverse 150	—	—					

3471

3471 Second dr. bust r. R. Second harp (hair across breast), 1696 (two varieties)
OCTAVO ....   *Each unique*

3472

3472 Third dr. bust, r. R. First harp, 1696 OCTAVO 60   175   600
1696 TRICESIMO ....   *Extremely rare*

	F	VF	EF		F	VF	EF
	£	£	£		£	£	£

3473 Crown. second harp, 1697 NONO 500 1250 9500

3474

		F	VF	EF
3474	**Crown.** Third bust variety r. R. Third harp, 1700 DVODECIMO 65	175	550
	1700 D. TERTIO..80	250	800
	1700 ANN⊙error 250	—	—
	1700 ⅭECIMO error	*Extremely rare*	
3475	**Halfcrown.** R. Small shields, 1696 OCTAVO 40	100	275
	— 1696 DECⱯS error 120	350	—
3476	— B *(Bristol)* below bust, 1696 OCTAVO...................................45	120	375

Chester Mint	Exeter Mint
3477	3478

		F	VF	EF
3477	— C *(Chester)* below bust, 1696 OCTAVO 100	275	575
3478	— E *(Exeter)* below bust, 1696 OCTAVO 125	325	750
3479	— N *(Norwich)* below bust, 1696 OCTAVO 65	175	350
3480	— y *(York)* below bust, 1696 OCTAVO..95	275	575

3481

3481 Halfcrown R. Large shield, early harp, 1696 OCTAVO 45 120 275

	F £	*VF* £	*EF* £		*F* £	*VF* £	*EF* £

3482 Halfcrown. — B (*Bristol*) below bust, 1696 OCTAVO 50   150   275
3483 — — C (*Chester*) below bust, 1696 OCTAVO 60   175   375
3484 — — E (*Exeter*) below bust, 1696 OCTAVO 70   225   475
3485 — — N (*Norwich*) below bust, 1696 OCTAVO 95   275   625
3486 — — y (*York*) below bust, 1696 OCTAVO...............65   175   400
— — — 1696 y (*York*), Scots Arms at date ....   *Extremely rare*
— — y over E 1696 ....   *Extremely rare*

3487 3488
Bristol Mint

3487 Halfcrown. R. Large shields, ordinary harp
1696 OCTAVO 120   400   900   1697 — GRR for GRA ...   *Extremely rare*
1697 NONO...............40   100   225   1697/6 — 85   250   500
3488 — — B (*Bristol*) below bust, 1697 NONO...............45   125   350
1697 — no stops on reverse...............60   150   400
3489 — — C (*Chester*) below bust
1696 OCTAVO 95   275   650   1697 NONO...............50   150   350

3490 3496
Exeter Mint

3490 — — E (*Exeter*) below bust
1696 OCTAVO 95   275   650   1697 NONO...............40   120   325
1696 NONO ....   *Extremely rare*   1697 — TⱯTAMEN error   *Extremely rare*
1697 OCTAVO...............   *Extremely rare*   1697 E over C or B under bust *Extremely rare*
3491 — — N (*Norwich*) below bust
1696 OCTAVO 100   325   750   1697 NONO...............50   150   350
1697 OCTAVO...............   *Extremely rare*   1697 — Scots Arms at date   *Extremely rare*
3492 — — y (*York*) below bust,
1697 NONO...............40   120   325   1697 OCTAVO ....   *Extremely rare*
3493 Second dr. bust r. (hair across breast), 1696 OCTAVO...............   *Unique*

	F £	VF £	EF £		F £	VF £	EF £

3494 Halfcrown. Dr. bust R. Modified large shields

1698 OCTAVO	*Extremely rare*			1699 — Lion of			
1698 DECIMO 40	100	275		Nassau inverted	*Extremely rare*		
1698/7 —	*Extremely rare*			1700 DVODECIMO...40	120	300	
1698 UNDECIMO	*Extremely rare*			1700 D. TERTIO 50	150	375	
1699 UNDECIMO 70	200	450		1700 — DECAS error 85	225	500	
1699 — Inverted A's for				1701 D. TERTIO 50	150	375	
V's on edge 100	300	—		1701 — no stops			
1699 — Scots Arms at date	*Extremely rare*			on reverse............75	200	450	

3495 – elephant and castle below bust, 1701 D. TERTIO .... *Fair* 450
3496 – R. Plumes in angles, 1701 D. TERTIO 125   350   800

First bust   Third bust   Third bust variety

Exeter Mint   3497   3504
3500   1st bust   2nd bust

3497 Shilling. First dr. bust

1695 30	75	200		1697 20	50	110	
1696 20	50	110		1697 E/A in DEI	*Extremely rare*		
1696 no stops on reverse 40	85	225		1697 GRI for GRA error	*Extremely rare*		
1696 MAB for MAG error	*Extremely rare*			1697 Arms of Scot/Ireland			
1696 GVLIEMVS error..	*Extremely rare*			transposed	*Extremely rare*		
1696 GVLIELMAS error	*Extremely rare*			1697 Irish Arms at date ..	*Extremely rare*		
1696 GVLELMVS:	*Extremely rare*			1697 no stops on reverse 30	80	200	
1696 2nd L over M	*Extremely rare*			1697 GVLELMVS error.	*Extremely rare*		
1696-1669 error	*Extremely rare*						

3498 — B (*Bristol*) below bust

1696 30	70	175		1697 30	75	200	

3499 — C (*Chester*) below bust

1696 30	75	200		1697 30	75	200	
1696 R/V in GRA	*Extremely rare*						

3500 — E (*Exeter*) below bust

1696 30	75	200		1697 30	75	200	

3501 – N (*Norwich*) below bust

1696 30	75	200		1697 30	75	200	

3502 — y (*York*) below bust

1696 30	75	200		1697 Arms of Scot./Ireland			
1697 30	75	200		transposed	*Extremely rare*		
1697 Arms of France/Ireland							
transposed	*Extremely rare*						

	F £	*VF* £	*EF* £		*F* £	*VF* £	*EF* £

3503　Shilling. Y (*York*) below bust

1696 40	80	225	1697 40	80	200
1696 Y over Λ	*Extremely rare*				

3504　Second dr. bust r. (hair across breast), 1696 ....　*Unique*

3505 3rd bust	3507 Chester Mint	3511 3rd bust var.

3505　Third dr. bust r., 1697..20	50	110
3506　— B (*Bristol*) below bust, 1697 40	90	225

3507　— C (*Chester*) below bust

1696 90	225	500	1697 no stops on reverse50	100	300
1697 FR.A error..........50	100	350	1697 Arms of Scotland		
1697 35	75	200	at date.....................	*Extremely rare*	

3508　— E (*Exeter*) below bust,

1696	*Extremely rare*		1697 40	80	225

3509　— N (*Norwich*) below bust, 1697 40	80	225

3510　— y (*York*) below bust

1696	*Extremely rare*		1697 40	80	225

3511　Third bust variety r.

1697 GΛLIELMVS error	*Extremely rare*		1697 GVLIELMΛS error	*Extremely rare*	
1697 20	50	110	1698 30	75	200

3512　— B (*Bristol*) below bust, 1697 40	80	225
3513　— C (*Chester*)　below bust, 1697..80	200	500
3514　— R. Plumes in angles, 1698 90	225	550

Third bust

Fourth bust

Fifth bust

3515
4th bust

3516
5th bust

	F £	VF £	EF £		F £	VF £	EF £
3515 Shilling Fourth dr. bust ('flaming hair') r.							
1698 60		175	500	1699 60		175	500
1698 No stop on reverse .	*Extremely rare*						
3516 Fifth dr. bust (hair high) r.							
1699 50		100	280	1700 Tall O's no stops			
1700 30		60	125	on reverse...........45		75	175
1700 Circular small				1701 50		100	250
Os in date 35		65	140				
3517 — R. Plumes in angles							
1699 70		175	450	1701 70		175	400

3518

1st bust
3520

		F £	VF £	EF £
3518	— R. Roses in angles, 1699 80		225	500
3519	— plume below bust, 1700 850		—	—

First bust

Third bust

Early harp.
large crown.

Later harp,
small crown.

	F £	VF £	EF £		F £	VF £	EF £
3520 Sixpence. First dr. bust r. R. early harp							
1695 35		75	225	1696/5 25		60	140
1696 15		35	85	1696 no stops on			
1696 French Arms at date	*Extremely rare*			obverse...............20		50	120
1696 Scots Arms at date..	*Extremely rare*			1696 DFI for DEI	*Extremely rare*		

	F	VF	EF		F	VF	EF
	£	£	£		£	£	£

3521 **Sixpence.** — — B *(Bristol)* below bust, 1696 ....20　40　100

　　　　— — 1696 B over E..　*Extremely rare*

3522 — — C *(Chester)* below bust, 1696.................................30　65　175

3523 — — E *(Exeter)* below bust, 1696................................35　75　225

3524 — — N *(Norwich)* below bust, 1696 ....30　60　150

3525 — — y *(York)* below bust, 1696 ....20　50　125

3526 — — Y *(York)* below bust, 1696 ....35　75　225

　　　　— — — 1696 no stops on obverse ....50　125　—

3527 — R. Later harp, large crowns, 1696 ....45　100　250

　　　　— — — 1696 no stops on obverse ....50　125　275

3528 — — — B *(Bristol)* below bust

1696 ....40　100　250　　1697 ....35　75　225

1696 no stops on

obverse ....50　120　250

3529 — — — C *(Chester)* below bust, 1697..........................40　100　250

3530 — — — E *(Exeter)* below bust, 1697.............................40　100　250

3531 — — small crowns

1696 ....40　90　225　　1697 Arms of France/Ireland

1697 GVLIELMVS.....50　125　225　　　　transposed ....　*Extremely rare*

1697 ....18　35　100

Bristol Mint
3532

3532 — — — B *(Bristol)* below bust

1696 ....50　125　275　　1697 ....30　65　150

1696 no stops on　　　　　　　　　　　　1697 B over E.............40　100　200

obverse ....50　125　275

3533 — — — C *(Chester)* below bust

1696 ....50　125　350　　1697 Irish shield at date..　*Extremely rare*

1697 ....25　55　150

3534 — — — E *(Exeter)* below bust,

1697 ....30　65　175　　1697 E over B ....　*Extremely rare*

3535 — — — N *(Norwich)* below bust

1696 ....50　125　300　　1697 ....　*Extremely rare*

1697 GVLIEMVS.......20　40　110

3536 — — — y *(York)* below bust,

1697 ....45　100　250　　1697 Irish shield at date..　*Extremely rare*

2nd bust
3537

Chester Mint
3540

	F £	VF £	EF £		F £	VF £	EF £
3537 Sixpence. Second dr. bust r.							
1696	200	375	—	1696 GVLELMVS	200	400	—
1697 GVLIELMⱯS	*Extremely rare*			1697	75	175	400
1697 G/I in GRⱯ	*Extremely rare*			1697 GR/DE in GRA	*Extremely rare*		
1697 GVLIEMVS	*Extremely rare*						

3537A Third dr. bust, r. early harp, large crowns. E *(Exeter)* below bust, 1696 ...... *Extremely rare*

3537B — — — Y *(York)* below bust, 1696 .... *Extremely rare*

	F £	VF £	EF £		F £	VF £	EF £
3538 Third dr. bust, r., R. Later harp, large crowns							
1697 GVLIEIMVS	Extremely rare						
1697	15	30	85	1699	45	120	275
1697 GⱯLIELMVS	*Extremely rare*			1700	20	35	75
1698	20	35	75	1701	25	45	125
3539 — — B *(Bristol)* below bust,							
1697	30	65	175	1697 IRA for FRA	*Extremely rare*		
3540 — — C *(Chester)* below bust, 1697 40					85	225	
3541 — — E *(Exeter)* below bust, 1697 50					125	300	
3542 Third dr. bust, r. R. Small crowns,							
1697	25	45	125	1698 G/D for GRA	*Extremely rare*		
3543 — — C *(Chester)* below bust, 1697 35					75	200	
3544 — — E *(Exeter)* below bust, 1697 30					65	175	
3545 — — Y *(York)* below bust, 1697 45					100	275	
3546 — — R. Plumes in angles							
1698	25	60	150	1699	30	60	175
3547 — R. Roses in angles,							
1699	45	100	250	1699 GⱯLIELMVS	*Extremely rare*		
3548 — plume below bust, 1700 600					—	—	
3549 Fourpence. R. 4 crowned							
1697		*Unique*		1700	11	18	45
1698	14	20	55	1701	14	20	55
1699	11	18	45	1702	10	18	40
3550 Threepence. R. 3 crowned							
1698	11	18	45	1701 GBA for GRA	15	25	50
1699	12	20	50	1701 small lettering	11	18	45
1700	11	18	45	1701 large lettering	12	20	45
3551 Twopence. R. Crown to edge of coin, large figure 2							
1698 12					20	50	
3551A – R Crown within inner circle of legend, smaller figure 2							
1699	9	15	40	1701	9	15	40
1700	9	15	40				

	F £	VF £	EF £		F £	VF £	EF £

3552 Penny. R. 1 crowned

1698 9	15	40	1699 10	16	45
1698 IRA for FRA error 12	25	50	1700 10	16	45
1698 HI.BREX error ...12	25	50	1701 9	15	40

3553

3553 Maundy Set. As last four. Uniform dates

1698 75	150	300	1700 90	200	350
1699 90	200	350	1701 75	150	300

COPPER

3554

3554 Halfpenny. First issue. R. Britannia with r. hand raised

1695 35	75	275	1697 25	65	225
1696 25	65	225	1698 35	85	300

3555 Second issue. R. Date in legend

1698 Stop after date 30	75	275	1699 No stop after date 25	65	225

3556 Third issue. R. Britannia with r. hand on knee

1699 25	65	225	1701 30	70	250
1700 25	65	225			

3557   3558

3557 Farthing. First issue

1695 35	95	350	1698 100	300	—
1696 30	80	325	1699 35	95	350
1697 25	70	300	1700 25	70	300

3558 Second issue. R. Date at end of legend

1698 Stop after date 40	125	450	1699 No stop after date 30	95	325

The Act of Union of 1707, which effected the unification of the ancient kingdoms of England and Scotland into a single realm, resulted in a change in the royal arms—on the Post-Union coinage the English lions and Scottish lion are emblazoned per pale on the top and bottom shields. After the Union the rose in the centre of the reverse of the gold coins is replaced by the Garter star.

Following a successful Anglo-Dutch expedition against Spain, bullion seized in Vigo Bay was sent to be minted into coin, and the coins made from this metal had the word VIGO placed below the Queen's bust.

GOLD

3560

Before Union with Scotland

	F	VF	EF		F	VF	EF
	£	£	£		£	£	£

3560 Five Guineas. Dr. bust l, regnal year on edge in words (e.g. 1705 = QVARTO)

1705 QVARTO 1450	2650	6500	1706 QVINTO........1250	2250	6000

3561   VIGO below bust, 1703 (Three varieties) SECVNDO ....— — 45000

3562   3564

3562 Guinea. Dr. bust l.

1702 250	600	1750	1706 350	750	2250
1705 350	750	2250	1707 400	850	2500

3563   VIGO below bust, 1703 ....2500 4500 —

3564 Half-Guinea. Dr bust l.

1702 250	600	1750	1705 250	600	1750

3565   VIGO below bust, 1703 ....1750 5000 —

3566

F	VF	EF		F	VF	EF
£	£	£		£	£	£

After Union with Scotland. The shields on the reverse are changed to Post-Union type

3566 Five Guineas. Dr. bust l., regnal year on edge in words 1706 QVINTO.1350   2500   5500

3567   3568

3567 — R. Narrower shields, tall narrow crowns, larger rev. lettering

1709 OCTAVO 1250   2200   5200

3568 — R. Broader shields

1711 DECIMO 1250	2200	5200	1714/3 D. TERTIO .1250	2200	5200
1713 DVODECIMO 1250	2200	5200	1714 D. TERTIO 1350	2500	5500

3569

3569 Two Guineas. Dr. bust l.

1709 500	1000	2250	1713 500	1000	2250
1711 500	1000	2250	1714/3 600	1250	2650

3570 Guinea. First dr. bust l.

| 1707 ....250 | 500 | 1100 | 1708 .... | *Extremely rare* | |

	3571				3574	
F	VF	EF		F	VF	EF
£	£	£		£	£	£

3571 Guinea. First dr. bust l. elephant and castle below

1707 450	1000	2500	1708	*Extremely rare*

3572 Second dr. bust l.

1707	*Extremely rare*		1709 250	550	1250
1708 225	450	1000			

3573 — elephant and castle below

1708 450	1000	2000	1709 400	900	1750

3574 Third dr. bust l.

1710 220	350	950	1713 220	325	900
1711 220	350	950	1714 220	325	900
1712 250	500	1250			

3575

3575 Half-Guinea. Dr. bust l.

1707 225	500	1200	1711 225	400	950
1708 275	550	1350	1712 225	450	1200
1709 200	400	950	1713 200	400	950
1710 200	400	950	1714 200	400	950

SILVER

3576

Before Union with Scotland

3576 Crown. VIGO below dr. bust, l., regnal year on edge in words (e.g. 1703 = TERTIO)

1703 TERTIO 175	500	1500

3577   3578

	F	VF	EF		F	VF	EF
	£	£	£		£	£	£

3577 Crown. Dr bust l. R. Plumes in angles, 1705 QVINTO 350   950   2500

3578 — R. Roses and plumes in angles

1706 QVINTO 120   350   750   1707 SEXTO 135   400   850

3579 Halfcrown. Dr. bust l. Regnal year on edge in words

1703 TERTIO 350   900   —

3580   3581

3580 VIGO below bust, 1703 TERTIO 75   175   400

3581 — R. Plumes in angles

1704 TERTIO............100   300   650   1705 QVINTO............85   225   550

3582

3582 — R. Roses and plumes in angles

1706 QVINTO 60   150   350   1707 SEXTO 50   120   300

	First bust				Second bust	
	F	*VF*	*EF*		*F*	*VF*	*EF*
	£	£	£		£	£	£

3583 Shilling. First dr. bust l. 1702 50   150   350

3584

3584 — R. Plumes in angles, 1702 70   175   400
3585 — VIGO below bust,
1702 60   160   375   1702 :ANNA ....   *Extremely rare*

3586   3592

3586 Shilling. Second dr. bust, l. VIGO below, 1703 50   125   300
3587 — plain
1704 350   700   —   1705 70   175   400
3588 — R. Plumes in angles
1704 75   200   450   1705 60   150   350
3589 — R. Roses and plumes in angles
1705 55   150   300   1707 55   150   325
3590 Sixpence. VIGO below dr. bust, l. 1703 30   65   125
3591 Dr bust l., R. Angles plain, 1705 45   100   225
3592 — R. Early shields, plumes in angles, 1705...35   85   175

3593   Early Shield   Late Shield

3593 – R. Late shields, plumes in angles, 1705 45   95   200
3594 – R. Roses and plumes in angles
1705 45   100   225   1707 35   75   150

	F	VF	EF		F	VF	EF
	£	£	£		£	£	£

3595 Fourpence. First dr. bust l. small face, curls at back of head point downwards.
R Small crown above the figure 4

1703	8	15	35	1704	6	12	30

3595A Second dr. bust l. larger face, curls at back of head point upwards

1705	8	15	35	1709	6	12	30
1706	6	12	30	1710	6	12	30
1708	6	12	30				

3595B – R Large crown with pearls on arch, larger serifs on the figure 4

1710	6	12	30	1713	6	12	30

3595C Second dr. bust l., but with re-engraved hair.

1710	6	12	30	1713	6	12	30

3596 Threepence. First dr. bust l., broader, tie riband pointing outwards. R. Crowned 3

1703	7 above crown 10	18	40	1703	7 not above crown 10	18	40

3596A Second dr. bust l., taller and narrow, tie riband pointing inwards

1704	8	15	35	1706	6	12	30
1705	8	15	35				

3596B Third dr. bust l., similar to first bust but larger and hair more finely engraved

1707	6	12	30	1710	6	12	30
1708	6	12	30	1713	6	12	30
1708/7	6	12	30	1713 mule with 4d obv.			
1709	6	12	30	die	10	20	50

3597 Twopence. First dr. bust l., as fourpence, R. Crown to edge of coin, small figure 2

1703	10	15	35	1705	6	11	26
1704	6	11	26	1706	7	12	28
1704	No stops on obv..10	15	35	1707	7	12	28

3597A Second dr. bust l., as fourpence, R Crown within inner circle of legend, large figure 2

1708	6	11	26	1710	6	11	26
1709	8	14	30	1713	6	11	26

3598 Penny. R. Crowned 1

1703	10	18	40	1709	8	15	35
1705	8	15	35	1710	12	20	45
1706	8	15	35	1713/0	10	18	40
1708	12	20	45				

3599

3599 Maundy Set. As last four. Uniform dates

1703	75	125	275	1709	75	125	250
1705	75	125	275	1710	80	140	300
1706	65	100	200	1713	70	115	225
1708	80	140	300				

After Union with Scotland

The shields on reverse are changed to the Post-Union types. The Edinburgh coins have been included here as they are now coins of Great Britain.

Edinburgh Mint
3600

	F	VF	EF		F	VF	EF
	£	£	£		£	£	£

3600 Crown. Second dr. bust, l. E (Edinburgh) below, regnal year on edge in words
(e.g. 1708 = SEPTIMO)

	F	VF	EF		F	VF	EF
1707 SEXTO 85	300	500		1708/7 — 100	375	600
1708 SEPTIMO 95	325	550				

3601 — plain

1707 SEPTIMO...........80	250	500		1708 SEPTIMO 110	350	—

3602 — R. Plumes in angles,

1708 SEPTIMO 125	400	750		1708 — BR for BRI	*Extremely rare*

3603

3603 Crown. Third dr. bust. l. R. Roses and plumes, 1713 DVODECIMO ..80   350   650

3604

	F	VF	EF		F	VF	EF
	£	£	£		£	£	£

3604 Halfcrown. R. Plain, regnal year on edge in words (e.g. 1709 = OCTAVO)

1707 SEPTIMO..........45	125	300	1709 OCTAVO 40	95	275
1708 SEPTIMO..........40	95	275	1713 DVODECIMO...50	125	300

3605 — E below bust

1707 SEXTO...............40	95	275	1708 SEPTIMO..........40	95	275
1707 SEPTIMO...............	*Extremely rare*		1709 OCTAVO 200	500	—

Edinburgh Mint
3606   3609

3606 — R. Plumes in angles, 1708 SEPTIMO 60   175   350

3607 — R. Roses and plumes in angles

1710 NONO 55	150	400	1714 D. TERTIO 50	150	375
1712 UNDECIMO 50	125	375	1714/3 — 100	250	500
1713 DVODECIMO ...60	175	400			

3608 Shilling. Second dr. bust, l. E *(Edinburgh)* below

1707 35	85	200	1708 70	175	350
1707 no stops on reverse	*Extremely rare*		1708 no rays to garter star	*Extremely rare*	

3609 — E* *(Edinburgh)* below

1707 70	200	400	1708/7	*Extremely rare*	
1708 45	120	250			

Third bust   Fourth bust

	F	VF	EF		F	VF	EF
	£	£	£		£	£	£

3610 Shilling Third dr. bust. l. R. Plain.

1707	25	55	125	1709	25	55	125
1708	20	50	100	1711	90	275	500

3611 — R. Plumes in angles

1707	40	95	250	1708	35	75	200

3612 — E below

1707	35	75	175	1708/7	75	175	350
1708	55	150	300				

3613 Second dr. bust l. R. Roses and plumes, 1708 .... 95 225 475

3614   3620
                                      Edinburgh Mint

3614 Third dr. bust l. R. Roses and plumes

1708	45	120	250	1710	25	55	125

3615 — 'Edinburgh' bust, E* below

1707		*Extremely rare*		1709	70	175	375
1708	65	150	350				

3616 — E below, 1709 .... 200 450 —

3617 Fourth dr. bust. l. R. Roses and plumes

1710	50	140	300	1714	25	60	125
1712	25	60	125	1714/3		*Extremely rare*	
1713/2	30	70	200				

3618 — plain, 1711 .... 20 50 100

3619 Sixpence. Normal dr. bust. l. R. Plain

1707	20	45	100	1711	20	40	75
1707 BR. FRA error		*Extremely rare*		1711 Large Lis	20	40	75
1708	25	50	110				

3620 — E *(Edinburgh)* below bust

1707	25	50	110	1708/7	40	90	175
1708	35	75	150				

3621 — E* *(Edinburgh)* below bust,

1708	35	85	175	1708/7	40	95	200

3622 'Edinburgh' bust, l. E* below, 1708 .... 40 95 200

3623

	F £	*VF* £	*EF* £		*F* £	*VF* £	*EF* £
3623 Normal dr. bust. l. R. Plumes in angles							
1707 20		50	125	1708 35		75	175
3624 — R. Roses and plumes in angles, 1710 35						75	200

COPPER

3625

3625 **Farthing.** Dr. bust l. 1714 175	250	375

GEORGE I, 1714-27

The coins of the first of the Hanoverian kings have the arms of the Duchy of Brunswick and Luneberg on one of the four shields, the object in the centre of the shield being the Crown of Charlemagne. The King's German titles also appear, in abbreviated form, and name him 'Duke of Brunswick and Luneberg. Arch-treasurer of the Holy Roman Empire, and Elector', and on the Guinea of 1714, 'Prince Elector'. A Quarter-Guinea was struck for the first time in 1718, but it was of an inconvenient size, and the issue was discontinued.

Silver coined from bullion supplied to the mint by the South Sea Company in 1723 shows the Company's initials S.S.C.; similarly Welsh Copper Company bullion has the letters W.C.C. below the King's bust; and plumes and an interlinked CC in the reverse angles. Roses and plumes together on the reverse indicate silver supplied by the Company for Smelting Pit Coale and Sea Coale.

GOLD

3626

	F	VF	EF		F	VF	EF
	£	£	£		£	£	£

3626 Five Guineas. Laur. head r. regnal year on edge in words (e.g. 1717 = TERTIO)

1716 SECVNDO	1400	2600	6000	1720 SEXTO	1500	2950	6500
1717 TERTIO	1500	2950	6500	1726 D. TERTIO	1400	2600	6000

3627

3627 Two Guineas. Laur. head r.

1717	500	1100	2500	1726	400	900	2250
1720	450	1000	2500				

	3628				3630	3631	
	F	VF	EF		F	VF	EF
	£	£	£		£	£	£

3628 Guinea. First laur. head r. R. Legend ends ET PR . EL (Prince Elector),

| 1714 | ....700 | 1250 | 2500 |

3629 Second laur. head, r. tie with two ends, R. normal legend 1715 275   650   1450

3630 Third laur. head, r. no hair below truncation

| 1715 | ....225 | 500 | 1250 | 1716 | ....250 | 600 | 1350 |

3631 Guinea. Fourth laur. head, r. tie with loop at one end

1716	200	550	1250	1720	200	550	1250
1717	225	600	1350	1721	225	650	1450
1718		*Extremely rare*		1722	200	550	1250
1719	200	550	1250	1723	225	600	1350

3632 — elephant and castle below

| 1721 | | *Extremely rare* | | 1722 | | *Extremely rare* | |

| | 3633 | | | | 3635 | | |

3633 Fifth (older) laur. head, r. tie with two ends

1723	225	600	1350	1726	200	550	1250
1724	225	600	1350	1727	250	650	1750
1725	225	600	1350

3634 — elephant and castle below, 1726 600   1500   —

3635 Half-Guinea. First laur. head r.

1715	200	400	750	1721		*Extremely rare*	
1717	175	350	650	1722	175	350	650
1718	150	300	600	1723		*Extremely rare*	
1719	150	300	600	1724	200	400	750
1720	225	450	800

3636 — elephant and castle below, 1721 ....   *Extremely rare*

| | 3637 | | | | 3638 | | |

3637 Second (older) laur. head r.

| 1725 | ....150 | 200 | 400 | 1727 | ....175 | 300 | 750 |
| 1726 | ....150 | 250 | 500 |

3638 Quarter-Guinea. 1718 60   100   200

SILVER

3639

	F £	VF £	EF £		F £	VF £	EF £

3639 Crown. R. Roses and plumes in angles, regnal year on edge in words (e.g. 1716 – SECVNDO)

	F	VF	EF		F	VF	EF
1716 SECVNDO 165	350	900		1720 — 225	575	1950
1718/6 QUINTO 195	375	1200		1726 D. TERTIO 225	500	1650
1720/18 SEXTO ,.... 195	400	1200				

3640 – R. SSC (South Sea Company) in angles, 1723 DECIMO 175   375   850

3641

3641 Halfcrown. R. Angles plain (pattern only), 1715 *FDC* £4000

3642   3643

3642 – R. Roses and plumes in angles, regnal year on edge in words (e.g. 1717 = TIRTIO)

	F	VF	EF		F	VF	EF
1715 SECVNDO 95	275	550		1717 TIRTIO 120	325	650
1715 Edge wording out				1720/17 SEXTO 95	275	550
of order 200	400	800		1720 — 250	750	1500
1715 Plain edge	*Extremely rare*					

3643 – R. SSC in angles, 1723 DECIMO 85   325   550

	F £	VF £	EF £		F £	VF £	EF £

3644 Halfcrown. R. Small roses and plumes, 1726 D. TERTIO 1250   2500   4000

3645 Shilling. First dr. bust. r. R. Roses and plumes in angles

1715 35	85	200	1720/18 85	250	250
1716 75	200	450	1721/0 40	110	250
1717 40	95	225	1721 — roses and plumes error *Extremely rare*		
1718 35	85	200	1722 40	95	225
1719 70	175	425	1723 55	150	325
1720 40	95	225			

3646 — plain (i.e. no marks either side)

1720 35	85	200	1721/0 100	225	550
1720 large O 40	95	225	1721/19 120	275	650
1721 90	200	500			

3647   3649

3647 – R. SSC in angles,

1723 25	45	85	1723 C/SS in 3rd		
1723 French Arms at			quarter............50	100	200
date 75	175	350			

3648 Second dr. bust, r. bow to tie. R. Similar, 1723 30   65   150

3649 — R. Roses and plumes in angles

1723 50	100	200	1726 400	800	—
1724 50	100	200	1727 375	750	—
1725 50	100	200	1727 no stops on rev.400	800	—
1725 no stops on rev...75	120	250			

3650   3651

3650 — W.C.C. (Welsh Copper Company) below bust

1723 225	450	1200	1725 225	450	1250
1724 225	450	1250	1726 225	450	1250

3651 Sixpence. R. Roses and plumes in angles

1717 45	100	250	1720/17 45	100	250
1717 Plain edge	*Extremely rare*				

	3652			3653		
	F	VF	EF		F	VF	EF
	£	£	£		£	£	£

3652 Sixpence. R. SSC in angles,

1723 20	40	75	1723 larger lettering ...25	45	85

3653 – R. Small roses and plumes, 1726 ....35 75 175

3654 Fourpence. Dr. bust r. R. crowned 4

1717 9	16	40	1723 9	16	40
1721 9	16	40	1727 12	20	45

3655 Threepence. R. crowned 3

1717 8	15	35	1723 9	16	40
1721 9	16	40	1727 small lettering 9	16	40

3656 Twopence. R. crowned 2

1717 6	12	22	1726 5	10	20
1721 5	10	20	1727 small lettering 8	14	25
1723 9	18	30			

3657 Penny. R. crowned 1

1716 5	9	18	1723 6	11	22
1718 5	9	18	1725 5	9	18
1720 5	9	18	1726 8	14	25
1720 HIPEX error.........8	18	30	1727 BRI·FR 8	14	25

3658

3658 Maundy Set. As last four. Uniform dates

1723 80	140	300	1727 75	130	275

COPPER

3659

3659 Halfpenny. 'Dump' issue

1717 25	70	275	1718 25	70	275

3660

	F £	VF £	EF £		F £	VF £	EF £
3660	**Halfpenny.** Second issue, second obverse, plain left shoulder strap, less hair to the right of tie knot						
1719	35	85	300	1722	30	70	250
1720	25	65	225	1723	25	65	225
1721	30	70	250	1724	25	65	225

3661   3662

3661	**Farthing.** 'Dump' issue, 1717				120	300	500
3662	Second issue						
1719	25	65	200	1722	30	75	250
1720	25	65	200	1723	30	75	250
1721	25	65	200	1724	30	75	250

Silver was coined only spasmodically by the Mint during this reign; and no copper was struck after 1754. Gold coins made from bullion supplied by the East India Company bear the Company's initials. Some of the treasure seized by Admiral Anson during his circumnavigation of the globe, 1740-4, and by other privateers, was made into coin, which had the word LIMA below the king's bust to celebrate the expedition's successful harassment of the Spanish Colonies in the New World. Hammered gold was finally demonetized in 1733.

GOLD

3664   3663A

	F £	VF £	EF £		F £	VF £	EF £
3663 **Five Guineas.** Young laur. head l. R. Crowned shield of arms, regnal year							
on edge in words (e.g. 1729 = TERTIO) 1729 TERTIO 1000		1950	4500				
3663A — R. Revised shield garnish							
1731 QVARTO 1000	1750	4750		1741/35 D. QVARTO 1000	2000	4750	
1735 OCTAVO 1000	1750	4750		1741 D. QVARTO....950	1950	4000	
1738 DVODECIMO 1000	1950	4750					
3664 — E.I.C. (East India Company) below, 1729 TERTIO 950		1950	4500				

3665   3667

3665 Old laur. head, l. LIMA below, 1746 D. NONO................................1000		1950	4750				
3666 — plain							
1748 V. SECVNDO ..950	1850	4000		1753 V. SEXTO 950	1850	4000	
3667* **Two Guineas.** Young laur. head l. R Crown with rounded arches							
1734/3 800	1750	—					
3667A – R. Crown with pointed arches, new type of shield garnishing							
1735 375	800	1750		1739 300	600	1200	
1738 350	600	1150					

* Beware recent forgeries

3668

	F £	VF £	EF £		F £	VF £	EF £
3668* Two Guineas. Intermediate laur. head l.							
1739 350		600	1250	1740 375		600	1250
3669* Old laur. head l.							
1748 375		750	1750	1753 475		950	2250

*Beware recent forgeries.
Overstruck dates are listed only if commoner than normal date or if no normal date is known.

3670 Guinea. First young laur. head, l. small lettering, 1727 500   1000   2500

3671				3674			
3671 — larger lettering, smaller shield							
1727 300		650	1900	1728 350		750	2000
3672 Second (narrower) young laur. head l.							
1730 300		650	1750	1732 300		650	1750
1731 250		550	1500				
3673 — E.I.C. below							
1729 450		1000	2250	1732 350		750	2000
1731 400		700	2000				
3674 — larger lettering on *obv*.							
1732 275		600	1500	1736 250		550	1500
1733 200		450	1250	1737 275		600	1650
1734 200		450	1250	1738 275		600	1650
1735 225		500	1350				
3675 — — E.I.C. below, 1732.....................350						750	2000
3676 Intermediate laur. head l.							
1739 200		450	1250	1741/39		*Extremely rare*	
1740 225		500	1350	1743		*Extremely rare*	
3677 — E.I.C. below, 1739.....................350						750	2000
3678 — larger lettering on *obv*., GEORGIUS							
1745 275						600	1500
3678A — as last but reads GEORGIVS							
1746 250						450	1250

| | 3679 | | | 3680 | | 3681A | | |

	F	VF	EF			F	VF	EF
	£	£	£			£	£	£

3679 Guinea. LIMA below, 1745 ....500 1000 2750

3680 Old laur. head l.

	F	VF	EF		F	VF	EF
1747 200	350	850	1753 175	275	750
1748 175	275	750	1755 200	375	900
1749 175	275	750	1756 175	250	700
1750 200	300	750	1758 150	225	650
1751 175	250	700	1759 150	225	650
1752 175	250	700	1760 175	250	700

3681 Half-Guinea. Young laur. head. l. R First shield

1728 200	450	1250	1729 250	500	1500

3681A – R. Modified garnished shield

1730 450	1000	—	1735		?exists
1731 300	700	2000	1736 200	450	1250
1732 250	500	1500	1737	Extremely rare	
1733		?exists	1738 175	400	1000
1734 175	400	1000	1739 175	400	1000

3682 — E.I.C. below

1729 300	700	2000	1732	Extremely rare	
1730 500	1000	—	1739	Extremely rare	
1731	Extremely rare				

3683 Intermediate laur. head l.

1740 300	700	2000	1745 300	700	2000
1743	Extremely rare				

3683A — as last but reads GEORGIVS, 1746 ....175 400 1000

| | 3684 | | | 3685 | |

3684 — LIMA below, 1745 ....500 1500 3000

3685 Old laur. head l.

1747 250	550	1500	1753 150	300	600
1748 150	325	700	1755 125	275	550
1749	Extremely rare		1756 125	275	550
1750 175	350	850	1758 125	275	550
1751 175	350	800	1759 120	250	500
1752 175	350	800	1760 120	250	500

SILVER

3686

	F £	VF £	EF £		F £	VF £	EF £

3686 Crown. Young dr. bust. l. R. Roses and plumes in angles, regnal year
on edge in words (e.g. 1736 = NONO)

	F	VF	EF		F	VF	EF
1732 SEXTO 120	350	700		1734 No A in ANNO 200	600	1200	
1732 Proof, plain edge *FDC* £2500				1735 OCTAVO 120	350	700	
1734 SEPTIMO 150	400	850		1736 NONO.............100	325	650	

3687 — R. Roses in angles

	F	VF	EF		F	VF	EF
1739 DVODECIMO .125	300	700		1741 D. QVARTO....100	300	600	

3688

3688 Old dr. bust l. R. Roses in angles, 1743 D. SEPTIMO 100   300   600
3689 — LIMA below, 1746 D. NONO 100   300   600

3690   3691

3690 — Plain (i.e. no marks either side)

1746 Proof only, VICESIMO *FDC* £2250

1750 V. QVARTO 150   350   700   1751 V. QVARTO....175   400   750

3691 Halfcrown. Young dr. bust l. R. plain (pattern only), 1731 *FDC* £1950

	3692			3693	
F	*VF*	*EF*	*F*	*VF*	*EF*
£	£	£	£	£	£

3692 Halfcrown. Young dr. bust l. R. Roses and plumes, regnal year on edge in words
    (e.g. 1732 = SEXTO)

1731 QVINTO 65	200	500	1735 OCTAVO 75	225	550
1732 SEXTO 65	200	500	1736 NONO...............95	250	650
1734 SEPTIMO...........75	225	550			

3693 — R. Roses in angles

1739 DVODECIMO ...50	125	350	1741 D. QVARTO......60	150	400
1741 Large *obv.* letters 75	200	450	1741/39 — 120	300	600

3694 Old dr. bust. l. GEORGIUS R. Roses in angles

1743 D. SEPTIMO......45	100	300	1745 65	125	350
1745 D. NONO 45	100	300			

3695 — LIMA below 1745 D. NONO 35 85 175

3695A — as last but reads GEORGIVS

1746 D. NONO 35	85	175	1746/5 50	120	300

3696

3696 — R. Plain angles
1746 *proof only* VICESIMO *FDC* £850

1750 V. QVARTO 75	200	500	1751 V. QVARTO......90	250	650

3697

3697 Shilling. Young dr. bust. l. R. Plumes in angles

1727 50	175	450	1731 65	200	550

3698

	F £	VF £	EF £		F £	VF £	EF £

3698 Shilling. R. Roses and plumes in angles

1727	35	85	200	1731	35	85	200
1728	45	95	250	1732	45	95	250
1729	45	95	250				

3699 — larger lettering. R. Roses and plumes in angles

1734	30	70	175	1736/5	50	120	250
1735	30	70	175	1737	30	70	175
1736	30	70	175				

3700   3701

3700 — R. Plain, 1728 125   300   500
3701 — R. Roses in angles

1739	25	60	125	1741	30	65	140
1739/7		*Extremely rare*		1741/39	300	600	—
1739 smaller garter star	85	200	450				

3702   3703A

3702 Old dr. bust, l. GEORGIUS R. Roses in angles

1743	20	45	125	1745/3	50	150	250
1745	30	75	140	1747	25	65	125

3703 — LIMA below 1745 15   45   100
3703A– as last but reads GEORGIVS

1746	85	175	450	1746/5	100	200	500

3704 — R. plain angles

1746 Proof only *FDC* £500				1750 Wide O	50	100	250
1750	30	75	200	1751	50	150	300
1750/6	50	100	250	1758	15	25	40

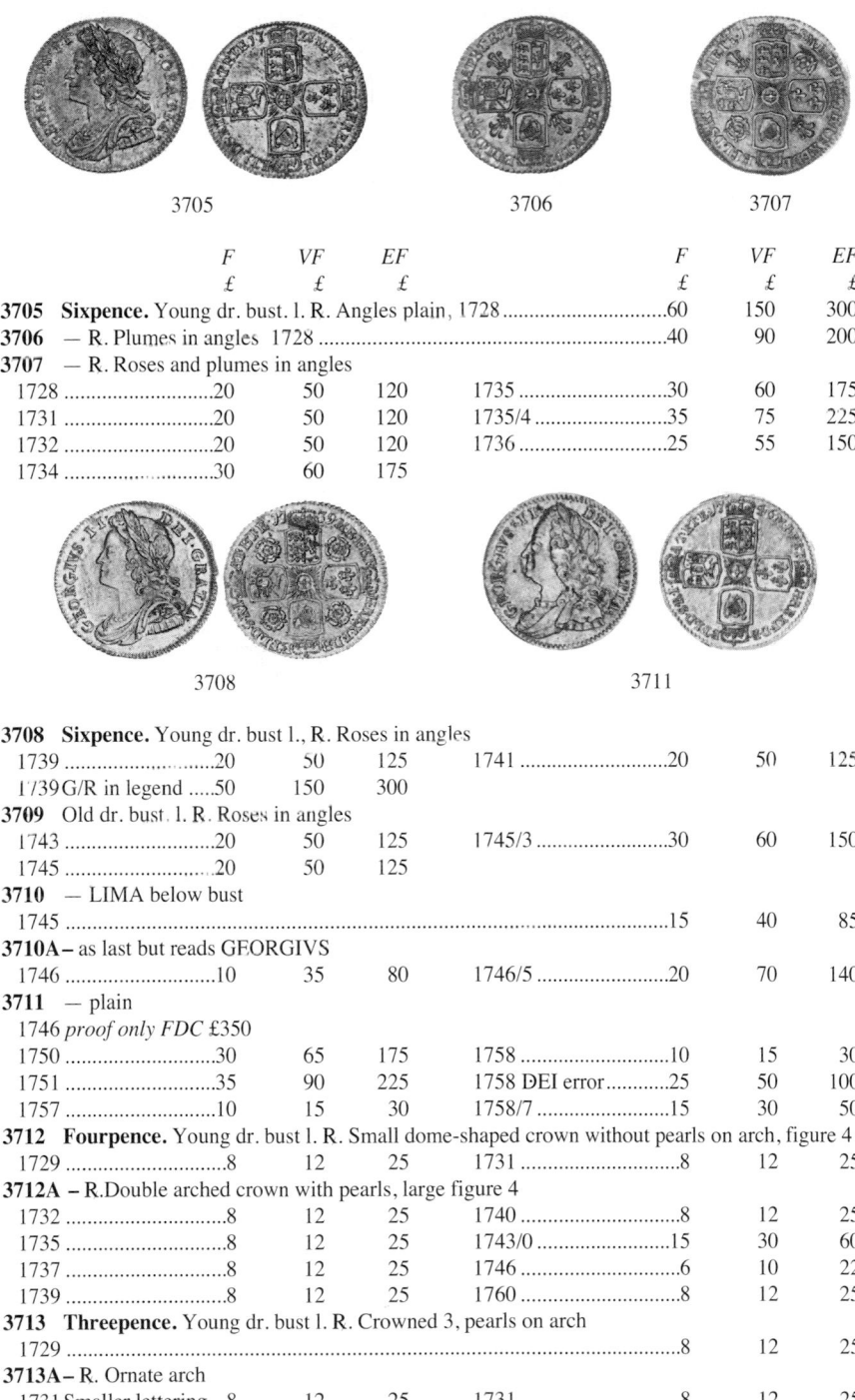

3705   3706   3707

	F	VF	EF		F	VF	EF
	£	£	£		£	£	£

3705 Sixpence. Young dr. bust. l. R. Angles plain, 1728 60   150   300
3706 — R. Plumes in angles 1728 40   90   200
3707 — R. Roses and plumes in angles

1728	20	50	120	1735	30	60	175
1731	20	50	120	1735/4	35	75	225
1732	20	50	120	1736	25	55	150
1734	30	60	175				

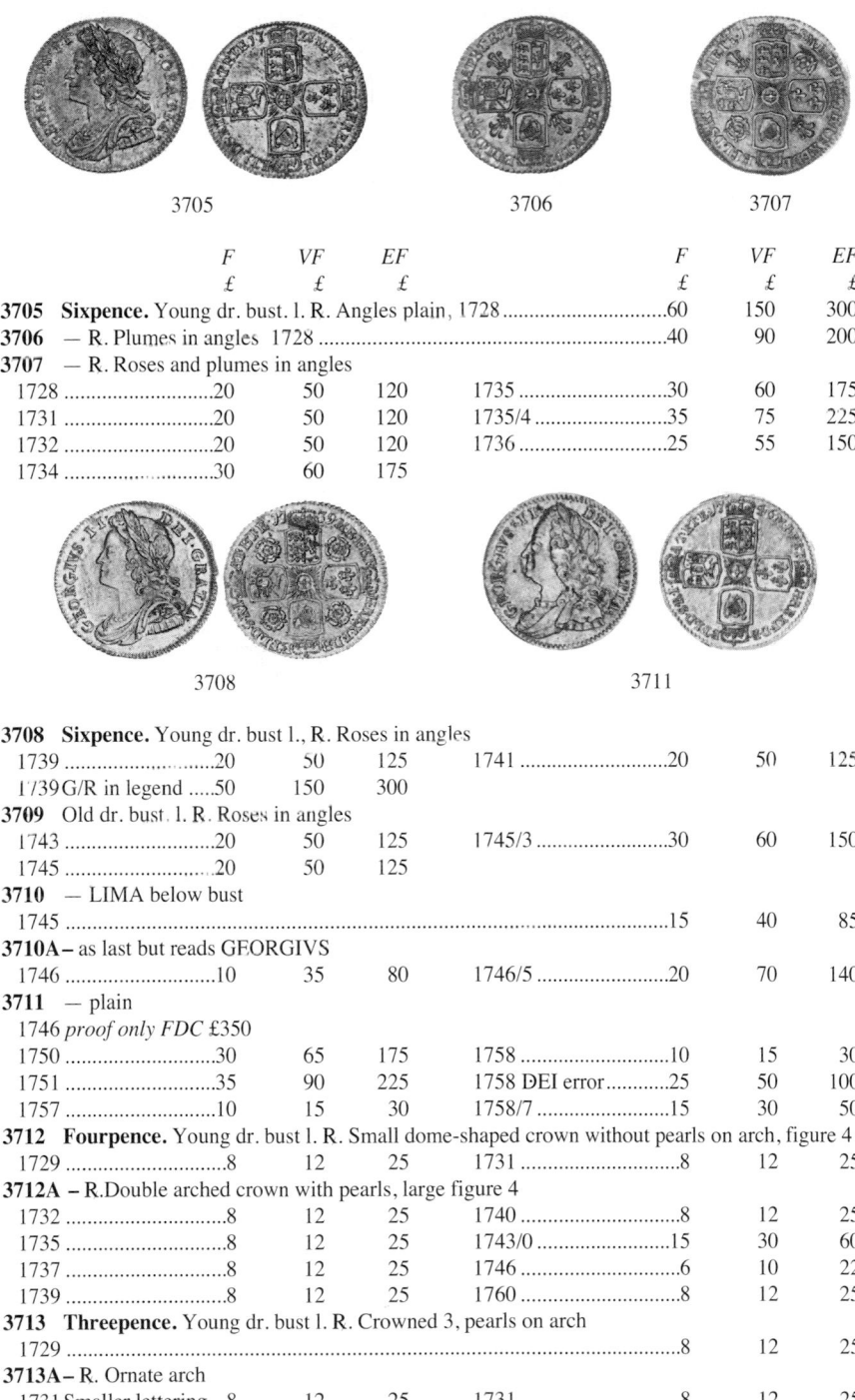

3708   3711

3708 Sixpence. Young dr. bust l., R. Roses in angles

1739	20	50	125	1741	20	50	125
1739 G/R in legend	50	150	300				

3709 Old dr. bust. l. R. Roses in angles

1743	20	50	125	1745/3	30	60	150
1745	20	50	125				

3710 — LIMA below bust

1745					15	40	85

3710A – as last but reads GEORGIVS

1746	10	35	80	1746/5	20	70	140

3711 — plain
1746 *proof only FDC* £350

1750	30	65	175	1758	10	15	30
1751	35	90	225	1758 DEI error	25	50	100
1757	10	15	30	1758/7	15	30	50

3712 Fourpence. Young dr. bust l. R. Small dome-shaped crown without pearls on arch, figure 4

1729	8	12	25	1731	8	12	25

3712A – R.Double arched crown with pearls, large figure 4

1732	8	12	25	1740	8	12	25
1735	8	12	25	1743/0	15	30	60
1737	8	12	25	1746	6	10	22
1739	8	12	25	1760	8	12	25

3713 Threepence. Young dr. bust l. R. Crowned 3, pearls on arch

1729					8	12	25

3713A – R. Ornate arch

1731 Smaller lettering	8	12	25	1731	8	12	25

	F	VF	EF		F	VF	EF
	£	£	£		£	£	£

3713B Threepence. R. Double arched crown with pearls

	F	VF	EF		F	VF	EF
1732 8	12	25		1743 Large lettering 6	10	22
1732 with stop over head10	15	30		1743 Small lettering 6	10	22
1735 8	12	25		1743 — stop over head.7	12	25
1737 6	10	22		1746 6	10	22
1739 6	10	22		1746/3 7	12	25
1740 6	10	22		1760 6	10	22

3714 Twopence. Young dr. bust l. R. Small crown and figure 2

1729 4	9	18		1731 4	9	18

3714A Twopence. Young dr. bust l. R. Large crown and figure 2

1732 4	9	18		1743/0 5	10	20
1735 4	9	18		1746 4	9	18
1737 4	9	18		1756 4	9	18
1739 5	10	20		1759 4	9	18
1740 8	14	25		1760 4	9	18
1743 4	9	18				

3715 Penny. Young dr. bust l. head. R. Date over small crown and figure 1

1729 6	12	20		1731 5	10	18

3715A Penny. R. Large crown dividing date

1732 5	10	18		1753/2 6	12	22
1735 6	12	22		1753 4	8	16
1737 6	12	20		1754 4	8	16
1739 5	10	18		1755 4	8	16
1740 5	10	18		1756 4	8	16
1743 5	10	18		1757 4	8	16
1746 5	10	18		1757 Colon after		
1746/3 6	12	22		GRATIA 6	12	22
1750 4	8	16		1758 4	8	16
1752 4	8	16		1759 4	8	16
1752/0 6	12	22		1760 6	12	22

3716

3716 Maundy Set. As last four. Uniform dates

	F	VF	EF		F	VF	EF
1729 60	100	200		1739 50	90	175
1731 60	100	200		1740 50	90	175
1732 50	90	175		1743 60	100	200
1735 50	90	175		1746 45	90	175
1737 50	90	175		1760 75	175	250

COPPER

3717

	F £	VF £	EF £		F £	VF £	EF £
3717 Halfpenny. Young Cuir. bust l.							
1729	15	45	140	1735	12	40	120
1730	12	45	125	1736	15	50	140
1731	12	40	120	1737	15	50	140
1732	12	45	125	1738	10	35	120
1733	12	40	120	1739	12	40	120
1734	12	40	120				
3718 Old Cuir. bust l., GEORGIUS							
1740	10	35	100	1744	10	35	100
1742	10	35	100	1745	10	35	100
1743	10	35	100				

3719

3719 Halfpenny. Old Cuir. bust l. GEORGIVS							
1746	10	30	100	1751	10	30	100
1747	10	35	120	1752	10	30	100
1748	10	35	120	1753	10	30	100
1749	10	30	100	1754	10	35	120
1750	10	35	120				

3720   3722

	F	VF	EF		F	VF	EF
	£	£	£		£	£	£
3720 Farthing. Young Cuir. bust l.							
1730 12	35	125	1735 10	30	100
1731 12	35	125	1736 12	35	125
1732 15	40	150	1737 10	30	100
1733 12	35	125	1739 10	30	100
1734 15	40	150			
3721 Old Cuir. bust. GEORGIUS							
1741 15	40	125	1744 10	25	95
3722 — GEORGIVS							
1746 8	25	85	1750 15	40	120
1749 15	40	120	1754 5	14	40

During the second half of the 18th century very little silver or copper was minted. In 1797 Matthew Boulton's 'cartwheels', the first copper Pennies and Twopences, demonstrated the improvement gleaned from the application of steam power to the coining press.

During the Napoleonic Wars bank notes came into general use when the issue of Guineas was stopped between 1799 and 1813, but gold 7s. pieces, Third-Guineas; were minted to relieve the shortage of smaller money. As an emergency measure Spanish 'Dollars' were put into circulation for a short period after being countermarked, and in 1804 Spanish Eight Reales were overstruck and issued as Bank of England Dollars.

The transition to a 'token' silver coinage began in 1811 when the Bank of England had 3s and 1s. 6d. tokens made for general circulation. Private issues of token money in the years 1788-95 and 1811-15 helped to alleviate the shortage of regal coinage. A change over to a gold standard and a regular 'token' silver coinage came in 1816 when the Mint, which was moved from its old quarters in the Tower of London to a new site on Tower Hill, began a complete re-coinage. The Guinea was replaced by a 20s. Sovereign, and silver coins were made which had an intrinsic value lower than their face value. The St. George design used on the Sovereign and Crown was the work of Benedetto Pistrucci.

GOLD

Early Coinages

3724

3723 Five Guineas. Pattern only, laur. bust r.

1770 *FDC* £45,000	1777 *FDC* £45,000
1773 *FDC* £45,000	

3724 Two Guineas. Pattern only, laur. bust r.

1768 *FDC* £22,500	1777 *FDC* £22,500
1773 *FDC* £22,500	

There are six different bust varieties for 3723 and 3724, for further details see Douglas-Morris Catalogue, November 1974, lots 127-132.

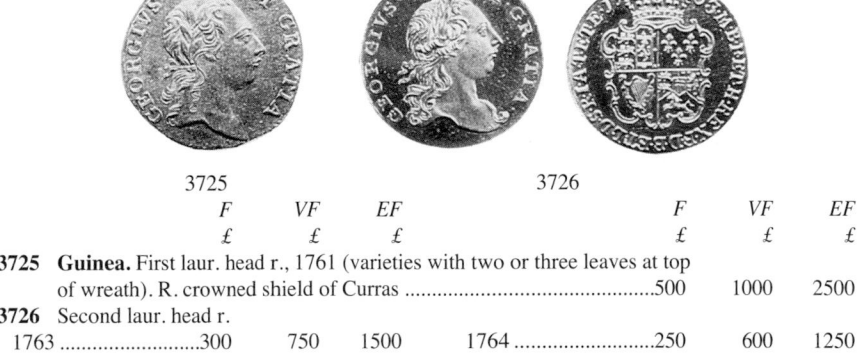

| 3725 | | | 3726 | | |

	F	VF	EF		F	VF	EF
	£	£	£		£	£	£

3725 Guinea. First laur. head r., 1761 (varieties with two or three leaves at top of wreath). R. crowned shield of Curras 500 1000 2500

3726 Second laur. head r.

| 1763 ....300 | 750 | 1500 | 1764 ....250 | 600 | 1250 |

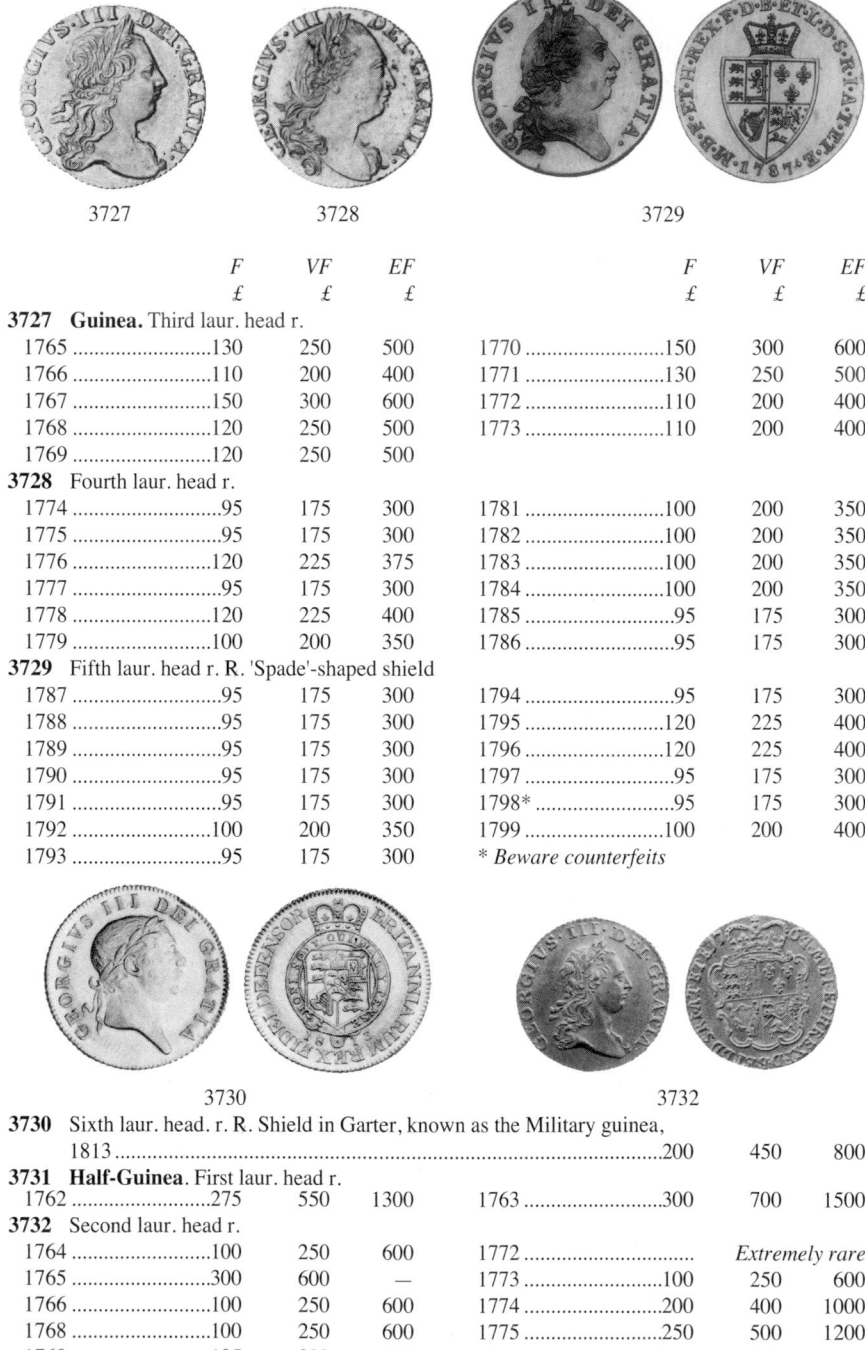

3727   3728   3729

	F £	VF £	EF £		F £	VF £	EF £
3727 Guinea. Third laur. head r.							
1765	130	250	500	1770	150	300	600
1766	110	200	400	1771	130	250	500
1767	150	300	600	1772	110	200	400
1768	120	250	500	1773	110	200	400
1769	120	250	500				
3728 Fourth laur. head r.							
1774	95	175	300	1781	100	200	350
1775	95	175	300	1782	100	200	350
1776	120	225	375	1783	100	200	350
1777	95	175	300	1784	100	200	350
1778	120	225	400	1785	95	175	300
1779	100	200	350	1786	95	175	300
3729 Fifth laur. head r. **R.** 'Spade'-shaped shield							
1787	95	175	300	1794	95	175	300
1788	95	175	300	1795	120	225	400
1789	95	175	300	1796	120	225	400
1790	95	175	300	1797	95	175	300
1791	95	175	300	1798*	95	175	300
1792	100	200	350	1799	100	200	400
1793	95	175	300	*Beware counterfeits*			

3730   3732

		F £	VF £	EF £
3730 Sixth laur. head. r. **R.** Shield in Garter, known as the Military guinea,				
1813		200	450	800
3731 Half-Guinea. First laur. head r.				
1762	275	550	1300	
1763	300	700	1500	
3732 Second laur. head r.				
1764	100	250	600	
1772		*Extremely rare*		
1765	300	600	—	
1773	100	250	600	
1766	100	250	600	
1774	200	400	1000	
1768	100	250	600	
1775	250	500	1200	
1769	125	300	750	

3733   3734   3735

	F	VF	EF		F	VF	EF
	£	£	£		£	£	£

3733   Half-Guinea Third laur. head (less fine style) r.

1774		*Extremely rare*		1775 400	850	2000

3734   Fourth laur. head r.

1775 75	150	300	1781 80	175	400
1776 75	150	300	1783 300	800	—
1777 70	125	275	1784 75	150	300
1778 80	175	350	1785 70	125	275
1779 100	200	500	1786 70	125	275

3735   Fifth laur. head. r. R. 'Spade' shaped shield, date below

1787 70	120	250	1794 75	150	300
1788 70	120	250	1795 100	200	450
1789 85	175	350	1796 75	150	300
1790 70	120	250	1797 70	125	250
1791 75	150	300	1798 70	125	250
1792 350	850	—	1800 125	350	—
1793 70	120	250			

3736   Sixth laur. head. r. R. Shield in Garter, date below

1801 50	75	125	1803 55	85	150
1802 55	85	150			

3737   Seventh laur. head. r. with short hair. R. As last

1804 50	75	125	1809 55	85	150
1805		*Extremely rare*	1810 55	85	150
1806 55	85	150	1811 100	200	400
1808 55	85	150	1813 75	150	300

3737   3738   3739

3738   Third-Guinea. First laur. head r. R. Crown, date in legend

1797 40	55	125	1799 45	75	175
1798 40	55	125	1800 40	55	125

3739   – R. Similar but date below crown

1801 40	55	125	1803 40	55	125
1802 40	55	125			

	3740				3741		
	F	*VF*	*EF*		*F*	*VF*	*EF*
	£	£	£		£	£	£

3740 Third-Guinea. Second laur. head r. with short hair, R. Similar

1804	40	55	125	1810	40	55	125
1806	40	55	125	1811	175	350	750
1808	40	55	125	1813	100	200	400
1809	40	55	125				

3741 Quarter-Guinea. 1762 50   85   175

For gold of the 'new coinage', 1817-20, see page 354.

SILVER

                       3742   3743

3742 Shilling. Young dr. bust, r. known as the 'Northumberland' shilling,
       1763 125   225   400
3743 Older dr. bust, R. No semée of hearts in the Hanoverian shield, 1787 ..15   25   35
3744 — No stop over head, 1787 20   35   60
3745 — No stops at date, 1787 25   45   75
3745A— No stops on *obv.*, 1787 90   300   600

no semée of hearts   with semée of hearts   3747

3746   — R. With semée of hearts, 1787 15   25   35
       1787 1/1 retrograde...30   75   150
3747   — No stop over head, 1798: known as the 'Dorrien and Magens' shilling *UNC* £4500
3748 Sixpence. R. Without semée of hearts, 1787 10   20   30
3749   — R. With semée of hearts, 1787 10   20   30

                       3749

3750   3751   3755

	F £	VF £	EF £		F £	VF £	EF £
3750 Fourpence. Young dr. bust r. R. Crowned 4							
1763	4	8	16	1772/0	5	9	18
1765	200	400	750	1776	4	8	16
1766	5	9	18	1780	4	8	16
1770	5	9	18	1784	5	9	18
1772	5	9	18	1786	6	10	20
3751 Older dr. bust. R. Thin 4 ('Wire Money'), 1792			10			20	35
3752 — R. Normal 4							
1795	5	8	16	1800	5	8	16
3753 Threepence. Young dr. bust r. R. Crowned 3							
1762	3	5	10	1772 small III	4	7	15
1763	3	5	10	1772 very large III	4	7	15
1765	150	300	650	1780	4	7	15
1766	5	9	1	1784	5	9	18
1770	5	9	18	1786	4	7	15
3754 Older dr. bust. r. R. Thin 3 ('Wire Money'), 1792			10			20	35
3755 — R. Normal 3							
1795	5	8	15	1800	5	8	15
3756 Twopence. Young dr. bust r. R. Crowned 2							
1763	6	10	15	1776	4	8	14
1765	100	250	550	1780	4	8	14
1766	4	8	14	1784	4	8	14
1772	4	8	14	1786	3	6	12
1772 second 7/6	5	9	18	1786 large obv. lettering	3	6	12
3757 Older dr. bust. r. R. Thin 2 ('Wire Money'), 1792			10			15	30
3758 — R. Normal 2							
1795	3	6	12	1800	3	6	12
3759 Penny. Young dr. bust r. R. Crowned 1							
1763	5	9	15	1779	4	7	12
1766	4	7	12	1780	5	9	15
1770	3	5	11	1781	3	5	11
1772	4	7	12	1784	3	5	11
1776	4	7	12	1786	3	5	11
3760 Older dr. bust. r. R. Thin 1 ('Wire Money'), 1792			8			15	25
3761 — R. Normal 1							
1795	3	5	12	1800	3	5	12
3762 Maundy Set. Young dr. bust. r. Uniform dates							
1763	50	95	175	1780	50	95	175
1766	50	95	175	1784	50	95	175
1772	50	95	175	1786	50	95	175
3763 — Older dr. bust. r. R. Thin numerals ('Wire Money'), 1792			90			140	275
3764 — R. Normal numerals. Uniform dates							
1795	40	80	125	1800	35	70	110

| 3765A | 3767 | 3766 |

Emergency Issue

		F	VF	EF
		£	£	£
3765	**Dollar.** Pillar type (current for 4s 9d). Spanish American 8 Reales, oval countermark with head of George III.			
	Mexico City Mint — ṁ	350	650	1250
	Bolivia, Potosi Mint – PTS monogram	650	1250	—
	Peru, Potosi Mint – LIMÆ monogram	600	1100	—
3765A	Portrait type, oval countermark.			
	Mexico City Mint — ṁ	95	200	350
	Bolivia, Potosi Mint — PTS monogram	110	300	—
	Chile, Santiago Mint — ṡ	500	1000	—
	Guatemala Mint — NG	400	850	—
	Spain, Madrid Mint	250	550	1250
	Spain, Seville Mint	200	450	1000
	Peru, Lima Mint — LIMÆ monogram	125	275	500
3765B	— Oval countermark on French Ecu		*Extremely rare*	
3765C	— Oval countermark on USA Dollar		*Of highest rarity*	
3766	— octagonal countermarks with head of George III			
	Mexico City Mint — ṁ	200	450	700
	Bolivia, Potosi Mint — PTS monogram	400	—	—
	Guatamala Mint — NG	650	1250	—
	Peru, Lima Mint — LIME monogram	250	500	1000
	Spain, Madrid Mint	350	750	—
	Spain, Seville Mint	400	850	—
3766A	— Octagonal countermark on French Ecu		*Of highest rarity*	
3766B	— Octagonal countermark on USA Dollar		*Extremely rare*	
3767	**Half-Dollar.** With similar oval countermark. Mints of Potosi, Santiago, Madrid & Seville ....*from* 100	225	425	
3767A	— Octagonal countermark		*Extremely rare*	

Bank of England Issue

3768

	F	VF	EF		F	VF	EF
	£	£	£		£	£	£

3768 Dollar. (current for 5s.). laur. and dr. bust of king. r. R.
Britannia seated l., several varieties occur

1804 75   150   300

These dollars were re-struck from Spanish-American 8-Reales until at least 1811. Dollars that show dates and Mint marks of original coin are worth rather more.

3769   3770

3769 Three Shillings. Dr and laur. bust in armour r. R. BANK / TOKEN /
3 SHILL. / date (in oak wreath)

1811	15	35	65	1812	15	35	65

3770 — Laureate head r. Top leaf between I/G R. As before but wreath of oak and olive

1812	15	35	65	1815	15	35	65
1813	15	35	65	1816	150	350	750
1814	15	35	65				

3771

3771 Eighteenpence. Dr. and laur. bust r. in armour R Bank/Token/Is. 6D./date (in oak wreath)

1811	10	25	55	1812	10	25	55

3772

	F	VF	EF			F	VF	EF
	£	£	£			£	£	£

3772 Eighteenpence. Laureate head r.

	F	VF	EF			F	VF	EF
1812	10	20	50	1815		10	20	50
1813	10	20	50	1816		10	20	50
1814	10	20	50					

3773 Ninepence. Similar, Laur. head 1812, R. 9D type (pattern only) *FDC* £800

3773A — — 1812, R. 9 pence type (pattern only) FDC .... *Extremely rare*

COPPER

First Issue — Tower Mint, London

3774   3775

3774 Halfpenny. Cuir. bust r. R. Britannia

	F	VF	EF			F	VF	EF
1770	12	35	80	1773		10	30	75
1771	10	30	75	1774		14	35	85
1772	10	30	75	1775		10	30	75
1772 GEORIVS error	35	75	125					

3775 Farthing. Similar

	F	VF	EF			F	VF	EF
1771	20	50	120	1774		12	30	75
1773	10	25	65	1775		12	30	75

Second Issue — Soho Mint. Birmingham 'Cartwheel' coinage

3776

3776 Twopence. Legends incuse on raised rim, 1797 15   65   150

3777

	VF £	EF £	UNC £		VF £	EF £	UNC £
3777 Penny. 1797. Similar					10	35	95

Halfpence and Farthings of this issue are patterns.

Third Issue—Soho Mint, Birmingham

		3778			3779		
3778 Halfpenny. Dr. bust r., 1799					9	30	75
3779 Farthing. 1799					6	22	60

Fourth Issue—Soho Mint, Birmingham

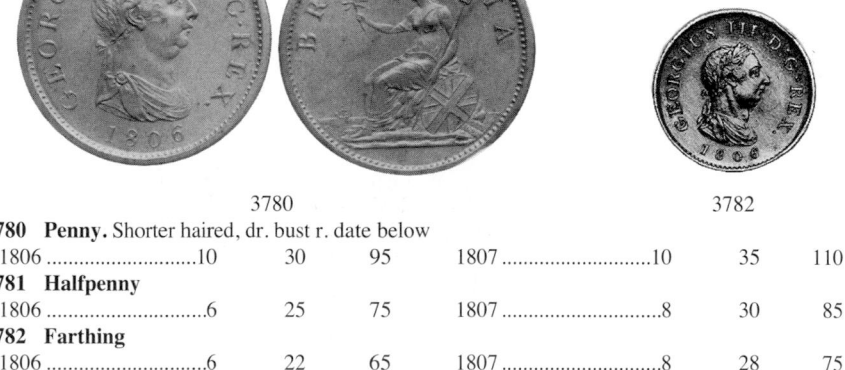

		3780				3782	
3780 Penny. Shorter haired, dr. bust r. date below							
1806	10	30	95	1807	10	35	110
3781 Halfpenny							
1806	6	25	75	1807	8	30	85
3782 Farthing							
1806	6	22	65	1807	8	28	75

Last or new coinage, 1816-20

The year 1816 is a landmark in the history of our coinage. For some years at the beginning of the 19th century Mint production was virtually confined to small gold denominations, regular full production being resumed only after the Mint had been moved from the Tower of London to a new site on Tower Hill. Steam powered minting machinery made by Boulton and Watt replaced the old hand-operated presses and these produced coins which were technically much superior to the older milled coins.

In 1816 for the first time British silver coins were produced with an intrinsic value substantially below their face value, the first official token coinage. The old Guinea was replaced by a Sovereign of twenty shillings in 1817, the standard of 22 carat (.916) fineness still being retained.

Engraver's and/or designer's initials:
    B.P. (Benedetto Pistrucci)

GOLD

3783   3784

3783   Five Pounds. 1820 (Pattern only) *FDC*..... £42,500

	F	VF	EF	UNC		F	VF	EF	UNC
	£	£	£	£		£	£	£	£

3784   Two Pounds. 1820 (Pattern only) *FDC*..... £12,500

3785   Sovereign. laur. head r. coarse hair, legend type A (Descending colon after BRITANNIAR, no space between REX and F:D:). R. St. George and dragon

	F	VF	EF	UNC		F	VF	EF	UNC
1817	100	175	450	600	1819			*Extremely rare*	
1818	110	200	500	700					

3785A — legend type B (Ascending colon after BRITANNIAR, space between REX and F:D:)

1818		110	200	500	700

3785B laur head r. Hair with tighter curls, legend type A. (as above)

1818	*Extremely rare*

3785C — legend type B. (as above)

			F	VF	EF	UNC
1818	*Extremely rare*	1820	100	175	450	600

3785   3785A   3785C

3786

	F	VF	EF	UNC		F	VF	EF	UNC
	£	£	£	£		£	£	£	£

3786 Half-Sovereign. laur head r. R. Crowned shield

1817	60	100	175	300	1820	65	110	200	350
1818	65	110	200	350					

SILVER

3787

3787 Crown. Laur. head r. R. Pistrucci's St. George and dragon within Garter

1818, edge	LVIII	22	55	165	350
1818 LVIII error edge inscription...			*Extremely rare*		
1818	LIX	22	55	165	350
1819 —	LIX	20	50	150	325
1819 —	LIX no stops on edge	45	100	200	500
1819/8	LIX	50	125	275	—
1819	LX	25	60	185	375
1820 —	LX	22	55	165	350
1820/19	LX	75	200	350	—

3788

3788 Halfcrown. Large laur. bust or 'bull' head r.

1816	20	45	100	200	1817	20	45	100	200
1817 D/T in DEI	30	75	—	—					

3789

	F £	VF £	EF £	UNC £		F £	VF £	EF £	UNC £

3789 Halfcrown. Small laur. head r.

1817	20	45	100	200	1818	25	50	120	225
1817 Reversed s's in garter	*Extremely rare*				1819	20	45	100	200
1818 Reversed s's in garter	*Extremely rare*				1820	30	65	150	325

3790   3791

3790 Shilling. laur head r. R. Shield in Garter

1816	10	15	30	55	1819/8	20	40	80	150
1817	10	18	35	60	1819	10	18	35	80
1817 GEOE error	100	200	350	—	1820	10	18	35	80
1818	20	40	95	175	1820 I/S in HONI	40	80	175	350
1818 High 8	30	75	120	225					

3791 Sixpence. laur head r. R. Shield in Garter

1816	6	12	25	50	1819 small 8	10	20	35	60
1817	8	15	30	55	1820	10	20	35	60
1818	10	20	35	60	1820 inverted 1	75	200	—	—
1819/8	12	25	40	70	1820 I/S in HONI	75	200	—	—
1819	10	20	35	60	1820 no colons on obv.	100	300	—	—

3792

	VF £	EF £	FDC £		VF £	EF £	FDC £

3792 Maundy Set. (4d., 3d., 2d. and 1d.)

1817		60	95	175	1820		60	95	175
1818		60	95	175					

3793	**— Fourpence.** 1817, 1818, 1820	*from*	14	30
3794	**— Threepence.** 1817, 1818, 1820	*from*	14	30
3795	**— Twopence.** 1817, 1818, 1820	*from*	8	15
3796	**— Penny.** 1817, 1818, 1820	*from*	8	14

The Mint resumed the coinage of copper farthings in 1821, and pennies and halfpennies in 1825. A gold Two Pound piece was first issued for general circulation in 1823.

Engraver's and/or designer's initials:
      B. P. (Benedetto Pistrucci)   W.W. P. (William Wellesley Pole)
      J. B. M. (Jean Baptiste Merlen)

GOLD

3797

3797 Five Pounds. 1826 Bare head l. R. Crowned shield and mantle, inscribed edge
    Proof *FDC* £7000

3798

	VF £	EF £	UNC £
3798 Two Pounds. 1823. Large bare head. l. R. St. George, inscribed edge.	375	600	950

3799 — 1826. Type as 3797 inscribed edge Proof *FDC* £2750

3800

3800 Sovereign. Laur. head. l. R. St. George

	F £	VF £	EF £	UNC £		F £	VF £	EF £	UNC £
1821	100	175	425	575	1824	100	175	450	600
1822*	100	175	450	600	1825	195	475	1150	—
1823	175	400	1000	—					

Beware counterfeits.

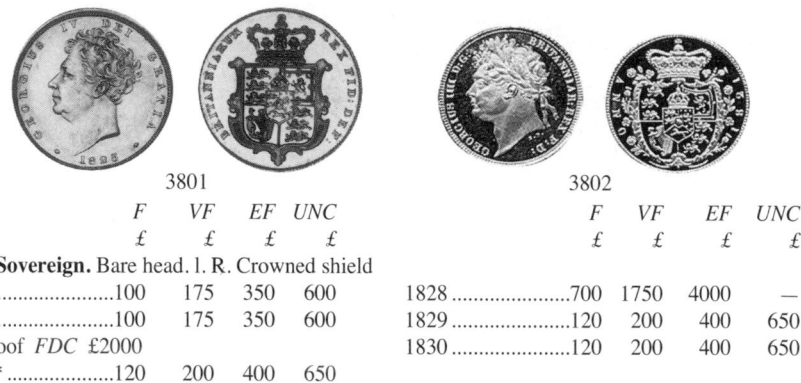

3801   3802

	F	VF	EF	UNC		F	VF	EF	UNC
	£	£	£	£		£	£	£	£

3801 Sovereign. Bare head. l. R. Crowned shield

1825	100	175	350	600	1828	700	1750	4000	—
1826	100	175	350	600	1829	120	200	400	650
— Proof *FDC* £2000					1830	120	200	400	650
1827*	120	200	400	650					

Beware counterfeits

3803   3804   3804A

3802 Half-Sovereign. Laur. head. l. R. Ornately garnished shield.

1821						300	700	1350	1950

3803 — R. Plain shield

1823	80	150	375	500	1825	70	125	325	450
1824	75	135	350	475					

3804 — Bare head. l. R. Garnished shield

1826	70	120	300	450	1827	70	120	300	450
— Proof *FDC* £1000					1828	65	110	275	425

3804A — with extra tuft of hair to l. ear, much heavier border

1826	70	120	300	450	1827	70	120	300	450
— Proof *FDC* £1000					1828	65	110	275	425

SILVER

3805

3805 Crown. Laur. head. l. R. St. George

1821, edge	SECUNDO	25	75	350	850
1821	SECUNDO Proof £1500				
1822 —	SECUNDO	30	90	400	950
— —	TERTIO	27	80	350	850

3806

3806 Crown. Bare head. l. R. Shield with crest inscribed edge, 1826 Proof *FDC* £2250

3807   3808

	F £	VF £	EF £	UNC £		F £	VF £	EF £	UNC £
3807 Halfcrown. Laur. head. l. R. Garnished shield									
1820 20		45	125	250	1823 — 400	1000	3500	—
1821 20		45	125	250				
1821 Heavier shield garnishing					20	45	140	275
3808 — R. Shield in garter and collar									
1823 20		45	125	275	1824 25	60	175	350

3809

3809 Bare head. l. R. Shield with crest

1824		*Extremely rare*			1826 Proof *FDC* £450			
1825 25	50	100	200	1828 30	85	200	425
1826 20	40	95	200	1829 25	75	175	375

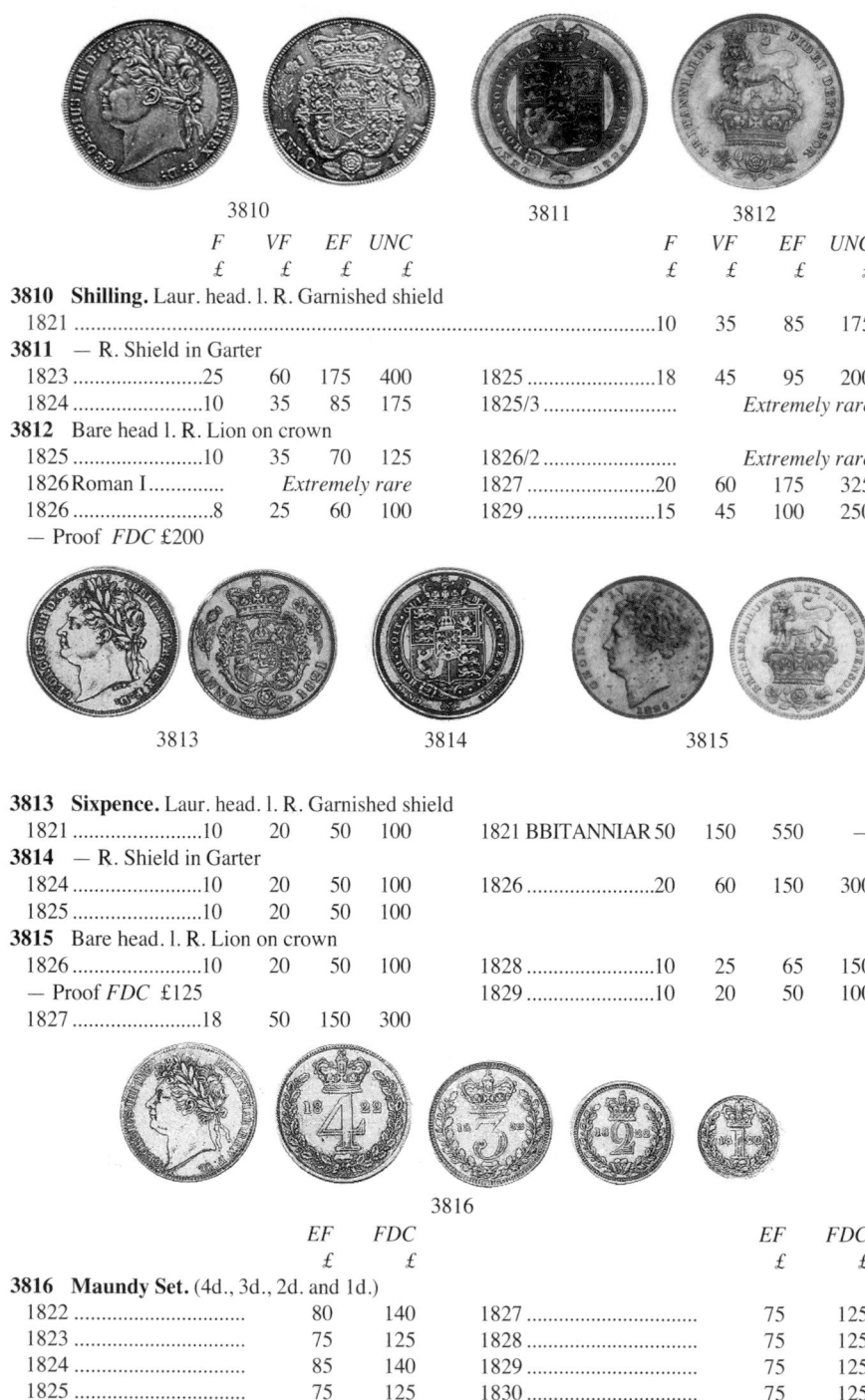

3810   3811   3812

	F	VF	EF	UNC		F	VF	EF	UNC
	£	£	£	£		£	£	£	£

3810 Shilling. Laur. head. l. R. Garnished shield

1821						10	35	85	175

3811 — R. Shield in Garter

1823	25	60	175	400	1825	18	45	95	200
1824	10	35	85	175	1825/3		*Extremely rare*		

3812 Bare head l. R. Lion on crown

1825	10	35	70	125	1826/2		*Extremely rare*		
1826 Roman I		*Extremely rare*			1827	20	60	175	325
1826	8	25	60	100	1829	15	45	100	250
— Proof *FDC* £200									

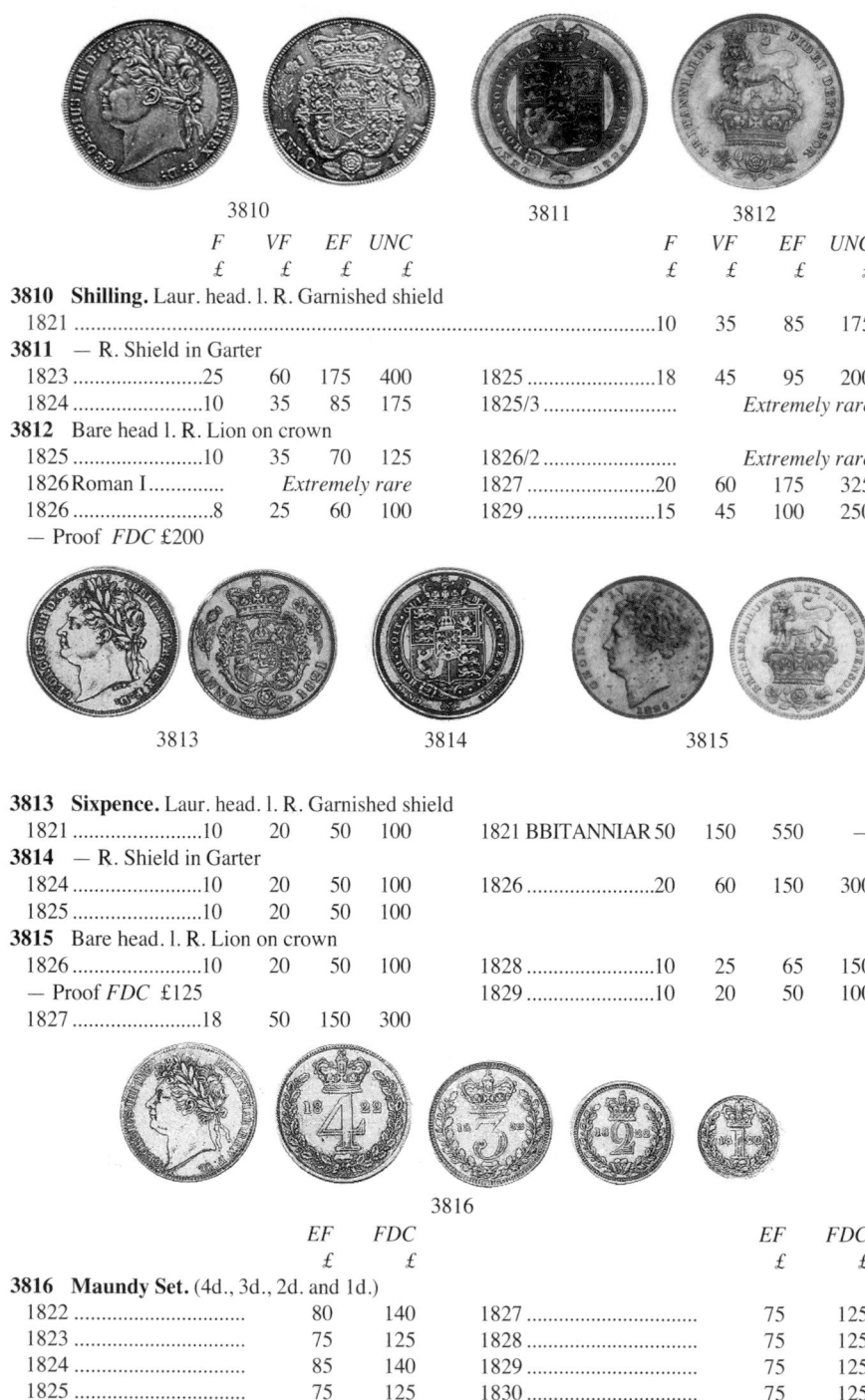

3813   3814   3815

3813 Sixpence. Laur. head. l. R. Garnished shield

1821	10	20	50	100	1821 BBITANNIAR	50	150	550	—

3814 — R. Shield in Garter

1824	10	20	50	100	1826	20	60	150	300
1825	10	20	50	100					

3815 Bare head. l. R. Lion on crown

1826	10	20	50	100	1828	10	25	65	150
— Proof *FDC* £125					1829	10	20	50	100
1827	18	50	150	300					

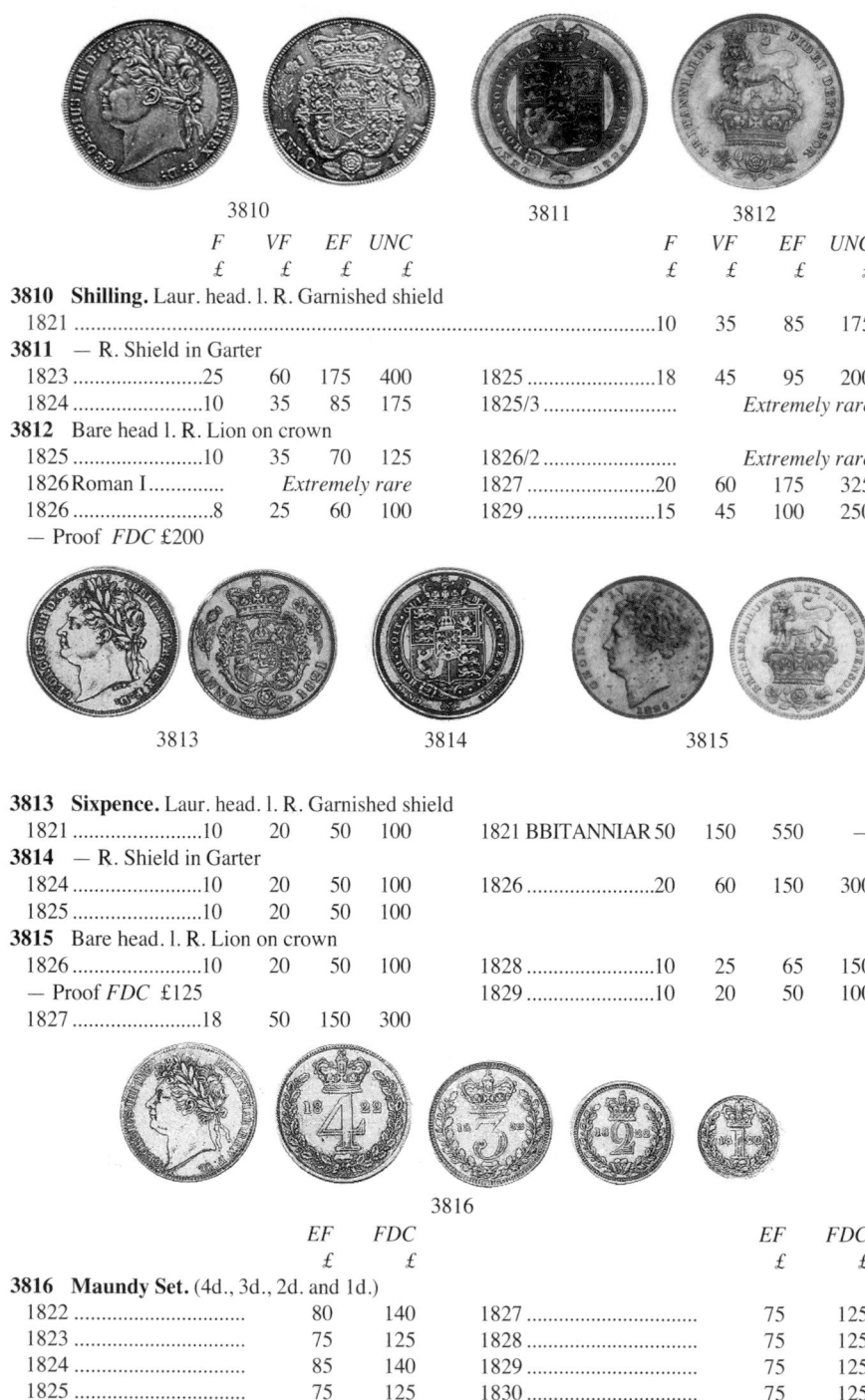

3816

	EF	FDC			EF	FDC
	£	£			£	£

3816 Maundy Set. (4d., 3d., 2d. and 1d.)

1822	80	140	1827	75	125
1823	75	125	1828	75	125
1824	85	140	1829	75	125
1825	75	125	1830	75	125
1826	75	125			

		EF	FDC
		£	£
3817	**Maundy Fourpence.** 1822-30 ....*from*	11	18
3818	— **Threepence**. small head, 1822...	25	40
3819	— — normal head, 1823-30 ....*from*	10	17
3820	— **Twopence.** 1822-30 ....*from*	9	12
3821	— **Penny.** 1822-30 ....*from*	7	10

COPPER

First Issue, 1821-6

3822   3824

	F	VF	EF	UNC			F	VF	EF	UNC
	£	£	£	£			£	£	£	£
3822 Farthing. Laur. and dr. bust l.										
1821 2		10	25	60		1825 2		10	25	55
1822 2		10	22	55		1826 5		15	35	85
1823 3		12	30	65						

3823   3827

Second issue, 1825-30

3823 Penny. Laur. head. l. R. Britannia

1825 12	30	80	250	1826 Proof *FDC £225*			
1826 10	30	70	250	1827 150	350	1000	—

3824 Halfpenny. Similar

1825 120	45	120	200	1826 Proof *FDC £175*			
1826 8	20	50	85	1827 10	25	60	100

3825 Farthing. Similar

1826 2	8	25	50	1828 2	8	30	70
— Proof *FDC £140*				1829 3	12	45	100
1827 3	8	35	75	1830 2	5	30	70

3826 Half-Farthing. (for use in Ceylon). Similar

1828 10	25	75	150	1830 10	25	75	150

3827 Third-Farthing. (for use in Malta). Similar

1827				15	40	75

Copper coins graded in this catalogue as UNC have full mint lustre.

PSI *Proof Set*, new issue, **1826.** Five pounds to Farthing (11 coins) *FDC* £18000
PSIA — — Similar, including Maundy Set (15 coins) *FDC* £18500

In order to prevent confusion between the Sixpence and Half-Sovereign the size of the latter was reduced in 1834, although the weight remained the same. The smaller gold piece was not acceptable to the public and in the following year it was made to the normal size. In 1836 the silver Groat was again issued for general circulation: it is the only British silver coin which has a seated Britannia as the type. Crowns were not struck during this reign for general circulation; but proofs or patterns of this denomination were made and are greatly sought after. Silver Threepences and Three-Halfpence were minted for use in the Colonies.

Engraver's and/or designer's initials:
　　W. W. (William Wyon)

GOLD

3828

3828　Two Pounds. 1831 (proof only). As illus...*FDC* £4250

	3829					3829B		
	F	*VF*	*EF*	*UNC*		*F*	*VF*	*EF*	*UNC*
	£	£	£	£		£	£	£	£

3829　Sovereign. First bust. r. top of ear narrow and rounded, nose to 2nd N of BRITANNIAR, fine obv. beading. R. Crowned shield.

| 1831 | 150 | 250 | 550 | 750 | 1832 | 125 | 200 | 525 | 750 |

— Proof *FDC £2250*

3829A — — WW without stops

| 1831 | | | | | | | | | *Extremely rare* |

3829B Second bust. r. top of ear broad and flat, nose to 2nd I in BRITANNIAR, coarser obv. beading.

1832*	125	195	450	675	1836	125	195	450	675
1833	125	195	450	675	1837	140	225	500	725
1835	125	195	475	700					

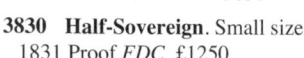

3830　　　　　　　　　　　　　　3831

3830　Half-Sovereign. Small size

1831 Proof *FDC* £1250

| 1834 | 100 | 200 | 475 | 750 |

* Beware of counterfeits

	F	VF	EF	UNC		F	VF	EF	UNC
	£	£	£	£		£	£	£	£

3831 Half-Sovereign. Large size

1835	100	200	450	700	1837	100	220	500	725
1836	120	250	550	750					

3832 *Obv.* struck from Sixpence. die in error, 1836 750   1250   2750   —

SILVER

3832   3833

3833 Crown. R. Shield on mantle, 1831 Proof only W.W. on trun. struck ↑↓ ....*FDC* £4750

1831 — W. WYON on trun. struck ↑↑ ....*FDC* £6500

1834 — W.W. on trun. struck ↑↓ ....*FDC* £9500

WW script

3834   WW block

3834 Halfcrown. WW in script on trun. R. Shield on mantle

1831 Proof *FDC* £450				1836/5	40	90	225	—
1834	20	50	125	300	1836	20	50	125	300
1835	30	90	200	500	1837	35	100	250	600

3834A — block WW on trun.

1834 40   120   325   —

3835   3836

3835 Shilling. R. Value in wreath

1831 Proof *FDC* £250				1836	20	40	100	200
1834	15	35	85	175	1837	28	60	150	350
1835	20	40	100	200					

3836 Sixpence. R. Value in wreath

1831	10	20	50	100	1835	10	20	50	100
— Proof *FDC* £175				1836	18	40	100	175
1834	10	20	50	100	1837	15	35	95	175

3837

	F £	VF £	EF £	UNC £		F £	VF £	EF £	UNC £
3837 Groat. R. Britannia seated									
1836	5	15	35	50	1837	10	20	40	60
3838 Threepence (for use in the West Indies). As Maundy threepence but with a dull surface									
1834	4	12	50	100	1836	4	12	50	100
1835	4	10	40	85	1837	10	20	60	125

3839

	F £	VF £	EF £	UNC £		F £	VF £	EF £	UNC £
3839 Three-Halfpence (for Colonial use). R. Value, Crowned in wreath									
1834	5	10	30	50	1836	6	15	35	60
1835/4	6	15	35	60	1837	15	35	100	200
1835	10	25	60	125					

3840

	EF £	FDC £		EF £	FDC £
3840 Maundy Set (4d., 3d., 2d. and 1d.).					
1831	100	200	1834	85	160
— Proof *FDC* £300			1835	85	160
1832	90	180	1836	100	200
1833	85	160	1837	100	200
3841 — Fourpence, 1831-7			*from*	11	20
3842 — Threepence, 1831-7			*from*	20	30
3843 — Twopence, 1831-7			*from*	8	13
3844 — Penny, 1831-7			*from*	9	14

COPPER

3845

	F £	VF £	EF £	UNC £		F £	VF £	EF £	UNC £
3845 Penny. No initials on trun.									
1831 18	50	120	400		1834 20	60	150	425
— Proof *FDC £250*					1837 45	110	250	600
3846 W.W on trun. 1831				30		85	200	500	
3847 Halfpenny. As penny									
1831 12	25	50	125		1834 12	25	50	125
— Proof *FDC £200*					1837 10	20	45	100

3847   3848

	F £	VF £	EF £	UNC £		F £	VF £	EF £	UNC £
3848 Farthing. Similar									
1831 2	10	30	50		1835 2	10	30	50
— Proof *FDC £150*					1836 5	15	40	75
1834 2	10	30	50		1837 2	10	30	50

	F £	VF £	EF £	UNC £
3849 Half-Farthing (for use in Ceylon). Similar				
1837 45	90	200	—
3850 Third-Farthing (for use in Malta). Similar				
1835 5	15	35	75

Copper coins graded in this catalogue as UNC have full mint lustre

3849   3850

PS2 *Proof* set. Coronation, **1831.** Two pounds to farthing (14 coins). *FDC* £16500

In 1849, as a first step towards decimalization, a silver Florin (¹/₁₀ th pound) was introduced, but the coins of 1849 omitted the usual *Dei Gratia* and these so-called 'Godless' Florins were replaced in 1851 by the 'Gothic' issue. The Halfcrown was temporarily discontinued but was minted again from 1874 onwards. Between 1863 and 1880 reverse dies of the gold and silver coins were numbered in the course of Mint experiments into the wear of dies. The exception was the Florin where the die number is on the obverse below the bust.

The gold and silver coins were redesigned for the Queen's Golden Jubilee in 1887. The Double-Florin which was then issued, was abandoned after only four years; the Jubilee Sixpence of 1887, known as the 'withdrawn' type, was changed to avoid confusion with the Half-Sovereign. Gold and silver were again redesigned in 1893 with an older portrait of the Queen, but the 'old head' was not used on the bronze coinage until 1895. The heavy copper Penny had been replaced by the lighter bronze 'bun' Penny in 1860. In 1874-6 and 1881-2 some of the bronze was made by Heaton in Birmingham, and these have a letter H below the date. From 1897 Farthings were issued with a dark surface.

Early Sovereigns had a shield-type reverse, but Pistrucci's St. George design was used again from 1871. In order to increase the output of gold coinage, branches of the Royal Mint were set up in Australia at Sydney and Melbourne and, later, at Perth for coining gold of imperial type.

Engraver's and/or designer's initials:

W. W. (William Wyon)
L. C. W. (Leonard Charles Wyon)
J. E. B. (Joseph Edgar Boehm)

T. B. (Thomas Brock)
B. P. (Benedetto Pistrucci, d.1855)

GOLD

Young Head Coinage, 1838-87

3851

3851 Five Pounds. 1839. Young filleted bust l. R. 'Una and the lion' (proof only) varieties occur, inscribed edge   *FDC* £18,500

3852

3852 Sovereign. First (small) young head. l. R. First shield. London mint

1838	85	250	450	750	1844	55	75	125	200
1839	125	300	900	1400	1845	55	75	125	200
— dre axis ↑↓ Proof *FDC* £2000					1846	55	75	125	200
1841	600	950	2750	—	1847	55	75	125	200
1842	55	75	125	200	1848	200	—	—	—
1843	55	75	125	200					

| 3852A | 3852B | 3852C |
| Leaves differently arranged | Narrow shield | Second large head |

	F	VF	EF	UNC		F	VF	EF	UNC
	£	£	£	£		£	£	f	£

3852A — R similar but leaves of the wreath arranged differently with tops of leaves closer to crown.
1838 ....1000 — — —

3852B — narrower shield. Considerably modified floral emblems, different leaf arrangement
1843 .... *Extremely rare*

3852C Second (large) head. l. W W still in relief. R. Shield with repositioned legend

	F	VF	EF	UNC			F	VF	EF	UNC
1848 ....—	65	110	175		1853 ....—	70	110	175
1849 ....—	65	110	175		1854 100	225	500	—
1850 ....—	65	115	200		1855 80	125	200	—
1851 ....—	65	110	175		1872 ....—	60	100	175
1852 ....—	60	100	175					

| 3852D | 3852E | 3852F/3853A |
| WW Incuse | Extra line in ribbon | 827 on truncation |

3852D — — WW incuse on trun.

1853 70	110	200	—		1858 ....—	70	140	225
— Proof *FDC £5000*					1859 ....—	65	100	175
1854 ....—	65	100	175		1860 ....—	65	95	175
1855 ....—	65	95	175		1861 ....—	65	95	175
1856 ....—	65	100	175		1862 ....—	65	95	175
1857 ....—	65	95	175		1863 ....—	65	95	175

3852E — — As 3852D 'Ansell' ribbon. Additional raised line on the lower part of the ribbon
1859 ....125 275 950 —

3852F — — As 3852D with die number 827 on trun.
1863 ....1650 3000 — —

3853
Die number location

3853B

	F £	VF £	EF £	UNC £		F £	VF £	EF £	UNC £
3853 — — As 3852D R. die number in space below wreath, above floral emblem									
1863		55	90	160	1868		55	90	160
1864		55	85	140	1869		55	85	140
1865		55	90	175	1870		55	100	195
1866		55	85	140					
3853A — — As 3853 with die number 827 on trun. R. die number is always no. 22									
1863						1500	2500	—	—
3853B — — WW in relief on trun. R. die number below wreath, above floral emblem									
1870		55	90	160	1873		55	90	160
1871		55	85	140	1874	600	1250	3000	—
1872		55	85	140					

Melbourne Mint mark
3854

Sydney Mint mark
3855

3854 Sovereign Second (large) head. l. WW in relief R. M below wreath for Melbourne Mint, Australia

		F	VF	EF	UNC			F	VF	EF	UNC
1872 M		65	125	225		1882 M	55	75	150	225	
1873 M		*Extremely rare*				1883 M	80	150	325	500	
1874 M		65	125	250		1884 M	55	75	150	225	
1879 M		*Extremely rare*				1885 M	55	75	150	225	
1880 M	200	650	2000	3500		1886 M	275	1000	2500	—	
1881 M	55	75	150	225		1887 M	200	500	1600	—	

3855 — — As 3854 R. with S below wreath for Sydney Mint, Australia

	F	VF	EF	UNC		F	VF	EF	UNC
1871 S	55	120	250		1881 S	55	120	250	
1872 S	55	120	250		1882 S	55	100	150	
1873 S	55	120	250		1883 S	55	100	150	
1875 S	55	120	250		1884 S	55	100	150	
1877 S	55	120	250		1885 S	55	110	160	
1878 S	55	120	200		1886 S	55	110	160	
1879 S	55	120	200		1887 S	55	110	160	
1880 S	55	120	250						

3855A Second (large) head WW incuse on trun. R. with S below wreath for Sydney Mint

			F	VF	EF	UNC
1871 S			75	100	160	325

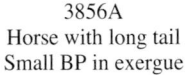

3856A	3856C
Horse with long tail	Horse with short tail
Small BP in exergue	No BP in exergue

	F	VF	EF	UNC		F	VF	EF	UNC
	£	£	£	£		£	£	£	£

3856 Soveriegn. First young head. l. WW buried in narrow trun. R. St. George.
London mint. Horse with short tail. Large BP in ex.

							F	VF	EF
1871							55	85	130

3856A — — As 3856 R. Horse with long tail. Small BP in ex.

	F	VF	EF			F	VF	EF
1871	55	75	120	1876		55	75	150
1872	55	75	130	1878		55	75	120
1873	55	75	120	1879	75	125	500	—
1874	60	85	150	1880		55	75	120

3856B — — As 3856 R. Horse with short tail, small BP in ex.

	F	VF	EF			F	VF	EF
1880	55	75	130	1885		60	85	130
1884	55	75	125					

3856C — — As 3856 R. Horse with short tail, no BP in ex.

				F	VF	EF
1880				55	75	120

3856D Sovereign. Second head. l. WW complete, on broad trun. R.
Horse with long tail, small BP in ex.

				F	VF	EF
1880				55	75	120

3856E — — As 3856D R. Horse with short tail. No BP in ex.

				F	VF	EF
1880				55	75	120

3856F — — As 3856E R. Horse with short tail, small BP in ex.

	F	VF	EF	UNC			F	VF	EF
1880	65	85	110	150	1885		60	85	130
1884	60	85	130						

3857	3857A
Melbourne Mint	Horse with short tail
WW buried in truncation	No BP in exergue

3857 — — First head. l. WW buried in trun. M below head for Melbourne Mint, Australia. R.
Horse with long tail, small BP

	F	VF	EF	UNC		F	VF	EF	UNC
1872 M	55	95	160	325	1877 M	55	100	325	
1873 M		85	150	325	1878 M	55	100	325	
1874 M		85	150	325	1879 M	55	100	250	
1875 M		85	150	275	1880 M	55	100	325	
1876 M		85	160	325	1881 M	55	100	325	

3857A — — As 3857 R. horse with short tail, no BP in ex.

	F	VF	EF			F	VF	EF
1881 M	60	120	250	1882 M		55	75	120

	F	VF	EF	UNC		F	VF	EF	UNC
	£	£	£	£		£	£	£	£

3857BSoveriegn. First head l. WW buried in trun. M below head for Melbourne Mint, Australia R. Horse with short tail, small BP in ex.

1882 M		55	75	120	1884 M		55	75	120
1883 M		55	75	120	1885 M		55	75	120

3857C— — Second head. l. WW complete on broad truncation. R. Horse with short tail, small BP in ex.

1882 M		55	75	120	1885 M		55	75	120
1883 M		55	75	140	1886 M		55	75	120
1884 M		55	75	120	1887 M		55	75	120

3858 Sovereign First head. l. WW buried in narrow trun. S below head for Sydney Mint, Australia, R. Horse with short tail, large BP in ex.

1871 S	60	80	120	250	

3858A— — As 3858 R. Horse with long tail, small BP in ex.

1871 S		70	120	250	1876 S		55	110	250
1872 S		70	140	250	1877 S			Extremely rare	
1873 S		70	140	300	1879 S	55	85	225	650
1874 S		60	100	200	1880 S		65	125	250
1875 S		60	100	175					

3858B — — As 3858 R. Horse with long tail, no BP in ex.

1880 S		55	120	250	1881 S		55	120	250

3858C
Sydney Mint
WW on broad truncation

3859
Type A1

3859A
Type A2

3858C Sovereign. Second head. l. WW complete on broad trun. R. Horse with long tail, small BP in ex.

1880 S		70	125	350

3858D — — As 3858C R. Horse with short tail, no BP in ex.

1881 S		55	120	400	1882 S		55	75	110

3858E — — As 3858D R. Horse with short tail small BP in ex.

1882 S		55	75	110	1885 S		55	75	110
1883 S		55	75	110	1886 S		55	75	110
1884 S		55	75	110	1887 S		55	75	110

3859 Half-Sovereign. Type A1. First (smallest) young head. l. R. First shield

1838	60	95	225	400	1850	105	225	750	—
1839 die axis ↑↓ Proof only FDC £1250					1851		75	175	300
1841	65	100	275	450	1852	65	90	200	350
1842		75	150	275	1853		70	150	275
1843	65	100	275	450	— Proof FDC £3000				
1844	60	75	225	400	1854			Extremely rare	
1845	120	300	950	—	1855		75	160	275
1846	60	85	225	400	1856		75	160	275
1847	60	85	225	400	1857	65	90	200	350
1848	60	85	225	400	1858	65	90	200	350
1849		75	175	300					

3859A Type A2, Second (larger) young head. l. R. First shield

1858		70	160	275	1861		70	160	275
1859		70	160	275	1862		750	—	—
1860		70	160	275	1863		70	160	275

3860	3860C	3860D	3860E
Die number location		Type A3	Type A4

	F	VF	EF	UNC		F	VF	EF	UNC
	£	£	£	£		£	£	£	£

3860 Half-Sovereign. Type A2, as last R. die number below shield

1863	...65	90	225	400	1867		70	150	275
1864		70	150	275	1869		70	150	275
1865		70	150	275	1870	...60	80	160	275
1866		70	150	275	1871		70	150	275

3860A — R. Re-engraved shield legend and rosettes closer to border, coarse boarder teeth both sides, with die number below shield

1870	...85	200	550	—	1871	...85	200	550	—

3860B R. As last but with normal border teeth and no die number below shied

1871 .... *Extremely rare*

3860C — obv. with repositioned legend, nose now points to T in VICTORIA. R Similar to last but with die number below shield

1871	...105	225	650	—	1872	...90	200	550	—

3860D Type A3, Third (larger still) young head l. R. As 3860A, with die number below shield

1872		70	150	275	1875		65	150	250
1873		70	150	275	1876		65	150	250
1874		75	150	275	1877		65	150	250

3860E Type A4. Fourth young head l. hair ribbon now narrow. R. As last with die number below shield

1876		65	140	250	1878		65	140	250
1877		65	140	250	1879	...60	85	275	450

3860F Type A5. Fifth young head l. in very low relief. R. As last with die number below shield

1880							75	275	450

3861	3862
Type A5	Sydney Mint

3861 Obv. as last. R. Cross on crown buried in border. Legend and rosettes very close to heavy border, no die number below shield

1880		75	165	300	1884		65	125	200
1883		65	135	200	1885		65	125	200

3862 Type A2, Second (larger) young head l. R. First shield with S below shield for Sydney Mint, Australia

1871 S ....60 125 500 —

3862A — obv. with repositioned legend, nose now points to T in VICTORIA. R Re-engraved shield, S below shield

1872 S ....70 150 550 —

3862B Type A3. Third (larger still) young head l. R. As last

1875 S ....60 125 500 —

	F £	VF £	EF £	UNC £		F £	VF £	EF £	UNC £

3862C Half-Sovereign. Type A4. Fourth young head l. hair ribbon now narrow. R. As last

1879 S 75   180   600   —

3862D Type A5. Fifth young head,l. in low relief. R as last.

1882 S   550   —   —   1883 S 75   140   525   —

3862E — R. Cross on crown buried in border. Legend and rosettes very close to heavy border, S below shield

1880 S 70   180   700   —   1883 S 50   95   575   —

1881 S 90   220   700   —   1886 S 60   175   575   —

1882 S 180   550   —   —   1887 S 60   140   650   —

Melbourne Mint
3863

3863 Type A. Third (larger still) young head l. R. Re-engraved shield with M below shield for Melbourne Mint, Australia

1873 M 65   100   500   —   1877 M 65   160   700   —

3863A Type A4, fourth young head l. hair ribbon now narrow. R. As last

1877 M 60   160   700   —   1882 M 80   150   650   —

3863B Type A5. Fifth young head l. in low relief. R. As last

1881 M 120   250   750   —   1885 M 120   400   1250   —

1882 M 80   120   650   —   1886 M 80   200   800   —

1884 M 95   160   650   —   1887 M 100   450   —   —

Jubilee Coinage, 1887-93

3864

3864* Five Pounds. R. St. George 1887 400   500   600   750
— Proof *FDC* £2250

3864A* R. St George, S on ground for Sydney Mint, Australia 1887S............   *Extremely rare*

* *Beware recent forgeries*

3865   3866

	EF	UNC		F	VF	EF	UNC
	£	£		£	£	£	£

3865* Two Pounds. Similar 1887 150   200   275   350
— Proof *FDC* £800
3865A* R. St George, S on ground for Sydney Mint, Australia 1887S..........   *Extremely rare*
3866* Sovereign. Normal JEB designer's initials on trun. R. St. George. London Mint
1887   70   95   1888   70   95
3866A — with tiny JEB designer's initials on truncation
1887 ....,....   *Extremely rare*
3866B Repositioned legend. G: of D:G: now closer to crown. Normal JEB designer's initials on trun.
1887 Proof *FDC* £550 .   1889   70   95
1888   70   95   1890   70   95
3866C Obv. as last. R. Horse with longer tail
1891   70   95   1892   70   95

3867   3869
Melbourne Mint

3867 With small spread JEB designer's initials on trun. R. M on ground for Melbourne Mint, Australia
1887M..   90   150
3867A With normal JEB designer's initials on trun. 1887M   65   90
3867B Repositioned legend. G: of D: G: now closer to crown. Normal JEB initials on trun.
1887M   65   90   1889M   65   90
1888M   65   90   1890M   65   90
3867C Obv. as last. R. Horse with longer tail
1891M   65   90   1893M   65   90
1892M   65   90
3868 With small spread JEB initials on trun. R. S on ground for Sydney Mint, Australia
1887S   100   300   550
3868A With normal JEB designer's initials on trun. 1888S   75   100
3868B Repositioned legend. G: of D:G: now closer to crown. Normal JEB initials on trun.
1888S...........................   75   100   1890S...........................   65   90
1889S...........................   65   90
3868C Obv. as last. R. Horse with longer tail
1891S...........................   65   90   1893S........................   65   90
1892S...........................   65   90
3869 Half-Sovereign. Obv. normal JEB designer's initials. on trun. R. High shield
1887   50   75   1890   110   200   —
— Proof *FDC* £225
* Beware recent forgeries

	VF	EF	UNC		F	VF	EF	UNC
	£	£	£		£	£	£	£

3869A Half-Sovereign. Small close JEB designer's intitials. on trun. R. High shield
1887 100   200   —

3869B Normal JEB initials. on trun. R. Lower shield, date therefore spread apart
1890 100   200   —   1892 100   200   —

3869C No JEB initials on trun. R. High Shield
1887 100   200   —   1891 100   200   —
1890 .... BV   50   85   1892 100   200   —

3869D As last. R. Lower shield, date therefore spread apart
1890 .... BV   50   85   1892 .... BV   50   85
1891 .... BV   70   100   1893 .... BV   80   110

3870 Small very spread JEB initials on trun. R. High shield, M below for Melbourne Mint, Australia
1887M...100   225   450   1000

3870A Small close JEB initials on trun. R. As last
1887M...100   225   450   1000

3870B Normal JEB initials on trun. R. Lower shield, date therefore spread apart
1893M...125   275   600   —

3871 Small very spread JEB initials on trun. R. High shield S below for Sydney Mint, Australia
1887S 95   200   500   —

3871A Small close JEB initials on trun. R As last.
1887S 95   200   500   —

3871B Normal JEB initials on trun. R. Lower shield, date therefore spread apart,
S below for Sydney Mint, Australia
1889S 95   200   450   —

3871C Normal JEB initials on trun. R. High shield, S below for Sydney Mint, Australia
1891S 100   225   450   1000

3871D No JEB initials on trun. R. As last
1891S 100   225   450   1000

Old Head coinage, 1893-1901

3872

3872* Five Pounds. R. St. George and dragon
1893 400   675   975   1250
— Proof *FDC* £2750

* Beware recent forgeries

3873   3874

	EF £	UNC £		F £	VF £	EF £	UNC £
3873* Two Pounds. Similar							
1893				150	250	400	550
— Proof *FDC* £1000							
3874 Sovereign. R. St. George, London Mint							
1893		85	1898				75
— Proof *FDC* £600			1899				75
1894		75	1900				75
1895		75	1901				75
1896		75					
3875 — R. St. George. M on ground for Melbourne Mint, Australia							
1893 M		75	1898 M				75
1894 M		75	1899 M				75
1895 M		75	1900 M				75
1896 M		75	1901 M				75
1897 M		75					

* *beware recent forgeries*

3876   3877
Perth Mint mark   Sydney Mint mark

3876 — — P on ground for Perth Mint, Australia				
1899 P	110	200	1901 P	120
1900 P		120		
3877 — — S on ground for Sydney Mint, Australia				
1893 S		75	1898 S	75
1894 S		75	1899 S	75
1895 S		75	1900 S	75
1896 S		95	1901 S	75
1897 S		75		

3878

F	VF	EF	UNC		F	VF	EF	UNC
£	£	£	£		£	£	£	£

3878 Half-Sovereign. R. St. George. London Mint

1893		.50	85	1897			50	85
— Proof *FDC* £450				1898			50	85
1894		.50	85	1899			50	85
1895		.50	85	1900			50	85
1896		.50	85	1901			50	85

3879 — — M on ground for Melbourne Mint, Australia

1893 M	.850	—	—	—	1899 M	.80	150	500	—
1896 M	.80	150	500	—	1900 M	.80	150	500	—

3880 — — P on ground for Perth Mint, Australia

1899 P......................... Proof only *unique*   1900 P..................400 650   —   —

3881 — — S on ground for Sydney Mint, Australia

1893 S	.100	200	600	—	1900 S		90	400	—
1897 S	.60	100	300	—					

SILVER

Young head coinage

3882

3882 Crown. Young head. l. R. Crowned shield, regnal year on edge in Roman figures (eg 1847 = XI)

1839 Proof only *FDC* £3000

	F	VF	EF	UNC
1844 Star stops VIII	.30	95	600	1200
1844 Cinquefoil stops VIII	.30	95	600	1200
1845 Star stops VIII	.30	95	600	1200
1847 XI	.35	120	750	1500

	3883				3885 Type 'A¹'		
F	*VF*	*EF*	*UNC*	*F*	*VF*	*EF*	*UNC*
£	£	£	£	£	£	£	£

3883*Crown. 'Gothic' type, as illustration; inscribed edge,
mdcccxlvii=1847 Undecimo on edge 200   400   600   1250
— Proof, Plain edge *FDC* £1650

*Beware of recent forgeries.

3884 — mdcccliii=1853. Septimo on edge Proof *FDC* £4000

3885 Halfcrown. Type A¹. Young head l. with one ornate and one plain fillet binding hair. WW in
relief on trun.

1839 250   750   2000   1839 Proof plain edge.   *FDC* £600

3886 Type A² Similar, but two ornate fillets binding hair. — 1839 Proof *FDC* £1500

3886A Type A²ᐟ³ Similar, Two plain fillets, WW relief, plain edge Proof *FDC* £2500

3887 — Type A³. Two plain fillets. WW incuse on trun.

1839 300	850	2500	—	1840 30	75	275	450

3888 — Type A⁴. Similar but no initials on trun.

1841 85	300	750	1250	1848/6 60	150	500	1000
1842 25	75	250	450	1848 25	250	700	1150
1843 30	100	350	600	1849 large date 30	80	300	500
1844 20	50	200	350	1849 small date......40	100	375	650
1845 20	50	200	350	1850 25	70	300	550
1846 20	50	200	350	1853 Proof *FDC* £1000			

	3889				3890		

3889 — Type A⁵. As last but design of inferior workmanship

1874 12	25	75	150	1881 12	25	75	150
1875 12	25	75	150	1882 15	30	90	175
1876 15	30	90	175	1883 12	25	75	150
1876/5 30	50	200	400	1884 12	25	75	150
1877 12	25	75	150	1885 12	25	75	150
1878 12	25	75	150	1886 12	25	75	150
1879 15	35	110	200	1887 15	30	90	175
1880 12	25	80	150				

3890 Florin. 'Godless' type A (i.e. without D.G.), WW behind bust

1848 Plain edge (Pattern) *FDC* £550				1849 WW obliterated35	70	175	300
1849 18	35	85	175				

	F	VF	EF	UNC		F	VF	EF	UNC
	£	£	£	£		£	£	£	£

3891 Florin. 'Gothic' type B[1]. Reads brit:, WW below bust, date at end of obverse legend in gothic numerals (1851 to 1863)

	F	VF	EF	UNC		F	VF	EF	UNC
mdcccli		*Extremely rare*			mdccclvi	20	50	135	250
mdccclii	18	40	100	200	mdccclvii	20	45	110	225
mdcclii, ii/i	18	40	100	200	mdcclviii	20	45	110	225
mdccliii	18	40	100	200	mdccclix	20	45	110	225
— Proof *FDC £1100*					mdccclx	25	50	135	250
mdcccliv	225	500	1750	—	mdccclxii	35	120	300	600
mdccclv	18	45	110	225	mdccclxiii	55	200	650	1000

3892

3892 — Type B[2]. As last but die number below bust (1864 to 1867)

	F	VF	EF	UNC		F	VF	EF	UNC
mdccclxiv	20	45	110	225	mdccclxvi	25	50	135	250
— heavy flan		*Extremely rare*			mdccclxvii	30	70	175	300
mdccclxv	20	45	110	225					

3893 Type B[3]. Reads britt:, die number below bust (1868 to 1879)

	F	VF	EF	UNC		F	VF	EF	UNC
mdccclxviii	20	50	135	250	mdccclxxiv	20	45	110	225
mdccclxix	20	45	110	225	mdccclxxiv iv/iii	25	65	140	250
mdccclxx	20	45	110	225	mdccclxxv	20	45	110	225
mdccclxxi	20	45	110	225	mdccclxxvi	20	45	110	225
mdccclxxii	18	40	85	175	mdccclxxvii	20	45	110	225
mdccclxxiii	18	40	85	175	mdccclxxix		*Extremely rare*		

3894 — Type B[4]. As last but with border of 48 arcs and no WW below bust

1877 mdccclxxvii ....   *Extremely rare*

3895 — Type B[5]. Similar but 42 arcs (1867, 1877 and 1878)

	F	VF	EF	UNC		F	VF	EF	UNC
mdccclxvii		*Extremely rare*			mdccclxxviii	20	45	110	225
mdccclxxvii	20	45	110	225					

3896 — Type B[5/6]. As last but no die number below bust (1877, 1879)

	F	VF	EF	UNC		F	VF	EF	UNC
mdccclxxvii		*Extremely rare*			mdccclxxix		*Extremely rare*		

3897 — Type B[6]. Reads britt:, WW; 48 arcs (1879)

mdccclxxix 20   45   110   225

3898 — Type B[7]. As last but no WW, 38 arcs (1879)

mdccclxxix 20   45   110   225

3899 — Type B[3/8]. As next but younger portrait (1880)

mdccclxxx..   *Extremely rare*

3900 — Type B[8]. Similar but 34 arcs (1880 to 1887)

	F	VF	EF	UNC		F	VF	EF	UNC
mdccclxxx	20	45	110	225	mdccclxxxiv	18	40	95	200
mdccclxxxi	18	40	95	200	mdccclxxxv	18	40	95	200
mdccclxxxi xxri	25	65	120	250	mdccclxxxvi	18	40	95	200
mdccclxxxiii	18	40	95	200					

3901 — Type B[9]. Similar but 46 arcs

1887 mdccclxxxvii 25   50   150   250

3902 Shilling. Type A[1]. First head l., WW on trun.

	F	VF	EF	UNC		F	VF	EF	UNC
1838	10	25	90	135	1839	10	25	90	135

| F | VF | EF | UNC | | F | VF | EF | UNC |
| £ | £ | £ | £ | | £ | £ | £ | £ |

3903 Shilling Type A². Second head, l. WW on trun. (proof only), 1839 *FDC £225*

3904

3904 — Type A³. Second head, l. no initials on trun.

1839 10	25	75	125	— Proof *FDC £400*				
1840 15	50	125	200	1854 50	150	450	800
1841 15	50	125	200	1854/1 150	500	1200	—
1842 10	20	60	100	1855 10	20	50	100
1843 15	30	95	150	1856 10	20	50	100
1844 10	20	60	100	1857 10	20	50	100
1845 10	20	70	120	1857 REG F:Ɔ:error125	275	500	—
1846 10	20	60	100	1858 10	20	50	100
1848 over 6 45	100	400	600	1859 10	20	50	100
1849 15	25	70	120	1860 15	25	80	135
1850 120	400	1000	—	1861 15	25	80	135
1851/49 150	500	1200	—	1862 20	40	110	175
1851 30	85	250	400	1863 25	60	225	400
1852 10	20	55	100	1863/1 75	175	350	—
1853 10	20	50	85					

3905 — Type A⁴. As last, R. Die number above date

1864 10	20	50	100	1866 BBITANNIAR50	125	250	—
1865 10	20	50	100	1867 10	20	55	110
1866 10	20	50	100					

3906 — Type A⁵. Third head, l. R. No die number above date

1867 Proof	*Extremely rare*	1867 Proof plain edge	*Extremely rare*

3906A   Die number location

3906A — Type A⁶. Third head, l. R. Die number above date

1867 45	100	450	—	1874 8	18	45	90
1868 10	25	50	100	1875 8	18	45	90
1869 18	35	70	140	1876 12	30	55	110
1870 18	35	70	140	1877 8	18	45	90
1871 8	18	45	90	1878 8	18	45	90
1872 8	18	45	90	1879 25	60	175	300
1873 8	18	45	90					

3907 — Type A⁷. Fourth head, l. R. No die number above date

1879 10	20	50	85	1884 8	15	30	70
1880 8	15	30	75	1885 8	12	25	65
1881 8	15	30	75	1886 8	12	25	65
1882 15	40	80	135	1887 10	25	60	125
1883 8	15	30	75					

3908 Sixpence. Type A[1]. First head l.

	F £	VF £	EF £	UNC £		F £	VF £	EF £	UNC £
1838	8	15	40	65	1852	4	12	40	70
1839	8	15	40	65	1853	6	14	35	60
— Proof *FDC* £175					— Proof *FDC* £300				
1840	8	15	45	75	1854	50	120	400	700
1841	8	18	50	100	1855	6	14	35	75
1842	8	15	40	85	1855/3	12	25	50	100
1843	8	15	40	85	1856	7	15	40	85
1844 Small 44	6	14	35	75	1857	7	15	40	85
1844 Large 44	10	25	50	100	1858	7	15	40	85
1845	7	15	40	85	1859	6	14	35	75
1846	6	14	35	755	1859/8	10	20	40	90
1848	30	75	300	450	1860	7	15	40	8
1848/6 or 7	40	90	350	500	1862	30	80	300	450
1850	7	15	40	85	1863	18	50	200	350
1850/3	15	30	80	150	1866			*Extremely rare*	
1851	7	15	40	85					

3909
Die number location

3912
Type 'A[5]'

3909 — Type A[2]. First head, R. die number above date

	F	VF	EF	UNC		F	VF	EF	UNC
1864	7	15	40	85	1866	7	15	40	85
1865	8	18	50	100					

3910 — Type A[3]. Second head, l. R. die number above date

	F	VF	EF	UNC		F	VF	EF	UNC
1867	10	18	55	110	1875	5	12	35	75
1868	10	18	55	110	1876	10	18	60	125
1869	10	20	80	150	1877	5	12	35	75
1870	10	20	80	150	1878	5	12	35	75
1871	7	15	40	85	1878 DRITANNIAR	30	80	275	—
1872	7	15	40	85	1878/7	35	100	300	—
1873	5	12	35	75	1879	10	18	60	125
1874	5	12	35	75					

3911 — Type A[4]. Second head, l. No die number

	F	VF	EF	UNC		F	VF	EF	UNC
1871	8	16	50	90	1879	7	15	40	75
1877	7	15	40	75	1880	8	16	50	90

3912 — Type A[5]. Third head l.

	F	VF	EF	UNC		F	VF	EF	UNC
1880	5	10	30	50	1884	5	10	25	45
1881	5	10	25	45	1885	5	10	25	45
1882	10	25	60	110	1886	5	10	25	45
1883	5	10	25	45	1887	4	8	20	40

3913

	F	VF	EF	UNC		F	VF	EF	UNC
	£	£	£	£		£	£	£	£

3913 Groat (4d.). R. Britannia seated r.

	F	VF	EF	UNC		F	VF	EF	UNC
1838	2	8	22	40	1846	4	10	32	55
1838/∞	3	16	35	75	1847/6 (or 8)	25	75	225	—
1839	3	9	28	45	1848/6	25	10	225	60
1839 die axis ↑↑ Proof *FDC* £125					1848	3	9	25	45
1839 die axis ↑↓ Proof *FDC* £200					1848/7	5	10	30	60
1840	3	9	25	45	1849	3	9	25	45
1840 small round o	5	15	30	65	1849/8	5	10	30	60
1841	4	10	35	55	1851	20	65	175	300
1842	4	10	32	55	1852	35	90	250	400
1842/1	5	15	35	75	1853	40	100	300	450
1843	4	10	32	55	— Proof *FDC* £300 milled edge				
1843 4 over 5	8	20	40	85	1854	3	9	25	45
1844	4	10	32	55	1855	3	9	25	45
1845	4	10	32	55					

Threepence. R. Crowned 3; as Maundy threepence but with a less prooflike surface

3914

3914 Type A[1]. First bust, young head, high relief, ear fully visible.

R Tie ribbon closer to tooth border, cross on crown further from tooth border, figure 3

	F	VF	EF	UNC		F	VF	EF	UNC
1838*	5	10	50	85	1851	5	10	50	90
1838 BRITANNIAB		*Extremely rare*			1851 5 over 8	10	20	80	—
1839*	5	18	65	120	1852*	60	175	400	—
— Proof (see Maundy)					1853	10	25	75	150
1840*	5	14	60	100	1854	5	10	50	90
1841*	5	18	66	120	1855	5	18	65	120
1842*	5	18	65	120	1856	5	10	45	85
1843*	5	12	50	85	1857	5	18	65	120
1844*	5	18	65	120	1858	5	10	45	85
1845	3	8	35	70	1858 BRITANNIAB		*Extremely rare*		
1846	10	20	75	150	1858/6	10	20	80	—
1847*	50	150	350	600	1858/5	8	18	65	—
1848*	40	125	325	—	1859	5	10	45	85
1849	5	18	65	120	1860	5	18	65	120
1850	3	8	40	65	1861	5	10	45	85

Issued for Colonial use only.

　　　3914A　　　　　　　　3914C　　　　　　　3914D

	F	VF	EF	UNC		F	VF	EF	UNC
	£	£	£	£		£	£	£	£

3914A Threepence. Type A². First bust variety, slightly older portrait with aquiline nose

	F	VF	EF	UNC		F	VF	EF	UNC
1859	5	10	45	85	1865	5	18	65	120
1860	5	10	45	85	1866	5	10	45	85
1861	5	10	45	85	1867	5	10	45	85
1862	5	10	45	85	1868	5	10	45	85
1863	5	18	65	120	1868 RRITANNIAR ..		*Extremely rare*		
1864	5	10	45	85					

3914B — Type A³. Second Bust, slightly larger, lower relief, mouth fuller, nose more pronounced, rounded truncation

	F	VF	EF	UNC
1867	5	18	65	120

3914C Threepence. Type A⁴. Obv. as last. R. Tie ribbon further from tooth border, cross on crown nearer to tooth border

	F	VF	EF	UNC		F	VF	EF	UNC
1867	5	18	65	120	1874	3	8	30	55
1868	5	18	65	120	1875	3	8	30	55
1869	10	20	75	140	1876	3	8	30	55
1870	4	12	50	85	1877	4	10	40	65
1871	5	14	55	100	1878	4	10	40	65
1872	5	14	55	100	1879	4	10	40	65
1873	3	8	30	55	1884	3	6	25	50

3914D — Type A⁵. Third bust, older features, mouth closed, hair strands leading from 'bun' vary

	F	VF	EF	UNC		F	VF	EF	UNC
1880	4	10	40	65	1885	3	6	25	50
1881	3	6	25	50	1886	3	6	25	50
1882	5	10	50	95	1887	4	10	40	65
1883	3	6	25	50					

3914E Twopence. Young head. R Date divided by a crowned 2 within a wreath

	F	VF	EF	UNC		F	VF	EF	UNC
1838	3	7	18	30	1848	5	10	22	40

3915 Three-Halfpence. (for Colonial use). R. Value, etc.

	F	VF	EF	UNC		F	VF	EF	UNC
1838	5	12	25	45	1843	3	6	15	35
1839	4	10	20	40	1843/34	8	20	70	125
1840	8	22	65	100	1860	6	18	50	85
1841	5	14	30	60	1862	6	18	50	85
1842	5	14	30	60					

3916

	EF £	FDC £		EF £	FDC £
3916 Maundy Set. (4d., 3d., 2d. and 1.)					
1838	60	100	1858	55	90
1839	70	120	1859	55	90
— Proof *FDC* £300			1860	50	80
1840	70	120	1861	50	80
1841	80	140	1862	50	80
1842	70	120	1863	50	80
1843	70	120	1864	50	80
1844	70	120	1865	50	80
1845	60	100	1866	50	80
1846	80	140	1867	50	80
1847	70	120	1868	50	80
1848	70	120	1869	55	90
1849	80	140	1870	45	75
1850	50	85	1871	45	75
1851	50	85	1872	45	75
1852	60	100	1873	45	75
1853	60	100	1874	45	75
— Proof *FDC* £350			1875	45	75
1854	60	100	1876	45	75
1855	60	100	1877	45	75
1856	55	90	1878	45	75
1857	55	90	1879	45	75
1880	45	75	1884	45	75
1881	45	75	1885	45	75
1882	45	75	1886	45	75
1883	45	75	1887	50	85
3917 — Fourpence, 1838-87 ....*from*	6	10			
3918 — Threepence, 1838-87 ....*from*	12	22			
3919 — Twopence, 1838-87 ....*from*	6	10			
3920 — Penny, 1838-87 ....*from*	5	8			

Maundy Sets in the original dated cases are worth approximately £10, and £5 for undated cases more than the prices quoted.

Jubilee Coinage 1887-93

3921

	F	VF	EF	UNC			F	VF	EF	UNC
	£	£	£	£			£	£	£	£

3921 Crown. R. St. George and dragon

	F	VF	EF	UNC			F	VF	EF	UNC
1887	15	25	40	75		1889	15	25	40	75
— Proof *FDC* £375						1890	15	30	60	95
1888 narrow date	15	30	60	95		1891	15	30	65	120
1888 wide date	35	75	175	—		1892	20	40	80	150

3922

3922 Double-Florin (4s.). R. Cruciform shields. Roman I in date

	F	VF	EF	UNC
1887	12	20	30	50
— Proof *FDC* £250				

3923 — R. Similar but Arabic 1 in date

	F	VF	EF	UNC			F	VF	EF	UNC
1887	12	20	30	50		1889	12	20	30	55
— Proof *FDC* £175						1889 inverted 1 for I in				
1888	12	20	35	60		VICTORIA	25	50	120	225
1888 inverted 1 for I in						1890	12	20	35	60
VICTORIA	25	50	120	225						

3924   3925

	F £	VF £	EF £	UNC £		F £	VF £	EF £	UNC £

3924 Halfcrown. R. Shield in garter and collar

1887	7	12	20	40	1890	10	18	45	70
— Proof *FDC* £100					1891	10	18	45	70
1888	10	15	35	60	1892	10	18	45	70
1889	10	18	45	70					

3925 Florin. R. Cruciform shields, sceptres in angles

1887	5	8	15	25	1890	10	25	60	120
— Proof *FDC* £75					1891	20	50	125	250
1888	6	12	22	35	1892	20	45	110	220
1889	6	12	24	40					

3926   3927

3926 Shilling. Small head. R. Shield in Garter

1887	3	5	10	18	1888/7	5	9	18	30
— Proof *FDC* £55					1889	35	90	300	450

3927 Large head. R. As before

1889	5	9	25	40	1891	5	10	35	50
1890	5	10	30	45	1892	5	10	35	50

3928   3929   3930

3928 Sixpence. JEB designer's initials below trun. R. Shield in Garter (withdrawn type)

1887	2	5	10	15	1887 JEB on trun.	15	40	85	150
1887 R/V in					—Proof *FDC* £40				
VICTORIA	10	35	75	125					

3929 — R. Value in wreath

1887	2	5	10	15	1891	5	10	18	35
1888	4	8	15	25	1892	5	10	18	35
1889	4	8	15	25	1893	100	350	1000	—
1890	4	8	16	30					

	F £	VF £	EF £	UNC £		F £	VF £	EF £	UNC £
3930 Groat (for use in British Guiana). R. Britannia seated									
1888	8	20	35	60					
3931 Threepence. As Maundy but less prooflike surface									
1887	—	1	3	7	1890	1	3	7	12
— Proof *FDC* £30					1891	1	3	7	12
1888	2	5	12	20	1892	2	5	12	20
1889	1	3	7	12	1893	15	40	95	175

3932

	EF £	FDC £		EF £	FDC £
3932 Maundy Set. (4d., 3d., 2d. and 1d.)					
1888	50	75	1891	50	75
1889	50	75	1892	50	75
1890	50	75			
3933 — Fourpence, 1888-92 ...*from*				9	13
3934 — Threepence, 1888-92 ...*from*				10	20
3935 — Twopence, 1888-92 ...*from*				5	10
3936 — Penny, 1888-92 ...*from*				5	10

Maundy Sets in the original dated cases are worth approximately £10 and £5 for undated cases more than the prices quoted.

Old Head Coinage 1893-1901

3937

	F	VF	EF	UNC
	£	£	£	£

3937 Crown. R. St. George. Regnal date on edge

		F	VF	EF	UNC
1893 edge LVI		15	30	100	200
— —	Proof *FDC* £400				
1893	LVII	25	60	175	350
1894 —	LVII	15	40	125	275
1894	LVIII	15	40	125	275
1895 —	LVIII	15	35	110	250
1895	LIX	15	35	110	250
1896 —	LIX	18	50	150	300
1896	LX	15	35	110	250
1897 —	LX	15	35	110	250
1897	LXI	15	35	110	250
1898 —	LXI	25	60	175	350
1898	LXII	15	40	125	275
1899 —	LXII	15	40	125	275
1899	LXIII	15	40	125	275
1900 —	LXIII	25	70	175	325
1900	LXIV	25	70	200	400

3938

	F	VF	EF	UNC		F	VF	EF	UNC
	£	£	£	£		£	£	£	£

3938 Halfcrown. R. Shield in collar

	F	VF	EF	UNC		F	VF	EF	UNC
1893	8	15	30	60	1897	8	15	30	60
— Proof *FDC* £120					1898	9	16	35	70
1894	10	18	50	90	1899	9	16	35	70
1895	9	16	35	70	1900	12	28	50	85
1896	9	16	35	70	1901	8	15	30	60

3939

	F £	VF £	EF £	UNC £		F £	VF £	EF £	UNC £

3939 Florin. R. Three shields within Garter

1893	5	10	30	50	1897	6	12	30	55
— Proof *FDC* £100					1898	6	15	35	65
1894	8	16	50	85	1899	6	12	30	55
1895	7	18	40	65	1900	10	25	50	85
1896	6	12	30	55	1901	5	15	30	50

3940A   3941

3940 Shilling. R. Three shields within Garter, small rose

1893	4	8	15	30	1894	5	10	20	45
1893 small lettering	6	15	30	50	— Proof *FDC* £65				

3940A Second reverse, larger rose

1895	4	9	18	40	1899	4	9	20	40
1896	4	9	18	35	1900	10	18	30	65
1897	4	9	18	35	1901	4	9	15	30
1898	4	9	18	35					

3941 Sixpence. R. Value in wreath

1893	3	6	12	25	1897	4	8	12	25
— Proof *FDC* £45					1898	4	8	12	25
1894	5	10	16	30	1899	4	8	14	25
1895	4	8	12	25	1900	8	16	25	40
1896	4	8	12	25	1901	4	8	12	20

3942 Threepence. R. Crowned 3. As Maundy but less prooflike surface

1893	1	2	5	12	1897	1	2	6	15
— Proof *FDC* £35					1898	1	2	6	15
1894	1	3	7	18	1899	1	2	5	12
1895	1	3	7	18	1900	3	5	10	20
1896	1	2	6	15	1901	1	2	5	12

3943

	EF £	FDC £		EF £	FDC £
3943 Maundy Set. (4d., 3d., 2d. and 1d.)					
1893	40	55	1898	40	55
1894	45	60	1899	50	60
1895	40	55	1900	75	100
1896	40	55	1901	40	55
1897	40	55			
3944 — **Fourpence.** 1893-1901 .... *from*				5	9
3945 — **Threepence.** 1893-1901 .... *from*				10	17
3946 — **Twopence.** 1893-1901 .... *from*				5	8
3947 — **Penny.** 1893-1901 .... *from*				5	8

Maundy Sets in the original dated cases are worth approximately £5 more than the prices quoted.

3948

Young Head Copper Coinage, 1838-60

	F £	VF £	EF £	UNC £		F £	VF £	EF £	UNC £
3948 Penny. R. Britannia									
1839 Bronzed proof *FDC* £275					1853	5	12	30	60
1841	5	10	30	60	— Proof *FDC* £275				
1843	35	100	400	—	1854	5	12	30	60
1844	10	15	40	80	1855	5	12	30	60
1845	15	25	75	150	1856	25	50	125	350
1846	10	20	60	120	1857	5	10	30	60
1847	8	15	40	80	1858	5	10	30	60
1848/7	5	15	35	75	1859	5	10	30	60
1849	50	150	450	—	1860/59*	175	450	950	—
1851	10	20	60	120					

*The 1860 large copper pieces are not to be confused with the smaller and commoner bronze issue with date on reverse (nos. 3954, 3956 and 3958).

3949

	F £	VF £	EF £	UNC £		F £	VF £	EF £	UNC £
3949 Halfpenny. R. Britannia									
1838.........................5	12	25	50	1852.........................8	18	35	75
1839 Bronzed proof *FDC* £150				1853.........................3	8	15	30
1841.........................4	10	20	45	— Proof *FDC* £150			
1843.......................25	45	90	200	1854.........................3	8	15	30
1844.........................6	15	30	60	1855.........................3	8	15	30
1845.......................50	95	300	—	1856.........................5	15	30	65
1846.........................8	18	35	75	1857.........................4	10	20	40
1847.........................8	18	35	75	1858.........................5	10	25	55
1848/7.....................8	18	35	75	1859.........................5	10	25	55
1851.........................5	15	30	65	1860*.........................	—	2750	—

Overstruck dates are listed only if commoner than normal date, or if no normal date is known.

3950

3951

	F £	VF £	EF £	UNC £		F £	VF £	EF £	UNC £
3950 Farthing. R. Britannia									
1838.........................5	10	25	45	1850.........................5	10	25	50
1839.........................4	8	20	40	1851.......................10	20	45	95
— Bronzed proof *FDC* £120				1852.......................10	20	45	95
1840.........................4	8	20	40	1853.........................5	10	25	50
1841.........................4	8	20	40	— Proof *FDC* £275			
1842.......................15	35	85	150	1854.........................5	10	25	50
1843.........................4	8	20	40	1855.........................5	10	30	55
1844.......................45	100	250	—	1856.........................8	20	40	85
1845.........................5	10	25	50	1857.........................5	10	25	50
1846.........................8	15	40	80	1858.........................5	10	25	50
1847.........................5	10	25	50	1859.......................10	20	45	95
1848.........................5	10	25	50	1860*......................—	—	3000	—
1849.......................30	60	150	—				
3951 Half-Farthing. R. Value								
1839.........................5	10	28	50	1852.........................4	10	35	50
1842.........................5	10	28	50	1853.........................5	15	40	75
1843...........................	5	12	25	— Proof *FDC* £250			
1844...........................	3	10	20	1854.........................8	25	65	100
1847.........................4	8	22	40	1856.........................8	25	65	100
1851.........................5	10	35	50				

*These 1860 large copper pieces are not to be confused with the smaller and commoner bronze issue with date on reverse (nos. 3954, 3956 and 3958).

	3951				3952		3953		

	F	VF	EF	UNC			F	VF	EF	UNC
	£	£	£	£			£	£	£	£

3952 Third-Farthing (for use in Malta). R. Britannia

1844						.20	35	75	140

3953 Quarter-Farthing (for use in Ceylon). R. Value

1839	...10	18	35	55	1853	...10	20	40	65
1851	...10	20	40	65	— Proof *FDC* £700				
1852	...10	18	35	55					

Copper coins graded in this catalogue as UNC have full mint lustre.

Bronze Coinage, 'Bun Head' Issue, 1860-95

3954

3954 Penny. R. Britannia

1860 Beaded border ..3	15	40	90	1873	...5	15	40	95
1860 Toothed border .2	10	35	75	1874	...5	15	55	140
1861	...2	10	35	75	1875	...2	10	35	85
1861 6 over 8	*Extremely rare*			1877	...2	10	35	85
1861 8 over 6	*Extremely rare*			1878	...3	15	50	140
1862	...2	10	35	75	1879	...2	7	25	65
1862 8 over 6	*Extremely rare*			1880	...3	15	65	120
1862 Halfpenny numerals	*Extremely rare*			1881	...4	15	50	140
1863	...2	10	35	75	1882*		*Extremely rare*		
1863 Die number below	*Extremely rare*			1883	...3	10	35	75
1863 Slender 3	*Extremely rare*			1884	...2	8	25	50
1864 4 with upper serif20	75	250	500	1885	...2	8	25	50
1864 crosslet 4 ...25	85	300	550	1886	...2	10	25	60
1865	...8	20	65	150	1887	...2	8	25	50
1865/3	...40	100	200	500	1888	...2	10	25	60
1866	...5	15	45	95	1889	...2	8	20	50
1867	...8	25	65	150	1890	...2	8	20	50
1868	...15	35	100	275	1891	...2	7	18	45
1869	...50	175	400	950	1892	...2	8	20	50
1870	...8	25	75	175	1893	...2	8	20	50
1871	...25	75	250	400	1894	...3	15	40	80
1872	...5	15	40	95					

* not to be confused with Heaton Mint (see over page)

H Mint mark location
3955

3956

	F	VF	EF	UNC		F	VF	EF	UNC
	£	£	£	£		£	£	£	£

3955 Penny. R. Britannia, H Mint mark below date – (struck by Ralph Heaton & Sons, Birmingham)

	F	VF	EF	UNC		F	VF	EF	UNC
1874 H 5	20	50	100		1881 H 3	15	35	80
1875 H 35	95	300	—		1882 H 2	10	25	60
1876 H 2	15	35	75		1882/1 H 10	25	60	120

3956 Halfpenny. R. Britannia

	F	VF	EF	UNC		F	VF	EF	UNC
1860 Beaded border ..1	5	20	45		1874 5	25	85	225
1860 Toothed border .2	10	30	75		1875 1	6	30	70
1861 1	5	20	45		1877 1	6	30	70
1861 6 over 8		*Extremely rare*			1878 3	15	50	150
1862 1	4	15	40		1879 1	5	20	50
1862 Die letter to left .					1880 2	7	30	75
of lighthouse		*Extremely rare*			1881 2	7	30	75
1863 small 3 2	6	35	80		1883 1	7	30	75
1863 large 3 2	6	35	80		1884 1	4	15	40
1864 2	10	40	90		1885 1	4	15	40
1865 3	15	50	150		1886 1	4	15	40
1865/3 40	100	200	400		1887 1	4	12	35
1866 2	10	40	90		1888 1	4	15	40
1867 3	15	50	150		1889 1	4	15	40
1868 2	10	45	100		1889/8 10	20	50	100
1869 10	40	150	275		1890 1	4	12	35
1870 2	8	35	80		1891 1	4	12	35
1871 15	50	175	300		1892 1	6	30	70
1872 2	7	30	75		1893 1	4	15	40
1873 2	10	40	90		1894 1	7	30	70

3957 — R. Britannia, H Mint mark below date — (struck by Ralph Heaton & Sons, Birmingham)

	F	VF	EF	UNC		F	VF	EF	UNC
1874 H 1	5	30	60		1881 H 1	5	30	60
1875 H 2	6	35	80		1882 H 1	5	30	60
1876 H 1	5	30	60					

3958   3960

	F £	VF £	EF £	UNC £		F £	VF £	EF £	UNC £
3958 Farthing. R. Britannia									
1860 Beaded border	5	20	40		1878		2	10	20
1860 Toothed border ...	3	15	30		1879 Large 9		5	15	35
1861	3	18	35		1879 Normal 9		2	10	20
1862	3	18	35		1880		3	20	40
1863 20	45	125	300		1881		2	10	25
1864 4 with no serif.....	5	25	50		1883 2	10	30	60
1864 4 with serif.........	8	30	60		1884		1	8	18
1865	3	18	35		1885		1	8	18
1865/2	10	25	70		1886		1	8	18
1866	3	15	30		1887		2	12	25
1867	4	20	45		1888		2	10	20
1868	4	20	45		1890		2	10	20
1869	10	30	70		1891		1	8	18
1872	3	18	35		1892 2	10	30	60
1873	2	12	35		1893		1	8	18
1875 10	20	50	100		1894		2	10	20
1877 Proof only £2000					1895 10	20	50	100

Bronze coins graded in this catalogue as UNC have full mint lustre

3959 — R. Britannia. H Mint mark below date — (struck by Ralph Heaton & Sons, Birmingham)

	F £	VF £	EF £	UNC £		F £	VF £	EF £	UNC £
1874 H 2	5	15	35		1876 H Normal 6 5	10	30	60
1874 H G over N's obv	*Extremely rare*				1881 II 2	5	12	30
1875 H	2	8	15		1882 H 2	5	12	30
1876 H large 6 10	25	60	100						

3960 Third-Farthing (for use in Malta). R. Value

	F £	VF £	EF £	UNC £		F £	VF £	EF £	UNC £
1866 1	3	10	25		1881 2	4	12	30
1868 1	3	10	25		1884 1	3	10	25
1876 2	4	12	30		1885 1	3	10	25
1878 1	3	10	25						

Old Head Issue, 1885-1901

3961

3961 Penny. R. Britannia

	F £	VF £	EF £		F £	VF £	EF £
1895	2	6	30	1898	3	10	35
1896	2	5	25	1899	2	5	25
1897	2	5	25	1900		8	20
1897 O'NE flawed	*Extremely rare*			1901		3	10

3961 'High Tide'
Horizon is level with folds in robe

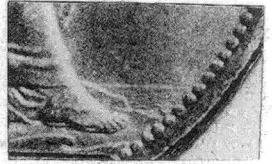

3961A 'Low Tide'
Horizon is level with hem line of robe

	VF £	EF £	UNC £		VF £	EF £	UNC £
3961A Penny. As last but 'Low tide', 1895					35	125	250
3962 Halfpenny. Type as Penny. R. Britannia							
1895	2	6	15	1899		5	12
1896	2	5	12	1900		8	15
1897	2	5	12	1901		2	5
1898	2	5	12				
3963 Farthing. R. Britannia. Bright finish							
1895	2	5	10	1897	2	5	12
1896	2	5	10				

3962

3964

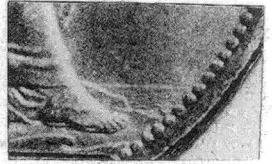

3964 — Dark finish							
1897	2	5	10	1900	3	8	15
1898	2	5	9	1901		2	5
1899	2	5	9				

Proof Sets

PS3 Young head, **1839.** 'Una and the Lion' Five Pounds, and Sovereign to Farthing
(15 coins) ....*FDC* £27,500

PS4 — **1853.** Sovereign to Half-Farthing, including Gothic type Crown
(16 coins) ....*FDC* £22,500

PS5 Jubilee head. Golden Jubilee, **1887.** Five pounds to Threepence (11 coins) .*FDC* £5,500

PS6 — — **1887.** Crown to Threepence (7 coins) ....*FDC* £1000

PS7 Old head, **1893.** Five Pounds to Threepence (10 coins) ....*FDC* £6,500

PS8 — — **1893.** Crown to Threepence (6 coins) ....*FDC* £1100

EDWARD VII, 1901-10

Five Pound pieces, Two Pound pieces and Crowns were only issued in 1902. A branch of the Royal Mint was opened in Canada at Ottawa and coined Sovereigns of imperial type from 1908.

Unlike the coins in most other proof sets, the proofs issued for the Coronation in 1902 have a matt surface in place of the more usual brilliant finish.

Designer's initials: De S. (G. W. De Saulles)
B. P. (Benedetto Pistrucci, d. 1855)

GOLD

3965

	VF	EF	UNC
	£	£	£

| 3965 | **Five Pounds.** 1902. R. St. George..500 | 625 | 750 |

3966 — Proof. 1902. *Matt surface FDC* £750

3966A — Proof 1902S. S on ground for Sydney Mint, Australia................... *Extremely rare*

3967   3969

	EF	UNC
	£	£

| 3967 | **Two Pounds.** 1902. Similar ....175 | 250 | 300 |

3968 — Proof. 1902. *Matt surface FDC* £300

3968A — Proof 1902S. S on ground for Sydney Mint, Australia................... *Extremely rare*

3969 Sovereign. R . St. George. London mint

1902 Matt proof *FDC* £110		1906	75
1902	75	1907	75
1903	75	1908	75
1904	75	1909	75
1905	75	1910	75

3970 — C on ground for Ottawa Mint, Canada

| 1908 C (Satin proof only) *FDC* £2250 | | 1910 C .... | 90 | 175 |
| 1909 C .... | 90 | 175 | | |

	UNC		*UNC*
	£		£

3971 Sovereign. R. St. George M on ground for Melbourne Mint, Australia

1902 M	75	1907 M	75
1903 M	75	1908 M	75
1904 M	75	1909 M	75
1905 M	75	1910 M	75
1906 M	75		

3972 — P on ground for Perth Mint, Australia

1902 P	75	1907 P	75
1903 P	75	1908 P	75
1904 P	75	1909 P	75
1905 P	75	1910 P	75
1906 P	75		

3973 — S on ground for Sydney Mint, Australia

1902 S	75	1906 S	75
— Proof	*Extremely rare*	1907 S	75
1903 S	75	1908 S	75
1904 S	75	1909 S	75
1905 S	75	1910 S	75

3974

	VF	*EF*	*UNC*		*VF*	*EF*	*UNC*
	£	£	£		£	£	£

3974 Half-Sovereign. R. St. George. London Mint

1902 Matt proof *FDC £70*				1906		40	55
1902		40	55	1907		40	55
1903		40	55	1908		40	55
1904		40	55	1909		40	55
1905		40	55	1910		40	55

3975 — M on ground for Melbourne Mint, Australia

1906 M	40	60	140	1908 M		60	150
1907 M	40	60	140	1909 M		60	140

3976 — P on ground for Perth Mint, Australia

1904 P	150	500	—	1909 P	125	400	—
1908 P	150	600	—				

3977 — S on ground for Sydney Mint, Australia

1902 S	50	125	250	1906 S	40	100	175
— Proof		*Extremely rare*		1908 S	40	100	175
1903 S	40	100	175	1910 S	40	100	175

SILVER

3978

	F	VF	EF	UNC
	£	£	£	£

3978 Crown. R. St. George and dragon

1902 ....25 50 75 100

3979 — *matt proof FDC £100*

3980

	F	VF	EF	UNC
	£	£	£	£

3980 Halfcrown. R. Crowned Shield in Garter

1902	10	20	45	75
— Matt proof *FDC* £70				
1903	65	175	450	900
1904	45	125	350	700
1905*	175	400	850	1500

1906	20	45	125	300
1907	20	45	125	300
1908	25	50	200	400
1909	20	45	150	350
1910	15	35	100	200

3981 Florin. R. Britannia standing on ship's bow

1902	5	10	40	65
— Matt proof *FDC* £60				
1903	10	25	80	175
1904	12	30	90	225
1905	40	95	350	600

1906	10	25	80	175
1907	10	30	90	225
1908	15	40	150	300
1909	15	40	125	250
1910	10	20	65	125

*Beware of recent forgeries.

3981	3982	3983

	F	VF	EF	UNC		F	VF	EF	UNC
	£	£	£	£		£	£	£	£

3982 Shilling. R. Lion rampant on crown

	F	VF	EF	UNC		F	VF	EF	UNC
1902	3	8	30	50	1906	5	10	35	75
— Matt proof *FDC* £40					1907	5	10	40	90
1903	8	20	75	175	1908	10	20	75	200
1904	8	15	65	125	1909	10	20	75	200
1905	50	150	400	750	1910	3	10	30	60

3983 Sixpence. R. Value in wreath

	F	VF	EF	UNC		F	VF	EF	UNC
1902	3	5	20	35	1906	4	10	25	60
— Matt proof *FDC* £30					1907	5	10	30	65
1903	4	10	25	60	1908	5	12	35	70
1904	6	15	40	85	1909	4	10	30	65
1905	5	12	30	70	1910	3	5	20	35

3984 Threepence. As Maundy but dull finish

	F	VF	EF	UNC		F	VF	EF	UNC
1902	2	5	10		1907	1	7	25	45
1903	1	7	25	45	1908	1	2	10	25
1904	3	7	35	60	1909	1	7	25	45
1905	2	7	25	45	1910		1	10	30
1906	2	7	25	45					

3985

	EF	FDC		EF	FDC
	£	£		£	£

3985 Maundy Set (4d., 3d., 2d. and 1d.)

	EF	FDC		EF	FDC
1902	40	55	1906	40	50
— Matt proof *FDC* £50			1907	40	50
1903	40	50	1908	40	50
1904	40	50	1909	50	75
1905	40	50	1910	50	75

	EF	FDC
	£	£

3986 — **Fourpence.** 1902-10 ....*from*   5   9
3987 — **Threepence.** 1902-10 ....*from*   5   11
3988 — **Twopence.** 1902-10 ....*from*   5   8
3989 — **Penny.** 1902-10 ....*from*   6   9

Maundy sets in the original dated cases are worth approximately £5 more than the prices quoted.

BRONZE

3990A

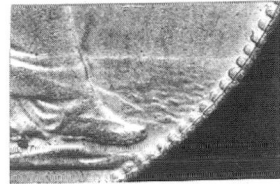

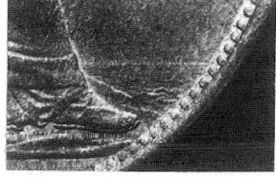

3990 'High Tide'   3990A 'Low Tide'

	VF	EF	UNC		F	VF	EF	UNC
	£	£	£		£	£	£	£
3990 Penny. R. Britannia								
1902 1	4	10	1906 2		8	25
1903 Normal 3 2	8	25	1907 2		8	25
1903 Open 3 20	50	—	1908 2		8	25
1904 3	12	30	1909 2		8	25
1905 2	10	27	1910 1		7	20

3990A — R. As last but 'Low tide', 1902 5   10   30   50

3991

	VF £	EF £	UNC £		F £	VF £	EF £	UNC £

3991 Halfpenny. R. Britannia

	VF	EF	UNC			F	VF	EF	UNC
1902	...1	4	10		1907	...1	5		15
1903	...2	8	20		1908	...1	5		15
1904	...2	8	25		1909	...2	8		25
1905	...2	8	25		1910	...2	7		20
1906	...2	8	20						

3991A — R. As last but 'Low tide', 1902 10   25   40   65

3992   3993

3992 Farthing. Britannia. Dark finish

		EF	UNC				VF	EF	UNC
1902	....	3	8		1907	...1	5		12
1903	...1	5	12		1908	...1	5		12
1904	...2	7	15		1909	...1	5		12
1905	...1	5	12		1910	...2	7		15
1906	...1	5	12						

3993 Third-Farthing (for use in Malta).

1902   5   10

No proofs of the bronze coins were issued in 1902

Proof Sets

PS9   Coronation, **1902.** Five Pounds to Maundy Penny, matt surface, (13 coins) *FDC*   £1,400
PS10 — **1902.** Sovereign to Maundy Penny, matt surface, (11 coins) ....*FDC*   £500

GEORGE V, 1910-36

Paper money issued by the Treasury during the First World War replaced gold for internal use after 1915 but the branch mints in Australia and South Africa (the main Commonwealth gold producing countries) continued striking Sovereigns until 1930-2. Owing to the steep rise in the price of silver in 1919/20 the issue of standard (.925) silver was discontinued and coins of .500 silver were minted.

In 1912, 1918 and 1919 some Pennies were made under contract by private mints in Birmingham. In 1918, as Half-Sovereigns were no longer being minted, Farthings were again issued with the ordinary bright bronze finish. Crown pieces had not been issued for general circulation but they were struck in small numbers about Christmas time for people to give as presents in the years 1927-36, and in 1935 a special commemorative Crown was issued in celebration of the Silver Jubilee.

As George V died in January, it is likely that all coins dated 1936 were struck during the reign of Edward VIII.

Designer's initials:

B. M. (Bertram Mackennal)   P. M. (Percy Metcalfe)
K. G. (Kruger Gray)   B. P. (Benedetto Pistrucci; d. 1855)

GOLD

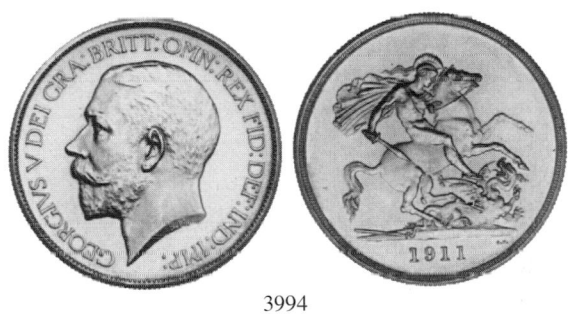

3994

	FDC
	£
3994 Five Pounds.* R. St. George, 1911 (Proof only)	1200
3995 Two Pounds.* R. St. George, 1911 (Proof only)	600

3996

	VF	EF	UNC
	£	£	£

3996 Sovereign. R. St. George. London Mint

				VF	EF	UNC
1911	75		1915			75
— Proof FDC £225			1916			85
1912	75		1917*		1500	2750	—
1913	75		1925			70
1914	75					

Forgeries exist of these and of most other dates and mints.

	VF £	EF £	UNC £		VF £	EF £	UNC £

3997 Sovereign. R. St George, C on ground for the Ottawa Mint, Canada

		VF £	EF £	UNC £			VF £	EF £	UNC £
1911 C			85	110	1917 C			85	110
1913 C		90	400	—	1918 C			85	110
1914 C		125	250	—	1919 C			85	110
1916 C*		3000	6000	—					

Beware of recent forgeries

3997 Canada Mint mark	3998 India Mint mark	4004 South Africa Mint mark

3998 — I on ground for Bombay Mint, India 1918 75

3999 — M on ground for Melbourne Mint, Australia

		VF £	EF £	UNC £			VF £	EF £	UNC £
1911 M				75	1920 M		950	2000	—
1912 M				75	1921 M		1250	3500	—
1913 M				75	1922 M		1200	3250	—
1914 M				75	1923 M				75
1915 M				75	1924 M				75
1916 M				75	1925 M				75
1917 M				75	1926 M				75
1918 M				75	1928 M		575	1750	—
1919 M				90					

4000 — small head

		VF £	EF £	UNC £			VF £	EF £	UNC £
1929 M		500	1750	—	1931 M		150	300	—
1930 M		95	175	—					

4001

4001 — P on ground for Perth Mint, Australia

		VF £	EF £	UNC £			VF £	EF £	UNC £
1911 P				75	1920 P				75
1912 P				75	1921 P				75
1913 P				75	1922 P				75
1914 P				75	1923 P				75
1915 P				75	1924 P		60	85	100
1916 P				75	1925 P		90	110	150
1917 P				75	1926 P		250	500	800
1918 P				75	1927 P		90	125	225
1919 P				75	1928 P		75	90	110

	VF £	EF £	UNC £		VF £	EF £	UNC £

4002 Sovereign. — — small head

| 1929 P | | | 75 | 1931 P | | | 75 |
| 1930 P | | | 75 | | | | |

4003 — S on ground for Sydney Mint, Australia

1911 S			75	1919 S			75
1912 S			75	1920 S			*Extremely rare*
1913 S			75	1921 S	600	1350	—
1914 S			75	1922 S	3000	9500	—
1915 S			75	1923 S	2000	4000	—
1916 S			75	1924 S	425	850	1250
1917 S			75	1925 S			75
1918 S			75	1926 S	4500	12500	—

4004 — SA on ground for Pretoria Mint, South Africa

1923 SA		1400	2500	1926 SA			75
1923 SA Proof *FDC* £450				1927 SA			75
1924 SA		2250	—	1928 SA			75
1925 SA			75				

4005 — — small head

| 1929 SA | | | 75 | 1931 SA | | | 75 |
| 1930 SA | | | 75 | 1932 SA | | | 90 |

4002

4006

4006 Half-Sovereign. R. St. George. London Mint

1911		35	50	1913		35	50
— Proof *FDC* £175				1914		35	50
1912		35	50	1915		35	50

4007 — M on ground for Melbourne Mint, Australia

| 1915 M | 45 | 70 | 125 |

4008 — P on ground for Perth Mint, Australia

| 1911 P | 45 | 70 | 100 | 1918 P | 175 | 400 | 550 |
| 1915 P | 45 | 70 | 100 | | | | |

4009 — S on ground for Sydney Mint, Australia

1911 S	45	70	90	1915 S	35	50	60
1912 S	45	70	90	1916 S	35	50	60
1914 S	40	60	75				

4010 — SA on ground for Pretoria Mint, South Africa

| 1923 SA Proof *FDC* £350 | | | | 1926 SA | | 35 | 50 |
| 1925 SA | | 35 | 50 | | | | |

SILVER

First Coinage. Sterling silver (.925 fine)

4011

	F £	VF £	EF £	UNC £		F £	VF £	EF £	UNC £
4011 Halfcrown. R. Crowned shield in Garter									
1911	5	18	35	85	1915	4	10	22	50
— Proof *FDC* £70					1916	4	10	22	50
1912	6	20	50	95	1917	5	15	35	65
1913	8	28	60	100	1918	4	10	22	50
1914	4	10	22	50	1919	5	15	35	65

4012

	F £	VF £	EF £	UNC £		F £	VF £	EF £	UNC £
4012 Florin. R. Cruciform shields									
1911	5	10	30	70	1915	6	12	25	50
— Proof *FDC* £60					1916	4	10	20	50
1912	5	15	40	75	1917	6	12	25	60
1913	8	25	60	100	1918	4	10	20	50
1914	4	10	20	50	1919	6	12	25	60
4013 Shilling. R. Lion rampant on crown, within circle									
1911	2	8	16	30	1915		4	16	30
— Proof *FDC* £40					1916		4	16	30
1912	4	12	28	50	1917		5	18	35
1913	8	15	40	70	1918		4	16	30
1914	3	10	20	35	1919	4	10	25	45

4013   4014

	F £	VF £	EF £	UNC £		F £	VF £	EF £	UNC £
4014 Sixpence. R. Similar									
1911	2	8	15	25	1916	2	8	15	25
— Proof *FDC* £30					1917	5	15	30	55
1912	4	10	22	40	1918	2	8	15	25
1913	5	12	28	45	1919	4	10	20	35
1914	2	8	15	25	1920	4	10	22	40
1915	2	8	15	25					
4015 Threepence. As Maundy but dull finish									
1911	1		4	14	1916	1		3	10
1912	1		4	14	1917	1		3	10
1913	1		4	14	1918	1		3	10
1914	1		4	14	1919	1		3	10
1915	1		4	14	1920	1		4	12

4016

	EF £	FDC £		EF £	FDC £
4016 Maundy Set (4d., 3d., 2d. and 1d.)					
1911	45	65	1916	45	65
— Proof *FDC* £70			1917	45	65
1912	45	65	1918	45	65
1913	45	65	1919	45	65
1914	45	65	1920	45	75
1915	45	65			
4017 — Fourpence. 1911-20 ....*from*				7	11
4018 — Threepence. 1911-20 ....*from*				8	12
4019 — Twopence. 1911-20 ....*from*				6	10
4020 — Penny. 1911-20 ....*from*				7	11

Second Coinage. Debased silver (.500 fine). Types as before.

	F £	VF £	EF £	UNC £		F £	VF £	EF £	UNC £
4021 Halfcrown.									
1920.....................4	8	20	50		1924.....................5	10	30	60
1921.....................5	10	25	60		1925...................20	50	150	250
1922.....................4	8	20	50		1926.....................5	10	30	65
1923.....................3	5	12	30		1926 No colon after OMN		75	120
4022 Florin.									
1920.....................3	8	25	45		1924.....................4	10	32	60
1921.....................3	8	25	45		1925...................25	45	100	175
1922.....................3	6	20	40		1926.....................3	10	32	60
1923.....................2	5	16	35					
4023 Shilling.									
1920.....................3	6	18	35		1924.....................3	8	22	40
1921.....................4	10	22	55		1925.....................5	10	40	70
1922.....................3	6	18	35		1926.....................3	6	14	35
1923.....................2	5	16	30					
4024 Sixpence.									
1920.....................2	4	10	20		1923.....................3	6	16	35
1921.....................2	4	10	20		1924.....................2	4	10	20
1922.....................2	5	12	25		1925.....................2	4	12	25

4025

4026

	F	VF	EF	UNC		F	VF	EF	UNC
4025— new beading and broader rim									
1925.....................2	4	10	20		1926.....................2	4	12	20
4026 Threepence.									
1920........................	1	3	10		1925...................—	2	14	20
1921........................	1	3	10		1926.....................1	3	15	25
1922........................	1	10	16					

	EF £	FDC £		EF £	FDC £
4027 Maundy Set. (4d., 3d., 2d. and 1d.)					
1921	40	65	1925	40	65
1922	40	65	1926	40	65
1923	40	65	1927	40	65
1924	40	65			
4028 — **Fourpence.** 1921-7 ....*from*	8	11
4029 — **Threepence.** 1921-7 ....*from*	8	12
4030 — **Twopence.** 1921-7 ....*from*	6	10
4031 — **Penny.** 1921-7..*from*	7	11

2nd coinage   3rd coinage
                               Modified Effigy

Third Coinage. As before but modified effigy, with details of head more clearly defined. The BM on truncation is nearer to the back of the neck and without stops; beading is more pronounced.

	F £	VF £	EF £	UNC £		F £	VF £	EF £	UNC £
4032 Halfcrown.									
1926	5	10	30	50	1927	4	7	18	30
4033 Shilling.									
1926	2	4	14	20	1927	2	6	20	30
4034 Sixpence.									
1926		3	8	14	1927	2	4	10	18
4035 Threepence.									
1926						1	5	20	

Fourth Coinage. New types, 1927-36

4036

4036 Crown. R. Crown in wreath

1927	−15,030 struck Proof only *FDC £125*				1932	−2395 struck	85	120	200	300
1928	−9034 struck	35	75	110	185	1933	−7132 struck	35	75	110	185
1929	−4994 struck	35	75	110	185	1934	−932 struck	200	450	600	950
1930	−4847 struck	35	75	110	185	1936	−2473 struck	65	100	175	275
1931	−4056 struck	35	85	130	200						

4037   4038

	F £	VF £	EF £	UNC £		F £	VF £	EF £	UNC £

4037 Halfcrown. R. Shield

1927 Proof only *FDC* £35

	F	VF	EF	UNC
1928......................2	5	10	15
1929......................2	5	10	15
1930....................10	25	85	175
1931......................2	5	10	18

	F	VF	EF	UNC
1932......................4	8	15	30
1933......................2	5	10	16
1934......................4	10	25	45
1935......................	5	10	15
1936......................	3	8	12

4038 Florin. R. Cruciform shields, sceptre in each angle

1927 Proof only *FDC* £40

	F	VF	EF	UNC
1928......................	3	10	16
1929......................	3	10	16
1930......................2	5	10	20
1931......................2	5	10	20

	F	VF	EF	UNC
1932....................20	40	95	225
1933......................	3	10	20
1935......................	3	10	15
1936......................	2	8	14

4039   4040

4039 Shilling. R. Lion rampant on crown, no inner circles

	F	VF	EF	UNC
1927......................2	4	15	25
— Proof *FDC* £25			
1928......................	3	10	15
1929......................	3	10	15
1930......................3	6	20	35
1931......................2	4	10	15

	F	VF	EF	UNC
1932......................2	4	10	16
1933......................	3	10	15
1934......................2	5	16	25
1935......................	3	10	15
1936......................	3	8	14

4040 Sixpence. R. Three oak sprigs with six acorns

1927 Proof only *FDC* £18

	F	VF	EF	UNC
1928......................	2	4	8

	F	VF	EF	UNC
1929......................	2	4	8
1930......................	2	4	8

4041 — closer milling

	F	VF	EF	UNC
1931......................2	3	8	16
1932......................2	4	14	22
1933......................2	3	8	14

	F	VF	EF	UNC
1934......................2	3	10	18
1935......................	2	6	12
1936......................	2	4	8

4042   4043

	F	VF	EF	UNC		F	VF	EF	UNC
	£	£	£	£		£	£	£	£

4042 Threepence. R. Three oak sprigs with three acorns

	F	VF	EF	UNC		F	VF	EF	UNC
1927 Proof only *FDC £35*					1933			1	5
1928	1	3	14	30	1934			1	5
1930	1	3	14	30	1935			1	5
1931			1	5	1936			1	5
1932			1	5					

	EF	FDC		EF	FDC
	£	£		£	£

4043 Maundy Set. As earlier sets

	EF	FDC		EF	FDC
1928	40	65	1933	40	65
1929	45	70	1934	40	65
1930	40	65	1935	45	70
1931	40	65	1936	45	70
1932	40	65			

The 1936 Maundy was distributed by King Edward VIII

		EF	FDC
4044 — **Fourpence.** 1928-36 .... *from*		8	12
4045 — **Threepence.** 1928-36 .... *from*		9	12
4046 — **Twopence.** 1928-36 .... *from*		7	11
4047 — **Penny.** 1928-36 .... *from*		8	13

Silver Jubilee Commemorative issue

4048

	VF	EF	UNC
	£	£	£
4048 Crown. 1935. R. St. George, incuse lettering on edge –714,769 struck ...10	10	15	20
1935 — error edge		*Extremely rare*	
4049 — Specimen striking issued in box			35
4050 — raised lettering on edge 2,500 struck.Proof (.925 Æ) *FDC £225*			
— error edge inscription Proof *FDC* £750			
— Proof in gold –28 struck £10,000			

BRONZE

H Mint mark location – 4052

4052

KN Mint mark location – 4053

	F £	VF £	EF £	UNC £		F £	VF £	EF £	UNC £
4051 Penny. R. Britannia									
1911			5	15	1918			5	15
1912			5	15	1919			5	15
1913			8	20	1920			5	15
1914			5	15	1921			5	15
1915			5	15	1922			15	25
1916			5	15	1926			20	35
1917			5	15					

4052 — R. Britannia, H (Heaton Mint, Birmingham, Ltd.) to l. of date

	F £	VF £	EF £	UNC £		F £	VF £	EF £	UNC £
1912 H		2	35	75	1919 H		8	85	175
1918 H		10	100	175					

4053 — R. Britannia KN (King's Norton Metal Co.) to l. of date

	F £	VF £	EF £	UNC £		F £	VF £	EF £	UNC £
1918 KN	3	15	125	250	1919 KN	3	18	150	300

4054 — modified effigy

	F £	VF £	EF £	UNC £		F £	VF £	EF £	UNC £
1926	10	45	350	650	1927			3	8

4055 — small head

	F £	VF £	EF £	UNC £		F £	VF £	EF £	UNC £
1928			3	8	1933			*Extremely rare*	
1929			3	8	1934			10	22
1930			5	10	1935			2	8
1931			5	14	1936			1	5
1932			12	25					

4056 Halfpenny. R. Britannia

	F £	VF £	EF £	UNC £		F £	VF £	EF £	UNC £
1911			5	15	1919			5	15
1912			5	15	1920			5	15
1913			5	15	1921			5	15
1914			5	15	1922			7	20
1915			5	15	1923			5	15
1916			5	15	1924			5	15
1917			5	15	1925			5	15
1918			5	15					

4057 — modified effigy

	F £	VF £	EF £	UNC £		F £	VF £	EF £	UNC £
1925			8	22	1927			5	15
1926			6	20					

4056   4058

	EF £	UNC £		EF £	UNC £
4058 Halfpenny. Small head					
1928	2	8	1933	2	8
1929	2	8	1934	4	15
1930	2	8	1935	2	8
1931	2	8	1936	1	5
1932	2	8			

4059   4062

4059 Farthing. R. Britannia. Dark finish

1911	3	7	1915	4	10
1912	2	5	1916	2	5
1913	2	5	1917	1	3
1914	2	5	1918	9	18

4060 — Bright finish, 1918-25 1   3

4061 — Modified effigy

1926	1	3	1932	0.50	2
1927	1	3	1933	1	3
1928	1	3	1934	2	5
1929	1	3	1935	2	5
1930	1	3	1936	0.75	3
1931	1	3			

4062 Third-Farthing (for use in Malta). R. Value

1913 7   12

Proof Sets

PS11 Coronation, **1911.** Five pounds to Maundy Penny (12 coins) ...... *FDC* £2,400
PS12 — **1911.** Sovereign to Maundy Penny (10 coins) ...... *FDC* £700
PS13 — **1911.** Half crown to Maundy Penny (8 coins) ...... *FDC* £350
PS14 New type, **1927.** Wreath type Crown to Threepence (6 coins) ...... *FDC* £250

Abdicated 10 December. Created Duke of Windsor (1936-72)

No coins of Edward VIII were issued for currency within the United Kingdom bearing his name and portrait. The Mint had commenced work on a new coinage prior to the Abdication, and various patterns were made. No Proof Sets were issued for sale and only a small number of sets were struck.

Coins bearing Edward's name, but not his portrait, were issued for the colonial territories of British East Africa, British West Africa, Fiji and New Guinea. The projected U.K. coins were to include a Shilling of essentially `Scottish' type and a nickel brass Threepence with twelve sides which might supplement and possibly supersede the inconveniently small silver Threepence.

Designer's initials:

H. P. (T. Humphrey Paget)   B.P. (Benedetto Pistrucci, d. 1855)
K. G. (Kruger Gray)   M. K. (Madge Kitchener)
W. P. (Wilson Parker)

4063

4063 Proof Set

Gold, £5, £2 and £1, 1937 .... *not issued*

Silver Crown, Halfcrown, Florin, Scottish shilling, sixpence and threepence, 1937   *not issued*

£

Sovereign,.. *Extremely rare*
Crown,... *Extremely rare*
Halfcrown,... *Extremely rare*
Florin,... *Extremely rare*
Shilling,... *Extremely rare*
Sixpence,.. *Extremely rare*
Threepence,... *Extremely rare*

Nickel brass. Threepence, 1937 .... *not issued*
Bronze. Penny. Halfpenny and Farthing, 1937 .... *not issued*

Pattern

4064 Nickel brass dodecagonal Threepence, 1937. R. Thrift plant of more
naturalistic style than the modified proof coin. A small number of these
coins were produced for experimental purposes and a few did get into
circulation   *Extremely rare*

GEORGE VI, 1936-52

Though they were at first issued concurrently, the twelve-sided nickel-brass Threepence superseded the small silver Threepence in 1942. Those dated 1943-4 were not issued for circulation in the U.K. In addition to the usual English 'lion' Shilling, a Shilling, of Scottish type was issued concurrently. This depicts the Scottish lion and crown flanked by the shield of St. Andrew and a thistle. In 1947, as silver was needed to repay the bullion lent by the U.S.A. during the war, silver coins were replaced by coins of the same type and weight made of cupro-nickel. In 1949, after India had attained independence, the title IND:IMP (*Indiae Imperator*) was dropped from the coinage. Commemorative Crown pieces were issued for the Coronation and the 1951 Festival of Britain.

Designer's initials:
K. G. (Kruger Gray)
H. P. (T. Humphrey Paget)

B. P. (Benedetto Pistrucci, d. 1855)
W. P. (Wilson Parker)

GOLD

4074   4076

	FDC £
4074 Five Pounds. Bare head l. R. St. George, 1937. Proof	575
4075 Two Pounds. Similar, 1937. Proof	350
4076 Sovereign. Similar, 1937. Proof	425
4077 Half-Sovereign. Similar, 1937. Proof	150

SILVER

First coinage. Silver, .500 fine, with title IND:IMP

4078

	VF £	EF £	UNC £
4078 Crown. Coronation commemorative, 1937. **R.** Arms and supporters	10	15	22

4079 — — Proof *FDC* £35

    — — Frosted 'VIP' Proof £250

           4080   4081

	EF £	UNC £		UNC £
4080 Halfcrown. R. Shield				
1937		7	1942	6
— Proof *FDC* £10			1943	7
1938	4	18	1944	5
1939		7	1945	5
1940		7	1946	5
1941		7		
4081 Florin. R. Crowned rose, etc.				
1937		6	1942	5
— Proof *FDC* £10			1943	5
1938	4	15	1944	5
1939		5	1945	5
1940		5	1946	5
1941		5		

           4082   4083

4082 Shilling. 'English'. **R.** Lion rampant on large crown				
1937		5	1942	5
— Proof *FDC* £8			1943	5
1938	3	15	1944	5
1939		5	1945	4
1940		5	1946	4
1941		5		

	EF £	UNC £		VF £	EF £	UNC £

4083 Shilling. 'Scottish'. R. Lion seated facing on crown

	EF £	UNC £		VF £	EF £	UNC £
1937		5	1942			5
— Proof *FDC* £8			1943			5
1938	3	15	1944			5
1939		5	1945			4
1940		6	1946			4
1941		6				

4084   4085

4084 Sixpence. R. GRI crowned

	EF £	UNC £		EF £	UNC £
1937		4	1942		3
— Proof *FDC* £5			1943		3
1938	2	6	1944		3
1939		4	1945		3
1940		4	1946		3
1941		4			

4085 Threepence. R. Shield on rose

	EF £	UNC £		VF £	EF £	UNC £
1937		3	1941		1	5
— Proof *FDC* £5			1942*	3	10	18
1938		3	1943*	3	10	20
1939	3	10	1944*	8	20	35
1940		5	1945*			*Extremely rare*

For colonial use only.

4086

	FDC £		FDC £

4086 Maundy Set. Silver, .500 fine. Uniform dates

	FDC £		FDC £
1937	60	1942	65
— Proof *FDC* £65		1943	65
1938	65	1944	65
1939	65	1945	65
1940	75	1946	65
1941	65		

FDC FDC
£ £

	FDC £
4087 — **Fourpence.** 1937-46 .... *from*	10
4088 — **Threepence.** 1937-46 .... *from*	10
4089 — **Twopence.** 1937-46 .... *from*	10
4090 — **Penny.** 1937-46 .... *from*	14

Second coinage. Silver, .925 fine, with title IND:IMP (Maundy only)
4091 Maundy Set (4d., 3d., 2d. and 1d.). Uniform dates

1947	65	1948	65

4092 — **Fourpence,** 1947-8	10
4093 — **Threepence,** 1947-8	10
4094 — **Twopence,** 1947-8	10
4095 — **Penny,** 1947-8	14

Third coinage. Silver, .925 fine, but omitting IND:IMP. (Maundy only)
4096 Maundy Set (4d., 3d., 2d. and 1d.). Uniform dates

1949	65	1951	65
1950	80	1952	65

The 1952 Maundy was distributed by Queen Elizabeth II.

4097 — **fourpence,** 1949-52 .... *from*	10
4098 — **threepence,** 1949-52 .... *from*	10
4099 — **twopence,** 1949-52 .... *from*	10
4100 — **penny,** 1949-52 .... *from*	14

CUPRO-NICKEL

Second coinage. Types as first (silver) coinage, IND:IMP.

	UNC £		UNC £
4101 Halfcrown. R. Shield			
1947	5	1948	5
4102 Florin. R. Crowned rose			
1947	5	1948	5
4103 Shilling. 'English' type			
1947	5	1948	4
4104 — 'Scottish' type			
1947	5	1948	4
4105 Sixpence. R. GRI crowned			
1947	4	1948	3

Third coinage. Types as before but title IND:IMP. omitted

4106

	UNC £		VF £	EF £	UNC £

4106 Halfcrown.

	UNC £		VF £	EF £	UNC £
1949	6	1951			8
1950	15	— Proof *FDC* £10			
— Proof *FDC* £15		1952		*Extremely rare*	

4107 Florin.

	UNC £		VF £	EF £	UNC £
1949	8	1951			8
1950	15	— Proof *FDC* £10			
— Proof *FDC* £15					

4108 Shilling. 'English' type

	UNC £		VF £	EF £	UNC £
1949	7	1951			7
1950	15	— Proof *FDC* £7			
— Proof *FDC* £12					

4109 — 'Scottish' type

	UNC £		VF £	EF £	UNC £
1949	9	1951			8
1950	15	— Proof *FDC* £8			
— Proof *FDC* £12					

4110

4110 Sixpence. As illustration

	UNC £		VF £	EF £	UNC £
1949	5	1951			5
1950	10	— Proof *FDC* £5			
— Proof *FDC* £8		1952	2	12	35

Festival of Britain issue

4111

	EF	UNC
	£	£
4111 Crown. R. St. George, 1951. *Proof-like*	4	8
— — Frosted 'VIP' Proof £200		

NICKEL BRASS

First issue, with title IND:IMP.

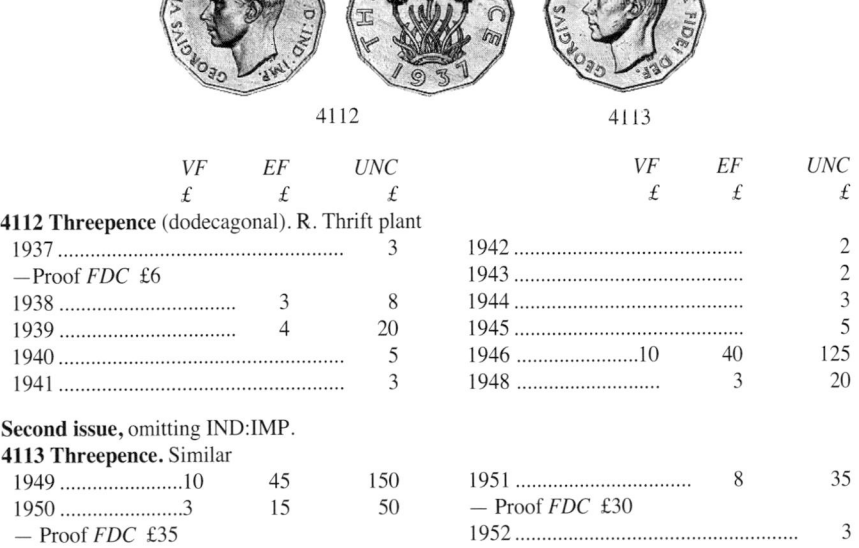

4112   4113

	VF	EF	UNC		VF	EF	UNC
	£	£	£		£	£	£
4112 Threepence (dodecagonal). R. Thrift plant							
1937			3	1942			2
—Proof *FDC* £6				1943			2
1938		3	8	1944			3
1939		4	20	1945			5
1940			5	1946	10	40	125
1941			3	1948		3	20

Second issue, omitting IND:IMP.
4113 Threepence. Similar

	VF	EF	UNC		VF	EF	UNC
1949	10	45	150	1951		8	35
1950	3	15	50	— Proof *FDC* £30			
— Proof *FDC* £35				1952			3

BRONZE

First issue, with title IND:IMP.

4114

	UNC £		UNC £

4114 Penny. R. Britannia r.

1937	2	1944	9
— Proof *FDC* £8		1945	7
1938	3	1946	7
1939	5	1947	2
1940	6	1948	2

4115   4116

4115 Halfpenny. R. Ship l.

1937	2	1943	2
— Proof *FDC* £5		1944	2
1938	3	1945	3
1939	4	1946	4
1940	6	1947	3
1941	2	1948	2
1942	2		

4116 Farthing. R. Wren l.

1937	1	1943	0.80
— Proof *FDC* £5		1944	0.80
1938	2	1945	0.80
1939	0.80	1946	0.80
1940	1	1947	0.80
1941	0.95	1948	0.95
1942	0.95		

Second issue, without IND.IMP. Types as before

	VF £	EF £	UNC £		VF £	EF £	UNC £

4117 Penny.

1949 2   1951 6   12   20
1950 8   20   35   — Proof *FDC* £18
— Proof *FDC* £20   1952 Proof only .....   *Unique*

4118   4119

4118 Halfpenny.

1949 5   1951 5
1950 8   — Proof *FDC* £5
— Proof *FDC* £10   1952 3

4119 Farthing.

1949 1   1951 1
1950 2   — Proof *FDC* £5
— Proof *FDC* £10   1952 1

The coins dated 1952 were issued during the reign of Elizabeth II.

Proof Sets

PS15 Coronation, **1937.** Five pounds to Half-sovereign (4 coins) ....*FDC*   £1400
PS16 — **1937.** Crown to Farthing, including Maundy Set (15 coins) ....*FDC*   £125
PS17 Mid-Century, **1950.** Halfcrown to Farthing (9 coins).................................*FDC*   £65
PS18 Festival of Britain, **1951.** Crown to Farthing (10 coins)..............................*FDC*   £65

ELIZABETH II, acc. 1952

The earliest coins of this reign have the title BRITT:OMN, but in 1954 this was omitted from the Queen's titles owing to the changing status of so many Commonwealth territories. The minting of 'English' and 'Scottish' shillings was continued. A Coronation commemorative crown was issued in 1953, another crown was struck on the occasion of the 1960 British Exhibition in New York and a third was issued in honour of Sir Winston Churchill in 1965. A very small number of proof gold coins were struck in 1953 for the national museum collections, but between 1957 and 1968 gold sovereigns were minted again in quantity for sale in the international bullion market and to counteract the activities of counterfeiters.

Owing to inflation the farthing had now become practically valueless; production of these coins ceased after 1956 and the coins were demonetized at the end of 1960. In 1965 it was decided to change to a decimal system of coinage in the year 1971. As part of the transition to decimal coinage the halfpenny was demonetized in August 1969 and the halfcrown in January 1970. (See also introduction to Decimal Coinage.

Designer's initials:

A. V. (Avril Vaughan)
B. P. (Benedetto Pistrucci, D. 1855)
B. R. (Bruce Rushin)
C. T. (Cecil Thomas)
D. C. (David Cornell)
E. F. (Edgar Fuller)
G. L. (Gilbert Ledward)
I. R. B. (Ian Rank-Broadley)
J. M. M. (John Mills)
M. G. (Mary Gillick)
M. M. D. (Mary Milner Dickens)
M. N. (Michael Noakes)
M. R. (Michael Rizzello)
N. S. (Norman Sillman)
P. N. (Philip Nathan)
R. D. M. (Raphael David Maklouf)

R. E. (Robert Elderton)
W. G. (William Gardner)
W. P. (Wilson Parker)
R. D. (Ron Dutton)
J. M. (Jeffrey Matthews)

Other designers whose initials do not appear on the coins:
Christopher Ironside
Arnold Machin
David Wynne
Professor Richard Guyatt
Eric Sewell
Oscar Nemon
Leslie Durbin
Derek Gorringe

PRE-DECIMAL ISSUES

GOLD

First coinage, with title BRITT.OMN, 1953. *Proof only*

4120 Five Pounds. R. St. George	*None issued for collectors*
4121 Two Pounds. Similar	*None issued for collectors*
4122 Sovereign. Similar	*None issued for collectors*
4123 Half-Sovereign. Similar	*None issued for collectors*

Second issue, BRITT.OMN omitted

4125

4124 Sovereign. laur. head r. R. St. George, fine graining on edge
1957 .... BV

4125 Sovereign. Similar, but coarser graining on edge

1958	BV	1965	BV
1959	BV	1966	BV
1962	BV	1967	BV
1963	BV	1968	BV
1964	BV		

SILVER

The Queen's Maundy are now the only coins struck regularly in silver.
The location of the Maundy ceremony is given for each year.

First issue, with title BRITT:OMN:

FDC
£

4126 Maundy Set (4d., 3d., 2d. and 1d.), 1953. St Paul's	300
4127 — Fourpence. 1953	50
4128 — Threepence. 1953	50
4129 — Twopence. 1953	50
4130 — Penny. 1953	100

Second issue, with BRITT:OMN: omitted

4131

FDC
£

4131 Maundy Set (4d., 3d., 2d. and 1d.). Uniform dates

1954 *Westminster*	65	1963 *Chelmsford*	65
1955 *Southwark*	65	1964 *Westminster*	65
1956 *Westminster*	65	1965 *Canterbury*	65
1957 *St. Albans*	65	1966 *Westminster*	65
1958 *Westminster*	65	1967 *Durham*	65
1959 *Windsor*	65	1968 *Westminster*	65
1960 *Westminster*	75	1969 *Selby*	65
1961 *Rochester*	65	1970 *Westminster*	75
1962 *Westminster*	65		

4132 — Fourpence. 1954-70	*from*	10
4133 — Threepence. 1954-70	*from*	10
4134 — Twopence. 1954-70	*from*	10
4135 — Penny. 1954-70	*from*	14

CUPRO-NICKEL
First issue, 1953, with title BRITT.OMN.

4136

	EF	UNC	PROOF FDC
4136 Crown. Queen on horseback. R. Crown in centre of emblematical cross, shield of Arms in each angle, 1953	£ 6	£ 7	£ 25

— — Frosted 'VIP' proof £250

4137   4138

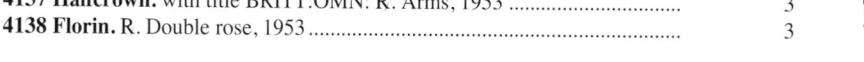

4137 Halfcrown. with title BRITT:OMN: R. Arms, 1953	3	9
4138 Florin. R. Double rose, 1953	3	7

4139   4140   4141

4139 Shilling. 'English'. R. Three lions, 1953	1	6
4140 — 'Scottish'. R. Lion rampant in shield, 1953	1	6
4141 Sixpence. R. Interlaced rose, thistle, shamrock and leek, 1953	0.70	5
4142 Set of 9 uncirculated cu-ni, ni-br and Æ coins (2/6 to 1/4d.) in Royal Mint plastic envelope	25	

Second issue, similar types but omitting BRITT.OMN.

4143	4144

	EF	UNC
	£	£
4143 Crown, 1960. Bust r. R. As 4136	3	5
— — Similar, from polished dies (New York Exhibition issue).........................	6	18
— — 'VIP' *Proof,* frosted design *FDC* £200		
4144 — Churchill commemorative, 1965. As illustration. R. Bust of Sir Winston		
Churchill r.		1
— — Similar, "Satin-Finish". VIP *Specimen*		350

4145 Halfcrown. R. As 4137

Year	EF	UNC	Year	EF	UNC	Year	EF	UNC
	£	£		£	£		£	£
1954	3	15	1960		3	1965		1
1955		4	1961		1	1966		0.60
1956		5	1961 Polished die		5	1967		0.60
1957		2	1962		1	1970 Proof *FDC* £3		
1958	3	12	1963		1			
1959	5	20	1964		3			

4146

4146 Florin. R. As 4138

Year	EF	UNC	Year	EF	UNC
1954	5	35	1962		1
1955		3	1963		1
1956		3	1964		1
1957	5	35	1965		1
1958	4	15	1966		1
1959	5	30	1967		1
1960		2	1970 Proof *FDC* £3		
1961		2			

	EF	UNC		UNC
	£	£		£

4147 Shilling. 'English' type. R. As 4139

Year		EF	UNC	Year	UNC
1954			2	1961	0.75
1955			2	1962	0.50
1956			6	1963	0.25
1957			1	1964	0.30
1958		1	12	1965	0.30
1959			1	1966	0.30
1960			1	1970 Proof *FDC* £2	

4148 — 'Scottish' type. R. As 4140

Year		EF	UNC	Year	UNC
1954			2	1961	3
1955			3	1962	1
1956			5	1963	0.25
1957		1	12	1964	0.50
1958			1	1965	0.50
1959		1	12	1966	0.30
1960			1	1970 Proof *FDC* £2	

4149 Sixpence. R. As 4141

Year	EF/UNC	Year	UNC
1954	3	1962	0.30
1955	1	1963	0.25
1956	1	1964	0.20
1957	0.65	1965	0.15
1958	0.75	1966	0.15
1959	0.35	1967	0.15
1960	0.75	1970 Proof *FDC* £2	
1961	0.50		

NICKEL BRASS

First issue, with title BRITT.OMN.

4152   4153

4152 Threepence (dodecagonal). R. Crowned portcullis, 1953 1
— Proof *FDC* £5

Second issue (omitting BRIT.OMN)

4153 Similar type

Year	EF/UNC	Year	UNC
1954	3	1962	0.30
1955	4	1963	0.20
1956	4	1964	0.20
1957	2	1965	0.20
1958	5	1966	0.15
1959	2	1967	0.15
1960	2	1970 Proof *FDC* £2	
1961	0.40		

BRONZE

First issue, with title BRITT.OMN.

4154   4155

	VF	EF	UNC	Proof FDC
	£	£	£	£
4154 Penny. R. Britannia (only issued with Royal Mint set in plastic envelope), 1953	0.60	2.50	5	6
4155 Halfpenny. R. Ship, 1953			2	4
4156 Farthing. R. Wren, 1953			1.25	3

Second issue, omitting BRITT.OMN.

	UNC		UNC
	£		£
4157 Penny. R. Britannia (1954-60 *not issued*)			
1954	*Unique*	1965	0.10
1961	0.50	1966	0.10
1962	0.15	1967	0.10
1963	0.15	1970 Proof *FDC £3*	
1964	0.10		

4158 Halfpenny. R. Ship (1961 *not issued*)			
1954	1.75	1962	0.10
1955	0.80	1963	0.10
1956	0.70	1964	0.10
1957	0.60	1965	0.10
1958	0.35	1966	0.10
1959	0.25	1967	0.10
1960	0.15	1970 Proof *FDC £2*	

4156   4159

	EF	UNC
	£	£
4159 Farthing. R. Wren		
1954 ... 1	1956 Rev. with thin rim ... 1	3
1955 Rev. with thin rim ... 1		

Proof Sets

PS19 Coronation, **1953.** Crown to Farthing (10 coins) .... *FDC*   55
PS20 'Last Sterling', **1970.** Halfcrown to Halfpenny plus medallion .... *FDC*   15

All prices quoted assume coins are in their original case. Issued by the Royal Mint in official case from 1887 onwards, but earlier sets were issued privately by the engraver. All pieces have a superior finish to that of the current coins.

		No. of coins	FDC £
PS1	**George IV, 1826.** New issue, Five Pounds to Farthing ....(11)		18,000
PS1A	— — Similar to above, including Maundy Set ....(15)		18,500
PS2	**William IV, 1831.** Coronation, Two Pounds to Farthing ....(14)		16,500
PS3	**Victoria, 1839.** Young head. "Una and the Lion" Five Pounds and Sovereign to Farthing...(15)		27,500
PS4	— **1853.** Sovereign to Half-Farthing, including Gothic type Crown(16)		25,000
PS5	— **1887.** Jubilee bust for Golden Jubilee, Five Pounds to Threepence ....(11)		5,500
PS6	— **1887.** Silver Crown to Threepence ....(7)		1,000
PS7	— **1893.** Old bust, Five Pounds to Threepence ....(10)		6,500
PS8	— **1893.** Silver Crown to Threepence ....(6)		1,100
PS9	**Edward VII, 1902.** Coronation, Five Pounds to Maundy Penny. Matt finish to surfaces..(13)		1,400
PS10	— **1902.** Sovereign to Maundy Penny. Matt finish.........................(11)		500
PS11	**George V, 1911.** Coronation, Five Pounds to Maundy Penny.........(12)		2,400
PS12	— **1911.** Sovereign to Maundy Penny..(10)		750
PS13	— **1911.** Silver Halfcrown to Maundy Penny ....(8)		350
PS14	— **1927.** New Coinage. Wreath type Crown to Threepence ....(6)		250
PS15	**George VI, 1937.** Coronation. Five Pounds to Half-Sovereign.........(4)		1,400
PS16	— **1937.** Coronation. Crown to Farthing, including Maundy Set .....(15)		125
PS17	— **1950.** Mid-Century, Halfcrown to Farthing...................................(9)		65
PS18	— **1951.** Festival of Britain, Crown to Farthing..............................(10)		65
PS19	**Elizabeth II, 1953.** Coronation. Crown to Farthing ....(10)		55
PS20	— **1970.** "Last Sterling" set. Halfcrown to Halfpenny plus medallion..(8)		15

A decision to adopt decimal currency was announced in March 1966 following the recommendation of the Halsbury Committee of Enquiry which had been appointed in 1961. The date for the introduction of the new system was 15 February 1971 and it was evident that the Royal Mint facilities which had been located on Tower Hill for more than 150 years would be unable to strike the significant quantities of coins required on that site. The Government therefore decided to build a new mint at Llantrisant in South Wales.

The new system provided for three smaller bronze coins and very large numbers were struck and stock piled for D-Day but the five and ten new pence denominations with the same specifications as the former shilling and florin were introduced in 1968. A further change was the introduction of a 50 new pence coin to replace the ten shilling banknote.

In 1982 and 1983 two more new coins were introduced; the 20 pence which helped to reduce demand for five and ten pence pieces, and the first circulating non-precious metal £1 coin which replaced the bank note of the same value.

Increasing raw material costs, and inflation also play a part in the development of a modern coinage system and a smaller 50 pence was introduced in the autumn of 1997. The bimetallic circulating £2 was postponed due to some technical problems associated with vending and similar machines. It is planned to release the coin this year.

For the collector, many of these changes have been accompanied by special issues often in limited editions struck in precious metal. New designs, particularly on the £1 coins, have added interest to the coins that circulate, and may hopefully stimulate new collectors.

In the period since decimalisation there has been a marked increase in the issue of commemorative coins. The crown size pieces, which by virtue of their size allow much scope for interesting designs seem to be reserved for the commemoration of Royal events or anniversaries, and other denominations such as the £2 and the 50 pence have honoured other interesting themes.

The major change in the coinage in 1998 is the new, and fourth, portrait of H. M. The Queen. Designed by Ian Rank-Broadley, a whole new series has started which will stimulate interest among collectors everywhere.

GOLD

| 4201 | 4204 |

4201　Five pounds. As illustration

| 1980 Proof *FDC** £425 | 1982 Proof *FDC** £450 |
| 1981 Proof *FDC* (Issued: 5,400)** £450 | 1984 Proof *FDC* (Issued: 905) £450 |

4202　As 4201 but, 'U' in a circle to left of date
1984 (Issued: 15,104) *Unc* £400

4203　Two pounds

| 1980 Proof *FDC** £225 | 1983 Proof *FDC* (Issued: 12,500)** £200 |
| 1982 Proof *FDC** £225 | |

* *Coins marked thus were originally issued in Royal Mint Sets.*
** *Numbers include coins sold in sets.*

4204 Sovereign. As illustration

1974	Unc BV	1981	Unc BV
1976	Unc BV	— Proof *FDC* (Issued: 32,960) £95	
1978	Unc BV	1982	Unc BV
1979	Unc BV	— Proof *FDC* (Issued: 20,000) £95	
— Proof *FDC* (Issued: 50,000) £95		1983 Proof *FDC* (Issued: 21,250)** £95	
1980	Unc BV	1984 Proof *FDC* (Issued: 12,880) £95	
— Proof *FDC* (Issued: 81,200) £95			

4205 Half-sovereign

1980 Proof *FDC* (Issued: 76.700) £60	1983 Proof FDC (Issued: 19,710)** £60
1982	Unc BV	1984 Proof FDC (Issued: 12,410) £60
— Proof FDC (Issued: 19,090) £60	

* *Coins marked thus were originally issued in Royal Mint sets*
** *numbers include coins sold in sets*

SILVER

	FDC		*FDC*
	£		£

4211 Maundy Set (4p, 3p, 2p and 1p). Uniform dates. Types as 4131

1971 *Tewkesbury Abbey*	55	1986 *Chichester Cathedral*	55
1972 *York Minster*	55	1987 *Ely Cathedral*	75
1973 *Westminster Abbey*	55	1988 *Lichfield Cathedral*	75
1974 *Salisbury Cathedral*	55	1989 *Birmingham Cathedral*	75
1975 *Peterborough Cathedral*	55	1990 *Newcastle Cathedral*	75
1976 *Hereford Cathedral*	55	1991 *Westminster Abbey*	75
1977 *Westminster Abbey*	65	1992 *Chester Cathedral*	75
1978 *Carlisle Cathedral*	55	1993 *Wells Cathedral*	75
1979 *Winchester Cathedral*	55	1994 *Truro Cathedral*	75
1980 *Worcester Cathedral*	55	1995 *Coventry Cathedral*	80
1981 *Westminster Abbey*	55	1996 *Norwich Cathedral*	85
1982 *St. David's Cathedral*	55	1997 *Bradford Cathedral*	90
1983 *Exeter Cathedral*	55	1998 *Portsmouth Cathedral*	95
1984 *Southwell Minster*	55	1999 *Bristol Cathedral*	100
1985 *Ripon Cathedral*	55		

4212	**— fourpence,** 1971-96 ....*from*	13
4213	**— threepence,** 1971-96 ....*from*	13
4214	**— twopence,** 1971-96 ....*from*	13
4215	**— penny,** 1971-96 ....*from*	15

The place of distribution is shown after each date.

NICKEL-BRASS

4221   4222

	UNC £
4221 One pound (Royal Arms design). Edge DECUS ET TUTAMEN	
1983	3
— Specimen in presentation folder (issued: 484,900)	5
— Proof *FDC** £5 — Proof piedfort in silver *FDC* (Issued: 10,000) £115	
— Proof in silver *FDC* (Issued: 50,000) £25	
4222 One pound (Scottish design). Edge NEMO ME IMPUNE LACESSIT	
1984	2
— Specimen in presentation folder (Issued: 27,960)	5
— Proof *FDC** £5 — Proof piedfort in silver *FDC* (Issued: 15,000) £45	
— Proof in silver *FDC* (Issued: 44,855) £21	

CUPRO-NICKEL

4223   4224

	UNC £		UNC £		UNC £
4223 Fifty new pence (seven-sided). R. Britannia r.					
1969	2	1976	2	1979	2
1970	4	— Proof *FDC** £2		— Proof *FDC** £3	
1971 Proof *FDC** £4		1977	2	1980	2
1972 Proof *FDC** £5		— Proof *FDC** £2		— Proof *FDC** £2	
1974 Proof *FDC** £3		1978	2	1981	2
1975 Proof *FDC** £3		— Proof *FDC** £3		— Proof *FDC** £2	

4224 Accession to European Economic Community. R. Clasped hands, 1973 .... 1.50

     — Proof *FDC*** £3

* *Coins marked thus were originally issued in Royal Mint sets as shown on page 457.*

** *Issued as an individual proof coin and in the year set shown on page 457.*

4225

4225 Fifty (50) pence. 'New' omitted. As illustration
1982 2   1983 2   1984* 3
— Proof *FDC** £2   — Proof *FDC** £2   — Proof *FDC** £2

4226

4226 Twenty-five pence. Silver Wedding Commemorative, 1972 .... 1.25
— Proof *FDC** (in 1972 Set, See PS48) £4
— Silver proof in case *FDC* (Issued: 100,000) £24

4227

UNC
£

4227 Twenty-five pence Silver Jubilee Commemorative, 1977 .... 0.75
— Specimen in presentation folder 2
— Proof *FDC** (in 1977 Set, See PS53) £4
— Silver proof in case *FDC* (Issued: 377,000) £22
* *Coins marked thus were originally issued in Royal Mint sets*

4228

4228 Twenty-Five pence Queen Mother 80th Birthday Commemorative, 1980 .... 1.25
— Specimen in presentation folder.. 2
— Silver proof in case *FDC* (issued: 83,672) £32.50

4229

4229 Twenty-five pence. Royal Wedding Commemorative, 1981 .... 1.25
— Specimen in presentation folder... 2
— Silver proof in case *FDC* (Issued: 218,142) £30

4230

	UNC £		*UNC* £		*UNC* £
4230 Twenty (20) pence. R crowned rose					
1982	0.40	1983..........................	0.40	1984..........................	0.40
— Proof *FDC** £2		— Proof *FDC** £1		— Proof *FDC** £1	
— Proof piedfort					
in silver *FDC* (Issued: 10,000) £40					

* *Coins marked thus were originally issued in Royal Mint sets*

4231 4232

4231 Ten new pence. R. Lion passant guardant.

1968	0.30	1974	0.40	1978 Proof *FDC** £4	
1969	0.30	— Proof *FDC** £1		1979	0.50
1970	0.30	1975	0.50	— Proof *FDC** £2	
1971	0.40	— Proof *FDC** £1		1980	0.75
— Proof *FDC** £2		1976	0.50	— Proof *FDC** £1	
1972 Proof *FDC** £3		— Proof *FDC** £1		1981	0.75
1973	0.40	1977	0.50	— Proof *FDC** £1	
— Proof *FDC** £2		— Proof *FDC** £2			

4232 Ten (10) pence. As illustration

1982*	3	1983*	3	1984*	2
— Proof *FDC** £1		— Proof *FDC** £2		— Proof *FDC** £1	

4233 4234

4233 Five new pence. R. Crowned thistle

1968	0.20	1974 Proof *FDC** £2		— Proof *FDC** £1	
1969	0.30	1975	0.20	1979	0.20
1970	0.30	— Proof *FDC** £1		— Proof *FDC** £1	
1971	0.20	1976 Proof *FDC** £2		1980	0.20
— Proof *FDC** £2		1977	0.20	— Proof *FDC** £1	
1972 Proof *FDC** £2		— Proof *FDC** £1		1981 Proof *FDC** £1	
1973 Proof *FDC** £2		1978	0.20		

4234 Five (5) pence. As illustration

1982*	2	1983*	2	1984*	2
— Proof *FDC** £2		— Proof *FDC** £2		— Proof *FDC** £1	

* *Coins marked thus were originally issued in Royal Mint sets.*

BRONZE

	4235			4236	

	UNC £		UNC £		UNC £

4235 Two new pence. R. Plumes

1971	0.10	1976	0.20	— Proof *FDC** £1	
— Proof *FDC** £1		— Proof *FDC** £1		1980	0.15
1972 Proof *FDC** £2		1977	0.10	— Proof *FDC** £1	
1973 Proof *FDC** £2		— Proof *FDC** £1		1981	0.15
1974 Proof *FDC** £2		1978	0.30	— Proof *FDC** £1	
1975	0.20	— Proof *FDC** £1			
— Proof *FDC** £1		1979	0.15		

4236 Two (2) pence. As illustration

1982*	1	— Error. R. as 4235	£250	1984*	1
— Proof *FDC** £1		— Proof *FDC** £1 ..		— Proof *FDC** £1	
1983*	1				

 (4237, 4238, 4239, 4240 illustrations)

4237	4238	4239	4240

4237 One new penny. R. Crowned portcullis

1971	0.10	1975	0.20	— Proof *FDC** £1	
— Proof *FDC** £1		— Proof *FDC** £1		1979	0.10
1972 Proof *FDC**£2		1976	0.20	— Proof *FDC** £1	
1973	0.20	— Proof *FDC** £1		1980	0.10
— Proof *FDC** £1		1977	0.10	— Proof *FDC** £1	
1974	0.20	— Proof *FDC** £1		1981	0.20
— Proof *FDC** £1		1978	0.20	— Proof *FDC** £1	

4238 One (1) penny. As illustration

| 1982 .... | 0.10 | 1983 .... | 0.20 | 1984* .... | 1 |
| — Proof *FDC** £1 | | — *FDC** £1 .... | | — Proof *FDC** £1 | |

4239 Half new penny. R. Crown

1971	0.10	1975	0.25	— Proof *FDC** £1	
— Proof *FDC** £1		— Proof *FDC** £1 ..		1979	0.10
1972 Proof *FDC** £2		1976	0.20	— Proof *FDC** £1	
1973	0.20	— Proof *FDC** £1 ..		1980	0.10
— Proof *FDC** £1		1977	0.10	— Proof *FDC** £1	
1974	0.20	— Proof *FDC** £1 ..		1981	0.20
— Proof *FDC** £1		1978	0.10	— Proof *FDC** £1	

4240 Half (1/2) penny. As illustration

| 1982 .... | 0.10 | 1983 .... | 0.25 | 1984* .... | 2.00 |
| — Proof *FDC** £1 | | — Proof *FDC** £1 .. | | — Proof *FDC** £2 | |

* *Coins marked thus were originally issued in Royal Mint sets.*

The new effigy was designed by Raphael David Maklouf, FRSA. It is the third portrait of the Queen to be used on UK coinage, the previous change of portrait being in 1968 with the introduction of decimal coins. The designer's initials R.D.M. appear on the truncation. There is no portrait change on the Maundy coins (see 4211-4215).

GOLD

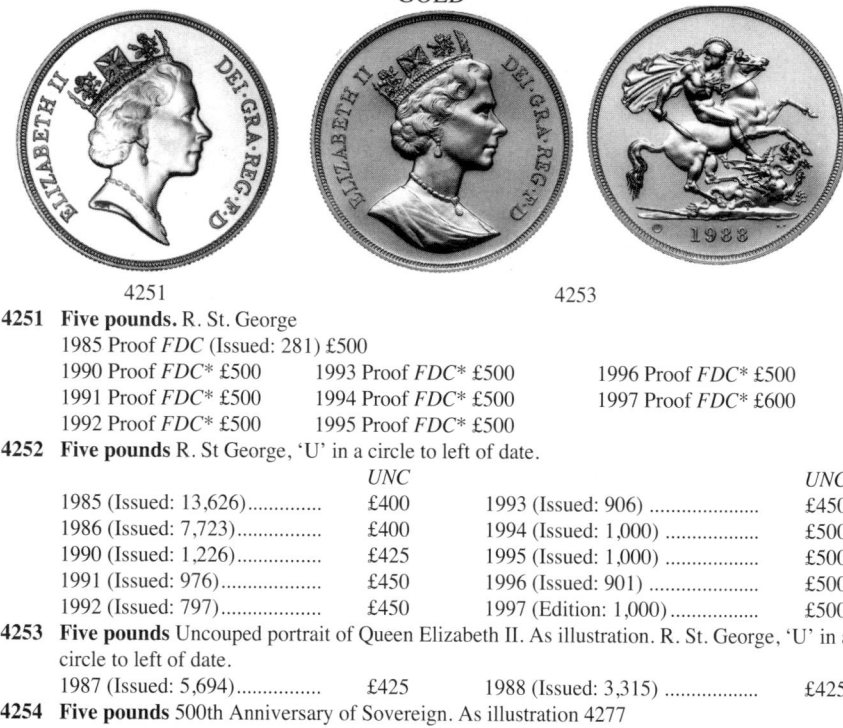

4251   4253

4251   Five pounds. R. St. George

1985 Proof *FDC* (Issued: 281) £500

1990 Proof *FDC** £500	1993 Proof *FDC** £500	1996 Proof *FDC** £500
1991 Proof *FDC** £500	1994 Proof *FDC** £500	1997 Proof *FDC** £600
1992 Proof *FDC** £500	1995 Proof *FDC** £500	

4252   Five pounds R. St George, 'U' in a circle to left of date.

	UNC		*UNC*
1985 (Issued: 13,626)..............	£400	1993 (Issued: 906)	£450
1986 (Issued: 7,723)................	£400	1994 (Issued: 1,000)	£500
1990 (Issued: 1,226)................	£425	1995 (Issued: 1,000)	£500
1991 (Issued: 976)...................	£450	1996 (Issued: 901)	£500
1992 (Issued: 797)...................	£450	1997 (Edition: 1,000).................	£500

4253   Five pounds Uncouped portrait of Queen Elizabeth II. As illustration. R. St. George, 'U' in a circle to left of date.

1987 (Issued: 5,694)................	£425	1988 (Issued: 3,315)	£425

4254   Five pounds 500th Anniversary of Sovereign. As illustration 4277

1989 (Issued: 2,937)................	£450	— — Proof *FDC** £500	

4261   Two pounds. R. St. George

1985 Proof *FDC** £200	1991 Proof *FDC* (Issued: 620) £225
1987 Proof *FDC* (Issued: 1,801) £175	1992 Proof *FDC* (Issued: 476) £225
1988 Proof *FDC* (Issued: 1,551) £175	1993 Proof *FDC* (Issued: 414) £225
1990 Proof *FDC* (Issued: 716) £200	1996 Proof *FDC* £250

4263   Two pounds 500th Anniversary of Sovereign. As illustration 4277

1989 Proof *FDC* (Issued: 2,000) £250

The 1986 £2, 1994 £2 and two types of 1995 £2 commemorative coins in gold previously listed as 4262, 4264, 4265 & 4266 respectively are now shown in the section commencing 4311 with their respective types in other metals.

4271   Sovereign. R. St. George

1985 Proof FDC (Issued: 11,393) £105	1992 Proof FDC (Issued: 4,772) £160
1986 Proof FDC (Issued: 5,079) £110	1993 Proof FDC (Issued: 4,349) £160
1987 Proof FDC (Issued: 9,979) £110	1994 Proof FDC (Issued: 4,998) £160
1988 Proof FDC (Issued: 7,670) £110	1995 Proof FDC (Issued: 7,500) £160
1990 Proof FDC (Issued: 4,767) £150	1996 Proof FDC (Issued: 7,500) £160
1991 Proof FDC (Issued: 4,713) £150	1997 Proof FDC (Edition: 7,500) £160

* Coins marked thus were originally issued in Royal Mint sets. Where numbers of coins issued or the Edition limit is quoted, these refer to individual coins. Additional coins were included in sets which are listed in the appropriate section.

4272 Sovereign. 500th Anniversary of Sovereign. As illustration 4277
1989 Proof *FDC* (Issued: 10,535) £175

4277

4276 Half-sovereign. R. St. George

1985 Proof *FDC* (Issued: 9,951) £65	1992 Proof *FDC* (Issued: 3,783) £80
1986 Proof *FDC* (Issued: 4,575) £65	1993 Proof *FDC* (Issued: 2,910) £85
1987 Proof *FDC* (Issued: 8,187) £65	1994 Proof *FDC* (Issued: 5,000) £85
1988 Proof *FDC* (Issued: 7,074) £65	1995 Proof *FDC* (Issued: 4,900) £85
1990 Proof *FDC* (Issued: 4,231) £80	1996 Proof *FDC* (Issued: 5,730) £85
1991 Proof *FDC* (Issued: 3,588) £80	1997 Proof *FDC* (Issued: 7,500) £85

4277 Half-sovereign 500th Anniversary of Sovereign. As illustration 4277
1989 Proof *FDC* (Issued: 8,888) £80

4281

	UNC £		UNC £
4281 Britannia. One hundred pounds. (1oz of fine gold) R. Britannia standing.			
1987.................................	BV	— Proof *FDC* (Issued: 626) £350	
— Proof *FDC* (Issued: 2,486) £350		1989	BV
1988.................................	BV	— Proof *FDC* (Issued: 338) £350	
4282 Britannia. One hundred pounds. (1oz of fine gold alloyed with silver) R. Britannia standing.			
1990.................................	BV	— Proof *FDC** £450	
— Proof *FDC* (Issued: 262) £350		1994	BV
1991.................................	BV	— Proof *FDC** £450	
— Proof *FDC* (Issued: 143) £400		1995	BV
1992.................................	BV	— Proof *FDC** £500	
— Proof *FDC** £450		1996	BV
1993.................................	BV	— Proof *FDC** £500	

Where numbers of coins are quoted, these refer to individual coins. Additional coins were included in sets which are listed in the appropriate section.

* *Coins marked thus were originally issued in Royal Mint sets.*

4283

4283 Britannia. One Hundred pounds. (1 oz of fine gold, alloyed with silver) R. Standing figure
of Britannia in horse drawn chariot. 10th Anniversary of Britannia issue
1997 Proof *FDC* (Edition: 1,000) £545

4286

4286 Britannia. Fifty pounds. (1/2oz of fine gold). R. Britannia standing.

1987...................................... BV	— Proof *FDC** £160	
— Proof *FDC* (Issued: 2,485) £160	1989	BV
1988...................................... BV	— Proof *FDC** £175	

4287 Britannia. Fifty pounds. (1/2oz of fine gold, alloyed with Silver)
R. Britannia standing.

1990...................................... BV	— Proof *FDC** £250	
— Proof *FDC** £200	1994	BV
1991...................................... BV	— Proof *FDC** £250	
— Proof *FDC** £200	1995	BV
1992...................................... **	— Proof *FDC** £250	
— Proof *FDC** £250	1996	BV
1993...................................... BV	— Proof *FDC** £250	

4288

4288 Britannia. Fifty pounds. (1/2 oz fine gold, alloyed with silver) R. Standing figure of
Britannia in horse drawn chariot 10th Anniversay of Britannia issue
1997 Proof *FDC** £300

4291   4296

4291 Britannia. Twenty five pounds. (1/4oz of fine gold). R. Britannia standing.

1987.. BV   — Proof *FDC** £85
— Proof *FDC* (Issued: 3,500) £85   1989 .... BV
1988.. BV   — Proof *FDC** £100

4292 Britannia. Twenty five pounds. (1/4oz of fine gold alloyed with silver).
R. Britannia standing.

1990.. BV   — Proof *FDC** £135
— Proof *FDC** £120   1994 .... BV
1991.. BV   — Proof *FDC** £135
— Proof *FDC** £135   1995 .... BV
1992.. BV   — Proof *FDC** £135
— Proof *FDC** £135   1996 .... BV
1993.. ***   — Proof *FDC** £135

4293

4293 Britannia. Twenty five pounds. (1/4 oz fine gold, alloyed with silver) R. Standing figure of
Britannia in horse drawn chariot. 10th Anniversary of Britannia issue
1997 Proof *FDC* (Edition: 2,500) £135

4296 Britannia. Ten pounds. (1/10oz of fine gold). R. Britannia standing.

1987.. BV   — Proof *FDC* (Issued: 2,694) £50
— Proof *FDC* (Issued: 3,500) £50   1989 .... BV
1988.. BV   — Proof *FDC* (Issued: 1,609) £55

4297 Britannia. Ten pounds. (1/10oz of fine gold alloyed with silver). R. Britannia standing.

1990.. BV   — Proof *FDC* (Issued: 997) £65
— Proof *FDC* (Issued: 1,571) £65   1994 .... **
1991.. BV   — Proof *FDC* (Issued: 994) £65
— Proof *FDC* (Issued: 954) £65   1995 .... BV
1992.. *   — Proof *FDC* (Issued: 1,500) £65
— Proof *FDC* (Issued: 1,000) £65   1996 .... BV
1993.. BV   — Proof *FDC* (Issued: 2,379) £65

* Coins marked thus were originally issued in Royal Mint sets.
** Issues of bullion quality coins of these years were modest and coins should command a premium
*** Extremely small numbers issued.

4298

4298 **Britannia. Ten pounds.** (1/10 oz fine gold, alloyed with silver) R. Standing figure of Britannia in horse drawn chariot. 10th Anniversary of Britannia issue
1997 Proof *FDC* (Edition: 5,000) £65

SILVER

4300

4300 **Britannia. Two pounds.** (1 oz fine silver) R. Standing figure of Britannia in horse drawn chariot. 10th Anniversary of Britannia issue
1997 Proof *FDC* (Edition: 20,000) £35

4300A

4300A **Britannia. One pound.** (1/2 oz of fine silver) R. Standing figure of Britannia in horse drawn chariot. 10th Anniversary of Britannia issue
1997 Proof *FDC** £25

* Coins marked thus were originally issued in Royal Mint Sets.

4300B

4300B Britannia. Fifty pence. (1/4 oz of fine silver) R. Standing figure of Britannia in horse drawn chariot. 10th Anniversary of Britannnia issue
1997 Proof *FDC** £20

4300C

4300C Britannia. Twenty pence. (1/4 oz of fine silver) R. Standing figure of Britannia in horse drawn chariot. 10th Anniversary of Britannia issue
1997 Proof *FDC* (Edition: 50,000) £15

CUPRO-NICKEL

4301

	UNC
	£
4301 **Five pounds (crown).** Queen Mother 90th birthday commemorative. 1990	8
— Specimen in presentation folder (Issued: 45,250)	10
— Proof in silver *FDC* (Issued: 56,102) £38	
— Proof in gold FDC (Issued: 2,500) £600	

* Coins marked thus were originally issued in Royal Mint Sets.

4302

4302 Five pounds (crown). 40th Anniversary of the Coronation. 1993................................ 7
— Specimen in presentation folder.. 9
— Proof *FDC* (in 1993 set, see PS77)* £9
— Proof in silver *FDC* (Edition: 100,000) £32
— Proof in gold *FDC* (Edition: 2,500) £650

4303

4303 Five pounds (crown). 70th Birthday of Queen Elizabeth II. R. The Queen's personal flag, the
Royal Standard, the Union Flag, two pennants bearing the dates '1926' and '1996' all against
a backdrop of Windsor Castle. Edge: VIVAT REGINA ELIZABETHA.
1996.. 7
— Specimen in presentation folder.. 9
— Proof (in 1996 set, See PS83) *FDC** £12
— Proof in silver *FDC* (Edition: 70,000) £32
— Proof in gold *FDC* (Issued: 2,127) £650

* *Coins marked thus were originally issued in Royal Mint Sets.*

4304

4304 Five pounds (crown). Golden Wedding of Queen Elizabeth II and Prince Philip. Conjoint
portraits of The Queen and Prince Philip. R. Royal Arms and Arms of Prince Philip
surmounted by St. Edward's crown which divides the dates 1947 and 1997 20 November, and
an anchor below with the denomination.

1997..   7
— Specimen in presentation folder...   9
— Proof *FDC* (in 1997 set, See PS85)* £12
— Proof in silver *FDC* (Edition: 75,000) £32
— Proof in gold *FDC* (Edition: 2,750) £650

NICKEL-BRASS

4311

	UNC		*UNC*
	£		£

4311 Two pounds. R. St. Andrew's cross surmounted by a thistle of Scotland. Edge XIII
COMMONWEALTH GAMES SCOTLAND 1986   3
— Specimen in presentation folder   5   — Proof in silver *FDC* (Issued: 59,779) £20
— .500 silver (Issued: 58,881)   12   — Proof in gold *FDC* (Issued: 3,277) £200
— Proof *FDC** £6

* Coins marked thus were originally issued in Royal Mint Sets.

4312   4313

4312 **Two pounds** 300th Anniversary of Bill of Rights. R Cypher of William and Mary, House of Commons mace and St. Edward's crown.

1989...   4   — Proof in silver *FDC* (Issued: 25,000) £23
— Specimen in presentation folder   5   — Proof piedfort in silver *FDC** £45
— Proof *FDC** £6

4313 **Two pounds** 300th Anniversary of Claim of Right (Scotland). R. As 4312, but with crown of Scotland.

1989...   8   — Proof in silver *FDC* (Issued: 24,852) £23
— Specimen in presentation folder   10   — Proof piedfort in silver *FDC** £45
— Proof *FDC** £10

4314

4314 **Two pounds** 300th Anniversary of the Bank of England. R: Bank's original Corporate Seal, with Crown & Cyphers of William III & Mary II. Edge SIC VOC NON VOBIS.

1994...   3   — Proof piedfort in silver *FDC* (Issued: 9,569) £50
— Specimen in presentation folder   5   — Proof in gold *FDC* (Issued: 1,000) £400
— Proof *FDC** £6..................   — gold error. Obverse as 4251 (Included in
— Proof in silver *FDC* (Issued: 27,957) £30   above) £700

* Coins marked thus were originally issued in Royal Mint sets.

4315

UNC
£

4315 Two pounds 50th Anniversary of the End of World War II. R: A Dove of Peace.
Edge 1945 IN PEACE GOODWILL 1995
1995 3
— Specimen in presentation folder 4
— Proof *FDC* *£6 ....   — Proof piedfort in silver *FDC* (Edition: 10,000) £50
— Proof in silver *FDC* (Edition: 50,000) £30 — Proof in gold *FDC* (Edition: 2,500) £375

4316

4316 Two pounds 50th Anniversary of the Establishment of the United Nations. R: 50th
Anniversary symbol and an array of flags. Edge NATIONS UNITED FOR PEACE
1945-1995.
1995 3
— Specimen in presentation folder 4
— Proof in silver *FDC* (Edition: 175,000) £30   — Proof in gold *FDC* (Edition: 17,500) £350
— Proof piedfort in silver *FDC* (Edition: 10,000) £50

4317

4317 Two pounds European Football Championships. R: A stylised representation of a football.
Edge: TENTH EUROPEAN CHAMPIONSHIP.
1996 3
— Specimen in presentation folder 4
— Proof *FDC** £6 ....   — Proof piedfort in silver *FDC* (Edition: 10,000) £55
— Proof in silver *FDC* (Edition: 50,000) £26 — Proof in gold *FDC* (Issued: 2,098) £295

* Coins marked thus were originally issued in Royal Mint Sets.

4318

<table>
<tr><td></td><td>UNC</td><td>UNC</td></tr>
<tr><td></td><td>£</td><td>£</td></tr>
</table>

4318   **Two pounds** Bimetallic currency issue. R. Four concentric circles representing the Iron Age, 18th century industrial development, silicon chip, and Internet. Edge: STANDING ON THE SHOULDERS OF GIANTS

1997...   3
  — Specimen in presentation folder...   6
  — Proof *FDC** £6
  — Proof in silver FDC (Edition: 30,000) £29
  — Proof piedfort in silver *FDC* (Edition: 10,000) £50
  — Proof in gold *FDC* (Edition: 2,500) £325

                                 4331   4332

4331   **One pound** (Welsh design). Edge PLEIDIOL WYF I'M GWLAD

1985...   2
  — Specimen in presentation folder (Issued: 24,850)
  — Proof *FDC** £5
  — Proof in silver *FDC* (Issued: 50,000) £21
  — Proof piedfort in silver *FDC* (Issued: 15,000) £45

1990...   3
  — Proof *FDC** £6
  — Proof in silver *FDC* (Issued: 23,277) £21

4332   **One pound** (Northern Irish design). Edge DECUS ET TUTAMEN

1986...   2
  — Specimen in presentatioon folder (Issued: 19,908)...   4
  — Proof *FDC** £4
  — Proof in silver *FDC* (Issued: 37, 958) £20
  — Proof piedfort in silver *FDC* (Issued: 15,000) £45

1991...   3
  — Proof *FDC** £6
  — Proof in silver *FDC* (Issued: 22,922) £20

* *Coins marked thus were originally issued in Royal Mint sets.*

4333 4334

4333 One pound (English design). Edge DECUS ET TUTAMEN
1987 2
— Specimen in presentation folder (Issued: 72,607)
— Proof *FDC** £6
— Proof in silver *FDC* (Issued: 50,000) £20
— Proof piedfort in silver *FDC* (Issued: 15,000) £45
1992 3
— Proof *FDC** £6
— Proof in silver *FDC* (Issued: 13,065) £21

4334 One pound (Royal Shield). Edge DECUS ET TUTAMEN
1988 3
— Specimen in presentation folder (Issued: 29,550) 5
— Proof *FDC** £6
— Proof in silver *FDC* (Issued: 50,000) £25
— Proof piedfort in silver *FDC* (Issued: 10,000) £45

4335 One pound (Scottish design). Edge NEMO ME IMPUNE LACESSIT (Illus. as 4222)
1989 .... 3 — Proof in silver *FDC* (Issued: 22,275) £20
— Proof FDC* £6 — Proof piedfort in silver *FDC* (Issued: 10,000) £50

4336 One pound (Royal Arms design). Edge DECUS ET TUTAMEN (Illus. as 4221)
1993 .... 3 — Proof in silver *FDC* (Issued: 16,526) £30
— Proof FDC* £6 — Proof piedfort in silver *FDC* (Edition: 12,500) £50

4337 4338 4339 4340

4337 One pound (Scottish design). R: Lion rampant within a double tressure. Edge NEMO ME
IMPUNE LACESSIT
1994 .... 2 — Proof in silver *FDC* (Issued: 25,000) £50
— Specimen in presentation folder 3 — Proof piedfort in silver *FDC* (Edition: 11,722) £50
— Proof *FDC** £6

4338 One pound (Welsh design). R. Heraldic dragon Edge PLEIDIOL WYF I'M GWLAD
1995 .... 2 — Proof in silver *FDC* (Issued: 27,445) £23
— Specimen in presentation folder 3 — Proof in piedfort in silver *FDC* (Issued: 8,458) £50
— Proof *FDC** £5

* Coins marked thus were originally issued in Royal Mint sets.

4339 **One pound** (Northern Irish design). R. A Celtic cross incorporating a pimpernel at its centre.
Edge DECUS ET TUTAMEN

1996..	2	— Proof in silver *FDC* (Issued: 25,000) £24
— Specimen in presentation folder	3	— Proof piedfort in silver *FDC* (Issued: 10,000) £50
— Proof *FDC** £6		

4340 **One pound** (English design) R. Three lions. Edge: DECUS ET TUTAMEN.

1997..	2	— Proof in silver *FDC* (Edition: 30,000) £25
— Specimen in presentation folder	5	— Proof piedfort in silver *FDC* (Edition: 10,000) £45
— Proof *FDC** £6		

4351

4351 **Fifty pence.** R. Britannia r. (4341)

1985	5	— Proof *FDC** £3....		1995*.........................		3
— Proof *FDC** £3		1990*.........................	4	— Proof *FDC** £4	
1986*	3	— Proof *FDC** £5....		1996*.........................		3
— Proof *FDC** £3		1991*.........................	4	— Proof *FDC** £4	
1987*	3	— Proof *FDC** £5....		— Proof in silver *FDC** £15	
— Proof *FDC** £3		1992*.........................	4	1997.........................		3
1988*	3	— Proof *FDC** £5....		— Proof *FDC** £4	
— Proof *FDC** £4		1993*.........................	4	— Proof in silver *FDC** £24	
1989*	4	— Proof *FDC** £4			

4352

4352 **Fifty pence** Presidency of the Council of European Community Ministers and completion of
the Single Market. R Conference table top and twelve stars

1992-1993	5	— Proof piedfort in silver *FDC* (Issued: 10,993) £45
— Proof *FDC** £5..................		— Proof in gold *FDC* (Issued: 1,864) £400
— Proof in silver *FDC** (Issued: 26,890) £24		

4352A — Specimen in presentation folder with 1992 date 4351 5

* *Coins marked thus were originally issued in Royal Mint sets.*

4353

4353 **Fifty pence** 50th Anniversary of the Normandy Landings on D-Day. R: Allied Invasion Force.

1994... 1
— Specimen in presentation folder 2
— Proof FDC* £5

— Proof in silver FDC (Issued: 40,000) £30
— Proof piedfort in silver FDC (Issued: 10,000) £50
— Proof in gold FDC (Issued: 1,877) £375

4354 **Fifty pence** R. Britannia: diam 27.3mm

1997... 1
— Proof FDC* £4

— Proof in silver FDC (Edition: 35,000) £27
— Proof piedfort in silver FDC (Edition: 10,000) £46

4361

4361 **Twenty pence.** R. Crowned double rose

1985	— Proof FDC* £3	1994 ....
— Proof FDC* £2	1990	— Proof FDC* £3
1986* 1	— Proof FDC* £3	1995 ....
— Proof FDC* £2	1991	— Proof FDC* £3
1987	— Proof FDC* £3	1996 ....
— Proof FDC* £2	1992	— Proof FDC* £3
1988	— Proof FDC* £3	— Proof in silver FDC* £15
— Proof FDC* £3	1993	1997 ....
1989	— Proof FDC* £3	— Proof FDC* £3

4366

	UNC £		UNC £		UNC £

4366 **Ten pence.** R. Lion passant guardant

1985*	3	1988*	3	1991*	4
— Proof FDC * £2		— Proof FDC* £3		— Proof FDC* £3	
1986*	2	1989*	4	1992*	3
— Proof FDC* £2		— Proof FDC* £3		— Proof FDC* £4	
1987*	3	1990*	4	— Proof in silver FDC* £14	
— Proof FDC* £3		— Proof FDC* £3			

* Coins marked thus were originally issued in Royal Mint sets.

4367

4367   Ten pence R Lion passant guardant: diam. 24.5mm

1992......................................   1995......................
— Proof *FDC** £3.................   — Proof *FDC** £2
— Proof in silver *FDC** £14..   1996......................
— Proof piedfort in silver *FDC** (Issued: 14,167) £30   — Proof *FDC** £2
1993*......................................   — Proof in silver *FDC** £15
— Proof *FDC** £2.................   1997......................
1994*......................................   — Proof *FDC** £2
— Proof *FDC** £2.................

4371

4371   Five pence. R. Crowned thistle

1985*................   1   — Proof *FDC** £2....   1990*........................   2
— Proof *FDC** £1   1988..........................   — Proof *FDC** £3
1986*................   1   — Proof *FDC** £2....   — Proof in silver *FDC**   £12
— Proof *FDC** £1   1989..........................
1987 ....   — Proof *FDC** £2

4372

4372   Five pence. R. Crowned thistle: diam 18mm

1990 ....   1992 ....   — Proof *FDC** £2
— Proof *FDC** £2   — Proof *FDC** £2....   1996..........................
— Proof in silver *FDC** £12   1993*..........................   — Proof *FDC** £2
— Proof piedfort in silver   — Proof *FDC** £2....   — Proof in silver *FDC** £15
   FDC (Issued: 20,000) £25   1994..........................   1997..........................
1991 ....   — Proof *FDC** £2....   — Proof *FDC** £2
— Proof *FDC** £2   1995..........................

* *Coins marked thus were originally issued in Royal Mint sets.*

BRONZE

4376 4381

4376 Two pence. R. Plumes

1985	1988	1991 ....
— Proof *FDC** £1	— Proof *FDC** £1....	— Proof *FDC** £1
1986	1989	1992* ....
— Proof *FDC** £1	— Proof *FDC** £1....	— Proof *FDC** £1
1987	1990	
— Proof *FDC** £1	— Proof *FDC** £1	

4381 One penny. R. Portcullis with chains

1985	1988	1991 ....
— Proof *FDC** £1	— Proof *FDC** £1....	— Proof *FDC** £1
1986	1989	1992* ....
— Proof *FDC** £1	— Proof *FDC** £1....	— Proof *FDC** £1
1987	1990	
— Proof *FDC** £1	— Proof *FDC** £1	

COPPER PLATED STEEL

4386 Two pence R. Plumes

1992	— Proof *FDC** £1....	— Proof *FDC** £1
1993	1995	— Proof in silver *FDC** £15
— Proof *FDC** £1	— Proof *FDC** £1....	1997 ....
1994	1996	— Proof *FDC** £1

4391 One penny R. Portcullis with chains

1992	— Proof *FDC** £1....	— Proof *FDC** £1
1993	1995	— Proof in silver *FDC** £15
— Proof *FDC** £1	— Proof *FDC** £1....	1997 ....
1994	1996	— Proof *FDC** £1

* *Coins marked thus were originally issued in Royal Mint sets.*

GOLD

4400

4400 Five pounds. R. St George
1998 Proof *FDC** £650   1999 Proof *FDC** £650

4410 Five pounds. R. St. George, 'U' in a circle to left of date
1998 £300

4420 Two pounds. R. St. George
1998 Proof *FDC** £300   1999 Proof *FDC** £300

4430 Sovereign. R. St. George
1998 Proof *FDC* (Edition: 10,000) £160   1999 Proof *FDC* (Edition 10,000) £150

4440 Half sovereign. R. St. George
1998 Proof *FDC* (Edition: 7,500) £85   1999 Proof *FDC* (Edition 7,500) £85

4450

4450 Britannia. One Hundred pounds. (1oz fine gold, alloyed with silver) R. Standing figure of Britannia
1998 Proof *FDC** £550   1999 Proof *FDC** £550

4460

4460 Britannia. Fifty pounds. (1/2 oz of fine gold, alloyed with silver) R. Standing figure of Britannia
1998 Proof *FDC** £300   1999 Proof *FDC** £300

* Coins marked thus were originally issued in Royal Mint sets.

4470

4470 Britannia. Twenty five pounds. (1/4 oz of fine gold, alloyed with silver) R. Standing figure of Britannia
1998 — Proof *FDC* (Edition: 1,000) £135   1999 — Proof *FDC* £135

4480 Britannia. Ten pounds. (1/10 oz of fine gold, alloyed with silver) R. Standing figure of Britannia
1998 — Proof *FDC* (Edition: 5,000) £65   1999 — Proof *FDC* £65

SILVER

4500

4500 Britannia. Two pounds. (1 oz of fine silver) R. Standing figure of Britannia
1998 .... £10
— Proof *FDC* (Edition: 20,000) £35

4501 Britannia. Two pounds. (1 oz of fine silver) R. Standing figure of Britannia in horse drawn chariot (Illus. as 4300)
1999 .... £10

4510

4510 Britannia. One pound. (1/2 oz of fine silver) R. Standing figure of Britannia
1998 — Proof *FDC** £25

4520

4520 Britannia. Fifty pence. (1/4 oz of fine silver) R. Standing figure of Britannia
1998 — Proof *FDC** £20

4530

4530 Britannia. Twenty pence. (1/10 oz of fine silver) R. Standing figure of Britannia
1998 — Proof *FDC* (Edition: 10,000) £15
* *Coins marked thus were originally issued in Royal Mint sets.*

CUPRO-NICKEL

4550

4550 Five pounds (crown). Prince of Wales 50th Birthday. R. Portrait of The Prince of Wales with
the inscriptions 'The Prince's Trust' and 'Helping young people to succeed' on a ribbon at
the base of the portrait with the denomination 'Five Pounds' and the dates 1948 and 1998.
1998 .... £7
— Specimen in presentation folder £10
— Proof *FDC* (in 1998 set, see PS 87)* £12
— Proof in silver *FDC* (Edition: 35,000) £33
— Proof in gold *FDC* (Edition: 2,000) £600

4551

4551 **Five pounds** (crown). Diana, Princess of Wales Memorial. R. Portrait of Diana, Princess of Wales with the inscription 'In memory of Diana, Princess of Wales' with the denomination 'Five Pounds' and the dates 1961 and 1997

1999 .... £7
  — Specimen in presentation folder £10
  — Proof *FDC* (in 1999 set, see PS 89)* £12
  — Proof in silver *FDC* (Edition: 350,000) £33
  — Proof in gold *FDC* (Edition: 7,500) £600

4552

4552 **Five pounds** (crown). Millennium commemorative. R. In the centre, on a patterned circle, a representation of the British Isles with a pair of clock hands emanating from Greenwich, set at 12 o'clock with the inscription 'Anno Domini' with the denomination 'Five Pounds' and the dates 1999 and 2000

1999 .... £7
  — Specimen in presentation folder £10
  — Proof in silver *FDC* (Edition: 75,000) £33
  — Proof in gold *FDC* (Edition: 2,500) £600

NICKEL-BRASS

4570

4570 Two pounds. Bimetallic currency issue. R. Four concentric circles, representing the Iron Age, 18th century industrial development, silicon chip and Internet. Edge: STANDING OF THE SHOULDERS OF GIANTS

1998 .... £4
— Proof *FDC** £6
— Proof in silver *FDC* (Edition: 25,000) £29
— Proof PIEDFORT in silver *FDC* (Edition: 10,000) £50

4571

4571 Two pounds. Rugby World Cup. R. In the centre a rugby ball and goal posts surrounded by a styalised stadium with the denomination 'Two Pounds' and the date 1999

1999
— Specimen in presentation folder £6
— Proof *FDC* (in 1999 set, see PS 89)* £6
— Proof in silver *FDC* (Edition: 25,000) £29
— Proof piedfort in silver *FDC* (Edition: 10,000) £50
— Proof in gold *FDC* (Edition: 2,000) £300

* Coins marked thus were originally issued in Royal Mint sets.

4590

4590 **One pound** (Royal Arms design). Edge: DECUS ET TUTAMEN (Illus. as 4221)
1998
— Proof *FDC** £6
— Proof in silver *FDC* (Edition: 25,000) £25
— Proof piedfort in silver *FDC* (Edition: 10,000) £45
4591 **One pound.** (Scottish lion design). Edge: NEMO ME IMPUNE LACESSIT (Illus as 4337)
1999
— Proof *FDC** £6
— Proof in silver *FDC* (Edition: 25,000) £25
— Proof piedfort in silver *FDC* (Edition: 10,000) £45
4610 **Fifty pence. R.** Britannia. (Illus. as 4351)
1998
— Proof *FDC** £3
1999
— Proof *FDC** £3

4611

4611 **Fifty pence. R.** Celebratory pattern of twelve stars reflecting the European flag with the dates 1973 and 1998 commemorating the 25th Anniversary of the United Kingdom's membership of the European Union and Presidency of the Council of Ministers.
1998
— Proof *FDC** £5
— Proof in silver *FDC* (Edition: 25,000) £25
— Proof piedfort in silver *FDC* (Edition: 10,000) £45
— Proof in gold *FDC* (Edition: 1,500) £250

* Coins marked thus were originally issued in Royal Mint sets.

4612

4612 Fifty pence. R. A pair of hands set against a pattern of radiating lines with the words Fiftieth
Anniversary and the value 50 pence with the initials NHS.
1998
— Specimen in presentation folder £3
— Proof *FDC** £5
— Proof in silver *FDC* (Edition: 25,000) £25
— Proof piedfort in silver *FDC* (Edition: 10,000) £45
— Proof in gold *FDC* (Edition: 1,500) £250

4630 Twenty pence. R. Crowned double rose. (Illus. as 4230)
1998
— Proof *FDC** £3
1999
— Proof *FDC** £3

4650 Ten pence. R. Lion passant guardant. (Illus. as 4232)
1998
— Proof *FDC** £3
1999
— Proof *FDC** £3

4670 Five pence. R. Crowned thistle. (Illus. as 4234)
1998
— Proof *FDC** £3
1999
— Proof *FDC** £3

* Coins marked thus were originally issued in Royal Mint sets.

COPPER PLATED STEEL

4690 Two pence. R. Plumes. (Illus. as 4376)
1998
— Proof *FDC** £3

4710 One pence. R. Portcullis with chains. (Illus. as 4381)
1998
— Proof *FDC** £3

* Coins marked thus were originally issued in Royal Mint sets

Uncirculated Sets

PS21 — 1982	Uncirculated (specimen) set in Royal Mint folder, 50p to $^1/2$p, new reverse type, including 20 pence (Issued: 205,000)	(7)	9
PS22 — 1983	'U.K.' £1 (4221) to $^1/2$p (Issued: 637,100)	(8)	15
PS23 — 1984	'Scottish' £1 (4222) to $^1/2$p (Issued: 158,820)	(8)	13
PS24 — 1985	'Welsh' £1 (4331) to 1p, new portrait of The Queen (Issued: 102,015)	(7)	13
PS25 — 1986	Commonwealth Games £2 (4311) plus 'Northern Irish' £1 (4332) to 1p, ((Issued: 167,224)	(8)	14
PS26 — 1987	'English' £1 (4333) to 1p, (Issued: 172,425)	(7)	12
PS27 — 1988	'Arms' £1 (4334) to 1p, (Issued: 134,067)	(7)	15
PS28 — 1989	'Scottish' £1 (4335) to 1p, (Issued: 77,569)	(7)	15
PS29 — 1989	Bill of Rights and Claim of Right £2s (4312 and 4313) in Royal Mint folder (Issued: not known)	(2)	9
PS30 — 1990	'Welsh' £1 (4331) to 1p plus new 5p, (Issued: 102,606)	(8)	15
PS31 — 1991	'Northern Irish' £1 (4332) to 1p, (Issued: 74,975)	(7)	15
PS32 1992	'English' £1 (4333), 'European Community' 50p (4352) and Britannia 50p, 20p to 1p plus new 10p (Issued: 78,421)	(9)	15
PS33 — 1993	'UK' £1 (4336), 'European Community' 50p to 1p ((Issued: 56,945)	(8)	20
PS34 — 1994	'Bank' £2 (4314), 'Scottish' £1 (4337) and 'D-Day' 50p (4353) to 1p, (Issued: 177,971)	(8)	15
PS35 — 1995	'Peace' £2 (4315) and 'Welsh' £1 (4338) to 1p (Issued: 105,647)	(8)	15
PS36 — 1996	'Football' £2 (4317) and 'Northern Irish' £1 (4339) to 1p (Issued: 86,501)	(8)	15
PS37 — 1997	'Bimetallic' £2 (4318), 'English' £1 (4340) to 1p plus new 50p (Issue figure not yet available)	(9)	15
PS38 — 1998	'Bimetallic' £2 (4570), 'UK' £1 (4590) and 'EU' 50 pence (4611) to 1 pence	(9)	12
PS39 — 1998	'EU' and Britannia 50 pence (4611 and 4610) in Royal Mint folder.	(2)	6
PS40 — 1999	'Bimetallic' £2 (4571), 'Scottish' £1 (4591) to 1p	(8)	11

Proof Sets

PS47 — 1971	Decimal coinage set, 50 new pence ('Britannia' to $^1/2$ new pence, plus medallion in sealed plastic case with card wrapper (Issued: 350,000)	(6)	10
PS48 — 1972	Proof 'Silver Wedding' Crown struck in c/n (4226) plus 50p to $^1/2$p (Issued: 150,000)	(7)	12
PS49 — 1973	'EEC' 50p (4224) plus 10p to $^1/2$p, (Issued: 100,000)	(6)	10
PS50 — 1974	Britannia 50p to $^1/2$p, as 1971 (Issued: 100,000)	(6)	8
PS51 — 1975	50p to $^1/2$p (as 1974), (Issued: 100,000)	(6)	8
PS52 — 1976	50p to $^1/2$p, as 1975, (Issued: 100,000)	(6)	8
PS53 — 1977	Proof 'Silver Jubilee' Crown struck in c/n (4227) plus 50p to $^1/2$p, (Issued: 193,000)	(7)	10
PS54 — 1978	50p to $^1/2$p, as 1976, (Issued: 86,100)	(6)	12
PS55 — 1979	50p to $^1/2$p, as 1978, (Issued: 81,000)	(6)	10
PS56 — 1980	50p to $^1/2$p, as 1979, (Issued: 143,000)	(6)	9
PS57 — 1981	50p to $^1/2$p, as 1980, (Issued: 100,300)	(6)	9
PS58 — 1982	50p to $^1/2$p including 20 pence (Issued: 106,800)	(7)	10
PS59 — 1983	'U.K.' £1 (4221) to $^1/2$p in new packaging (Issued: 107,800)	(8)	17
PS60 — 1984	'Scottish' £1 (4222) to $^1/2$p, (Issued: 106,520)	(8)	15
PS61 — 1985	'Welsh' £1 (4331) to 1p, (Issued: 102,015)	(7)	15
PS62 — 1985	As last but packed in deluxe red leather case (Included above)	(7)	20
PS63 — 1986	Commonwealth games £2 (4311) plus 'Northern Irish' £1 (4332) to 1p, (Issued: 104,597)	(8)	18

PS64 — **1986**	As last but packed in deluxe red leather case (Included above)	(8)	23
PS65 — **1987**	'English' £1 (4333) to 1p, (Issued: 88,659)	(7)	20
PS66 — **1987**	As last but packed in deluxe leather case (Included above)	(7)	24
PS67 — **1988**	'Arms' £1 (4334) to 1p, (Issued: 79,314)	(7)	25
PS68 — **1988**	As last but packed in deluxe leather case (Included above)	(7)	29
PS69 — **1989**	Bill of Rights and Claim of Right £2s (4312 and 4313), 'Scottish' £1 (4335) to 1p, (Issued: 85,704).............................	(9)	28
PS70 — **1989**	As last but packed in red leather case, (Included above)	(9)	32
PS71 — **1990**	'Welsh' £1 (4331) to 1p plus new 5p, (Issued: 79,052)...........	(8)	27
PS72 — **1990**	As last but packed in red leather case (Included above)..........	(8)	32
PS73 — **1991**	'Northern Irish' £1 (4332) to 1p, (Issued: 55,144)	(7)	27
PS74 — **1991**	As last but packed in red leather case (Included above)..........	(7)	33
PS75 — **1992**	'English' £1 (4333), 'European community' 50p (4352) and Britannia 50p, 20p to 1p plus new 10p, (Issued: 44,337)	(9)	28
PS76 — **1992**	As last but packed in red leather case (Issued: 17,989)	(9)	33
PS77 — **1993**	'Coronation Anniversary' £5 struck in c/n (4302), 'U.K.' £1 (4336), 50p to 1p, (Issued: 43,509).............................	(8)	30
PS78 — **1993**	As last but packed in red leather case (Issued: 22,571)	(8)	35
PS79 — **1994**	'Bank' £2 (4314), 'Scottish' £1 (4337), 'D-Day' 50p (4353) to 1p, (Issued: 44,643)...	(8)	28
PS80 — **1994**	As last but packed in red leather case (Issued: 22,078)	(8)	34
PS81 — **1995**	'Peace' £2 (4315), 'Welsh' £1 (4338) to 1p, (Issued: 42,842) .	(8)	29
PS82 — **1995**	As last but packed in red leather case (Issued: 17,797)	(8)	35
PS83 — **1996**	Proof '70th Birthday' £5 struck in c/n (4303), 'Football' £2 (4317), 'Northern Irish' £1 (4339) to 1p, (Issued: 46,295).......	(9)	30
PS84 — **1996**	As last but packed in red leather case (Issued: 21,286)	(9)	35
PS85 — **1997**	Proof 'Golden Wedding' £5 struck in c/n (4304), 'Bimetallic' £2 (4318), 'English' £1 (4340) to 1p plus new 50p (Edition: 100,000)	(10)	33
PS86 — **1997**	As last but packed in red leather case (Included above)..........	(10)	40
PS87 — **1998**	Proof £5 'Prince of Wales 50th Birthday', struck in c/n (4550), 'Bimetallic' £2 (4570), 'UK'. £1 (4590), 'EU' 50 pence (4611) to 1 pence. (Edition: 100,000).................................	(10)	33
PS88 — **1998**	As last, but packed in red leather case. (Edition – included in above)	(10)	40
PS89 — **1999**	Proof £5 'Diana, Princess of Wales', struck in c/n (4551), 'Bimetallic' 'Rugby' £2 (4571), 'Scottish' £1 (4591) to 1p. (Edition: 100,000)	(9)	34
PS90 — **1999**	As last, but packed in red leather case. (Edition included in above)	(9)	40

Silver Sets

PS96 — **1989**	Bill of Rights and Claim of Right £2s (4312 and 4313), Silver piedfort proofs (Issued: 10,000).....................................	(2)	85
PS97 — **1989**	As last but Silver proofs (Issue figure not known)	(2)	42
PS98 — **1990**	2 x 5p Silver proofs (4371 and 4372), (Issued: 35,000)	(2)	24
PS99 — **1992**	2 x 10p Silver proofs (4366 and 4367), (Not known)..............	(2)	28
PS100 — **1996**	25th Anniversary of Decimal Currency (4339, 4351, 4361, 4367, 4372, 4386, 4391) in Silver proof (Edition: 15,000)	(7)	100
PS101 — **1997**	2 x 50p silver proofs (4351 and 4354) (Edition: 25,000)	(2)	48
PS102 — **1997**	Britannia proofs, £2 – 20 pence (4300, 4300A, 4300B, 4300C) (Edition: 15,000)...	(4)	85
PS103 — **1998**	Britannia proofs, £2 – 20 pence (4500, 4510, 4520, 4530) (Edition: 10,000)	(4)	85
PS104 — **1998**	'EU' and 'NHS' Silver proofs (4611 and 4612)......................	(2)	50

Gold Sovereign Proof Sets

PS111 — **1980**	Gold £5 to half-sovereign (4201, 4203-4205) (Issued: 10,000)	(4)	700
PS112 — **1981**	U.K. Proof coin Commemorative collection. (Consists of £5, sovereign, 'Royal Wedding' Crown (4229) in silver, plus base metal proofs 50p to 1/2p), (Not known)	(9)	600
PS113 — **1982**	Gold £5 to half-sovereign (Issued: 2,500)	(4)	750
PS114 — **1983**	Gold £2, sovereign and half-sovereign, (Not known)	(3)	325
PS115 — **1984**	Gold £5, sovereign and half-sovereign, (Issued: 7,095)	(3)	600
PS116 — **1985**	Gold £5 to half-sovereign (4251, 4261, 4271, 4276) (Issued: 5,849)	(4)	750
PS117 — **1986**	Gold Commonwealth games £2, (4311) sovereign and half-sovereign (Issued: 12,500)	(3)	325
PS118 — **1987**	Gold £2 (4261), sovereign and half-sovereign (Issued: 12,500)	(3)	325
PS119 — **1988**	Gold £2 to half-sovereign (Issued: 11,192)	(3)	325
PS120 — **1989**	Sovereign Anniversary Gold £5 to half-sovereign (4254, 4263, 4272, 4277), (Issued: 5,000)	(4)	900
PS121 — **1989**	Gold £2 to half-sovereign (Issued: 7,936)	(3)	450
PS122 — **1990**	Gold £5 to half-sovereign (as 1985 issue), (Issued: 1,721)	(4)	775
PS123 — **1990**	Gold £2 to half-sovereign (as 1988 issue), (Issued: 1,937)	(3)	375
PS124 — **1991**	Gold £5 to half-sovereign (Issued: 1,336)	(4)	850
PS125 — **1991**	Gold £2 to half-sovereign (Issued: 1,152)	(3)	400
PS126 — **1992**	Gold £5 to half-sovereign (Issued: 1,165)	(4)	875
PS127 — **1992**	Gold £2 to half-sovereign (Issued: 967)	(3)	425
PS128 — **1993**	Gold £5 to half-sovereign with silver Pistrucci medal in case (Issued: 1,078)	(5)	900
PS129 — **1993**	Gold £2 to half-sovereign (Issued: 663)	(3)	425
PS130 — **1994**	Gold £5, £2 (as 4314), sovereign and half-sovereign (Issued: 918)	(4)	1050
PS131 — **1994**	Gold £2, (as 4314), sovereign and half-sovereign (Issued: 1,249)	(3)	500
PS132 — **1995**	Gold £5, £2 (as 4315), sovereign and half-sovereign (Issued: 718)	(4)	1100
PS133 — **1995**	Gold £2 (as 4315), sovereign and half-sovereign (Issued: 1,112)	(3)	500
PS134 — **1996**	Gold £5 to half-sovereign (as 1992 issue) (Issued: 742)	(4)	1100
PS135 — **1996**	Gold £2 to half-sovereign (as 1992 issue) (Issued: 868)	(3)	500
PS136 — **1997**	Gold £5, £2 (as 4318), sovereign and half-sovereign (Edition: 1,000)	(4)	1175
PS137 — **1997**	Gold £2 (as 4318) to half-sovereign (Edition: 1,250)	(3)	500
PS138 — **1998**	Gold £5 to half sovereign (4400, 4420, 4430, 4440) (Edition: 1,500)	(4)	1175
PS139 — **1998**	Gold £2 to half sovereign (4420, 4430, 4440) (Edition: 2,000)	(3)	495
PS140 — **1999**	Gold £5, £2 (as 4571), sovereign and half sovereign (Edition: 1,000)	(4)	1175
PS141 — **1999**	Gold £2 (as 4571), sovereign and half sovereign (Edition: 1,250)	(3)	495

Britannia Series

PS147 — **1987**	Britannia Gold Proofs £100, £50, £25, £10 (4281, 4286, 4291, 4296), (Issued: 10,000)	(4)	625
PS148 — **1987**	Britannia Gold Proofs £25, £10 (4291 and 4296) (Issued: 11,100)	(2)	125
PS149 — **1988**	Britannia Proofs £100 – £10 (as 1987 issue) (Issued: 3,505)	(4)	625
PS150 — **1988**	Britannia Proofs £25, £10 (as 1987 issue) (Issued: 894)	(2)	125
PS151 — **1989**	Britannia Proofs £100 – £10 (as 1987) (Issued: 2,268)	(4)	675
PS152 — **1989**	Britannia Proofs £25, £10 (as 1987 issue) (Issued: 451)	(2)	150
PS153 — **1990**	Britannia Proofs, £100-£10, gold with the addition of silver alloy (4282, 4287, 4292, 4297) (Issued: 527)	(4)	775
PS154 — **1991**	Britannia Proofs, as PS153 (Issued: 509)	(4)	775
PS155 — **1992**	Britannia Proofs, as PS153 (Issued: 500)	(4)	900
PS156 — **1993**	Britannia Proofs, as PS153 (Issued: 462)	(4)	900
PS157 — **1994**	Britannia Proofs, as PS153 ((Issued: 435)	(4)	900

APPENDIX 1

SOME COIN DENOMINATIONS

Gold

Angel	Eighty pence (6s. 8d.) from 1464; later 7s. 6d., 8s., 10s. and 11s.
Angelet or 1/2 Angel	Forty pence (3s. 4d.) from 1464, later 3s. 9d., 4s., 5s., 5s. 6d.
Aureus	Roman currency unit (originally 1/60th lb), discontinued A.D. 324 and superceded by the Solidus.
Britain Crown	Five shillings, 1604-12; 5s. 6d. (66d.) 1612-19.
Broad	Twenty shillings, Cromwell, 1656.
Crown	Five shillings, from 1544 (and see below and Britain Crown above).
Crown of the Rose	Four shillings and six pence, 1526.
Crown of the Double Rose	Five shillings, 1526-44.
Florin (Double Leopard)	Six shillings, Edward III.
George Noble	Eighty pence (6s. 8d.) 1526.
Gold 'Penny'	Twenty to twenty-four pence, Henry III.
Guinea	Pound (20s.) in 1663, then rising to 30s. in 1694 before falling to 21s. 6d., 1698-1717; 21s., 1717-1813.
Halfcrown	Thirty pence, 1526 intermittently to 1612; 2s. 9d. (33d.), 1612-19.
Helm (Quarter Florin)	Eighteen pence, Edward III.
Laurel	Twenty shillings, 1619-25.
Leopard (Half Florin)	Three shillings, Edward III.
Noble	Eighty pence (6s. 8d., or half mark), 1344 -1464.
Pound	Twenty shillings, 1592-1600 (see also Unite, Laurel, Broad, Guinea and Sovereign).
Quarter Angel	Two shillings, 1544 -7 and later 2s. 6d.
Rose Noble (Ryal)	Ten shillings, 1464 -70.
Rose-Ryal	Thirty shillings, 1604 -24.
Ryal	Ten shillings, Edward IV and Henry VII; fifteen shillings under Mary and Elizabeth I (see also Spur Ryal).
Solidus	Roman currency unit (1/72nd lb) from A.D. 312; it superceded the Aureus and is the 's' of the £.s.d.
Sovereign	Twenty shillings or pound, 1489-1526 (22s. 6d., 1526-44), 1544-53, 1603-04 and from 1817 (see also Pound, Unite, Laurel, Broad and Guinea, and Fine Sovereign below).
'Fine' Sovereign	Thirty shillings, 1550-96 (see also Rose-Ryal).
Spur-Ryal	Fifteen shillings, 1605-12; 16s. 6d., 1612-25.
Stater	Name commonly given to the standard Celtic gold coin.
Third-Guinea	Seven shillings, 1797-1813.
Thistle Crown	Four shillings, 1604-12; 4s. 5d., 1612-19.
Thrymsa	Early Anglo-Saxon version of the late Roman tremissis (one-third solidus).
Triple Unite	Three pounds, Charles I (Shrewsbury and Oxford only, 1642-4).
Unite	Twenty shillings, 1604-12 and 1625-62; 22s., 1612-19.

Silver (and Cupro-Nickel)

Antoninianus	Roman, 2 denarii in A.D. 214 (later debased to bronze).
Argenteus	Roman, a revived denarius.
Crown	Five shillings, 1551-1965.
Denarius	Roman, originally 10 then 16 asses (25 to the Aureus), later debased: the 'd' of the £.s.d.
Double Florin	Four shillings from 1887-1890.
Farthing	Quarter penny, 1279-1553.
Florin	Two shillings, from 1849-1967.
Groat	Four pence, 1279 – c. 1300 and 1351-1662 (Halfgroat from 1351). 'Britannia' groat, 1836-55 (and 1888 for Colonial use only). See also Maundy money.
Halfcrown	Thirty pence (2s. 6d.), 1551-1967.
Halfpenny	Intermittently, c. 890-c. 970, c. 1108, short cross and, more generally, 1279-1660.
Maundy money	Four, three, two and one penny pieces, from 1660.
New pence	Decimal coinage: 50p from 1969, 25p. (crown) 1972 and 1977, 1980, 1981, 10p. and 5p. from 1968. 'New' removed in 1982.
Quinarius	Roman, half denarius or 8 asses; later debased.
Penny (pl. pence)	Standard unit of currency from c. 775/780 A.D until 1800.
Sceat	Early Anglo-Saxon, small, thick penny.
Shilling	Twelve pence, 1548-1966.
Siliqua	Roman, 1/24th solidus.
Sixpence	From 1551-1967.
Testern (Portcullis money)	One, two, four and eight testerns for use in the Indies (and equal to the Spanish 1, 2, 4 and 8 reales); 1600 only.
Testoon	Shilling, Henry VII and VIII.
Threefarthings	Elizabeth I, 1561-82.
Threehalfpence	Elizabeth I, 1561-82, and for Colonial use, 1834-62.
Threepence	From 1551-1944 (then see Maundy money).
Twenty pence	Decimal coinage from 1982.

Copper, Bronze, Tin, Nickel-Brass, etc.

As	Roman, an early unit of currency; reduced in size and equal to 1/16th of a denarius in Imperial times.
Centenionalis	Roman, replaced the depleted follis in A.D. 346.
Dupondius	Roman, brass two asses or one-eighth of a denarius.
Farthing	Quarter penny: Harrington, Lennox, Richmond, Maltravers and 'rose' farthings, 1613-49; regal issues, 1672-1956 (tin, 1684-92).
Follis	Roman, silver-washed bronze coin, 1/5th an argenteus, introduced c. A.D. 290, later debased.
Half Farthing	Victoria, 1842-56 (and for Colonial use 1828-39).
Halfpenny	From 1672 to 1967 (tin, 1685-92).

New Pence	Decimal coinage; 2p., 1p. and 1/2p. from 1971. 'New' removed from 1982.
Penny	From 1797 to 1967 (previously a silver coin).
Pound	Decimal coin from 1983.
Quadrans	Roman, quarter as or 1/64th of a denarius.
Quarter Farthing	For Colonial use only, 1839-53.
Semis	Roman, half as or 1/32nd of a denarius.
Sestertius	Roman, brass four asses or a quarter denarius.
Third Farthing	For Colonial use only, 1827-1913.
Threepence	Nickel-brass, 1937-67.
Twopence	George III, 'Cartwheel' issue, 1797 only. From 1971 Decimal only.
Mark	Various denominations have been used as moneys of account for which no actual coin existed e.g. the 'mark' was 160 pennies or two thirds of a pound.

APPENDIX II

A SELECT NUMISMATIC BIBLIOGRAPHY

Listed below is a selection of general books on British numismatics and other works that the specialist collector will need to consult.

General Books:
BROOKE, G. C. *English Coins*. 3rd ed., 1966.
CHALLIS, C. E. (ed.) *A New History of the Royal Mint*. 1992
GRUEBER, H. A. *Handbook of the Coins of Great Britain and Ireland*. Revised 1970
KENYON, R. Ll. *Gold Coins of England*. 1884
NORTH, J. J. *English Hammered Coinage,* Vol. I, c. 650-1272. 1994; Vol. II, 1272-1662. 1991
SUTHERLAND, C. H. V. *English Coinage, 600-1900*. 1972

Specialist Works:
ALLEN, D. *The Origins of Coinage in Britain: A Reappraisal*. Reprint 1978
ALLEN, D. F. *The Coins of the Coritani*. (SCBI no. 3) 1963
ALLEN, D. F. *English Coins in the British Museum: The Cross-and-Crosslets* (*'Tealby'*) *type of Henry II*. 1951
ARCHIBALD, M. M. and BLUNT, C. E. *British Museum. Anglo-Saxon Coins. Athelstan to the reform of Edgar. 924-c 973*. 1986
ASKEW, G. *The Coinage of Roman Britain*. (1951) Reprinted 1980.
BESLY, E. M. *Coins and Medals of the English Civil War*. 1990
BLACKBURN, M. A. S. *Anglo-Saxon Monetary History*. 1986
BLUNT, C. E. and WHITTON, C. A. *The Coinages of Edward IV and of Henry VI (Restored)*.
BLUNT, C. E., STEWART, B.H.I.H. and LYON, C.S.S. *Coinage in Tenth-Century England. From Edward the Elder to Edgar's Reform*. 1989
BRAND, J.D. *The English Coinage 1180-1247: Money, Mints and Exchanges* 1994
BROOKE, G. C. *English Coins in the British Museum: The Norman Kings*. 1916
BROWN, I. D. and DOLLEY, M. *Bibliography of Coin Hoards of Great Britain and Ireland 1500-1967*. 1971
CARSON, R. A. G. *Mints, Dies and Currency. Essays in Memory of Albert Baldwin*. 1971
DE JERSEY, P. *Coinage in Iron Age Armorica*. 1994
DOLLEY, R. H. M. (ed.). *Anglo-Saxon Coins; studies presented to Sir Frank Stenton*. 1964
GRIERSON, P. and BLACKBURN, M. A. S. *Medieval European Coinage, vol. 1, The Early Middle Ages*. 1986
HOBBS, R. *British Iron Age Coins in the British Museum*. 1996
KEARY, C. and GREUBER, H. *English Coins in the British Museum: Anglo-Saxon Series*. 1887, reprinted, 1970, 2 volumes.
LAWRENCE, L. A. *The Coinage of Edward III from 1351*.
LINECAR, H. W. A. *The Crown Pieces of Great Britain and the British Commonwealth*. 1962
— — *English Proof and Pattern Crown-Size Pieces*. 1968

MACK, R. P. *The R. P. Mack Collection, Ancient British, Anglo-Saxon and Norman Coins.* (SCBI no. 20) 1973

MANVILLE, H. E. *Encyclopedia of British Numismatics. Numismatic Guide to British and Irish Periodicals 1731-1991.* 1993

MANVILLE, H. E. and ROBERTSON, T. J. *An Annotated Bibliography of British Numismatic Auction Catalogues from 1710 to the Present.* 1986

MARSH, M. A. *The Gold Half Sovereign.* 1982

MARSH, M. A. *The Gold Sovereign.* 2nd Edition 1999

NORTH, J. J. *Edwardian English Silver Coins 1279-1351. (SCBI 39)* 1989

NORTH, J. J. and PRESTON-MORLEY, P. J. *The John G. Brooker Collection: Coins of Charles I. (SCBI 33)* 1984

PECK, C. W. *English Copper, Tin and Bronze Coins in the British Museum, 1558-1958.* 1970

RAYNER, P.A. *The English Silver Coinage from 1649.* 5th ed. 1992

REECE, R. *Coinage in Roman Britain,* 1987.

ROBINSON, Dr. B. *The Royal Maundy.* 1992

RUDING, REV. R. *Annals of the Coinage of Great Britain.* 3rd Edition 1840

SEAR, D. R. *Roman Coins and their Values.* 3rd Edition (1988) Reprinted 1997, 1998

SEAR, DAVID R. *The History and Coinage of the Roman Imperators 49-27 BC.* 1998

THOMPSON, J. D. A. *Inventory of British Coin Hoards, A.D. 600-1500.* 1956

VAN ARSDELL, R. *Celtic Coinage of Britain.* 1989.

VAN ARSDELL, R. D. *The Coinage of the Dobunni.* 1994

WHITTON, C. A. *The Heavy Coinage of Henry VI.*

WOODHEAD, P. *English Gold Coins 1257-1603. The Herbert Schneider Collection, vol. 1 (SCBI 47)* 1996

WREN, C. R. *The Short-cross coinage 1180-1247. Henry II to Henry III. An illustrated Guide to Identification.* 1992

— — *The Voided Long-Cross Coinage 1247-1279. Henry III and Edward I.* 1993

— — *The English Long-Cross Pennies 1279-1489. Edward I-Henry VII.* 1995

For further references to British hammered coinage see *Sylloge of Coins of the British Isles*, a serial publication now comprising 50 volumes cataloguing collections in private hands and institutions. For full list of the 50 volumes published to date in this series, please contact Spink at the address below.

Other authoritative papers are published in the *Numismatic Chronicle, British Numismatic Journal and Spink's Numismatic Circular.* A complete book list is available from Spink & Son Ltd., Book Department, 5 King Street, St James's, London SW1Y 6QS. Tel: 0171 747-6951. Fax: 0171 747 6920

LATIN OR FOREIGN LEGENDS ON ENGLISH COINS

A DOMINO FACTUM EST ISTUD ET EST MIRABILE IN OCULIS NOSTRIS.
(This is the Lord's doing and it is marvellous in our eyes: *Psalm 118.23.*) First used on
'fine' sovereign of Mary.

AMOR POPULI PRAESIDIUM REGIS. (The love of the people is the King's
protection.) Reverse legend on angels of Charles I.

ANNO REGNI PRIMO, etc. (In the first year of the reign, etc.) Used around the edge of
many of the larger milled denominations.

CHRISTO AUSPICE REGNO. (I reign under the auspice of Christ.) Used extensively in
the reign of Charles I.

CIVIUM INDUSTRIA FLORET CIVITAS. (By the industry of its people the State
flourishes.) On the 1951 Festival Crown of George VI.

CULTORES SUI DEUS PROTEGIT. (God protects His worshippers.) On gold double
crowns and crowns of Charles I.

DECUS ET TUTAMEN. (An ornament and a safeguard: Virgil, *Aenid, v.*262.) This
inscription on the edge of all early large milled silver was suggested by Evelyn, he
having seen it on the vignette in Cardinal Richelieu's Greek Testament, and of course
refers to the device as a means to prevent clipping. This legend also appears on the edge
of U.K. and Northern Ireland one pound coins.

DIEU ET MON DROIT. (God and my right.) On halfcrowns of George IV and later
monarchs

DIRIGE DEUS GRESSUS MEOS. (May the Lord direct my steps.) On the 'Una' Five
pounds of Queen Victoria.

DOMINE NE IN FURORE TUO ARGUAS ME. (O Lord, rebuke me not in Thine anger:
Psalm 6, 1.). First used on the half-florin of Edward III and then on all half-nobles.

Domi*N*us *Deus Omnipotens* REX. (Lord God, Almighty King.) Viking coins.

DUM SPIRO SPERO. (Whilst I live, I hope.) On the coins struck at Pontefract Castle
during the Civil War after Charles I had been imprisoned.

EXALTABITUR IN GLORIA. (He shall be exalted in glory.) On all quarter-nobles.

EXURGAT DEUS ET DISSIPENTUR INIMICI EIUS. (Let God arise and let His
enemies be scattered: *Psalm* 68, 1.) On the Scottish ducat and early English coins of
James I (VI) and was chosen by the King himself. Also on Charles I, civil war, and
Declaration coins,

FACIAM EOS IN GENTEM UNAM. (I will make them one nation: *Ezekiel, 37, 22.)* On
unites and laurels of James I.

FLORENT CONCORDIA REGNA. (Through concord kingdoms flourish.) On gold unite
of Charles I and broad of Charles II.

HANC DEUS DEDIT. (God has given this, i.e. the crown .) On siege-pieces of Pontefract
struck in the name of Charles II.

HAS NISI PERITURUS MIHI ADIMAT NEMO. (Let no one remove these [letters] from
me under penalty of death.) On the edge of crowns and half-crowns of Cromwell.

HENRICUS ROSAS REGNA JACOBUS. (Henry united the roses, James the kingdoms.)
On English and Scottish gold coins of James I (VI).

HONI SOIT QUI MAL Y PENSE. (Evil to him who evil thinks.) The Motto of the Order
of the Garter, first used on the Hereford (?) halfcrowns of Charles I. It also occurs on
the Garter Star in the centre of the reverse of the silver coins of Charles II, but being so
small it is usually illegible; it is more prominent on the coinage of George III.

ICH DIEN. (I serve.) Aberystwyth Furnace 2d, and Decimal 2p. The motto of The Prince
of Wales.

INIMICOS EJUS INDUAM CONFUSIONE. (As for his enemies I shall clothe them with shame: *Psalm* 132, 18.) On shillings of Edward VI struck at Durham House, Strand.

JESUS AUTEM TRANSIENS PER MEDIUM ILLORUM IBAT. (But Jesus, passing through the midst of them, went His way: *Luke iv. 30.*) The usual reverse legend on English nobles, ryals and hammered sovereigns before James I; also on the very rare Scottish noble of David II of Scotland and the unique Anglo-Gallic noble of Edward the Black Prince.

JUSTITIA THRONUM FIRMAT. (Justice strengthens the throne.) On Charles I half-groats and pennies and Scottish twenty-penny pieces.

LUCERNA PEDIBUS MEIS VERBUM EST. (Thy word is a lamp unto my feet: *Psalm 119, 105.*) Obverse legend on a rare half-sovereign of Edward VI struck at Durham House, Strand.

MIRABILIA FECIT. (He made marvellously.) On the Viking coins of (?) York.

NEMO ME IMPUNE LACESSIT. (No-one provokes me with impunity.) On the 1984 Scottish one pound. Motto of The Order of the Thistle.

NUMMORUM FAMULUS. (The servant of the coinage.) The legend on the edge of the English tin coinage at the end of the seventeenth century.

O CRUX AVE SPES UNICA. (Hail! O Cross, our only hope.) On the reverse of all half-angels.

PAX MISSA PER ORBEM. (Peace sent throughout the world.) The reverse legend of a pattern farthing of Anne.

PAX QUÆRITUR BELLO. (Peace is sought by war.) The reverse legend of the Cromwell broad.

PER CRUCEM TUAM SALVA NOS CHRISTE REDEMPTOR. (By Thy cross, save us, O Christ, our Redeemer.) The normal reverse of English angels.

PLEIDIOL WYF I'M GWLAD. (True am I to my country.) Used on the 1985 Welsh one pound. Taken from the Welsh National Anthem.

POST MORTEM PATRIS PRO FILIO. (After the death of the father for the son.) On siege-pieces struck at Pontefract in 1648 (old style) after the execution of Charles I.

POSUI DEUM ADJUTOREM MEUM. (I have made God my Helper: *comp. Psalm* 54, 4.) Used on many English and Irish silver coins from Edward III until 1603. Altered to POSUIMUS and NOSTRUM on the coins of Philip and Mary.

PROTECTOR LITERIS LITERÆ NUMMIS CORONA ET SALUS. (A protection to the letters [on the face of the coin], the letters [on the edge] are a garland and a safeguard to the coinage.) On the edge of the rare fifty-shilling piece of Cromwell.

QUÆ DEUS CONJUNXIT NEMO SEPARET. (What God hath joined together let no man put asunder: *Matthew 19, 6.*) On the larger silver English and Scottish coins of James I after he succeeded to the English throne.

REDDE CUIQUE QUOD SUUM EST. (Render to each that which is his own.) On a Henry VIII type groat of Edward VI struck by Sir Martin Bowes at Durham House, Strand.

RELIGIO PROTESTANTIVM LEGES ANGLIÆ LIBERTAS PARLIAMENTI. (The religion of the Protestants, the laws of England, the liberty of the Parliament.) This is known as the 'Declaration' and refers to Charles I's declaration to the Privy Council at Wellington, 19 September, 1642; it is found on many of his coins struck at the provincial mints during the Civil War. Usually abbreviated to REL:PROT:LEG: ANG:LIB:PAR: ROSA SINE SPINA. (A rose without a thorn.) Found on some gold and small coins of Henry VIII and later reigns.

RUTILANS ROSA SINE SPINA. (A dazzling rose without a thorn.) As last but on small gold only.

SCUTUM FIDEI PROTEGET EUM or EAM. (The shield of faith shall protect him, or her.) On much of the gold of Edward VI and Elizabeth.

SIC VOC NON VOBIS (Thus we labour but not for ourselves). 1994 £2 Bank of England.

TALI DICATA SIGNO MENS FLUCTUARI NEQUIT. (Consecrated by such a sign the mind cannot waver: from a hymn by Prudentius written in the fourth century, entitled 'Hymnus ante Somnum'.) Only on the gold 'George noble' of Henry VIII.

TIMOR DOMINI FONS VITÆ. (The fear of the Lord is a fountain of life: *Proverbs, 14, 27.)* On many shillings of Edward VI.

TVAETUR UNITA DEUS. (May God guard these united, i.e. kingdoms.) On many English Scottish and Irish coins of James I.

VERITAS TEMPORIS FILIA. (Truth, the daughter of Time.) On English and Irish coins of Mary Tudor.

Some Royal Titles:

REX ANGL*orum*—King of the English.

REX SAXONUM OCCIDENTA LIM —King of the West Saxons.

DEI GRA*tia* ANGL*iae* ET FRANC*iae* Domi*N*us HYBerniae ET AQVITaniae—By the Grace of God, King of England and France, Lord of Ireland and Aquitaine.

D*ei GRAtia Magnae Britanniae, FRanciae ET Hiberniae REX Fidei Defensor BRunsviciensis ET Luneburgen-sis Dux, Sacri Romani Imperii Archi-THesaurarius ET ELector=*By the Grace of God, King of Great Britain, France and Ireland, Defender of the Faith, Duke of Brunswick and Luneburg, High Treasurer and Elector of the Holy Roman Empire.

BRITANNIARUM REX —King of the Britains (i.e. Britain and British territories overseas).

BRITT:OMN:REX:FID:DEF:IND:IMP: —King of all the Britains, Defender of the Faith, Emperor of India.

VIVAT REGINA ELIZABETHA — Long live Queen Elizabeth. On the 1996 £5 Queen's 70th birthday £5 crown.

APPENDIX IV

NUMISMATIC CLUBS AND SOCIETIES

Coins News is the major monthly numismatic magazine. Spink's *Numismatic Circular* is long established, its first issue appeared in December 1892, and is now published 10 times a year. There are many numismatic magazines which carry articles of interest, such as the *CNG Review* and the *S & B Bulletin*. Many local clubs and societies are affiliated to the British Association of Numismatic Societies, (B.A.N.S) which holds an annual Congress. Details of your nearest numismatic club can be obtained from the Hon. Secretary, Philip Mernick, British Association of Numismatic Societies, c/o Bush, Boake Allen Ltd. Blackhorse Lane, London E17 5QP.

The two principal learned societies are the Royal Numismatic Society, c/o Department of Coins and Medals, the British Museum, Great Russell Street, Bloomsbury, London WC1 3DG, and the British Numismatic Society, c/o Graham Dyer, The Royal Mint, Llantrisant, Pontyclun, mid Glamorgan, Wales. Both these societies publish an annual journal.

MINTMARKS AND OTHER SYMBOLS ON ENGLISH COINS

A Mintmark (*mm.*), is a term borrowed from Roman and Greek numismatics where it showed the place of mintage; it was generally used on English coins to show where the legend began (a religious age preferred a cross for the purpose). Later, this mark, since the dating of coins was not usual, had a periodic significance, changing from time to time. Hence it was of a secret or 'privy' nature; other privy marks on a coin might be the code-mark of a particular workshop or workman. Thus a privy mark (including the *mintmark.*) might show when a coin was made, or who made it. In the use of precious metals this knowledge was necessary to guard against fraud and counterfeiting.

Mintmarks are sometimes termed 'initial marks' as they are normally placed at the commencement of the inscription. Some of the symbols chosen were personal badges of the ruling monarch, such as the rose and sun of York, or the boar's head of Richard III, the dragon of Henry Tudor or the thistle of James I; others are heraldic symbols or may allude to the mint master responsible for the coinage, e.g. the *mm.* bow used on the Durham House coins struck under John Bowes and the WS mark of William Sharrington of Bristol.

A table of mintmarks is given on the next page. Where mintmarks appear in the catalogue they are sometimes referred to only by the reference number, in order to save space, i.e. *mm. 28* (=mintmark Sun), *mm.28/74 (=mm.* Sun on obverse, *mm.* Coronet on reverse), *mm. 28/- (=mm.* Sun on obverse only).

MINTMARKS AND OTHER SYMBOLS

1 Edward III, Cross 1 (Class B+C).
2 Edward III, broken Cross 1 (Class D).
3 Edward III, Cross 2 (Class E)
4 Edward III, Cross 3 (Class G)
5 Cross Potent (Edw. III Treaty)
6 Cross Pattee (Edw. III Post Treaty Rich. III).
7 (a) Plain of Greek Cross.
   (b) Cross Moline.
8 Cross Patonce.
9 Cross Fleuree.
10 Cross Calvary (Cross on steps).
11 Long Cross Fitchee.
12 Short Cross Fitchee.
13 Restoration Cross (Hen. VI).
14 Latin Cross.
15 Voided Cross (Henry VI).
16 Saltire Cross.
17 Cross and 4 pellets.
18 Pierced Cross.
19 Pierced Cross & pellet.
20 Pierced Cross & central pellet.
21 Cross Crosslet.
22 Curved Star (rayant).
23 Star.
24 Spur Rowel.
25 Mullet.
26 Pierced Mullet.
27 Eglantine.
28 Sun (Edw. IV).
29 Mullet (Henry V).
30 Pansy.
31 Heraldic Cinquefoil (Edw. IV).
32 Heraldic Cinquefoil (James I).
33 Rose (Edw. IV).
34 Rosette (Edw. IV).
35 Rose (Chas. I).
36 Catherine Wheel.
37 Cross in circle.
38 Halved Sun (6 rays) & Rose.
39 Halved Sun (4 rays) & Rose.
40 Lis-upon-Half-Rose.
41 Lis-upon-Sun & Rose.
42 Lis-Rose dimidiated.
43 Lis-issuant-from-Rose.
44 Trefoil.

45 Slipped Trefoil, James I (1).
46 Slipped Trefoil, James I (2).
47 Quatrefoil.
48 Saltire.
49 Pinecone.
50 Leaf (-mascle, Hen. VI).
51 Leaf (-trefoil, Hen. VI).
52 Arrow.
53 Pheon.
54 A.
55 Annulet.
56 Annulet-with-pellet.
57 Anchor.
58 Anchor & B.
59 Flower & B.
60 Bell.
61 Book.
62 Boar's Head (early Richard III).
63 Boar's Head (later Richard III).
64 Boar's Head, Charles I.
65 Acorn   (a) Hen. VIII
               (b) Elizabeth.
66 Bow.
67 Br. (Bristol, Chas. I).
68 Cardinal's Hat.
69 Castle (Henry VIII).
70 Castle with H.
71 Castle (Chas. I).
72 Crescent   (a) Henry VIII
               (b) Elizabeth.
73 Pomegranate. (Mary; Henry VIII's is broader).
74 Coronet.
75 Crown.
76 Crozier   (a) Edw. III
              (b) Hen. VIII.
77 Ermine.
78 Escallop (Hen. VII).
79 Escallop (James I).
80 Eye (in legend Edw. IV).
81 Eye (Parliament).
82 Radiate Eye (Hen. VII).
83 Gerb.
84 Grapes.
85 Greyhound's Head.
86 Hand.
87 Harp.
88 Heart.
89 Helmet.
90 Key.
91 Leopard's Head.

91A Crowned Leopard's Head with collar (Edw. VI).
92 Lion.
93 Lion rampant.
94 Martlet.
95 Mascle.
96 Negro's Head.
97 Ostrich's Head.
98 P in brackets.
99 Pall.
100 Pear.
101 Plume.
102 Plume. Aberystwyth and Bristol.
103 Plume. Oxford.
104 Plume. Shrewsbury.
105 Lis.
106 Lis.
107 Portcullis.
108 Portcullis, Crowned.
109 Sceptre.
110 Sunburst.
111 Swan.
112 R in brackets.
113 Sword.
114 T (Henry VIII).
115 TC monogram.
116 WS monogram.
117 y or Y.
118 Dragon (Henry VII).
119 (a) Triangle
     (b) Triangle in Circle.
120 Sun (Parliament).
121 Uncertain mark.
122 Grapple.
123 Tun.
124 Woolpack.
125 Thistle.
126 Figure 6 (Edw. VI).
127 Floriated cross.
128 Lozenge.
129 Billet.
130 Plume. Bridgnorth or late declaration
131 Two lions.
132 Clasped book.
133 Cross pomee.
134 Bugle.
135 Crowned T (Tournai, Hen VIII)
136 An incurved pierced cross

The reign listed after a mintmark indicates that from which the drawing is taken. A similar mm. may have been used in another reign and will be found in the chronological list at the beginning of each reign.

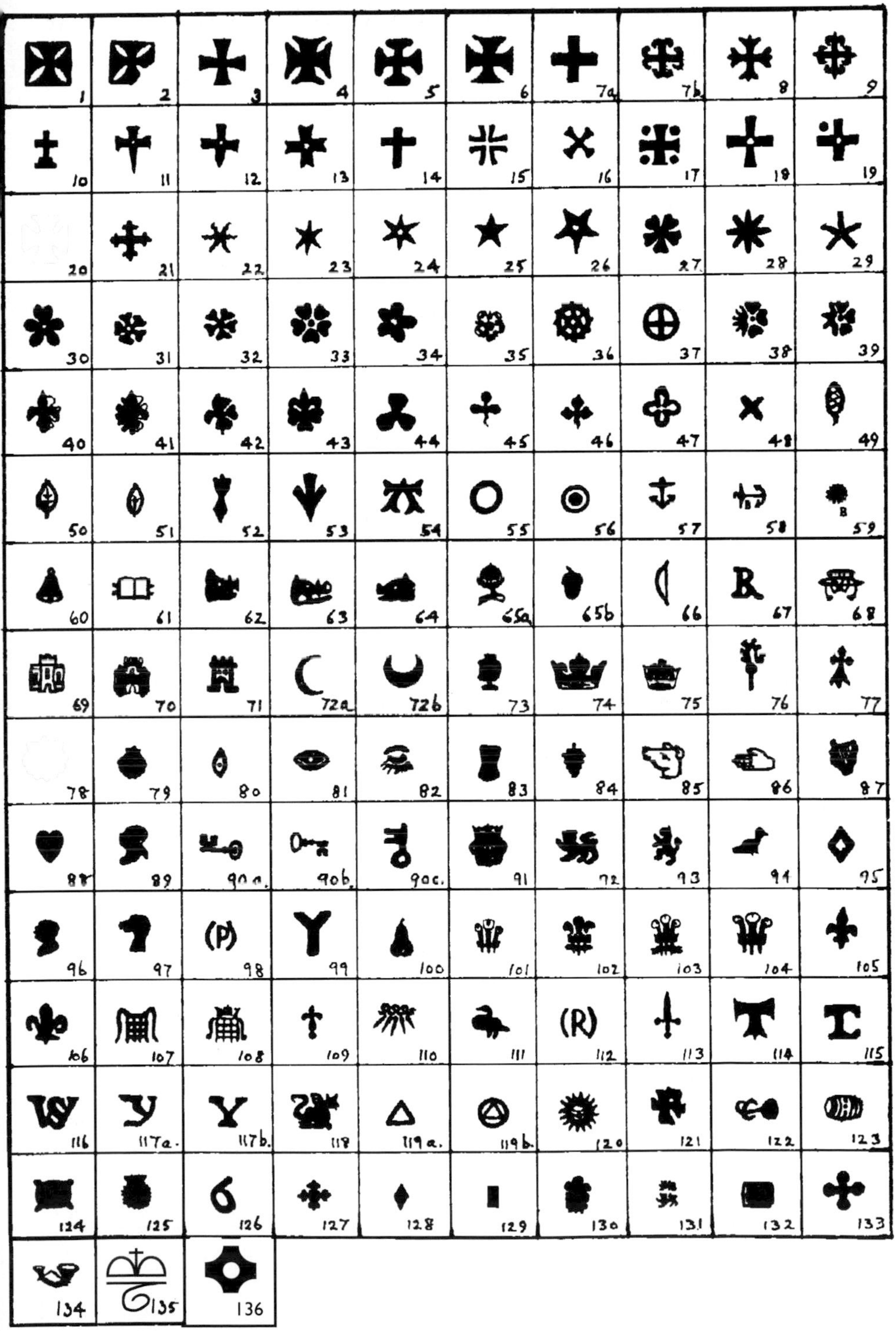
1 2 3 4 5 6 7a 7b 8 9
10 11 12 13 14 15 16 17 18 19
20 21 22 23 24 25 26 27 28 29
30 31 32 33 34 35 36 37 38 39
40 41 42 43 44 45 46 47 48 49
50 51 52 53 54 55 56 57 58 59
60 61 62 63 64 65a 65b 66 67 68
69 70 71 72a 72b 73 74 75 76 77
78 79 80 81 82 83 84 85 86 87
88 89 90a. 90b. 90c. 91 92 93 94 95
96 97 98 99 100 101 102 103 104 105
106 107 108 109 110 111 112 113 114 115
116 117a. 117b. 118 119a. 119b. 120 121 122 123
124 125 126 127 128 129 130 131 132 133
134 135 136

ALPHABETICAL INDEX
OF RULERS AND COIN ISSUES